PowerPoint and Mail Quick Reference

W9-CAX-386

PowerPoint Shortcut Keys

Command	Shortcut
Formatting Commands	
Bold	Ctrl+B
Center paragraph	Ctrl+E
Change font	Ctrl+Shift+F
Change point size	Ctrl+Shift+P
Copy	Ctrl+select and drag
Italic	Ctrl+I
Justify paragraph	Ctrl+J
Left-align paragraph	Ctrl+L
Plain text	Ctrl+Shift+Z
Right-align paragraph	Ctrl+R
Select a paragraph	Triple-click on it
Select a word	Double-click on it
Select all objects, slides, or text	Ctrl+A
Select any amount of text	Drag while pressing left mouse button
Toggle case	Shift+F3
Underline	Ctrl+U
Outlining Commands	
Collapse text under a heading	Alt+Shift+minus
Demote a paragraph	Alt+Shift+→
Display character formatting	/
Expand text under a heading	Alt+Shift+plus
Insert tab in text box	Ctrl+Tab
Move selected paragraph(s) down	Alt+Shift+↓
Move selected paragraph(s) up	Alt+Shift+↑
Promote a paragraph	Alt+Shift+←
Show all text and headings	Alt+Shift+A
Show heading level	Alt+Shift+*heading number*
Slide Show Commands	
Advance slides on mouse click	M
Advance to hidden slide	H
Advance to next slide	Click or spacebar or N or → or ↓ or PgDn
End show	Esc or Ctrl+Break or minus
Erase screen annotations	E
Go to slide	*Slide number+↵*

Command	Shortcut
Slide Show Commands (continued)	
Go to slide 1	Hold both mouse buttons down for 2 seconds
Return to previous slide	Click right mouse button or Backspace or P or ← or ↑ or PgUp
Show/hide the pointer	A or =
Stop/restart automatic show	S or plus
Toggle black screen	B or period
Toggle white screen	W or comma
Use new time	T
Use original time	O

Mail Shortcut Keys

Command	Shortcut
Compose a new message	Ctrl+N
Delete selected mail item	Ctrl+D
Display a list of user directories on Mail system	Ctrl+L
Display members of Personal Address Book	Ctrl+P
Find a member in current user directory	Ctrl+F
Forward message to another user	Ctrl+F
Move message to another folder	Ctrl+M
Reply to sender and all recipients of an open message	Ctrl+A
Reply to sender of an open message	Ctrl+R
View next mail item in folder	Ctrl+>
View previous mail item in folder	Ctrl+<

For every kind of computer user,
there is a SYBEX book.

All computer users learn in their own way. Some need straightforward and methodical explanations. Others are just too busy for this approach. But no matter what camp you fall into, SYBEX has a book that can help you get the most out of your computer and computer software while learning at your own pace.

Beginners generally want to start at the beginning. The **ABC's** series, with its step-by-step lessons in plain language, helps you build basic skills quickly. For a more personal approach, there's the **Murphy's Laws** and **Guided Tour** series. Or you might try our **Quick & Easy** series, the friendly, full-color guide, with **Quick & Easy References**, the companion pocket references to the **Quick & Easy** series. If you learn best by doing rather than reading, find out about the **Hands-On Live!** series, our new interactive multimedia training software. For hardware novices, there's the **Your First** series.

The **Mastering and Understanding** series will tell you everything you need to know about a subject. They're perfect for intermediate and advanced computer users, yet they don't make the mistake of leaving beginners behind. Add one of our **Instant References** and you'll have more than enough help when you have a question about your computer software. You may even want to check into our **Secrets & Solutions** series.

SYBEX even offers special titles on subjects that don't neatly fit a category—like our **Pushbutton Guides**, our books about the Internet, our books about the latest computer games, and a wide range of books for Macintosh computers and software.

SYBEX books are written by authors who are expert in their subjects. In fact, many make their living as professionals, consultants or teachers in the field of computer software. And their manuscripts are thoroughly reviewed by our technical and editorial staff for accuracy and ease-of-use.

So when you want answers about computers or any popular software package, just help yourself to SYBEX.

For a complete catalog of our publications, please write:

SYBEX Inc.
2021 Challenger Drive
Alameda, CA 94501
Tel: (510) 523-8233/(800) 227-2346 Telex: 336311
Fax: (510) 523-2373

SYBEX is committed to using natural resources wisely to preserve and improve our environment. As a leader in the computer book publishing industry, we are aware that over 40% of America's solid waste is paper. This is why we have been printing the text of books like this one on recycled paper since 1982.

This year our use of recycled paper will result in the saving of more than 15,300 trees. We will lower air pollution effluents by 54,000 pounds, save 6,300,000 gallons of water, and reduce landfill by 2,700 cubic yards.

In choosing a SYBEX book you are not only making a choice for the best in skills and information, you are also choosing to enhance the quality of life for all of us.

TALK TO SYBEX ONLINE.

The
COMPACT GUIDE *to*
MICROSOFT® OFFICE
Professional

RON MANSFIELD

SYBEX®   *San Francisco* ■ *Paris* ■ *Düsseldorf* ■ *Soest*

ACQUISITIONS EDITOR: Joanne Cuthbertson
DEVELOPMENTAL EDITOR: Sarah Wadsworth
PROJECT EDITOR: Doug Robert
EDITORS: Abby Azrael, Guy Hart-Davis, Brenda Kienan, Doug Robert
TECHNICAL EDITORS: Erik Ingenito, Tanya Strub, and Celeste Grinage
BOOK DESIGNER: Suzanne Albertson
CHAPTER ART: Helen Bruno
TYPESETTER: Deborah Maizels
PRODUCTION COORDINATOR: Janet K. Boone
INDEXER: Ted Laux
COVER DESIGNER: DesignSite
COVER PHOTOGRAPHER: David Bishop

Library of Congress Card Number: 94-68438
ISBN: 0-7821-1604-3

Manufactured in the United States of America
10 9 8 7 6 5 4 3

To Nancy, Adam, and Murphy
Thanks for being so patient and supportive

Acknowledgments

Wow. It seems to take fewer weeks but more people to create a computer book these days! I'd like to thank here as many of the participants as I can name, and to thank anyone else down the line whose name I've missed or whose contribution was made anonymously. Starting at the top, I'd like to thank Editor-in-Chief R. S. Langer, a man of his word and a lover of books, for keeping me in mind to tackle the large projects.

Developmental Editor Sarah Wadsworth gets the credit for prescribing many of the book's new features, like the "Whole New Way to Work" sections and the button tables at the beginning of each part, and for her encouragement in adapting the book to reflect the package's integrative approach.

Then the Editors—Doug Robert, Abby Azrael, Guy Hart-Davis, and Brenda Kienan—had the unenviable job of making sense of my misspelled instructions and keeping the project rolling and on track, smoothing out the details in the process. Technical Editors Erik Ingenito, Tanya Strub, and Celeste Grinage took pains to weed out technical inaccuracies. Deborah Maizels spent long hours typesetting the book, and Janet Boone and Elisabeth Dahl spent even longer proofreading it. Suzanne Albertson designed the book, and a whole team of Production Artists, led by Rhonda Holmes, pulled the parts together. Frank Seidel provided timely assistance with the last of the Toolbar Reference tables. Finally, Ted Laux produced the excellent index you'll find at the back. Thanks to all.

Contents
at a Glance

Contents

Compact Guide to MS Office

Compact Guide to MS Office

Compact Guide to MS Office

Compact Guide to MS Office

Compact Guide to
MS Office

Compact Guide to MS Office

Compact Guide to MS Office

Compact Guide to
MS Office

Compact Guide to MS Office

Compact Guide to MS Office

Introduction

Today you can purchase several of Microsoft's award-winning programs for what any one of them would have cost a few years ago. Here's what you get when you buy Microsoft Office Professional:

- Microsoft Office Manager (MOM)
- Word for Windows
- Excel
- PowerPoint
- A Mail workstation license
- Access

There's also a version of Office called "Standard version," which leaves out the Access application. You can save a little money by getting that version if you're sure you'll never need the database management tools provided by Access, but the difference in price is less than the cost of buying Access later if you find out you could really use it, so I'd suggest springing for the Professional version.

One of the best things about Office is that Microsoft has standardized the look and feel of the component applications. For instance, most of the menus and the top menu choices in Word, Excel, and PowerPoint are arranged identically. Also, all of the programs in the Office collection share common modules for things like spell-checking and special text effects. This means that you'll spend a lot less time *learning*, and a lot more time *enjoying* your new programs.

The recent addition of *OfficeLinks* makes it easy to share text, data, and graphics among the Office programs. This is due in large part to Microsoft's latest Object Linking and Embedding technology (OLE 2). For example, to include an Excel chart in a Word document, you need only drag it from an Excel window into the desired location in a Word window. This industry standard is evolving to also let you exchange information with other conforming programs, both Microsoft and non-Microsoft. While it's not totally seamless, the ideal of the fully integrated Office package is getting close.

Microsoft Office also offers these benefits:

- Microsoft Office includes an Office toolbar that lets you switch quickly from one program to another.
- New IntelliSense technology provides Tip Wizards that "watch" you work and offer time-saving suggestions for the current context.
- Cue Cards—on-screen guides—offer basic instructions for complex tasks like charting, creating form letters, and presentations.
- If you like, you can read a new Tip of the Day each time you start any of the programs. This is a painless way to gain additional skills and confidence a step at a time.

About This Book

Compact Guide to Microsoft Office covers the essential skills for using all the Office programs, separately and as a team. The examples and reference materials are designed to get you up and running in minutes. We've tried to make the guide small enough to carry along with your portable computer, yet complete enough to use as an everyday desktop reference.

How This Book Is Organized

This Compact Guide is divided into seven parts, an installation appendix, and a toolbar reference section. Each part has its own thumb tab, making it easy to find the sections on the different programs. At the beginning of each part, you will find special charts explaining the application's toolbar buttons. You can use these as a quick reference to the program's features and shortcuts. (The toolbar charts are also gathered into an extended reference section at the end of the book for your convenience.)

In each part, you'll find examples of the program at work, plus step-by-step instructions for all the essential features. Throughout the first six parts you will also find highlighted sections titled "A Whole New Way to Work," which illustrate working with more than one program at a time and discuss issues involved with sharing information across applications. The seventh part of the book presents Object Linking and Embedding, the big hitters in the integration department, in more detail.

Part One: Welcome to Microsoft Office

Part One provides the basic information you'll need to work efficiently with the Microsoft Office Manager: menus, dialog boxes, and online help. You will also learn what's available to you as an Office user for exchanging information among the applications.

Part Two: Word Processing with Word for Windows

In Part Two you will learn everything you need to know to create, format, and print documents in Word for Windows, perhaps the most important program in the Office package, and the one you'll probably consider your "home base." Version 6 of this word-processing application is a major upgrade to an already full-featured program. (In fact, it's an upgrade from Version 2.0c; there were no Versions 3, 4, and 5 for Windows.) If you have already used a previous version, you'll find a lot here to make your work even easier and faster, including how to use Word's sophisticated mail-merge and macro capabilities.

Part Three: Working with Excel

In Part Three you will see how you can use Microsoft's latest version of Excel to compute and keep track of all sorts of interdependent data. You'll learn not only how to have Excel perform complex calculations, but also how to display your data in eye-pleasing charts and graphs. Once you've gotten the hang of it, spice up your work by including graphics and special annotations, and speed up your work with macros. Use Excel's Scenario Manager to automatically generate various "what-if" conditions, and when you've found the optimum balance, import your results into Word or PowerPoint for a polished presentation.

Part Four: Presenting with PowerPoint

There was a time when you could stand up, speak your piece, get a yes or a no, and sit down. But it's the nineties now, and you are expected to give "awesome" meeting presentations to the MTV generation. Your audience expects to be dazzled. They want to see color, motion, and special effects. To a large extent how a presentation *looks* is often as important as what it *says*.

PowerPoint is Microsoft's answer to that need. It will help you create good-looking overhead transparencies, 35mm slides, and even video slide shows. And while it is true that most of what PowerPoint does can also be done by Word and Excel, PowerPoint streamlines a few of the tasks, and provides some handy prefabricated layouts, color schemes, and font choices.

Part Five: Delivering Information with Microsoft Mail

Microsoft Mail makes it possible for networked users to exchange messages and files. Depending on your network, you can communicate with other users in the same department, the same building, or stretched world-wide. Here you will find out how to use Mail to join the e-mail revolution.

Part Six: Managing Your Data with Access

As you will see in the chapters describing Word's mail-merge features, Excel's database tools, and PowerPoint's outlining features, Office provides many different ways to collect and organize business and personal information. But while PowerPoint is fine for small projects, and Word and Excel are great for small to medium projects, you may still need the extra features, speed, and flexibility provided by a full-featured database management system. Microsoft Access Version 2 is a major package in its own right, and perhaps the main reason you bought Microsoft Office Professional in the first place. In this part of the book I'll show you how to use Access to your best advantage, with both simple and complex examples, and an eye toward cutting through the sometimes confusing terminology connected with DBMS (oh yeah, I mean, "database management systems").

Part Seven: Sharing Info with OLE

Throughout the other parts of this book you'll run into specially marked sections ("A Whole New Way to Work") illustrating techniques for sharing information among Offices's component programs. This last part of the book presents a more detailed look at the opportunities and, realistically, the limits of, the two most powerful ways to share information between documents—Object Linking and Embedding. Known collectively as OLE, these techniques are available to all of the component programs of Microsoft Office. With OLE you could create a graph in Excel or Microsoft Graph and then insert it in a Word document or PowerPoint slide presentation, and if the data in the graph changes over time you can choose whether you want the graph in the Word or PowerPoint presentation to show the changes automatically or simply to serve as a snapshot of the way things were when you first inserted it. With OLE, you're not even limited to using programs from the Office package.

Conventions Used in This Book

We've used some standard conventions and typographer's tricks to make this book easier to read. While most of them will be obvious, you should scan the next few paragraphs just in case.

Keyboard Notations

To simplify instructions and make them easier to follow, we've used a special kind of shorthand notation:

- Whenever you need to hold down one key, then press another, you'll see the keys separated by plus signs. For instance, Ctrl+S means hold down the Ctrl key while pressing the S key.

- Boldface text usually indicates text you are expected to type.

- Some keys (the arrow keys and the Enter key, to be precise) are indicated by symbols, especially in lists where we're trying to save space. The symbol for the Enter key is a crooked arrow, ↵, as found on many keyboards.

So, if you are being asked to type a file name and then press the Enter key in an example, you'll read something like

Type **readme.doc** then press ↵.

The ➤ Symbol for Menu Commands

As a shortcut and an eye-catcher, we've used a special convention to indicate menu commands. When we want you to choose a menu command, it will follow this pattern: *menu name* ➤ *command*. For instance, "Choose File ➤ Save" is a shorter, neater way of saying, "Choose the File command from the menu bar, then choose the Save command from the File menu." Sometimes you'll even see a sequence of commands that goes three or four levels deep into subcommands.

Toolbar Button References

One of the coolest things about the latest versions of all the Office programs is their *toolbars*. These contain buttons you can click on with your mouse to carry out many of the most common tasks within each program. They can even be customized to show only the buttons you want, or you can add additional commands to specific buttons. At the beginning of each part of the book, we've listed just about all of the buttons available for that program and described how each one is used. The toolbar charts are also gathered into an extended reference section at the end of the book for your convenience.

If Microsoft Office is not yet installed on your computer, refer to Appendix A for installation instructions.

There's a lot of ground to cover, so let's get right to it! Don't forget, if you run into any difficulties, check the index to see if your topic is dealt with further elsewhere in the book. Failing that, feel free to write me, care of SYBEX, with any suggestions or (shudder) corrections. We're all trying to keep up with the latest releases, but a few mistakes might have crept in at the last minute, so let me know!

Welcome to
Microsoft Office

In Part One you will begin to understand how Microsoft
Office is organized and integrated. You'll learn the names and
functions of the various Office components, and you'll learn
how to use the Microsoft Office Manager. You will also learn
how to use some of the tools shared by all the Office applications, such as online help, the Windows Clipboard, and, most
importantly, OLE—Object Linking and Embedding.

Microsoft Office Toolbar Reference

BUTTON	DESCRIPTION
Buttons on the Microsoft Office Manager Toolbar	

Launches or switches to Microsoft Word.

Launches or switches to Microsoft Excel.

Launches or switches to Microsoft PowerPoint.

Launches or switches to Microsoft Mail.

Launches or switches to Microsoft Access.

You can add non-Office buttons, like this one for the Windows File Manager.

Brings down the Microsoft Office menu.

Introducing
Microsoft Office

Office

Microsoft Office Professional is a hefty collection of programs and other files that all work together. Office includes five of Microsoft's flagship applications:

Word   A full-featured word processor that you can use to create letters, memos, reports, newsletters, manuals, and just about any other kind of document.

Excel   A spreadsheet program that allows you to organize, analyze, and graph information on your computer.

PowerPoint   A presentation graphics program that you can use to create slides, overhead transparencies, handouts, and speaker notes.

Mail (workstation license)   A mail application that enables you to send and receive electronic messages.

Access   A powerful relational database program that you can use to store, retrieve, and organize information.

Office makes it easy to transfer information from one application to another. This means that you can combine text, data, and graphics created in different programs into a single compound document. And, since the Office applications share a common look and feel, once you've learned how to use one of the Office components, it's easy to learn the others.

You'll need anywhere from 16 to more than 70 MB of hard disk space to install Microsoft Office and its various components. This is over and above the disk space needed for Windows and DOS. Moreover, you'll probably need disk space for your documents, Print Manager's spool files, and so forth. It is possible to do minimum installations of the various Office components by eliminating advanced features, sample files, etc. Appendix A can help you understand disk requirements, installation options, memory, and other installation considerations.

Which Application Should You Use?

There are often several ways to accomplish a task using the Microsoft Office applications. For instance, you can add up tables of numbers in Word using Word's Sum function, or you can create a list of numbers in Excel, add them up using Excel's Sum function, and then paste or link the results into the Word document. You can use Excel's database feature to maintain a mailing list for use with Word, or you can use Word's Mail Merge Helper or a dedicated database program like Access. For some mass mailings, you may be better off using Access both for the list maintenance and the actual creation of the form letters.

Here are some tips to help you choose a starting point for your project:

- If the project is primarily a written report, manual, or other publication where page formatting and appearance are important, start with Word and insert other elements from Excel and elsewhere as needed. This is particularly important if you'll need a table of contents and an index in the document. Use Word's templates, predefined styles, and Wizards to give the document a professional look.

- If you plan to create slides from your project, start with Word and use its outline feature. This will make it easy to import your work into PowerPoint where you can create slides.

- For very small databases (like mailing lists with a few hundred names and addresses), use Word tables or Word's Mail Merge Helper.

- Large databases with hundreds or thousands of records are often best left to Access and similar database management programs with the power to find, update, and report rapidly.

- Databases requiring numerical summaries, subtotals, graphs, and complex arithmetic manipulation are often best created in Excel (but don't rule out Access for these projects, if you have Office Professional).

TIP If at all possible, try to make room on your hard disk for at least the "Typical" installation of the Office components you've purchased. Later, after you've had a chance to experiment, you can delete things you never use.

Besides the main components (Word, Excel, PowerPoint, Mail, and, if you have Office Professional, Access), Office provides smaller programs that help you check spelling, evaluate a document's grammar, create drawings, and much more. And, if you've done a typical or complete installation, your hard disk will also contain sample documents provided by Microsoft, templates that speed creation of everyday documents, and even some graphic files (clip art) that you can use to embellish your work.

Overview of the Office Components

Whether you work for a multinational corporation, run a small business from home, or help out in the community when not carpooling the kids, Microsoft Office can make you more productive. But first, you'll need to know all the ways it can be of assistance. So let's get a quick overview of each Office component before we settle into the specifics of the various programs. Let's start with Word.

Overview of Microsoft Word

Microsoft Word is a legendary word-processing program. You can use it for anything from simple, daily correspondence to impressive desktop-publishing projects. As you can see from Figure 1.1, Word is as comfortable with graphics as it is with text:

In addition to more traditional menus and keyboard shortcuts, Microsoft Word includes *toolbars*. Word's Standard and Formatting toolbars are shown in Figure 1.1. These toolbars contain *buttons* that you can click to perform

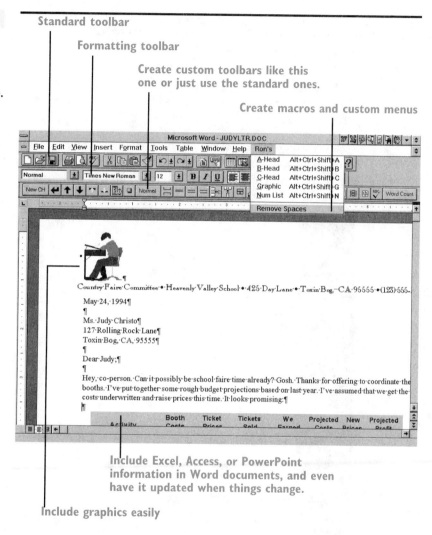

FIGURE 1.1

Word is a powerful word-processing package that is remarkably easy to use.

Standard toolbar

Formatting toolbar

Create custom toolbars like this one or just use the standard ones.

Create macros and custom menus

Include Excel, Access, or PowerPoint information in Word documents, and even have it updated when things change.

Include graphics easily

common tasks like centering text or printing and saving your work. Once you've developed your own working style, you can even make *custom* toolbars like the one I created in Figure 1.1. You can also add new menu choices (like the menu called Ron's) to make you more efficient.

Word provides a macro capability, of course, which helps you automate repetitive tasks.

Word's designers have created a collection of *templates* and *Wizards* to help with everyday tasks. For instance, there are "canned" letters (templates) covering such topics as employee issues and overdue payments. To create a letter or memo, you can often start with one of these templates and personalize it for your needs rather than typing the whole thing from scratch. Other templates help you create manuscripts, press releases, reports, and even resumes and school papers.

Wizards are even more powerful than templates. These assistants ask you questions about your next project and do much of the grunt work for you. As an example, you can create a 12-month calendar by answering only five questions!

	Sun	Mon	Tue	Wed	Thu	Fri	Sat
	1	2	3	4	5	6	7
	8	9	10	11	12	13	14
January	15	16	17	18	19	20	21
	22	23	24	25	26	27	28
	29	30	31				
1995							

Here you can see the first page of a typical Wizard-created calendar. Wizards let you add graphics, change the orientation of the pages and more. Other Wizards help create more personalized legal documents like pleadings, newsletters, meeting agendas, etc.

For serious publication projects, you'll want to take advantage of Word's ability to quickly create headings, a table of contents, indexes, and more. There's a wonderful spelling checker, an on-line thesaurus, and other authoring tools. An *AutoFormat* feature will even examine your plain text and embellish it with complimentary typestyles, formatting choices and so forth. Take a look at the same document before and after auto formatting (see Figure 1.2)

FIGURE 1.2

Word's AutoFormat feature examines and automatically embellishes your plain text—compare BEFORE.TXT in the top window and AFTER.TXT in the bottom window.

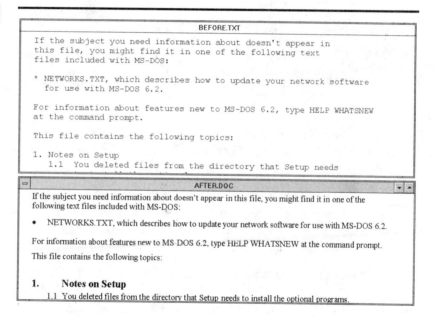

Additional features simplify the age-old task of printing envelopes and labels. You'll find predefined settings for most common envelope sizes and label stocks. You can use on-screen addresses from your current document, or create and use stored address lists. So next time you need a single envelope or a dozen laser-printed labels, they will be only a click or two away. You might actually be able to toss out that old Selectric!

Finally, we can't move on without mentioning Word's powerful *mail-merge* features that let you do much more than send personalized junk mail. Here too, Wizards make your life much easier, assisting in everything from setting up "data documents" (names and addresses, perhaps), to formatting your merged documents.

Overview of Microsoft Excel

Microsoft Excel was designed from the ground up for graphical (Windows and Macintosh) users. It was meant to be mouse-driven, and it shows. Perhaps that's what makes Excel the premiere Windows spreadsheet program. Notice the similarity between it and Microsoft Word in Figure 1.3.

Many of Excel's menus will remind you of others you'll see throughout the Office collection. Excel sports toolbars as well. Here too, you can personalize the program to fit the way you work.

Since so many spreadsheet projects involve multiple subjects, Excel lets you assign multiple sheets to a single file. So, when budgeting, for instance, it's a snap to create a separate sheet for each branch office or department, each on its own worksheet, then consolidate the results.

Notice the *Tip Wizard* at the bottom of Figure 1.3. When you display the Wizard, it watches as you work and makes suggestions for alternate ways to accomplish your goals. It's a little spooky, but very helpful. Be sure to give it a try.

Automatic formatting tools help you develop just the look you want for important reports and presentations. There are buttons for common tasks like adding dollar signs and commas to cells. You can create borders and add shading

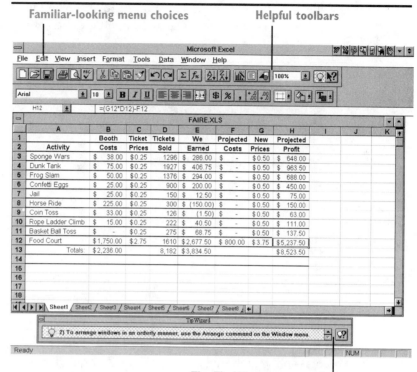

Designed with a
mouse in mind,
Excel will remind
you of Word.

Familiar-looking menu choices   **Helpful toolbars**

**The Tip Wizard can watch you
work and make suggestions**

manually or let Excel's *AutoFormat* feature take charge. Like its Word counter-
part, Excel AutoFormat has a number of predefined color, shading, and font
schemes that you can use as-is or modify to suit your own taste.

Excel sports a bejillion built-in, industry-specific *functions* that will be useful
to scientists, bankers, and homemakers. Functions make quick work of setting
up complex equations. There's a *Function Wizard* to help you sort this out, not
to mention a massive amount of on-line help.

Charts and graphs are a snap (or perhaps I should say a click). The chart shown
here was made by simply selecting the cells to be included and answering a

few questions from Excel's *Chart Wizard*. Too bad you can't see the stunning on-screen colors the Wizard selected when I created this:

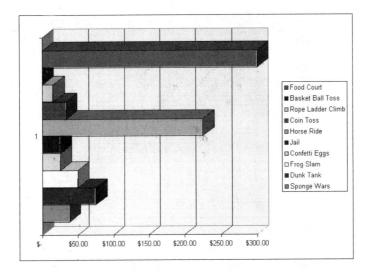

Besides including charts and graphs in your Excel spreadsheets, you can add artwork—photographs, drawings, clipart, logos, and more.

Excel includes features that help you develop and explore complex what-if scenarios. You'll be able to create cross-tab reports. Excel also offers database tools, though, if you have Microsoft Office Professional, you'll probably find Access more to your liking.

You've already seen a hint of the integration possible with Excel. It's easy to use all or part of a spreadsheet in your Word or PowerPoint documents. The reverse is also true. Access data can be exported easily to Excel, and vice versa.

Overview of PowerPoint

PowerPoint is a presentation tool that will help you capture and hold people's attention, whether in a big meeting or a one-on-one presentation. You use PowerPoint to create *slides*. The slides can be arranged to make *presentations*. In addition, you can print *handouts* and *speaker's notes*. Again, notice the familiar-looking menus and toolbars in Figure 1.4.

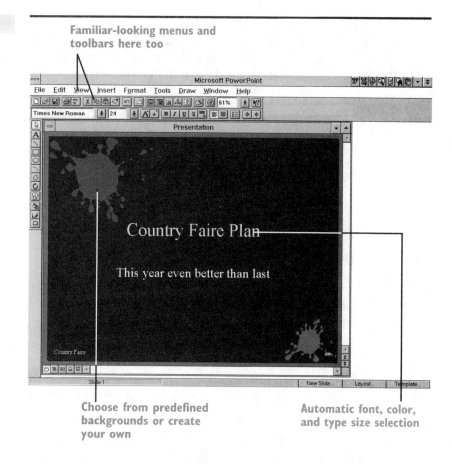

FIGURE 1.4

PowerPoint lets you quickly create complete compelling presentations.

PowerPoint's designers have provided a wealth of predefined slide formats, useful for 35mm slides, overhead transparencies, on-screen computer presentations and printouts. You can use the designs as-is or modify them. PowerPoint takes care of the formatting issues so that you can concentrate on the content of your presentations.

And, speaking of content, there's an *AutoContent Wizard* that helps prepare commonly given presentations. Do you need to break bad news? Run a training session? Report your progress? The AutoContent Wizard can begin the presentation, even providing outlines and major topic headings for you. All you need to do is add your own thoughts and specific facts. It's faster than microwaving frozen lasagna!

Rearranging presentations has never been easier. When you switch to *Slide Sorter View*, PowerPoint lets you drag slides around, delete unwanted slides, hide those "just-in-case" facts and play until you are happy with the results. PowerPoint worries about the details like renumbering:

As you might have guessed, PowerPoint presentations can include things from Word, Excel, and Access. Yes, that chart and spreadsheet are from the Word and Excel Country Fair documents. PowerPoint supports sound objects (as do the other Office programs), so if you are a multimedioid, you can have your computer sing and dance to keep people awake.

It is also a snap to *export* PowerPoint material to Word documents. Microsoft's long-touted *Whole New Way to Work* is actually beginning to become a reality.

When you get ready to rehearse, watch your computer screen. PowerPoint will time your talk as you give it. You can turn your finished presentations into slides or pass them around to other computer users via disks or a network for their own private viewing. A number of third parties will convert your PowerPoint files into film, often overnight if you send the files via modem.

Overview of Microsoft Access

It's a simple data collector. It's a development system for hard-core consultants and system developers. Microsoft Access attempts to be all things to all people and it's not a bad set of compromises. While there are simpler database

Office

programs, and while real computer wonks will probably find something to complain about, Access is in truth a pretty nice balance of power and simplicity.

As you can see from Figure 1.5, Access is a database program that helps you collect information in tables (collections of rows and columns) that you design. It then lets you scroll through the information on screen, sort it, print it, and so on. You can design on-screen (and printed) forms. Reports can contain subtotals, averages, and numerous other computations. When you need to find specific information, you *query* Access. It responds by showing you just the information you've asked for in an agreeable layout of your own design.

FIGURE 1.5

Access is a relational database for both beginners and experts.

Consistent menus and toolbars will make you feel right at home here too

Create your own forms

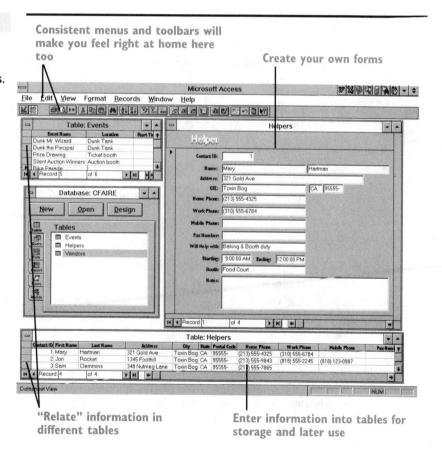

"Relate" information in different tables

Enter information into tables for storage and later use

By enabling you to use *multiple tables* in the same database, Access lets you break your information up into manageable chunks, then *relate* the various pieces when it needs to be combined.

Like Word, Excel, and PowerPoint, Access has Wizards, this time helping you set up different *kinds* of databases. Wizards know a lot about databases and can provide you with suggested designs for contacts databases, customer lists, employee records, and dozens of other business and personal database applications. For example, have you ever wanted to get a handle on your garden? Ask the Wiz to help you set up a database for that purpose. Dieting? Wine collector? Video buff? Setting up an order entry system for your new business? The Wiz has been there and done that.

You can create custom *buttons* and macros in Access so that even casual users can perform complex data manipulations. Naturally enough, Access knows how to import and export information. It knows how to use graphics, sound, and other twentieth-century information sources.

Access is a lot like the game of chess. You can learn the basics in an evening, then spend the rest of your life exploring and discovering the Zen of it all.

Overview of Microsoft Mail

By now you must be dying to pick up your mouse and get clicking, so I'll just *mention* that Microsoft Office also comes with a Microsoft Mail licensee. So, if you are on a network, and you use Microsoft Mail around your shop, you can instantly become a legal MS Mail user. Office makes it easy to use MS Mail to route documents (such as Word and Excel files) to others on your network for review and comment, as you will see later in this book. But for now, since you can't pass what you don't have, let's figure out how to create some documents!

The Microsoft Office Group

When you install Microsoft Office or any of its individual components, the installer will suggest that you create a *Microsoft Office group*. If you agree (which is the default, and an excellent idea), you will wind up with a program group visible from your Windows Program Manager. It will contain icons like the ones shown in Figure 1.6.

Office

FIGURE 1.6

Typical Office group
icons

Program
icons

Setup icons

Double-click on
these to read
the latest help
information

**For an overview of Windows techniques, turn to Appendix B.
There you will find a quick reference to help you arrange
windows, manage files, and start and quit Windows.**

The icons in the Microsoft Office group make it easy to run the programs,
make changes to program setups, and read last minute "readme" files provided
by Microsoft. The principal programs themselves (Word, Excel, etc.) will be
installed in their own directories (C:\WINWORD, C:\EXCEL, etc.).

**Immediately after installing Office or any new Office
component, double-click on the related Readme icons in the
group window (Office Readme Help, Word Readme Help, and
so forth). Then browse the resulting screens. Use the Print
Topic command in the File menu to print information of
interest.**

The Office Manager

You can run the various Office components (Word, Excel, Access, etc.) *without* the Office Manager by simply double-clicking on any of the program icons
in the Microsoft Office group. But there's a better way. The Microsoft Office

Manager displays a handy toolbar and menus to make it easy to run programs and to switch from one program to another.

Starting the Office Manager

After a normal Office installation, your Windows StartUp group will contain an Office Manager icon like this one:

This will be in addition to the Office Manager icon in the Microsoft Office group.

If your StartUp group contains such an icon, the Office Manager will run automatically each time you start Windows. (You can also run the Office Manager manually by double-clicking on its icon in the Microsoft Office group window or in the StartUp window.)

Office Cue Cards

The first two times you start the Office Manager, you will see a Cue Cards window that will welcome you to Office and act as an online guide as you explore. It will look something like Figure 1.7.

Click on the various buttons and phrases to learn more about Microsoft Office. The Menu button takes you back to the first Cue Card screen, and the Back button moves you back one screen at a time. To close the Cue Cards window, double-click the Control-menu box in the upper left corner (see Figure 1.7). To visit Cue Cards again, use the Office menu described later in this chapter.

FIGURE 1.7

The Office Cue Cards window will appear the first two times you start the Office Manager.

Double-click to close the Cue Cards window

Click on buttons to learn more

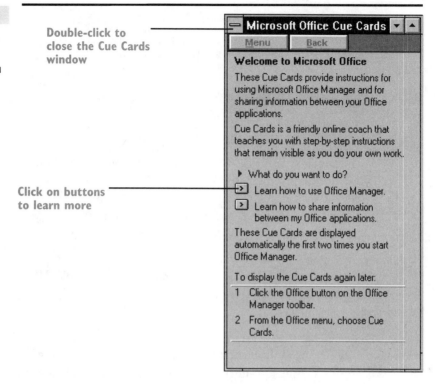

The Office Manager Toolbar

Whenever the Office Manager is running, you'll see an Office Manager toolbar. The exact appearance and location of this toolbar are under your control. The first time you use Office, you'll probably see small toolbar buttons near the top-right corner of your screen.

Clicking once on an Office Manager toolbar button with the primary (usually the left) mouse button will:

- Run the corresponding program if it is not already running.
- Switch you to that program if it is already running.

For instance, clicking on the Word button will either run Word or switch you to Word if Word is already running.

Toolbar Appearance and Location

As mentioned earlier, when you first install and run the Office Manager, you'll see a tiny toolbar like this near the upper right corner of your screen:

This is called the *Small Buttons* version of the Office Manager toolbar. It is always located in the menu bar at the top of your screen unless you specify a different location using the Office Customize command (explained later in this chapter) or you switch to *Regular* or *Large* buttons (also explained later in this chapter).

The number and kind of buttons in your toolbar will depend upon which Microsoft products you have installed. In this example, Word, Excel, Power-Point, and Access have been installed. The far right toolbar button is for the Office Manager itself.

TIP   **If you forget the purpose of a toolbar button, just move the mouse pointer over the button and wait a moment. The name of the button will appear on-screen, thanks to a feature called <u>ToolTips</u>.**

Office Manager Menus

There are two Office Manager menus. One is reached by pointing to the Office Manager toolbar button and pressing the *right* mouse button. The other menu is reached by pointing to the same toolbar button and clicking with the *left* mouse button.

The Right–Mouse-Button Menu

Unless you've swapped the functions of your mouse buttons (as many left-handed people do), clicking the right—or nonprimary—mouse button will display a menu that looks something like this:

This menu lets you change the appearance of your Office Manager toolbar. For example, by selecting Regular Buttons or Large Buttons, you get a larger toolbar that you can move and reshape. The Regular and Large Buttons toolbars will remind you of small windows. The difference between Office Manager toolbar windows and regular windows is that the toolbar windows will always try to remain topmost as you work. Here's what a typical Large Buttons version of the Office Manager toolbar looks like:

To move a Regular or Large Buttons toolbar around on your screen, point to the title bar and drag. Reshape it by pointing to an edge of the toolbar, then when the mouse pointer changes shape, drag the toolbar to a new shape, as shown here:

 TIP Stick with the Small Buttons option in the beginning. The moveable Regular and Large Buttons toolbars can get in your way when you work, and they can be a distraction when you're first learning Office techniques.

The remaining Office Manager menu choices offered by the right mouse button include Customize, Minimize, Cue Cards, and Help for Office Manager:

Customize Lets you add, delete, and rearrange buttons and menu items. You can also use this option to specify a new location for the Small Buttons version of the Office toolbar. Here, too, I suggest you leave things as they are for the moment. Later, when you decide to experiment, read the Customize command's online Help. (See Chapter 2 to learn how to use Help.)

Minimize Minimizes the Office Manager toolbar.

Cue Cards Displays the Cue Cards window, discussed earlier in this chapter.

Help for Office Manager Launches online Help for the Microsoft Office Manager. (See Chapter 2 for more about online Help.)

The Left–Mouse-Button Menu

Pointing to the Office toolbar button and pressing the primary (usually the left) mouse button reveals a different menu. Here's a typical example of what you will see:

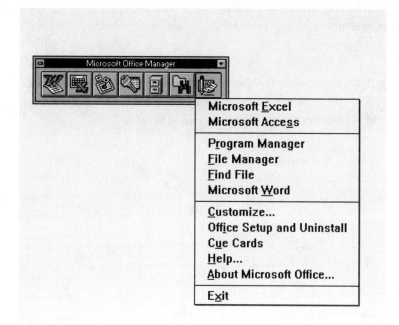

This menu lists programs that you can quickly load or switch to. In addition to Office programs like Word, Excel, PowerPoint, and Access, you will see choices such as Program Manager, File Manager, and Print Manager. Here, too, you can add, delete, and rearrange menu choices using the Customize command.

The Office Setup and Uninstall command lets you add or remove Office components (such as programs or clip art). The Cue Cards and Help options, discussed earlier, also appear in this Office menu. The About Microsoft Office option displays the version number, licensee's name (yours, one would hope), a serial number, system statistics, and other good stuff.

Quitting Office Manager

When you exit Windows, the Office Manager program quits automatically. The Exit choice on either Office menu also quits the Office Manager and removes the Office Manager toolbar from your screen. If you've displayed the regular or large Office Manager toolbar buttons, you can exit the Office Manager by double-clicking on the Control-menu box in the upper-left corner of the Office window.

TIP If you exit the Office Manager accidentally, double-click on its icon in the Office group in Program Manager or in the Windows StartUp group to restart it.

2

Common Office Tools and Techniques

T here are a number of common threads that run through Microsoft Word, Excel, and the other Office components. In this chapter you will learn menu, dialog box, and keyboard techniques that you can use with all the Office programs. You will also learn about the online Help system, which works virtually the same way in all the Office applications. The small, external programs that come with Office, like Microsoft Graph and WordArt, will be covered later on in this book.

Microsoft Office provides many techniques for moving information between programs. These include using the Clipboard, the Insert File command, and Object Linking and Embedding (OLE). These techniques are discussed in Chapter 3, in Part Seven, and in sidebars throughout the book.

NOTE Techniques that vary among the Office applications are explained fully in the application-specific sections of this book. See Chapters 4–12 for information on Word, Chapters 13–23 for Excel, Chapters 24–28 for PowerPoint, Chapters 29 and 30 for Mail, and Chapters 31–41 for Access.

Switching from One Application to Another

In Chapter 1 you learned how to use the Microsoft Office Manager toolbar and menus to move from application to application. Another way to switch from one application to another is by holding down the Alt key and then pressing the Tab key. When you do this, you will see the name of a different running program in the center of your screen each time you press Tab. When you see the name of the program you wish to use next, release the Alt key and you will switch over to that program.

Sizing and Arranging Windows

When you're working on a complex project, you may have two or more windows open on your screen at the same time. These can be two windows from the same program (two Word windows, for instance) or windows from different programs (such as Word and Excel). Figure 2.1 shows an example of this.

Office

FIGURE 2.1

A Word window and an Excel window open on the screen

A Word window   Scroll bars   An Excel window

NOTE   Notice in Figure 2.1 how the menu bars fold to fit inside narrow windows. You can use the horizontal scroll bars, if necessary, to see parts of your document that are hidden.

You can use standard Windows techniques to move and resize windows (for example, drag the corners of windows). Consult Appendix B or your Windows documentation if you need additional information on this topic. To return a window to its normal, full-screen width, click on the ▲ symbol in the upper-right corner of the window.

Working with Menus

Figure 2.2 shows a typical Office application menu. To display a menu, just point with your mouse to a title in the application's menu bar and click your left mouse button once. In most cases, you can then execute a command by clicking on its name in the menu.

Notice in Figure 2.2 that some menu commands end in an ellipsis (...). The ellipsis tells you that when you choose that menu command, you will be presented with a dialog box where you will need to make additional choices

FIGURE 2.2

A typical menu. To display a menu, point to a title in the application's menu bar with your mouse and click once.

Edit	
Can't Undo	Ctrl+Z
Can't Repeat	Ctrl+Y
Cut	Ctrl+X
Copy	Ctrl+C
Paste	Ctrl+V
Paste Special...	
Clear	Delete
Select All	Ctrl+A
Find...	Ctrl+F
Replace...	Ctrl+H
Go To...	Ctrl+G
AutoText...	
Bookmark...	
Links...	
Object	

before the command can be executed. For instance, when you choose File ➤ Print…, the Print dialog box will appear on your screen, offering you a variety of Print options to choose from.

When you pull down a menu, some of the options on the menu may be dimmed, or light gray. Dimmed menu choices are unavailable until you do something else. For instance, if you have not made any changes to a document, the Undo command on the Edit menu will be dimmed, because there are no changes to be undone.

Using Menus without a Mouse

You can often make choices from menus without using your mouse. There are two ways to do this.

Some commands (like Paste, Copy, and Cut) have keyboard shortcuts. These are listed next to their names. In Figure 2.2, you can see that the shortcut for Cut is Ctrl+X, the shortcut for Copy is Ctrl+C, and the shortcut for Paste is Ctrl+V. Not all menu choices have these keyboard shortcuts. However, you can assign your own shortcuts from within a program by customizing. (You'll learn about customizing in later chapters.)

If you don't mind learning some multistep keyboard shortcuts, you can reach virtually any menu option from the keyboard. This is particularly handy if your mouse dies or your aircraft tray table is too small for your portable *and* your mouse. All menu choices contain names with an underlined letter (for example, Paste and Paste Special). You can select these options by pressing the Alt key and then typing the necessary sequence of underlined letters. For instance, to choose the Paste Special command from the Edit menu, you would press and release the Alt key, then type E (for Edit), then S (for Paste Special).

Shortcut Menus

Also available in Word, Excel, PowerPoint, and Access are *shortcut menus* that you can display by pointing to items on the screen and clicking the right (or nonprimary) mouse button. The available menu choices depend on the item you are clicking on. You'll learn more about these handy menus later in the book.

Working with Dialog Boxes

Many of Microsoft's dialog boxes now have handy, easy-to-use *tabs*. Simply click on a tab at the top of the dialog box to reveal additional options. For instance, the dialog box in Figure 2.3 has three tabs: Toolbars, Menus, and Keyboard.

FIGURE 2.3

Many dialog boxes have tabs that reveal additional choices. In this example, the Menus tab is foremost. You could click on the Toolbars tab or the Keyboard tab to see more options.

Click on arrows or type letters to scroll

Type in boxes like these or click on arrows to see a list

When the Menus tab is foremost, you will see only the options relevant to menus. If you were to click on the Toolbars tab, the Menu choices would drop back and you would see the Toolbar choices.

You can usually use the Tab key to move from place to place in a dialog box. You can also use underlined letters in dialog boxes as keyboard shortcuts.

You can use the Tab key to reach buttons in dialog boxes too. Watch the outlines surrounding the buttons darken as you tab from one to the next. To select a button with a dark outline, press ↵. In Figure 2.3, for example, pressing ↵ would select the Close button.

TIP Many dialog boxes contain Description boxes like the one in the Customize dialog box shown in Figure 2.3. Look to these for useful explanations of dialog box options.

Getting Help

It's a little ironic that the Microsoft Office has so many online Help features that it takes several pages of a book to describe them. Generally, you'll find three kinds of online Help:

- Topic-specific Help
- Screen-element Help
- Help for users of competitive products (WordPerfect or Lotus 1-2-3, for instance)

In addition, Microsoft offers product support over the telephone, via fax, and through CompuServe and other bulletin board services. There is also TTY assistance for the hearing-impaired. Since Word's Help feature does a good job of explaining itself, I'll just touch on it in the sections below.

Starting Online Help

You can start online Help for a particular application from within that application by pressing the F1 function key. In addition, the Office applications have Help menus. Here's Word's Help menu:

Help menus give you the opportunity to search for Help on a particular topic, see previews of features, and, in some cases, witness examples and demonstrations. Help menus also offer online Help for users experienced with competitive products.

The Help Contents Window

To see an overview of the online Help available for a product, choose Help ➤ Contents. You'll see a window listing the various types of Help available, as in the Excel example shown in Figure 2.4.

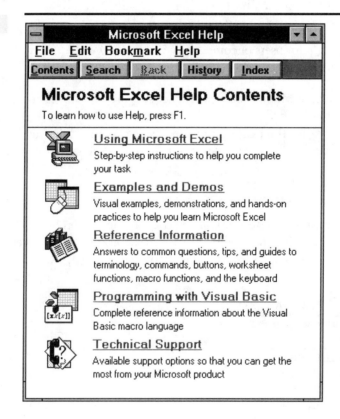

In the Help Contents window, you can click on underlined words or icons corresponding to the type of help you want. For example, to see demonstrations of Excel at work, click on the Examples and Demos icon.

Along the top of the Help Contents window is a row of buttons to help you navigate through the Help system:

Contents   Takes you back to the Help Contents screen.

Search   Lets you search for specific words (for example, *print*).

Back   Takes you to the previous Help screen.

History   Lists previous Help topics you have visited.

Index   Displays an alphabetic list of Help topics.

Examples and Demos

When you choose Examples and Demos, you'll see a list of choices, as shown in Figure 2.5. Click on the button next to the type of demonstration you want to see. You may be offered additional choices before the demo actually runs. Eventually, you'll see an overview of the demonstration and several on-screen buttons that let you run the demonstration, close (quit) the demonstration, and go back to earlier topics.

 TIP   Some words in Help headings and Help text are underlined, and appear in a different color if you have a color monitor. Clicking on these entries will lead you to additional Help.

Searching for Specific Words of Wisdom

The Help ➤ Search for Help on command lets you enter specific words and phrases which you would like information about. For instance, to find out more about printing, you could do this:

1. Choose Help ➤ Search for Help on.

2. Type the search word or phrase of interest (**print**, for example). The Office program you are running will show you a list of possible topics, as shown in Figure 2.6.

FIGURE 2.5

The Examples and Demos screen offers a list of topics to choose from. These are the topics available in Excel.

Microsoft Excel Examples and Demos

Examples and Demos

Working in Workbooks	Formatting a Chart
Selecting Cells, Choosing Commands	Using Charts to Analyze Data
Using Toolbars	Organizing Data in a List
Entering Data	Using Pivot Tables
Creating Formulas and Links	Performing What-If Analysis
Editing a Worksheet	Outlining a Worksheet
Formatting a Worksheet	Using Templates
Creating Graphic Objects	Troubleshooting and Annotating
Printing	Sharing and Importing Data
Creating a Chart	Using Visual Basic

Close

3. Click the Show Topics button to see a list of hints.

4. Double-click on a listed topic to read it (or click once to select the topic and then click the Go To button).

Competitive Help

If you are familiar with WordPerfect, Lotus 1-2-3, or other competitive products, you can often get help that compares these products to their Microsoft counterparts. For instance, Microsoft Word offers help for WordPerfect users. To access WordPerfect Help, follow these steps:

1. Make sure WordPerfect Help has been installed and enabled.

2. Choose Help ➤ WordPerfect Help.

FIGURE 2.6

The Search dialog box lets you search for Help on specific topics

3. Find the topic of interest in the scrolling list, as shown below:

4. Point and click on a topic to read about it.

5. Use the buttons at the bottom of the window to see demos and explore other Help options. For instance, here are the Help options for WordPerfect users running Microsoft Word:

6. Press Escape or use the Close button to quit Help.

Pointing to Get Online Help

You can often get help by pointing with your mouse to items on the screen. For instance, when you point to a button in a toolbar, the function of that button will be displayed on-screen. (This is the ToolTips feature.)

You can also use the Help buttons on the Office applications' Standard toolbars. The mouse pointer will change into an arrow with a question mark. When you point and click with that pointer, you get online Help. Here's an example:

1. Click the Help button on the Standard toolbar (shown at left). Your mouse pointer will become a giant question mark with an arrow. (Press Escape if this happens by mistake.)

Office

2. Using your mouse, point to the item of interest and click. In the illustration below, I'm pointing to Excel's Comma Style button.

3. Read the resulting Help text or click the buttons in the Help window to narrow in on the information of interest. Figure 2.7 shows the Help screen for Excel's Comma Style button. (You may need to scroll to read the entire text.)

FIGURE 2.7

The Help screen for Excel's Comma Style button

4. Click the Contents button or press **C** to see the topics list again. Or choose File ➤ Exit to quit Help.

Getting Online Help in Dialog Boxes

Many dialog boxes contain Help buttons. Use these buttons when you get stumped or when you want to learn more about a dialog box's capabilities. For example, the Help button in Word's Page Setup dialog box (shown in Figure 2.8) will explain the hundreds of page-setup options available.

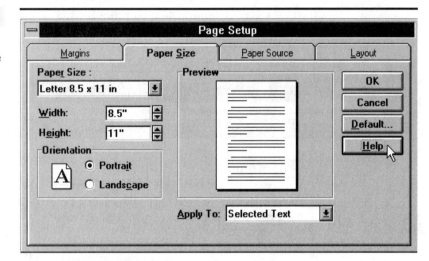

Printing Online Help

You can often print online Help topics by selecting the Print Topic command in the Help window's File menu. Make sure your printer is set up and ready.

Quitting Online Help

When you're done using online Help, just press Alt+F4 to close the Help windows. Or you can double-click in the Help window's Close box, found in the upper-left corner of Help windows.

Microsoft Product Support Services

When you really get stuck, Microsoft's huge technical support staff can be a big help. They provide technical note–downloading services, CompuServe forums, prerecorded voice message support, and even real, live people to answer your questions.

The first step, as they say in tech support circles, is to "Read Your Friggin' Manuals." People who don't read their manuals are referred to as RYFMs. If you can't find the answers you need in online Help or your manuals or books like this one, it's time to call out the big guns.

Finding Out about Tech Support Options

Microsoft is changing the way it supports users, and things that were once free are now often quite expensive. To find out more about available support options, use the Technical Support command on the Help menu.

When you choose Help ➤ Technical Support, a list of support topics will appear on your screen. You can read and print these topics just as you would any other Help information.

  Microsoft Technical support is not always free. Be sure you understand the costs before obtaining support.

3

Sharing Information with Microsoft Office

W indows makes it possible to pass information from one program to another so you don't have to recreate the information. And Microsoft Office provides many alternatives for sharing and exchanging information. In this chapter, we'll take a look at the most fundamental methods: the Clipboard, the new interprogram drag-and-drop facility, and the Insert File command. Later, when you've learned the basics of the individual Office applications, you can turn to Part Seven for coverage of more advanced integration features, including Object Linking and Embedding (OLE2).

TIP Throughout this book you will find sidebars that demonstrate how the Office applications work together. These examples illustrate why Microsoft has dubbed the Office "A Whole New Way to Work."

The Clipboard

If you've used Windows programs before, you've probably used the Clipboard to move things from place to place within a document. You can also use the Clipboard to move things *between* different programs. This is a particularly convenient way to transfer information if your computer supports 386 Enhanced mode and lets you switch between multiple programs without quitting and restarting them. For instance, if you use the Windows Calculator accessory, you can copy the results of your calculations to the Clipboard, switch to Word or Excel, and paste the calculation results into a Word paragraph or an Excel worksheet cell. It is also possible to move things to and from *non-Windows* programs via the Clipboard. You can copy an entire screen's contents or just selected portions.

Since many programs use unique control codes, characters, and graphics formats, the results of pasting can be a little unpredictable at times. Windows, together with all Windows-savvy applications, does a pretty good job of minimizing these often perplexing differences, but the farther you get off the

A WHOLE NEW WAY TO WORK

Alternatives to the Clipboard

Before we explore basic copying and pasting between programs using the Clipboard, it's worth mentioning that there are other ways to move data from one application into another. For instance, to turn an entire WordPerfect or Lotus 1-2-3 document into a Word or Excel document, your best bet is usually to rely on Word's and Excel's ability to open and convert these non-Microsoft files *directly*.

Some programs offer industry-standard ways to export and import data without using the Clipboard at all. For instance, many database and word processing programs import and export ASCII files. Then there's Word's Import Picture command, which will open, convert, and import graphic files even if you don't have the program used to create them. Specialized importing and exporting features like these can sometimes provide a quicker, more accurate way to move information from place to place.

As mentioned earlier, there's a new interprogram drag-and-drop capability that lets you select things in one program and then drag those items (or copies of those items) to another window—even in another application. This is another feature that does not use the Clipboard. (See "Drag-and-Drop," later in this chapter.)

Finally, there's Object Linking and Embedding, which you'll learn about later in this book. Object Linking and Embedding is the best technique to use when you're dealing with information that you want to update continually and keep current in multiple files.

But for simple, occasional movement of text and graphics, you can't beat the plain old Clipboard.

beaten path, the more likely you are to have problems. When pasting from a non-Windows program into a Windows program, you may need to experiment, and possibly even do some manual reformatting to obtain the desired results.

Using the Clipboard to Cut, Copy, and Paste

As you may already know, you place things on the Clipboard by first *selecting* them, then either *copying* or *cutting* the selected items to the Clipboard. Once an item has been placed on the Clipboard, you can move or copy it elsewhere by *pasting* it.

NOTE   **Techniques that vary among the Office applications (such as selecting) are explained fully in the application-specific sections of this book. Please refer to Chapters 4–12 for information on Word, Chapters 13–23 for Excel, Chapters 24–28 for PowerPoint, Chapters 29 and 30 for Mail, and Chapters 31–41 for Access.**

The Clipboard is a *temporary* storage area, and its contents are *replaced* each time you copy or cut something new. There is only *one* Clipboard in Windows, even if you are running multiple programs in 386 Enhanced mode. Thus, if you are using Word and you copy something (say, a paragraph), then switch to Excel and copy something else (like a formula), when you switch back to Word, your Clipboard will contain the formula but *not* the paragraph. The paragraph will be in paragraph heaven. Even the Undo command usually can't bring it back.

Clipboard contents also disappear whenever you quit Windows or turn off your computer. Clipboard contents can be saved to disk, however. This process is discussed later in this chapter.

Copying and Pasting Portions of a Window

The steps for copying are identical in Word, Excel, PowerPoint, and other well-designed Windows applications. The same is true of cutting and pasting. You can copy or cut (and then paste) text, graphics, other objects, or combinations thereof.

Start by selecting whatever it is you want to copy or cut, then choose Edit ➤ Copy or Edit ➤ Cut. (The keyboard shortcuts for copying and cutting are Ctrl+C and Ctrl+X, respectively.) The Copy command leaves the original item(s) intact and places a copy of the item(s) on the Clipboard.

Cut removes the selected item(s), placing the item(s) on the Clipboard. (Choosing Edit ➤ Undo *immediately* will usually restore items you've accidentally cut.)

When you choose the Paste command (Edit ➤ Paste, or Ctrl+V), the contents of the Clipboard are inserted into the active document at the insertion point. If you are cutting or copying from one program (let's call it the *source* program) and pasting into another program (the *destination*), you'll need to have both programs running (or at least available) and then switch from the source to the destination program before pasting. In Windows 386 Enhanced mode this can be as easy as pressing the Alt+Tab key combination repeatedly until you see the name of the program you want to use. You can also arrange your screen so that you can see both programs' windows, then just point to the one you want to paste into. When running in Standard mode, however, you will need to quit the source program and load the destination program. Ah, progress...

Exactly what happens when you paste depends upon a number of factors. First of all, not every application can accept everything you might place on the Clipboard. If you try to paste a graphic into a Windows program that cannot accept graphics, for instance, you will fail.

Typically, you'll want to paste things into applications that use different formats and formatting commands. Sometimes Windows and the programs you are using can work around these differences; other times they can't. Occasionally, the results are better than you might expect. For instance, when you copy a range of cells from an Excel worksheet into a Word document, Word automatically creates a table of the appropriate size to accommodate the contents of the pasted cells. Figure 3.1 illustrates this.

Sometimes, the results of pasting can be downright mysterious. For example, pasted items may look bizarre because they don't fit the destination document's margins or styles. Occasionally, pasted items will look fine when you view them on-screen, then have line- and page-ending problems when you print them. This usually happens because of differences in screen and printer fonts. Check your work after pasting and, as always, *save your work* before making major alterations with the Paste command.

TIP   Some programs (like Word and Excel) have AutoFormat commands. Try using these to reformat items that don't look right after pasting. And be patient when you paste between programs. It can take a moment or two—your machine may only <u>appear</u> to be locked up.

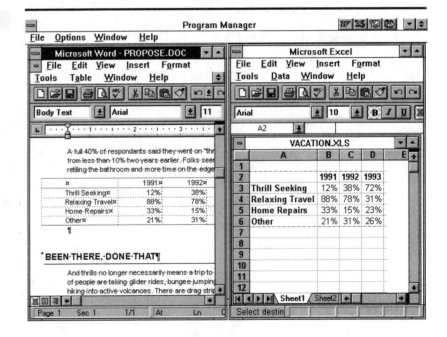

The Paste Special Command

While the regular Paste command is often all you'll need, sometimes the Edit menu's Paste Special command proves useful.

When you copy or cut things to the Clipboard, the source program often sends the information to the Clipboard in more than one format. When you use the Paste command, the destination application pastes the Clipboard contents using *its* default format, which is often—but not always—the best format.

The Paste Special command provides you with a dialog box containing an ever-changing list of data types. For instance, when the Clipboard contains a bitmapped graphic, you might see choices like *Picture* and *Microsoft Drawing Object*. If the Clipboard contains text, you're likely to see choices like *Microsoft Word Object*, *Formatted Text*, *Unformatted Text*, and so on.

Choosing one of these different formats changes the way the item is pasted, thereby converting the Clipboard contents when you paste. Pick the desired format from the list, then click Paste to place a converted copy of the item at the insertion point. (The Paste Link options that sometimes appear are discussed later in this chapter.)

Copying and Pasting an Entire Screen or Window

When your applications permit, you can copy the entire contents of your screen or just the contents of the active window to the Clipboard as a bitmapped graphic. This is a quick-and-dirty way to create illustrations for programming documentation. While the illustrations may lack much of the sophistication of true screen captures, you may find the trick useful.

Actual steps will vary from program to program. Generally, to begin, make sure that the screen contains exactly what you wish to capture. Next, press the PrtSc key (Print Screen) on your keyboard, or perhaps Alt+PrtSc or Shift+PrtSc on some keyboards. (Some keyboard types require Shift or Alt combinations since they don't recognize plain PrtSc or Alt+PrtSc combinations.) This should capture the entire screen. Try either Shift+PrtSc or Alt+PrtSc to capture just the active window rather than the entire screen. To see what works, use the Clipboard Viewer accessory program, described in the next section.

Once you've placed a bitmapped image on the Clipboard, you can paste it to any application that accepts bitmaps, including Word, Excel, and PowerPoint. (Using screen dumps like these with Excel's and PowerPoint's slide show features can help you create simple training slide shows.)

The Clipboard Viewer

The Windows Clipboard Viewer lets you see what's on the Clipboard. You can save the Clipboard contents to disk, retrieve previously saved Clipboard files, and clear the Clipboard. The Clipboard Viewer is normally found in the Program Manager's Main group (its icon looks like a tiny clipboard). Figure 3.2 shows how the Clipboard Viewer displays different types of Clipboard contents.

TIP If you find the Clipboard Viewer very useful, you may want to place it in your Windows StartUp group. That way, it will be loaded automatically each time you start Windows.

Viewing in Different Formats

The Clipboard Viewer's Display menu often lets you view text, graphics, and most other items in a variety of different formats. The Owner option shows the item as it would appear in the program that created it. Other viewing options vary with the item being viewed. To return to the format that was displayed when you opened the Viewer, choose Display ➤ Auto.

Saving Clipboard Contents to Disk

You can save Clipboard contents as disk files by using the Save As command on the Clipboard Viewer's File menu. You'll see a Save As dialog box. Get in the habit of noticing where Windows intends to save the file. Change the path if you like. Clipboard files are normally saved with the extension .CLP. It's a good idea to stick with this extension, to facilitate searches for an elusive file.

FIGURE 3.2

The Clipboard Viewer lets you esamine the contents fo the Clipboard.

Retrieving Clipboard Files

The File ➤ Open command in the Clipboard Viewer will bring up a standard Open dialog box and let you pick files saved with the Clipboard Viewer's Save As command. When you open a saved Clipboard file this way, the existing contents of the Clipboard will be replaced with the contents of the newly opened file. You will have the opportunity to confirm that that's OK.

Clearing the Clipboard's Contents

Sometimes you'll want to clear the contents of the Clipboard. If the Clipboard contains a large item in several formats, this is a way to free up RAM.

To clear the Clipboard, first display its contents with the Clipboard Viewer. Then press the Del key, or use the lonely Delete command on the Edit menu. There's no Undo command, so think twice or thrice before you delete.

 To remove a large item from the Clipboard without running the Clipboard Viewer, you can copy something small to the Clipboard. For example, you can select a single space in a Word document and copy that to the Clipboard, and it will remove whatever was there before.

Using the Clipboard with Non-Windows Applications

It is often possible to paste non-Windows items into Windows documents and vice versa. The steps are only slightly more involved than moving things between two Windows programs. You use additional commands found on the Control menu when running a non-Windows program in a DOS window. For instance, in Figure 3.3 I used the DOS command **TYPE README.TXT** to place some DOS text on the screen in a DOS window. Then I copied a portion of the text to the Clipboard and pasted it into Word for Windows. The specific steps involved are explained below.

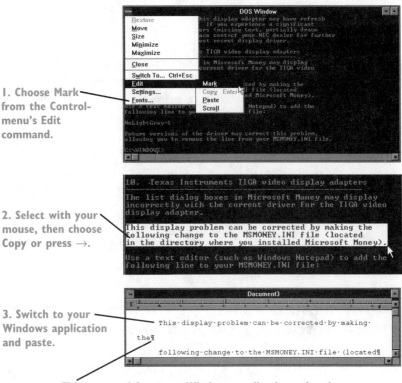

FIGURE 3.3

It is often possible to move things to and from non-Windows programs via the Clipboard.

Office

1. Choose Mark from the Control-menu's Edit command.

2. Select with your mouse, then choose Copy or press →.

3. Switch to your Windows application and paste.

Things pasted from non-Windows applications often have unwanted carriage returns that will need to be edited

Copying and Pasting Non-Windows Items to Windows

Here are the general steps for copying non-Windows items to a Windows application in 386 Enhanced mode:

1. Run the DOS program in a window (press Alt+↵, if necessary).

2. Choose Edit from the window's control menu.

3. Choose Mark from the submenu.

4. Select the item(s) in the DOS window that you want to copy.

5. Press ↵ to copy the item(s) to the Clipboard.

6. Switch to your Windows application and choose Edit ➤ Paste (or Ctrl+V).

TIP

Unless your non-Windows application uses the Alt+spacebar key combination for something else, you can often use Alt+spacebar to bring up the non-Windows Control menu. From there you should be able to reach the Edit command.

Notice that when you paste, things are not always exactly as you'd like them. At the bottom of Figure 3.3 the text came in just fine and was reformatted to match the Word document's current style (double-spaced Courier). But look at that paragraph mark (¶) smack in the middle of the sentence. That happens because there was a carriage return at that point in the DOS text to make it fit the DOS screen. You may need to correct things like this after you paste.

Copying and Pasting Windows Items to Non-Windows Applications

Not all non-Windows programs can accept formatted text or graphics. Check the documentation of your non-Windows applications, or experiment on non-critical copies of your DOS files.

Here are the general steps for copying and pasting to non-Windows applications, assuming that you are using 386 Enhanced mode:

1. Run the DOS program in a window (press Alt+↵, if necessary).

2. Run the Windows program that contains the items you want to paste.

3. Place the items of interest on the Clipboard (choose Edit ➤ Copy or Edit ➤ Cut).

4. Switch to the DOS window and place the insertion point or its equivalent where you want the items to be inserted.

5. Choose Edit from the window's Control menu.

6. Choose Paste from the submenu, and see what happens...

Drag-and-Drop

With Microsoft's drag-and-drop feature (once a Word-only tool) you can move or copy items by selecting them with your mouse and then dragging them from place to place on your screen. Drag-and-drop now lets you drag selected items from one window to another, even between applications. Here are the steps:

1. Arrange the source and destination windows on your screen so that you can see both.

2. Select the item or items you want to move or copy.

3. Point to the selected object you wish to move or copy. If you're in Excel, point to the edge of the selected area so that the mouse pointer becomes an arrow.

4. To *move* the selected item, hold down the primary mouse button and drag into the destination window. To *copy the selected item, hold down the Ctrl key while you drag. The mouse pointer will change shape (it will have a small box added to it when you move, or a box and a plus sign when you copy).*

5. Point to the desired destination location and release the mouse button. Be patient. In a moment the item will move.

Drag-and-drop will work with most applications that support Object Linking and Embedding. It might even work with non-Microsoft programs. Try it.

TIP Drag-and-drop is turned on when you first install most Microsoft applications, but many programs let you turn it off since some people don't like it. Check the Options settings if you are having trouble with drag-and-drop. For instance, the Edit tab in Excel's Options dialog box contains its drag-and-drop control. Check online Help for assistance.

The Insert File Command

Microsoft Word has an Insert File command (Insert ➤ File) that lets you import documents. Imported text is placed at the insertion point in the destination file. If you have installed the necessary filters, Word will even convert non-Word documents, maintaining much of the original formatting.

A Whole New Way to Work

Throughout this book you will find sidebars that demonstrate how the Office applications work together. These examples illustrate why Microsoft has dubbed Office "A Whole New Way to Work."

To make it easier for you to locate topics and turn straight to the examples you need, Table 3.1 lists these sidebars by title and page number. The icons in the table show you which applications are involved in the example.

TABLE 3.1: A Whole New Index of Sidebars

Applications	Sidebar	Page
🇼 🇽 🇵 🇲 🇦	Which Application Should You Use?	5
	Alternatives to the Clipboard	43
🇼	Linking Multiple Word Documents	111
🇼 🇽 🇵 🇲 🇦	OLE Tips for Word	132
🇼 🇽	Creating Excel Tables in Word Documents	227
🇼	Special Effects with WordArt	264
🇼	Creating Vertical Text	270
🇽 🇵 🇲 🇦	Spelling in Other Office Applications	300

TABLE 3.1: A Whole New Way to Work: Index of Sidebars

Applications	Sidebar	Page
	Creating Presentations from Word Outlines	323
	Planning Your Data Document	382
	Using Excel Worksheets with Mail Merge	388
	Using Word Text in Excel Worksheets	428
	OLE Tips for Excel	520
	WordArt in Excel Worksheets	574
	Troubleshooting OLE Links	632
	OLE Tips for PowerPoint	644
	Converting PowerPoint Slides to Word Reports	681
	Word Tables in PowerPoint	701
	Excel Charts in PowerPoint	717

PART TWO

Word Processing with Word for Windows

In this part you'll learn a lot about using Word for Windows, perhaps the most important program in the Office package. Version 6 of this word-processing application is a major upgrade to an already full-featured program. If you have already used a previous version, you'll find a lot here to make your work even easier and faster.

Word Toolbar Reference

BUTTON	DESCRIPTION

Buttons on Word's Standard Toolbar

Opens a new document. [File ➤ New] *Shortcut:* Ctrl+N

Opens an existing document. [File ➤ Open] *Shortcut:* Ctrl+O or Ctrl+F12

Saves your work. [File ➤ Save] *Shortcut:* Ctrl+S or Shift+F12

Prints one copy using default settings. [Similar, but not identical to, File ➤ Print]

Switches to Print Preview. [File ➤ Print Preview] *Shortcut:* Ctrl+F2 or Alt+Ctrl+i

Checks spelling. [Tools ➤ Spelling] *Shortcut:* F7

Cuts selected material and places it on the Clipboard. [Edit ➤ Cut] *Shortcut:* Ctrl+X or Shift+Delete

Copies selected items to Clipboard. [Edit ➤ Copy] *Shortcut:* Ctrl+C or Ctrl+Insert

Pastes (inserts) Clipboard contents at insertion point. [Edit ➤ Paste] *Shortcut:* Ctrl+V or Shift+Insert

Copies character formatting.

Provides a list of actions that can be undone. [Similar, but not identical to, Edit ➤ Undo] *Shortcut:* Ctrl+Z or Alt+Backspace

Provides a list of actions that can be redone. [Similar, but not identical to, Edit ➤ Redo] *Shortcut:* Ctrl+Y or Alt+Enter

Automatically formats the document. [Format ➤ AutoFormat]

BUTTON	DESCRIPTION

Buttons on Word's Standard Toolbar (continued)

Creates or inserts AutoText entries. [Similar, but not identical to, Edit ➤ AutoText] *Shortcut:* F3 or Alt+Ctrl+V

Inserts (helps you create) new tables. [Table ➤ Insert Table]

Inserts MS Excel worksheet objects. [Insert ➤ Object ➤ Microsoft Excel 5.0 Worksheet]

Lets you define number of text columns. [Similar, but not identical to, Format ➤ Columns]

Shows and hides the Drawing toolbar.

Lets you create new charts (MS Graph Objects). [Insert ➤ Object ➤ Microsoft Graph 5.0]

Toggles display of paragraph marks and other nonprinting characters.

(Help tool) Lets you point to see on-screen command help and text property information. *Shortcut:* Shift+F1

Buttons on Word's Drawing Toolbar

Creates straight lines.

Creates rectangles.

Creates ellipses.

Creates arcs.

Creates freeform shapes.

Word Toolbar Reference

BUTTON	DESCRIPTION
Buttons on Word's Drawing Toolbar (continued)	

Creates text boxes.

Creates callouts.

Lets you format callouts.

Lets you choose fill colors.

Lets you choose line colors.

Lets you choose line styles.

Lets you select drawing objects or surround objects by dragging.

Brings selected drawn objects forward.

Moves selected drawn objects back.

Brings selected objects in front of text.

Moves selected drawn objects behind text.

Groups selected items.

Ungroups selected items.

Flips selected items from left to right (horizontally).

Flips selected items from top to bottom (vertically).

Rotates selected objects 90 degrees to the right.

Lets you reshape freeform objects by dragging points.

Establishes a grid to which objects are attracted.

BUTTON	DESCRIPTION

Buttons on Word's Drawing Toolbar (continued)

Aligns multiple drawn objects.

Opens a new picture object window or inserts selected drawing into a picture object.

Inserts a new frame or encloses selected objects in a frame. [Insert ➤ Frame]

Buttons on Word's Formatting Toolbar

Toggles Bold formatting. [Format ➤ Font ➤ Bold (on Font Style list)] *Shortcut:* Ctrl+B or Ctrl+Shift+B

Toggles Italic formatting. [Format ➤ Font ➤ Italic (on Font Style list)] *Shortcut:* Ctrl+i or Ctrl+Shift+i

Toggles single underline formatting. [Format ➤ Font ➤ Single (on Underline list)] *Shortcut:* Ctrl+U or Ctrl+Shift+U

Makes selected paragraph(s) left-aligned. [Format ➤ Paragraph ➤ Left (on Alignment list)] *Shortcut:* Ctrl+←

Centers selected paragraph(s). [Format ➤ Paragraph ➤ Centered (on Alignment list)] *Shortcut:* Ctrl+E

Makes selected paragraph(s) right-aligned. [Format ➤ Paragraph ➤ Right (on Alignment list)] *Shortcut:* Ctrl+R

Aligns (justifies) left and right sides of selected paragraph(s). [Format ➤ Paragraph ➤ Justified (on Alignment list)] *Shortcut:* Ctrl+J

Creates numbered lists. [Similar, but not identical to, Format ➤ Bullets and Numbering (Numbered tab)]

Word Toolbar Reference

BUTTON	DESCRIPTION

Buttons on Word's Formatting Toolbar (continued)

Creates bulleted lists. [Similar, but not identical to, Format ➤ Bullets and Numbering (Bulleted tab)] *Shortcut:* Ctrl+Shift+L

Decreases indent or promotes headings one level. *Shortcut:* Ctrl+Shift+M

Increases indent or demotes headings one level. *Shortcut:* Ctrl+M

Shows and hides the Borders toolbar.

Buttons on Word's Borders Toolbar

Changes top border of selected item(s). [Format ➤ Borders and Shading ➤ Borders tab]

Changes bottom border of selected item(s). [Format ➤ Borders and Shading ➤ Borders tab]

Changes left border of selected item(s). [Format ➤ Borders and Shading ➤ Borders tab]

Changes right border of selected item(s). [Format ➤ Borders and Shading ➤ Borders tab]

Changes inside border(s) of selected item(s). [Format ➤ Borders and Shading ➤ Borders tab]

Changes outside (surrounding) border of selected item(s). [Format ➤ Borders and Shading ➤ Borders tab]

Removes borders from selected item(s). [Format ➤ Borders and Shading ➤ Borders tab ➤ None]

BUTTON	DESCRIPTION

Buttons on Word's Forms Toolbar

Button	Description
ab	Inserts a text field.
☒	Creates a box field.
	Creates a drop-down field.
	Displays the Text Forms Field Options dialog box.
	Inserts a new table. [Table ➤ Insert Table]
	Inserts a frame. [Insert ➤ Frame]
	Lets you shade fields.
	Lets you protect forms. [Tools ➤ Protect Document ➤ Forms option]

Buttons on Word's Database Toolbar

Button	Description
	Edits or creates a data form from a list or table.
	Lets you add, remove, or rename fields.
	Adds a new, blank record to a database.
	Deletes selected records from a database.
	Sorts lists in ascending order.
	Sorts lists in descending order.
	Inserts a database. [Insert ➤ Database]
	Updates selected fields. *Shortcut:* F9 or Alt+Shift+U

Word Toolbar Reference

BUTTON	DESCRIPTION

Buttons on Word's Database Toolbar (continued)

	Displays Find In Field dialog box.
	Switches to a mail merge main document.

Buttons on Word's MailMerge Toolbar

	Toggles between displaying merge fields and actual data.
	Displays your first record from the data source.
	Takes you to the previous record in the data source.
	Takes you to the next record in the data source.
	Takes you to the last record in the data source.
	Runs Mail Merge Helper and creates a main document. [Tools ➤ Mail Merge]
	Checks for mail merge errors. *Shortcut:* Alt+Shift+K
	Merges to a new Word document. *Shortcut:* Alt+Shift+N
	Merges to your printer. *Shortcut:* Alt+Shift+M
	Displays the Merge dialog box.
	Displays the Find In Field dialog box.
	Opens or takes you to the data source for editing. *Shortcut:* Alt+Shift+E

4

Word Basics

Y ou'd be hard-pressed to name a word-processing feature not included in Microsoft Word for Windows version 6. Usually, Word provides two or three different ways to accomplish the same task. Beginners will find the program easy to use and very logically organized. Power users will discover new capabilities and possibilities each time they run it. So whether you are a first-time word-processing novice or a battle-scarred WordStar and WordPerfect pro, you won't be disappointed. Let's take a look.

Starting Word

To start Word, click the Word button in the Office Manager toolbar or double-click on the Word program icon in Windows. Figure 4.1 shows both options.

You can also switch to File Manager and double-click on a Word for Windows *document* icon to start Word:

This will launch Word and immediately open the document so you can get right to work.

FIGURE 4.1

To start Word, click on the Office Manager's Word button or double-click on the Word program icon.

Double-click on the Word program icon to start Word

You can also click on the Office Manager's Word button to start Word

 TIP

If you always work on the same document or same type of document, put a copy of the document's icon (or template icon) in your Windows StartUp folder. Then, each time you start Windows, it will start Word and open the desired document or document template.

Your final option is to start Word and Windows from the DOS prompt by typing **win**, any necessary pathnames, and an optional document file name. For example, if you wanted to use a document called CLIENTS.DOC from your EXAMPLES directory you could type:

```
C:\WIN \WINWORD\ EXAMPLES CLIENTS.DOC┘
```

Notice the required spaces after the program names WIN and WINWORD.

Tip of the Day

You will see a Tip of the Day (shown in Figure 4.2) each time you start Word. Most are very useful; a few are even entertaining. Click OK when you've finished reading the tip. You can see additional tips by clicking the appropriate buttons in the Tip of the Day window. To stop tips from appearing, click in the Show Tips at Startup box to remove the X. You can see tips any time you like by choosing Tip of the Day from Word's Help menu.

Creating New Documents When Word Is Running

Whenever you start Word for Windows, it opens a new, untitled, "normal" document so that you can begin a new project from scratch (unless you specified a Word file name or double-clicked a document icon to start Word). If you want to start a new project with Word already running, simply choose File ➤ New. You will see the New dialog box shown in Figure 4.3.

Word gives you a choice of document templates and Word Wizards designed to minimize repetitive formatting tasks. You'll learn more about templates and Wizards in Chapter 9.

FIGURE 4.3

The New dialog box

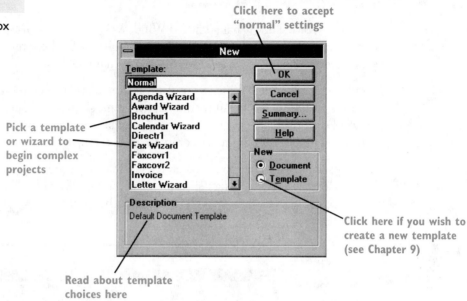

Click here to accept "normal" settings

Pick a template or wizard to begin complex projects

Click here if you wish to create a new template (see Chapter 9)

Read about template choices here

If you simply click OK, Word will open a new, untitled document window using the standard or "normal" settings. Each new window opened this way in a session is sequentially numbered (Document1, Document2, and so on).

TIP You can also open a new, untitled document window by pressing Ctrl+N or by clicking on the dog-eared–document icon located on the Standard toolbar.

Opening Preexisting Documents when Word Is Running

To open a Word document when Word for Windows is running, choose File ➤ Open. Use the drop-down list below the scrollable list to open the appropriate disk or scroll through the directory list. Double-click on the desired file name to open the document.

The Parts of a Word Window

An active Word window has standard Windows scroll bars, a title bar, zoom boxes, a menu bar, and so on. (If you are unfamiliar with these terms and concepts, take a moment to review your Windows manuals.)

In addition to the usual Windows tools, you should see a ruler, toolbar, a flashing insertion point, and possibly some of the items shown in Figure 4.4. Word for Windows now has many toolbars, and you may see up to eight at one time on-screen (although two is more common and practical).

You may see more or fewer buttons on the toolbar than those illustrated in Figure 4.4. Don't worry. The exact size and shape of your Word for Windows workspace will vary with your screen size and other factors.

FIGURE 4.4

The Word workspace

The Menu Bar

Normally, the top of your screen will contain traditional Windows-style menus in a menu bar. When you point to a menu title with the mouse pointer and click once, the menu will drop. Clicking on the desired command in a menu tells Word to execute that command. Commands with ellipses (...) after their names will ask you for additional information before they go to work. Dimmed commands cannot be used until other functions have been performed.

Many commands can be executed by holding down specific key combinations (often called *hot keys*). As with other Windows programs, these keyboard shortcuts are usually listed next to command names in menus. For instance holding down the Ctrl key and pressing the P key is the same as choosing File ➤ Print.

The Mouse Pointer

Your mouse pointer should look like an I-beam and you should be able to move it freely about the screen. The pointer will change shapes when it passes over certain parts of the Word for Windows workplace. For instance, it turns into a large arrow at the edges of Word windows.

The Insertion Point

The *insertion point* or cursor denotes where text, graphics, and other items will be placed when you type or insert them. The insertion point is a tall, skinny, blinking vertical stick.

  Beginners sometimes forget to press the mouse button after pointing with the I-beam. Don't confuse the I-beam with the insertion point! First you use the I-beam to point to where you want the insertion point placed. Then you must press and release the mouse button to move the insertion point.

Toolbars

Word for Windows provides over a dozen different toolbars, although you'll normally display only two or three at any one time. Microsoft's "factory settings" display only the Standard and Formatting toolbars (shown in Figure 4.4). The other toolbars include:

- Standard
- Formatting
- Borders

- Database
- Drawing
- Forms
- Microsoft
- Word for Windows 2.0

Toolbars contain buttons, drop-down menus, and other controls that help you quickly alter the appearance and arrangement of documents by executing a variety of Word for Windows commands.

For example, you can use the Formatting toolbar's Bold button to make text bold, or its drop-down font menus to pick a font and size. Point to the buttons containing arrows (next to the font and type size menus) to see drop-down lists of choices. You can also type font names or sizes directly into the font and size boxes.

The paragraph mark (¶) button (shown at left) on the Standard toolbar alternately shows and hides paragraph marks, tab marks, space marks (the little dots), and other nonprinting items.

You can display any available toolbar by right-clicking on any toolbar displayed on your screen and selecting the toolbar from the drop-down menu that appears.

The Ruler

The ruler lets you quickly change margins and indents. The ruler lets you alter the appearance of multiple paragraphs or just the paragraph containing the insertion point. To display or hide the ruler, choose View ➤ Ruler.

Status Area

The *status area* at the bottom of your Word window gives additional information about your work. It's always present unless you choose the Full Screen view.

Designing Your Document

You should start each new project by thinking about the document's overall design and final appearance. Word for Windows gives you on-screen clues about how your document will look on paper. If you give Word some basic information, such as the paper size and kind of printer you will be using, it can show you line endings, page endings, the relative size and placement of text, graphics, margins, and so on. In order to do this, Word needs some information from you—such as the paper size and kind of printer you will be using. The Page Setup dialog box, shown in Figure 4.5, allows you to give Word all the information it needs.

FIGURE 4.5

The Page Setup
dialog box

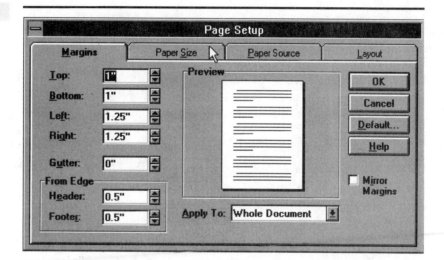

To display the Page Setup dialog box, choose File ➤ Page Setup. Click on the tabs at the top of the dialog box to see additional choices. Type new settings in the text boxes or click on the arrows and other tools to make changes. Once you tell Word your desires, it changes the on-screen appearance of margins, the ruler, and other settings to accommodate and reflect your design.

It is always a good idea to input (at least preliminary) printer, paper, margin, and other document-design decisions before you start typing.

Typing Text

Don't worry if you make typing mistakes; they are easy to fix. Watch the screen as you type. Notice that when you reach the end of a line, Word for Windows automatically begins a new line for you.

This feature is called automatic word wrap, and it eliminates the need to press ↵ until you want to start a new paragraph.

America·is·restless.·In·a·recent·survey·of·10,000·people·between·the·ages·of·
21·and·65·it·became·clear·that·we·all·like·to·get·that·adrenaline·flowing.·Take·
a·look·at·these·fascinating·survey·results:¶
¶

Typing Habits to Break

If you learned to type on a typewriter or even an old word processor, chances are you have established habits that will be counterproductive in your use of Word for Windows. Here are a few habits you should try to break:

- Do not use the Tab key or the spacebar to indent paragraphs. Instead, use the indent control in Word's ruler (the top "handle" at the left side of the ruler).

- Never use the spacebar to center or otherwise position text. Use the center-alignment button on the Standard toolbar instead.

- Don't use the spacebar to make columns. Instead use tabs, Word's multi-column features, or tables.

- Do not manually space paragraphs with carriage returns. Use Word's paragraph spacing instead.

- Do not hit ↵ repeatedly to start a new page. Instead, use Word's Insert Page Break command.

Selecting Text

Word lets you do a lot with text after you've typed it. You can change its appearance, move it around, delete it, and copy it. The first step is *always* to tell Word which text you want to work with. This is done by *selecting* it. Word has many, many ways to select text. For instance, you can drag your mouse pointer over the text while holding down the primary mouse button. There are shortcuts for selecting individual words, lines, sentences, and paragraphs, which you will read about in a moment.

Depending on your system configuration, selected text will either change color or be surrounded by a gray or black background. That's how you know what you have selected. If you are a new Windows user, practice selecting other words, sentences, and single characters with the mouse.

Selecting with a Mouse

It is easy to select different blocks of text and even graphics with the mouse. Here are the techniques:

Selecting Entire Words

Double-click anywhere on a word to select the entire word and the space that follows it:

America·is·restless.·In·a·recent·survey·of·10,000·people·between·the·ages·of·
21·and·65·it·became·clear·that·we·all·like·to·get·that·adrenaline·flowing.··Take·
a·look·at·these·fascinating·survey·results:¶
¶

To select adjacent words, drag after double-clicking on the first word of interest. Entire words will be selected when you drag this way.

Selecting Entire Lines

To select entire lines, follow these steps:

1. Move the mouse pointer to the *selection bar* (an invisible strip running down the extreme left edge of the document window). The mouse pointer will change from the I-beam to an arrow.

America·is·restless.·In·a·recent·survey·of·10,000·people·between·the·ages·of·21·and·65·it·became·clear·that·we·all·like·to·get·that·adrenaline·flowing.·Take·a·look·at·these·fascinating·survey·results:¶
¶

2. Click the primary mouse button only once. The entire *line* to the right of where you've clicked will be selected.

Continue dragging down to select additional lines.

Selecting Entire Sentences

Hold down the Ctrl key while you click anywhere in the sentence of interest:

This also selects the sentence's punctuation mark and the space following the sentence, if there is one. Drag after you click this way to select additional sentences.

Selecting Entire Paragraphs

The quickest way to select a paragraph with your mouse is to *triple-click* anywhere in the paragraph. Point anywhere in the paragraph and quickly press and release the mouse button three times in succession. Use the following steps to select paragraphs using the selection bar.

1. Move the mouse pointer to the selection bar (the invisible strip running down the extreme left edge of the document window). The pointer will become an arrow.

2. Double-click. The adjacent paragraph will be selected.

Selecting Your Entire Document

To select the entire document, follow these steps:

1. Move the mouse pointer to the selection bar at the left edge of the document and the pointer will become an arrow.

2. Hold down the Ctrl key and click. The entire document will be selected. Alternately, you can triple-click on the selection bar to select the whole document.

Selecting Graphics and Other Objects

Click anywhere within the graphic or other object. You'll see a border—usually with *handles* (small black boxes) surrounding the selected object:

America·is·restless.·In·a·recent·survey·of·10,000·people·between·the·ages·of· 21·and·65·it·became·clear·that·we·all·like·to·get·that·adrenaline·flowing.·Take· a·look·at·these·fascinating·survey·results:¶

Selecting Variable Units of Text

Sometimes you'll want to select just a single character or parts of a text string. Here are some techniques to use.

Dragging to Select   To select adjacent bits of text, follow these steps:

1. Point to the place where you want selection to begin.

2. Hold down the primary mouse button and drag in any direction.

3. When the pointer hits a screen boundary (top, bottom, or side) the document will scroll as highlighting continues.

4. Release the mouse button when you've selected the desired area.

 Word now provides an option called Automatic Word Select. You select as many or as few characters of the first word you want to change. Then, when you drag over to the next word, the <u>entire</u> second word is selected. <u>You must hold down Alt to select partial words</u> when Automatic Word Select is on (and it is on by default). You can turn this option off in the Edit tab in the Options dialog box (select Tools ➤ Options to display the Options dialog box).

Shift-Clicking to Select Large Areas   To select large blocks of continuous text, follow these steps:

1. Point to the place where you want selection to begin.

2. Click to place the insertion point there.

3. Point to the end of the desired area (scroll if necessary) and press Shift while you click.

4. Release the mouse button.

Selecting Rectangular Areas

To select rectangular areas (like columns in a tabbed list), hold down the Alt key while you drag the mouse.

Selecting in Tables

You can select characters, words, and other items in table cells using Word's usual mouse and keyboard features. In addition, Word also provides *table-specific* selection tools enabling you to choose whole cells, entire rows, columns, or areas.

Selecting Single Cells   The area between the first character in a cell and the left edge of the cell is called the *cell selection bar*. Click on it to select the contents of the entire cell. You can also select an entire cell by dragging with the mouse. Just be sure you include the end-of-cell mark in your selection.

Selecting Columns   To select a column, move the mouse pointer to the area at the top of a column called the *column selection bar*. You'll know you've arrived when the pointer changes into a large, down-pointing arrow. Click to select the entire column.

Holding down the Alt key while clicking anywhere in a column will also select the entire column. Selecting the bottom or top cell in a column and dragging up or down is somewhat tedious, but will also work.

Selecting Rows   Double-clicking any cell selection bar will select the entire row. You can also select the left-most or right-most cell in a row and drag it.

Selecting Adjacent Groups of Cells   To select groups of adjacent cells, either drag through the cells or click in one cell and Shift+click in the others.

Selecting the Whole Table   To select an entire table, hold down the Alt key and double-click anywhere in the table. If your document contains multiple tables and they are not separated by paragraph marks, this technique will select all adjacent tables.

Do *not* use Word's Select All command to select a table, since this will also select paragraph marks and other things *outside* of the table.

Word

Selecting with the Keyboard

You can also select text with keyboard shortcuts. Here's a summary of the shortcuts:

TO INCREASE A SELECTION...	PRESS...
one character to the right of the insertion point	Shift+→
one character to the left of the insertion point	Shift+←
to the start of a word	Ctrl+Shift+←
to the end of a word	Ctrl+Shift+→
to the start of a line	Shift+Home
down one line	Shift+↓
up one line	Shift+↑
to the end of a paragraph	Ctrl+Shift+↓
to the start of a paragraph	Ctrl+Shift+↑
down one screen	Shift+PgDn
up one screen	Shift+PgUp
to the document's end	Ctrl+Shift+End
to the start of the document	Ctrl+Shift+Home
to a vertical block of text	Ctrl+Shift+F8 and arrow keys

 TIP To select an entire document, use the Ctrl+A keyboard shortcut.

Deleting Text

There are several ways to delete unwanted text. If you spot a mistake right after typing it, pressing the backspace key will remove unwanted characters and spaces. You can also delete text by selecting it and then pressing the Delete key or by using the Clear command on Word's Edit menu.

Undo

Word watches as you work. It remembers which steps you last took. When asked, it can frequently undo your errors. The exact name of the Undo choice on the Edit menu changes as you work. Sometimes it says Undo Typing. Other times it says Undo Formatting (see Figure 4.6) or Undo Sort, or some such.

Edit	
Undo Formatting	**Ctrl+Z**
Repeat Formatting	**Ctrl+Y**
Cut	Ctrl+X
Copy	Ctrl+C
Paste	**Ctrl+V**
Paste Special...	
Clear	**Delete**
Select All	**Ctrl+A**
Find...	**Ctrl+F**
Replace...	**Ctrl+H**
Go To...	**Ctrl+G**
AutoText...	
Bookmark...	
Links...	
Object	

There are three ways to undo:

- Edit ➤ Undo reverses your last action; choose Edit ➤ Undo again to reverse the action before that, and so on.
- If you press Ctrl+Z repeatedly, it will reverse previous actions.

■ The Undo toolbar button and its associated drop-down list menu let you undo multiple actions in sequence.

To undo multiple actions or selected actions, use the drop-down list reached with the button shown at left.

1. Reveal the list by pointing to and clicking on the Undo list arrow.

The last thing you've done will be on the top of the list.

2. Click on an item to undo it, or drag to select and undo a sequence of actions.

3. If you accidentally undo the wrong things, use the Redo list to the right of the Undo list to undo your Undo.

Redo

Use the Redo command to undo an Undo. To redo your last action only, choose Edit ➤ Redo, press the keyboard shortcut (F4), or click the Redo button on the Standard toolbar.

To redo multiple actions or selected actions, use the drop-down list reached with the button shown at left.

1. Reveal the list by pointing to the Redo list arrow. The last thing you've undone will be on the top of the list.

2. Click on an item to redo (undo the Undo) or drag to select a sequence of actions.

3. If you accidentally redo the wrong things, use the Undo list to the right of the Redo list to undo your Redo.

Occasionally, you will see a Can't Undo message indicating that your most recent action cannot be undone. That's why it is a good idea to save your work early and often.

Repeat

Sometimes, after you've done something repeatable (like formatting or typing) you will find a Repeat command on Word's Edit menu. The shortcut is the F4 function key. Repeat watches you work and attempts to remember and recreate your actions on demand.

Like Undo, Repeat's name changes depending on what you have last done, and it works with most Word for Windows actions immediately after you take them. Experiment.

TIP There are often better ways to repeat actions. For instance, Word provides a format "paintbrush" that you may find easier to use when repeating format changes. (See Chapter 5 for details of the Format Painter feature.)

Inserting Text

Word offers several ways to insert new text into an existing document. The most straightforward approach is to move the insertion point to the desired location and start typing. Word accommodates the new text by pushing the existing text to the right and down as necessary.

You start by placing the mouse pointer (the I-beam) where you want to begin inserting text. Next, press and release the mouse button to move the insertion point to the desired position.

Replacing Text

Word can combine the steps of deleting unwanted text, positioning the insertion point, and inserting replacement text. Highlight the unwanted text and start typing. The old text disappears and the new text snakes across the screen as you type it.

Formatting Text

Let's take a quick look at a few of Word's most often used ways to modify the appearance of text. They include toolbars, menus, and keyboard shortcuts. See Chapter 5 for a more complete discussion of Word's formatting capabilities.

Using the Formatting Toolbar

Word's Formatting toolbar contains a number of text formatting buttons. To see a button's function, move the mouse pointer over the button and hold it there momentarily. The button's name will appear, as shown in Figure 4.7.

Toolbars let you make style changes by clicking buttons or pulling down single-level menus, rather than going to the more crowded menu bar. As always, you must select text before working with it.

To change the appearance of characters (making them bold or italicized, for instance), first select them, then click the appropriate button on the Formatting toolbar.

Aligning Text with the Formatting Toolbar

Notice the group of four buttons to the right of the Underline button in the Formatting toolbar:

These let you specify left-aligned, centered, right-aligned, or fully justified text, respectively.

These paragraph formatting buttons and similar formatting tools work on entire paragraphs. Simply place the insertion point in the paragraph to be affected before using the button. To change multiple paragraphs simultaneously, select them first.

Copying and Moving

Word for Windows supports all of the usual Windows techniques for copying and moving information. It also provides a feature called *drag-and-drop*, a handy one-step, mouse-assisted mover.

Using Cut, Copy, and Paste

The traditional way to move or duplicate items in Windows programs is to select them, cut or copy them to the Clipboard, move the insertion point to the new position, and paste them in. You can even copy into different applications—from Word to Excel, for instance. See Chapter 3 for details.

1. Start by selecting the desired text.

2. Choose Edit ➤ Cut or press the Ctrl+X shortcut. You can also click the Cut button (shown here) on the Standard toolbar.

3. The selected text will disappear from the screen and will be placed on the Clipboard.

4. Now place the insertion point at the desired location (point and click).

5. Paste, using Edit ➤ Paste or the Ctrl+V shortcut. Text will flow to the right and down as the Clipboard's contents move into place. You can also click the Paste button (shown here) on the Standard toolbar.

Copying from One Word Document to Another

Since you can open and work on multiple Word documents at the same time, it is easy to move things from one document to another. First, arrange your workspace by clicking and dragging the size boxes in the lower-right corners of windows to adjust their size and shape. You can move windows around by pointing to their title bars and dragging them. Once you have arranged the windows to your liking, you can easily move back and forth simply by clicking in the window of interest. See Figure 4.8.

FIGURE 4.8

Arranging windows for easy access

While it is possible to have many windows in view at the same time, you can have only one *active* window. It is easy to tell which is the active window—it's the top one with the highlighted title bar.

See the sidebar "Linking Multiple Word Documents" at the end of this chapter for information on linking data in Word files.

Using Word's Window Menu

Sometimes your screen may not be big enough to display multiple Word documents in useful sizes. Word provides the Window menu for these instances. The Window menu lists the open documents and lets you switch between them. A checkmark indicates the active window. Using this menu, you can activate one window to copy information, go back to the Window menu to activate and display another window, and then paste.

TIP The Window menu's Arrange All command will display and arrange all open windows at once.

The contents of your Clipboard usually stay the same when you switch from program to program, as long as you do not turn off or restart your computer. Thus, you can copy items from a spreadsheet, quit the spreadsheet program, launch Word, and paste the spreadsheet information into your Word document. Or you can run more than one program at once and use the Clipboard to pass information back and forth without quitting any of the programs.

Advanced users will also want to explore other pasting options such as Object Linking and Embedding (OLE) and the Insert File command, explained in Chapter 3. These advanced techniques make it possible to keep multiple documents up-to-date when data change. See Part Seven for more information about OLE.

Word

Using Drag-and-Drop

Word's drag-and-drop feature lets you highlight text or other movable objects and drag them to a new location. To move text with drag-and-drop, follow these steps:

1. Select the desired text or other item.

2. Release the mouse button, if necessary, then point to the selected item(s) and press and hold down the mouse button. Watch the mouse pointer. It will change to look like the one in Figure 4.9.

FIGURE 4.9

The drag-and-drop mouse pointer

3. When you see the pointer change to its drag-and-drop shape, drag the pointer while holding down the mouse button until the insertion point is at the desired location.

4. Release the mouse button. The selected item should move.

5. Undo immediately (press Ctrl+Z) if things didn't go right.

Drag-and-drop copying works just like drag-and-drop moving, with one exception: You hold down the Ctrl key while you work.

Hotspots

You can bring up dialog boxes, windows, and other tools of interest by double-clicking at appropriate areas (called *hotspots*) in Word for Windows. Figure 4.10 shows many of them. There may even be some undocumented hotspots you can discover on your own.

FIGURE 4.10

Word's hotspots and
their functions

Opens Page Setup dialog box

Opens Indent and Spacing tab in
Paragraph dialog box

Toggles split window

Opens headers or footers

Opens footnote window

Opens
annotation
window

Allows you to
edit drawings

Opens
WordPerfect Help

Opens Section dialog box

Opens the Revisions
dialog box

Opens the Go To dialog box

Opens the application used to
create the object

Starts Macro Recorder

Page Setup Dialog Box Hotspot

If you click on the small square box at the right end of the Ruler, you'll see
the Document dialog box used to control header, footer, and other measurements precisely.

When in Page Layout view, if you double-click in the margins at the corners
of your document you will also see the Document dialog box.

Footnote Window Hotspots

To reveal a footnote window, simply double-click on a footnote reference mark.

The Go To Dialog Box Hotspot

To bring up the Go To dialog box, useful for navigating in big documents, double-click on a page or section number in the status area at the lower-left portion of the document window.

Section Hotspot

Double-click on section break marks to reveal the Page Setup dialog box. It contains section break information.

Mouse Shortcut Menus

Frequently, when you point to items on the screen and press the nonprimary (usually the right) mouse button, you'll see a shortcut menu of commands that you can issue with your mouse (see Figure 4.11).

The available choices change depending on what's selected and what's possible at the moment.

Navigating with Your Mouse

Word for Windows offers navigational tools that let you move quickly to the desired part of even huge documents. Several views make it easy to see what your document will look like without printing it. Other views are available to simplify and speed up the creation of rough drafts and outlines. In addition, you can hide and show elements such as paragraph marks (¶) and the little dots between words that denote spaces. Let's take a look at your scrolling options.

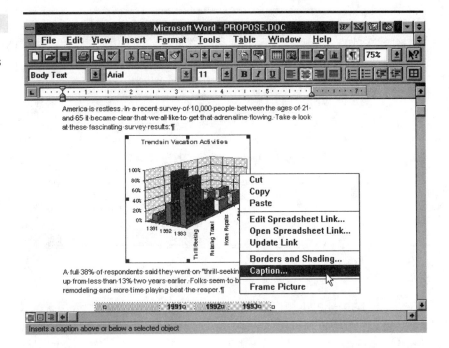

FIGURE 4.11

The mouse shortcut menus offer commands related to the object you right-click on. Here, the object is a spreadsheet link, so spreadsheet link–related commands appear on the shortcut menu.

Scrolling in a Window

Most documents are too big to be displayed in their entirety on your screen. You reveal unseen portions of your document by scrolling to bring parts of the document into view while temporarily hiding other parts. Usually, you'll scroll up and down to see long documents, but you will sometimes need to scroll left and right to see different parts of wide documents. There are many ways to scroll.

Scrolling with the Scroll Arrows

When you click on a scroll arrow you will see a different part of your document. For instance, suppose you are looking at page two of a three-page document. If you click on the up scroll arrow (located near the top-right of the active window), you will move a little nearer to the beginning of the document. See Figure 4.12.

Clicking on the down-pointing arrow will take you closer to the end of the document. (Typically, one click moves you up or down about one line.) The

FIGURE 4.12

Using the scroll tools
to reveal portions of
your document that
have scrolled out of
view

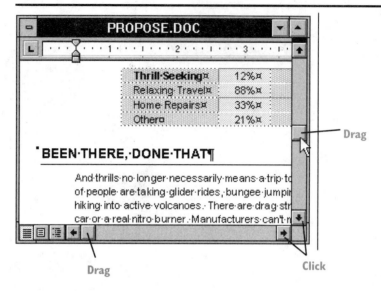

Drag

Drag   Click

right- and left-pointing arrows let you see corresponding portions of wide
documents.

 If you click and hold down the mouse button while pointing
to any of the four scrolling arrows, your document will
scroll continuously until you reach the end of the document
or release the mouse button. But there are better ways to
scroll long distances. Read on.

Scrolling by Clicking in the Scroll Bars

Clicking in the shaded areas of scroll bars (as opposed to clicking on the scroll
arrows themselves) scrolls approximately one screen's worth. The exact scroll
distance will vary with your screen and document window size. Experiment.

Scrolling with the Scroll Boxes

The square boxes in the horizontal and vertical scroll bars can be used to
move great distances quickly. For instance, if you are looking at the first page
of a 100-page document, the scroll box will be at the top of the vertical scroll
bar. Dragging it with your mouse exactly halfway down the scroll bar will

bring page 50 into view; dragging it three-quarters of the way will take you to page 75; and so forth. Horizontal scroll boxes can be used the same way to scroll wide documents quickly.

Obviously it is difficult to drag to the exact middle or three-quarters position on the scroll bar. Use the scroll boxes to get you in the neighborhood, then use other scrolling tools to fine-tune.

  It's easy to forget to move the insertion point when you bounce from place to place in a document by scrolling or using the navigational tricks discussed in this chapter. Get into the habit of repositioning and then looking for the insertion point before you type, paste, or do other potentially destructive things.

Navigating with Your Keyboard

Word for Windows offers many, many keyboard shortcuts for navigating. You can just scroll using keyboard commands, or you can scroll and move the insertion point at the same time. Be sure you understand the difference!

Moreover, frequently if you hold the Shift key down while using keyboard shortcuts, you will select text in addition to scrolling and moving the insertion point. For example, pressing the Ctrl+→ key combination moves the insertion point to the beginning of the next word; while Ctrl+Shift+→ selects the current word starting at the insertion point and the space following it.

There should be a keyboard shortcut that lists all of Word's keyboard-navigation shortcuts, but there isn't. Table 4.1 is the next-best thing.

Use the numbers on the numeric keypad (with Num Lock off) for the tasks listed in Table 4.1. Home, End, Page Up, Page, and Page Down keys are not available on all Ctrl keyboards. If you ever memorize all of Word's keyboard shortcuts, you are spending too much time with Word for Windows. Take a very long vacation.

TABLE 4.1: Keyboard Shortcuts for Moving, Scrolling, and Editing

Scrolling	
TO MOVE TO...	**PRESS...**
Up	↑ or **8** (keypad)
Down	↓ or **2** (keypad)
Left	← or **4** (keypad)
Right	→ or **6** (keypad)
Previous Word	Ctrl+← or Ctrl+**4** (keypad)
Next Word	Ctrl+→ or Ctrl+**6** (keypad)
Beginning of line	**7** (keypad)
End of line	**1** (keypad)
Previous sentence	Ctrl+**7** (keypad)
Next sentence	Ctrl+**1** (keypad)
Next page	Ctrl+Page Down
Previous page	Ctrl+Page Up
Beginning of current paragraph	Ctrl+↑ or Ctrl+**8** (keypad)
Beginning of next paragraph	Ctrl+↓ or Ctrl+**2** (keypad)
Top of window	Home or Ctrl+**5** (keypad)
Bottom of window	End
Start of document	Ctrl+Home or Ctrl+**9** (keypad)
End of document	Ctrl+End or Ctrl+**3** (keypad)
Scroll up one screen	Page Up or **9** (keypad)
Scroll down one screen	Page Down or **3** (keypad)
Scroll up one line	* (asterisk on keypad)
Scroll down one line	+ (plus sign on keypad)

TABLE 4.1: Keyboard Shortcuts for Moving, Scrolling, and Editing (continued)

In Tables or Page Layout View

TO MOVE TO...	PRESS...
First table cell or page element	Ctrl+Alt+7
End of table or last page element	Ctrl+Alt+1
Next cell in table	Tab or Ctrl+Alt+3
Previous cell in table	Shift+Tab or Ctrl+Alt+9
Next page element	Ctrl+Alt+3
Previous page element	Ctrl+Alt+9
Cell or page element above	Ctrl+Alt+8
Cell or page element below	Ctrl+Alt+2
Cell or page element to the left	Ctrl+Alt+4
Cell or page element to the right	Ctrl+Alt+6

Editing

TO DO THIS...	PRESS...
Select the entire document	Ctrl+A
Delete character before cursor or selected text	Delete (Backspace)
Delete character after cursor or selected text	Ctrl+Alt+F or Del
Delete previous word	Ctrl+Alt+Delete (Backspace)
Delete next word	Ctrl+Alt+G
Insert formula character	Ctrl+Alt+\ (backslash)
Copy text	Ctrl+Alt+C
Move text	Ctrl+Alt+X

Word

TABLE 4.1: Keyboard Shortcuts for Moving, Scrolling, and Editing (continued)

Editing	
TO DO THIS...	**PRESS**...
Insert glossary entry	Ctrl+Delete
Copy formats	Ctrl+Alt+V
Insert special character (symbol)	Ctrl+Alt+Q
Copy as picture	Ctrl+Alt+D

  Be careful when using the numeric keypad to navigate. For instance, if you select some text, then press the asterisk key (*) by accident when you meant to hit the PgUp key on the keypad, your text will be replaced with an asterisk! Or, if Num Lock is accidentally turned on, when you press the ↑ key (or any other arrow key), the selected text will be replaced with the number corresponding to the key you've pressed. Some users avoid the numeric-pad navigation shortcuts for these reasons.

The Go To Command

When editing big documents, particularly when you have a marked-up paper copy in your hand, it is useful to be able to scoot quickly to a particular page or to a specific page within a certain section. If you know page (and section) numbers, Word for Windows makes this easy. Word can also take you to specified lines, bookmarks, annotations, footnotes, endnotes, fields, tables, graphics equations, and objects. This is all accomplished in the Go To dialog box, reached with the Edit ➤ Go To command or the F5 function key.

In single-section documents or documents in which page numbers do not re-start in each section, just type the desired page number and press ↵ or click the Go To button. Quicker than you can say *amen*, Word will take you to the requested page and place the insertion point at the beginning of the first line on the page. Here are the steps:

1. Press the F5 function key or choose Edit ➤ Go To.

2. Type the desired page number when you see the dialog box.

3. Press ↵. Word will take you to the requested page.

4. Close the Go To dialog box with the Close button or close box or press Esc.

5. Get back to work.

If your document is broken into sections with page numbers that restart in new sections, you must specify section numbers in the Go To dialog box. To specify a section number in the Go To dialog box, type an **S**. For instance, typing **S4** would take you to the beginning of Section 4 (assuming your document has a Section 4).

To specify a particular page and section, type **P**, the page number, **S**, and the section number. Thus, **P3S5** would take you to the third page in the fifth section. **S5P3** will do the same thing.

You can also go to a particular section by selecting Section in the Scrolling list and then typing the desired section number. Once in the desired section, you can use Go To again to get to the appropriate page within the section.

You can also use the Go To command to move forward or backward a specific number of pages. And you can use it to go to the end of a document, even if you don't know the last page number. Here's a list of things you can do with the Go To dialog box and samples of typical entries:

- Move to the beginning of the document (0)
- Move to the next page (+ or leave blank)
- Move to the last page (enter any number greater than the number of pages in the document)
- Move to a specific page number (4 or P4)
- Move to a specific page within a specific section (P4S3)
- Move to the first page of a specific section (S3)
- Move forward a specified number of pages—3, for example (+3)
- Move back a specific number of pages—5, for instance (−5)

TIP   **Double-clicking on the Page Number portion of the status area will bring up the Go To dialog box.**

The Go Back Feature

Here's a handy but often confusing gizmo. When you are editing, it is sometimes necessary to bounce from one part of a document to another part of the same document. Or, if you have two different documents open, you may find yourself repeatedly moving from one document to the other.

Word for Windows remembers the last three places you have edited plus the current insertion point location. The Go Back feature lets you quickly move to those edit points. Simply press Shift+F5 (or Ctrl+Alt+Z) repeatedly to cycle you through the last three insertion point locations. The Go Back command is not on Word's standard menus, but you can add it or even create a toolbar button for it.

Incidentally, simply moving the insertion point somewhere in a document does not necessarily add that point to the places in the Go Back list. Generally, you need to edit something there.

Using Find to Navigate

Word's Find command is a great way to move to an area needing work. For instance, if you are looking at a printout containing a typo you want to fix, use the Find command to get to the corresponding spot on your screen. Here are the basics:

1. Press Ctrl+F or choose Edit ➤ Find to bring up the Find dialog box.

2. Enter the text you wish to find, then press ↵. Word will search (usually down from the insertion point) and show you the first occurrence of the specified text.

3. Click on Next or press ↵ to move to the next occurrence, if that's not the occurrence you want.

4. If necessary, answer Yes (press ↵) when Word asks if it should search from the beginning of the document.

5. When you find what you need, close the Find dialog box or click in the document window to activate it.

6. Edit away.

Views

Word for Windows can show you your document with varying levels of detail to make things easier to visualize or quicker to work with. These different display options are called *views*. Word provides five different views:

- Normal view
- Page Layout view
- Outline view
- Print Preview
- Split screen

Switching Views

Word for Windows has a View menu that you can use to select Normal, Outline, or Page Layout views.

Three buttons in the bottom-left corner of Word's status area let you quickly switch views. They are (from left to right) Normal view, Page Layout view, and Outline view. You might wish to switch views as you read about them.

Switching to Print Preview either requires a trip to the File menu or the use of a not-so-intuitive keyboard shortcut (Alt+F, V).

Normal View

Unless you are very patient, or have a *very* fast computer with a large screen, use Normal view for most of your heavy-duty text entry and editing. Word's other views respond noticeably slower to typing, editing, and scrolling.

Normal view keeps repagination and screen redraw delays to a minimum. It shows your text as you have typed it, and displays graphics where you've inserted them (which is not necessarily where they'll print).

It does not show side-by-side column positioning, footers, headers, or the printing position of framed items. Columns are shown at their actual width, but not side-by-side. Automatic page breaks are shown as dotted lines. Manual page breaks, if you've defined any, are shown as darker lines containing the words *Page Break*, while section breaks are double dark lines with the words *End of Section*, and so on.

NOTE If you have instructed Word for Windows to number lines, the numbers will not appear in Normal view. Use Print Preview to see line numbers.

Editing in Normal View

You can create and edit text, columns, and graphics as usual in Normal view. To work on headers or footers, though, you must open Header or Footer windows from the View menu.

Page Layout View

In Page Layout view, the screen resembles a white sheet of paper, or at least a portion of a sheet (see Figure 4.13).

Look closely at the top and left edges of the screen in the illustration. You will see a dark background that Word for Windows places behind the "paper." On a large enough screen, you will see the whole page. On smaller screens or when using a large paper setting in Page Setup, you may need to scroll to see these representations of the paper's edges.

FIGURE 4.13

Page Layout view

Editing in Page Layout View

Generally, you edit as usual in Page Layout view. Text and graphics are positioned where they will print. Headers and footers can be both seen and edited. Click in a header, footer, or body text to position the insertion point. Page breaks, be they automatic or forced, are represented by new pages on the screen rather than by dashed lines in the text. You can scroll from page to page, as you'd expect.

Hidden Text in Page Layout View

If you have hidden text in your document and you reveal it, Page Layout view will display line and page endings adjusted to include the hidden text. This may not correspond to pages that you print if the Print dialog box's Print Hidden Text box is unchecked. In order to see what your pages will look like without the hidden text, you must hide the text by unchecking the Show Hidden Text box in the Preferences dialog box.

Headers and Footers in Page Layout View

You can see headers and footers in Page Layout view. To edit, click anywhere in a header or footer. It will "undim" and be surrounded by a dashed line. The Header and Footer toolbar will also appear if it's not already on your screen.

To add date or time entries and page numbering to headers and footers, use the buttons on the Header and Footer toolbar. You can format text in headers just as you would anywhere else in a Word for Windows document. For instance, to right-align header text, place the insertion point in the text (or select multiple lines in the header) and use the Align Right button on the Formatting toolbar.

 NOTE Unlike in earlier versions of Word for Windows, if you have requested numbered lines, the numbers will appear in Page Layout view.

Outline View

If your document is properly formatted, switching to Outline view lets you quickly navigate and reorganize even large, complex documents. Outline view allows you to see the entire contents of the document, just chapter headings, or just section headings, and so on.

Print Preview

Print Preview is more than just another way to view documents. Choose File ➤ Print Preview or use Ctrl+Alt+I or Ctrl+F2.

Depending on your screen size and settings, you will see either an unreadable bird's-eye view of a page or two (like the one in Figure 4.14), or you will see a full, readable page.

FIGURE 4.14

Print Preview gives you a bird's-eye view of one, two, or many pages at once.

Prints
Lets you zoom in and out
Shows a single page
Determines the number of pages on-screen
Toggles rulers
Shrinks page to fit screen
Full screen
Takes you back to the view you were using

Take you to Normal, Page Layout, or Outline views

For a more complete discussion of Print Preview, see "Using Print Preview before Printing" later in this chapter.

 The button that looks like a magnifying glass and a piece of paper on the Standard toolbar will switch you to Print Preview mode. Use the Close button in Print Preview (or press Esc) to bring you back to whatever view you were in previously.

Split Screen View

Regardless of which view you prefer, you can profit from using Word's split-screen feature (see Figure 4.15). You can use the split-screen to keep two widely separated portions of a document in view at the same time. To split the screen, simply point to the small black rectangle in the upper-right corner of your Word document window. The pointer will change to the Split-bar pointer. Drag the Split-bar pointer down to divide the screen.

When you release the mouse button, your screen will split into two independent windows, each with its own scroll bar. To return to a single screen, double-click the Split-bar or drag it to just below the title bar. This takes some practice. Alternatively, you can use the keyboard shortcut Alt+Shift+C.

FIGURE 4.15

Point to the thick black line. The pointer will change shape, indicating that you can drag the black bar to create a split window.

Drag to split screen

When you unsplit the screen, the portion that the insertion point was in becomes the only screen. This can be a nuisance if you actually wanted to be in the other portion of text! So be sure that the insertion point is in the correct pane before you unsplit.

Why Split Screens?

With the screen split, you can see two parts of your document at once. Use this feature to refer to different portions of a document as you write or to speed copying, cutting, and pasting. But there's another powerful reason to use split screens.

You can use a different view in each portion of the split screen. For instance, you might want to speed scrolling and editing by working in a window pane set to Normal view while watching the effects of your changes in a Page Layout view pane, as shown in Figure 4.16.

View Defaults

Normal view is the default for new documents unless you change the default to Page View by using the View tab of the Options dialog box (choose Tools ➤ Options to display the Options dialog box). Word for Windows remembers the view you were using when you last saved a document and opens the document in that view. If you opened a new document in Normal view, did some work, switched to Page Layout view, saved, and exited, the next time you opened the document it would appear in Page Layout view.

Showing Paragraph Marks, Spaces, Etc.

Word for Windows can display helpful nonprinting characters to let you see what's going on. Examples include:

- Paragraph marks (¶)
- Dots denoting spaces
- Arrows denoting tab characters

Word

FIGURE 4.16

A screen split between Normal and Page Layout views

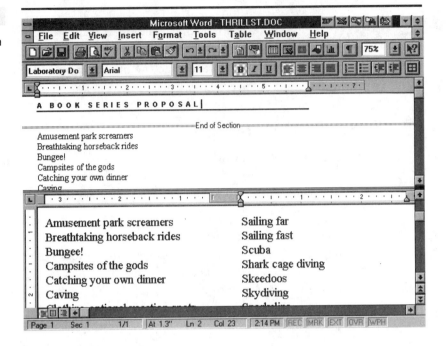

- Dashed lines for page breaks
- Text and graphic boundaries

I like to leave these on, although turning them off can sometimes help you better visualize the final appearance of a document. To toggle the display of these items, click the button that looks like a paragraph mark (¶) on the Standard toolbar. (It's near the right edge.)

Zooming

The little drop-down list near the right end of the Format toolbar is called the Zoom Control. It lets you zoom in and out to see bigger or smaller on-screen representations. It does not affect printing size. For instance, the Page Width choice, shown in Figure 4.17, lets you see both page edges.

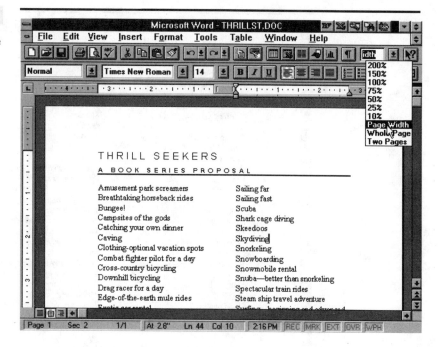

FIGURE 4.17

The Page Width choice

Full Screen—Seeing Just Your Work

The View ➤ Full Screen command, or the corresponding button that you'll find in Print Preview, removes all the usual workspace clutter and fills your screen with your current document (see Figure 4.18). You'll also see a very small window containing the Full button, which allows you to return to the prior view. You can also use the Alt+V+U keyboard shortcut.

Saving Documents the First Time

When you first type and stylize a document, it exists only on your screen and in your computer's volatile RAM (random-access memory). If you were to switch off the computer or experience a power failure or other malfunction, your work would be forever lost. By saving your work to disk as you go, you can pick up where you have left off without losing your changes.

FIGURE 4.18

A full screen

THRILL SEEKERS
A BOOK SERIES PROPOSAL

Amusement park screamers	Sailing far
Breathtaking horseback rides	Sailing fast
Bungee!	Scuba
Campsites of the gods	Shark cage diving
Catching your own dinner	Skeedoos
Caving	Skydiving
Clothing-optional vacation spots	Snorkeling
Combat fighter pilot for a day	Snowboarding
Cross-country bicycling	Snowmobile rental
Downhill bicycling	Snuba—better than snorkeling
Drag racer for a day	Spectacular train rides
Edge-of-the-earth mule rides	Steam ship travel adventure
Exotic car rental	Surfing—beginning and advanced
Exotic food	Thrilling hot-air rides
Eye-to-eye with tropical fish	Thrilling sunrises and sunsets
Ferry rides you'll never forget	Traveling as an air courier
Flying upside down	Unbelievable sights
Full-motion flight simulators	Unusual places to stay
Getting the best helicopter rides	Virtual-reality experiences
Glider rides	Volcanoes
Hang-gliding lessons	Whale watching
Ice-climbing	Waterskiing
Jetski rentals	White-water canoeing
Kayaking	White-water rafting
Meeting other thrill seekers	Wildlife photography tours

TIP Save every fifteen minutes or whenever you are interrupted by phone calls or visitors. You can even set Word for Windows to do the saving for you.

The Ctrl+S keyboard shortcut is a convenient way to save without visiting the File menu. The Save button shown at left, which can be found in the Standard toolbar, will also start the Save process.

The Save As dialog box, shown in Figure 4.19, tells you where Word for Windows plans to store your work and requests a name for the file. It also gives you many other Save options.

Start by noticing where Word proposes to put your document. This is a very important habit to establish.

It's not a good idea to clutter up your Word for Windows directory with a lot of documents, so create some directories specifically for Word documents.

FIGURE 4.19

The Save As dialog box

Telling Word Where to Save Your Document

Like any good Windows program, Word lets you specify save locations. You do this by picking the desired location from the Directories list located just to the right of the File Name list in the Save As dialog box (see Figure 4.19). Use the Drives list to switch drives, if necessary.

Naming Word Documents

Type a name for your document in the File Name: box, then simply click the Save button. Names can be up to eight characters and must conform to the DOS file naming rules (no spaces, asterisks, etc.). It's a good idea to use the extension .DOC for all of your Word documents unless you understand and know how to use the Windows Associate feature. Read more about this feature in your Windows documentation.

Pressing ↵ will have the same effect as clicking Save. With Word, like most Windows programs, pressing ↵ will execute the button with the bold border in the active dialog box.

Word

One way or the other, Word for Windows will save your document and, if the Summary Info feature is turned on, you will see the Summary Info dialog box in Figure 4.20 with blanks in many places. The information it collects is optional and can be added later, if you like.

Providing Summary Information

You needn't type anything in the Summary Info dialog box, and you can prevent it from even appearing. But if you plan to keep many documents on your hard disk, and particularly if you will be storing things on a crowded network server, it is a good idea to use this handy feature. It will help you quickly locate projects with the File ➤ Find File command when you want to round them up for later use.

Once you have saved a document's summary information, you will not be asked for it again when you save your work. Choose File ➤ Summary Info to view or modify summary information.

To prevent the Summary Info dialog box from appearing when you save a new document, choose Tools ➤ Options, click on the Save category, and click in the Prompt For Summary Info box to uncheck it.

FIGURE 4.20

The Summary Info dialog box

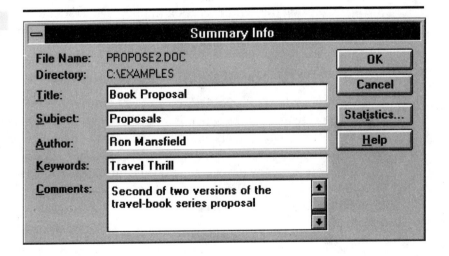

A WHOLE NEW WAY TO WORK

Linking Multiple Word Documents

You can use Object Linking and Embedding to link two Word documents if you like. For example, you could create one document containing an in-house distribution list and link it to memos or memo templates. Then, when the distribution list changes, your new memos will contain the latest distribution list.

The illustration below shows a distribution list linked to a memo.

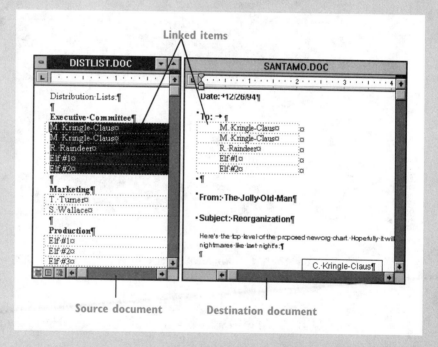

Source document   Destination document

Word

Here are the general steps:

1. Create and open both Word documents.
2. Select the source material to be linked (the Executive distribution list table in this example).

3. Copy the source material (select Edit ➤ Copy, click the Copy button, or press Ctrl+C).

4. Switch to the destination document (click in it or use the Window menu to move to it).

5. Link the material to the destination document by selecting Edit ➤ Paste Special. Make sure the Paste Link option is selected in the Paste Special dialog box (as illustrated here).

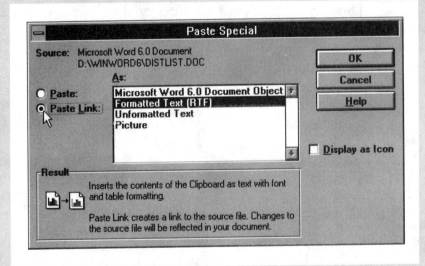

6. Format the incoming information if necessary in the destination document.

Thereafter, when you open the destination document (the memo draft, in this case), Word will insert the current information from the source document (the distribution list).

Consider using tables for things like the distribution list, since tables can minimize indentation and other formatting problems you'll sometimes encounter when linking. See Part Seven for more information on Object Linking and Embedding.

Saving as You Work

Once you've named a document and specified a place to save it, you won't see the Save As or Summary dialog boxes when you save unless you request them. A quick trip to File ➤ Save or better still, the key combination Ctrl+S, will save your work whenever you desire. So will clicking the Save button on the Standard toolbar.

Quitting and Restarting Word

There are several ways to quit Word. You can choose File ➤ Exit or double-click on the Control box in the upper-left corner of the main Word window.

If you have made any changes since the last time you saved, Word will ask if you want them saved. Select Yes to save changes, No to ignore the most recent changes, or Cancel to abort your exit request and return to word processing. After you have satisfied Word that you have saved everything of value, Word will quit.

  Word needs to do some housekeeping when you exit. For instance, Word updates its settings files and asks if you want to save last-minute changes to your documents. When you use Word's File ➤ Exit command or attempt to exit Windows, this housekeeping will proceed smoothly. But if you use the power switch on your computer (or simply unplug it) without first exiting Word and Windows, you may damage a document file or lose valuable changes to your Word settings.

Minimizing Instead of Quitting

You can run Word *minimized*, which gets the program "out of the way" without actually exiting it. See your Windows documentation for details.

Accessing Recent Projects Quickly

Once you have saved some Word for Windows documents, Word remembers their names and locations and lists them at the bottom of your File menu (see Figure 4.21).

FIGURE 4.21

The names of the last files you worked on are stored at the bottom of the File menu. By default, Word lists the last four files; you can change this number to between 0 and 9 by entering a number in the Recently Used File List on the General tab of the Options dialog box (Tools ➤ Options).

File	
New...	Ctrl+N
Open...	Ctrl+O
Close	
Save	Ctrl+S
Save As...	
Save All	
Find File...	
Summary Info...	
Templates...	
Page Setup...	
Print Preview	
Print...	Ctrl+P
1 PROPOSE2.DOC	
2 THRILLST.DOC	
3 PROPOSE.DOC	
4 FAX.DOC	
Exit	

Choose the file of interest and Word will attempt to locate and load it. If you have changed the document's name or moved it since your last Word session, Word may ask for help locating it.

By default, Word lists your last four documents. To specify longer or shorter lists, choose Tools ➤ Options, click on the General tab, and specify the desired number of entries in the Recently Used File List box.

Printing

 If you only have one printer and it is properly installed and ready to go, and you just want to print a single copy of the current document, just press the Print button, shown at left, on the Standard toolbar.

The status area will chart Word's progress as it prints. Page numbers and a little animated printer icon will tell you how many pages have been sent to the printer or to the Windows background printing feature.

While printing can be as simple as previously described, it is a good idea to get into the habit of visiting the Page Setup dialog box, and possibly the Print dialog box, whenever you begin to create a new document—particularly if you work with a variety of printers, paper sizes, and document designs. If you wait until you have finished working on your document to choose a printer, your page and line endings may change considerably from those you initially saw on your screen. This can be a minor annoyance or a major disaster.

For example, if you write a long document, create a table of contents, then change printer models or choose different printing features, you will find that line and page endings may change. This will require you to redo the table of contents. Otherwise it will not agree with the printed pages. The following printer decisions affect pagination and should be selected or determined when you begin a project:

- Page Setup options (like paper source)
- Printer model
- Paper size
- Reduction/enlargement (scaling)
- Page orientation
- Margins
- Gutters
- Larger print area
- Printing/not printing hidden text
- Printing/not printing footnotes and endnotes
- Font substitution options

Other changes affect the appearance of printed pages, but have little impact on pagination.

If you have only one printer and it works properly, you can skip ahead to the section "Choosing Print Dialog Box Options".

Choosing a Printer

To choose a printer:

1. Choose File ➤ Print or use the Ctrl+P shortcut. You will see the dialog box shown in Figure 4.22.

FIGURE 4.22

The Print dialog box

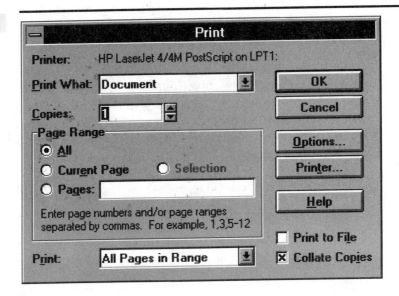

2. Click on the Printer button to reach the Print Setup dialog box, shown in Figure 4.23. It will list your printer models.

3. Point and click in the scrollable list to select the desired printer.

4. If the printer you've chosen has options (lighter/darker, letter quality vs. draft, etc.) you can usually reach them by clicking the Options button.

FIGURE 4.23

The Print Setup dialog box lists the available printers.

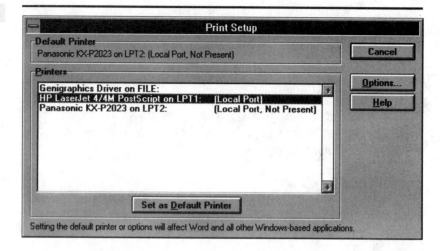

5. When you are done making choices, return to the Print Setup dialog box (if you aren't already there) and click the Close box to select the printer and options.

6. You will be returned to the Print dialog box.

Choosing Print Dialog Box Options

The Print dialog box will show you which printer is selected. Use this dialog box to make decisions, such as how many copies of which pages you need.

Choosing What to Print

Normally, you'll want to print all or part of your document. But sometimes you'll want to print other things, such as the document's annotations or other settings information. Use the drop-down list to pick any of the following options:

- Document (discussed in this chapter)
- Summary Info (discussed in the "Providing Summary Information" earlier in this chapter)
- Annotations (discussed in the "Annotations" section in Chapter 10)
- Styles (discussed in the "Styles and the Style Gallery" section in Chapter 5)

- AutoText entries (typing shortcuts; discussed in the "AutoText" section in Chapter 10)
- Key assignments (keyboard shortcuts)

Copies

To specify more than one copy of whatever you intend to print, either type a number in the Copies box or click on the up or down arrows next to the box to scroll and choose a number.

Page Range

To print the entire page range, make sure the All button is darkened (the default). Click on the little button next to All, if necessary, to darken it.

To print just the page in your document currently containing the insertion point, click on the Current Page button.

To print selected text, first select it, then bring up the Print dialog box and use the Selection button in the Page Range area. This choice will be dimmed unless you've selected something in your document.

To print a range of pages (pages 6–10 in a 50-page document, for instance), type the first and last desired page number in the Pages text box. Separate the numbers with hyphens (**6-10,** for instance).

To print specific pages, list them separated by commas (**3,5,8,** for example). Ranges and single pages can be combined, so **6-10,13,19,83** will work as well.

Print All, Odd, or Even

Normally, Word prints all pages in order, but if you are planning to do "manual" two-sided printing or you have other reasons to separate odd and even pages, use the drop-down Print list at the bottom of the Print dialog box to specify Odd Pages or Even Pages. For example, you might first print all odd numbered pages, then put those pages back in the printer to print the even numbered pages on the other side.

Print to File

It's possible to print to disk files instead of to a printer. Use this technique when you want to take a document to a service bureau for typesetting or other special services. It is a very good idea to do a test run before trying this technique for rush work, since there are many land mines. Consider providing your service bureau copies of the actual Word document files instead of (or in addition to) print files. Here are the steps for printing to a file:

1. Edit and polish your document as usual.
2. Consider printing a paper copy.
3. Open the Print dialog box with File ➤ Print or Ctrl+P.
4. Check the Print to File box in the Print dialog box.
5. Click OK. You'll see the Print to File dialog box.
6. Pick a drive from the Drives list.
7. Pick a directory as needed.
8. Name the file in the Output File Name box.
9. Click OK to create the file.

  Print files can get pretty big, particularly if they contain graphics. Consider printing small ranges of pages to multiple files if you need to transport print files on floppies. You'll need to experiment, since the actual number of bytes-per-page can vary widely, even between several pages in the same document.

Collate Copies

If you request multiple copies (five copies of a ten-page document, for instance) and you don't choose the Collate Copies option, Word will print all five page 1's, then all five page 2's, and so on. You'll need to hand-collate them to make orderly sets.

The Collate Copies option prints five "books," each one complete and in order. This may or may not increase overall printing time depending on your printer and a number of other factors.

Choosing Your Paper Source

If your printer has two paper sources (two trays or a tray and a "pass-through," for instance), Word can switch sources as needed. Use the First Page, Other Pages, and perhaps Apply To choices found under the Paper Source tab in the Page Setup dialog box.

Other Printing Options

There are other printing options available. They can be reached by choosing the Print tab in Word's Options dialog box, shown in Figure 4.24.

FIGURE 4.24

Printing Options on the Print Tab of the Options dialog box

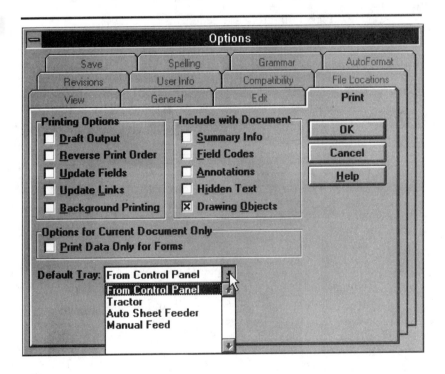

You can display the Options dialog box either by choosing Tools ➤ Options or by pressing the Options button in the Print dialog box. Most of these settings remain in place once you change them and are used for each new printing job until you change them.

Draft Output

This option can speed up printing. Its effect varies from printer to printer. Usually everything is printed in a single font, as efficiently as possible, and at the expense of appearance. It is often faster to print draft dot-matrix copy than fancy laser copy.

Reverse Print Order

Use Reverse Print Order when you want pages to come out last-to-first. This is handy for some printers that "stack" pages in the wrong order.

Update Field and Update Links

As you learned in Chapter 3, this is how you determine when and if things get updated before printing.

Background Printing

An X in this option box causes Word to use the Windows Background printing feature. Theoretically, it lets you work on other things while your document prints in the background. In real life it often makes your computer so sluggish that you'll end up taking a break anyway. If you keep getting printing errors or low memory messages while printing, try turning off background printing.

You can turn on background printing from the General tab in the Options dialog box.

1. Choose Tools ➤ Options.
2. Click the Print tab, if necessary, to reveal printing options.
3. Make sure there is an X in the Background Printing box (click if necessary).

4. Click OK and print as usual. Your documents will print in the background while you're working on other things.

Include with Document

The Include with Document choices in the Print tab of the Options dialog box are pretty self-explanatory. An X causes data to be delivered with the printed pages (summary info, annotations, etc.). Click on an X to remove it and prevent the item from printing.

Current Document Options

The options that will appear here vary with the contents of your document. For instance, you may be given the option to print data without printing forms.

Tray Choice

Use this choice to force something other than the standard tray choice for special printing jobs (e.g., a cover letter on your business letterhead). The selected printer must have more than one paper source for this to be useful.

Checking the Status of a Print Job

TIP

A great Windows shortcut to know is Alt+Tab. If you hit this key combination, Windows switches you to the next open application. If you have several open applications, repeatedly pressing Alt+Tab will cycle through them.

With background printing at work, you can use the Print Manager to check and change the status of multiple print jobs. Follow these steps:

1. Switch to the Print Manager window (hold down the Alt key and press Tab as many times as necessary to display the Print Manager name in the center of your screen, then release the keys).

2. Click to select the job or jobs you wish to cancel or reschedule.

3. Click on the appropriate button (Pause, Resume, Cancel, etc.).

4. Use Print Manager's menus for other options.

5. To return to Word for Windows, hold down the Alt key and press Tab as many times as necessary.

For more information about background printing with the Windows Print Manager, use the Print Manager's on-line help and see your Windows documentation.

Aborting Printing

To stop printing prematurely, press the Esc key repeatedly until the printing status information disappears from your screen. Even after the print status information disappears, your printer may print a few pages that were sent prior to print cancellation, since many printers contain their own memory (called a *buffer*). Check your printer manual for ways to quickly clear the printer's memory if this annoys you.

If you are using background printing, you will probably need to visit the Print Manager, as described earlier in this chapter, and cancel the job there.

Using Print Preview before Printing

You can use Print Preview to see a screen representation of your document prior to printing it. Print Preview will give you an excellent idea of where the text will print on the paper. Unlike in previous versions of Word for Windows, you can now edit this text. You will be able to see margins as well. If your document contains headers, footers, line numbers, and other embellishments you will see them, too. Using Print Preview will allow you to make adjustments to any of these settings *before* printing, thus saving paper and time.

The buttons along the top of the screen let you control many of Print Preview's functions. As always, if you forget a button's function, simply point to it without clicking to reveal button help. Here is a general description of each button.

 Print Button   This button prints a single copy of the document without taking you to the Print dialog box. (If you really want to visit the Print dialog box, choose File ➤ Print or use the Ctrl+P shortcut.)

Magnifier   The Magnifier button lets you zoom in to better read small portions of the page and zoom out to get a bird's eye view of one or more pages. It also toggles you in and out of the edit mode, as you will see momentarily.

 One Page   This button displays a single page even if you are working with a multi-page document.

 Multiple Pages   The Multiple Pages button lets you specify the number of miniaturized pages you'll see on-screen. Pressing this button reveals a matrix that you drag across to design your screen display. Choices range from a single page to 3×6 (18) pages.

 Zoom Control   The Percentage text box and related zoom list are called the *Zoom controls*. They tell you the current zoom percentage and let you pick a variety of zoom options from a drop-down list.

 View Ruler   The View Ruler button is used to toggle the rulers that you use to see and change margin settings.

 Shrink to Fit   When you press the Shrink to Fit button, Word attempts to tighten up documents that end with a mostly white page.

To undo proposed changes, use the Ctrl+Z shortcut or File ➤ Undo Shrink to Fit. Occasionally, Word can't shrink your document and will tell you so.

 Close Button   The Close button takes you back to the previous view.

 Full Page   The Full Page button removes most of the Print Preview clutter (menu bar, status line, etc.) so you can see a bigger version of your document. Pressing the Full Page button a second time returns the hidden controls.

 Help Button   The Help button will turn your pointer into a question mark. Point to the item of interest (the vertical ruler, for instance) to read any available help. Double-click on the Help window's Close box or Press Esc to quit help.

Moving Margins in Print Preview

Here is a quick trick you can try in Print Preview:

1. Type some text.

2. Display the rulers if they are not already on-screen by clicking on the View Rulers button.

3. Point to the vertical ruler on the left edge of your screen. Notice how the pointer gets smaller and has an up and down-pointing head, as shown in Figure 4.25.

4. Hold down the primary (usually the left) mouse button and notice the dashed margin line.

5. While holding down the mouse button, drag down to specify a new top margin while watching the dashed line.

Word

The pointer becomes a double-headed arrow when you move margins in Print Preview

6. Release the mouse button and Word will adjust the margin, moving the text down.

You can use the same basic techniques to move the left and right margins.

Leaving Print Preview

Use the Close button to leave Print Preview and return to your previous view. The three standard view buttons (Normal, Page Layout, and Outline) are also available in the lower-left corner of the status area of Print Preview.

Printing Envelopes

Word can print addresses on envelopes by looking for the addresses in your documents (the inside address of a letter for instance), or you can type an address in the Envelopes and Labels dialog box, shown in Figure 4.26.

FIGURE 4.26

The Envelopes and Labels dialog box

You reach the Envelopes and Labels dialog box with the Tools ➤ Envelopes and Labels command. The dialog box lets you:

- Print envelopes containing one-time addresses that you type into the dialog box itself.
- Copy an address from your document for envelope printing.
- Type envelope addresses, then insert them into your letters or other Word documents.

Including Graphics on Envelopes

You can print graphics on envelopes. It's a great way to add logos, special messages, business reply art, and so on. Here are the general steps:

1. Select the Envelope tab in the Envelopes and Labels dialog box reached with Tools ➤ Envelopes and Labels.

2. Click on either the Add To Document or Change Document button.

3. Switch to Page Layout if not already there.

4. Paste or create a graphic and frame it (using the Insert ➤ Frame command), then move it into position as you would any other framed item.

5. Make any other changes that you like (rearrange or reformat lines of text in the inside address, for instance).

At this point, the envelope is one-of-a-kind, and in a separate section at the top of your current document. You can either save the document and print the envelope along with the rest of the document or save the document as a template for repeated use. But there's one other possibility. If you want the artwork to appear on *all* of your envelopes, you can select the art and create a special AutoText entry called EnvelopeExtra 1 or EnvelopeExtra 2. (See the "AutoText" section in Chapter 10 to learn about AutoText.)

Setting Up a Return Address

If your envelopes have preprinted return addresses, you can skip this task. But if you want to use plain envelopes and have Word print your return address in the upper-left corner of envelopes, do this:

1. Choose the printer you plan to use if you have more than one.

2. Open the Envelopes and Labels dialog box by choosing Tools ➤ Envelopes and Labels.

3. Click on the Envelope tab if it is not foremost. You'll see the Envelopes and Labels dialog box.

4. If Word finds an address in the current open Word document, you will see it in the Delivery Address portion of the dialog box.

5. Type your return address in the large box labeled Return Address. (Word may have filled out part of the address already using your Word User Info.)

6. When you are happy with the spelling and appearance of your return address, try test printing on a plain #10 ($4\frac{1}{8} \times \frac{1}{2}''$) envelope. Word assumes that you can center-feed envelopes in your printer. If that's not possible, click on the envelope in the Feed section of the dialog box to bring up the Envelope Options dialog box.

7. Select a combination that will work with your printer, then click OK.

8. Place an envelope in your printer.

9. Back in the Envelopes tab of the Envelopes and Labels dialog box, click Print to ensure that envelopes will print properly.

Suppressing Return Addresses

If you always plan to use envelopes that contain preprinted return addresses, you can leave the Return Address area blank. Or you can type a return address but click to place an X in the Omit box if you use preprinted envelopes sometimes and plain ones at other times.

Printing Envelopes with New Addresses

You can either type an envelope address directly into the Envelopes and Labels dialog box or select an address in your letter or other Word document, then open the Envelopes and Labels dialog box. Here are the general steps for envelope printing:

  Word will often make a guess as to what it thinks should be the delivery address. Generally, it makes pretty good guesses, but if you don't have an address or if it is ambiguous where you want the correspondence sent, you may have to help out.

1. Select the address in your document if there is one.
2. Open the Envelopes and Labels dialog box by choosing the Tools ➤ Envelopes and Labels command.
3. If you selected an address in step 1, you'll see it in the dialog box; if not, type an address in the Delivery Address box.
4. Insert an envelope in your printer.
5. Click on the Print button.

Adding an Envelope Page to Documents

Click on the Add To Document button in the Envelopes and Labels dialog box to add an envelope page to the beginning of your document. Word takes care of all the details.

Changing Addresses

Once you've inserted an envelope page in your document you can change the envelope and inside address at any time. Here's how:

1. Open the document.
2. Make the address change in the inside address.

Alternatively, you could

1. Open the Envelopes and Labels dialog box (Tools ➤ Envelopes and Labels).
2. Click the Change Document button. The envelope will be changed.

WARNING

If you change the Delivery Address in the Envelopes and Labels window, then click the Change Document button, Word will update the envelope but not the inside address, so be careful. It's better to make the change in the document, not the Envelopes and Labels window.

Envelope Sizes, Fonts, and Other Options

Word lets you specify envelope sizes (both standard and custom), fonts used for delivery, return addresses, and more. The options are selected in two tabs located in the Envelope Options dialog box.

Bar Codes to Speed Postal Delivery

If you are planning to send mail within the United States, you can ask Word to print bar codes on your envelopes. These will speed automated mail sorting. Two coding techniques are provided—POSTNET for regular mail and FIM-A for "courtesy reply" mail. Place an X in the box or boxes you desire. Word will do the rest.

Printing Labels

Label printing is a lot like envelope printing except you have even more options. For instance, you can print single labels or sheets of labels. Word "knows" the dimensions for many different industry-standard stocks from Avery and others. For instance, you'll find Word knows how to print:

- Audio tape labels
- Business card perf stock
- Diskette labels

- File folder labels
- Mailing (address) labels
- Name tags
- Postcards
- Ready indexes
- Rotary (Rolodex) cards
- Shipping labels
- Video tape labels
- WorkSaver tabs

Simple label printing is a lot like envelope printing. Here are the general steps:

1. Select the address in your document if it has one.

2. Open the Envelopes and Labels dialog box with the Tools ➤ Envelopes and Labels command.

3. Click on the Labels tab if it is not already foremost. You'll see some options.

4. If you selected an address in step 1 or if Word finds one on its own, you'll see it in the dialog box; if not, type an address in the big box.

5. Choose the desired options in the main Labels tab. To print a single label on a multilabel sheet, click on Single Label and specify the row and column location of the label. Choose to print or not print the bar code and return address.

6. To select different label sizes, click either on the picture of a label or the Options button. You'll see the available choices.

7. Pick the label maker, label product number, and printer type. Press the Details button to see more choices.

8. Fine tune Top and Side margins here if your printer prints *all of the labels of the current type too high or too far left or right. The other settings are probably correct if you've selected the correct label type back in step 6. When you have made all your choices, Click OK once or twice as necessary to return to the Label tab of the Envelopes and Labels dialog box.*

9. Insert a label or sheet of labels in your printer. (Make sure the label isn't too small for your printer.)

10. Click on the Print button.

Normally, you can put partially used sheets of laser labels through your printer once or twice more, but you run the risk of jamming and possibly damaging your printer. It's often better to print full sheets and file the unused labels for the next time you mail something to the same recipient.

A WHOLE NEW WAY TO WORK

OLE Tips for Word

■ You can resize, crop, change text appearance, and otherwise embellish linked and embedded objects just as if they were ordinary elements created by Word.

■ Use frames to position things like linked charts and graphics. That way, you'll be able to flow text around them, anchor them where you like, and so on.

■ If you insert an object such as an Excel chart as a picture, double-clicking on it in Word will reveal Word's Drawing tools. You can use these tools to modify the appearance of the object in the word document. This will not change the object at its source.

■ When sharing information between Word and Excel, it is often easier to create a table in Excel. It is possible to go the other way, however. Word table cells can be linked to Excel worksheet cells, with Word as the source and Excel as the destination.

■ If you paste a paragraph from Word to Excel, the paragraph will occupy a single column with sentences in separate rows.

5

Formatting Your Text and Documents

Word offers almost too many ways to change the appearance of your documents. You can embellish individual characters, change the indentation of paragraphs, adjust the white space between lines and paragraphs, and much more. So far in this book, you've already done some formatting with Word's toolbars. In this chapter, we'll take a look at other techniques worth knowing.

AutoFormat

AutoFormat inspects your document and suggests formatting changes that you can accept or reject. You can use it on newly typed documents, or on old Word or non-Word text files.

With AutoFormat, Word can locate and reformat headings, change straight quotes to curly quotes, and more. Here are the general steps:

1. Open or create the document you wish to AutoFormat. Figure 5.1 shows an unformatted text document from my DOS subdirectory. It's called DOS 6 README.TXT. You probably have something similar on your hard disk.

2. Choose Format ➤ AutoFormat.

3. If you wish to change the way AutoFormat works, click the Options button. Click to tell which formatting tasks you don't want it to perform. For instance, if you don't want Word to preserve any styles you've already applied, click to remove the X from the appropriate box.

4. When you have specified any necessary changes to Word's usual AutoFormatting habits, click OK to be taken back to the AutoFormat dialog box.

FIGURE 5.1

An unformatted text
document ready for
AutoFormat

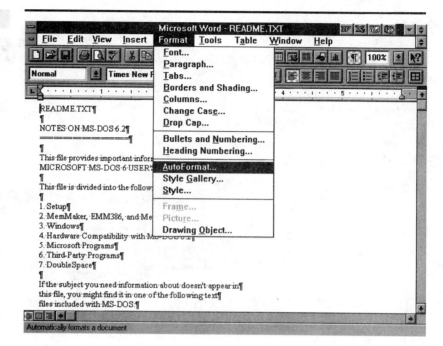

5. Click OK in the AutoFormat dialog box. Word will go to work. It can
take a while; watch the Status area for a progress report.

6. You will see the changed document (notice things like changes in the appearance of headings) and an AutoFormat dialog box (see Figure 5.2).

7. To see and review each proposed change, choose Review Changes, or to
apply different "canned" formatting via the Style Gallery, click the Style
Gallery button. You can review the changes in the style gallery by clicking
on choices in the scrolling Template list. (See the end of this chapter for
more about styles.) Here, for instance, I've used the Manual1 template
styles (see Figure 5.3). Notice the newly indented numbered list.

8. Inspect your finished product carefully to be sure that you got what you
wanted. You may need to polish Word's work with the techniques described in the rest of this chapter.

FIGURE 5.2

The changed document with the AutoFormat dialog box. You can now choose to review each proposed change, apply different formatting, accept all the changes, or reject all the changes.

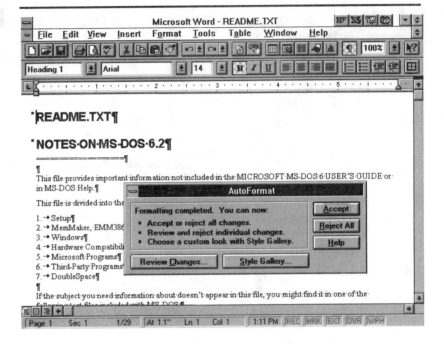

FIGURE 5.3

Here I've used the Manual1 template styles. Notice the newly indented numbered list.

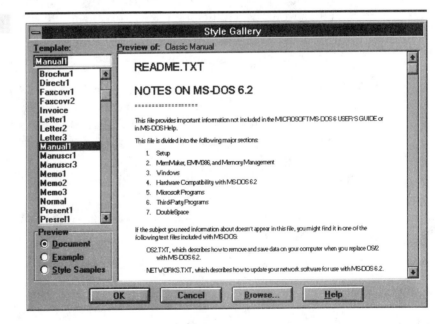

formatting Characters

Word's Formatting toolbar contains a number of text-formatting buttons. There are other toolbars containing formatting buttons. (Remember, if you forget a button's function, move the mouse pointer over the button and hold it there momentarily. The button's name will appear.)

You can also use keyboard shortcuts to alter the appearance of characters. And there are dialog boxes containing character-formatting choices. The most useful is the Font dialog box (Format ➤ Font) shown in·Figure 5.4.

FIGURE 5.4

The Font dialog box offers the most character-formatting choices.

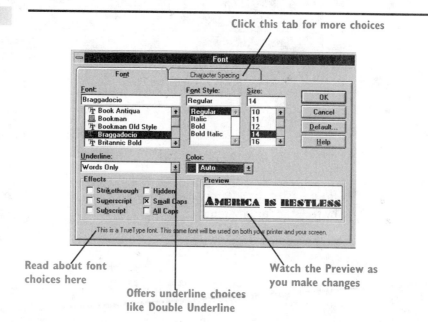

Click this tab for more choices

Read about font choices here

Offers underline choices like Double Underline

Watch the Preview as you make changes

Changing Fonts and Font Sizes

To change fonts and font sizes, select text, then:

■ Use the drop-down Font and Size lists on the Formatting toolbar, as shown in Figure 5.5.

Word

CHAPTER 5

FIGURE 5.5

Using toolbars to pick
fonts, sizes, and much
more

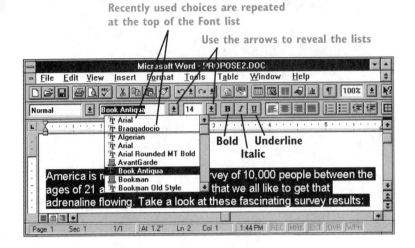

- Type the name of the desired font or size directly into the Font or Size name boxes on the Formatting toolbar, then press ↵.

- Choose Format ➤ Font and select a font or size from the Font dialog box.

- Press Ctrl+] or Ctrl+[to increase or decrease the size one point at a time (respectively).

- Press Ctrl+Shift+>> or Ctrl+Shift+<< to increase or decrease the size by the standard increments listed in Word's various Font size lists.

To Boldface Selected Text

Click the Bold button on the Formatting toolbar; use one of the keyboard shortcuts (Ctrl+B or Ctrl+Shift+B); or check the Bold check box in the Font Style list in Word's Font dialog box (reached by Format ➤ Font).

To Italicize Selected Text

Click the Italic button on the Formatting toolbar; use one of the keyboard shortcuts (Ctrl+I or Ctrl+Shift+I); or enable the Italic option in the Font Style list in Word's Font dialog box.

To Underscore Selected Text

 Click the Underline button on the Formatting toolbar (for single, continuous underline), use the keyboard shortcut Ctrl+U, or choose None, Single, Words Only, Double, and Dotted from the options in the Underline list in Word's Font dialog box.

To Produce Superscripts and Subscripts

To produce superscripts and subscripts, use the shortcuts Ctrl+= and Ctrl+Shift+= or bring up the Character Spacing tab of the Font dialog box (Format ➤ Font) and choose either Raised or Lowered.

 TIP Word lets you add Superscript and Subscript buttons to your toolbars to make this even easier. Go into Chapter 11 to find out about customizing toolbars.

To Expand or Condense Selected Text

Open the Character Spacing tab in the Font dialog box (Format ➤ Font) and choose Expanded or Condensed from the Spacing list.

Changing Case

To change case, select Format ➤ Change Case. This opens the Change Case dialog box (see Figure 5.6), which offers (and demonstrates) five choices of case.

FIGURE 5.6

The Change Case
dialog box

Word

For instance, UPPERCASE changes all selected characters to uppercase letters, and the choice UPPERCASE itself appears all uppercase in the dialog box. Title Case changes the first letter of each selected word to uppercase, as illustrated in the dialog box.

The Title Case feature is not context-sensitive, so it capitalizes prepositions and articles, including *of*, *the*, and so on. To change case with this feature, follow these steps:

1. Select the text you wish to change.
2. Choose Format ➤ Change Case.
3. Choose the desired case option.
4. Click OK.

When you change case using the Change Case dialog box, the characters themselves change to the specified case. It is just as if you had retyped them using the new capitalization scheme. Undo works here.

The All Caps Option

The All Caps feature in the Font dialog box changes only the appearance of letters without actually changing the letters themselves. Unlike Format ➤ Change Case, the All Caps option lets you type in lowercase and see uppercase letters as you work. Follow these steps:

1. Select the text you wish to change, or position the insertion point for typing.
2. Choose Format ➤ Font.
3. Check the All Caps check box.
4. Click OK. Selected and/or subsequently typed case will appear in uppercase, but the underlying text will retain its actual capitalization.

Using the Small Caps Option

The Small Caps option in the Font dialog box can create some very interesting effects. Remember that applying the Small Caps formatting option to text containing Wingdings will usually capitalize the dingbats, thereby changing the characters that appear and print. If this happens, select dingbats and re-move Small Caps formatting. Use Edit ➤ Replace to do this if you have many changes to make.

Drop Caps

Drop caps, also called *initial caps*, are decorative first letters or words that have been stylized, and are usually bigger than surrounding text. Here's an example:

I n a recent survey of 10,000 people between
the ages of 21 and 65 it became clear that we
all like to get that adrenaline flowing. Take
a look at these fascinating survey results:

To create drop caps, select Format ➤ Drop Caps to open the Drop Cap dialog box.

  Drop caps work with single-spaced text only—they won't work in tables, headers, or footers. You won't be able to see the position of drop caps or create them in Outline view. You can't place drop caps in the margins of multicolumn documents, but you can place them within text in multicolumn documents. Narrow indents sometimes screw up the automatic drop cap feature.

That said, here are the general steps:

1. Format the body text the way you like it. Be sure you are happy with things like margins, fonts, and so on. Single-space the text.

2. Select the character or characters you want to drop, and choose the Format ➤ Drop Cap command. If you are not in Page Layout view, Word will prompt you to switch. You'll see the Drop Cap dialog box (see Figure 5.7).

FIGURE 5.7

The Drop Cap
dialog box

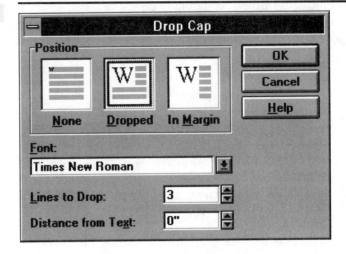

3. If you want to use a different font for the drop cap, choose it from the drop-down Font menu.

4. The Lines to Drop box proposes the number of lines the cap will drop. For instance, 3 li means that the drop cap will be three lines tall and drop alongside the first three lines of text. Pick the desired number of lines from the drop-down line list.

5. Choose the Dropped option for traditional-looking drop caps or choose the In Margin option to place drops in the margin.

6. When you click OK, Word places the specified text into a frame and positions the frame for you.

7. Use the character, frame, and paragraph tools, if you dare, to modify Word's settings.

 You can use the Format ➤ Drop Cap command to drop graphics as well. Paste a graphic at the beginning of a line of text, drag, and if necessary, make it reasonably small. Then, with the graphic selected, use Format ➤ Drop Cap.

Format Painter

Use the Format Painter to copy character formatting from place to place:

1. Select the text containing the formatting you wish to copy.

2. To copy the formatting to one location, click once on the Format Painter button on the Standard toolbar. (To copy to several locations, double-click.) The mouse pointer will change to a paintbrush.

3. Select the text you wish to format.

4. If you double-clicked in step 2, press Escape when you've finished using the Format Painter.

Formatting Paragraphs

Your English teachers probably taught you that paragraphs are collections of sentences on a related topic; Word uses a somewhat more liberal definition. A Word paragraph can be a single text character, a graphic, or even a blank line consisting only of the paragraph mark (¶), which appears in your document when you press the ↵ key. Paragraph-formatting features are an important part of Word's arsenal.

Each Word paragraph in your document can be uniquely formatted, and need not contain text.

Creating Paragraphs

Each time you press ↵, you create a new paragraph. It's that simple. When you open a new document, Word applies the default paragraph settings stored as a style called Normal. It formats each new paragraph the same way until and unless you tell it to do otherwise.

Word paragraphs can be simple blank "lines" or complex collections of indentation, tab, line spacing and other settings. A paragraph's attributes are stored with its paragraph mark. Deleting the mark removes a paragraph's formatting. To create new paragraphs, press ↵.

To modify the appearance of a single paragraph, simply place the insertion point anywhere in the paragraph (with the mouse, point and click). To modify multiple paragraphs, select all or parts of each paragraph to be changed.

Splitting One Paragraph into Two

Position the insertion point where you want to break the paragraph and press ↵. Watch out for extraneous spaces!

Joining Paragraphs

Select the paragraph mark that separates them and press the spacebar. Look out for extra spaces or tabs.

Forcing a New Line without Creating a New Paragraph

Press **Shift+↵**. This inserts a *new line* mark, pushing text down to the next line, but does *not* create a new paragraph. This can be important when you are working with sophisticated styles.

Deleting a Paragraph

To delete a paragraph, double-click in the left margin to select the doomed paragraph and press the **Backspace** key. This will delete the paragraph *and* its ¶ mark. Alternately, you can select all text in the paragraph except the ¶ and delete it, which will leave the ¶ mark with its formatting information.

Think twice when deleting paragraphs. You can delete just the contents of a paragraph or delete the contents and the paragraph marker. If you delete the marker, text above the old paragraph will take on the characteristics of the remaining paragraph below it. This is by design, and is not a bug. If you accidentally delete a paragraph mark and create a problem, the Undo command (Edit ▶ Undo or Ctrl+Z) will usually return your heart rate to normal.

Modifying the Appearance of Paragraphs

To modify the appearance of paragraphs, use the ruler, the Formatting toolbar, and the Paragraph dialog box or one of Word's paragraph-formatting shortcut key combinations.

To Indent Paragraphs Automatically

Drag the top half of the triangular indent marker on the ruler to the right to the desired position:

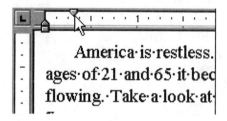

Alternatively, use the keyboard shortcut (**Ctrl+M**), or select Format ➤ Paragraph and enter a setting in the First Line indent box in the Paragraph dialog box.

Increasing or Decreasing Indents by One Tab Stop

Use the Increase Indent and Decrease Indent buttons on the Formatting toolbar.

Hanging Indents

To create a hanging indent (an indent that sticks out beyond the paragraph), drag the top half of the triangular indent marker to the left to the desired position, as shown in Figure 5.8.

You can also use the keyboard shortcut **Ctrl+T**, or select Format ➤ Paragraph and enter a setting in the First Line indent box in the Paragraph dialog box that is *farther* left than the indent of the paragraph as a whole.

FIGURE 5.8

Creating a hanging indent

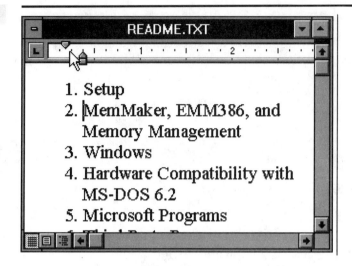

Indenting with Keyboard Shortcuts

Word offers various keyboard shortcuts that move the left indent marker. Some of these are additive commands and can create nested paragraphs. For example, pressing Ctrl+M three times will move the indent position in three stops.

INDENT ACTION	KEYBOARD SHORTCUT
Center	Ctrl+E
Justify	Ctrl+J
Left align	Ctrl+L
Right align	Ctrl+R
Left Indent	Ctrl+M
Remove left indent	Ctrl+Shift+M
Create hanging indent	Ctrl+T
Reduce hanging indent	Ctrl+Shift+T

Creating Bulleted Lists

 Select the items in your list, then click the Bullets button on the Formatting toolbar, which automatically creates a hanging indent and places bullets to the left of the text (see Figure 5.9).

Creating a bulleted list by using the Bullets button

Creating Automatically Numbered Lists

 Select the items in your list, then click the Numbering button on the Formatting toolbar, which automatically creates a hanging indent and places numbers to the left of the text (see Figure 5.10).

Centering, Right-Alignment, and Left-Alignment

Select the paragraph(s) you wish to align, then use one of the four paragraph alignment buttons on the Formatting toolbar (Left, Right, Center, or Justify), as shown in Figure 5.11. (Justify aligns text with both the left and right margins or indents.)

FIGURE 5.10

Creating a numbered
list by using the
Numbering button

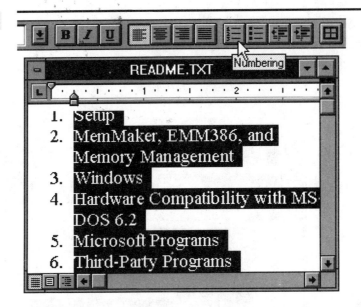

FIGURE 5.11

Using the Center
button to center text

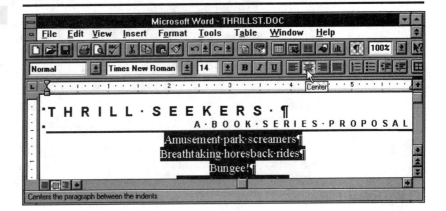

Formatting with the Paragraph Dialog Box

Choose Format – Paragraph to reach the Paragraph dialog box shown in Figure 5.12. (Alternatively, double-click on any indent marker.) The Paragraph dialog box lets you:

- Precisely specify inter-line spacing (single, double, etc.).
- Precisely specify inter-paragraph spacing (space before and after paragraphs).
- Dictate exact indentation measurements.
- Turn off line numbering for specific paragraphs.
- Specify text alignment (left, centered, right, or justified).
- Specify text flow guidelines (widows, orphans, etc.).
- Suppress hyphenation.

  Widows are short lines (typically a single word) at the ends of paragraphs. Orphans are the first lines of paragraphs that print by themselves at the bottom of a page.

You can often use different units of measure for the same specification when entering measurements in the Paragraph dialog box. For instance, you can specify line height in points (pt), lines (li), inches (in), picas (pi), or centimeters (cm). Each possible numeric entry in the Paragraph dialog box has a default unit of measure that is shown in each entry box.

 Line Spacing shows a unit of measure when you select At Least or Exactly. When you select Multiple, you can enter a number and Word will assume you mean li.

In United States versions of Word, the default for horizontal measurements, such as indents, is inches. The default unit of measure for line and paragraph spacing is points. (There are 72 points per inch.)

FIGURE 5.12

Reach the Paragraph dialog box by selecting Format ➤ Paragraph or by clicking hotspots. Both tabs of the Paragraph dialog box are shown here. Click on Widow/Orphan Control in the Text Flow tab to keep the first line of a paragraph from appearing by itself at the bottom of a page.

You can make entries in the Paragraph dialog box without specifying units of measure if you know the default unit of measure for each type of entry. For instance, the default for line spacing is points. Here's the rub. If you enter 2, Word will assume you mean 2 points, not double spacing. To specify double spacing you'd need to enter 2 li (or specify Double in the Line Spacing box). When you are uncertain about the default unit of measure for a paragraph specification, to play it safe, always enter the abbreviation for the unit of measure.

Line Spacing

Individual line spacing is easy to change. You can change the space between lines, and the space above and below paragraphs.

Adjusting the Space between Lines

The Indents and Spacing tab of the Paragraph dialog box provides a drop-down list for simple but effective control of the space between lines under most circumstances. The preview area demonstrates the relative effect of single, one-and-a-half, and double line spacing. Single spacing causes 12-point line spacing, $1\frac{1}{2}$-line spacing is 18 points, and double-spaced lines will be 24 points apart.

When you use these choices, Word will compensate for graphics, superscripts, and large or small type sizes. To force exact line spacing, use the At Least or Exactly choices described in a moment.

Single Spacing Text

To single-space text, follow these steps:

1. Single spacing is Word's default spacing. To reapply it to text spaced some other way, place the insertion point in a paragraph or select multiple paragraphs.

2. Press Ctrl+1 or choose Single in the Paragraph dialog box's Line Spacing menu. Selected text and subsequent typing will be single spaced.

Double Spacing Text

To double-space text, follow these steps:

1. To apply double spacing to text spaced some other way, place the insertion point in a paragraph or select multiple paragraphs.

2. Press Ctrl+2 or choose Double in the Paragraph dialog box's Line Spacing menu. Selected text and subsequent typing will be double spaced.

Line-and-a-Half Spacing

To apply line-and-a-half spacing to text spaced some other way, follow these steps:

1. Place the insertion point in a paragraph or select multiple paragraphs.

2. Press Ctrl+5 or choose 1.5 Lines in the Paragraph dialog box's Line Spacing list. Selected text and subsequent typing will be one-and-a-half–line spaced.

Specifying Exact Line Heights

Word automatically sets the appropriate amount of white space between lines for you unless you tell it to do otherwise. It even compensates for different-sized characters on the same line by setting line spacing to the tallest character.

But sometimes you'll want to specify exact line spacing for one or more paragraphs. Increasing the spacing by a nonstandard amount can help you fill unused space when your copy runs a little short. Specifying slightly less than normal space between lines can help keep text from running on to the top of an extra page.

Here's how to specify exact paragraph spacing:

1. Place the insertion point in a paragraph or select multiple paragraphs.

2. Open the Paragraph dialog box (choose Format ➤ Paragraph or double-click on any indent marker).

3. Choose Exactly or At least from the Line Spacing drop-down list.

4. Enter a specification, and unit of measure (2.5 li, 26 pt, 1.5 in, 22 cm, etc.) in the At box. Watch the preview as you work.

5. Click OK to make the specified spacing change.

TIP If the tops or bottoms of characters are cut off, you may have set a line height that is too small. Revisit the Paragraph dialog box and increase the height.

Space before and after Paragraphs

The Spacing box in the Paragraph dialog box (Format ➤ Paragraph) lets you define the amount of white space Word places before and after paragraphs. You can enter spacing settings in points (pt), inches (in), centimeters (cm), or lines (li). Thus, 12 points would be entered as **12pt**, 25 centimeters would be entered as **25cm**, and so on.

You can give each paragraph unique before and after spacing if you wish. One advantage to adding space this way is that the spacing before and after paragraphs does not change when you change the point size of your text. Another advantage is that you can use different spacing combinations for different purposes.

Headings often have different spacing requirements from body text, for instance. You may wish to create different before and after spacing designs for figures and figure captions as well.

As you will learn soon, you can save unique spacing specifications as part of a *style*, making it easy to keep the look of your documents consistent.

Word

TIP If a paragraph has space added after it, and the paragraph beneath it has space added before, the white space between them will be the <u>combination</u> of the two settings. For example, if one paragraph has 12 points of spacing after it and its successor has 6 points of spacing before, the white space between will be 18 points.

Adding White Space before Paragraphs

To add a single line of white space before a paragraph, place the insertion point in a paragraph (or select multiple paragraphs) and press Ctrl+0 (zero). (To remove single lines of white space originally created with Ctrl+0, press Ctrl+0 a second time.)

To enter a specific amount of space before a paragraph:

1. Place the insertion point in a paragraph or select multiple paragraphs.

2. Double-click on any indent marker to open the Paragraph dialog box.

3. Enter new Before dimensions in the Spacing area in lines, inches, picas, etc., then click OK. Selected paragraphs and subsequent ones will have additional amounts of white space before them.

Fine-Tuning Paragraph Spacing

While the ruler buttons are fine for most occasions, you may need to visit the Paragraph dialog box occasionally to get just the right look. Select Format ➤ Paragraph, then enter appropriate specifications in the Spacing Before and After boxes to fine tune. You can observe the effect of your changes in the Preview box. Click OK when you are satisfied.

Space Before and Page Tops

When you print, Word ignores the Space Before setting in paragraphs that automatic pagination places at the top of a page. If you force a page or section break, however, Word retains this extra space. It will also retain the additional space if you check the Page Break Before option in the Pagination section of the Paragraph dialog box.

Margins and Gutters

The white space around the edges of a Word page are determined primarily by margin and optional gutter settings. (Gutters add extra white space for bound documents.) You can use one set of margin and gutter settings for an entire document, or you can define different settings for different pages in your document. Your choice of paper size, paper orientation (portrait vs. landscape), margin, and gutter settings work together to determine the size and shape of the text area of pages.

Larger margins and gutter settings decrease the available text area while increasing the surrounding white space on each page.

Since margin settings (and Page Setup information) all affect pagination, it is a good idea to define these dimensions right when you begin a new project. This will give you a better grasp of the page count and overall look of the document as you work. You can always fine-tune margin settings just before final printing.

When printing two-sided documents, you may want to use Word's Mirror Even/Odd margin feature and possibly add gutters to place extra white space near the center of your book. (Note that it is convention to have odd-numbered pages on the right and even on the left—just look at any book!) If you plan to have different left and right margins in a two-sided document (a wide left and narrow right, for instance), it is useful to think of these as *inside* and *outside* margins rather than left and right margins, since the wide margin will be on the left side of odd-numbered pages but on the right of even-numbered pages.

If you use headers and footers, you will want to know how they interact with margin settings. Word makes this all fairly painless. When setting margins, bear in mind that some printers cannot print at the extreme edges of a page.

Don't confuse Word's margin settings with its paragraph indentation feature. A Word *page* can have only one user-specified left *margin* setting and only one user-specified right margin setting, but each *paragraph* on the page can have a different left and right *indentation* setting.

Indents are *added* to margin settings. That is to say, if you specify a 1.0″ left margin and a $1/2$″ left indent, your text will print $1\frac{1}{2}$″ from the left margin. If you set a 1.0″ right margin and indent the right edge of a paragraph 1.0″, the text will stop 2.0″ from the right edge of the page.

Changing Document Margins

Word gives you three ways to set margins. The most straightforward method is to use the Margins portion of the Page Setup dialog box, reached with the File ➤ Page Setup command.

You can also drag margins using the rulers in Print Preview. This lets you see the results of margin changes after a slight repagination delay.

Finally, you can drag new margins with the rulers in Page Layout view. The margin brackets are located on the ruler. Let's look at all three techniques, starting with the dialog box.

Follow these general steps to change margins from within the Document dialog box:

1. Place the insertion point on the page where you want margin settings to be changed (unless you plan to use the Whole Document choice).

2. Choose File ➤ Page Setup.

3. If need be, change paper size and orientation by using the Paper Size tab.

4. Switch to the Margins tab if it is not already displayed.

5. Current settings are shown in the various margin dimension boxes.

6. Type the dimensions you desire, or click the little triangles to increase and decrease settings. The Preview will change as you work.

7. When satisfied, click OK.

Dimensional settings in most Word dialog boxes can be expressed in inches (in), points (pt), centimeters (cm), picas (pi), and, frequently, lines (li). For instance, to set a top margin's height to 12 points, you would type **12pt** in the Top margin box; to set a one-and-one-half–line top margin, you'd type **1.5li**, etc.

NOTE While you can type other measurements, Word will convert them to the default measurement when you close the dialog box. You change the default measurement in the General tab of the Options dialog box (Tools ➤ Options).

Dragging Margin Brackets on the Ruler

Word's new rulers display margins as dark gray areas that you can drag to change the document's margins. Don't confuse this with dragging to create indents, which is similar but has a very different effect. Follow these steps:

1. Change to Page Layout view if you're not there already.

2. If the ruler is not displayed, choose View ➤ Ruler.

3. Point to the transition area on the ruler where gray becomes white. The mouse pointer will become a two-headed arrow.

4. Drag the margin to the desired position with your mouse. Watch the ruler's dimensions change as you drag.

Alternate Facing (Mirror) Margins

Select the Mirror Margins feature in the Margins tab of the Page Setup dialog box (File ➤ Page Setup) when you want different left and right margin widths and your final output will be two-sided. Word makes inside margins of odd- and even-numbered pages the same size; and does the same with the outside margins of odd and even pages. This is how you get white space on the appropriate side of even and odd, two-sided pages.

When adjusting margins in Print Preview, if you've chosen the Mirror Odd/Even feature, display two pages in Print Preview so that you can see the different margins.

Gutters Facilitate Binding

Gutter margins—additional white space in the inside margins—compensate for the paper tucked away in the binding of a two-sided book that would be unreadable. The gutter width, which you specify in the Margin tab of the

Page Setup dialog box (File ➤ Page Setup), reduces the text area. Instead of using gutters, you might simply want to increase the size of the inside margins to accommodate binding.

Printing in the Margins

You can place text, graphics, and page numbers in margins by using indent markers. You can drag indent markers into margins, and text or graphics will follow. You can also use Insert ➤ Frame to place things in margins. (See Chapter 8 to find out how to use frames.)

To See What Formatting Choices Are at Work

Click the Help button on the Standard toolbar and point at the characters of interest. A balloon box will appear, containing information about the paragraph and character styling (see Figure 5.13).

FIGURE 5.13

To see formatting information for text, click the Help button on the Standard toolbar, then click on the text.

Columns

To quickly arrange your text into columns, click the Columns button on the Formatting toolbar and drag it to select from one to six columns, as shown in Figure 5.14.

FIGURE 5.14

To arrange your text into columns, click the Columns button and drag to select a number of columns.

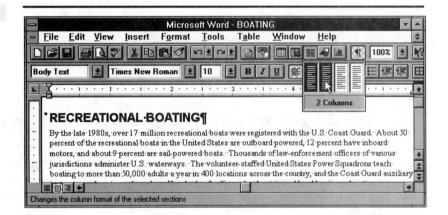

When you release the mouse button, Word automatically determines the appropriate width of columns and the amount of white space between columns based on the page and document settings (see Figure 5.15).

FIGURE 5.15

Word automatically determines the appropriate width of columns and the amount of white space between them.

TIP

> To avoid unsightly column widths and spacing, change your margins, page size, orientation, indents, and related settings before you set your text in columns. For greater control over the look and number of columns, use the Columns dialog box (Format ➤ Columns), where you can preview the results of choices made.

Using Multiple-Column Designs in a Document

To create different columns (even on the same page), select the text to be "columnized" and specify column settings with the toolbar button or the Columns dialog box. Word will apply the settings *only to the selected text* and will insert necessary breaks automatically (see Figure 5.16).

FIGURE 5.16

Select text and specify the desired number of columns. Word takes it from there.

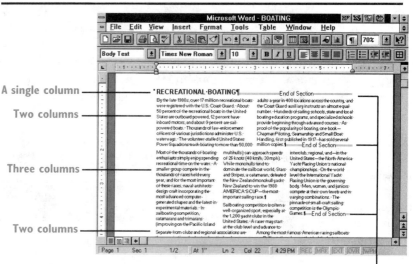

A single column

Two columns

Three columns

Two columns

Word inserts column section breaks for you

Changing Column Widths

To change column widths, drag columns to different widths using margin markers. Start by placing the insertion point in the desired column and, in Page Layout view, display the rulers if they aren't already on screen. Click on the Margin Marker button in the ruler to display the margin markers, then drag any marker and the columns will adjust to their new width:

Decorative Lines between Columns

To add decorative lines between columns, place the insertion point in a column that you wish to decorate. Then choose Format ➤ Columns to open the Columns dialog box and check the Line Between check box (see Figure 5.17).

Forcing Column Breaks

Place the insertion point where you want the column break, then choose Insert ➤ Break, specify Column, and click OK. To remove breaks, highlight them and press Delete.

To Even Out Uneven Columns

Place the insertion point after the last character in the text and choose Insert ➤ Break. Choose Continuous in the Sections area. Then click OK and the column bottoms will align.

FIGURE 5.17

The Columns dialog box. Check the Line Between check box to add decorative lines between columns.

Removing Columns Document-Wide

 Select all of the text, then use the Standard toolbar's Columns button to specify a single column.

Removing One of Several Column Specifications

Place the insertion point in the unwanted column and then use the Columns toolbar button on the Standard toolbar to redefine the number of columns.

Borders and Shading

 You can apply various border treatments and shading to single paragraphs or groups of paragraphs. You can also put borders around graphics. Don't limit yourself to boxes. Use the Border feature to create lines as shown in Figure 5.18.

FIGURE 5.18

Use the Borders tools to create effects like these.

Borders needn't be *boxes*. Use them to create *lines* like this one.

←

Lines *above* attract attention

Make thick lines from thin, shaded paragraphs...

Lines below set things off

Consider leaving off left & right sides

Tables often look better with borders too.		

Creating Lines with the Border Command

Format ➤ Borders and Shading can be used to create lines as well as boxes. You adjust the horizontal *length* of borders or lines by adjusting a paragraph's width with indent markers or the Paragraph dialog box. It's also easy to control the distance between text and border lines. You can use borders to surround paragraphs, framed objects (like graphics), and tables.

The Border Toolbar

You can quickly add borders by using the Borders toolbar (see Figure 5.19).

1. Place the insertion point in the paragraph of interest, or select elements to be formatted—multiple paragraphs, graphics, etc.

2. Adjust indents if necessary to define the desired width for the borders.

FIGURE 5.19

Use the Borders
toolbar for quick
borders and shading.

3. Reveal the Borders toolbar by clicking the Borders button on the For-matting toolbar or by selecting View ➤ Toolbars and checking the Bor-ders check box.

4. With the Borders toolbar open, choose the desired line thickness from its drop-down list. You will see the changes in your document as you work.

5. Click on the button corresponding to the desired border (No Border, Outside, Inside, Right, Left, Bottom, or Top).

6. Pick shading if you like from the drop-down shading list.

7. Admire your work.

You can mix line thicknesses and shading by reselecting different parts of the project and using different settings. Read on.

Custom Borders and Lines

For more complex border and shading projects, select Format ➤ Borders and Shading and use the Paragraph Borders and Shading dialog box shown in Fig-ure 5.20.

The border sample changes to represent the border you are creating. You spec-ify lines (add and remove them) by clicking on border guides. They look like dotted *T*s and *L*s. Clicking on any of the three horizontal guides toggles hori-zontal lines on and off. Clicking on vertical guides toggles them on and off.

The *selection markers*, the little triangles that appear and disappear, show you which border lines will be affected when you click a border guide. Don't worry—this will begin to make sense when you experiment on your own.

If you've selected multiple paragraphs (or tables), you'll be able to place lines between the different paragraphs (or table rows) thanks to those center border

The Paragraph
Borders and Shading
dialog box

guides. And, as you've seen in the examples, you can specify the line widths used for borders or even combine different line styles in the same project. Here are the general steps for custom borders:

1. Place the insertion point in the paragraph of interest, or select elements to be formatted—multiple paragraphs, graphics, etc.

2. Select Format ➤ Borders and Shading to open the Paragraph Borders and Shading dialog box.

3. Click on the appropriate border guides in the sample to turn them on or off.

4. Click on the line type or types you wish. Watch your document change as you work.

Increasing the Space between Borders and Text

To add extra space between the text contained within borders and the borders themselves, specify a measurement (in points) in the From Text portion of the Borders tab of the Paragraph Borders and Shading dialog box. You can do this when you are designing the border, or select an existing border and change the spacing later by visiting the Paragraph Borders and Shading dialog box.

Controlling Border Width

A paragraph's indents (and the document's margins) control the width of a border. To change the border, select the paragraph(s) containing the border formatting and change the indents.

Shading

You can add shading to paragraphs with or without borders. Use shading to create forms or just to add decoration. Be aware, however, that shading can look pretty raggedy on many printers. Test-print some samples before spending hours shading your favorite form or resume.

You can use either the Borders toolbar or the Paragraph Borders and Shading dialog box to add and change shading. To add paragraph shading, pick a shading percentage from the drop-down Shading menus, or enter the first number of a percentage in the entry box. For example, to choose a 40% shading, type **4** in the shading list box and press ↵. The smaller the percentage, the lighter the shading—100% is solid black.

For settings that begin with the same number (e.g., 5 and 50), typing the number acts as a toggle. For example, typing **5** once selects 5; typing it a second time selects 50.

While you can remove borders and shading either with the Borders toolbar or the Paragraph Borders and Shading dialog box, the toolbar's easier. Here are the general steps for using the Paragraph Borders and Shading dialog box:

1. Place the insertion point in the paragraph of interest, or select elements to be shaded—multiple paragraphs, graphics, etc.

2. Open the Paragraph Borders and Shading dialog box with the Format ➤ Borders and Shading command.

3. Click on the Shading tab.

4. Scroll through the Shading list and select a percentage.

5. You will see the effects of your work in the Preview box.

6. Click OK.

7. Be sure to test print new designs.

Removing Borders and Shading

To remove borders and shading:

1. Select the objects with the borders or shading you wish to remove.

2. Display the Borders toolbar (View ➤ Toolbars).

3. Click on the No Border button (it's the rightmost button).

4. If shading has been applied, choose Clear from the Shading list, or type c in place of the displayed percentage and press ↵.

Page Breaks

Page breaks are the places in your document where one page ends and a new page begins. Many things affect where page breaks will occur. Factors include the size of your paper, margin settings, paragraph formats, and section breaks. Word automatically computes and displays page breaks as you add and delete information. You can view page breaks in all views prior to printing. Breaks appear as dotted lines in Normal and Outline views. Since both Page Layout view and Print Preview simulate sheets of paper, page breaks are easy to see in those views as well.

You can force your own page breaks—for instance, to start new chapters on a new page. Generally speaking, only force page breaks after you have done all of your other formatting.

Forcing Page Breaks

To force a page break, you insert manual page breaks. In Normal and Outline views, these look thicker than Word's automatic page breaks and contain the words *Page Break*.

To insert a manual page break, place the insertion point where you want the break, then press Ctrl+↵. Alternatively, select Insert ➤ Break to open the Break dialog box, make sure the Page Break button is selected (the default), then click OK. You'll see a thick manual page break line on your screen. Text or graphics below the manual page break will appear on the next page of your document.

Moving and Deleting Page Breaks

You can delete manual breaks like text. (You cannot delete automatic breaks placed by Word.) Select a manual break line and press Delete. Alternatively, use Edit ➤ Replace to search for manual breaks and replace them with nothing.

Repagination

In order to display and print page breaks properly, Word must recalculate page endings after you've made changes. Normally this is done automatically in the background whenever Word can steal some otherwise unused computer time. This process is called *automatic repagination*. Since page endings affect certain other features, Word always repaginates when:

- You ask it to print.
- You are in Print Preview or Page Layout view.
- You compile a Table of Contents or Index.

To turn off automatic repagination (and speed up Word on slower computers or when working on large documents), follow these steps:

1. Choose Tools ➤ Options.
2. Click on the General tab if it's not already in view.

3. Clear the X from the Background Repagination check box. (You won't be able to do this if you are in Page Layout view.)

4. Click OK to close the Options dialog box.

5. Word will repaginate only when you are in a view that requires it. To force repagination, switch to Page Layout, Print Preview, or issue a Print request.

Sections

Word's section features can help you organize large projects this way, of course, but they do much more. Word sections are designed to let you change major formatting features at places you decide in your document.

Sections need not be used only for books or reports. It's a shame sections aren't called zones or something less ambiguous.

You must start a new section whenever you need to:

- Change page orientation within a document.
- Change margins in part of a document.
- Turn line numbering on or off.
- Change footnote appearance or suppress notes.
- Change the appearance of headers and footers.
- Change the format, position, or progression of page numbers.

While the exact sequence of events will vary with your project and needs, in general you will:

1. Place the insertion point where you want a new section to begin.
2. Select Insert ➤ Break to create the new section.
3. Make the desired formatting and other changes for that section.
4. Perhaps create other sections farther down in the document.

You'll see practical applications of sections in a moment. There are no hard and fast rules about *when* to create new sections. Experienced Word users often create ten or twenty sections in a short document. Others use a single section for an entire 100-page report.

Occasionally, Word will insert section breaks for you—when creating an automatic table of contents, for instance. Mostly, you'll insert them yourself.

Inserting Section Breaks

To insert a section break, follow these steps:

1. Place the insertion point where you want the break.

2. Choose Insert ➤ Break. Choose one of the types of Section Breaks in the Break dialog box, and click OK.

This places a double-dotted, non-printing line containing the words *End of Section* at the insertion point on your screen. The status area reflects section numbers as you move the insertion point or scroll to pages in the new section.

Sections as Chapter Elements

It is very common to create a new section for each chapter in a large publishing project, such as a manuscript or report. This makes it possible to change header and footer information like chapter names. If you were creating an employee handbook, Chapter One's header might contain the words *Welcome, new employees,* while the headers in Chapter Two might say *Your health plan explained,* and so forth.

Sections also make it possible to customize page numbers within chapters. Your document's frontmatter might be numbered in lowercase Roman numerals (i, ii, iii, etc.). Page numbers within chapters might contain chapter-related numbers that restart at the beginning of each chapter (1-1, 2-1, and so on). As you'll recall, you can use different page-numbering styles in each section of your document, and you can restart page numbering at the beginning of any new section.

Setting Sections with the Layout Tab in Page Setup

You can set sections using the Layout tab of the Page Setup dialog box (see Figure 5.21). To reach the Layout tab, double-click on the section break at the end of the section you wish to change; or place the insertion point in the section and choose File ➤ Page Setup, then click on the Layout tab.

FIGURE 5.21

The Layout tab of the Page Setup dialog box.

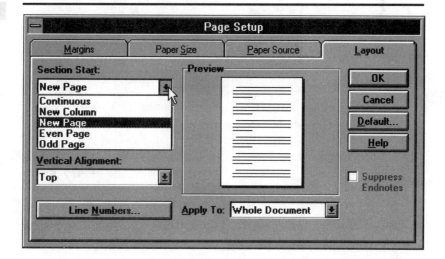

Many of the choices in the Layout tab are covered elsewhere in this book, but the Section Start drop-down menu of the dialog box contains a number of section-specific items worth exploring.

The options listed in the Section Start drop-down menu are the same as those in the Break dialog box (reached by choosing Insert ➤ Break).

This is how you tell Word where you want it to start printing the various sections of your document. You can make a different choice for each section. Here's what the options do:

Continuous   (The default setting.) Text from preceding sections will occupy the same page as the designated section, if there is enough room for the text from both sections.

New Column	In multicolumn formats, Word breaks a column when it encounters a section mark. It prints the subsequent text at the top of a new column.
New Page	Word will always start new sections on new pages with this choice.
Even Page	Word starts printing the new section on an even-numbered page, even if it means leaving an odd-numbered page blank.
Odd Page	Word will start the new section on an odd numbered page. Use this to ensure that new sections start on right-hand pages when designing documents for two-sided printing.

The Apply To portion of the Layout tab lets you tell Word how far to go with your requested changes:

This Section	Changes affect only the section containing the insertion point.
This Point Forward	Changes affect the document from the insertion point to the end.
Whole Document	Changes affect the whole document.

Copying Section Breaks

Section-formatting information is stored with section breaks much the same way paragraph formatting is stored with paragraph marks, and you can copy section information by copying and pasting section breaks. You can even place section breaks as AutoText items. (AutoText is explained in Chapter 10.)

Section breaks differ from paragraph marks (¶), in that a section break controls the information *below* it, while a paragraph mark controls the information that precedes it.

Click on a break to select it. An insertion point will straddle the break line. You may find it easiest to do this in Normal view. Once the break is selected, you can then copy, cut, etc.

Deleting Section Breaks

Select a section break as just described. Then press the Backspace or Delete key. Text after the removed section break will take on the characteristics of the preceding material. It may take a moment for Word to reformat and re-paginate the document. Watch the status line and be patient.

Changing Page Orientation with Breaks

Section Breaks make it possible for you to mix portrait and landscape page orientations in the same document. For instance, you could have a three-page memo with pages one and three in portrait mode (the text, perhaps) and the middle page in landscape mode (a wide spreadsheet, perhaps).

Word flips headers, footers, page numbers and other marginalia for you unless you override this. Therefore, if you've placed page numbers at the bottom of your pages, the landscape page(s) will have numbers at the right edge of the paper so that they read like the rest of the (flipped) text on the page(s). Here are the general steps:

1. Position the insertion point where you want the break.
2. Choose Insert ➤ Break.
3. Choose the Next Page Option.
4. Click OK.
5. Move the insertion point to where you want the orientation to change again (if you do)—the beginning of page 3 in our example.
6. Insert another section break there.
7. Position the insertion point in the new section you've created.

8. Visit the Layout tab in Page Setup (double-click in an unmarked part of the ruler or choose File ➤ Page Setup).

9. Make other page layout choices in the other Page Setup tabs.

10. Preview and then print your work.

Styles and the Style Gallery

Styles are collections of paragraph and character formatting decisions that you or others make and save using meaningful names. Styles make it easy for you to reuse complex paragraph formats without laboriously recreating them each time. Built-in styles are available in all Word documents, and each document can have its own collection of custom styles.

Applying Styles from the Formatting Toolbar

Since Word comes with built-in styles, you can easily apply them to one or more paragraphs. Here are the general steps:

1. Either place the insertion point in a paragraph or select several paragraphs.

2. Scroll through the drop-down style list on the Formatting toolbar to pick the desired style (see Figure 5.22). The available items in the list will vary from document to document for reasons you'll soon understand.

3. Click on a style name to apply it to the selected text. Your text will be reformatted using the selected style.

4. Use Edit ➤ Undo if you don't like the results.

When the drop-down list is long, type the first letter of the style's name. The list will scroll to the proximity of your desired style.

FIGURE 5.22

Applying styles from
the Formatting styles
toolbar

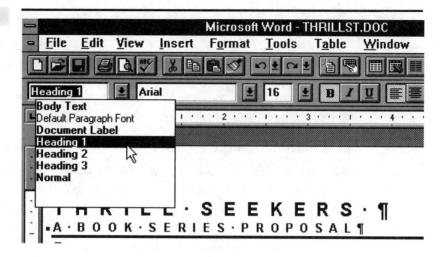

Applying Styles from the Keyboard

A few of the commonly used styles have their own keyboard shortcuts. To use
them, select text or place the insertion point in the paragraph to be stylized
and use one of the following key combinations:

Style	Press
Normal	Ctrl+Shift+N
Heading 1	Alt+Ctrl+1
Heading 2	Alt+Ctrl+2
Heading 3	Alt+Ctrl+3
List Bullet	Ctrl+Shift+L
Style Shown in Toolbar	Ctl+Shift+S

The Edit ➤ Repeat keyboard shortcut (Ctrl+Y) works when applying styles.
After you apply a style once, you can move the insertion point to other paragraphs and press Ctrl+Y to apply the new style where needed.

You can no longer type the first few characters of a style name to apply it as
you could in earlier Word versions.

Defining Your Own Styles from the Formatting Toolbar

You can define your own styles, and many experienced users do that. But before spending hours reinventing the wheel, check out the styles already provided by Word. When you have satisfied yourself that you need something that doesn't exist, try the following steps:

1. Display the Formatting toolbar if it is not already in view.

2. Place the insertion point in the formatted paragraph whose style you'd like to capture. Make any last-minute changes in style.

3. As shown here, click *once* on the style box (the name portion of the drop-down style-name list). The style box will be highlighted, indicating that you can type a new style name.

4. Type a meaningful style name and press ↲. Word will save the style information and add the new name to the drop-down style list for the current document.

Choosing Suitable Style Names

Style names can be up to 253 characters long, but shorter is often better. Names can contain any legal characters except backslashes (\ ), braces ({ }), or semicolons (;). Word cares about capitalization in style names. For example, *Figure* and *figure* are two different names. Try to be consistent when naming similar styles in different documents.

The Style Dialog Box

The Style dialog box (Format ➤ Style) shown in Figure 5.23 lets you define new styles and rename, explore, list, or delete existing ones.

To define a style via the Style dialog box, follow these steps:

1. Place the insertion point in or select a paragraph containing the desired format.

2. Open the Style dialog box.

FIGURE 5.23

FIGURE 5.23

The Style dialog box

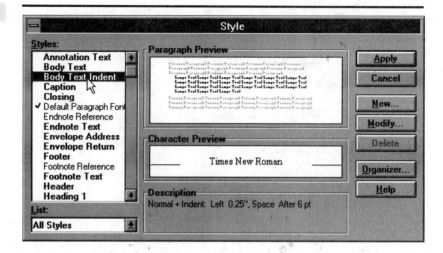

3. Click on the New button.

4. Type a legal style name in the box provided.

5. Click on OK to record the style.

Defining Keyboard Shortcuts for Styles

Word lets you assign keyboard shortcuts from the Modify Style dialog box (reached with the Modify button in the Style dialog box). You can also use the Keyboard tab of the Customize dialog box (reached with Tools ➤ Customize).

Basing One Style upon Another

Word lets you build upon styles, or base one upon another. Word watches as you develop new styles and bases new styles on the styles you modify. Unless you are careful, you can create quite a chain reaction this way. Experienced users try to create one or two base styles and tie most of the rest of their styles to those base styles, rather than basing each new style on the previous style. To base styles, follow these steps:

1. Choose Format ➤ Style to open the Style dialog box.

2. Select the style you plan to base on another.

3. Click the Modify button to open the Modify Style dialog box.

4. Choose a base style from the Based On list.

5. Make any other necessary changes in the Modify Style dialog box.

6. Click OK when you're done.

To add a style you've created to the template upon which the document you are working on is based, enable the Add to Template option in the Modify Style dialog box.

Next Style

Frequently, you can predict the order in which styles will be used. When you type letters, for instance, you know that the To style will always be used after the From style. In reports and manuals, headings are usually followed immediately by body text, and so on.

The Modify Style dialog box lets you specify which style Word will flip to when you finish typing a paragraph and press ↵. Often, you want a paragraph to be in the same style as its predecessor (this is the default setting) when creating styles. But you can specify different next styles:

1. Choose Format ➤ Style.

2. Select the style you plan to modify.

3. Click the Modify button.

4. When you see the Modify Style dialog box, choose a "next" style from the Style for Following Paragraph list.

5. Make any other necessary changes in the Modify Style dialog box.

6. Click OK when done.

Finding Out Which Styles Have Been Used

The obvious way to sniff out styles is to place the insertion point in the text of interest and look at the Formatting toolbar indicators (the style list, which buttons are depressed, and so on). But there are several easier ways to see which styles and character formatting have been applied. The first is to print out a style list.

Printing Out a Style List

It is often useful to have a printed list of styles and their descriptions. This can help you keep things consistent in a large organization, and it can help you troubleshoot formatting problems in complex documents. To print style information:

1. Open the document of interest.
2. Choose File ➤ Print (or press Ctrl+P).
3. Choose Styles from the drop-down Print What list (see Figure 5.24).
4. Click OK.

Word

The Style Gallery

This new feature lets you explore the seemingly endless collection of styles provided with Word's templates. Earlier in this chapter you saw one use of the Style Gallery (previewing the effect of a templates styles on your document).

By clicking the Style Samples button in the Style Gallery, you can see examples of all of the styles for a document or template. Check out how cool the Thrill Seekers list looks after reformatting with the Classic Resume template's styles (see Figure 5.25).

FIGURE 5.25

The Thrill Seekers list after reformatting with the Classic Resume template's styles

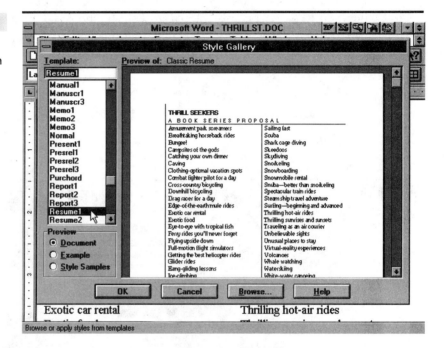

If you are currently working on a project, you can also see how the project would look if you applied styles from various templates. If you like what you see, you can even have Word automatically apply the styles to your current project. You do not need to have a project in the works to visit the Gallery, but if you think you might want to reformat something, open it first and make it the active Word project before you begin. Here are the general steps.

1. Open a Word project you think you might want to reformat.
2. Open the Gallery with the Format ➤ Style Gallery command.
3. Click the Style Samples button.
4. Pick a style from the Template list.

5. Wait a moment while Word displays the samples.

6. Choose different template names if you wish to see samples of other style collections.

7. Click the Document button if you want to see the styles automatically applied to the current document you have open (your current project).

8. Click OK to close the gallery *and apply the new styles* or Cancel to close the gallery without changing your document.

Displaying Style Names On-Screen

To keep track of which styles a document uses, you can display style information at the left edge of the screen in the *style area* (see Figure 5.26):

1. Switch to Normal or Outline view.

2. Choose Tools ➤ Options and select the View tab.

3. Pick a style area width (1″, perhaps) from the Style Area width section of the View tab, then click OK. Style names will appear at the left of the screen.

FIGURE 5.26

Using the style area to display style names

4. To remove them, repeat steps 1 through 3 but choose 0 (zero) for the Style Area Width.

When and Where Styles Are Saved

Styles are saved with your document and they are saved only when you save the document. This is yet another good reason to get in the habit of saving early and often. If your computer crashes after you've spent several hours setting up a complex collection of new styles, or if you accidentally click No in response to the *Do you want to save changes?* message box when you close a document, you will not be happy.

Word's Standard Styles

Word's designers have created hundreds of standard styles that are used by its footnote, outline, index, table-of-contents, page-numbering, header, and footer features.

Many of the templates for letters, brochures, newsletters, and other documents have their own predefined styles. Take some time now to open a few documents based on these templates and explore their styles. As a starter, try this:

1. Choose File ➤ New.
2. Scroll through the list and pick Report1. Take a few moments to look it over. Could you use this template as is? How might you modify it to make it more useful?

Styles that Word Applies Automatically

Word applies certain styles automatically, as listed here:

STYLE	WHEN WORD APPLIES THE STYLE
Annotation Text	Comments inserted by the Annotation command
Annotation Reference	Initials of person who inserted the comment
Caption	Captions and table and figure titles

STYLE	WHEN WORD APPLIES THE STYLE
Footer	In footers
Footnote Text	Text in a footnote or endnote
Endnote Text	Endnotes
Footnote Reference	Numbers and characters used as reference marks
Endnote Reference	Reference marks
Header	Header info
Index l–Index 9	Index entries created with the Index and Tables
Line Number	Automatic line numbers
Macro Text	Text of a WordBasic macro
Page Number	Automatic page numbers
TOC 1–TOC 9, Table of Contents	TOC entries
Table of Figures	Automatic figure numbering

Reapply/Redefine Styles

If you ask Word to apply a style to a paragraph that already uses that style (applying Normal to an already Normal paragraph, for instance); you will be visited by this strange and powerful dialog box:

To Restore Styles

This box serves two purposes. First it lets you reapply a style to a paragraph that you have inadvertently messed up. Suppose you accidentally dragged the first line indent marker in a Body paragraph and the paragraph no longer looks like the others. By choosing the Body style again from the Formatting toolbar you will get a chance to reapply your Body style and repair the errant paragraph. Follow these steps to restore a style:

1. Select the paragraph, paragraphs or characters you wish to restore.
2. Chose the desired style from the Formatting toolbar's list.
3. If asked to reapply or redefine, pick Reapply.
4. Click OK.

To Redefine a Style

The second use of this dialog box is to let you quickly redefine a style. Suppose you hate the first line indent you've used for body text. Change the indent in any one Body style paragraph, then pick Body from the Style list. Click on the Redefine button and click OK. Word will redefine the Body style using the new indent from your sample paragraph. All of your Body paragraphs will be changed. To redefine a style, follow these steps:

1. Select any paragraph or character formatted with the style to be changed.
2. Make the desired appearance changes (indents, underlining, etc.).
3. From the Formatting toolbar's list, choose the style *originally* used for the formatting.
4. When you see the Redefine/Reapply choice, choose Redefine.
5. Click OK.

Strange things sometimes happen when you redefine or reapply styles to manually embellished paragraphs, however. While the interaction of manually applied formatting and styles may seem almost random sometimes, it is not.

Deleting Styles

You cannot delete Word's built-in styles (headings and Normal, for instance), but you can remove custom ones you've created and many of the fonts provided with Word's templates. To delete unwanted styles, select them in the Style dialog box and click the Delete button.

You will be asked to confirm; press OK. All paragraphs formatted with a deleted style will revert to the document's Normal style. Follow these steps:

1. Open the Style dialog box with Format ➤ Style.
2. Click on the style you want to delete in the Styles list (scroll, if necessary).
3. Click Delete.
4. Click OK to confirm the deletion.
5. The style will be deleted from the current document.

  Undo does not restore deleted styles. Thus, you cannot undo (re-establish) a deleted style, but you can sometimes work around this. Save the document just before you attempt any style deletion. Inspect the document immediately after deleting styles. Do not save the document again until you are certain that the deletion of styles hasn't caused problems. If there are problems, close the document without saving (by answering No to the Save Changes? prompt). Reopen the document and your styles should all be intact. Better yet, experiment on a copy of your document.

Renaming Styles

You can rename styles in the Style dialog box:

1. Open the Style dialog box with the Format ➤ Style command.
2. Click on the style you want to rename in the Styles list (scroll, if necessary).
3. Click the Modify button.
4. You will see the Modify Style dialog box.

5. Edit the name in the Name box.

6. Make any other desired changes while in the Modify Style dialog box.

7. Click OK.

If you change a style's name to one that already exists in the document, the style that you have renamed will take on the characteristics of the pre-existing style. For instance if you have a double-spaced style called Draft and you change the name of a single-spaced style from Body to Draft, all of the paragraphs formatted as Body will be double-spaced and take on any other style characteristics associated with the original Draft style.

Remember—Word cares about capitalization when you name styles. The names *Salutation* and *salutation* are not the same.

Finding and Replacing Styles

Style-change junkies rejoice. You can search for and replace styles:

1. Open the Replace dialog box (Edit ➤ Replace or Ctrl+H).

2. Place the insertion point in the Find What box.

3. Choose Style from the drop-down Format menu. You will be presented with a list of possible styles in the Find Style dialog box.

4. Pick the style you wish to replace (Heading 2, for instance) and click OK. The name of the style will appear in the format portion of the Find What area.

5. Move the insertion Point to the Replace With portion of the dialog box.

6. Choose Style from the drop-down Format menu again.

7. Choose the new style from the resulting Replace Style dialog box list (Heading 1, for example).

8. Click OK.

9. Tell Word if you want to search the whole document (All), up from the insertion point, or down from the insertion point.

10. When you are ready, click Find Next and Replace, or Replace All, as appropriate. For instance to replace all Heading 2 style occurrences with Heading 1 styles, you'd pick Search All and Replace All.

Transferring Styles to Other Documents

After you've spent time setting up complex styles, it would be nice to reuse them in new projects. Word provides several ways to do this. For repetitive tasks, consider setting up Template documents containing styles. If you have just a style or two you want to copy from one document (the source) to another (the destination), follow these steps:

1. Select some text from the source document containing the style of interest and paste it into the destination document needing the style.

2. Word will bring over the style with the text.

Remember that if the destination document has a style name identical to the style being copied from the source, the destination document will reformat the incoming text rather than take on the new style. Moreover, if you copy more than fifty styles at once, the source document's entire style sheet will be automatically copied to the destination document.

You can also merge different style sheets, which copies unique styles from one document to another and modifies styles with identical names. Think of the document containing styles you want to copy as the *source* document and the document receiving the new styles as the *destination* document. Here's how to merge style sheets:

1. With styles properly named and saved, work in the destination document.

2. Open the Style dialog box with the Format ➤ Style command.

3. Click on the Organizer button to open the Organizer dialog box.

4. Pick the Styles tab if it is not already foremost.

5. The name of the source file should appear in the In list at the left side of the dialog box, and probably the file NORMAL.DOT will be specified as the destination or To file on the right of the dialog box. This is telling you that word wants to copy new styles to the NORMAL.DOT template so that it will be available in each new document that you open.

6. If you want to make the style or styles you are copying globally available, leave the To setting as NORMAL.DOT. If you want to add the style(s) to just a selected document or template, click the *right* Close File button (note that there are two). It will change to an Open File button. Choose the desired destination file using standard Windows file-opening techniques.

7. When the source and destination files have been properly identified, pick the styles you wish to copy in the left-hand scrolling list. Click to choose a single style, Shift+click to select ranges or hold down the Ctrl key while you selectively click on noncontiguous styles.

8. With the desired styles selected, click Copy.

9. Use the Delete or Rename keys as necessary.

10. Open other source or destination files as necessary, then click Close when you're done.

6

Working with Headers, Footers, and Footnotes

Sometimes it's helpful to print data, such as headers, footers, and footnotes, in the margins of your text. Word makes it easy for you to add these features to your documents and edit them. Read on to learn more about Word's Header, Footer, and Footnote features and how to use them.

What Are Headers and Footers?

Headers and *footers* are places to put repetitive information in a document's top and bottom margins—headers print at the top, footers at the bottom. You can use headers and footers to print something simple on each page, such as your name, or something complex, such as a graphic. Stylized text, dates, and automatic page numbering can all be included in headers and footers.

You can use identical headers and footers on all pages in your document, or you can specify different contents for each section of the document. Odd and even pages can have different designs if you wish. The first page of each document or each section can be unique.

In Word 6, header and footer editing always takes place in Page Layout view. You work right in the header and footer area of your document after double-clicking to undim it.

You can apply virtually any paragraph or character style to your headers and footers using the Formatting toolbar and rulers. They will repeat on all pages thereafter.

Once headers and footers have been added to a document, it is possible to see and edit them in Page Layout view. They are also displayed in Print Preview, but when you attempt to open a header or footer in Normal view or Print Preview, Word switches you to Page Layout view and displays the Header and Footer toolbar.

Creating Basic Headers and Footers

To enter a header that repeats on all pages in your document:

1. Choose View ➤ Header and Footer or double-click in the header area of the first page to be modified in Page Layout view or Print Preview.

2. Word will switch to Page Layout view if it is not already there and display the Header and Footer toolbar, shown in Figure 6.1.

FIGURE 6.1

Edit headers and footers right in Page Layout view. Use the Header and Footer toolbar for tasks such as automatic page numbering and time and date stamping.

Different sections can have different headers and footers

You can embellish text by boldfacing it, right-aligning it, etc.

Headers and footers expand as you add lines

Show/Hide
Document/Text
Go to Page Setup
Time Stamp
Page Numbers
Same as Previous (Copy)
Show Next Header or Footer
Show Previous Header or Footer
Switch between Headers and Footers

3. Create and edit header text as you would any other. You can paste graphics, apply styles, and otherwise format your work normally.

4. Use the automatic page-number, time-stamping, and date-stamping features described later in this chapter.

5. Double-click in the main document to return to work there.

You enter footers the same way as headers, except that you work in a Footer window:

1. Choose View ➤ Header and Footer or double-click in the footer area of the first page to be modified in Page Layout view or Print Preview. Word will switch to Page Layout view if it is not already there and display the Header and Footer toolbar.

   ■ If you chose View ➤ Header and Footer, Word will show you the header first. Click the Switch Between Header and Footer button to view the footer.

2. Create and edit footer text as you would any other. You can paste graphics, apply styles, and otherwise format your work normally.

3. Use the automatic page-number, time-stamping, and date-stamping features described later in this chapter.

4. Double-click in the main document to continue working there.

 NOTE You can use your regular document ruler or Formatting toolbar when working in header and footer windows. Margins, indents, tabs, and all the other tools work as you'd expect.

Creating Different Headers and Footers for Odd and Even Pages

To create different even and odd headers or footers:

1. Place the insertion point in the section where you want the odd/even effect to begin.

2. Open the Page Setup dialog box (double-click in a blank part of a ruler or choose File ➤ Page Setup) and click the Layout tab.

3. Check the Different Odd and Even choice in the Headers and Footers area, then click OK.

Creating Different Headers and Footers for the First Page

Word lets you create unique headers and footers for the first page of your document:

1. Place the insertion point in the section where you want the different first page.

2. Open the Page Setup dialog box (double-click in a blank part of a ruler or choose File ➤ Page Setup) and choose the Layout tab.

3. Check the Different First Page choice in the Headers and Footers area. You'll have different header and footer areas on first pages. Their names will be visible in Page Layout view.

4. Create different headers and footers for the first page in Page Layout view.

Word

Putting Page Numbers in Headers and Footers

Word offers a variety of tools to help you automatically number pages. You can choose from many page numbering format and style choices and position page numbers nearly anywhere that pleases you. Let's explore these features and discuss the effects of document sections and pagination on page numbering.

TIP If you plan to break a document into multiple sections, you may want to insert page numbers before you split the document into sections. Otherwise, you will have to repeat the page-numbering process for each section of your document.

Word provides two page-numbering techniques. Both have advantages and disadvantages. Normally, you will use only one for a particular document—otherwise, you might end up with two or more sets of page numbers!

Using the Header and Footer Toolbar to Add Page Numbers

To add page numbers using the header/footer toolbar:

1. Open a header or footer by double-clicking on it in Page Layout view.

2. Click on the page numbering button in the Header and Footer toolbar. Word will insert a number in your header or footer at the insertion point.

3. Like anything else placed in headers and footers, page numbers can be stylized, repositioned, surrounded with borders, accompanied by text, and otherwise embellished.

Word uses the standard header or footer style to format page numbers placed therein. You can override this by applying additional character and paragraph formats or by changing the standard header or footer style (see Chapter 5 to learn about styles).

Headers and footers have tab stops, which you may find useful for positioning page numbers.

Using the Page Numbers Command

Word's new Insert ➤ Page Numbers command provides a wider variety of numbering options. It reveals the Page Numbers dialog box and lets you quickly reach the Page Number Format dialog box.

1. Place the insertion point in the section you want to number.

2. Display the Page Numbers dialog box, shown in Figure 6.2, by choosing Insert ➤ Page Numbers.

3. Word suggests placing page numbers in the bottom-right corner of your document ($1/2''$ from the bottom and right edges of the paper), but you can specify different positions with the Position and Alignment drop-down menus. Watch the Preview area as you work.

4. Choose whether you want a page number on the first page by clicking to add or remove the corresponding X.

5. Either click OK or click on the Format button to review other page numbering options.

FIGURE 6.2

The Page Numbers dialog box

Using Page Numbering Formats and Styles

Word supports four page-number formats, all of which are available regardless of which page-numbering technique you use:

1. Standard Arabic numbers (1, 2, 3…)—the default
2. Capital Roman numerals (I, II, III…)
3. Capital letters (A, B, C…)
4. Lowercase formats (i, ii, iii… and a, b, c…)

To specify number formats:

1. Choose Insert ➤ Page Numbers.
2. Click the Format button in the Page Numbers dialog box, shown in Figure 6.2 above.
3. In the Page Number Format dialog box, choose the format you want from the drop-down list and choose OK.

You can use Word's many character and paragraph embellishment features to spruce up page numbers. Pick the font of your choice, make numbers bold, align them, put boxes around them. You can have text appear next to the numbers (*Page-1*, for instance).

After inserting page numbers, switch to Page Layout view and change their appearance.

Documents containing multiple sections can have different formats in each section. That's both good and bad news. If you want all sections to have the same format, you will want to pick a format before you break up the document. Otherwise you must place the insertion point in each section and pick the same format for every one. Plan ahead.

Adding Chapter Numbers to Page Numbers

If you use Word's standard heading styles, and if you use one of the headings for chapter titles, you can have Word include chapter headings with your page number (*2-36*, for instance.) You can specify one of four separators—hyphens, periods, colons, or em dashes.

You set up chapter page numbering in the Page Number Format dialog box, in the section called Use Separator.

Specifying the Starting Page Number

Word lets you specify the starting page number in four different ways:

■ You can suppress the first page number (for example, on multipage letters) but then have 2 on the second page, 3 on the third, etc. To do so, uncheck the Show Number on First Page check box in the Page Numbers dialog box.

■ You can restart each new section in a multisection document with 1. To do so, place the insertion point in any section, check the Start At box in the Page Number Format dialog box, specify the number each section will start with, and then click OK.

■ You can print your first page without a number (a cover page, for instance) and then have the second page begin from 1. To do so, uncheck the Show Number on First Page check box in the Page Numbers dialog box, then enter 0 in the Start At box in the Page Number Format dialog box.

■ You can start page numbering with a number other than 1, like 25 or 100. This is helpful when you are combining your work with other documents. To do so, enter the starting number in the Start At box in the Page Number Format dialog box.

Removing Page Numbers

To remove page numbers, simply open the header or footer containing unwanted page numbers and delete one. The rest of the page numbers in the section will disappear.

Word

To delete all the page numbers in a multisection document, follow these steps:

1. Open a header or footer containing page numbers.

2. Choose Edit ➤ Select All or use the Ctrl+A shortcut.

3. Delete a page number. The rest will disappear.

Date and Time Entries

To insert the current date or time:

1. Position the insertion point.

2. Choose Date and Time from the Insert menu.

3. Pick the appropriate format from the scrolling list.

4. Click OK.

If the Insert As field box is checked, Word will update the date and time entry whenever you print the document. The Header and Footer pane also contains buttons for inserting times and dates.

Creating Footnotes and Endnotes

Word lets you create *footnotes* or *endnotes* (notes appearing at the end of your document) and personalize their appearance. For footnotes, follow these steps:

1. Place the insertion point where the footnote marker is needed (after the words *aboard a ship* in our example).

2. Choose Insert ➤ Footnote.

3. You can dismiss the Footnote and Endnote dialog box, shown in Figure 6.3, by clicking OK, since Word's defaults are fine for this project.

4. In Normal view, a second window pane opens where you do the footnote typing (see Figure 6.4). In Page Layout view, you type right where the footnote will print—usually between the text and footer (see Figure 6.5).

FIGURE 6.3

The Footnote and
Endnote dialog box

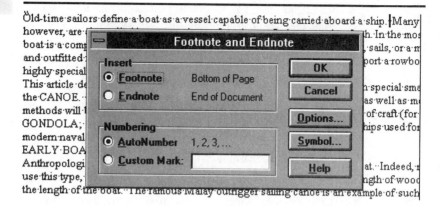

FIGURE 6.4

The footnote window

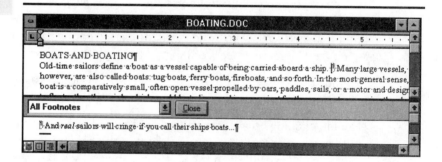

FIGURE 6.5

Entering footnotes in
Page Layout view

5. In either case, the insertion point automatically moves to the proper place for you to type the footnote. Type it.

6. To return to the main document, move the insertion point with the mouse or press Ctrl+Alt+Z.

Viewing Footnotes

Footnotes are always displayed in Page Layout view and Print Preview. If they are not visible in Normal or Outline view, choose View ➤ Footnotes to open a footnote window.

If you are constantly entering or referring to footnotes in Normal view, you can leave the footnote window visible while you work. Scrolling in your document will cause corresponding scrolling in the footnote window. Use the footnote scroll bars if necessary to view notes. You can resize the footnote window to suit your taste and screen size by dragging the bar separating the two windows the same way you resize other Word split screens (point to the split box and drag).

To hide the footnote window, choose View ➤ Footnotes again or click the Close button.

Double-clicking on a footnote marker in your document will display the footnote pane and place the insertion point at the beginning of the footnote. If necessary, Word will open the footnote pane and scroll to the appropriate note. Also, moving the insertion point in the footnote pane will cause the main document to scroll to the reference.

NOTE **Whenever you insert or delete footnotes, Word renumbers the others accordingly.**

Working with Entire Footnotes

You can copy, move, or delete entire footnotes as easily as you would a single character.

1. Select the footnote marker of interest in the document text.

2. Cut, copy, paste, or drag-and-drop the footnote mark.

3. Word does the rest. If you have Numbering turned on, Word will update the numbers in your text and in the corresponding footnotes. If you copy and paste a mark, a corresponding new footnote will magically appear in the right spot in your footnotes. Deletion works as you would expect.

Editing Footnote Text

Visit the footnote pane in Normal view, or the footnote itself in Page Layout view. Cut, paste, and drag-and-drop away to your heart's content. (Note that you cannot cut a footnote's entire text; you must cut the footnote mark in text if you wish to delete or move it.)

Personalizing Footnotes

You can personalize footnotes by using Insert ➤ Footnote and the Note Options dialog box:

1. Choose Insert ➤ Footnote.

2. Click the Symbol button to bring up the Symbol dialog box. Click on the desired symbol to change the footnote symbol character.

3. Click on Options to bring up the Note Options dialog box, shown in Figure 6.6.

4. Click to switch to the All Footnotes tab, if necessary.

5. Specify note placement, number formats, starting numbers, and starting points.

6. Click OK.

For more ways to personalize footnotes, check on-line help and my book *Mastering Word 6 for Windows*, from SYBEX.

FIGURE 6.6

The Note Options
dialog box

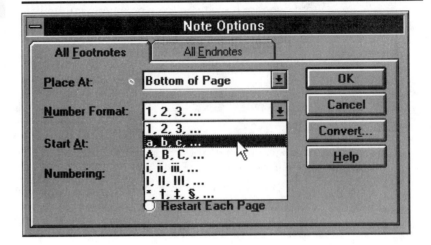

7

Tabs, Tables, and Sorting

∎

Microsoft Office provides many ways to create and format tabular information (lists of items in columns). Although you can use Word as a typewriter and press Tab as needed to create columns, you can take a giant step up from that basic approach by using Word's Table features. However, I'd be remiss not to mention Excel as a possible option for such tasks. See the sidebar at the end of this chapter for details of how to use Excel tables in Word. We've already touched on linking and embedding Excel information, and you'll learn more in Part Three. This chapter deals entirely with Word.

Tabs

Tabs are great for creating quick, relatively simple lists; and tabs do some things in Word you can't do on a typewriter. For instance, they can help you exchange Word data with spreadsheets, databases, and other programs. Each paragraph in a Word document can have the same or different tab settings. Word offers five specialized types of *tab stop*:

Left	Like the plain vanilla ones you find on your old Smith Corona: Text typed at these tab stops bumps up against the left edge of the stop.
Center	Center your text around the tab stop.
Right	Position whatever you type to the left of the tab stop. This is a great way to type long lists of numbers and have them line up.

Decimal   Align columns of numbers on the decimal point and are perfect for simple financial reports.

Bar   Creates nice, thin vertical lines that separate columns. These aren't actual tab stops—that is, you cannot use them to align text—but they can be placed and moved like stops. You can only specify bar tabs from the Tabs dialog box.

Each type of tab helps you align text, and they are particularly useful for making simple columnar lists. Figure 7.1 illustrates the types of tab.

FIGURE 7.1

Tab stop buttons and
the tab stops they
create

Click the Tab Stop button
to change its type

Left

Center

Right

Decimal

With Show ¶ turned on, you'll see fat arrows indicating each tab character you type:

```
Animas        →    12675·Colony·Street  →  Chino     →  CA →91710  →  800-800-5885¶
Apple·Credit  →    4440·Willow·Road     →  Pleasanton→CA →94566  →  800-367-1334¶
Ashton-Tate   →    20101·Hamilton·Ave   →  Torrance  →  CA →90502  →  800-437-4329¶
```

Setting Custom Tab Stops

In the United States, at least, Word starts each new document by default with tab stops set at one-half-inch intervals. You can create custom tabs to replace these.

Tab stops are always stored with the paragraph mark for each paragraph, thus all of the rules about paragraph markers apply. If, for example, you set tab stops once and type ↵ at the end of each typing line, each new paragraph (line) will use the same tab stops as the preceding one, until you tell Word otherwise.

Setting Tab Stops with the Ruler

You can set custom tabs as you type or you can use the standard tabs initially and then go back to fine-tune. Here are the general steps.

1. With the ruler in view, click the button at the left edge of the horizontal ruler repeatedly until it shows the icon for the desired tab stop type (Left, Right, Decimal, or Center).

2. Click on the ruler where you want to place a tab stop. If you make a mistake, drag the stop off the ruler and try again.

3. When you type, press the Tab key to move the insertion point to the new tab positions.

Moving Tab Stops on the Ruler

To move tab stops before you've entered text, simply point to the stop you need and drag to the right or left.

NOTE   If you have already entered text that uses the tab stops you want to move, first select all of that text before moving the tab stop.

Setting Tab Stops with the Tabs Dialog Box

Although using the ruler is easy, you may want to use the Tabs dialog box (shown in Figure 7.2) for some projects. It provides ways to set tab stops precisely and it offers some additional tab-related options. To reach the Tabs dialog box, choose Format ➤ Tabs or click the Tabs... button in the Paragraph dialog box.

FIGURE 7.2

Use the Tabs dialog box for precision work.

Remember to select all the intended text and paragraph markers before you move tab stops. Undo (Ctrl+Z) will save you when you forget.

Units of Measure in the Tab Dialog Box

Measurements in the Tabs dialog box are assumed to be in inches unless you type another legal abbreviation (**cm** for centimeter, **pt** for point, or **pi** for pica). As an example, 5 *cm* would position a tab stop 5 centimeters from the left margin.

There is also an Alignment section in the Tabs dialog box, where you can change current tab stop types. This is the only place where you can select a bar tab.

Adding Tab Leader Characters

Leader characters make it easy to read wide, sparsely populated lines without losing your place. Word's leader characters are dots, dashes, and solid lines (see below). You set them in the Tabs dialog box.

> None (Type 1)
> ....Dots (Type 2)
> ----------------Dashes (Type 3)
> _____Solid (Type 4)

To create leaders, follow these steps:

1. Select the paragraph(s) you want to pretty up.

2. Click on the tab where you want the leaders.

3. Choose the leader style you desire from the Tabs dialog box.

4. Click OK.

You can apply this effect when defining new tab stops or you can double-click on existing stops to bring up the Tabs dialog box as an afterthought.

Default Tab Stop Positions

The Word standard settings specify tabs every half inch (*0.5 in*). You can change this for a single document by changing the setting in the Tabs dialog box. To forever change default tabs, change and save stops in the NORMAL template.

Clearing Tab Stops

You can drag the occasional tab off the ruler if you don't need it. The Tabs dialog box provides facilities for clearing multiple tabs at once—you can clear all the tabs at one time by clicking Clear All or choose a specific tab in the Tab Stop Position and click the Clear button to remove it.

Entering and Editing Tabular Data

Once you have set up tab stops, simply press the Tab key to reach the stop and begin typing. Word will position the text as you type. If you are typing at a center or right stop, text will flow appropriately as you type. When you type at decimal stops the insertion point sits to the left of the decimal position until you hit the period key; then it hops to the right side. To leave an entry blank, simply tab past it by pressing the Tab key.

Tables

Tables help you organize complex columnar information. Use them to create such diverse documents as forms, television scripts, financial reports, parts catalogs, and résumés. You can insert tables anywhere you need them in Word documents. Word's table feature and the terminology used to describe it will remind you of a spreadsheet.

Word tables consist of horizontal *rows*, and vertical *columns* (see Figure 7.3). You do the typing in areas called *cells*. Cells can contain text, numbers, or graphics. The text in cells is edited and embellished as usual with Word's Formatting toolbar and ruler.

A number of table-specific features let you control the size, shape, and appearance of cells. Border and shading features are available. It is also easy to insert and delete rows and columns.

FIGURE 7.3

Tables consist of cells arrayed in rows and columns.

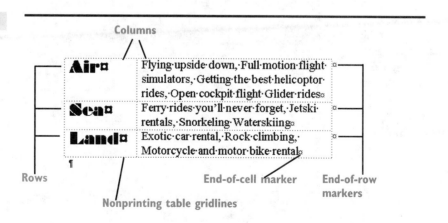

Tables can be created from existing text without needless retyping. Or, you can use the table feature to organize information and then convert your table to text. You can even import and export spreadsheet data. A feature called the Table Wizard helps you automate table creation, but we'll wait to discuss it until after you understand the manual process. That's because you will often want to fine-tune the Wizard's results; so you'll need to become a wizard also.

The dotted lines around each cell represent *nonprinting table gridlines*. You can add printing borders with the Format ➤ Borders And Shading command. The larger dots are end-of-cell and end-of-row marks. Click the Show ¶ button in the Standard toolbar to reveal them.

Creating a Simple Table

To create a table with the Table button, follow these steps:

1. Place the insertion point where you want to insert a table (ideally, *not* at the very beginning of a new, otherwise empty document).

2. With the Standard toolbar in view, click the Table button, then drag while holding down the mouse button to highlight the number of rows and columns you want in your table (see Figure 7.4).

FIGURE 7.4

In this figure, I'm inserting a new table below an existing empty table. At this point, I've dragged the mouse pointer down from the Table button to highlight the number of rows and columns I want.

3. When the displayed grid represents the desired number of rows and columns, release the mouse button. Word will insert an empty table at the insertion point when you release the mouse button.

Creating a Table Using the Table Menu

You can use the Table ➤ Insert Table command to create more complex tables with the Insert Table dialog box.

Unless you specify a column width in the Column Width box, Word computes a column width automatically, taking into consideration the available text area in your document and the number of columns you've specified. Initially, all table columns are the same width, but you can change column widths using techniques described later in this chapter.

Entering and Editing Text in a Table

With only a few exceptions, you navigate, enter, and edit table text just as you do any other Word text. Use your mouse or arrow keys to position the insertion point, then type normally. Think of cells as *miniature pages*, and the cell borders as *margins*. Word will automatically wrap text within the cell as you reach the right edge. Rows will automatically grow taller as necessary to accommodate your typing.

To move from cell to cell within a table, either use your mouse or use the Tab key to go forward and Shift+Tab to go backward. The insertion point will move down to the beginning of the next row when you press Tab in the right-most column (thus, it jumps from the right down to the left); and it will move to the end of the previous row when you Shift+Tab past the leftmost column (thus it jumps from the left up to the right). If you press Tab in the last cell of the last row, you will create a new row.

You can apply the usual character formatting to all or selected characters in a table. The familiar toolbar, ruler, and menu features all work here.

A cell can contain more than one paragraph. You create paragraphs in the usual way, and you can apply all of Word's paragraph formats to paragraphs in cells. Since cells can contain multiple paragraphs, they can also contain multiple paragraph formats. Thus, within a single cell, you can have several different indent settings, tab settings, line-spacing specifications, styles, etc.

Selecting in Tables

As you've just seen, you can select characters, words, and other items in table cells using Word's usual mouse and keyboard features. In addition, Word also provides *table-specific* selection tools enabling you to choose whole cells, entire rows, columns, or areas.

The area between the first character in a cell and the left edge of the cell is called the *cell selection bar.* When you point to it the mouse pointer changes directions (points to the right).

Clicking on it selects the contents of the entire cell. You can also select an entire cell by dragging with the mouse. Just be sure you include the end-of-cell mark in your selection.

To select a column, move the mouse pointer to the area called the *column selection bar* at the top of a column. You'll know you've arrived when the pointer changes into a large, down-pointing arrow.

Holding down the Alt key while clicking anywhere in a column will also select the entire column. Selecting the bottom or top cell in a column and dragging up or down is somewhat tedious, but will also work.

Selecting Rows

Double-clicking any cell selection bar will select the entire row. Selecting the leftmost or rightmost cell in a row and dragging will also work.

Selecting Adjacent Groups of Cells

To select groups of adjacent cells, either drag through the cells or click in one cell and Shift+click in the others.

Selecting the Whole Table

To properly select an entire table, hold down the Alt key and double-click anywhere in the table. If your document contains multiple tables and they are not separated by paragraph marks, this technique will select all adjacent tables.

Do *not* use Word's Select All command to select a table, since this will also select paragraph marks and other things *outside* the table. Instead, use Table ➤ Select Table or press Alt+5 on the numeric keypad (NumLock has to be off for this to work).

Word

Table Borders and Shading

An easy way to dress up a table is to add printing borders and shading, as shown below. Select the cell or cells you wish to embellish, then use the line thickness portion of the Borders toolbar. Pick the desired combination of line thicknesses and apply the borders just as you would add them to Word paragraphs. Add shading to some or all of the cells.

Air	Flying upside down, Full motion flight simulators, Getting the best helicoptor rides, Open cockpit flight, Glider rides
Sea	Ferry rides you'll never forget, Jetski rentals, Snorkeling Waterskiing
Land	Exotic car rental, Rock climbing, Motorcycle and motor bike rental

Test-print any shading you intend to use before getting carried away. It often looks different on paper than it does on your screen. For example, compare the 20% screen in the previous "screen shot" with this printed output of the same document:

Air	Flying upside down, Full motion flight simulators, Getting the best helicopter rides, Open cockpit flight, Glider rides
Sea	Ferry rides you'll never forget, Jetski rentals, Snorkeling, Waterskiing
Land	Exotic car rental, Rock climbing, Motorcycle and motor bike rental

Adding Rows

To add a new row *at the end of an existing table*, place the insertion point anywhere in the last cell (the one in the lower-right corner of your table) and press Tab.

To insert a row *in the middle of a table*, place the insertion point in the row *below* where you want the new row and select Table ➤ Insert Rows. Word will insert a new row using the styles of the cells immediately above.

Changing Row Heights

Normally, Word sets the height of each row automatically to accommodate the cell containing the tallest entry. For instance, if one cell in a row needs 2.0″ to accommodate the text or graphic it contains, all of the cells in that row will be 2.0″ high. All cells in a row must be the same height, but different rows can have different heights.

Dragging a Row to New Heights

To adjust the height of a row, follow these steps:

1. Click anywhere in the row you wish to resize.

2. Move the pointer to the vertical ruler at the left edge of the screen, watching the pointer as you move it.

3. When it becomes an up-and-down arrow, use it to drag the row to the desired height.

4. Release the mouse button.

Word

Resizing Rows with Cell Height and Width

You can also overrule Word's automatic row-height (and column-width) settings via the Table ➤ Cell Height and Width command. This is one way to create forms with fixed-size entry areas.

There is no standard keyboard shortcut for this command, but experienced table typists often add their own. To resize cells, follow these steps:

1. Place the insertion point anywhere in the row whose height you wish to specify. If you want multiple rows to share the same height, select all of them.

2. Choose Table ➤ Cell Height and Width.

3. Click on the Row tab if necessary to reveal its choices:

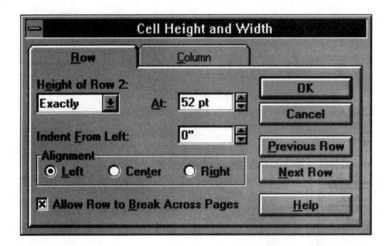

4. Use the drop-down list to choose Auto, At Least, or Exactly.

5. Enter the desired dimension in points, inches, centimeters, and so on. (The default is points.)

6. To change settings for previous or next rows, click the Previous or Next buttons.

7. Click OK to make the change and close the dialog box.

If the exact height you specify is too small to accommodate the biggest entry in a row, the excessive text or a portion of the entry will be cropped when printed. Simply increase the row height if this is undesirable.

Changing the Spacing between Rows

To change the amount of white space between rows—not the *height* of rows—select the rows, choose Format ➤ Paragraph and specify the before and after spacing (see Chapter 5 for details).

Deleting Rows

To delete a row or rows of cells, select the row(s) to be deleted, then use the Table ➤ Delete Rows command. This will delete both the rows themselves (the cells) and their contents (text or graphics or whatever). To delete the *contents* of cells but leave the cells intact, use Word's usual text-deletion tricks (select text or graphics and press Del, for instance).

Inserting Columns

To insert a single column in the middle of a table:

1. Select the column to the *right* of where you want the new column to appear.

2. Click the Table button in the Standard toolbar (notice how its name has changed to Insert Columns) or choose Table ➤ Insert Columns. Word will add a new column but will not change the width of the earlier columns to accommodate it.

3. In order to make the enlarged table fit on your page, you will probably need to adjust margins or column widths (described in a moment), or change page orientation. New columns retain the format of the old right-most columns, but borders will not transfer.

To insert multiple columns, select as many existing columns as you want to insert new ones to the right of the desired location of the new columns—if you want to add three columns, select the three existing columns to the right of the desired insertion point—then click on the Table button. Word will insert three columns.

Inserting Columns at the Right Edge of a Table

To insert a column at the right edge of a table, select an end-of-row marker, click on the Table button in the Standard toolbar (notice how its name has changed to Insert Cells), pick Insert Entire Column in the Insert Cells dialog box, and click OK.

Deleting Columns

To delete columns, select the column or columns to be removed and choose Table ➤ Delete Columns.

Changing Column and Cell Widths

You can change the widths of entire columns or selected cells within columns. You can make most changes by dragging column markers on the table scale in the ruler or you can make precision adjustments in the Table Cells dialog box.

To change the width of one or more *cells only*, select them and visit the Cell Height and Width dialog box (Table ➤ Cell Height and Width). Specify a new width in the Columns tab.

Changing Column Widths with the Ruler

To change the width of an entire column:

1. Point to a column boundary so that the pointer changes shape.

2. Drag the column-width marker:

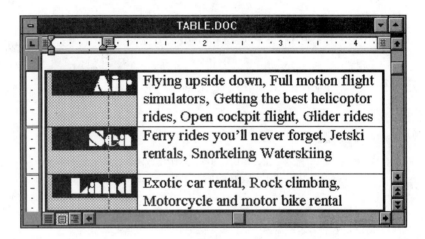

3. Watch the dotted line and ruler settings, then release the mouse button when it reaches the desired width.

   ■ If you hold down the Shift key while dragging, the column to the right changes size to make up the difference while the table's overall width remains unchanged. (Note that this affects two columns: the one being dragged and one whose width is encroached upon.)

   ■ If you hold down Ctrl while dragging, *all* columns to the right change size, but the table's overall width does not.

   ■ You can also drag the *column markers* on the ruler to change column widths. (Just don't accidentally drag the cells' indent markers instead.)

Changing Cell Widths with the AutoFit Button

The AutoFit button attempts to make cells surround their contents snugly. Use it after you've entered all the information in your table, or after you are done adding or deleting items. Follow these steps:

1. Select the cells you wish to resize (or, more often, the entire table).

2. Choose Table ➤ Cell Height and Width.

3. Click the Column tab if it is not already in view.

4. Click the AutoFit button. Word will snug up the selected cells.

Merging Cells

Use the Merge Cells feature to combine the contents of multiple cells—for example, to make a heading in one cell span an entire table or a selected group of columns. You select the cells to merge, then choose Table ➤ Merge Cells, and the contents of the designated cells will merge. You may need to reformat text merged this way.

Unmerging Cells

To split (unmerge) cells, place the insertion point in a merged cell and choose Table ➤ Split Cells. You'll be asked how many cells you want after the split.

Changing the Space between Columns

Word assigns cell widths based on the available text area and the number of columns you request. In the process, it sets aside a small amount of unprintable space between each cell (or within, actually). This space takes away from the usable cell space. For instance, a $1\frac{1}{2}''$ column with $\frac{1}{4}''$ column spacing would have $1\frac{1}{4}''$ of usable space in the middle of each cell.

To change the space between columns, follow these steps:

1. Select the columns of interest.

2. Select Table ➤ Cell Height and Width to open the Cell Height and Width dialog box, then choose the Columns tab.

3. Type a new specification in the Space Between Columns box, or use the arrows to flip through suggested choices.

4. Click OK.

AutoFormatting Tables

Word 6's new Table ➤ Table AutoFormat command attempts to pick cell settings that make a presentable table. Whether it succeeds or not will vary with the project it's given and your definition of success. Personal taste plays a role too.

Here are the basic steps for using Table AutoFormat:

1. Enter, edit, spell-check, reorganize, and otherwise finish with your table.

2. Save your document to disk.

3. Select the entire table (Table ➤ Select Table or Alt+5 on the numeric keypad with NumLock off).

4. Choose Table ➤ Table AutoFormat to open the Table AutoFormat dialog box (see Figure 7.5).

5. Preview the format choices from the scrolling list by highlighting their names one at a time. The up- and down-arrow keys are handy here.

6. Pick a style by highlighting it and click OK.

Pay particular attention to how Word handles row and column headings in the preview examples. Note that most of the canned styles assume that the top row will be column headings (months or years, for instance); and the left-most column will be row headings of some kind (itemized expense items, for instance). Turn these effects on and off with their corresponding checkboxes in the Apply Special Formats To area of the Table AutoFormat dialog box. You can also turn off many of the AutoFormat effects (borders, shading, etc.) the same way.

FIGURE 7.5

The Table AutoFormat
dialog box

 NOTE Use Table ➤ Table AutoFormat to format tables, not Format ➤ AutoFormat.

Converting Tables to Text and Vice Versa

Sometimes you'll start a project using tabs and wish you'd created a table—or a coworker will give you some tabbed text. Other times, you will want to export things you've typed using Word's table feature for use with database and other programs that expect tab- or comma-separated (delimited) input. Word has solutions for all these contingencies.

Word makes it quite easy to convert back and forth from tables to text. You may need to do some cleanup before or after conversion though. Always work on copies of your documents when you do this!

Converting Text to Tables

To convert text to a table, highlight the text you want to turn into a table. Choose Table ➤ Convert Text to Table... and click the appropriate option button in the resulting dialog box. Here's an explanation of the choices:

Tab	Lines of text separated by paragraph marks or line breaks will become rows in your table. Tab-separated strings of text within those lines will become cell entries in the row. Word will automatically create the necessary number of columns based on the maximum number of tabs in a line.
Comma	Lines of text separated by paragraph marks or line breaks will become rows in your table. Comma-separated strings of text within those lines will become cell entries in the row. Word will automatically create the necessary number of columns based on the maximum number of commas in a line. Beware of commas that might create unintentional cells.
Paragraphs	Word will propose a single column and create as many rows as you have paragraphs. Changing the number of columns will distribute paragraphs among the columns from left to right. In a two-column layout, the first paragraph would end up in the top-left cell of the new table, the second paragraph in the top-right cell, the third in the left cell of row two, and so on.

Converting Tables to Text

To convert an existing table to text, select the table cells you wish to convert, or Alt+double-click to select the whole table. Choose Table ➤ Convert Table To Text. Word will display a Table To Text dialog box, which asks if you want the table converted to paragraphs, tab-delimited text, or comma-delimited text. Pick one.

Choosing the paragraph option will convert each old table cell into at least one paragraph: If the table's cells contain multiple paragraphs, the paragraph marks are retained during the conversion, so some cells will create more than one new paragraph.

If you pick the comma or tab options, Word will convert each row of your table into one paragraph. Cells from the tables will be separated within the paragraphs by tabs or commas.

The Table Wizard

The Table Wizard (see Figure 7.6) will ask you some questions and format your table. Here are the basic steps to using this Wizard:

1. Place the insertion point where you want the table. Tap ↵ once or twice if you've just opened a new document.

2. Choose Table ➤ Insert Table.

3. Click the Wizard button in the resulting dialog box. You will be presented with a number of screens asking you questions.

4. Look at each choice *carefully*, and study the examples if they are given. Don't confuse *rows* and *columns* when the Wizard gives you choices. Try to imagine *your* data in the sample table formats.

FIGURE 7.6

The Table Wizard
dialog box

5. Click on the Next button after each choice or the Back button to back up one screen.

6. When the Wiz runs out of questions, click Finish. You'll be presented with the Table AutoFormat dialog box (which you read about earlier).

7. Cruise the format samples until you find just the right mood, then click OK.

Sorting

Word can sort lines of tabular text, items you've entered in tables, or even paragraphs in a document. The Sort command can be helpful when preparing data files for Word's Print Merge feature.

  As with some other Word features, Sort can make substantial changes to your document (read: ruin your hard work if you didn't save it first), so save before you sort. DON'T save _after_ you sort until you've scanned the document to see if the sort worked as you intended. For extra security, consider running the sort on a copy of your document rather than the original.

Sorting with the Database Toolbar

The Database toolbar contains some sorting buttons, among other things. To sort rows of text, select them and click on either the Sort Ascending or Sort Descending button. Word will perform its sort based on the first letter(s) at the left of each line. If the first row (line) of text is bold or otherwise seems like it might be part of a label, Word will not move that row.

To sort items in a table with the Database toolbar, follow these steps:

1. Save your work, just in case.

2. Place the insertion point in the column that you want to use as the "sort by" column.

Word

3. Click the Ascending or Descending sort button. This displays the Sort dialog box (see Figure 7.7).

4. Word will sort the entire table (all columns), leaving labels untouched.

FIGURE 7.7

The Sort dialog box
on top of a Word table

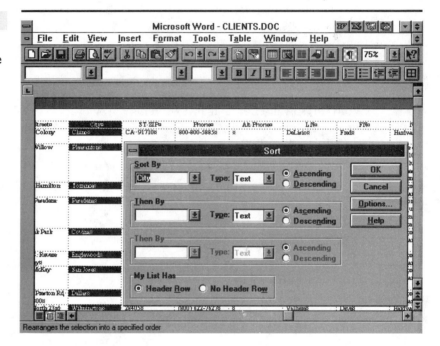

Sorting with the Sort Text Command

Word's Table ➤ Sort Text command will attempt to sort selected text alphabetically, numerically, or chronologically at your request. Sorts can be up to three levels "deep." It can be used in freeform text, but is much more powerful when used with a table. To sort a table with this command, follow these steps:

1. Save your work, just in case.

2. Place the insertion point in the table you wish to sort.

3. Pick Table ➤ Sort Text. Word will highlight (select) the entire table, and you will see the Sort dialog box.

4. If you have labels at the top of your table, choose the option My List Has Header Row. There will be up to three drop-down lists containing the column labels (if you have them) or column numbers.

5. Specify the sort order by choosing the desired column for each sort level.

6. Choose a sort order for each column.

7. Tell Word if the data in each column are text, numbers, or dates by choosing from the Type drop-down lists.

8. Click OK and Word will sort.

If you want the sort to be case-sensitive, or if you are sorting things that are not in a table, click the Options button in the Sort dialog box and make the appropriate choices in the Sort Options dialog box.

Alternatives to Word

For big sorting projects, check out Excel's database features (see the chapters on Excel later in this book) or full-fledged databases like Microsoft Access.

A WHOLE NEW WAY TO WORK

Creating Excel Tables in Word Documents

The Excel button in Word's Standard toolbar lets you create Excel worksheets right in Word documents. You define the size of the worksheet, and Word temporarily replaces the Word menus with Excel menus. Here's how it works:

1. Position the Word insertion point where you want to create the worksheet.

2. Click on the Excel button in Word's Standard toolbar.

3. Drag with your mouse as shown below to define the desired number of rows and columns in the worksheet, then release the mouse button.

4. In a while, Word will insert Excel worksheet cells and the menu bar will contain Excel commands as shown here. Don't worry if the worksheet temporarily covers up part of your text as you work.

A WHOLE
NEW WAY
TO WORK

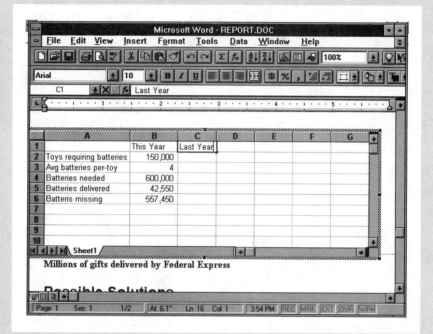

5. Create the worksheet labels and formulas using the techniques in Part Three of this book. Spell-check the worksheet cells from within Excel.

6. Click outside of the worksheet area to insert the finished worksheet object into the Word document at the insertion point.

7. If necessary, double-click on the worksheet itself (the Worksheet object) in your Word document to edit it.

8

Working with Graphics

ord for Windows lets you draw, place, resize, reposition, and embellish graphics. You can work with your own drawings, charts from Excel, PowerPoint and other software packages, photos from scanners, and just about any other computer-compatible art form. In fact, Microsoft Office even comes with some clip art and a clip art viewer you can use to get your graphics library started.

> **TIP**
>
> **Microsoft Office actually comes with two art collections— one in the WINWORD\CLIPART directory and another collection reached from the ClipArt Gallery. You'll see how to combine the two collections later in this chapter.**

You can simply *paste* graphics or place them in *frames*. As you'll soon see, the use of frames makes it easier for you to reposition and work with graphics. OLE is also a possibility. See Chapter 3 for more information about OLE.

There are plenty of new graphics-related buzzwords and standards to learn. In fact, another book the size of this one could be written just on those subjects. But this chapter contains all you'll need to start creating your own art and using free or low-cost clip art.

Importing Graphics

Like text, computer art can be stored in disk files. Unfortunately, different drawing packages, scanners, and other graphics tools create files in their own unique formats. Word for Windows comes with a number of built-in translation utilities (called *filters*) that can convert graphics from many sources, allowing you to insert them in Word for Windows documents. At a minimum, you will be able to work with the following graphic formats. (Their usual file extensions are listed after their names:)

- AutoCAD 2-D (DXF)
- Computer Graphics Metafile (CGM)
- CompuServe GIF (CGM)
- CorelDRAW (CDR)
- DrawPerfect (WPG)
- Encapsulated PostScript (EPS)
- HP Graphic Language (HGL)
- Kodak Photo CD (PCD)
- Lotus 1-2-3 (PIC)
- Macintosh PICT (PCT)
- Micrografx Designer 3/Draw Plus (DRW)
- PC Paintbrush (PCX)
- TIFF (Tagged Image File Format—TIF)
- Windows Bitmap (BMP)
- Windows Metafile (WMF)

If you don't see the format you need here, contact Microsoft technical support. They may be able to provide you with new filters, give you some work-around tips, or refer you to makers of graphics conversion programs.

Other Sources of Clip Art

If you don't have the time or inclination to draw your own art, you can purchase compatible clip-art disks from mail-order firms and retail software dealers like Egghead. Many companies and nonprofit groups also distribute low-cost or free shareware and public-domain clip art. Check local computer user groups and on-line art libraries like the ones provided by America Online and CompuServe. If you have a scanner, you can convert printed images to Word-compatible art. Be sure you understand and honor any copyright restrictions when you use other people's art.

Word

Using the Insert Picture Command

The easiest way to get hooked on graphics is to import a picture or two. Here's how:

1. Start by creating or opening a document.

2. Place the insertion point where you want the picture to appear.

3. Choose Insert ➤ Picture to bring up the dialog box shown in Figure 8.1.

4. Click Preview Picture to enable the preview option.

5. Browse by clicking on directories and files until you see something you like.

FIGURE 8.1

Use the Insert ➤ Picture command to insert disk-resident graphic files.

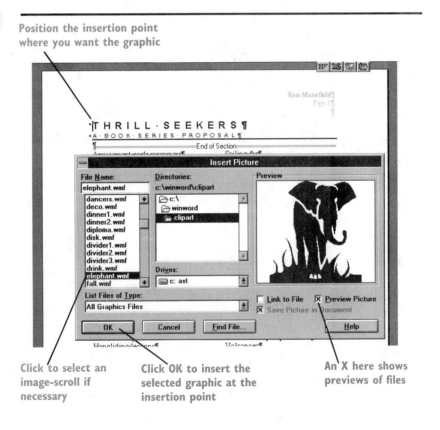

Position the insertion point where you want the graphic

Click to select an image-scroll if necessary

Click OK to insert the selected graphic at the insertion point

An X here shows previews of files

6. When you find your favorite graphic, click OK to insert it. Here's ele-phant.wmf from the c:\winword\clipart directory:

 T H R I L L   S E E K E R S
A B O O K S E R I E S P R O P O S A L

Amusement park screamers   Parasailing
Breathtaking horesback rides   Pontoon planes
Bungee!   Racecar lessons from the pros

7. Reposition and perhaps resize or otherwise embellish the image. You will learn more about these options later in this chapter.

TIP In addition to the Word for Windows clip art folder, chances are you have other graphic images on your hard disk. For instance, your Windows directory probably has a dozen or so bitmap files (files ending in BMP). Use Find File's scrollable lists to locate files of interest. When you see one, click on the name to highlight it, then click the Preview Picture button to get an idea of what it will look like. If you use graphics regularly or have a large collection, you may prefer the new ClipArt Gallery, described next.

ClipArt Gallery

The Office ClipArt Gallery is reached from the Insert Object command. It offers "categories" of art and some other intriguing features.

To use the ClipArt Gallery:

1. Start by creating or opening a document.

2. Place the insertion point where you want the picture to appear.

3. Choose Insert ➤ Object.

4. When you see the Object dialog box, click the Create New tab if necessary and then scroll to pick Microsoft ClipArt Gallery.

5. Click OK. You will see the ClipArt Gallery dialog box shown in Figure 8.2.

FIGURE 8.2

Use the ClipArt Gallery to preview and insert disk-resident graphic files.

6. Browse by clicking on categories of interest and scrolling to view *thumbnails* (miniature copies) of graphics in the gallery.

7. Double-click on a thumbnail or click once on it and once on OK to insert a full-sized copy of the image at the insertion point in your Word document.

THRILL SEEKERS
A BOOK SERIES PROPOSAL

Amusement park screamers   Pontoon planes
Breathtaking horesback rides   Racecar lessons from the pros

8. Reposition and perhaps resize or otherwise embellish the image. You will learn more about these options later in this chapter.

Maintaining the Gallery

You can add other images to the gallery by using the gallery's Add and Refresh buttons in the Options dialog box shown in Figure 8.3, reached via the

FIGURE 8.3

Add and remove gallery items with the Options dialog box.

Clean up the gallery after adding and deleting files

Click the Help button to read about maintaining your gallery

Use the Add button to add new pictures

Options button. Learn more by reading the associated on-line help in the Options dialog box.

Using Your Clipboard to Insert Art

If you already have a drawing program that you use to create and edit artwork, it is possible to copy your work to the Clipboard, then paste it into a Word for Windows document. Here are the steps:

1. Switch to or run the drawing program.

2. Select the art of interest.

3. Copy it to the Clipboard (Ctrl+C).

4. Switch to or start Word (you may first have to quit or minimize the drawing program to run Word).

5. Move the insertion point to the desired location in your Word document.

6. Paste the graphic with the Edit ➤ Paste command or Ctrl+V.

Resizing Graphics with Your Mouse

When you click on a graphic in a Word for Windows document to select it, the picture will be surrounded by a box containing eight handles—one in each corner and one on each side of the outline box. The mouse pointer will turn into a two-headed arrow.

NOTE If you size something (a graphic, for example) proportionally, as the size changes, the width and height retain the same proportions relative to each other. That is, if the height gets three times larger, the width will get three times larger as well.

To increase or decrease the size of the entire graphic *proportionally*, drag a *corner* handle diagonally, releasing it when you are happy with the size.

To distort a dimension, use the handles on the *edges* of the graphic outline to stretch (distort) the graphic, as shown in Figure 8.4. Use Undo if you are unhappy with the results.

FIGURE 8.4

Drag center handles to distort, corner handles to resize proportionally.

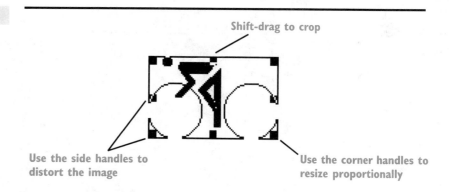

Shift-drag to crop

Use the side handles to distort the image

Use the corner handles to resize proportionally

Cropping Graphics with Your Mouse

To crop a document (hide part of it), hold down the Shift key while you drag any of the handles to create the desired effect. The mouse pointer will turn into a square with a line through it.

Adding Space around Graphics

To add space around a graphic, hold down the Shift key and drag handles away from the graphic. Use Undo to restore the original size.

Sizing and Cropping Graphics with the Picture Command

The Format ➤ Picture command reveals the Picture dialog box, shown in Figure 8.5. It contains information about a selected picture's original size and any cropping or resizing that's been done.

FIGURE 8.5

Use the Picture dialog box to see what you've done; you can modify or undo resizing and cropping settings here.

You can also use this box to specify new size and cropping dimensions. The Reset button returns a graphic to its original size and uncrops it.

Using Word's Drawing Features

To create a new drawing using the Word for Windows drawing features:

1. Open a new or existing Word document.

2. Place the insertion point where you want your new art to be inserted.

3. Click on the Standard toolbar's Drawing button, shown at left. (Or, if you have a Word document containing a graphic you want to modify, double-click on the graphic.)

4. You'll see the Drawing toolbar, illustrated in Figure 8.6.

You'll use a series of buttons, menu commands, and your mouse to draw, resize, and rearrange shapes, lines, and text.

FIGURE 8.6

Use the Drawing toolbar to create new drawings and edit existing ones.

TIP You might want to reshape the Drawing toolbar to facilitate moving it around and keeping it out of the way. Drag an edge of the toolbar to change its shape from wide and short to tall and skinny, for instance, as shown in Figure 8.7.

FIGURE 8.7

You can change the shape of the toolbar by dragging any side.

Drawing Objects

First click on a shape button or line button (line, ellipse, circle, etc.) in the Drawing toolbar, then use your mouse to create lines or shapes. For instance, to create rectangles for an organizational chart, you would click on the Rectangle tool and drag with your mouse to create a rectangle of the desired shape and size. (Hold down the Shift key while dragging to create squares.)

Use the Ellipse tool for ovals and circles. (Hold down the Shift key while dragging to create precise circles.)

To create polygons, choose the Freeform tool, then click and drag repeatedly until you are done. For example, to make a triangle, you would click once to anchor the first point and drag to create the first side. Click again to anchor the second point and drag again. Click to anchor the third point, then drag

back to the starting point and click one last time to complete the triangle.

  To change the shape of a polygon, select it using the techniques described next, then click the Reshape tool on the Drawing toolbar. Handles will appear at each intersection of the shape. Drag them as necessary to create the desired shape.

Selecting Objects

To select rectangles or other drawing elements (lines, text, etc.), click on the arrow button at the top of the drawing tool stack, then point to the item you want to move.

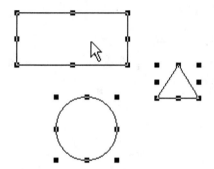

Hold down the Shift key to select multiple objects. The Edit ➤ Select All command selects all text and pictures. Selected objects are surrounded by small handles. Click outside of any selected object to deselect all selected objects.

Text in Drawings

You can create text for drawings either in *text boxes* or in frames. Creating text in frames will be discussed later in this chapter. To create a text box:

1. Click on the toolbar's Text Box button.

2. Drag the text box to the desired size and shape. Make it a little bigger than you think it needs to be to accommodate the text you will type.

3. Type the word **Marketing** (the insertion point's already in the box, so there's no need to position it).

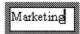

4. If necessary, you can increase the size of a text box by dragging, just as if it were any other graphic object.

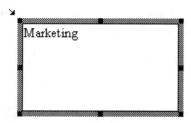

Text in boxes is automatically surrounded by lines unless you eliminate them. You will learn how to do so later in this chapter.

Embellishing Text in Drawings

You can embellish text (make it bold, center it, change type styles, and so on) and you can combine the effects using most of Word's formatting tools. For example, here's a box with two typefaces, some bold characters, and a bulleted list, created with the Bullets button on the Format toolbar.

Marketing Department
- Sandra Lexington
- William Johnson
- Karin Danialson
- Bobbi Wrightwood

More or Less Space between Text and Box Lines

To increase or decrease the space between the text and text box lines:

1. Select the text box.

2. Choose Format ➤ Drawing Object.

3. Select the Size and Position tab. You'll see the choices illustrated in Figure 8.8.

FIGURE 8.8

Use the Drawing Object dialog box to add white space in a text box.

4. Specify a new internal margin by typing a new setting in the appropriate box or using the up and down arrow keys. For instance, here's the marketing text box with 6 points (6pt) of internal margin:

> **Marketing Department**
> - Sandra Lexington
> - William Johnson
> - Karin Danialson

Eliminating Text Box Lines

To eliminate the lines surrounding the text box, follow these steps:

1. Select the box or boxes by clicking or shift-clicking.

2. Use the Drawing toolbar's Line Color button to reveal the line color palette.

3. Click on None (at the top), as shown here:

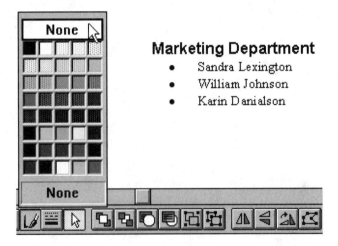

Moving Objects

To move objects, follow these steps:

1. Select the item or items to be moved.

2. Point to one of the selected items with your mouse pointer, avoiding the object's handles.

3. The pointer will change, now looking like an arrow with four heads.

Marketing Department

- Sandra Lexington
- William Johnson
- Karin Danialson

4. Drag with your mouse and watch as an outline of the object(s) proposes a new location.

5. Release the mouse button to complete the move.

Grid Lines

Word's drawing feature has optional *invisible gridlines* that make it easy to align objects. These gridlines make dragging a little jerky when the Snap To Grid feature is enabled. The gridlines act like magnets and moved objects migrate to them. For precise, smooth moves, turn the Snap To Grid feature off. You can also change the spacing and origin of grids. Press the Snap To Grid button, shown below, to reveal the Snap To Grid dialog box, shown in Figure 8.9.

Word

FIGURE 8.9

Use the Snap To Grid
dialog box to change
the spacing and origin
of grids.

To turn off the snap feature, click to remove the X from the Snap To Grid box. Even if the grid is turned off, you can still use it whenever you wish by holding down the Alt key while you drag.

Use the other tools in the dialog box to change the grid's dimensions and starting point with respect to the upper-left corner of the window.

Layers

You can construct objects from multiple elements placed near, on top of, or beneath one other. For instance, the books.wmf file shown here contains a number of separate elements that you can rearrange, delete, or use separately.

Objects piled on top of each other in drawings are said to be *layered*. You can select items and use the Bring To Front or Send To Back buttons on the Drawing toolbar to arrange layers to your liking.

Grouping and Ungrouping

Sometimes you'll want to turn multiple drawing parts into a single object. This makes it easier to move and resize complex elements (see Figure 8.10). Simply select all of the elements of interest by shift-clicking, then use the Group button on the Drawing toolbar.

TIP   Only elements of <u>drawings</u> can be grouped and ungrouped. Bitmap images (like those found in Microsoft's free ClipArt Gallery) are not drawings.

FIGURE 8.10

Grouping objects makes them easy to keep together.

Henceforth, all of the items will act as a single item, as you can see here:

The items will act as a unit until you select the group and choose Draw ➤ Ungroup.

Reorienting Objects

 To flip objects, select them and choose Draw ➤ Rotate/Flip. Choose one of the three Flip and Rotate buttons, shown at left, on the Drawing toolbar.

Duplicating Objects

Once you've created an object, you can select, copy, and paste it to save time. Consider grouping complex collections of lines and shapes and text before duplicating them.

Pictures vs. Drawing Objects

There are two general types of graphic images—drawings like the ones created and discussed in this chapter and "pictures" or "painted" images created with paint programs. Drawings are made up of individual elements—lines, circles, etc. Painted images are generally treated as one large collection of dots. Files that end with the extension .BMP are bitmap "paintings." So are many Windows Metafiles (.WMF). Word for Windows can use both drawings and bitmaps, but if you want to edit them, you must do so in a special window. Suppose you want to change the color and shading of the ornamnt1.wmf file in the winword6/clipart directory. Here are the steps:

1. Position the insertion point where you want the graphic to appear in your Word document.

2. Choose Insert ➤ Picture and locate the desired file (ornamnt1.wmf), as shown in Figure 8.11.

3. Click OK to insert the graphic. It will appear in the Word document, but most of the Drawing toolbar buttons won't work. You can confirm this by watching the Status area as you point to the various buttons.

Word

FIGURE 8.11

Find the graphic file you wish to edit.

4. Double-click on the graphic to open a picture window. You'll see the graphic, a *picture boundary*, and a small dialog box:

5. If the graphic isn't surrounded by the picture boundary, click on the Reset Picture Boundary button to move the picture into the boundary, as shown here:

6. Edit the picture. (Shift-click to select all elements and use the Fill Color button on the Drawing toolbar to choose 20% gray, as illustrated here:)

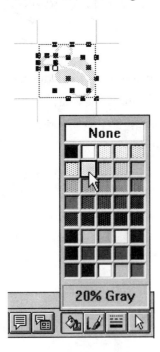

7. When done editing, click the Close Picture button in the little Picture window. The edited graphic will be placed in your Word for Windows document at the insertion point.

Rotating and Flipping Objects

To rotate or flip objects, select them and use the Flip Horizontal, Flip Vertical, and Rotate Right buttons on the Drawing toolbar.

NOTE These buttons won't work on Text boxes. Use WordArt, described later in this chapter, to manipulate the orientation of text.

Callouts

You can use callouts to label graphics in Word for Windows documents. Here are the steps:

1. Create or import a graphic.

2. Click the Callout button, shown at left, on the Drawing toolbar.

3. Click where you want the callout arrow to point.

4. Drag to where you want to position the text and then release the mouse button. The callout will appear.

5. Type any text you want to show in the callout, then select the text and change its appearance if you like.

6. Select the callout box and resize it if you wish.

7. Drag the box and line as desired to reposition them.

8. To change the design of the callout box, use the Callout Defaults dialog box, shown in Figure 8.12. Reach it with the Format Callout button, shown at left.

NOTE If you select a callout and then click on Format Callout, changes you make will affect that callout and the defaults, but not any other existing callouts.

FIGURE 8.12

Use the Callout
Defaults dialog box to
change the design of
the callout box.

Word

filling

To fill drawn items with different colors or shades of gray, follow these steps:

1. Select the desired item(s).

2. Choose the button shown at left from the Drawing toolbar to bring up the Fill Color palette.

3. Click to select the desired fill color.

Line Colors and Shades of Gray

To change the color or shade of lines:

1. Select the desired item(s).

2. Choose the button shown at left from the Drawing toolbar to bring up the line palette.

3. Click to select the desired line color.

255

Line Sizes and Arrowheads

To change the size of lines and arrowheads:

1. Select the desired line(s).

2. Choose the button shown at left from the Drawing toolbar to bring up the line palette.

3. Click to select the desired line type.

4. Choose More to bring up the Line tab in the Drawing Defaults dialog box, illustrated in Figure 8.13.

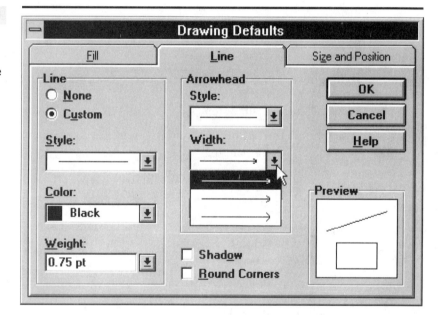

Using Frames to Position Objects

If you simply paste a graphic into a Word for Windows document (without framing it), it is treated like a character. You can place the graphic between characters, move it from one line to another, copy it, delete it, and so on. But it is a slave to elements like line and paragraph specifications, margins, indents, and such. To have maximum control over graphics and other document elements, you should place them in frames.

Frames can contain either graphics, text, or both. Frames let you precisely position objects virtually anywhere in your document. And you can tell Word for Windows to flow your unframed text around frames, as illustrated in Figure 8.14. Frames can contain graphics, Excel charts, Word text, or any combination thereof. In fact, it may be helpful to think of frames as pages within a page that you can move, resize, and embellish.

To use frames, you create them, insert objects into them, then size and position them either with your mouse or with the Frame dialog box. Normally, you'll want to work with framed items in Page Layout view or Print Preview so that you can easily see and move them.

Word

FIGURE 8.14

Use frames to contain and position both text and graphics. Notice how frames make room for themselves in text.

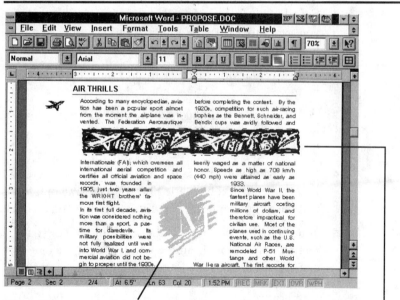

Text will wrap around framed objects   **Framed objects can span columns**

> **TIP** It's a good idea to turn on hidden paragraph marks when working with frames. If they are not visible, click on the Show/Hide¶ button in the Standard toolbar. It looks like a ¶ mark.

Inserting Frames and Framing Objects

You can either insert an empty frame and then place something in it or you can select something and frame it. In either case, you use the Insert ➤ Frame command *or* the Insert Frame button, shown at left.

Inserting Empty Frames

Here are the steps for creating a new, empty frame:

1. Start by switching to Page Layout view if you are not already in it. (If you forget to do this, Word for Windows will ask if it can switch views for you.)

2. Click the Drawing toolbar's Insert Frame button or choose Insert ➤ Frame.

3. Your pointer will change to a crosshair. Drag to create a frame of the approximate size and shape you desire, located about where you want it to be placed.

4. Shortly after you release the mouse button, you'll see a frame surrounded by a border. If you have the Show/Hide paragraph feature enabled, you will see a paragraph mark within the frame and an anchor outside of it.

5. You can either type text in the resulting frame (you'll learn how in a moment), paste things from the Clipboard, or use one of the Insert menu commands, such as the Picture and Object commands.

Framing Existing Objects

If you already have something in your document that needs framing, you can do so by following these steps:

1. Switch to Page Layout view if you are not there already.

2. Select the item or items to be framed.

3. Use either the Frame button on the Drawing toolbar or choose Insert ➤ Frame.

4. Your selected item(s) will be surrounded by a frame, and you'll see a paragraph mark and an anchor, as illustrated here, if you have clicked the Show/Hide ¶ button.

Framed items and their frames can be resized just as you resize graphics. Drag their handles. If you accidentally frame the wrong thing or too many or too few things, or accidentally distort the size or shape of a graphic, use Undo to reverse your mistakes.

TIP If you start the framing process (choose Insert ➤ Frame) and change your mind, cancel it by pressing Esc.

Positioning Framed Items with a Mouse

The dirt-simple way to position frames is to drag them with your mouse while in Page Layout view or Print Preview. Follow these steps:

1. Place the pointer anywhere within the frame and watch the pointer.

2. The pointer will change to include a 4-headed arrow.

Word

3. Press down on the primary mouse button and drag the frame to the upper-left corner of the text.

4. Release the mouse button.

5. Soon after you release the mouse button the frame will take up residence in its new location. Text will move out of the way for the frame and the anchor icon will move as well.

You can continue to drag the framed graphic around to suit yourself. Switch to Print Preview and try moving it there too. Remember—you'll need to click on the Magnifier button in Print Preview first to let you edit the document.

A frame is always anchored to a paragraph. When you position a frame by dragging it, it is initially anchored to its closest paragraph. When you move it, the anchor moves to the next nearest paragraph. To see where a frame's anchor is, select the frame and look for the anchor icon.

As you add or delete text in your document the framed item stays with its paragraph. A frame always appears on the same page with its paragraph.

This is often the desired effect. But what if you want to keep a framed item on a particular page, or a specific distance from a particular paragraph?

Positioning Framed Items with the Frame Dialog Box

When you want to position frames precisely or force a frame to position itself relative to other things that might move, choose Format ➤ Frame. You will see the Frame dialog box, shown in Figure 8.15.

When you select a frame and open this dialog box, you will see the current size and position of the frame. You can specify new size and position settings for the frame in inches (in), centimeters (cm), points (pt), or picas (pi). You can change the units of measurement by using the General tab in the Options dialog box (reached by choosing Tools ➤ Options).

FIGURE 8.15

The Frame dialog box

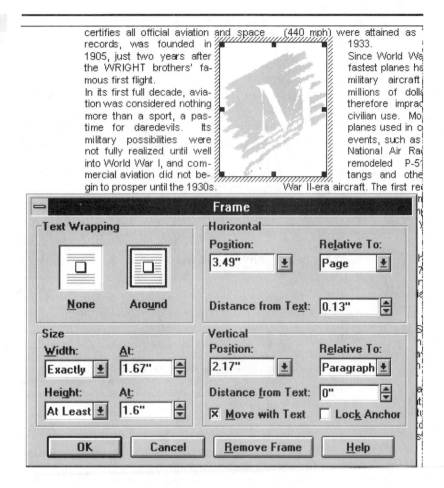

Aligning Frames with Reference Points

The Frame dialog box also provides a mind-boggling array of positioning and reference options. For instance, you can force a frame to always remain in the exact horizontal and vertical center of a page, even when you change margins or page sizes. Or you can tell Word for Windows to keep a frame a specified distance from margins or columns. Finally, you can anchor a frame to text, so when the text moves, the frame accompanies it. Place a check mark in the Move With Text box to accomplish this.

Text and Frames

Frames and text can be used together several ways. Besides framing text, you can position frames relative to text or have text flow around frames. Here are a few ways to work with frames and text.

Placing Text in Frames

You can use frames as small text windows that can be moved anywhere in your document. For instance, here the heading "Been There, Done That" has been framed and moved into the document's margin. (You may want to remove the frame borders when you do this.)

BEEN·
THERE,·
DONE·
THAT¶

And·thrills·no·longer·necessarily·means·a·trip·to·Disneyland.·A·growing·number·of·people·are·taking·glider·rides,·bungee·jumping,·being·gored·by·bulls·and·hiking·into·active·volcanoes.·There·are·drag·strips·where·you·can·race·your·own·car·or·a·real·nitro·burner.·Manufacturers·can't·make·downhill·snowboards·fast·enough·to·keep·up·with·the·demand.·Barnstormers·are·back,·and·you·can·ride·along·with·them.·They'll·even·provide·the·leather·cap,·goggles·and·scarf!¶

If the Move With Text option is checked in the Frame dialog box, the headings will stay with their paragraphs when your document is edited.

A quick way to create lots of marginal headings like this is to create one, then *redefine the document's heading style(s)* on the basis of the example. All of your headings will be framed and placed in the margin quicker than you can say "Bungeeee!" When framing existing *text*, Word for Windows will make the frame big enough to accommodate all of the text you've selected. If you paste text into an existing frame, make sure the frame is big enough to prevent "weird word wrap," a problem that arises when you specify large line indents or place long words in narrow frames. If the text you insert changes into a long vertical string of characters, try resizing the frame to make the text legible.

Feel free to use all of Word's text formatting tools in Frames. You can have multiple paragraphs in frames.

Word's Formatting toolbar and ruler work in frames. You can change type sizes and styles, center, justify, and otherwise fool with text in frames. Even Word's spelling checker peeks into them.

Inserting Text in Framed Graphics (Captioning)

If you want to add a caption to a framed graphic, select the frame, then press ↵. You'll see a new paragraph mark in the frame. Type the caption. Stylize the text if you like. The caption will stay with the frame when you move it.

How Framed Items Appear in Different Views

Framed items can be seen where they will print when displayed in Print Preview and Page Layout view. When you switch to Normal or Outline views, framed items will appear within the page boundaries where they will print, but not necessarily in their printing positions. You can easily spot framed items in Normal and Outline views.

Selecting and Deleting Framed Items

It's possible to delete frames *and their contents* by simply selecting the frame and then cutting (Ctrl+X) or pressing the Delete key. (Select a frame by pointing and clicking with your mouse. Eight dark black handles and a black line will appear around the frame when you've selected it.)

To remove a frame but not its contents, select the frame and click the Remove Frame button in the Frame dialog box (reached by choosing Format ➤ Frame). If you use this method to remove a frame with a printing border but not its contents, the frame's *border* will remain. Delete it or change it as described next.

Word

Deleting or Changing Frame Borders

Frames are created without printing borders, but these can be added and altered.

1. Select a framed object in Page Layout view by clicking on the object.

2. Use the Format ➤ Shading command to add, change, or remove the border. For instance, clicking on the None icon in the Preset area of the Border dialog box removes a frame's border.

 TIP There is also a border button on the Standard toolbar. It's on the right end and looks like a four-pane window.

Repeating Framed Items on Multiple Pages

To repeat the same framed object on multiple pages, create them in headers or footers.

A WHOLE NEW WAY TO WORK

Special Effects with WordArt

You can use WordArt, an intriguing little program installed with Word for Windows, to create unusual-looking text objects (for example, company logos), and then put them into your projects. In this example, we'll create a WordArt object to use in a Word document.

1. Open or create a document in Page Layout view.

2. Place the insertion point where you want the WordArt object to appear.

3. Choose Insert ➤ Object.

A WHOLE NEW WAY TO WORK

4. Double-click to pick MS WordArt from the scrolling list in the Create New tab:

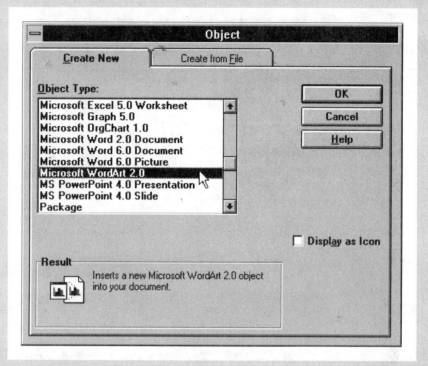

5. Either type new text or paste text from the Clipboard into the resulting dialog box. Then click Update Display to insert it into your document.

6. Notice that the menu bar has changed: it has a drop-down list of special effects. Experiment with the fonts, sizes, styles, alignment, and other options. You'll see a preview as you work, but it can take a moment for the screen to update fully. Don't panic if you see gnarly-looking "interim" images. The fonts supplied with WordArt are bitmap, and may be hard to read in small sizes or appear jagged if they get too big. The following shows some text formatted with the Wave effect.

7. When you are happy with the result, click on Update Display, and WordArt will paste your concoction into your active Word for Windows document at the insertion point.

8. Click in the document to close WordArt.

9. Frame the finished object to make it easier to move.

10. Reposition it like any other framed item.

11. Go show someone!

> **A WHOLE NEW WAY TO WORK**
>
> Any of the art and WordArt that you create using the techniques in this chapter can be placed in other documents created with Excel, PowerPoint, and other OLE-capable programs. As usual, you can have changes to the art object reflected automatically in the destination document(s), depending on whether the object is embedded or linked when it is placed.

Captions

If you write long documents with numbered figures, tables, and other elements you will love this new feature! It automatically numbers things, lets you label them, then renumbers them if you move them or otherwise change their sequence in a document. There are a variety of appearance options as well.

Adding Captions

You can either manually caption the occasional item or turn on automatic captioning. To manually caption:

1. Select the item to be captioned.
2. Choose Insert ➤ Caption.
3. You'll see the Caption dialog box.
4. Word proposes a caption label that you can accept as-is or edit. For example, you can type descriptive text.
5. You can change the default appearance options by visiting the Position List and Numbering dialog box.
6. Click OK to insert the label. Be patient; it takes a moment.

To automatically add captions to items of a particular type (all drawings, for instance), use the AutoCaption dialog box, reached with the AutoCaption button in the Caption dialog box. Word for Windows can recognize and automatically caption the following types of files:

- Most graphic files
- Microsoft drawings
- Microsoft equations
- Microsoft Graphs
- Microsoft WordArt
- Inserted Word documents
- Paintbrush pictures
- Sounds
- And much more

To automatically caption items, follow these steps:

1. Choose Insert ➤ Caption.
2. Click AutoCaption.
3. Pick a type of item to automatically caption. You can pick more than one type for the same caption label (for instance, you can pick Microsoft drawings and Word pictures). Inserting either will have the same effect.
4. Pick a label type from the Use Label list or create your own with the New Label button.
5. Pick a position for the label (above or below the item).
6. Change the numbering scheme if you like.
7. Repeat steps 3 through 6 for each different type of caption you want.
8. Click OK.

After you've turned on AutoCaption and defined the appearance options, Word for Windows will automatically label any insertion that meets the Auto-Caption criteria.

If you move a figure and its label, Word for Windows will not immediately update the figure labels. But it *will* update figure numbers whenever you ask to print or switch to Print Preview. To force an immediate update, select all of your text (Ctrl+A) and press F9.

To revise a caption, just edit it like any other text. To change all of the captions of a given type (*Figure* to *FIG*, for instance), select a caption in text, visit the Caption or AutoCaption dialog box, and pick a different label from the Use Label List.

To create new label types (*FIG*, for example), use the New Label button in the Caption and AutoCaption dialog boxes.

Including Chapter and Other Numbers in Captions

You can include chapter and similar numbers in automatic captions if you like. Here are the steps:

1. Format all of the main headings (chapters, for example) as Heading Style 1.

2. Choose Format ➤ Heading Numbering. Make sure a numerical numbering style is in use (not Chapter One, for instance).

3. Visit either the Caption or AutoCaption dialog box.

4. Choose the Numbering button.

5. When you see the Caption Numbering dialog box, choose Include Chapter Numbers.

6. Back out by clicking OK as needed.

Word

A WHOLE NEW WAY TO WORK

Creating Vertical Text

WordArt is the program to use if you want to include the occasional piece of vertical text in one of your projects. To include vertical text in a Word document, for example, follow these steps:

1. Open or create a document in Page Layout view.
2. Place the insertion point on a new line near where you want the vertical text to appear.
3. Choose Insert ➤ Object.
4. Pick MS WordArt from the scrolling list in the Create New tab.
5. Either type new text or paste text from your Clipboard in the resulting dialog box, then click Update Display to insert it into your document.
6. Choose a font (Arial in this example).
7. Rotate the text 90 degrees using the Rotate button.
8. Click in the Word for Wkindows document itself to close WordArt.
9. Select the rotated text by dragging.

Competitions are organized for antique aircraft, such as the still numerous World War II-era Steerman biplane, and for experimental aircraft, including many bizarre designs powered by small automobile engines.
The holder of the most individual records for powered flight is Jacqueline CO-CHRAN, with more than 250 for speed, distance, altitude, and innovator flights.
POWERLESS FLIGHT

**A WHOLE
NEW WAY
TO WORK**

10. Frame the selected object by using Insert ➤ Frame. The frame will move to the left of your screen.

11. Reposition it like any other framed item—in the upper-right corner of the page, for instance. Remember that if you drag it too close to the edge of a page, your printer may not be able to print it.

Word

9

Templates, Wizards, and Sample Documents

Templates are read-only documents containing styles and other design elements that you can use to create or restyle your own documents. *Wizards* are like computerized assistants. Like you, Wizards also use templates to create documents, after asking some questions and making a few design decisions on their own. *Sample documents* are examples created by Microsoft to show you what can be done. They are great learning tools. Table 9.1 shows a list of the template, Wizard, and sample files supplied with Word.

If you did a complete installation, these files are all located in their own subdirectory called TEMPLATE.

Look for the TEMPLATE subdirectory in your Word for Windows directory. Let's begin our tour with templates.

TABLE 9.1: Word's Templates, Wizards, and Sample Documents

TEMPLATES	WIZARDS	SAMPLE DOCUMENTS
BROCHUR1.DOT	AGENDA.WIZ	CLASSIC1.WZS
DIRECTR1.DOT	AWARD.WIZ	CLASSIC2.WZS
FAXCOVER1.DOT	CALENDAR.WIZ	CLASSIC3.WZS
FAXCOVER2.DOT	FAX.WIZ	CLASSIC4.WZS
INVOICE.DOT	LETTER.WIZ	MODERN1.WZS
LETTER1.DOT	MEMO.WIZ	MODERN2.WZS
LETTER3.DOT	NEWSLTTR.WIZ	MODERN4.WZS
MANUAL1.DOT	PLEADING.WIZ	
MANUSCR1.DOT	RESUME.WIZ	
MANUSCR3.DOT	TABLE.WIZ	
MEMO1.DOT		
MEMO2.DOT		

Templates

There are at least four different ways to use templates:

- Start new projects based on templates shipped with Word.
- Modify existing projects by choosing templates and *completely reformat* your work in the template's styles.
- Copy *selected* styles from templates for use in your projects.
- Create and save new templates of your own creation.

Template Types

Word's standard templates come in up to four different "flavors." Microsoft refers to these as *Template Types*:

- Classic (type 1)
- Contemporary (type 2)
- Typewriter (type 3)
- Elegant (type 4)

The different types give documents different moods. For instance, a Classic Letter template uses Times Roman while a Contemporary letter uses Arial. The Company Name style in the Contemporary letter template includes a border, while the Classic type does not, and so on.

By always using templates of the same type, you can give your work a consistent look. And when creating your documents using templates, you can copy the existing styles. See Chapter 5 for more about styles.

Not all templates come in all types. For instance, there is only one Elegant document titled RESUME4.DOT. Here's a summary of the rest:

TEMPLATE TYPE	CLASSIC	CONTEMPORARY	TYPEWRITER
Brochure	BROCHUR1.DOT		
Directory	DIRECTR1.DOT		
Fax cover sheet	FAXCOVR1.DOT	FAXCOVR2.DOT	
Invoice		INVOICE.DOT	
Letter	LETTER1.DOT	LETTER2.DOT	LETTER3.DOT
Manual	MANUAL1.DOT		
Manuscript	MANUSCR1.DOT		MANUSCR3.DOT

TEMPLATE TYPE	CLASSIC	CONTEMPORARY	TYPEWRITER
Memo	MEM01.DOT	MEM02.DOT	MEM03.DOT
Normal	NORMAL.DOC		
Presentation	PRESENT1.DOT		
Press release	PRESREL1.DOT	PRESREL2.DOT	PRESREL3.DOT
Purchase order	PURCHORD.DOT		
Report	REPORT1.DOT	REPORT2.DOT	REPORT3.DOT
Resume	RESUME1.DOT	RESUME2.DOT	
Thesis	THESIS1.DOT		
Timesheet	WEEKTIME.DOT		

Using Templates

Once you know what each template looks like, you can quickly start projects by picking a template whenever you start a new project. Just pick it by name from the Template list in the New dialog box (shown in Figure 9.1).

Then you simply add your own text by clicking on the appropriate areas of the template and replacing the labels with your own words (see Figure 9.2).

But first, it's helpful to know what the various templates look like. You could load each one and take a look, but there's an easier way.

Exploring Templates

Use the Style Gallery, reached with the Format ➤ Style Gallery command, to preview templates. Here are the steps:

1. Open a new document with the File ➤ New command.
2. Choose NORMAL (the Default template).

FIGURE 9.1

Pick a template from
the Template list.

FIGURE 9.2

Personalizing a
template

▪ Memorandum¶

▪**DATE:** → September 30, 1993¶

▪**TO:** → John, Paul, George and Ringo¶

▪**FROM:** → [*Names*]¶

▪**RE:** → [*Subject*]¶

▪**CC:** → [*Names*]¶
▪

[*Type your memo text here*]¶

3. Choose Format ➤ Style Gallery. You will see a window like the one in Figure 9.3.

4. Pick the template that you want to see from the scrolling list. Click on Browse if you have template files in a different directory.

NOTE Remember: Classic templates end in 1, Contemporary templates end in 2, Typewriter templates end in 3, and Elegant templates end in 4.

FIGURE 9.3

You can preview templates in the Style Gallery.

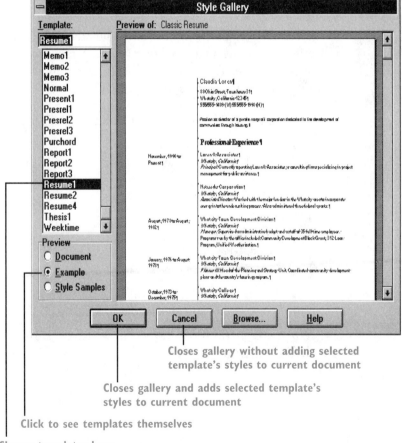

Closes gallery without adding selected template's styles to current document

Closes gallery and adds selected template's styles to current document

Click to see templates themselves

Choose templates here

5. Click the Example button in the Preview area to see a preview of the template's appearance.

6. Scroll to make sure you see the entire template; templates are often several pages long.

7. Click Style Samples to see the names of styles displayed in the styles themselves. Unfortunately these are often too small to read.

8. When you are done, click Cancel. (Clicking OK copies the styles to your current document but does not load the other template elements—boilerplate text, etc.)

Modifying Templates

You can change templates just as you would any other Word documents. The only difference is one additional step you must take when saving your work. Suppose you wanted to update the Classic letter template to include your company logo. Follow these steps to see how:

1. Use the File ➤ New command to open the Letter1 template (see Figure 9.4).

2. Make the changes, such as adding your logo and other embellishments.

[Company·Name]¶
- *[Street·Address]¶*
- *[City, ·State/Province·Zip/Postal·Code]¶*

3. Print out a sample and check your work.

4. When you are satisfied, choose File ➤ Save As. You will see the Save As dialog box, shown in Figure 9.5.

FIGURE 9.4

Opening the Letter1
template

FIGURE 9.4

Opening the Letter1
template

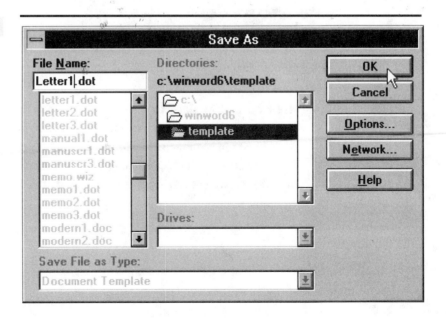

FIGURE 9.5

Saving your work

5. Type the exact same file name as the old template if you want to replace the old template or type a new file name if you want to keep *both* the old and new (make sure to type the extension .DOT if you choose a new file name).

Prewritten Business Letters

Word comes with a number of prewritten letters for various occasions. Figure 9.6 shows an example. They all end with the file extension .DOT and you can find them in the Letters subdirectory within your Word directory. Whether the letters will work for you is a matter of taste and circumstance.

FIGURE 9.6

A prewritten business letter

141·Kinsford·Avenue¶
Anytown,·WA··6999¶

Dear·Mr·Picard,¶

What·could·be·better·than·Word·version·2?·That's·easy·—·Word·version·6!¶

Although·you·might·find·it·hard·to·believe,·we·have·significantly·improved·Word,·adding·<u>safety·and·operating·features</u>·that·make·it·faster·and·easier·to·<u>prepare·potatoes</u>.¶

The·new·<u>Tater·Dicer·Mark·II*plus*</u>·offers·the·following:¶

To use the letters, replace the underlined phrases with your own information, then delete the underlining.

TIP

Use Find and Replace to speed the task of changing items like product names that repeat many times in the same document. To remove underlining, consider using the Select All command (Ctrl+A) and toggling all underlining off at once by clicking the Underline button in the Formatting toolbar.

Here's a list of form letters provided with Word:

LETTER DESCRIPTION	FILENAME
Price increase announcement	CSTMRR03.DOT
Apology for delay	CSTMRC03.DOT
Collection letter	CRED01.DOT
Credit report request	CREDll.DOT
Customer complaint	CSTMRC01.DOT
Direct mail	MKTG07.DOT
Lease expiring	SPACE03.DOT
Letter to Mom	OTHER10.DOT
Press release	ADPR01.DOT
Resume cover letter	EMPRL02.DOT
Returning product letter	SUPPL14.DOT
NSF check (request for payment)	CRED05.DOT
Thanks for inquiry	MKTG02.DOT
Thanks for job application	EMPRL03.DOT
Thanks for the suggestion	CSTMRR05.DOT

Tips for Using Templates

Word often gets information from the User Information entered with the User Info tab in the Options dialog box (reached with the Tools ➤ Options command). Make sure your info is up to date by visiting that tab.

In templates with inside addresses, signature blocks, and other multi-line items, consider the Shift+↵ trick to keep lines all in the same paragraph. This eliminates unwanted space before each address line, for example.

Switching types (from typewriter to Classic, for instance) can give your documents a whole new look. And you can mix and match styles by copying selected styles from other documents.

Some of the more complex templates (like MANUAL1.DOT) use a wealth of word features including tables of contents and index entries.

Don't forget other time-savers such as the Tools ➤ Envelopes and Labels command. They work with templates too.

Wizards—The Computer Wants Your Job

Wizards ask you questions, then use your responses to design documents for you. Take the Calendar Wizard for instance. You start Wizards with the File ➤ New command. Pick the Calendar Wizard from the scrolling list and the screen shown in Figure 9.7 will appear.

FIGURE 9.7

The Calendar Wizard

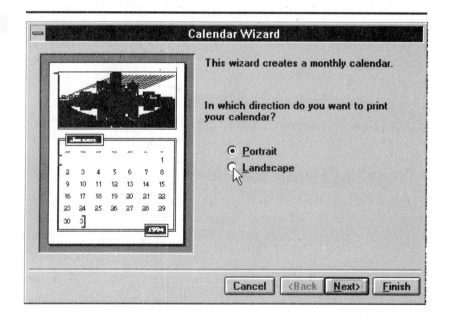

As shown in Figure 9.8, you'll be asked questions about your hopes and dreams for the new document. Do you want portrait or landscape orientation? Would you like to leave room for a picture or other graphic? Do you want fries with that? You get the idea.

FIGURE 9.8

The Wizard will ask you questions about your new document.

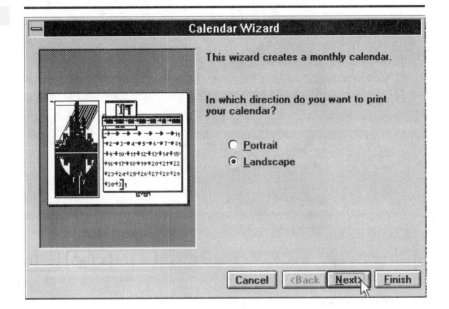

All the while, Word shows you a preview, making changes as you answer questions. The preview allows you to try several different settings in each window to see which you prefer. Eventually the Calendar Wizard tires of this and, when you click the Finish button, it works its magic (see Figure 9.9).

FIGURE 9.9

The Wizard's work

CHAPTER TEN

10

Writers' Tools

In this chapter, we'll cover the ways in which Word can make you a better author. If you are intrigued by what you read here, consider picking up an additional "Word-only" book such as my *Mastering Word 6 for Windows*, which contains additional information and many more examples and illustrations.

Typing Symbols and Special Characters

Word for Windows makes it easy to type special characters and symbols not listed on your keycaps but available in most fonts. Use the Symbol feature or keyboard shortcuts.

The Symbol Command

The dialog box shown in Figure 10.1 appears whenever you choose Insert ➤ Symbol. It has two tabs.

It shows you all available characters in the current font. Clicking on a symbol shows you a magnified, more readable version. Double-clicking inserts the character at the insertion point in your document. (Alternatively, you can click on a character and then click on the Insert button, but that's more work.)

TIP Once you've clicked to magnify a character in the Symbol dialog box, you can see magnified views of others by navigating with the arrow keys. This can eliminate the need for a lot of precision clicking. Also, once a character is highlighted, you can insert it by hitting ↵.

FIGURE 10.1

The two tabs in the Symbol dialog box (reached by choosing Insert ➤ Symbol) offer many symbols and special characters.

To see which symbols are available in different fonts, simply choose a font from the Font menu in the Formatting toolbar and use the Insert – Symbol command to view the choices. Or, if the Symbol dialog box is already open, pick a font from the Font list in the dialog box.

The Special Characters tab provides a scrolling list of commonly used symbols and characters. Here too, double-clicking inserts the character at the insertion point.

The Special Characters tab in the Symbol window also lets you see (and change) keyboard shortcuts.

Typing Symbols from the Keyboard

If you know the appropriate key combinations, you can enter them directly from the keyboard without using the Symbol feature. Different fonts sometimes have different key combinations, so consult the documentation that comes with your fonts or use the Insert ➤ Symbol command to learn the combinations. Table 10.1 shows commonly used special characters and their keyboard shortcuts.

Wingdings and Dingbats

Use the little pictures found in the Wingdings font to embellish documents. Wingdings are great as bullets, list separators, and border decorations. Use the Insert ➤ Symbol command to see and insert them.

International and Accented Characters

To type accented international characters (like the ñ in La Cañada) you use three keys. First you hold down the Alt key plus a key to tell your computer which accent to apply, then you press the character key for the character you wish to accent. For example, to umlaut an o, do the following:

1. Hold down the Ctrl key and press the : key.

2. Release both keys.

3. Press the o (or Shift+O) key to get a small (or capitalized) umlauted o (ö).

Incidentally, you can't accent just any old characters. Table 10.2 shows you the possibilities and their key combinations.

TABLE 10.1: Special Characters and Their Keyboard Shortcuts

NAME	SAMPLE	KEYS	NOTES
Angstroms	Å	Ctrl+Shift+@+A	
Bullet	•	Alt+0149	
Cent sign	¢	Ctrl+/,c	
Copyright	©	Ctrl+Alt+C	
Dagger	†	Alt+1034	
Degrees	°	Alt+1086	
Double close quote	"	Alt+0148	Use AutoCorrect instead
Double open quote	"	Alt+0147	Use AutoCorrect instead
Ellipsis	…	Alt+Ctrl+.	
em dash	—	Alt+Ctrl+Num-	Usually longer than a hyphen
en dash	–	Ctrl+Num-	
Function, f-stop	ƒ	Alt+0131	
Logical not	¬	Alt+0172	
Mu (lowercase)	μ	Alt+0181	Aka micro
Much greater than	»	Ctrl+à,>	Also European close quote
Much less than	«	Ctrl+à,<	Also European open quote
Paragraph mark	¶	Alt+0182	
Plus or minus	±	Alt+0177	
Pound (currency)	£	Alt+0163	

TABLE 10.1: Special Characters and Their Keyboard Shortcuts (continued)

NAME	SAMPLE	KEYS	NOTES
Registered	®	Alt+Ctrl+R	AutoCorrect for (R)
Section mark	§	Alt+0167	
Single close quote	'	Ctrl+à,'	Use AutoCorrect instead
Single open quote	'	Ctrl+à,à	Use AutoCorrect instead
Trademark	™	Alt+Ctrl+T	
Yen (currency)	¥	Alt+0165	

TABLE 10.2: Keyboard Shortcuts for Accented Characters

NAME	SAMPLE	KEYS
Acute	áéíóú ÁÉÍÓÚ	Ctrl+' (apostrophe), letter
Circumflex	â ê î ô û ÂÊÎÔÛ	Ctrl+^, letter
Diaresis	ä ë ï ö ü ÄËÏÖÜ	Ctrl+;, letter
Grave	àèìòù ÀÈÌÒÙ	Ctrl+', letter
Tilde	ãñõ ÃÑÕ	Ctrl+~, letter

Bulleted List Command

There's a button on the Standard toolbar that looks like a bulleted list. It places plain old bullets in front of selected paragraphs and creates hanging indents. The feature uses the current font.

Bulleting Existing Paragraphs

To bullet existing paragraphs, follow these steps:

1. Select the paragraph or paragraphs you wish to format.

2. Click the Bullets button, shown at left. Word will create hanging indents and insert bullets in front of each selected paragraph.

Typing New Bulleted Lists

To type new bulleted lists, follow these steps:

1. Click the Bullets button on the Standard toolbar or choose Format ➤ Bullets and Numbering. A bullet appears.

2. Type an entry and press ↵. A new bullet appears on the next line.

3. Repeat step 2 and continue until you've finished the list.

4. When finished, click the Bullets button to deactivate the feature.

Changing Bullet Styles

Word for Windows offers an astonishing array of bullet list options. You can even choose your own, nonstandard bullet characters. Here are the steps:

1. Select your list if you've already typed it.

2. Choose Format ➤ Bullets and Numbering.

3. Click to pick a style you like.

4. Click OK to change the style of the selected list.

5. Type additional list items or a new list, as necessary.

"Smart" or Typographer's Quotes

Word for Windows can automatically place curly quotes in documents when you type straight quotes. These *smart* quotes give your work a typeset look.

Word

Turn the option on before typing, since Word will not automatically change quote marks you've already typed.

1. Use the Tools ➤ Options command to display the Options dialog box.

2. Click on the AutoFormat tab to display the AutoFormat options.

3. Enable Smart Quotes by clicking to place an X in the option box.

4. Subsequently, when you type quotes, Word will convert them to curly opening and closing quotes (assuming that your chosen font has these characters).

 If you are creating a document that you plan to export (for use with different word-processing software, perhaps), turn off the Smart Quotes feature before creating documents containing quotes. Otherwise you risk confusing the other programs with strange codes instead of quotation marks.

Spelling Checker

The first time you use the Spelling checker, it's a good idea to ensure that it is set to use the proper dictionary—English (US) in the United States. Here are the steps:

1. Choose Tools ➤ Language.

2. Scroll to the desired language—probably English (US)—and select it by double-clicking or clicking once on the name and once on OK.

3. Click the Default button.

4. Answer Yes to the confirmation prompt.

5. Click on OK.

You can format certain text (foreign language or technical, for example) as "no proofing" text, which means Word will skip it during spell checks. If you don't instruct Word for Windows to use a dictionary, you might think Word has spell-checked your document and found nothing wrong. Your only clue will be a casual note that text formatted with "no proofing" has been skipped.

Start the Spelling checker with the F7 shortcut or by picking Tools ➤ Spelling. The Spelling dialog box, shown in Figure 10.2, appears.

 If there are no mistakes in the text you ask Word to check, you won't see the Spelling dialog box—Word will pop up a message box saying The spelling check is complete.

FIGURE 10.2

Word can spell-check all or part of your documents.

Unless you've selected only a portion of your document to check, Word for Windows scans down, beginning at the insertion point, and will then ask if you want to go back to the top of the document to continue checking.

The Spelling checker looks for words that it cannot find in its open dictionaries. When it spots a word that it can't match, Word highlights the questionable characters, scrolls the document so that you can see the problem word in context, and offers you a number of choices.

Typing Your Own Changes

If you want to change a misspelled word only once:

1. Type a replacement in the highlighted Change To box.

2. Press ↵ or click the Change button. Word will replace the problem text with the new text you have typed in the Change To box and then continue spell-checking.

To change the word throughout the document that you are checking, click Change All instead of pressing ↵ or clicking Change. If the new word you've typed is something you want Word for Windows to recognize in all of your documents, see the section "Custom or User Dictionaries" later in this chapter.

Word's Suggested Changes

If you have enabled the suggestions feature (check the Always Suggest option in the Spelling tab of the Options dialog box), Word for Windows will usually list one or more possible spellings, placing what it thinks is the best guess in the Change To box. If the default is not enabled, you can always ask for suggestions by clicking Suggest. Other suggestions, if any, will be listed in the scrollable Suggestions box. It may take a moment for Word to find alternative words. You'll know Word is finished looking for suggestions when you see either (End of Suggestions) or (No Suggestions) in the Suggestions list.

If you agree with Word's best guess, simply click the Change button to change this occurrence or use the Change All button to change this and all succeeding occurrences of the word. The Spelling checker will replace the word and continue examining your document.

Word's best guess is usually, but not always, right. If one of the alternative suggestions is correct, simply double-click on the desired word to replace the misspelled word, or click once on the desired word in the list to move it to the Change To box, then click the Change or Change All button as necessary.

Overruling Suggestions

Sometimes Word won't make correct suggestions, or you might want to correct the problem yourself without retyping the entire word or phrase. For instance, Word for Windows may spot two run-together words. When it has no suggestions, Word for Windows moves the problem text to the Change To box, where you can edit it yourself (by placing a space between the two words, for instance).

Ignoring Flagged Words

Sometimes Word for Windows will spot a word that is properly spelled but is not in Word's open dictionaries. Proper nouns, technical jargon, and typesetting codes are examples.

If you want Word for Windows to ignore the text only once, click the Ignore button. Word will leave the word or other text string as you typed it and continue to spell-check. To ignore the word throughout the document you are checking, click Ignore All. (If the word is something you want to ignore in all of your documents, you may want to add it to a custom dictionary, discussed next.)

NOTE If you tell Word to ignore a word in the morning, it will ignore the word all day, in each document you check, unless you exit Word or use the Reset "Ignore All" List button in the Spelling tab of the Options dialog box.

Custom or User Dictionaries

Most of the words used by the Spelling checker are located in a dictionary that comes with your Word for Windows program. You cannot make changes to this dictionary.

You can, however, maintain one or more of your own *custom* dictionaries. Word checks only open dictionaries. The more dictionaries you have open, the slower the spell check will be.

The Standard Custom Dictionary

When you install Word for Windows, the installation program places an empty Custom Dictionary in your WINDOWS/MSAPPS/PROOF subdirectory. The default name for the dictionary is CUSTOM.DIC. It is opened and used whenever you spell-check, unless you instruct Word otherwise. This is where you will want to keep most proper nouns, trademark names, etc.

Word for Windows will place words in the Custom Dictionary whenever you click the Add button while spell-checking. (The first time you add a word, you may be asked to create a custom dictionary.) Normally Word for Windows places words in a dictionary called CUSTOM.DIC in the PROOF subdirectory of the MSAPPS subdirectory. You can overrule this default use of the Custom Dictionary by using the drop-down Add Words To list to specify a different dictionary.

Custom dictionaries handle capitalization as follows. If you add a word to a dictionary as all lowercase, it will be recognized later, regardless of whether it is typed as all lowercase, all uppercase, or with an initial capital letter. If you enter a word with only the first letter capitalized, Word will recognize the word when it later appears in all caps or with a leading cap, but will question the word if it is all lowercase. Unusual capitalizations like VisiCalc will be questioned unless they are stored in the dictionary exactly as they should appear.

Creating Additional Custom Dictionaries

If you work on unusual projects that involve technical jargon, typesetting codes, etc., you might want to create one or more additional, specially named custom dictionaries, which you can turn on or off in the Spelling tab of the Options dialog box. To create a new custom dictionary, follow these steps:

1. Visit the Spelling tab in the Options dialog box either by choosing Tools ➤ Options or by clicking the Options button in the Spelling dialog box. Figure 10.3 shows the Spelling tab.

2. Click New to create a new dictionary. You will be prompted for a dictionary name.

FIGURE 10.3

Place an X next to custom dictionaries of interest.

3. Type a new name containing up to 32 characters.

4. Open the folder where you want to store the dictionary (it is best to keep custom dictionaries with the main dictionary).

5. Click Save.

Opening and Closing Custom Dictionaries

To make a dictionary available to the Spelling checker, it must be open. Place Xs next to both custom dictionaries in Figure 10.3 to make both open and available for the Spelling checker to use. Click in the box next to the desired dictionary to open or close it. An X means it's open.

To open dictionaries that are not in the folder containing the main dictionary, click the Add button. Show Word for Windows where the desired dictionary is, using standard Windows directory-navigation techniques.

Editing Custom Dictionaries

To add items to a custom dictionary, click the Add button when the Spelling checker encounters a word of interest, or type a Word for Windows document containing all of the words you want to add, then spell-check the document, adding each unrecognized word.

If you accidentally add a word to a custom dictionary, it is a good idea to delete it, since extra words mean more searching time during your spell checks. And if you add misspelled words, they will no longer be challenged by the checker. Here's how to remove words from a custom dictionary:

1. Choose the dictionary you wish to edit from the Spelling tab in the Options dialog box (reached by choosing Tools ➤ Options).
2. Click the Edit button.
3. A dialog box will appear offering to let you edit the dictionary as a regular Word document. Click Yes.
4. Close the Options dialog box.
5. Edit the dictionary.
6. Save it with the Save command (Ctrl+S) and close it.

Spelling in Other Office Applications

Excel, PowerPoint, and other Microsoft applications also have spelling checkers. Their actual features and dialog boxes may differ from Word's, but they can all share the *same* custom dictionaries. Read more about these other spelling checkers in Parts Three and Four.

AutoCorrect

The primary reason for AutoCorrect is to fix typos like *teh* when you meant to type *the*. Word for Windows will watch you type and change words for you.

NOTE AutoCorrect moves into action every time you press the spacebar, the Tab key, or the ↵ key after entering a letter or a word. If the previous word is stored as an AutoCorrect entry, AutoCorrect changes it; if it is not stored as an AutoCorrect entry, nothing happens.

You can create your own entries or use predefined entries. For instance, if you type **(r)** or **(R)**, Word will replace those characters with the Registered symbol, ®.

To use the built-in entries, you just type along as usual. Word for Windows will make changes when it thinks they are needed. You can see a list of the current autocorrections by scrolling in the AutoCorrect dialog box (reached with the Tools ➤ AutoCorrect command), shown in Figure 10.4.

Other Uses of AutoCorrect

In addition to correcting typos, you can use AutoCorrect to convert "shorthand" into longer text strings. For instance, you could tell Word for Windows

FIGURE 10.4

See and change AutoCorrect entries in the AutoCorrect dialog box.

AutoCorrect

☒ Change 'Straight Quotes' to 'Smart Quotes'
☒ Correct TWo INitial CApitals
☐ Capitalize First Letter of Sentences
☒ Capitalize Names of Days

| OK |
| Cancel |
| Help |

☒ Replace Text as You Type

Replace: With: ◉ Plain Text ○ Formatted Text

(r)	®
adn	and
don;t	don't
i	I
incl	include
occurence	occurrence

| Add |
| Delete |

Word

that you want it to replace aka with also known as, or replace mwg with Mr. William Gates, and so on. You can even insert text and graphics this way. Type sylogo for instance, and insert the SYBEX logo (see "Creating Your Own AutoCorrect Entries," next).

AutoCorrect will *always* make the replacement when you type a defined string of characters followed by a space, a tab, or a carriage return (↵). *AutoText*, which you will read more about later, waits for you to press the F3 key or click on the toolbar button before it takes over.

Creating Your Own AutoCorrect Entries

When creating your own AutoCorrect entries, there is one potential land-mine, which is that AutoCorrect will always blindly replace certain text strings with other text strings. So, try to use names that are uncommon yet easy to remember. Consider preceding all of your many entry names with some unusual character that will never appear in normal text, like a backslash (*add* for instance). Names can be up to 31 characters long. That said, here are the steps:

1. Open the AutoCorrect dialog box with the Tools ➤ AutoCorrect command.

2. Type the "name" (the text string you wish to replace) in the Replace box.

3. Type the replacement in the With box (or see the tip that follows).

4. Click Add.

5. Make any other entries or changes.

6. Click OK when done.

TIP   If you select the text (or graphics and other things) you want to use as the replacement item before you open the AutoCorrect dialog box, it will appear in the With portion of the box when it opens. If the items are formatted, you'll be given the choice of pasting the items as formatted or not.

Editing AutoCorrect Entries

To modify an AutoCorrect entry, follow these steps:

1. Correct the entry in a document.
2. Choose Tools ➤ AutoCorrect to open the AutoCorrect dialog box.
3. Type the old Replace name.
4. When the Replace button undims, click it.
5. Answer Yes to the "Do you want to redefine?" question.
6. The entry will be updated.

Deleting AutoCorrect Entries

To delete an AutoCorrect entry, follow these steps:

1. Choose Tools ➤ Autocorrect to open the AutoCorrect dialog box.
2. Select the victim.
3. Click the Delete button. The entry will be deleted.

Automatic Correction

In addition to fixing mistakes as you type them, you can run the AutoCorrect feature at any time to inspect and clean up documents. Use the AutoCorrect dialog box to choose the options you wish Word to use.

AutoText

AutoText is the replacement for Word's old Glossary command. It's an easy way to store and retrieve "boilerplate" text, graphics, addresses, letter closings, memo distribution lists, tables, logos, and just about anything else that you can create with Word for Windows.

You can store AutoText entries with the NORMAL template so that they are always available or with other templates for specialty projects.

Word

Creating AutoText Entries

Simply select whatever it is you wish to memorialize, then choose Edit ➤ AutoText. Or click the toolbar button for AutoText, shown at left, on the Standard toolbar. If you want to store the paragraph formatting with the entry, be sure to include paragraph marks in your selection. (Even if you store an entry *with* paragraph formatting, you can later insert the entry *without* formatting if you wish.) Click Add.

Saving AutoText Entries

To save AutoText entries, follow these steps:

1. Before you save an entry, you are given a chance to review and change the automatic entry name assigned by Word for Windows. To change the name, just type a new one in the name box. Names can be up to 32 characters long and spaces are permitted.

2. If you want an entry to be available whenever you use Word, leave the default choice All Documents (Normal.dot) in the drop-down "availability" list. To attach an entry to a different template, pick one from the drop-down list.

3. Click the Add button.

It is often good to select the space *after* text being memorialized as an AutoText entry (that is, the single space created by the spacebar, not the blank line created by the paragraph return). Then you won't have to type a space each time you insert the entry later.

Using AutoText Entries

Once you've saved some AutoText entries, you can insert them using several different techniques. Always begin by placing the insertion point where you want the entry to be placed. If you need spaces or tabs or anything else before the entry, it is easiest to type them first. When the insertion point is properly positioned, do one of the following:

- Type all or part of an AutoText entry's name and then click the AutoText toolbar button.

- Type all or part of an AutoText entry's name and then press the F3 function key.

- Type all or part of an AutoText entry's name and then type Alt+Ctrl+V.

- Choose Edit ➤ AutoText (you'll see a preview), then double-click to select an entry from the scrolling name list. Instead of double-clicking, you could also click once and then click the Insert button or press ↵.

In any event, Word for Windows will insert the entry. Edit it as you would any other text, graphic, or other document element.

Forcing Plain Text

You can have an AutoText entry take on the appearance of the text at the insertion point in the current document, even if you saved it with its own formatting. To do so, choose Plain Text in the Insert As box of the AutoText dialog box.

Editing AutoText Entries

To edit an entry, follow these steps:

1. Insert the entry in a document.

2. Edit and reformat it as necessary.

3. Select the corrected entry and any necessary punctuation, paragraph marks, spaces following, etc.

4. Visit the AutoText dialog box (Edit ➤ AutoText).

5. Rename the entry, if necessary.

6. Click the Add button.

7. Answer Yes to the "Do you want to redefine?" question.

Deleting AutoText Entries

Deleting AutoText entries is as simple as you'd expect (and hope). Follow these steps:

1. Choose Edit ➤ AutoText to open the AutoText dialog box.

2. Select the doomed item from the scrolling list.

3. Look in the Preview box or insert the entry and check to be *certain* that this is the entry you wish to delete.

4. Click Delete.

Grammar Checker

Word offers grammar and style checking, which is no match for a human editor, but worth mentioning nonetheless. Start the Grammar checker by choosing Tools ➤ Grammar.

Unless you select a portion of your document, Word will attempt to check the whole thing. Working from the insertion point, Word will highlight a portion of your prose (usually a sentence) and evaluate it. There may be a slight delay. If Word spots questionable spellings, you will be given the opportunity to correct them or tell Word to ignore them. Once spelling issues have been dealt with, Word will use its Grammar dialog box to point out questionable style and grammar issues. The text being considered is listed in the scrolling Sentence box. See *Mastering Word 6 for Windows* and on-line help for details.

Word Count and Other Statistics

The Word Count command is found in the Tools menu. Simply choose the command to start the process.

Tools ➤ Word Count will scan an entire document or just text you've selected. It counts pages, words, characters, paragraphs, and lines. If you place an X in the appropriate box it will include footnote and endnote text when counting. It does *not* count words in headers and footers. You must display invisible text to count it.

Tables of Contents

Word for Windows will help you create a *table of contents* (TOC) for your documents. If you format your headings using Word's standard heading styles or Outline feature, the Insert ➤ Index and Tables command will quickly compile (create) a simple but very usable table of contents and place it in a new section at the beginning of your document.

It is also possible to manually select items to appear in your table of contents. You do this by identifying words and phrases in your document using hidden text codes called *TOC Entry* codes. You can control the appearance of the table of contents as well. Your TOC can have one or multiple levels.

The Insert ➤ Index and Tables command and the hidden *Index Entry* codes work together to produce equally simple or distinctive *indexes* at the end of your document.

Creating a Table of Contents

To create a table of contents, follow these steps:

1. Begin by formatting your document's headings with Word's standard-heading styles. (These styles can be added to your Formatting toolbar's drop-down style list by visiting the Style dialog box. Be sure to hold down Shift when clicking on the Formatting toolbar's style drop-down list.

2. When you have typed and proofed your document and are happy with margins, headers, footers, and other design elements (especially those that affect page breaks), pick Insert ➤ Index and Tables.

3. Choose the Table of Contents tab, shown in Figure 10.5, if it is not already foremost.

4. Preview the available formats by clicking in the Formats list and watching the Preview area. Pick one.

5. Choose the number of levels you wish to include in the TOC.

Word

6. If you wish to include a tab leader (dashes or dots, for instance), choose the style from the drop-down list.

7. Click OK or press Enter. Word will compile the new TOC. It starts by repaginating your document. Then it will begin the TOC at the insertion point.

If you've already created a TOC for the document, Word will ask if you want to replace it. If you choose No, you will end up with *two* TOCs at the beginning of your document (or wherever the insertion point was). This is a way to create two levels of content detail like the Contents at a Glance and regular TOC at the beginning of this book.

Including Non-Heading Styles in Your TOC

Word for Windows now lets you easily specify non-heading styles for inclusion in your TOC. For example, suppose you create and define a style called Chapters, and you want it to be "above" Heading 1 in your TOC. Use the TOC options to accomplish this.

1. Create and define styles for items you wish to include in the TOC.

2. Format the material using these styles.

3. Open the Table of Contents tab in the Index and Tables dialog box (reached with Insert ➤ Index and Tables).

4. Click on the Options button.

5. You will see a scrolling list of all of the styles in the current document.

6. Assign "levels" to the styles you wish to include in the TOC.

7. Make any other formatting choices and create the TOC as usual.

Changing a TOC's Appearance

You can edit the resulting TOC as you would any other text in your document. Feel free to embolden characters, change line spacing, etc. As you'd expect, changing the style definitions for styles 1 through 9 will change the appearance of your TOC. Here's how to change style definitions:

1. Choose Insert ➤ Index and Tables to visit the Table of Contents tab in the Index and Tables dialog box.

2. Pick Custom Style from the Formats list.

3. Click the Modify button. You will see the Style dialog box.

4. Pick the style you wish to modify by clicking on it in the scrolling list.

5. Click the Modify button. You'll see the Modify Style box.

6. Make the desired changes to the style using the drop-down lists and the Format button (which takes you to familiar formatting dialog boxes).

7. "Back out" to the Index and Tables dialog box and click OK.

Some of the TOC styles apply elements like all caps and small caps formatting for different levels. Some styles include underlines. Remove one or the other format and redefine the style using standard Word techniques.

Restricting Levels

If you want to suppress the printing of all of the levels past a certain point (everything after 5, for instance), specify the levels you wish to print in the Show Levels portion of the Table of Contents tab. You can also turn levels on and off with the Table of Contents Options dialog box.

Updating a Table of Contents

You should update a TOC after you've made changes to your document. You'll be given the choice of just changing page numbers or updating the entire TOC.

Creating an Index

Automatic indexes are created using hidden codes sometimes called *XE* or *Index Entry* codes. Word for Windows compiles indexes on demand and places them at the end of your document in new sections that it creates for this purpose. Index entries can include the contents of headers and footers if you wish.

Marking Index Entries

Word for Windows now makes it easy to create an index. Simple indexes can be created by selecting text, issuing the Alt+Shift+X keyboard shortcut, and choosing a few options. Word then compiles and stylizes an index and places it at the document's end. Here are the steps:

1. Start by making sure that you are done proofing, fiddling with margins and page endings, and the like.

2. Select (highlight) a word or phrase you want to use as an index entry.

3. Press Alt+Shift+X.

4. You'll see the Mark Index Entry dialog box, shown in Figure 10.6.

5. Click Mark to mark just this entry, or Mark All to mark all occurrences. (Word will scan the document, mark all occurrences, and the status area will tell you how many were found.) Edit the entry and add a subentry. You can also include a cross reference (*See...*) at this time.

6. The Mark Index dialog box remains visible so that you can scroll to other text and mark it, or simply type words to be indexed into the Main Entry section of the dialog box.

7. Repeat steps 2 through 6 until you have specified all desired entries.

FIGURE 10.6

The Mark Index Entry
dialog box

8. Click on Close to close the dialog box.

9. Place the insertion point where you want the index (typically at the end of your document).

10. Choose Insert ➤ Index and Tables.

11. Visit the Index tab of the Index and Tables dialog box.

12. Pick an index style using the scrolling Preview area as your guide.

13. Double-click on the name of the desired style or click once on a style name and once on OK.

14. Word will repaginate the document and then create an index that will be placed at the insertion point.

Updating Indexes

Each time you visit and close the Index tab in the Index and Tables dialog box, Word for Windows will ask if you want to replace (recompile) the selected index. Click Yes if you do (and you probably will want to).

Here's an index-updating shortcut worth knowing:

1. Click anywhere in the index to select it.

2. Press the right mouse button to display the shortcut menu.

3. Choose Update Field. Word will repaginate and then recompile and update the index.

Formatting Indexes

The easy way to change the appearance of index entries is to pick a different index format choice from the scrolling Formats list in the Index tab of the Index and Tables dialog box. Watch the Preview area of the dialog box as you shop. It is also possible to change the standard index styles (Index 1–Index 9).

Creating Automatic Indexes

It is possible to have Word for Windows automatically index a document without your needing to visit the text manually. You do this by creating a list of terms you wish to index (called a *concordance* list). Here are the steps:

1. Create a new document with the FileNew command.

2. Insert a two-column table (with the Table button, perhaps).

3. Type all index entries in the first column. They must be identical to text Word will find in the document you intend to index. Capitalization counts. (*Network Troubleshooting* might be a typical entry.)

4. In the second column, type all index entries as you wish them to appear in the index (*Troubleshooting: network*, for instance).

5. Save the document.

6. Open the document to be indexed.

7. Choose Insert ➤ Index and Tables.

8. Visit the Index tab of the Index and Tables dialog box.

9. Click the AutoMark button.

10. Choose the concordance file from the resulting Open dialog box.

11. Click OK.

Tables of Authorities

Word can help you automatically create tables of authorities. It provides commonly used categories, including:

■ Cases

- Statutes
- Other Authorities
- Rules
- Treatises
- Regulations
- Constitutional Provisions

You can control the appearance of the entries and the table itself. Word will even help you seek out items to be included in your table.

Creating TOA Entries

Always type a long citation as your first entry in a legal document—*Mansfield v. Numan, 45 Wn 2d 412 (1994)*, for instance. Subsequent entries can be short versions like *Mansfield v. Numan*. Once you've typed all the entries:

1. Scroll to the first long entry.

2. Select it.

3. Press Alt+Shift+I to bring up the Mark Citation dialog box.

4. Type your selected text in both the Selected Text and Short Citation boxes.

5. Edit the long Citation and format it if you like; you may use only the keyboard shortcuts here (Ctrl+B, Ctrl+I, etc.).

6. Pick a category (Cases, for example).

7. Edit the short Citation so that it matches those in your document, *Mansfield v. Murphy*, for instance.

8. Click the Mark button to visit each potential citation or mark All to automatically mark them.

9. To find the next citation to mark, click Next Citation. Word will search for legalese (*v.*, *in re*, etc.) and display possible citations. When you find one, repeat steps 2 through 8.

10. When you've marked all the citations, click Close.

Creating the Actual Table of Authorities

To format and compile the actual table, visit the Table of Authorities tab in the Index and Tables dialog box. Follow these steps:

1. Choose Insert ➤ Index and Tables. You'll see the Index and Tables dialog box.

2. Pick a format from the Format list.

3. If you want Word to replace five or more page references with *passim*, choose that option.

4. Click OK. Word will compile the table.

Updating a Table of Authorities

Place the insertion point anywhere in the table of authorities, then press F9. Word will update the table to include any recent insertions, deletions, etc.

Custom Styles and Categories

Word lets you change the appearance of the styles used for TOAs. It also lets you create and edit category names. Consult the on-line help for details.

Tables of Figures

Word will help you create tables of figures and other elements based on captions and bookmarks. Assuming you've captioned documents with the Insert ➤ Caption command, the process is quite simple:

1. Place the insertion point where you want the table to appear.

2. Choose Insert ➤ Index and Tables.

3. Display the Table of Figures tab if it is not in view.

4. Select the desired caption label from the scrolling list.

5. Select a format for the table.

6. Visit the Table of Figures Options dialog box if necessary to pick the style you want Word to use as the basis of the table.

7. Back in the Table of Figures tab, make other option choices (Show page numbers, etc.).

8. Click OK. Word will compile a table and place it at the insertion point.

Updating a Table of Figures

Place the insertion point anywhere in the table of figures, then press F9. Word will update the table to include any recent insertions, deletions, etc.

Outlines

Word's *Outline* view, located on the View menu (Ctrl+Alt+O), is really more than a view. It's a collection of tools designed to help you plan, create, and re-organize long documents. It does this by letting you expand or contract the amount of detail you see on your screen. Figure 10.7 illustrates this.

Word

FIGURE 10.7

Outline view lets you get a bird's-eye view of large documents

The lower half of Figure 10.7 shows a document in Outline view with all of the body text collapsed (not revealed). Since only paragraph headings are visible in the bottom window, it's easy to see the overall organization (the outline) of the document. Outline view lets you control how much detail you see. For instance, you can view the first line of text following each heading if you wish.

Notice also that headings in Outline view are indented, giving you a better idea of the document's organization. Each new level is indented $\frac{1}{4}$" from the preceding one.

It's a snap to reorganize documents in Outline view. If you want to move all of the paragraphs having to do with Landing gear so they appear before Tail, simply drag the Landing gear heading using the Outline view's special pointer. This will move all corresponding paragraphs, called *subtext*.

Finally, you can quickly promote or demote portions of your document using the Outline view tools found on the Outline toolbar.

Styles and Outlines

In order to use Outline view, your headings need to be formatted using Word's standard-heading styles (heading 1 through heading 9). If you didn't use these styles when you created a document, it is easy to reformat with them. And, as you probably know, you can change the appearance of standard headings if you don't like Word's standard styles.

The Outline View's Toolbar

Outline view provides a number of unique tools. They are found on the Outline toolbar, shown in Figure 10.8. There is a new pointer shape indicating the pointer's ability to move large collections of text. It looks like a compass.

FIGURE 10.8

The Outline toolbar

On-screen text is often underlined with an unusual line style. Text that is underlined on-screen will not be underlined when printed. Rather, on-screen underlining indicates that there is collapsed subtext beneath the text.

Plus Signs, Dashes, and Boxes

Large plus signs, dashes, and boxes appear next to many headings in Outline view. Boxes tell you that you are looking at body text; pluses indicate headings containing subtext; and minuses denote headings without subtext.

Finally, Outline view includes the Outline toolbar, with its special heading and body-text symbols.

Creating and Editing Outlines

When you start typing a new document in Outline view, Word for Windows assumes the first thing you want to type is a level 1 heading. Each new paragraph you type will take on the heading level of the previous paragraph.

One strategy is to type all of your top-level headings first, and then go back and insert headings in progressively lower heading levels. Another approach is to type all your document's headings in sequence, promoting and demoting as you go. It is even possible to type the entire document (all headings and text) in Outline view, without doing a traditional outline first.

The approach you choose is largely a matter of personal preference. In any scenario, you will need to know how to promote and demote headings and text.

Promoting and Demoting

The two arrows at the left end of the Outline toolbar are used to promote and demote headings. Place the insertion point in the heading you wish to promote or demote. Click the right arrow to demote. Figure 10.9 shows an example of this process.

Figure 10.9 starts out with all headings at the same level. By selecting headings (like Parts of the Plane, Wings, Fuselage, Tail, etc.) and clicking on the

Word

FIGURE 10.9

Click on the arrows on the Outline toolbar to promote and demote headings and body text.

The Theory of Glider Flight
Parts of the Plane
Wings
Fuselage
Tail
Landing gear
Tow hook

The Theory of Glider Flight
Parts of the Plane
Wings
Fuselage
Tail
Landing gear
Tow hook

Demote (or Promote) button, you can change the relative importance of a heading and the underlying text. For instance, in the third section of Figure 10.9, you can see that Parts of the Plane has become a subheading of The Theory of Glider Flight. Moreover, the various plane parts have been demoted further, to subheadings of Parts of the Plane.

Outlining Existing Documents

To outline existing documents, follow these steps:

1. Open your document in Outline view. You will see the first line of each paragraph.

2. Place the insertion point in each heading and promote or demote them as desired.

3. Save your work.

4. Use the viewing techniques described next to view, rearrange, and understand the organization of your document.

Expanding and Collapsing Outlines

One of the main reasons to use Outline view is to get a collapsed overview of a document's contents, such as the view shown in Figure 10.10. Do this by expanding and collapsing views with the numbers and buttons on the Out ine toolbar.

Clicking on the various numbered buttons reveals corresponding levels of detail. For instance, clicking on the number 3 button displays heading levels 1 through 3. Clicking on the number 4 button reveals an additional level of detail, and so on. The All Text button reveals your whole document and the Show First Line Only button displays the first line of text for each heading.

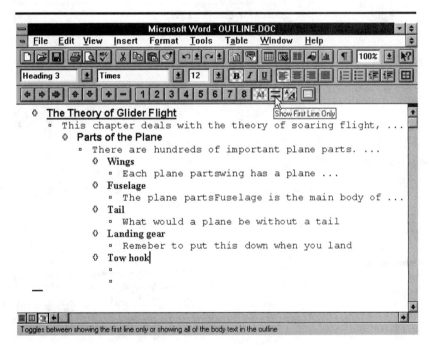

Split Views

You can split the screen and show your document in Normal view in one half of the window and Outline view in the other (see Figure 10.11). To split a window this way, double-click on the Split-bar. Then drag it up or down to change the size of the two areas. Double-clicking on the Split-bar in a split window returns you to a single window. Each part of the screen has its own scroll bars.

FIGURE 10.11

Splitting the screen lets you see your document both in Outline view and Normal or Page Layout view.

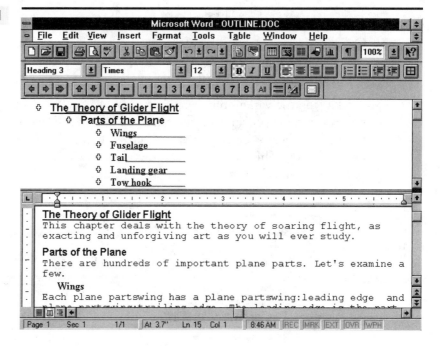

Moving Paragraphs

With the outline collapsed, you can move collections of paragraphs (also called *subtext*) by moving their associated headings. When you move a heading, *all* heads (i.e., those of lower head levels) and text below it will be moved along with it. This facilitates the movement of entire chapters without the need to highlight them. Think of this feature as drag-and-drop on steroids.

Placing the pointer over the left edge of a heading changes the pointer's shape. It will look like a compass. Click and drag, and a large right arrow will appear along with a dotted line (see Figure 10.12). Drag the line and the pointer to where you want to move the text. Release the mouse button and the document will be reorganized.

The up and down pointing arrows on the Outline toolbar will also move items up and down. Highlight the headings and then click on the appropriate arrow.

Dragging to Change Levels

You can also drag to change the indent level in Outline view. When you do, the pointer arrow changes and you'll see a guideline that indicates the pending indent level (see Figure 10.13).

FIGURE 10.12

Dragging headings and related text in Outline view

FIGURE 10.13

Change heading levels by dragging left or right.

Rearrange Tables by Dragging Rows

When you view a table in Outline view, it is possible to move rows by dragging them (see Figure 10.14). It's a great way to rearrange a table!

Numbering Headings in Outline View

You can number headings in Outline view just as you can in any other view. Here are the steps:

1. Choose Format ➤ Heading Numbering. You will see the Heading Numbering dialog box, shown in Figure 10.15.

Word

FIGURE 10.14

Drag table rows in
Outline view.

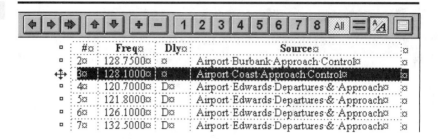

FIGURE 10.15

You can number para-
graphs in Outline view.

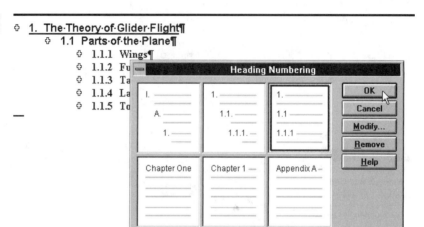

2. Click on a sample to select the numbering format you desire, or choose
Modify for custom numbering choices.

3. Click OK. Word will renumber immediately and whenever you rearrange your outline. Whenever you add a heading it will automatically be
numbered (see Figure 10.16).

FIGURE 10.16

Adding or moving
numbered paragraphs
in Outline view

⬦ **1.1.4 Landing·gear¶**
⬦ **1.1.5 Tow·hook¶**
▫ **1.2 Thermals—Rising·Hot·Air¶**

Creating Presentation from Word Outlines

If you've created Microsoft Word documents using Heading styles, you can often use these as the starting point for PowerPoint presentations, saving you the time and trouble of retyping information to create slides or overheads. It's worth investigating, but not when you have an important deadline looming. There are a couple of gotchas, as you will see in a moment. Here are the steps for using Word outlines:

1. Create a Word document using the styles Heading 1 through Heading 6 for the document's headings. Save your work. Do not use the fancier chapter headings and other styles offered by Word's Wizards, and do not use Heading styles 7–9. The illustration here shows an example of a Word document that could be imported successfully into PowerPoint.

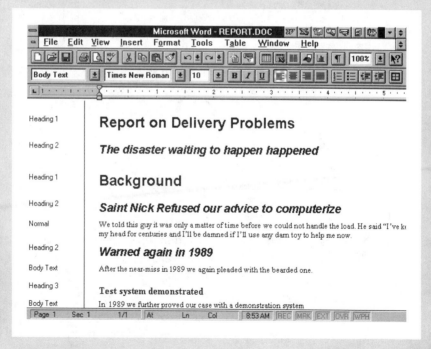

Word

2. Begin a new PowerPoint project or open an existing one.

3. Switch to the slide where you want the new information to be inserted (the slide after the title slide, perhaps). You may also want to switch to Outline view, although this is not required.

4. Choose *Insert Slides from Outline* on PowerPoint's Insert menu.

5. Show PowerPoint the location of the Word document file and click OK, as illustrated here.

6. PowerPoint will attempt to import the headings and create slides, starting a new slide whenever it encounters a Heading level 1 (which it uses as the title for a new slide). Heading 2 entries become the next level down on your slides, and so on.

7. Review the resulting slides and make desired changes in content, formatting, etc., just as you would with any other PowerPoint slides.

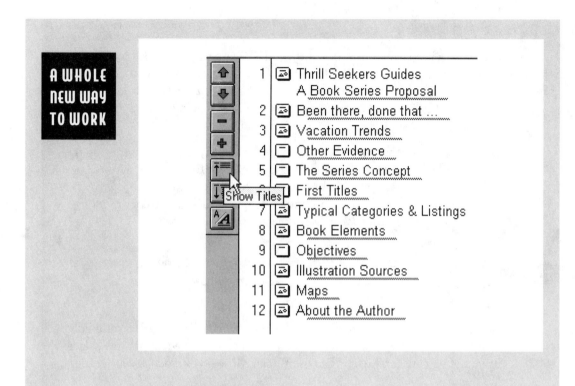

Outlines and Tables of Contents

Since Outlines use (assign) standard Word for Windows Heading styles to headings, you can quickly create a table of contents based on your outline. The TOC will include each heading from the outline.

Printing Outlines

Printing in Outline view creates a document containing only the levels you see on the screen. Collapse the document to the desired level and then use the File – Print command or the Ctrl+P shortcut. Even if just the first line of text appears, Word for Windows will print the whole paragraph.

Word
CHAPTER 10

find and Replace

Every contemporary word-processing product has a way to quickly locate and replace specific text strings (collections of words, numbers, and other characters). Lawyers use these features (sometimes called *global replace features*) to do things like finding each occurrence of *Marion Morrison* in a contract and replacing it with *John Wayne*.

Some typists enter shorthand or acronyms for lengthy items when they draft. Then, while polishing the document, they replace the shorthand with the actual text. For instance, you might initially type *DRD* in the draft of a government document, then have Word find and replace each occurrence of *DRD* with *Department of Redundancy Department*.

If you do a lot of this, consider using Word's AutoCorrect feature instead. It will replace acronyms as you type them.

Word provides two separate commands called Edit ➤ Find (Ctrl+F) and Edit ➤ Replace (Ctrl+H). Find is really just an evolutionary predecessor to Replace. In fact, if you are careful, you can use Replace instead of Find for everything.

With Word you can search for and then replace or remove special characters like paragraph marks, optional hyphens, or footnote-reference marks.

You can use wildcards in search requests to work around minor spelling variations. Asking Word to find **Sm?th**, for instance, would find both *Smith* and *Smyth*. You can search for ranges of numbers using a similar technique. Word's designers refer to this process as searching for *unspecified letters* and *unspecified digits*.

Occasionally, Word's Find and Replace features can be used to reformat documents. You might, for instance, search for all occurrences of two consecutive spaces and replace them with a single space. But Word can do much more than that. The Find and Replace commands can do the following:

- Help you find all or selected paragraphs formatted with a particular style and apply a different style.
- Remove things simply by telling Word to search for the item you wish to delete and replace it with nothing.

■ Search your entire document or selected portions. You specify the direction of the search (up or down).

The Art of Finding

The Find feature helps you quickly locate text, formats, special characters, and combinations thereof. It lets you search selected parts of your document or the whole enchilada. Simple find requests can locate text regardless of format.

New Word 6 features make it easy to ask Word to search for very specific things, like occurrences of the word *Liberace* formatted in bold, blue, 24-point Playbill.

You need not limit your searches to text. You can look for section marks, graphics, paragraph marks, and more. When using the Find command (as opposed to Replace), Word finds what you've requested, then scrolls to the found item and its surrounding text without modifying anything.

You must click in the document window to work with the found item. You can leave the Find dialog box out on your screen as you work, flipping between it and your document window. Figure 10.17 shows the Find dialog box.

Here's a general overview of the Find dialog box. (Details will follow.) To do a search:

1. Choose Edit ➤ Find.

2. Specify text and special characters (if any) to find.

3. Specify formatting characteristics (if any) to find.

FIGURE 10.17

The Find dialog box (reached by choosing Edit ➤ Find or pressing Ctrl+F) lets you specify search criteria.

4. Tell Word where to search and in which direction.

5. Use the Special menu to search for things like section breaks, paragraph marks, etc.

6. Check off any special search requests like Match Case or Find Whole Words Only.

7. Click Find Next to start the search.

8. When Word finds what you want, return to the document.

9. To find again, press = (the equals sign) on the numeric pad or the Enter key on the numeric keypad (if you're still in the document) or click the Find Next button in the dialog box.

Like any good computer program, Word takes your requests quite literally, so you will need to understand each Find option fully to locate exactly what you want.

For example, if Word searches using the criteria *B B King*, it will find *B B King*, but not *B.B. King*, *BB King*, or *Burger King*.

There are ways to get Word to find each of these text strings, of course. Just realize that you may need to carefully formulate and test your search strategy. In some cases, you will need to perform multiple searches to find similar but subtly different text strings.

Word will automatically search in headers and footers. For multi section documents, you may need to open and search headers and footers in each section. If you plan to search for items such as paragraph marks or hidden text, the hidden text must be visible on the screen.

TIP   **Consider proofing your document or at least running the Spelling checker before important, major searches. If you spell <u>banana</u> correctly six times and incorrectly once, Word will find only six of your seven bananas…**

Finding Text

Choose Edit ➤ Find or use the Ctrl+F shortcut. Move to the text area of the Find What box and type enough text (a maximum of 255 characters) for an accurate, unambiguous search. For instance, suppose you wanted to find the word *man*. Entering **man** in Find What would cause Word to find the words *man, Man, Mansfield, reprimand, manhole,* and *man* at the end of a sentence (followed by a period, question mark, etc.).

Placing a space after **man** in your find request would eliminate the unwanted *Mansfield, reprimand,* and *manhole,* but would also prevent you from finding *man* at the ends of sentences because periods, question marks, and such are not spaces.

That's the reason for the Match Whole Word Only checkbox in the Find dialog box. If you type **man** (no space) in the Find What area and check Match Whole Word Only, Word will locate only *man, Man,* and *man* at the end of sentences.

The Match Case checkbox instructs Word to look for exact capitalization matches. If you type **postscript** in the Find What area and check Match Case, Word will not find *POSTSCRIPT, PostScript,* or even *Postscript* at the beginning of sentences.

Extra spaces, nonbreaking spaces, and forced page breaks can also get in the way of searches. See the section "White Space" later in this chapter to learn how to work around this.

Finding Special Characters

The Special drop-down list is a convenient way to enter certain special characters like tab marks, nonbreaking spaces, etc. when constructing a search request. Place the insertion point in the Find What box where you want the special character to go, and choose the desired character from the drop-down list.

Find requests can combine regular text and special characters. For instance, you could ask Word to search for occurrences of *Bob* followed by two tab marks. Many of the special characters in the drop-down list are self-explanatory. Let's look more closely at the ones that are not. Some are extremely useful.

White Space Here's one to keep you awake nights. Suppose you are searching for two words together like *Microsoft Corporation*. Suppose further that sometimes you used nonbreaking spaces to separate the two words. Other times you've just typed regular spaces. Occasionally, you typed two spaces between the words by mistake. Unless you use Word's White Space feature, you will not find the occurrences of *Microsoft Corporation* containing nonbreaking spaces or two spaces!

So, to do it right, insert Word's White Space special character in your search string. In our example, you'd start by typing **Microsoft** in the Find What box. Then, without touching the spacebar, choose White Space from the Special menu. The White Space code (w) will appear next to **Microsoft**. Type *Corporation*. Your finished search string would be **MicrosoftwCorporation**. That should do it.

Any Letter   The Any Letter character lets you overcome some nasty problems too. Suppose you've used accented characters sometimes but not always. *La Cañada* and *La Canada* are not the same thing to Word when it searches. A search for **La Ca*ada** will find both. Enter the Any Letter character from the Special drop-down menu the same way you entered the White Space character.

Any Digit   This special character will sometimes help you find numbers within ranges. It might be helpful for finding specific groups of part numbers or zip codes.

NOTE   When using Any Digit once with the Replace feature, Word will find all occasions, but only highlight the first two digits. So, when you use Replace, you must handle this differently. With the Find feature, it doesn't matter.

For instance, the search string **99#** would find any number between *990* and *999*. The specification **1#** would find the combinations *101* and *11* in *111*. It would also find *1000*, but not *1,000*, since Word treats numbers as text, not numeric values, in searches like these. Commas confuse things. Ah, computers…

Finding Sound Alikes

Word can attempt to locate words that sound alike but are spelled differently (*smith* and *smyth, but* and *butt*, for instance). This is an imprecise art at best, since even words that are *spelled* the same *sound* different in various parts of any country. (If you doubt this, ask a Bostonian, New Yorker, and Chicagoan to pronounce the word *car*.)

At any rate, the Sounds Like option can sometimes round up useful word variations and misspellings.

Pattern Matching

To perform advanced searches for combinations of things (such as both *bet* and *bat*), you use *operators*. For instance, to find either *bet* or *bat*, you would place **b?t** in your Find What box and check Use Pattern Matching. If you forget to check Use Pattern Matching, the results will not be what you expect. Here's the list of operators you can use with Word and what they help you do:

OPERATOR	LETS YOU FIND
?	A single character: b?t finds bet and *bat*
*	Any string of characters: **b*d** finds *bed*, *befuddled*, and *blood*
[*characters*]	Any of the characters in brackets: **b[eo]d** finds *bed* and *bod* but not *bid*
[*character-character*]	Any character in the range: **b[a-i]d** finds *bed* and *bid* but not *bod*
[!*character*]	Any single character except the one in brackets: b[!i]d finds bed and bod but not bid
(!*Range of characters*)	Any single character *except* those in the specified range
character {**n**}	Any n occurrences of the preceding character: **ble{2}d** finds *bleed* but not *bled*
character {**n,**}	At least n occurrences of the preceding character: **b{1,}** finds *bled* and *bleed*
Character {**n,m**}	The specified range of characters: **10{2,3}** finds *100* and *1000* but not *10*

OPERATOR	LETS YOU FIND
character @	One or more occurrences of the preceding character: **ble@d** finds *bled* and *bleed*
<<*text*	The beginning of a word: **<man** finds *manhole* and *manage*
>>*text*	The end of a word. **in>** finds *in* and *herein* but not *interfere*

To search for characters used as operators ({, !, *, etc.), separate them with a backslash. For instance, to find the ampersand, search for *.

The Art of Replacing

To replace, follow these steps:

1. Save your work.
2. Choose Edit ➤ Replace or press Ctrl+H.
3. Create search criteria using the techniques discussed in the previous section.
4. Specify the desired replacement text, formats, etc.
5. Tell Word where to search and in which direction.
6. Click Find Next or Replace All to start the replacement.
7. Confirm the replacements.

  It is a good idea to save your work before using the Replace feature. If you are working on a complex, important project, you might want to use a copy rather than the original document since it is much easier to screw up a document with Replace than it is to repair it.

As you can see from Figure 10.18, the Replace dialog box looks like the Find dialog box, with additional features. Word lets you confirm each replacement before it happens, or it will find and replace without your intervention.

Just as you can search for text, formats, styles, and special characters, you can also replace them. For instance, you could replace *Marion Morrison* with *John Wayne*. (Don't you wish the Duke had kept his given name?)

Or you could change each occurrence of two consecutive paragraph marks to a single end-of-line marker, or change the style of certain paragraphs from chapter-heading style to appendix style. It is even possible to replace text with graphics. Here are examples of each technique.

FIGURE 10.18

The Replace dialog box (reached by choosing Edit ➤ Replace or pressing Ctrl+H) resembles the Find dialog box, with added features.

Replacing Text with Text

To simply replace text (like changing *Marion Morrison* to *John Wayne*) without altering formats or styles, start by entering the text to find and the desired replacement text. For instance, you might enter *Marion Morrison* in the Find What box and *John Wayne* in the Replace With box. Follow these steps:

1. Save your work.

2. Choose Edit ➤ Replace (Ctrl+H).

Visit the Search drop-down menu to tell Word if you want it to search the entire document or a selected portion, and so on.

  If there are any formats or styles listed under the Find What or Replace With boxes, click No Formatting with the insertion point in the appropriate place (Find What, Replace With, or both). This way, Word will not alter the style or format of the document.

4. When the replacement instructions are complete, click Find Next. Word will search the document (or selected portion) for things matching your Find criteria and propose the next replacement. The Replace button should undim and your document screen should scroll to reveal the first potential replacement point.

5. If you want Word to make the change it is proposing, click Replace. To skip the change, click Find Next. To make the change and let Word continue uninterrupted, click Replace All. Word will make the rest of the replacements nonstop, and probably too quickly for you to even see them. The status area in the lower-left corner of your document window will briefly flash the number of replacements made.

6. Check your work. You can use Undo if you have made any mistakes.

Replacing Formatting

Suppose you have italicized words scattered throughout your text and decide to change all of them to underlined words. Start by removing any text from the Find What and Replace With boxes. (This is because you want Word to find all italicized text, not just words in the Find What box that are italicized.) Then follow these steps:

1. Specify the character attributes you want Word to find (italics for example). You can do this in one of several ways. Always start by placing the insertion point in the Find What entry box. Then specify the Italic format from the Standard toolbar or pull down the Format list in the Replace dialog box. From there, choose Font, then click in the Italic option of the Font dialog box.

TIP You can use keyboard shortcuts or toolbar buttons to specify formatting as well. It is often much quicker.

The word *Italic* (or whatever) will appear beneath the Find What box.

2. Next go to the Replace With box and specify the new format (Underline in Figure 10.18). In order to prevent Word from changing the italic to italic underline, you may need to click the Formatting toolbar's italic button until the Replace With criteria read Italic: No Underline. Figure 10.18 shows the appearance of the critical parts of the dialog box when you are ready to go.

3. Let 'er rip! Either tell Word to Replace All or you can supervise by using the Replace and Find Next buttons.

Replacing Styles

If you want to change the style of certain paragraphs, the Replace command can help:

1. Click on the Format button.

2. Choose Styles.

3. You will see a list of your document's styles and descriptions.

4. Pick styles for both the find and replace criteria, then proceed as usual.

In this example, paragraphs formatted with the Heading 3 style will be reformatted using the Heading 2 style.

Combining Replacement Tasks

Within reason, it is possible to combine search and replace instructions to restrict actions. For instance, assuming you had a document with appropriate styles, you could italicize all occurrences of *Gone With The Wind* in the body text of your report, while leaving the same words alone when they appear in headings, tables-of-contents, and indexes.

You would do this by typing **Gone with the Wind** in the Find What box and restricting the find to the body text style. Then you'd have to type **Gone with** the Wind again in the Replace With box and specify Italic as the format. (If you forget to enter **Gone with the Wind** in the Replace With box, Word will replace occurrences of *Gone with the Wind* with nothing...) Computers are very obedient but not very clever. Undo should help, but work on *copies* of important documents just in case.

Search

Word has several methods to search your document for words you wish to either find or replace. These options are found under the Search drop-down menu in the Find and Replace dialog boxes. Up searches back toward the beginning of the document, while Down searches toward the end. All searches the entire document, as you would expect.

Using the Clipboard with Find and Replace

The Clipboard can be used for several interesting Find and Replace tasks. For instance, you can copy text from your document to the Clipboard, then paste it into the Find What or Replace With boxes. This is a great way to paste long passages or obscure characters like umlauted letters or math symbols. It is even possible to overcome the 255 character limitation this way.

Word also lets you replace text with graphics if you place the graphics on the Clipboard.

1. Copy a graphic to the Clipboard.

2. Visit the Replace dialog box.

3. Enter find criteria.

4. Place the insertion point in the Replace With portion of the dialog box.

5. Choose Clipboard Contents from the Special list.

6. Replace as usual.

Replacing Tips

Here are some tips for replacing:

- The Replace command uses considerable memory if you make a lot of changes. It is a good idea to perform a normal save after assuring that your replacements are satisfactory.

- Undo will undo all changes if you use Replace All, but only your last change if you have been supervising with the Find Next button.

- If you've used styles in your document, you may find it easier to make wholesale style changes by redefining or reapplying styles rather than using Replace.

- You can specify any character in Find or Replace strings by typing **n**, where *n* is the ASCII (decimal) code for the character of interest.

- Remember to click No Formatting when specifying new search criteria in the Find What and Replace With boxes.

- All of the special characters (paragraphs, tabs, etc.) are represented by two-character codes that you can enter into Find and Replace boxes from the keyboard. It's often the quick way to go. Here's a handy reference list. Notice that they must always be typed in lowercase:

CHARACTER	CODE
Paragraph mark	^p
Tab	^t
Annotation mark	^a
Any character	^?
Any digit	^#
Any letter	^$
Caret	^^
Column break	^n
Em dash	^+
En dash	^=

CHARACTER	CODE
Endnote mark	^e
Field	^d
Footnote mark	^f
Graphic	^g
Line break	^l
Manual page break	^m
Nonbreaking hyphen	^~
Clipboard contents	^c
Nonbreaking space	^s
Optional hyphen	^-
Section break	^b
White space	^w

How Replace Interacts with Styles

Be aware that just as manually applied formatting and styles interact when you change styles or formatting yourself, they interact when the Replace command makes changes.

Annotations

Word for Windows offers several ways to annotate. Hidden text was available in earlier Word versions, and remains in this one. It has been joined by *voice annotations*, a way to record and play back sounds attached to specific locations in Word for Windows documents if your computer is sound-capable.

Finally, Word's text annotation and Revisions features let you document changes as you work.

Using Hidden Text for Annotations

Authors often use hideable text to make notes to themselves or to colleagues. They leave the notes in view while working, then hide them when they print their work. To define text as hideable:

1. Select the desired text.

2. Visit the Font dialog box (choose Format ➤ Font).

3. Check Hidden in the Effects area.

4. Click OK to set.

5. When printing, click on Options in the Print dialog box (Edit ➤ Print) and check the Hidden Text option in the Include with Document section of the Options dialog box.

The keyboard shortcut to define text as hideable is Ctrl+Shift+H. This command toggles hidden text. If you use it with hideable text, the text will revert to nonhideable text.

Showing and Hiding Text

To show or hide text, follow these steps:

1. Use the View tab in the Options dialog box (reached with Tools ➤ Options).

2. Enable or disable the Hidden Text feature by clicking to add or remove an X.

3. Click OK.

Text Annotations

This feature lets you add reminders to yourself and notes to others collaborating on your document. The notes can be completely hidden, flagged, or displayed and printed. When you are done with them they can be deleted or incorporated into your final document. Annotations with Word for Windows couldn't be easier. Follow these steps:

1. Place the insertion point at the place in your document where you want to insert the annotation, or select the item you wish to discuss.

2. Pick Insert ➤ Annotation (*not* View ➤ Annotations).

3. You'll see the annotation window pane.

4. Word will insert initials (hopefully, yours) as hidden text.

5. Type the note.

6. Either choose Close or leave the pane visible as you work.

If you don't see your initials in the document or in the drop-down From list, visit the User Info tab in the Options dialog box and type your initials in the initials area. Click OK.

Viewing Annotations

You view annotations with the View ➤ Annotations command. (Notice that *this* command is plural while the one on the Insert menu is singular, since you insert annotations one at a time but can view several at once.)

1. Double-click on the annotation mark of interest in your document or use the View ➤ Annotations command. (If you don't see marks, reveal them with the Standard toolbar's ¶ button.)

2. To view the next or previous annotations, scroll in the annotations window.

3. To filter annotations so that you see only those from a particular author, pick the initials of interest from the annotation pane's drop-down list.

4. When you are done, close the Annotations pane with the Close button or leave it open while you work.

If the author of an annotation highlights document text or other elements when creating the note, those items will be highlighted again when you read the annotation. This is not the same thing as selecting prior to editing. If you wish to edit highlighted things, you'll still need to select them.

Editing and Protecting Annotations

You can change any existing annotation, even if you are not the author of the annotation. It is possible for authors to password-protect annotations (and re-vision marks) with the Tools ➤ Protect Document command. Here's how to protect your annotations and revisions:

1. Choose Tools ➤ Protect Document. The Protect Document dialog box will appear.

2. Choose the protection you desire (Annotations).

3. Enter a clever password.

4. Repeat it when Word asks.

5. Click OK or press ↵.

6. Remember it....

  Punctuation counts when entering passwords. <u>watergate</u>, <u>Watergate</u>, and <u>WATERGATE</u> are all different (and dumb) passwords. Beware of the Caps Lock key. Since Word no longer indicates in the status area whether Caps Lock is on or off, you have to be especially careful.

  Give some thought to your passwords. They should be easy for you to remember and difficult for others to guess. Your name or nickname is too easy. The word <u>password</u> is too obvious a choice. Names of old flames are good, unless they're well known to would-be password breakers. Favorite TV or movie characters are good with the same cautions. If you are a Trekki, people who know you will try words like <u>Spock</u> and <u>Kirk</u> early on in their rummaging.

Incorporating Annotations

You can copy and paste text from the annotation pane into the document. Drag-and-drop works here too!

Printing Annotations

To print just the annotations, visit the Print dialog box (Ctrl+P) and choose Annotations from the Print What list.

To print a document and its annotations, choose Document in the Print dialog box's Print What list, then click the Options button to reveal the Print Tab. Choose Annotations from the options list.

Moving and Removing Annotations

Move and delete annotations by treating their annotation marks as you would any other character in a document. Select them, drag-and-drop, delete, copy, etc. This assumes of course that the document is not password protected, or that you know the password.

Cross-Referencing

Cross-referencing lets you say things like *see Chapter 29 for details*, then have Word for Windows automatically update the reference if you change the chapter number. Cross-references are not limited to chapter numbers; they can refer to just about anything, including headings, footnotes, endnotes, captions, etc. You can cross-reference things in different documents, as long as they are in the same Master Document.

Creating Cross-References

1. Begin by typing the in-text reference followed by a quotation mark (**Parts of an Airplane**", for example).

2. Choose Insert ➤ Cross-reference. You'll see the Cross-reference dialog box.

3. Pick the Reference Type that will tie the in-text reference to the item you wish to reference. (Figure 12, for instance.)

4. Choose the item you wish to reference in the scrolling For Which list.

5. Click Insert. You'll see some new information at the insertion point. This is actually a field.

6. Click Close or make other cross references first, then close.

Once you've created cross-references, they will be updated when you switch to Print Preview or print. To update immediately at any time, select the entire document and press F9.

If you delete an item that is referenced, Word will alert you.

Thesaurus

The Thesaurus... command can help you add flavor and punch to your documents. Select the word you want to change, then open the Thesaurus dialog box either with the keyboard shortcut Shift+F7 or by choosing the Thesaurus command on the Tools menu. You'll see a dialog box like the one in Figure 10.19.

FIGURE 10.19

Word's Thesaurus can help you find the perfect word.

The Meanings section of the dialog box lists available meanings and parts of speech for the selected word. If antonyms (words with opposite meanings) are available, you'll see an Antonym choice as well.

1. Pick the meaning of interest, and you'll see a corresponding list of synonyms or antonyms in the box to the right of the Meanings list. Click on the closest meaning or Antonyms if that's a possibility. You'll see a list of choices in the box to the right of the Meanings box.

2. Clicking on a word places it in the Replace with box.

3. If you click the Replace button at this point, the new word will replace the selected one in your document.

4. To look for other words instead, click the Look Up button. This will display additional choices.

5. The Synonyms For list builds as you explore alternate words, and you can "go back" by clicking on the arrow and selecting an earlier word.

6. Clicking the Cancel button closes the Thesaurus without changing your selected word.

NOTE If the selected word is misspelled or unfamiliar to the Thesaurus feature, you will see a list of "close" words that may or may not be useful. You'll also see close words for some tenses of some words. For example, if you try to look up <u>carries</u>, the Thesaurus will suggest <u>carry</u>.

Incidentally, the Thesaurus sometimes recognizes phrases. Look what happens when I select the phrase *about to* (Figure 10.20).

FIGURE 10.20

Word's Thesaurus can recognize phrases as well as single words

Bookmarks

Bookmarks let you name specific points or areas of your document. Use bookmarks to identify the beginning of chapters, tables, spots that need work, the place where you left off, and so on. You can mark a place, a character, ranges of characters, graphics, or just about any other element in a Word document. You can then tell Word to go to those specific points without a lot of scrolling and searching.

To use bookmarks, you simply locate things of interest, define them as bookmarks, and visit them as necessary. Here are the general steps.

Defining Bookmarks

To define a bookmark, follow these steps:

1. Either move the insertion point to the item of interest, or select the item.

2. Choose <u>E</u>dit ➤ <u>B</u>ookmark... (Ctrl+Shift+F5). You'll see the Bookmark dialog box, shown in Figure 10.21.

FIGURE 10.21

Creating a bookmark

3. Give the bookmark a unique name consisting of up to 40 characters. Spaces are *not* allowed, so use an underscore instead, as illustrated in Figure 10.21. Numbers are allowed, but not for the first character of the bookmark—that has to be a letter.

4. Click Add. (If the button is dimmed, check to see that the name is less than 40 characters long and contains no spaces).

5. Create more bookmarks or close the box. Clicking on Add also closes the dialog box.

Going to a Bookmark

Once you've defined some bookmarks, you can go to them in one of two ways. If you select Edit ➤ Go To, you'll see a list of bookmarks in scrolling lists (as illustrated in Figure 10.22). Double-click on a bookmark's name to go there. If you click the Go To button in the in the Bookmark dialog box, however, Word will go to the selected bookmark without displaying the dialog box.

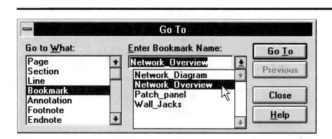

In the Bookmark dialog box, you can sort the list either by name or by the relative location of the bookmark in the document, as shown in Figure 10.23.

FIGURE 10.23

The Bookmark dialog box allows you to sort bookmarks by Location in the document rather than by Name (the default way)

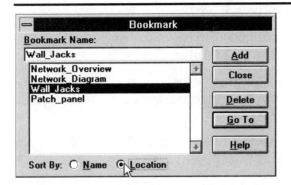

Displaying and Hiding Bookmarks

You can see little in-document markers that indicate the location of bookmarks. These large, square brackets indicate the beginning and ending of a bookmarked area. For instance, the entire heading *Patch Panel* is a bookmark, as shown here.

NOTE If you select text prior to setting a bookmark, you'll get something that looks like [selectedtext]. If you don't select text, though, you'll get something that looks like a big I.

As you can see, these markers can get in the way of the text, so you can turn them on and off by selecting or clearing the Bookmarks check box on the View tab of the Options dialog box (reached by choosing Tools ➤ Options), as shown in Figure 10.24.

FIGURE 10.24

To display bookmarks, check the Bookmarks check box on the View tab of the Options dialog box (View ➤ Options)

Working with Bookmarked Items

It's often easiest to work with bookmarked items and see the effect of your work if you have the bookmark markers displayed.

If you move a bookmarked item, the mark moves with it, even to another document (as long as this won't create a duplicate bookmark name in the destination document).

Deleting the entire text or other items between two bookmark markers deletes the bookmark as well. (Say that five times fast.)

To add things and have them included with the bookmark, insert them within the bookmark marks. To insert things and not have them included, place the insertion point to the right of the bookmark marker.

Deleting Bookmarks

To delete a mark but not the marked item(s), follow these steps:

1. Visit the Bookmark dialog box.
2. Choose the desired bookmark name.
3. Click the Delete key.
4. Click Close. The bookmark disappears and the previously marked items remain.

To delete a bookmark and the items it marks:

1. Turn on Bookmark markers in the View tab.
2. Select the item and both bookmark markers.
3. Delete as usual (Cut, press Delete, etc.). The mark and the items(s) will disappear.

Macros,
Custom Toolbars,
Keyboard Shortcuts,
and Menus

Word
CHAPTER 11

macro has now achieved international status as a dirty word in computing, a reputation quite unjustified. Macros are one of the most powerful features of Word 6, since they allow you to customize and automate your work to a high degree. Custom toolbars and menus let you further personalize Word. You can also add or change keyboard shortcuts to speed your work.

What Are Macros?

A macro is a series of Word commands grouped together as a single command to make everyday tasks easier. You can assign a macro to a toolbar, a menu, or a shortcut key and run it by simply clicking a button, selecting a menu choice, or pressing a key combination. Macros are recorded as instructions in Word's macro language, *WordBasic*. You can create a macro in two ways:

- Record a series of actions using the keyboard and mouse. This is the easiest way.

- Type a macro directly into a macro-editing window. This way you have more flexibility, and can include WordBasic instructions that you can't record using the keyboard and mouse.

For complicated macros, consider combining these two ways: Record as much as possible, then edit the result in the macro-editing window. Record further pieces, edit them, and add them as necessary.

Recording Macros

To record a macro, you start the Word macro recorder and record a sequence of actions. You then stop the recorder and edit the macro if need be. Then you can run the macro whenever you need to perform the same sequence of actions.

There are three ways to start the macro recorder:

- Double-click REC on the status bar (at the bottom of your screen). Yes, even though REC is dim, double-clicking works.... This is the quick and easy way.
- Select Tools ➤ Macro, then click the Record button in the Macro dialog box. Easy but slower.
- Click the Record button on the Macro toolbar if you have it displayed.

Here's how to record a macro:

1. Start the macro recorder by double-clicking REC on the status bar. The Record Macro dialog box will appear, as shown in Figure 11.1.

2. Enter a name for the macro in the Record Macro Name box.

   If you don't give your macro a name, Word will name it Macro1, Macro2, and so on. No spaces, commas, or periods allowed in the name.

FIGURE 11.1

The Record Macro dialog box

3. Enter a description of what the macro does in the Description box. This is optional but heavily recommended. Use up to 255 characters.

4. To assign the macro to a toolbar, a menu, or a keyboard shortcut, click the Toolbars, Menus, or Keyboard button.

5. If your current document is attached to a template other than NORMAL.DOT, drop down the Save Changes In list and select either that template or Normal.

6. Click OK, then perform the actions you want to record.

7. To stop recording the macro, click the Stop button on the Macro Record toolbar that appears when you start recording (shown here). The Macro Record toolbar will disappear.

Pausing while Recording the Macro

Word 6 allows you to suspend and resume recording a macro as suits you. If you reach some impasse in the procedure that you don't want to record for posterity, or just want to record isolated actions here and there as the fancy strikes you, here's what to do:

1. Click the Pause button on the Macro Record toolbar to pause recording.

2. Perform the actions you don't want to record.

3. Click the Pause button again to restart recording (just like a tape recorder).

Editing Macros

Here's how to edit a macro:

1. Select Tools ➤ Macro. The Macro dialog box will appear.

2. Select the list of macros to choose from by dropping down the Macros Available In box.

3. Choose the macro you want to edit, then click the Edit button. The macro-editing window will appear, displaying the text of the macro you chose.

4. Edit the macro.

Running a Macro

Once you have recorded your macro, you can assign it to a toolbar, a menu, or a shortcut key combination. You can then run it as you would a normal Word command or feature.

If you don't want to assign a macro to a toolbar, menu, or key combination—perhaps you simply have too many macros, or use some of them too seldom to merit having them available all the time—you can also run a macro by choosing Tools ➤ Macro, selecting the macro name in the Macro dialog box, and clicking the Run button.

If you've got everything right, your macro will perform the actions you taught it to do. If something is wrong, you may have to edit it.

Organizing Your Macros

Word 6's new Organizer dialog box (see Figure 11.2) greatly simplifies managing your macros. You can use it to move, copy, or rename a macro.

By default, macros are stored in the Global Template (NORMAL.DOT) and so are available for use with every Word document. However, you can store them in other templates if you wish. For example, if you have a macro that's only useful for annual reports, you might include it in your ANNUREPO template.

The Organizer dialog box lets you manage your macros easily.

Copying Macros from One Template to Another

Word 6 lets you easily copy macros from one template to another. So you can record or write a macro in the Normal template, then decide you only need it in your IMCLEVER template, and transfer it across:

1. Select File ➤ Templates. The Templates and Add-Ins dialog box will appear.

2. Click the Organizer button to display the Organizer dialog box.

3. Choose the Macros tab.

4. If necessary, close the open file, select the Open File button, and open the template or document containing the macro.

5. Select the macro you want to copy, then choose the Copy button.

6. Click the Close button when you've finished copying macros.

You can also get to the Organizer dialog box by selecting Tools ➤ Macro and clicking the Organizer button in the Macro dialog box.

Renaming a Macro

If you find you've given a macro a confusing name, you may want to rename it. Here's how:

1. Select Tools ➤ Macro. The Macro dialog box will appear.

2. Click the Organizer button. The Organizer dialog box will appear with the Macros tab selected.

3. In the left list box, choose the macro to rename. If necessary, choose a different template in the Macros Available In list box.

4. Click the Rename button. The Rename dialog box will appear:

5. Enter the new name for the macro and click OK. The macro will be renamed.

Deleting a Macro

Here's how to delete a macro that you no longer need—or one that doesn't work:

1. Select Tools ➤ Macro. The Macro dialog box will appear.

2. Highlight the macro to delete and click the Delete button.

3. Click Yes in the confirmation dialog box that Word pops up. The macro will be deleted.

4. Click the Close button to return to your document.

Word

Word's Automatic Macros

Even if you never get deeply into writing and using macros, you should look briefly at Word's five autoexecuting macros. With only a little effort, you can use these to set and restore screen preferences, open a bunch of documents, and generally make life a little more pleasant for you.

The five automatic macros are:

MACRO NAME	WHAT IT DOES	SUGGESTED USES
AutoExec	Runs when you start Word	Set general screen preferences; open a particular document
AutoNew	Runs when you open a new file based on its template	Set screen document for a particular template; change printers
AutoOpen	Runs when you open a file you created before	Return to last editing location (using GoBack)
AutoClose	Runs when you close a file (new or created before)	Prompt to back file up
AutoExit	Runs when you exit Word	Restore screen preferences for next use; reminders; valedictions

You can create automatic macros just as you do any other macros—by typing the commands into the macro-editing window (reached by selecting the Edit or Create button in the Macro dialog box), by recording a series of actions, or by a judicious mixture of the two.

The Macro Toolbar

When working with macros, you'll often want to use the Macro toolbar (see Figure 11.3). This contains 12 buttons and a name box and lets you manipulate macros in a variety of useful ways. Here's what the different parts of the Macro toolbar do.

TOOLBAR ITEM	WHAT IT DOES
Macro name box	Lists the name of the macro
Record	Turns recording a macro on or off
Record Next Command	Records the next command executed
Start	Starts running the current macro
Trace	Highlights each statement as the active macro executes it
Pause/Continue	Pauses or continues running the macro
Stop	Stops running the macro

FIGURE 11.3

The Macro toolbar

TOOLBAR ITEM	WHAT IT DOES
Step	Runs the active macro one step at a time
Step Subs	Runs the active macro one step at a time, considering subroutines one step
Show Variables	Lists the active macro's variables
Add/Remove REM	Adds or removes a REM (remark) at the beginning of each selected line in the active macro
Macro	Runs, creates, deletes, or revises a macro
Dialog Editor	Launches the macro Dialog Editor, a mini-application that you can use to design dialog boxes

For reasons of space, this chapter has only been able to skim the surface of macros, the macro language, and the benefits they can offer you. Consult on-line help and the big books for more information about macros.

Customizing Word's Toolbars

You can customize Word 6's toolbars to simplify the way you work. You can add and remove commands, macros, AutoText entries, and styles, and move buttons from one toolbar to another. You can even create custom toolbars. You can move toolbars to different positions on the screen or have them float freely above the document. You can move and resize a floating toolbar as if it were a window. In the following sections, we'll look at the different things you can do with toolbars.

Figure 11.4 shows my custom toolbar, which contains things I like to have at my fingertips. It's a combination of Word commands and macros; there are some custom graphics on a few of the buttons. I've labeled the buttons in Figure 11.4 to give you some ideas for making your own toolbars.

FIGURE 11.4

My favorite buttons run Word commands or macros. Others open new documents based on templates or insert AutoText items.

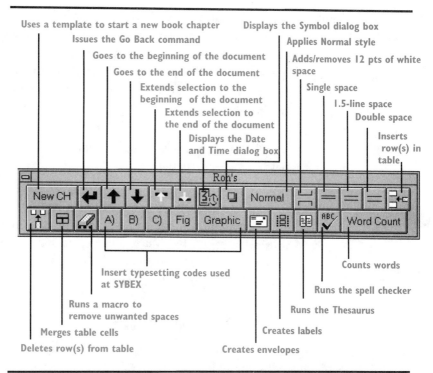

Uses a template to start a new book chapter
Issues the Go Back command
Goes to the beginning of the document
Goes to the end of the document
Extends selection to the beginning of the document
Extends selection to the end of the document
Displays the Date and Time dialog box

Displays the Symbol dialog box
Applies Normal style
Adds/removes 12 pts of white space
Single space
1.5-line space
Double space
Inserts row(s) in table

Insert typesetting codes used at SYBEX
Runs a macro to remove unwanted spaces
Merges table cells
Deletes row(s) from table
Creates envelopes
Creates labels
Runs the Thesaurus
Runs the spell checker
Counts words

FIGURE 11.5

The Toolbars dialog box. Check the check boxes for the toolbars you want to see.

Word

NOTE You can't display the Mail Merge toolbar unless you're running a mail merge. (Select Tools ➤ Mail Merge to fire up the Mail Merge Helper.) Likewise some of Word's other specialized toolbars—you can't display the Headers and Footers toolbar unless you're working in a header or footer, and so on.

To remove a toolbar from the screen, select View ➤ Toolbars and uncheck the appropriate check box, then click OK.

TIP To display and remove toolbars using the mouse, right-click on a displayed toolbar to display a shortcut menu and click to display an unchecked toolbar or to hide a checked toolbar. Click Toolbars or Customize to display the Toolbars or Customize dialog box, respectively.

Moving and Resizing Toolbars

You can place toolbars anywhere on your screen that suits you and resize them to a number of shapes.

To move a toolbar displayed at the top of the screen, click in blank space in it and drag it to where you want it. It'll change shape as soon as you drag it out of the toolbar area at the top of the screen. Alternatively, double-click in blank space in it to display it in its last floating position on the screen.

To return a toolbar to the top of the screen, click in blank space in it and drag it to the top of the screen, where it'll revert to its long and wide shape. Alternatively, double-click in blank space in it to flip it back up there.

To resize a toolbar, move the mouse pointer over one of its borders so that a double-headed arrow appears; then click and drag the border to the shape you want. Toolbar shapes adjust in jumps, not smoothly, so that they're the right size and shape for their buttons.

Changing the Predefined Toolbars

If you want, you can change Word's predefined toolbars. You might want to re-move buttons that you never use or change the command that an existing but-ton runs. Here's how:

1. Display the toolbar you want to change.
2. Choose Tools ➤ Customize. The Customize dialog box will appear.
3. Select the Toolbars tab (see Figure 11.6).
4. To add a button, select the right category in the Categories box, and then drag the button or item to where you want it on the toolbar.
5. To delete a button, drag the button off the toolbar and drop it in the dia-log box (or anywhere else where no toolbar is).
6. When you're done, click the Close button.

FIGURE 11.6

The Toolbars tab of the Customize dialog box

WARNING When you delete a built-in toolbar button, it'll still be available in the Customize dialog box. But when you delete a custom toolbar button, it's gone for good. Consider creating a storage toolbar for keeping unused buttons rather than deleting them permanently.

Moving or Copying a Toolbar Button

Here's how to move or copy buttons from one toolbar to another:

1. Select Tools ➤ Customize. The Customize dialog box will appear.

2. Select the Toolbars tab.

3. To move a button, drag it to where you want it on the same toolbar or on another toolbar.

4. To copy a button, hold down Ctrl and drag the button to where you want it on the same toolbar or on another toolbar. Word will automatically close the gap left (when you move a button) and shift the buttons along in the new location.

TIP To move a toolbar button quickly, without opening the Customize dialog box, hold down Alt and drag the button to where you want it. To copy a button, hold down Ctrl+Alt and drag the button to where you want it.

NOTE To add space before a button, go to the Toolbar tab in the Customize dialog box and drag a button a little way to its right. When you're done, close the dialog box. This seems pretty pointless unless you're <u>mega</u>clumsy with your mouse, and even then you'd be better off recalibrating the mouse's movements in the Control Panel.

Resetting a Built-In Toolbar

Here's how to restore a toolbar to its original settings:

1. Select View ➤ Toolbars. The Toolbars dialog box will appear.

2. Highlight the toolbar you want to restore, and then click the Reset button.

3. In the Reset Toolbar dialog box (see Figure 11.7), select the template in which to make the change, and then choose OK.

4. Click OK to close the Toolbars dialog box.

FIGURE 11.7

The Reset Toolbar dialog box

Creating a Custom Toolbar

If you find yourself using buttons on half-a-dozen different toolbars in the course of the day's work, or if you wish there were buttons for commands, macros, templates and other things that don't have them, you may want to create a custom toolbar that contains only the buttons you need. Here's how:

1. Select View ➤ Toolbars. The Toolbars dialog box will appear.

2. Click the New button. The New Toolbar dialog box will appear:

3. Type a name for the new toolbar in the Toolbar Name box.

4. Select the template in which to store the toolbar in the Make Toolbar Available To box, and then click OK. Word will display the Customize dialog box with the Toolbars tab selected and a new toolbar without buttons in its own toolbar window.

5. In the Categories box, select the category containing the first button to add to the new toolbar.

6. Drag the appropriate button to the new toolbar (see Figure 11.8).

7. Add further buttons as appropriate.

8. When you finish building your new toolbar, click the Close button.

Your new toolbar will appear in the Toolbars dialog box and in the shortcut menu produced by right-clicking a displayed toolbar.

FIGURE 11.8

Dragging a button to
the new toolbar

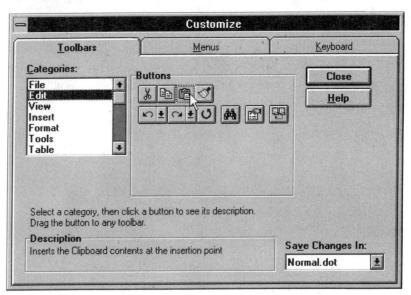

Deleting a Custom Toolbar

When you get sick of your custom toolbars, you can easily delete them:

1. Select View ➤ Toolbars to display the Toolbars dialog box.

2. Highlight the custom toolbar you want to delete and click the Delete button.

3. Click Yes in the confirmation dialog box.

 NOTE Word won't let you delete the toolbars it provides, only your custom toolbars.

Renaming a Custom Toolbar

You can rename a custom toolbar at any point:

1. Select File ➤ Templates. The Templates and Add-Ins dialog box will appear.

2. Click the Organizer button. The Organizer dialog box will appear.

3. Select the Toolbars tab (see Figure 11.9).

FIGURE 11.9

The Toolbars tab of the Organizer dialog box. Select the toolbar you want to rename.

Word

4. In the left or right box, highlight the toolbar to rename, and then click the Rename button.

5. In the Rename dialog box (shown below), enter a new name for the toolbar and click OK.

6. Click Close to close the Organizer dialog box.

Assigning an Item to a Toolbar Button

You can assign toolbar buttons to run commands, macros, fonts, AutoText entries, or styles. You can attach toolbars to specific templates, which gives you great flexibility.

To assign an item to a toolbar button:

1. Open a document based on the template containing the item you want to assign—or open the template itself.

2. Display the toolbar you want to change.

3. Select Tools ➤ Customize. The Customize dialog box will appear.

4. Choose the Toolbars tab (see Figure 11.10).

5. In the Save Changes box, select the template containing the item you want to assign to the toolbar.

6. In the Categories box, select the category containing the command to add. (The All Commands choice will list all of Word's commands.)

7. Drag the item name from the box to the right of the Categories box to the toolbar.

   ■ When you choose an item without a built-in button, you'll get a blank button on the toolbar, and Word will open the Custom

FIGURE 11.10

The Customize dialog
box with the Toolbars
tab selected

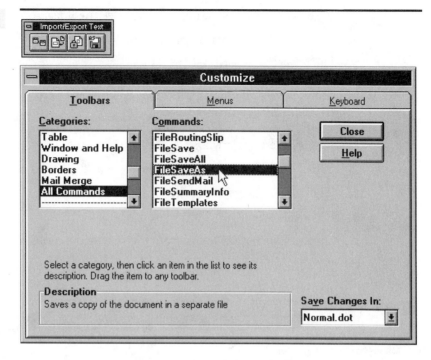

Button dialog box. (See the section "Creating a Custom Button,"
coming up in a moment).

8. Select a button, then click the Assign button, and then click Close.

Creating a Custom Button

You can create a custom toolbar button in two ways: Either create a new image in the Button Editor dialog box or copy an image from a graphics application and paste it onto a button. The latter's more fun, so let's look at it first:

1. Create the image in your graphics application and copy it to the Clipboard, preferably in bitmap or picture format.

2. Switch to Word and display the target toolbar.

3. Select Tools ➤ Customize.

4. In the Customize dialog box, select the Toolbars tab.

5. Right-click the toolbar button to receive the image.

6. Choose Paste Button Image from the shortcut menu.

7. Click the Close button.

If you don't have a graphics application, here's how to create (from a blank button) or modify a toolbar button:

1. Display the toolbar whose button you want to modify.

2. Select Tools ➤ Customize. The Customize dialog box will appear.

3. Click the Toolbars tab.

4. Right-click the button you want to modify.

5. Choose Edit Button Image from the shortcut menu. The Button Editor dialog box will appear (see Figure 11.11).

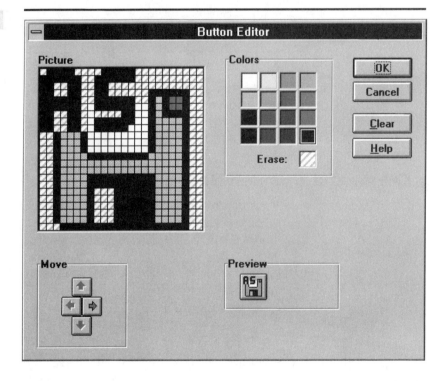

6. Change the button image to your liking. Click on the small boxes representing each pixel in the button face to add/remove or change a color. Watch the little sample as you work.

7. Choose Close when finished.

Restoring a Built-In Toolbar Button's Image

If you don't like the changes you made to the image on a button, you can easily restore it:

1. Display the toolbar whose button you want to change.

2. Select Tools ➤ Customize. The Customize dialog box will appear.

3. Select the Toolbars tab.

4. Right-click the button you want to restore.

5. Choose Reset Button Image from the shortcut menu.

6. Choose Close.

Enlarging Toolbar Buttons

You can enlarge the toolbar buttons to make them easier to see, or make them smaller so that more will fit on your screen. (You may want to remove unnecessary commands from the toolbars so all of your favorites will fit.)

To display large toolbar buttons:

1. Select View ➤ Toolbars to display the Toolbars dialog box.

2. Check the Large Buttons check box, and then click OK. Your toolbars will appear with large buttons, as illustrated in Figure 11.12.

To restore toolbar buttons to their normal size, select View ➤ Toolbars and uncheck the Large Buttons check box.

Word

FIGURE 11.12

The difference between toolbars with large buttons (above) and regular buttons (below)

Customizing Word's Menus

Word lets you control the appearance and arrangement of its menus. You can add, delete, and reposition menu items. You can also change the keyboard shortcuts for most menu items. You can use this flexibility to make your copy of Word extremely easy to use or to deliberately restrict someone's options. For example, you could prevent your default temp from applying any formatting to your precious documents.

Adding Menu Items

Here's how to customize Word's menus so they contain the commands, macros, fonts, AutoText entries, and styles you need most often:

1. Open a document based on the template containing the item you want to assign—or open the template itself.

2. Select Tools ➤ Customize. The Customize dialog box will appear.

3. Click the Menus tab (see Figure 11.13).

4. In the Save Changes In box, select the template in which the item is stored.

5. Select the category to which the item belongs in the Categories box.

6. Select the item you want to assign in the box to the right of the Categories box.

7. Choose the menu you want in the Change What Menu box.

FIGURE 11.13

The Menus tab in the
Customize dialog box

8. In the Position on Menu box, select (Auto) to let Word automatically position similar menu items together, select (At Top) or (At Bottom) to position the item at the top or bottom of the menu, or select the item below which to position the item if you want to position it within the menu list.

9. In the Name on Menu box, either accept the default name or type the name you want to appear. Put an ampersand (&) in front of the hot-key letter.

10. Click the Add button or Add Below button. (Word will offer you one or t'other.)

11. To close the Customize dialog box, click the Close button.

NOTE   To add a menu item separator bar, choose (Separator) in the Commands area of the Customize dialog box, position it as described above, and click the Add or Add Below button.

Removing Menu Items

Here's the quick way to remove items you don't need from menus:

 1. Press Ctrl+Alt+− (that's Ctrl+Alt+minus). The mouse pointer will change to a heavy horizontal line, as shown here.

 NOTE If you change your mind, press Esc to return the mouse pointer to normal.

2. Click the menu item you want to remove. It'll disappear.

This method is much more fun than using the Tools ➤ Customize dialog box, selecting the command to remove, and then clicking the Remove button, but that way works too.

NOTE To remove a menu item separator bar, choose (Separator) in the Commands area of the Customize dialog box and click the Remove button.

Restoring Built-In Menus to Their Original Settings

To quickly restore all built-in Word menus to their original state:

1. Select Tools ➤ Customize. The Customize dialog box will appear.

2. Choose the Menus tab.

3. Select the template to restore in the Save Changes In box.

4. Click the Reset All button.

5. Click Yes in the confirmation dialog box.

6. Click the Close button.

Think twice before restoring all menus, especially if you've made any significant changes. Consider backing up any superb pieces of customization so you can't trash them in an instant with the Reset All button.

Adding New Menus

Word 6 lets you add new menus—a great improvement over Word 2.0! You can add as many menus as you want, but they may not all fit on one line of menu bar. (In case you're wondering, yes, they wrap around onto a second line of menu bar.)

To add a new menu:

1. Select Tools ➤ Customize. The Customize dialog box will appear.

2. Choose the Menus tab.

3. Select the template for the new menu in the Save Changes In box.

4. Select the Menu Bar button. The Menu Bar dialog box will appear:

5. Enter the name for the menu in the Name on Menu Bar box. Use an ampersand (&) in front of a letter to designate a hot key.

6. Position the new menu using the Position on Menu Bar box:

■ To position it first, select First.

■ To position it last, select Last.

■ To position the menu after another menu, select the menu for it to appear after.

7. Click the Add button or Add After button (Word will offer you one or the other, depending on your choice in step 6) to add the menu.

8. Choose the Close button to close the Menu Bar dialog box, add items to the menu as described before, and choose the Close button again to close the Customize dialog box.

Renaming Menus

You can rename a menu so it suits your purposes better. Here's how:

1. Select Tools ➤ Customize. The Customize dialog box will appear.

2. Choose the Menus tab.

3. Select the template containing the menu you want to rename in the Save Changes In box.

4. Select the Menu Bar button. The Menu Bar dialog box will appear.

5. Select the menu to rename in the Position on Menu Bar box.

6. Type the new name in the Name on Menu Bar box.

7. Click the Rename button.

8. Click the Close button to close the Menu Bar dialog box, and then click the Close button on the Customize dialog box to close that too.

Customizing Word's Keyboard Shortcuts

You can get the most use from your keyboard by customizing Word's keyboard shortcuts. You can assign shortcut keys to commands, macros, fonts, AutoText entries, styles, and special characters. You want Ctrl+A to change selected text to 40-point Desdemona? *No problemo.* You need Ctrl+Shift+T to type "I was quite ecstatic to see you last night, darling!"? Read on, MacDuff!

Changing Keyboard Shortcuts

Here's how to see what your current keyboard shortcuts are and change them:

1. Select Tools ➤ Customize. The Customize dialog box will appear.
2. Select the Keyboard tab (see Figure 11.14).
3. In the Categories box, select the category containing the items you want.
4. In the box to the right of the Category box, select the command whose shortcut you want to view. The shortcut will appear in the Current Keys box.
5. Move to the Press New Shortcut Key box and press the keyboard shortcut you want to assign. Word will display the current assignation of that keyboard shortcut.
6. Click the Assign button to assign the shortcut key to the item.
7. Click the Close button to close the Customize dialog box.

FIGURE 11.14

The Keyboard tab
of the Customize
dialog box

375

TIP

Here's a shortcut: Press Ctrl+Alt++ (that's Ctrl+Alt+plus). The mouse pointer changes to a command symbol. Choose a menu command or click a toolbar button. Word will display the Customize dialog box showing the command you select. Follow steps 5 to 7 of the preceding list.

Deleting Shortcuts

By deleting shortcuts, you can prevent yourself or another user of your computer from performing unwanted actions. Here's how:

1. Select Tools ➤ Customize. The Customize dialog box will appear.
2. Choose the Keyboard tab.
3. Select the template containing the item whose shortcut you want to remove in the Save Changes In box.
4. In the Categories box, select the category containing the item.
5. In the box to the right of the Categories box, select the item.
6. Select the shortcut key to delete in the Current Keys box.
7. Click the Remove button.
8. Choose the Close button to close the Customize dialog box.

Reverting to Default Keyboard Shortcuts

Here's how to restore all shortcut key assignments to their original settings:

1. Select Tools ➤ Customize. The Customize dialog box will appear.
2. Choose the Keyboard tab.
3. Select the template containing the shortcut key assignments you want to restore in the Save Changes In box.
4. Click the Reset All button.
5. Choose Yes in the confirmation dialog box that Word throws at you.
6. Click the Close button to close the Customize dialog box.

12

Introduction
to Mail Merge

Word 6's Mail Merge feature lets you quickly create personalized correspondence and other documents by combining (*merging*) information from two different files. For instance, you could merge a list of names and addresses from one file (your *data document*) with a form letter in another file (your *main document*) to produce a number of personalized form letters. Or you could create catalogs, forms with variable information fields, or labels.

You insert data instructions (*fields*) in the main document wherever you want data from the data source to appear in your merged documents. For instance, for a letter, you could use fields to create suitable salutations for each one. Instead of writing plain old boring "Dear" to each recipient, you could have a salutation field in addition to the name field. Optionally, you could have a third field (to appear on the same line) of further greeting. This way, you could produce such salutations as "Hi, Joe Bob, how's it going?" and "My darling little Rosemary, how much you've grown this year!" as well as the staid "Dear Aunt Edna."

Once the main document and the data source are prepared, you're ready to merge them. The Mail Merge Helper lets you send merged documents directly to your printer or save them to a file for editing and later printing.

In either case, Word will automatically take care of things like word wrap and pagination for each new document. Figure 12.1 shows an overview of the elements in a mail merge project.

Thanks to Word 6's new Mail Merge Helper, merging is relatively painless, though you still need to pay plenty of attention to what you're doing. Some planning beforehand doesn't hurt either, but it's not absolutely essential. That said, let's get into it.

FIGURE 12.1

Mail merge projects require a data source (top) and a main document (bottom) to produce new documents that contain information from both.

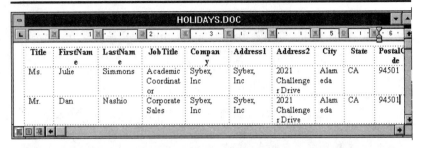

Title	FirstName	LastName	Job Title	Company	Address1	Address2	City	State	PostalCode
Ms.	Julie	Simmons	Academic Coordinator	Sybex, Inc	Sybex, Inc	2021 Challenger Drive	Alameda	CA	94501
Mr.	Dan	Nashio	Corporate Sales	Sybex, Inc	Sybex, Inc	2021 Challenger Drive	Alameda	CA	94501

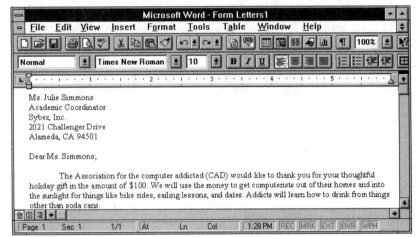

Ms. Julie Simmons
Academic Coordinator
Sybex, Inc.
2021 Challenger Drive
Alameda, CA 94501

Dear Ms. Simmons;

The Association for the computer addicted (CAD) would like to thank you for your thoughtful holiday gift in the amount of $100. We will use the money to get computerists out of their homes and into the sunlight for things like bike rides, sailing lessons, and dates. Addicts will learn how to drink from things other than soda cans.

NOTE Unfortunately, a book this size cannot cover all the variables involved in mail merges. Sometimes you'll find it easier to copy a form letter a few times and paste in the names and addresses of the recipients rather than perform an entire mail merge. Take a quick reality check before turning blindly to the Mail Merge Helper.

About Data Sources and Main Documents

Data sources are organized collections of information—databases—stored as Word tables. As you'll see in this chapter, Word 6's Mail Merge Helper leads you step by step through the creation of a new data source.

Word can also use data from other applications, such as Microsoft Excel or Microsoft Access. All data sources, no matter where they come from, contain *records* and *fields*. For instance, an employee data source would usually contain one record for each employee. This record would contain multiple fields—one field for the employee's first name, one for the middle initial, one for the last name, one for each part of the address, and so on.

Main documents, as mentioned above, contain the text of your project (the body of a letter, for instance), fields, and merge instructions.

Using Main Documents from Earlier Versions of Word

You can use main documents from earlier versions of Word for Windows—for example, version 2.0x—with no problem. Simply open the document in Word 6 and proceed as normal.

When you open a main document in Word 6, it will bring with it the association (to its data source) with which it was last saved. If you use a previously created main document, remember to attach to it any new data source that you want to use.

Using Main Documents from Other Applications

You can use a main document from other applications by opening that document in Word 6 and converting its contents to Word for Windows. However, field names and formatting from some applications may not translate well into Word for Windows format. Check the fields in your main document and adjust them if necessary before completing the merge.

If you experience problems, try pasting the main document into Word for Windows as plain text, then applying the formatting and entering the field names.

Using Data Sources from Other Applications

You can use data sources from other applications in your Word for Windows merges. For example, if you have data in a Microsoft Excel spreadsheet, you can insert either the whole worksheet or just a range of cells. If you have Microsoft Access, you can open a database and insert records from a table or a selection of records defined by a query.

After opening a data source in another application, make sure that the merge fields in your main document match those in the data source.

Creating Your First Mail Merge Project

The best way to learn how to create a print merge document is to try one. Consider working along as you read the rest of this chapter.

Project Overview

For each new mail-merge project, you'll need to:

- Create and proof the text of your main document
- Create a new data source
- Enter information into the data source
- Insert fields into your main document
- Check for design and data-entry errors
- Merge the data source and main document and print the merge documents

Since data sources in Word can be documents containing tables, you can add information and edit them at any time before doing the actual merge. Once you get comfortable with merging and its possibilities, feel free to do things in any workable order that pleases you.

While you don't need to type your main document first, it's often helpful to make a draft to get a sense of which information you will need from your data sources and where to insert it.

Word

NOTE If you already have a data source, simply open it or adapt it for the new project.

<table>
<tr><td>A WHOLE
NEW WAY
TO WORK</td><td>

Planning Your Data Document

</td></tr>
</table>

Designing a useful and easy-to-maintain data source is one of the most important parts of a new mail-merge project. With a little ingenuity, you can use the same data sources for a number of projects.

For instance, if you plan to use an employee data source to send letters or memos, you might want one field for the employee's full legal name and another for an informal salutation. That way you could address mailing envelopes to Dr. Buster Chops and have the salutation of the letters or memos read *Dear Chopster* or *Dear Dr. C.*

At first glance, it might seem a good idea to create a single field for all the address information needed for letters and labels. Then you could type everything—the recipient's name, company name, street address, city, state, and zip code—in that single field, insert that field in your main documents for form letters and envelopes, and merge merrily away. The problem with this comes when you need to break up the information you put in that field—for example, to produce a quick list of employees (without their full addresses) who live in a particular city who might appreciate ride-sharing.

It's far better to break your data up into multiple fields. Create separate fields for recipients' first and last names. Then you can use Word's Sort feature to produce alphabetized lists or labels sorted by last name. Break addresses down into five or six fields, as Word's Mail Merge Helper encourages you to do: street address, apartment number (if any), city, state, country (if you're international), and zip code. Putting city, state, country, and zip code in their own fields gives you enormous flexibility—you can easily find out who all your customers are in, say, Anaheim, Colorado, or Mexico.

Test your new design with small data documents containing a dozen or so representative records. Try your sample data source with a number of different main documents, or have an experienced print merge user look over your new design before you spend hours entering data into your first data source. Consider keeping sample main documents and data sources at hand in a test directory, so you can perform quick tests on new merge projects you put together.

Using the Mail Merge Helper

Word 6's Mail Merge Helper guides you through the steps of merging documents. The process seems a little convoluted the first time, but it works well. Once you've tried it once or twice, you'll be merging merrily with the best of them.

In the following sections, we'll discuss how to perform the different stages of a mail merge by using the Mail Merge Helper, since this is the easiest way to merge. We'll also indicate how you can proceed without using the Mail Merge Helper.

To start the Mail Merge Helper, select Tools ➤ Mail Merge. The Mail Merge Helper dialog box appears, as shown in Figure 12.2. Note the instructions in the box at the top telling you to click the Create button to set up the mail merge. Watch these instructions as you proceed with subsequent stages of the mail merge. If you're ever confused about what to do next, consult this box.

The first step in the mail merge is to create your main document, since the type of main document governs the subsequent choices you can make in the Mail Merge Helper. Form Letters, Mailing Labels, Envelopes, and Catalogs have different components, so the Mail Merge Helper offers you different choices of data source.

FIGURE 12.2

The Mail Merge
Helper dialog box.
Watch the instructions
in the top-left corner.

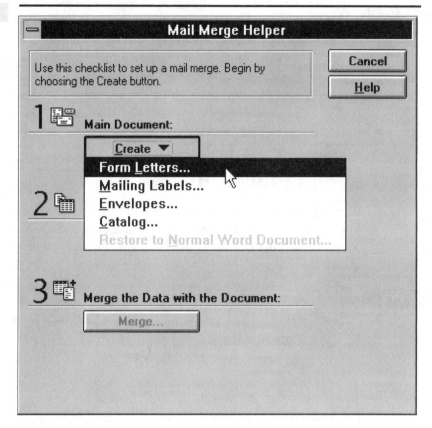

Starting Your Main Document

To start your main document, follow these steps:

1. Select the Create button to start creating your main document. A list will drop down offering you four choices—Form Letters, Mailing Labels, Envelopes, and Catalog.

2. Select the type of main document you want. A dialog box will appear offering you the choice of the active window or a new main document.

3. Select the window you want to use. If you're starting from a new document, or if the active window contains information for your main document, choose the Active Window button. If your active window contains valuable information that has nothing to do with the mail merge, choose the New Main Document button.

   ■ If you choose the New Main Document button, Word will open a new document. The previously active document stays open—Word does not save or close it.

Whichever button you chose, Word will return you to the Mail Merge Helper dialog box for the next stage of the mail merge, arranging the data source. You'll see that the space below the Create button now lists the information you've entered so far—the type of merge and the main document to use.

The information box at the top of the Mail Merge Helper dialog box tells you that the next step is to specify the data source. Let's do it.

Specifying the Data Source

Next, you need to specify the data source and arrange in it the fields that will be available to your main document for the merge.

1. Click the Get Data button to display a list of options for your data source.

2. If you already have a data source that you want to use, select Open Data Source. If you want to create the data source, select Create Data Source.

If you chose Open Data Source, skip ahead a section. If you chose Create Data Source, read the next section.

Creating a Data Source

The Create Data Source dialog box that appears when you choose Create Data Source contains a list of commonly used field names for the type of mail merge you're performing. Figure 12.3 shows the Create Data Source dialog box for form letters.

FIGURE 12.3

The Create Data Source dialog box offers a list of commonly used field names. Delete, add, and change fields here.

Adding a Field Name

Here's how to add field names to the list in the Field Names in Header Row box:

1. Type the name in the Field Name box.

Field names can be up to 40 characters long and can contain letters, numbers, and underscores (_). Field names cannot contain spaces and must start with a letter (not a number or an underscore). For example, What_We_Discussed_At_Yesterday's_Meeting is an acceptable field name (and might remind you better of the field's purpose than MeetingTopic), but 1994_May_15_Meeting is not. Bear in mind that the ends of very long field names may not show in the Field Names in Header Row box, so it can be confusing to have long field names that differ only at their ends.

2. Click the Add Field Name button. The new field name is added at the bottom of the list.

3. To move the new field name to a different position in the list, make sure it's highlighted and click the Move arrow buttons.

Removing or Modifying a Field Name

1. In the Field Names in Header Row box, highlight the field name you want to remove by clicking it with the mouse or by scrolling to it with the scroll bars or the down arrow. Then click the Remove Field Name button. The field name will be removed from the Field Names in Header Row list and will appear in the Field Name box.

2. To modify the field name, make your changes in the Field Name box and then click the Add Field Name button.

Rearranging Field Names

To rearrange the field names in the Field Names in Header Row box, highlight the field you want to move and click the Move up- and down-arrows beside the Field Names in Header Row box to move the highlight field up or down.

Saving Your Data Source

When you've finished adding, removing, and arranging fields, click OK to save your data source. In the Save Data Source dialog box that appears, enter a name for your data source file and select OK to save the file.

Word will save the data source file under the name you give and then return you to the Mail Merge Helper dialog box.

Opening a Data Source

To open an existing data source, select Open Data Source from the Get Data drop-down list. The Open Data Source dialog box that appears works just like the File Open dialog box: Select the document you want to use and click OK. Word will open the document and return you to the Mail Merge Helper dialog box.

> **NOTE** If you want to use a data source from another application, such as Microsoft Excel or Microsoft Access, simply choose it at this point and select the data records you want to use.

A WHOLE NEW WAY TO WORK

Using Excel Worksheets with Mail Merge

If you have collected information in Excel worksheets that you wish to use in a mail-merge project (like names and addresses, part numbers, pricing information, etc.), follow these general steps:

I. When the Mail Merge Helper asks for a data source, choose the Open Data Source option, as shown here:

A WHOLE NEW WAY TO WORK

2. When the Open Data Source dialog box appears, find the worksheet containing the data to be merged, then click OK. (Change the List File Types choice to MS Excel Worksheets if necessary to help narrow your search.)

3. The Mail Merge Helper will examine the specified worksheet and give you a list of named ranges, if any, and the opportunity to use one of those ranges or the entire worksheet as the data source.

4. The Mail Merge Helper will let you know if the data can be used as-is or if there are problems.

5. If there are no problems, the Mail Merge Helper will continue. To fix problems (redefine a range, or add labels that can be used as headers, and thus field names) use the techniques described in the Excel portion of this book.

Word

389

Editing the Data Source

Back in the Mail Merge Helper dialog box, you'll see that Word displays the name of the data source document beneath the Get Data button.

Word now checks your data source to see if it contains records. If it doesn't, Word will display a dialog box informing you of this and inviting you to edit the data source or the main document. Choose the Edit Data Source button to edit your data source.

Entering Your Records

In the Data Form dialog box that Word displays (see Figure 12.4), enter the details for each of your records by typing text into the boxes. Press Tab or ↵ to move from field to field. To move backwards, press Shift+Tab.

Here's how to alter the records in the Data Form dialog box:

- To add a new record, choose the Add New button.
- To delete a record, choose the Delete button.

FIGURE 12.4

Entering data in the Data Form dialog box

■ If you realize you've trashed a record (by entering data in the wrong place, or whatever), click the Restore button to return its entries to their previous state.

To Find a Record

Word's database functions offer great flexibility in searching. You can search for any word or part of a word in any of the fields.

To find a record, follow these steps:

1. Click the Find button. The Find in Field dialog box will appear.

2. Type the word or words you want to find in the Find What box.

3. Click the arrow at the right end of the In Field box to drop down the list of field names, and select the name of the field you want to search.

4. Click the Find First button. Word will search for and display the first record it finds containing the word or words in the selected field.

5. If this is the record you were looking for, click Close to close the Find in Field dialog box. If not, click the Find Next button to find the next occurrence of the text.

6. When you've finished entering or updating your records, click OK to close the data source and save the changes. Now you're ready to edit your main document.

If the Find in Field dialog box is hovering annoyingly over the field you're trying to read, grab it by clicking anywhere in its title bar, then drag it to a more convenient location on the screen.

Editing the Main Document

Main documents contain the following:

■ Text and punctuation.

■ Merge instructions and field names that Word uses to merge data.

Figure 12.5 shows a main document for our sample mail merge. We'll discuss the various elements in detail.

FIGURE 12.5

The main document for the mail-merge letter

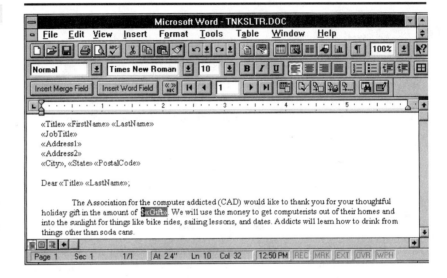

Text in Main Documents

Use Word 6's word-processing and graphics features to create the text and design elements for your main document. Add data instructions containing field names and other merge devices inserted as needed, as explained below.

Inserting Data Instructions

The Mail Merge Helper makes it easy to insert field names and other data instructions in your main documents. Just place the insertion point where you want to insert a data instruction, then pull down the appropriate list from the Mail Merge Toolbar and pick the item to insert.

Place the insertion point where you want to insert a field name, then click the Insert Merge Field button on the Mail Merge Toolbar to display the list of field names available in the associated data source. Next select the appropriate field name to insert it into the document. (The guillemets—«»—are inserted automatically with the field name.)

  When preparing the text of a main document, remember to include things like spaces between field names and any required punctuation following them. Running people's first and last names together will spoil the effect of your carefully personalized letters. You'll know the feeling if you've ever been renamed by Publishers' Clearing House.

As you'll see in a moment, you can use combinations of merge fields from the Insert Merge Field button and Word fields from the Insert Word Field button (both on the Mail Merge Toolbar), and text typed from the keyboard, to put together powerful merge instructions.

Testing and Proofing

Before firing up the Mail Merge Helper and churning out a whole batch of letters, proofread your work. Use Word's spell checker and grammar tools. Make any necessary corrections. Remember that Word will faithfully copy every error in your main document into every single copy it merges.

Next run the Mail Merge Helper's error-checking program. Choose the Check Errors button from the Mail Merge Toolbar. The Checking and Reporting Errors dialog box will appear.

You have several choices. Word will simulate the merge or actually do a merge and report errors. In either case, Word will check your data source and main document for errors (such as missing data fields in the data source and misspelled field names in your main document). If Word finds no errors, you will see a happy dialog box telling you that no mail merge errors have been found. If errors are found, correct them.

As a final check, consider merging some or all of your documents to a file and inspecting them, rather than printing them all at once. We'll look at how to do this in just a moment. First, let's look at Word's sorting and filtering features.

Sorting Merged Documents

Usually, records are merged in the order they occur in your data source; but Word 6's Mail Merge Helper lets you sort the records during the merge. In addition, Word lets you use filters to restrict merging to records containing certain data. (Filtering is discussed in the next section.)

To sort records before you perform a merge, follow these steps:

1. Open the Mail Merge Helper dialog box and choose the Query Options button. The Query Options dialog box will appear.

2. Click the Sort Records tab to enter your sorting preferences.

3. In the Sort By field that you want to use, click the down arrow, then select a field to sort by from the list that appears.

4. Select a field for one or both Then By fields if you want to refine your sort further.

5. When you've defined the sort to your satisfaction, click OK. If you mess things up, click the Clear All button to clear the fields and start again, or click Cancel to escape from the dialog box.

Filtering Merged Documents

If you're not content with sorting your records, you can filter them as well. Filtering gives you a lot of flexibility in removing from the merge records that for one reason or another you don't want to use. For instance, you can exclude records based on certain criteria.

Here's how to set up filtering:

1. Pull up the Mail Merge Helper dialog box and choose the Query Options button. The Query Options dialog box will appear.

2. Select the Filter Records tab.

3. In the Field column of the first row, choose the field you want to use as a filter.

4. In the Comparison column of the first row, drop down the list of filtering comparisons. This is what they do:

COMPARISON	EFFECT
Equal to	The contents of the data field you chose must match those of the Compare To box.
Not Equal to	The contents of the data field you chose must *not* match those of the Compare To box.
Less than	The contents of the data field you chose must be less than those of the Compare To box.
Greater than	The contents of the data field you chose must be greater than those of the Compare To box.
Less than or Equal	The contents of the data field you chose must be less than or equal to those of the Compare To box.
Greater than or Equal	The contents of the data field you chose must be greater than or equal to those of the Compare To box.
Is Blank	The merge field must be empty.
Is Not Blank	The merge field must not be empty.

5. In the second row, choose And or Or in the first column to include additional or complementary criteria for filtering.

6. Repeat steps 3, 4, and 5 for further rows as necessary to refine your criteria further.

7. When you've defined the filtering criteria to your satisfaction, select OK. If you mess things up, select Clear All to start again or Cancel to escape from the Query Options dialog box.

NOTE When you compare a data field that contains text, Word compares the sequence of characters based on the ANSI sort order. Since <u>antelope</u> precedes <u>zebra</u> alphabetically, Word considers it "less than" <u>zebra</u>. So if you wanted to retrieve data records for only the second half of the alphabet, you could specify LastName Is Greater Than M. If you mix numbers with letters, Word compares the numbers as though they were a sequence of text characters.

Printing Merged Documents

When you've specified any filtering and sort-ordering that you want, you're ready to run the mail merge.

1. Start the merge process by making your main document the active document (click in it if necessary).

2. Click the Merge button in the Mail Merge Helper dialog box to bring up the Merge dialog box.

3. You can either merge directly to your printer by selecting Printer in the Merge To: box, or you can have Word merge to a new, untitled document that will contain all of the merge documents by selecting New Document.

4. Select the Records to Be Merged by choosing All or From: and To:. If you choose From: and To:, specify the record numbers for the merge to start and stop at.

5. The default is not to print blank lines when data fields are empty. If you *do* want to print blank lines when the fields are empty—perhaps you have a reason, like to show gaps in your data source—choose the *Print blank lines when data fields are empty* option.

6. When all is set to your liking, click OK. The mail merge will finally take place.

When the mail merge is finished, close the Mail Merge Helper dialog box. If you merged to a new document, it should be on screen now. If you merged to a printer, the printer will be churning out your merged documents. Either way, check your output carefully before inflicting it on your victims. The law of mass mailing clearly states that you'll only notice an egregious error *after* you've mailed the whole batch.

If you have unsaved changes in your main document, Word will invite you to save them.

Specifying Header Options

The header row is the row of fields at the top of a data source that identifies each kind of information in the data source—the Title, FirstName, and Last-Name fields and so on.

Why would you want to reuse a header? Well, you could then use the same header source with more than one data source. If you can't change the merge fields in a data source to match the names of the merge fields in a main document (the file might be read-only), you can use a header source that contains matching merge fields.

To specify a header source:

1. Choose the Get Data button in the Mail Merge Helper dialog box and select Header Options. The Header Options dialog box will appear.

2. In the Header Options dialog box, choose Create to create a new header source. Or choose Open to open an existing header source, then skip ahead to step 5.

3. If you chose Create, the Create Header Source dialog box will appear. This works just like the Create Data Source dialog box we discussed under *Creating a Data Source*, earlier in the chapter. Add, remove, and rearrange the fields to your satisfaction, then click OK.

4. In the Save Data Source dialog box that appears, give your header source a name and click OK. You'll be returned to the Mail Merge Helper dialog box, and the header source you created will now appear under the Get Data button.

5. If you chose Open, the Open Header Source dialog box will appear. Select the header source you want to use and click OK. You'll be returned to the Mail Merge Helper dialog box, and the header source you created will now appear under the Get Data button.

Word

6. Word will check the header source against the data source and warn you if the data source contains too many data fields. The Merge button on the Mail Merge Helper dialog box will be dimmed, indicating that you cannot yet run the merge.

7. If the data source contains too many fields, edit the data source or header source.

Using Word's Merge Instructions

Word 6 provides a number of ways to change its behavior based on the contents of individual records in your data source. As you've just seen, it can eliminate unwanted blank lines in merged documents. It can insert special text if certain conditions are met, or stop during each merge to let you enter unique text from the keyboard. If you decide to use these features, be prepared to spend some time experimenting and troubleshooting. Here's a brief summary of the function of each part of the Mail Merge toolbar (see Figure 12.6).

FIGURE 12.6

The Mail Merge Toolbar

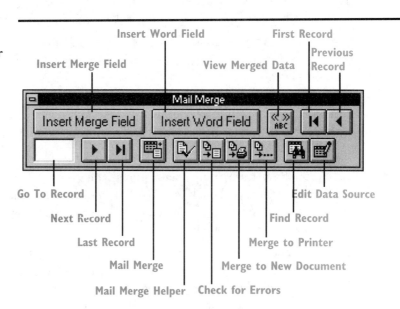

398

NAME	FUNCTION
Insert Merge Field	Inserts a merge field at the insertion point.
Insert Word Field	Inserts a Word field (e.g., ASK) at the insertion point.
View Merged Data	Toggles between viewing merge fields and the data that will appear in them.
First Record	Displays the first record in the data source.
Previous Record	Displays the previous record in the data source.
Go to Record	Enter the number of the record you want to go to in this box.
Next Record	Displays the next record in the data source.
Last Record	Displays the last record in the data source.
Mail Merge Helper	Displays the Mail Merge Helper.
Check for Errors	Displays the Check for Errors dialog box.
Merge to New Document	Merges the main document and data source to a new document.
Merge to Printer	Merges the main document and data source to a printer.
Mail Merge	Displays the Merge dialog box.
Find Record	Displays the Find Record dialog box.
Edit Data Source	Displays the Data Form dialog box.

Word

Merge-Printing Labels and Envelopes

You can also use Word 6's Mail Merge Helper to merge labels and envelopes. Since the procedures for merging labels and envelopes are very similar to those for form letters, we'll discuss them only briefly here.

Printing Labels on Laser Printers

The Mail Merge Helper makes merging labels on a laser printer dead simple. You use the Mail Merge Helper to create a main document containing a table with fixed-size cells and cell spacing that match the size and position of your blank labels, then insert merge instructions in each table cell. Here's how to do it:

1. Select Tools ➤ Mail Merge to fire up the Mail Merge Helper.

2. Click the Create button to drop down a list of options.

3. Select Mailing Labels from the drop-down list.

4. Arrange your data source as usual. Word will then invite you to set up your main document. In the Label Options dialog box that appears, make the appropriate choices for your printer and labels:

   ■ In the Printer Information box, select Laser or Dot Matrix as appropriate. If necessary, click the arrow to drop down the Tray list and select a different tray.

 Consider selecting a different Tray option when printing labels on a network. That way, you might be able to avoid having someone else print a 90-page report on your precious disk labels.

   ■ In the Label Products box, select the brand of labels you want: Avery Standard, Avery Pan European, or Other. (Other includes brands such as Inmac and RAJA.)

   ■ In the Product Number box, select the number for the labels you're using. If you don't know the number, consult the Label Information box to find out the size of the labels listed in the Product Number box. If you're still no wiser, measure your labels carefully and choose the closest match.

- For precise layout information on the labels, choose the Details button. In the dialog box that appears, make any necessary adjustments in the labels' margin, pitch, dimensions, and layout, then click OK.

5. When you've chosen the labels to use, choose OK to close the dialog box.

6. The Create Labels dialog box will appear. Enter the fields here by pulling down the Insert Merge Field list and selecting them in turn. Remember to include any necessary spaces and punctuation.

- To include a postal bar code, click the Insert Postal Bar Code button. In the Insert Postal Bar Code dialog box (shown below), enter the Merge Field with ZIP Code and Merge Field with Street Address in the appropriate boxes, then click OK.

Click OK when you're finished making choices in the Create Labels dialog box. Word will then enter your label fields into the main document.

7. Make any necessary adjustments to your main document (for example, adding ASK or FILL-IN fields).

8. Open the Mail Merge Helper dialog box and choose the Merge button to merge your data source with the main document. Choose whether to merge to a new document or to the printer. (You can also use the Merge to New Document and Merge to Printer buttons on the Mail Merge Toolbar here.)

9. Save your documents with meaningful names.

Printing Addresses on Envelopes

Word 6 offers the ability to print addresses on envelopes. This can be convenient for small numbers of envelopes; but as most laser printers require you to feed envelopes in by hand, printing large numbers of envelopes can be a slow business. Take a quick reality check before you arrange to print a whole slew of envelopes, and consider using mailing labels on the envelopes instead.

  Before starting to prepare envelopes, make sure your return address is correct. Choose Tools ➤ Options to display the Options dialog box. Click on the User Info tab to view (and if necessary change) the name and mailing address. Click OK when you're finished.

1. Select Tools ➤ Mail Merge to fire up the Mail Merge Helper.
2. Click the Create button to drop down a list of options.
3. Select Envelopes from the drop-down list.
4. Arrange your data source as usual. Word will invite you to edit your main document. In the Envelope Options dialog box that appears, make the appropriate choices for your envelopes:

   - On the Envelope Options tab, click the Font button in the Delivery Address box or the Font button in the Return Address box to change the font in which the addresses appear. If necessary, adjust the position of the delivery address or return address by entering From Top and From Left measurements in their boxes.

   - On the Printing Options tab, select the Feed Method and the tray to Feed From. Note that the default Feed From option is manual. For large numbers of envelopes, you'll be spending half the afternoon chez the printer.

  Word displays the name of your currently selected printer in the Printing Options tab of the Envelope Options dialog box. If need be, change the printer using File ➤ Print and then choosing the Printer button. If necessary, click the arrow to drop down the Tray list and select a different tray.

5. When you've chosen the envelope options and printing options, choose OK to close the dialog box.

6. The Envelope Address dialog box will appear. Enter the fields here by pulling down the Insert Merge Field list and selecting them in turn. Remember to include any necessary spaces and punctuation.

   ■ To include a postal bar code, click the Insert Postal Bar Code button. In the Insert Postal Bar Code dialog box, enter the Merge Field with ZIP Code and Merge Field with Street Address in the appropriate boxes, then click OK.

   Click OK when you're finished making your choices in the Envelope Address dialog box. Word will then enter your label fields into the main document.

7. Make any necessary adjustments to your main document.

8. Open the Mail Merge Helper dialog box and choose the Merge button to merge your data source with the main document. Choose whether to merge to a new document or to the printer. (You can also use the Merge to New Document and Merge to Printer buttons on the Mail Merge Toolbar.)

9. Save your documents with meaningful names.

Creating Catalogs with Mail Merge

As mentioned at the beginning of this chapter, you can use Word's Mail Merge Helper to create catalogs. What we didn't mention was that to make a catalog you follow the same procedure as for form letters. The only difference is that instead of selecting Form Letters from the Create drop-down list, you choose Catalog. Have a ball.

Restoring a Mail-Merge Document to a Normal Word Document

You can restore a mail-merge main document to a normal Word document when you've finished merging with it. This removes the association between the main document and its data source and header source (if it has one). The text of the main document does not change.

To restore a main document to a normal Word document, follow these steps:

1. Open the Mail Merge Helper dialog box by selecting Tools ➤ Mail Merge.

2. In the Main Document section, choose the Create button to display the list of options.

3. Choose the Restore to Normal Word Document option.

4. In the Restore to Normal Word Document dialog box that appears, choose Yes. The association between the main document and its data sources will be removed.

Tips, Techniques, and Troubleshooting

■ To change the appearance of merged characters—to make them bold or italic, or a larger point size—format their merge instructions in the main document. Merged characters take on the formatting of their merge instructions.

■ If you move your data source files, Word will ask you to relocate them before you can merge.

■ To print selected items from a longer data file, sort them and print just the range containing the desired records (from 10 to 30, for instance).

The following shortcut key combinations are available when merging documents using the <u>T</u>ools ➤ Mail Me<u>r</u>ge... command:

KEY COMBINATION	EFFECT
Alt+Shift+K	Preview a mail merge.
Alt+Shift+M	Merge a document.
Alt+Shift+N	Print the merged documents.
Alt+Shift+E	Edit a mail-merge data source.
Alt+Shift+Q	Sort and filter records.

Word

PART THREE

Working with Excel

In Part Three you will see how you can use Microsoft's latest version of Excel to compute and keep track of all sorts of interdependent data. You'll learn not only how to have Excel perform complex calculations, but also how to display your data in eye-pleasing charts and graphs. Once you've gotten the hang of it, spice up your work by including graphics and special annotations, and speed up your work with macros. Use Excel's Scenario Manager to automatically generate illustrative "what if" conditions, and when you've found the optimum balance, import your results into Word or PowerPoint for a polished presentation.

Excel Toolbar Reference

BUTTON	DESCRIPTION
Buttons on Excel's Standard Toolbar	

Opens a new workbook. [File ➤ New] *Shortcut:* Ctrl+N

Displays the Open dialog box to open a file. [File ➤ Open] *Shortcut:* Ctrl+O

Saves the current workbook. [File ➤ Save] *Shortcut:* Ctrl+S

Prints the current worksheet. [File ➤ Print] *Shortcut:* Ctrl+P

Displays each page as it will print. [File ➤ Print Preview]

Checks spelling in the current worksheet. [Tools ➤ Spelling] *Shortcut:* F7

Cuts the selection to the Clipboard. [Edit ➤ Cut] *Shortcut:* Ctrl+X

Copies the selection to the Clipboard. [Edit ➤ Copy] *Shortcut:* Ctrl+C

Pastes the Clipboard contents. [Edit ➤ Paste] *Shortcut:* Ctrl+V

Copies the format of the selection. [Edit ➤ Paste Special]

Reverses the last command or action. [Edit ➤ Undo] *Shortcut:* Ctrl+Z

Repeats the last command. [Edit ➤ Repeat] *Shortcut:* F4

Implements the SUM function. *Shortcut:* Alt+=

Displays the Function Wizard dialog box. [Insert ➤ Function] *Shortcut:* Shift+F3

BUTTON	DESCRIPTION

Buttons on Excel's Standard Toolbar (continued)

Arranges a selected list from minimum to maximum. [Data ➤ Sort]

Arranges a selected list from maximum to minimum. [Data ➤ Sort]

Runs the Chart Wizard. Click in the worksheet to display the Chart Wizard dialog box. [Insert ➤ Chart]

Draws a text box on the current sheet.

Displays the Drawing toolbar.

Displays the Tip Wizard, which shows hints about the current task.

Changes the pointer into the Help pointer. When double-clicked, displays the Search dialog box. [Help ➤ Search for Help on] *Shortcut:* Shift+F1.

Buttons on Excel's Chart Toolbar

Creates an embedded chart of the type displayed on the button. Click the drop-down list button to display a palette of available chart types to change the selected chart. This command is only available if the chart is activated—you must double-click on the chart to activate it. [Format ➤ Chart Type]

Changes the selected or active chart to the default chart type.

Runs the Chart Wizard to create or edit an existing chart. [Insert ➤ Chart]

Excel

Excel Toolbar Reference

BUTTON	DESCRIPTION

Buttons on Excel's Chart Toolbar (continued)

 Toggles major horizontal gridlines on and off the active chart. This command is only available on the activated chart's shortcut menu. [Shortcut menu ➤ Insert Gridlines]

 Toggles the display of the selected chart's legend.

Buttons on Excel's Formatting Toolbar

B   Applies bold formatting to selected characters. [Format ➤ Cells ➤ Font] *Shortcut:* Ctrl+B

I   Applies italic format to selected characters. [Format ➤ Cells ➤ Font] *Shortcut:* Ctrl+I

U   Applies a single underline to selected characters. [Format ➤ Cells ➤ Font] *Shortcut:* Ctrl+U

Aligns selected characters to the left of the cell, text box, button, or chart. [Format ➤ Cells ➤ Alignment] *Shortcut:* Ctrl+1, Alignment

Centers selected characters within a cell, text box, button, or chart. [Format ➤ Cells ➤ Alignment] *Shortcut:* Ctrl+1, Alignment

Aligns selected characters to the right of the cell, text box, button, or chart. [Format ➤ Cells ➤ Alignment] *Shortcut:* Ctrl+1, Alignment

Centers the contents of the first cell in a selection horizontally across selected cells. [Format ➤ Cells ➤ Alignment] *Shortcut:* Ctrl+1, Alignment

$ Applies the current currency style to selected cells. [Format ➤ Cells ➤ Number] *Shortcut:* Ctrl+1, Number

Buttons on Excel's Formatting Toolbar (continued)

%	Applies the current percent style to selected cells. [Format ➤ Cells ➤ Number] *Shortcut:* Ctrl+1, Number
,	Applies the current comma style to selected cells. [Format ➤ Cells ➤ Number] *Shortcut:* Ctrl+1, Number
+.0 .00	Adds a decimal place to the selection's number format. [Format ➤ Cells ➤ Number] *Shortcut:* Ctrl+1, Number
.00 +.0	Removes a decimal place from the selection's number format. [Format ➤ Cells ➤ Number] *Shortcut:* Ctrl+1, Number
	Adds the cell format displayed to the selected cell. Click the drop-down list button to display a palette of borders. [Format ➤ Cells ➤ Border] *Shortcut:* Ctrl+1, Border
	Changes the background color of the selection to the displayed color. Click on the drop-down list button to display a color palette. [Format ➤ Cells ➤ Patterns] *Shortcut:* Ctrl+1, Patterns
	Changes the color of the characters in the selection to the displayed color. Click on the drop-down list button to display a color palette. [Format ➤ Cells ➤ Font] *Shortcut:* Ctrl+1, Font

Buttons on Excel's Auditing Toolbar

	Draws an arrow from each cell that supplies a value to the formula in the active cell. [Tools ➤ Auditing ➤ Trace Precedents]
	Deletes the level of precedent tracer arrows farthest from the active cell.
	Draws arrows from the active cell to each cell that contains a formula using the value in the active cell. [Tools ➤ Auditing ➤ Trace Dependents]

Excel

Excel Toolbar Reference

BUTTON	DESCRIPTION

Buttons on Excel's Auditing Toolbar (continued)

	Deletes the level of dependent tracer arrows farthest from the active cell.
	Deletes all precedent and dependent tracer arrows in the worksheet. [Tools ➤ Auditing ➤ Remove All Arrows]
	Draws an arrow from each cell that might have caused the error in the active cell. [Tools ➤ Auditing ➤ Trace Error]
	Displays the Cell Note dialog box used to attach a note to the active cell. [Insert ➤ Note]
	Displays the selected cell's Info window. [Tools ➤ Options ➤ View]

Buttons on Excel's Drawing Toolbar

	Creates straight lines on a worksheet, macro sheet, or chart.
	Creates empty rectangles on a worksheet, macro sheet, or chart.
	Creates empty ellipses on a worksheet, macro sheet, or chart.
	Creates empty arcs on a worksheet, macro sheet, or chart.
	Creates empty freehand polygon objects on a worksheet, macro sheet, or chart.
	Creates empty text boxes on a worksheet, macro sheet, or chart.
	Creates arrows on a worksheet, macro sheet, or chart.
	Creates freehand lines on a worksheet, macro sheet, or chart.

Creates filled rectangles on a worksheet, macro sheet, or chart.

Creates filled ellipses on a worksheet, macro sheet, or chart.

Creates filled arcs on a worksheet, macro sheet, or chart.

Creates filled freeform polygons on a worksheet, macro sheet, or chart.

Creates blank buttons to which you can assign macros.

Changes the pointer into a selection arrow.

Places selected objects in front of any other objects. [Format ➤ Placement ➤ Bring to Front]

Places selected objects in back of any other objects. [Format ➤ Placement ➤ Send to Back]

Changes multiple selected objects into a single group. [Format ➤ Placement ➤ Group]

Divides a group into separate objects. [Format ➤ Placement ➤ Ungroup]

Changes the shape of a selected polygon.

Creates a dark border along the right and bottom edges of a selected object or range.

Changes the fill pattern and color in selected cells, chart items, or objects. [Format ➤ Cells ➤ Patterns; Format ➤ Selected *chart item* ➤ Patterns; or Format ➤ Cells ➤ Object ➤ Patterns] *Shortcut:* Ctrl+1, Patterns

Excel

Excel Toolbar Reference

BUTTON	DESCRIPTION

Buttons on Excel's Query and Pivot Toolbar

Displays the Pivot Table Wizard, used to create or edit a pivot table. [Data ➤ Pivot Table]

Changes the properties of the data area or options for a field. [Data ➤ PivotTable Field]

Divides a category group into separate items. [Shortcut menu ➤ Group and Outline ➤ Ungroup] (Right-click on the pivot table to display the shortcut menu.) *Shortcut:* Alt+Shift+←

Changes multiple items in a pivot table into a single grouped item. [Shortcut menu ➤ Group and Outline ➤ Group] *Shortcut:* Alt+Shift+→

Collapses the outer item in a row or column field to hide subordinate data. [Shortcut menu ➤ Group and Outline ➤ Hide Detail] *Shortcut:* Double-click on the item

Displays hidden subordinate data in a pivot table. [Shortcut menu ➤ Group and Outline ➤ Show Detail] *Shortcut:* Double-click on the item.

Copies each page of a pivot table to a different worksheet in the current workbook. [Shortcut menu ➤ Show Pages]

Updates the pivot table of the results of a query. [Shortcut menu ➤ Refresh Data]

13

Excel Basics

Excel

I f you've been using the same old spreadsheet program for years, you're in for a pleasant surprise. If you happen to be a newcomer to spreadsheets, you've made the right choice. Microsoft's Excel is a comfortable blend of old and new. Like Word, it is easy to learn and difficult to outgrow. Users of earlier versions of Excel as well as users of Lotus 1-2-3 or other spreadsheet programs will quickly feel right at home with Excel's familiar old features—and will grow to appreciate its powerful new ones.

The Usual Spreadsheet Features

Excel lets you create and quickly perform "what-if" analysis of complex, inter-related columnar reports, in work spaces called *worksheets* or *spreadsheets*. (I'll use the terms "spreadsheet" and "worksheet" interchangeably in this book.)

Worksheets are made up of *cells* arrayed in *rows* and *columns*—rows run across your screen and columns run down. You type or otherwise enter things like labels, numbers, and dates into cells. Excel rows are usually identified with numbers, and columns with letters. The *address* of a cell is a combination of the row and column labels. Thus, cell B5 would be the fifth cell down in the second column from the left of the worksheet.

You also create *formulas* (sometimes called *equations*) in cells. For instance, you might enter five different numbers in cells A1 through A5, then place a formula in cell A6 that adds those five numbers and displays the results in cell A6. Excel helps you quickly build formulas using your keyboard and mouse. Excel also provides Toolbar tools, menu choices, and functions you can employ to create and use complex formulas.

An almost overwhelming array of formatting features lets you "dress up" and print your final work product. A ChartWizard quickly converts your worksheet numbers and cell labels into all manner of impressive pie charts, line graphs, bar charts, three-dimensional charts, scatter charts, and other visual aids. There's even a way to create automated, on-screen slide shows displaying spreadsheet data and charts, complete with audio and special effects!

Windows Savvy

Because Microsoft designed Excel from the ground up as a Windows product, the program offers Windows features you've already learned about in other parts of this book. You edit Excel worksheet text using the same techniques you learned for Word. Many of the commands you'll use are located on the same menus as they are in Word. And Excel offers impressive compatibility with other Windows products. For instance, it's easy to insert graphics from most other Windows programs into Excel worksheets. It's also easy to paste Excel worksheet data and charts into PowerPoint or Word documents. Data collected in Excel worksheets can be used to create Word mail-merge data files, for example.

For most people the real Excel advantage is its usability. Microsoft has created powerful tools to speed spreadsheet construction, formatting, and use. Let's get an overview in this chapter, then create a first worksheet.

Overview of Excel Features

Figure 13.1 illustrates some of the most important new features in the current version of Excel.

Automatic Number Formatting Here's an example of an Excel power tool. If you type a dollar sign or percent sign when entering numbers, Excel will format the cells and numbers appropriately as you enter them. Thus, typing **$10.00** will cause Excel to format that cell and the rest of the cells in that row for dollars and cents.

Automatic Summation Usually Excel can determine where to place subtotals and totals, making it unnecessary for you to type and copy lengthy summary equations. For instance, if you enter five numbers in a column, then use

Excel

Excel

FIGURE 13.1

Excel offers a number of impressive new and improved features

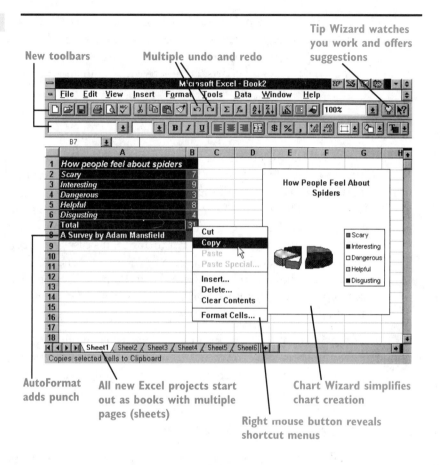

New toolbars

Multiple undo and redo

Tip Wizard watches you work and offers suggestions

AutoFormat adds punch

All new Excel projects start out as books with multiple pages (sheets)

Right mouse button reveals shortcut menus

Chart Wizard simplifies chart creation

Excel's Summation button on the Standard toolbar, Excel will automatically outline all five numbers and offer to create an equation that adds them up and to format and display the answer. This can be a real time-saver.

Automatic Worksheet Formatting Excel's *AutoFormat* feature presents sample formats from which you pick the desired spreadsheet appearance. The formats consist of combinations of type styles, 3-D shading, borders around related data, colors, and the like. Once you make your choice, Excel will apply the format to your whole spreadsheet or selected parts. It is usually smart enough to locate and highlight subtotals and totals for you. Adam's spider survey data in Figure 13.1, for example, have been formatted using Excel's List 1 AutoFormat style.

TIP   Since some printers won't reproduce all of Excel's automatic formats acceptably, and since some formats slow the printing process, you'll want to experiment with these features long before starting a project that needs to be completed on a tight deadline.

Built-In Spell-Checking   How many times have you handed out spreadsheets in an important meeting and noticed a typo or spelling error? Well, apparently this has happened in meetings at Microsoft too, since Excel now has a built-in spelling checker that can even share Word's *custom dictionaries*. This lets you keep unusual words like proper nouns and technical terms all in one place so that the spelling checker in both your word processor and your spreadsheet programs can recognize them.

Tip Wizard   The Tip Wizard displays a variety of helpful tips and techniques based on what you are doing.

All New Projects Start as Books   All new Excel projects start as multipage books. This makes it easier to create 3-D worksheets. For instance, if you are a retailer with multiple stores, you could have a sheet for each store and a top "consolidation sheet."

Shortcut Menus   Microsoft has finally found a powerful use for the right mouse button. Whether you are formatting a document, editing a cell, or working on a chart, commands appropriate to the work you are doing appear whenever you press the right mouse button.

Drag-and-Drop Worksheet Rearrangement   Do you want to move a group of cells? Excel's drag-and-drop feature lets you reposition selected portions of your spreadsheet by simply dragging them with your mouse, just as you do in Word. Properly written equations automatically adapt themselves to their new locations. It almost makes budgeting fun.

Excel

Function Wizard   The new Function Wizard takes the mystery out of complex formula creation. It leads you through the steps and variables required to use Excel's built-in functions.

Toolbars   Excel offers a variety of toolbars. If you don't find one you like, you can create your own, or modify Microsoft's. You are allowed to move many of the toolbars to different locations on your screen, then point-and-click to accomplish things like formatting numbers or creating charts. It's even possible for advanced users to create their own buttons and spreadsheet functions for the toolbar.

Intelligent AutoFill   Imagine creating an annual budget or other calendar-related project. How many times have you typed **January** then **February** and so on, slavishly visiting cell after cell? With the AutoFill feature, you need only type **January**, then highlight the next 11 cells by dragging with your mouse. Excel will automatically fill in **February, March,** and the rest of the months for you. This works on rows or columns. Moreover, AutoFill is intelligent: type **Jan 1994** and Excel will fill in **Feb 1994, Mar 1994,** etc. If the filling-in reaches the end of 1994, it will change the year to 1995 at the appropriate column or row. AutoFill's not limited to months and years, either. Type **Monday** and AutoFill will provide **Tuesday, Wednesday,** and so on. Type **Product 1** and Excel can fill in **Product 2** and on and on. Suppose you want headings with quarterly subtotals. Enter **January 94, February 94, March 94,** and **Quarter 1** as the first four cells, whereupon AutoFill will create the rest of the year or years, complete with properly numbered quarters.

Besides automatically filling row and column labels, AutoFill can help create forecasts based on sample data you provide. Enter expense dollar amounts for the first quarter and drag the mouse through the cells to fill them with similar estimates for the remainder of the year. If expenses go up from month to month within your sample quarter (or week or year or whatever), these trends will be reflected in the auto-filled cells. This works great for projections that must account for the fact that some months have four weeks while others have five (sometimes referred to as the "4-4-5 problem"). Obviously, you can later fine-tune Excel's automatic projections as needed.

Charting   Excel's Chart Wizard steps you through the many possible formatting choices, converting an often confusing process into a few simple steps.

There are numerous new chart types including some impressive 3-D charts that can be rotated with your mouse. This makes it easy for you to pick the best vantage point for viewing and printing your chart.

Lotus 1-2-3 Compatibility and Transition Aids   If you have a ton of Lotus 1-2-3 spreadsheets replete with complex macros, you're not alone. That's why Microsoft has provided a very satisfying Lotus file compatibility. Excel can load from or save to most popular 1-2-3 file formats, including WKS, WK1, WK3, FMT, and FM3. Generally, if your spreadsheet package (including Quattro Pro) can save in one of these formats, Excel can use your spreadsheets. With very few exceptions, macros you've created in 1-2-3 will also work in Excel. In addition, there is special online help for those suffering from Lotus withdrawal.

Improved Views   Excel lets you combine multiple worksheets and view them in outline form. For instance, you could have a forecast spreadsheet for each product line or each of your many offices, then combine the data contained in them to produce a "top" summary spreadsheet. Then, by expanding and collapsing the view of these data with View Manager, you can zero in on specific products and offices—or zoom back to see the whole enchilada.

Scenario Manager Helps You "What-If"   Scenario Manager generates tables of values as Excel tries different combinations of assumptions. Say you wanted to see the tax effects and net profit of selling your home at various prices and sales commission percentages. You could tell Excel's Scenario Manager the selling price and commission ranges to use, then see the results of multiple, automatic computations.

Presentation Features   Excel now offers a "slide show" feature that lets you create on-screen, sequential presentations. Your slide shows can contain spreadsheets, charts, graphics, and even sounds! There are "transitioning effects" that can be placed between slides. Examples include dissolves and wipes and venetian blinds like the ones TV weather forecasters use when switching from map to map. Shows are constructed by copying the various elements (spreadsheets, graphs, sounds, whatever) into a special document (a "script") while specifying the transition effects, length of time each slide will be displayed, and so on. The shows can run over and over again, automatically, or you can advance them manually. This is an excellent, low-cost way to create point-of-sale demonstrations in stores or to make your point at sales meetings or even to create professional-looking displays for trade shows.

TIP Consider using Microsoft PowerPoint for your presentations instead of (or in addition to) Excel's slide show feature— you may find PowerPoint easier, more flexible, and "prettier." Remember, you can always use OLE to place Excel information in your PowerPoint presentations without retyping.

Crosstabulation with Crosstab Wizard As you may know, spreadsheets can also be used as databases. For instance, you could create a spreadsheet containing the names, departments, and salaries of each of your employees. You might have one horizontal row for each worker, and a column titled *Name*, another *Department*, another *Sex*, and another *Salary*. Excel's Custom Report Wizard will then lead you through the necessary steps to create reports broken down the way you want them—like a report of salaries by department, or one by sex or by salary within departments, and so on. Here again, Microsoft's Wizards automate, simplify, and greatly speed the crosstabulation process.

Macros Macros are collections of automated steps that your program can perform for you. For instance, you could teach Excel to sort the information in a section of your spreadsheet, then print an updated report that you need regularly. Excel can learn the macro steps by "watching" you perform them and "recording" them in macro files on your disk. If you have Lotus 1-2-3 spreadsheets containing macros, chances are that Excel can successfully convert and use them.

Getting Started

The obvious way to start Excel is to click once on the Office Manager's Excel button. Or, you can double-click the Excel icon in the Office Manager toolbar. You can also double-click the Excel icon in Program Manager. Starting in either of these ways opens a new, untitled workbook.

You can also start Excel from File Manager either by double-clicking on EX-CEL.EXE in your Excel directory or by double-clicking Excel worksheet icons and related files (files with the extensions .XLA, .XLB, .XLC, .XLL, .XLM, .XLS, .XLT, or .XLW, and possibly others). This starts the program and displays the worksheet whose icon you clicked.

Parts of a Worksheet

As you can see in Figure 13.2, Excel follows most of Microsoft's Windows conventions. There are scroll bars, control boxes, menu bars, and so forth. There are some new tools in Excel windows as well. See if you can find them in Figure 13.2 as they are described here. (Your screen may look different, especially if someone else has used the program before you. That's because users have considerable control over the appearance of the workspace.)

FIGURE 13.2

Double-click on the Excel icon or on a related file icon to start Excel. You'll see either a new untitled worksheet or the worksheet you double-clicked on.

Name box (active cell address)

Formatting toolbar

Standard toolbar

Formula bar

The Tip Wizard toolbar

Text (labels)

The active cell

Drawing toolbar

Normally, you will see at least one or two toolbars (probably the Standard and Formatting toolbars shown at the top of Figure 13.2). You might also see other toolbars at the bottom or even in the middle of your worksheet. For instance, that's the Tip Wizard toolbar beneath the Formatting toolbar, and the Drawing toolbar near the lower right of the window.

By now you should know that worksheets consist of horizontal, numbered rows and vertical columns identified with letters. The resulting boxes are called *cells*, and the cell where you're working is called the *active cell*. It has a dark border around it, or sometimes appears ghostly white when you select cells around it. In Figure 13.2 cell B4 is the active cell. Notice that the address of the active cell is displayed in a box above the left edge of the worksheet.

When you type text or formulas (instructions Excel uses to compute results), you'll see your characters scroll across the *Formula bar* and in the active cell. There's normally a status bar at the bottom of your Excel window.

Using the Excel Tutorials

Excel contains two tutorials, each containing seven lessons. They are reached via the Help menu, by choosing Help ➤ Quick Preview and Help ➤ Examples and Demos. Microsoft estimates that it would take you about $2\frac{1}{4}$ hours to complete all of the lessons. Since lessons are broken down by topic and skill level, chances are you'll not need to visit all of them. For instance, users of earlier Excel versions will be able to skip the basics and go right to "What's New?" Lotus 1-2-3 converts have their own tutorials in Excel as well.

If you are already working on an Excel project when you decide to take the tutorials, Excel sets aside your work, restoring it when you quit the tutorials. The tutorials gives you hands-on exercises. Your time will be very well spent if you decide to run them.

Using Excel's Online Help

Like many other Windows programs, Excel offers extensive online help. Reach it either with the F1 function key or from the Help menu. Navigate the Help files as described in the Word section of this book.

By far the slickest online help can be had from the Tip Wizard. Click on the lightbulb button in the Standard toolbar and keep one eye on the resulting Tip toolbar as you work. It will give you tips on new ways to do what you do while you do it.

Help for 1-2-3 Users

As mentioned earlier, 1-2-3 users can get oriented quickly by choosing the Lotus 1-2-3 option on the Excel Help menu. (If you don't see this choice, rerun the Excel Setup program and add it to your installation of Excel.)

Creating a New Worksheet

The best way to learn Excel is to use it. If you haven't already done so, start the program. You should see a blank worksheet.

Page Setup First

Since Excel can show you page endings, as well as how much information will fit on each page as you work, it's a good idea to make Page Setup decisions right when you start a new project. Use the Page Setup command located on Excel's File menu. Page size, orientation, and header and footer dimensions are just a few of the things you can control with Page Setup. For your first project you may want to stick with Excel's default settings, but as a rule you will want to get in the habit of changing Page Setup settings when you start new worksheets.

The tabs on Excel's Page Setup dialog box (see Figure 13.3) will remind you of others that you've seen, except you'll be given choices like printing gridlines, the printing order of pages in reports that won't fit on one page, and so on. Use online help to learn more.

Excel

FIGURE 13.3

Excel's Page Setup
dialog box lets you
control many aspects
of what you print.

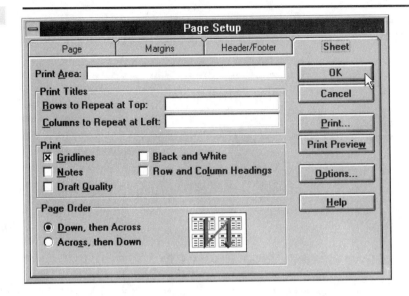

Selecting Cells

Before entering or editing cell contents, or before you can format or move
cells, they need to be selected. You can select single cells or *ranges* of cells.

Selecting Cells with a Mouse

To select a single cell, simply point-and-click in it. It becomes the active cell.
The following techniques, illustrated in Figure 13.4, are for rows, columns,
and ranges:

- Click on a row number to select the whole row.
- To select an entire column of cells, point to the column's heading.
- Click-and-drag to select a range of cells.
- Click on the empty button at the top-left corner of the workbook to se-
  lect the entire worksheet.

To select noncontiguous (nonadjacent) cells, or groups of cells, hold down the
Ctrl key and do any of the aforementioned selection tricks. For example, to

FIGURE 13.4

A mouse makes it easy
to select columns,
rows, or ranges of cells.

select rows 2 and 4 but not row 3, click on the number for row 2, then
Ctrl+click on 4.

Selecting Cells with the Keyboard

While you will probably want to use your mouse for most selections (it's speed-
ier), there are many keyboard selection tricks.

- If you've already selected a range of cells, Shift+spacebar selects the entire row or rows in which the cells are located.

- Ctrl+spacebar selects an entire column.

- Ctrl+Shift+spacebar selects the entire worksheet.

To *extend* selections in any direction, hold down the Shift key and press the
appropriate arrow key. The other navigational keys can be used to extend selections also. For instance, Shift+Ctrl+End extends the selection to the end
of your worksheet.

Excel

A WHOLE NEW WAY TO WORK

Using Word Text in Excel Worksheets

You can paste or drag-and-drop Word text into Excel worksheets. This can sometimes save you some retyping. Here's one approach:

1. Open the Word document containing the text and select the text of interest, as shown here:

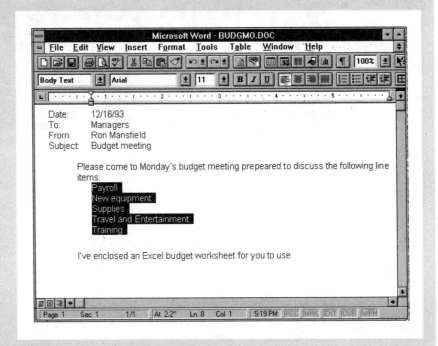

2. Open the Excel document.

A WHOLE NEW WAY TO WORK

3. If there is room on your screen, you can drag the text from Word to Excel by arranging the two windows. Here Word's on top and Excel's on the bottom:

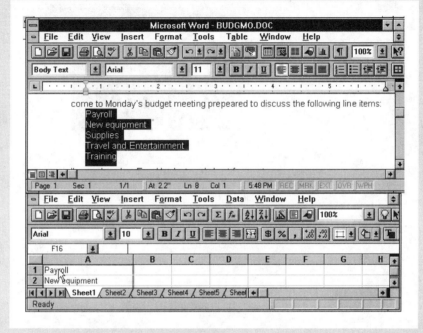

4. Click on the selected Word text.

5. Drag it to the first cell in the Excel worksheet that you want to contain the text. Releasing the mouse button will move the text from Word to Excel (or Ctrl-dragging will *copy* the text).

Excel

6. Format and work with the text in Excel using the techniques described in this and other Excel chapters.

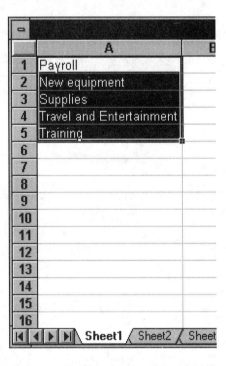

When you select Word text containing tabs, or Word tables, each time Excel encounters a tab or new table column, it will put the text in a new column in the worksheet. For example, if you copy the Word text **Item (tab) 1993 (tab) 1994** and paste or drag to cell A1 in an Excel Worksheet, *Item* would be placed in cell A1, *1993* in cell B2 and *1994*

Navigating with the Mouse and Keyboard

Use the same navigational tools I presented earlier in this book to move around in large worksheets. Scroll with the scroll bars, and use PgUp, Home, and related keys.

The Edit menu offers a number of other navigational aids. For instance, there is a Find command that will remind you of Word's—it lets you search for text strings, formulas, and other items of interest. You can name areas of your spreadsheet by choosing Insert ➤ Name ➤ Define and use the Go To command to quickly find them.

Navigating with the Go To Command

The Edit menu's Go To command can be used to find areas you've named. This makes it easy to jump around in large sheets. For instance, we've named two data-entry areas in the sample worksheet, and these names appear in the Go To dialog box (see Figure 13.5).

You'll learn more about labeling areas later in the Excel section of the book. For now, it's enough to be aware that it is both possible and handy to be able to name selected parts of a worksheet.

FIGURE 13.5

The Go To dialog box lets you quickly access named areas of your worksheets.

Excel

The Go To Special Button

The Go To Special dialog box (reached by choosing the Special button in the Go To dialog box) lets you select cells meeting specific criteria. For instance, you can specify all notes, formulas, blank cells, the last cell, etc. To inspect only a certain range of cells, first select only the cells of interest before using the Special button. To search the entire worksheet, select any single cell before using the button. Figure 13.6 shows the Go To Special dialog box.

FIGURE 13.6

The Go To Special dialog box lets you select cells that meet specific criteria.

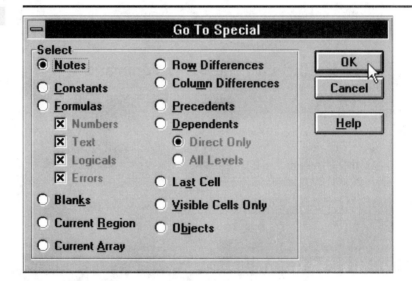

Entering and Editing Text

To enter the text used to label things in your worksheets, simply activate the cell where you want the text to appear (point to it and click), then begin typing. (When you enter text into a cell this way, the text is sometimes referred as a *constant value*, since you want it to remain the same until you change it yourself.)

As you start typing, the text will appear in the active cell *and* in the Formula bar. Pressing ↵ or clicking the checkmark button in the Formula bar concludes the text entry and places the text in the active cell. If you change your mind before you press ↵, you can press the Esc key or click on the X button in the Formula bar to cancel the entry. Figure 13.7 illustrates this.

You can type up to 255 characters per cell. After you've entered text, you can easily increase cell sizes later or word-wrap text to accommodate the entries, as you'll see in a moment.

Type in the Formula bar. click the checkmark or press ↵ to accept the entry. Press Esc or click the X button to cancel.

Cancels the entry

Enters what you've typed

Typing appears both here and in the active cell

Editing Text

If you spot an error while entering text, simply backspace to correct it. If you see an error after finishing the entry, activate the cell and edit the text—you can do this in the cell itself or in the Formula bar. Use your Windows text-editing skills here: Drag over the text you want to delete or correct, or double-click it, or select it using the keyboard. Move the insertion point around in the text on the Formula bar as necessary. When the corrections have been made, press ↵ or click the checkmark button.

Replacing Text

If you activate a cell containing text, then type new text and press ↵ or click the checkmark button, the new text will replace the old text.

Styling Text

You can change the appearance of both text and numbers in cells (make things bold or bigger, change fonts, and so on). Normally, all the text in a cell is affected, but you can choose to modify only portions by selecting them.

Excel

Use the buttons on the Formatting toolbar, and additional choices reached through the Cells command on the Format menu. The process of embellishing cell appearance is described in more detail later.

TIP The Format Cells dialog box can also be reached by right-clicking on the cell, and choosing Format Cells from the resulting menu.

Text Boxes

Besides typing text into cells, you can create *text boxes* and place them anywhere you like on your worksheets. They are a kind of graphic object. It's even possible to rotate text in text boxes, and draw arrows from text boxes to things the text describes. To create a text box, click the Text Box button, then use your mouse to drag a box of the desired size. Release the mouse button and type. You'll learn more about text boxes later.

Text Notes

Text notes are used to hold notes that you don't want to display on your worksheets. The notes are attached to cells, and can be viewed on-screen by yourself or coworkers.

Creating Notes

To create a note, start by selecting the appropriate cell. Then choose Note from the Insert menu, or press Shift+F2. Excel will display the Cell Note dialog box (see Figure 13.8). A red dot appears in the top-right corner of a cell that has a note attached to it.

Type the note in the Text Note box. Click OK to attach the note to the cell.

FIGURE 13.8

The Cell Note dialog box lets you attach a note to a cell.

Displaying and Printing Notes

Select the cell of interest, then press Shift+F2. You'll see the Cell Note dialog box. To print notes, visit the Page Setup dialog box, click on the Sheet tab, and select the Note option box.

Sound Notes

If you have a multimedia-equipped computer, you can record and play back audio notes by using the Sound Note buttons in the Cell Note dialog box.

Checking Spelling

Once you've entered the worksheet headings and other text (like chart labels), Excel's Spelling command on the Options menu will launch the spelling checker shown in Figure 13.9. (There is also a spelling button on the Standard toolbar.) This feature is similar to the Word spelling checker, though not identical.

If you have a custom Microsoft *Word* dictionary called CUSTOM.DIC in the default location, the MSAPPS\PROOF subdirectory of your WINDOWS directory on your hard disk, Excel will also use this custom dictionary. Otherwise, it will create its own.

Running the Spelling Checker

To check the spelling of your entire worksheet, run the spelling checker *without selecting a range of cells.* This checks labels, cell notes, embedded charts, text boxes, headers, and footers. It does *not,* however, check text created by formulas.

To check a small portion of the worksheet, select the appropriate range of cells. To check a single word, highlight it in the Formula bar and run the checker.

You can accept Excel's spelling suggestions, ignore them, type your own changes, or add words to the custom dictionary as you do in Word.

Undoing and Repeating Actions

Excel's Edit menu contains Undo and Repeat commands similar to Word's. There are the familiar Undo and Redo buttons on the Standard toolbar.

Usually, if you catch a mistake, a trip to the Undo command or use of the Ctrl+Z shortcut will fix it. The Repeat command was designed to duplicate your last action. On the Edit menu, the exact names of the Undo and Repeat commands change, based on your prior actions—for example, they may say Repeat Paste and Undo Paste. Sometimes you'll see gray "Can't Undo" or "Can't Repeat" commands, indicating that Excel is unable to undo or play back your most recent type of operation, at least under the current circumstances.

Entering and Formatting Numbers

Numbers are the raw materials for spreadsheets. They are often referred to as *constant values*, or simply *values*. You type numbers into the active cell by using either the number keys above the letter keys on your keyboard, or by using the numeric keypad in NumLock mode. Pressing the NumLock key toggles the numeric keypad between number and cursor-movement mode.

In addition to the numerals 0 through 9, you can enter the following special symbols when typing numbers:

+ – ( ) , . $ % E e

Excel ignores the plus sign in numeric entries, and considers a number to be negative if you precede it with a minus sign or hyphen or enclose it in parentheses. It treats commas and dollar signs correctly, and accepts numbers entered in scientific notation (**2.5E+2**, for instance).

When you enter dollar signs, percentages, or commas, Excel changes the number's *format*.

Number Formats

Within limits, Excel stores and calculates numbers at the precision you type them, but may display them slightly differently than you typed them. For instance, if you type

3.141592654

in a cell, that's what will be *stored* in the cell even if you *see* something else. For example, if you place that entry in a narrow cell, you might see **3.141593**. In this case, Excel displays the number at the maximum possible precision under the circumstances and rounds it up to display it. The actual appearance of the number changes with the *number format* defined for the cell. (Normally this affects neither the value itself nor other computations based on the number.)

You can control the precision with which numbers are displayed. All new worksheets start out with all of their cells formatted in *General* format, which attempts to show as much precision as possible. You can force cells to use other formats designed by Microsoft, or you can create your own formats.

Sometimes, the entry techniques that you use change the cell's number format automatically. For example, if you activate a cell in the General format, then type a number with a dollar sign, the cell's format will change from General to a currency format.

Typing a percent sign changes a cell's number format to a percentage with two decimal places (**10.05%**, for instance). There are scientific and fractional number formats as well. You can specify the number format for a cell or group of cells from the Number tab in the Format Cells dialog box shown in Figure 13.10. (Reach it from the Cells command on the Format menu.) Choose a category to reduce the number of formats displayed.

When Numbers Are Too Big for Their Cells

When a number is too big to be properly displayed in its cell, Excel often displays a series of pound signs (**######**) instead of the number. Other times, Excel will switch to scientific notation to accommodate a large number.

Making the column wider using techniques described in Chapter 15, or using a shorter number format, will solve the problem. For instance, when dealing with large sums of money, you can often save room in cells by using number formats that don't *display* pennies and decimal points, even if you enter them. They will still calculate correctly.

FIGURE 13.10

Pick a number format here or design your own. The same uses the contents of the active cell to show you what the number will look like.

A quick way to increase or decrease the number of displayed decimal places is to use the Toolbar buttons called Increase Decimal and Decrease Decimal. They are located on the Formatting toolbar and contain zeros, decimal points, and arrows. Each time you click, display precision is incremented or decremented one decimal place.

Entering and Formatting Dates and Times

You enter dates and times by typing them in most commonly accepted American formats. These include, but are not limited to:

11/7/93

11-Nov-93

Nov 7, 1993

8:10 PM

8:10:12 PM

20:10

20:10:12

11/7/93 20:10

You can even create your own date formats. For instance,

mmmm d, yyyy

will display **November 7, 1947**.

Excel will *store* entries like these as dates or times, and then *reformat* and *display* them using one of several predefined date formats.

How Excel Stores Dates and Times

Date and time entries are a slightly confusing topic, made tougher by Excel's desire to be all things to all people. If you ever plan to enter dates into cells, you should know the following.

Because Excel is often required to do date-and-time math (determine the number of days between two dates, or the number of hours between two time entries, for instance), it *stores* dates and times as *serial numbers* using January 1, 1900, as the starting date. Here's how it works:

The serial number 1 represents January 1, 1900; the serial number 2 stands for January 2, 1900. As I'm writing this chapter, we're coming up on serial number 34,550.

If you *reformat* a cell containing a date and display it as a number you will see the serial number instead of the date. Excel will still treat the cell's contents as a date for computations (but the cell will *look* strange to you).

Alas, not all computers use 1/1/1900 as the starting point for their date serial numbers. For example, Excel for Macintosh computers use 1904. Excel usually converts dates from Macintosh spreadsheets properly when importing and exporting, but check carefully when moving worksheets containing dates from one platform to another.

Forcing Numbers to Be Treated as Text

If you want Excel to treat numbers or time entries or date-like entries as text instead of numbers, you need to tell it to do so. Suppose, for instance, you want to enter the part number **12/63**. Excel would try to treat this as a date, and instead of seeing your part number in the cell you'd see **Dec-63** after you finished the entry. To prevent this, precede such entries with ' (the apostrophe or single quotation mark), which will not display or print. Alternatively, since Excel treats any cell containing non-numbers as text, the entries **#12/63**, **12/63B**, and even numbers preceded by a space (**12/63**) will be treated as text.

Entering and Editing Formulas

Formulas get the work done. When you want to add a column of numbers and see the results, or divide one number by another, or do any other computation, you must create formulas. Formulas are sometimes even used to manipulate text in worksheets.

Usually, you place the formula in the cell where you want to see the results. You type formulas in the Formula bar. Excel formulas always start with = (the *equal sign*), although die-hard Lotus users can cheat and use & (the *ampersand*) instead.

Remember the sample miles-per-gallon worksheet at the beginning of this chapter? It contains formulas to compute miles traveled by three trucks, miles per gallon, and cost per mile.

	A	B
1		**Truck 1**
2	Starting Odometer	1025.8
3	Ending Odometer	1455.2
4	**Miles Travelled**	=B3-B2
5		
6	**Cost Per Gallon**	1.35
7	**Gallons Used**	12.2
8	**Miles Per Gallon**	=B4/B7
9		
10	**Cost Per Mile**	=$B$6/B8

The mileage formula in cell B4 subtracts the starting odometer reading (located in cell B2) from the ending reading (in cell B3) to compute and display the mileage. Notice that the formula does this by referring to the two cell addresses B3 and B2. Whenever the contents of B3 or B2 change, Excel will automatically compute a new answer and display it in cell B4. That's the essence of worksheet computations! Formulas tell Excel what to do whenever the contents of specified cells change.

Use the View tab in the Tools ➤ Options dialog box to show all of your worksheet's formulas at once:

Excel's Tip Wizard just reminded me that the shortcut for displaying and hiding formulas is Ctrl+`. That's Ctrl plus the grave accent mark, usually located on the same key as the ~ (tilde) symbol. It toggles between displaying formulas and their answers.

Creating Formulas

If you've never used a mouse to create formulas before, you might want to fire up Excel and follow along with this description.

Start by activating the cell where you want to place the formula (point to B4, for instance). Next type either an equal sign or an ampersand to tell Excel you want to create a formula.

You can then either type the formula one character at a time, or *assemble* it using your mouse and keyboard. For instance, you could type **=B3-B2** and press ↵ to create the formula in B4—but it's often better to reach for the mouse. You could type the equal sign, then point to and click on cell B3 with your mouse. Cell B3 will be surrounded by a dashed outline (I like to call this "the marching ants"). The cell's address will appear in the Formula bar. This makes it unnecessary for you to *type* the address with the keyboard. Next, you'd type the minus sign for your equation, then point to and click on cell B2 with the mouse. Pressing ↵ finishes the formula. If you have entered values in cells B2 and B3, they will be subtracted from each other and their difference appears in cell B4.

Excel's Formula Operators

The *operators* you use in a formula tell Excel what you want to do (add two numbers, or compare things, for instance). For purposes of explanation, Excel operators can be divided into four general categories—*arithmetic*, *comparison*, *text*, and *reference*. Most of the time you will use arithmetic operators. The others can be useful for more complex projects.

Arithmetic Operators

You've already seen two arithmetic operators at work   the slash symbol / (division) and the hyphen or minus sign – (subtraction). Here's the standard collection:

+	addition
–	subtraction
*	multiplication
/	division
%	percentage
^	exponentiation

Simply include these at the appropriate places in your formulas to perform the desired calculation. For instance, the formula **=B5*10%** would compute 10% of the contents of cell B5. The equation **=B5^2** computes the square of cell B5's contents.

More complex formulas, like

```
=E6*B2-(B3*10%)
```

can be created by combining operators and using parentheses.

Comparison Operators

Comparison operators let you inspect two values and come to a conclusion about their relative values. They are usually coupled with Excel's *logical functions* (discussed in Chapter 17).

The operators are:

=	equal
>>	greater than
>>=	greater than or equal to
<<	less than
<<=	less than or equal to
<>	not equal to

At the risk of confusing you, here is an example of comparison operators at work with the logical function IF. Suppose you wanted to display an error message whenever the ending odometer reading in cell B3 was *smaller* than the starting reading in B2. The formula

```
=IF((B3<<B2),"Bad OD!",B3-B2)
```

would compare the contents of cells B2 and B3. If B3 is less than B2 the text *Bad OD!* is displayed instead of the negative (wrong) numeric mileage value. If the odometer readings pass the comparison test, the math is performed (B3–B2). (As I mentioned earlier, the topic of logical functions will be taken up more fully in the chapter on functions.)

Text Operator

Excel's only text operator is the ampersand (**&**). It is used to combine text. For instance, if you had the word **aero** in cell C7 and the word **plane** in C8, the formula **=C7&C8** would create the text string **aeroplane**.

Reference Operators

Finally, Excel offers reference operators. The most common reference is to a range of cells. For instance, the expression B1:C3 refers to cells B1, C3, and all the cells between them. You'll learn more about ranges later in this chapter.

Referencing Cells

When creating a formula, you will frequently refer to a *single cell*. For example, in a miles-per-gallon formula, you might refer to the cell containing miles traveled. Other times it is useful to refer to *ranges* of cells. In an annual budget, you might have twelve different cells, each containing totals for a different month. It's possible to refer to individual cells or all of the cells in the range.

You often specify references by clicking or dragging with your mouse (clicking on cell A1, or dragging from cell B1 to B4, for instance). Alternatively you can type references directly into formulas (like **A1** or **B1:B4**). When you create and duplicate formulas, Excel makes some assumptions about which cell or cells you wish to reference. You can often overrule these assumptions as you'll see in a moment. References can be *absolute*, *relative* or *mixed*. Let's consider a simplified budget exercise (see Figure 13.11) designed to illustrate various reference types and referencing techniques.

Single-Cell References

Single-cell references specify a specific cell. For instance, when building an new formula, if you wanted to include the 3-Year non-payroll costs from our example, you could either click upon cell B10, or type **B10** in the new formula. An important variation on this technique creates *absolute references*, and will be discussed momentarily.

Excel

FIGURE 13.11

A simplified budget

	A	B	C	D
1	**Proposed increase:**	10%		
2				
3				
4	**Item**	**Last Year**	**This Year**	**Next Year**
5	**Payroll**	$525,000	$600,000	$660,000
6	**Benefits**	$ 50,000	$ 70,000	$ 77,000
7	**Recruiting fees**	$ 6,000	$ 1,000	$ 1,100
8	**Total empl. costs**	$581,000	$671,000	$738,100
9				
10	**3-Yr Non-payroll costs**	$205,100		
11				

REFSMPL.XLS

Sheet1 / Sheet2 / Sheet3 /

Range References

To refer to a range of cells, you can either drag over the desired cells, or type the beginning and ending cell addresses in the range using colons to separate the beginning and ending cell addresses. For instance, to specify the group of six cells containing non-payroll costs in out example, you would either drag from cell B6 to D7 or type **B6:D7** into your formula. Incidentally, you can give *names* to ranges of cells like these and refer to the names in equations. For instance, you could name cells B6 through D7 *Nonpay* and place the range name **nonpay** in your formulas. This approach often makes it easier to understand and troubleshoot complex worksheets. Read more about this technique in Chapter 16.

TIP To reference an entire row, type its number twice, separated by a colon (2:2 for example). To specify an entire column, type the column's letter twice with a colon (A:A for instance).

Absolute versus Relative References

Sometimes you'll want to specify an exact cell not only for the first formula you create, but for others that will be modeled after it. This is particularly important when building formulas that you plan to copy. Suppose, in our example, we want to create a formula that increases Payroll expenses by a specified percentage over last year's spending. We could just include the cell address containing the percentage increase (B1) in our formula:

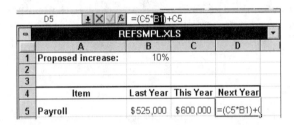

This would work fine until you tried to save some time by copying the formula for other rows using the techniques later in this chapter, or rearranged the worksheet. While *copying* the formula, Excel would increment (adjust) the reference to B1 as shown here. Thus the first formula will work and the others won't because they refer to cells other than B1:

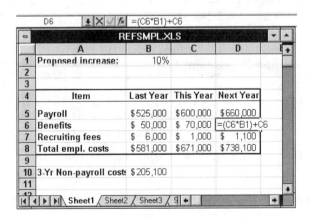

You'll learn more about this when you learn to duplicate formulas later, but here's the solution if you are familiar with the problem and just can't wait. To

Excel

assure that formulas always refer to a specific cell (like the one containing the mark-up percentage in our example), it is wise to make an *absolute* reference. Absolute addresses use dollar signs before both the row and column address. For instance, to create an absolute reference to cell B2, you would type **$B$2**.

Mixed References

Finally, it is worth mentioning that you can create mixed references that point to a specific column and a relative row (like **$A1**), or a specific row and a relative column (like **A$1**), or a specific worksheet and relative row and column. Again, this will make more sense when you start copying formulas.

Named References

As you'll see in Chapter 16, you can assign names to cells or ranges of cells. When you do that, you can use the names in your formulas. For instance, if you had a column named QTY and a column named Price, you could create a formula like **=QTY*PRICE**. Read more about this in Chapter 16.

Changing Reference Types in a Formula

Naturally, you can edit the reference by typing directly in a formula (to add or remove dollar signs, for instance). But there is an alternative:

1. Select the cell containing the formula to be changed.

2. In the Formula bar, select (highlight) the reference to be changed (**B1**, for example)

3. Press the F4 function key repeatedly, watching the reference change until you see the desired effect (**$B$1**, for example)

4. Tap the Enter key or click the Enter box to change the formula.

Changing Reference Style

By default, Excel uses letters for column references and numbers for row references (A1 for instance). It is possible, however, to use "R1C1" style referencing, as illustrated here:

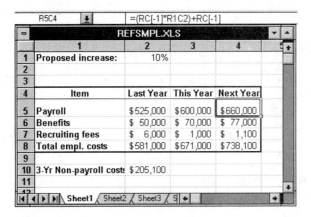

Notice that there are numbers both for columns and rows. Inspect the formulas in the example as well. When you choose this option, Row references in formulas must be preceded with the letter **R** and Column references with the letter **C**.

This is a method used in some competitive spreadsheet programs like Multi-Plan, so if you find it easier to use (or if your organization has standardized on this method), it's easy to change over to this reference style.

1. Choose Tools ➤ Options on Excel's Tools menu

2. Bring the General tab frontmost if it is not already in view.

3. Choose R1C1 on the Reference Style area of the dialog box.

4. Click OK. Excel will adjust all of your formula references automatically.

To switch back to "normal" Excel referencing, repeat steps 1 through 5, choosing A1 in step 3.

Order of Evaluation in Formulas

Whenever you add more than one operator to a formulas, Excel must decide which *operation* to perform first. Moreover, the *position* of the elements in your formula play a part. For example, the formula **=5+2*10** yields **25**, while **=10*5+2** yields **52**; which makes sense when you understand the order in which Excel performs operations. In the first example, Excel adds five to the product of 2 times 10. In the second example 10 is multiplied by 5 and its product (50) is added to 2, since addition occurs after multiplication. Here's a list of Excel's operators in the order Excel uses them:

OPERATORS	FUNCTION
:	Range specifiers
Space	Intersection (see on-line help)
,	Union
-	Negation (creating a negative number by using only one operand)
%	Percent
^	Exponentiation (raising to a power)
* or /	Multiplication or division
+ or -	Addition or subtraction
&	Joins text
= <> <= >= <>	The comparison operators

As you may recall from algebra class, you can often use parentheses and other tricks to force the correct order of evaluation. For instance, **=10*(5+2)** returns **70**.

Built-In Functions versus Hand-Built Formulas

Excel provides a number of built-in functions that automate otherwise time-consuming common tasks. For instance, there is a function that computes monthly loan payments given a loan amount, interest rates, and the length of your loan. Another function computes averages for specified groups of numbers. Other functions perform engineering or statistical tasks. There is also a Function wizard to help you sort out all the details. You'll learn more about functions in Chapter 17. But there is one worth learning about now. It's called the *SUM* function, and it can be reached with the Summation or SUM button on the standard Toolbar.

Suppose you wanted to add the column of numbers at the top of Figure 13.12. You *could* type the equation

=A2+A3+A4+A5

But the SUM function is a better way to get the sum of those figures.

As you can see at the bottom of Figure 13.12, pressing the SUM button caused Excel to propose a range of cells to include in its range (cell E1 through and including cell E4). "Marching ants" surround the cells to be included. The SUM equation also appears in the Formula bar, where you can accept or edit it. Pressing ↵ or clicking on the Formula bar's checkmark button will accept the proposed formula and display the answer in cell A6. The SUM button and related SUM function work on rows, columns, or arrays (described next).

FIGURE 13.12

Functions make quick work of laborious tasks like adding rows or columns of numbers

	A	B	C	D
1	10			
2	25			
3	65			
4	40			
5	=A4+A3+A2+A1			

A5   =A4+A3+A2+A1

	E	F
	10	
	25	
	65	
	40	
	=SUM(E1:E4)	

Arrays and Formulas

Formulas can include references to *arrays*, which are contiguous (adjacent) groups of numbers. For instance, in the example below, the SUM function will add up all the numbers in the six-cell array B2:C5.

When using the SUM function and similar tools to specify arrays, you can drag the marching ants with your mouse to include or exclude cells.

Lookup Tables

Lookup tables are special arrays that you create to help you look up and provide different cell contents as conditions warrant. For instance, you could create a lookup table like the one in cells A3 through B5 here:

```
=LOOKUP(A9,$A$3:$B$5)
```

	A	B
1		
2	Qty	Price
3	1	$ 1.00
4	100	$ 0.90
5	1000	$ 0.85
6		
7		
8	110	$ 0.90
9	1600	$ 0.85
10	1	$ 1.00
11		

LOOKUP.XLS

The lookup table itself consists of the range of cells A3:B5. Cells A3 through A5 contain quantities for each of three price breaks. Cells B3 through B5 contain the prices.

To demonstrate a lookup table at work, there are identical sample formulas in cells B8, B9 and B10. (The formula for cell B9 is shown in the illustration. It was created using the Insert Function command and resulting Function Wizard.) You'll learn more about this in Chapter 17.

Cells A8 through A10 contain different order quantities. As you can see from the illustration, the LOOKUP functions in the formulas places the appropriate price in cells B8 through B10 based on the quantities entered in cells A8 through A10. You can specify exact lookups or have Excel find the closest match as illustrated in this example.

Incidentally, you can use lookup tables with text as well as numbers. Here, Excel inserts different words based on order quantities:

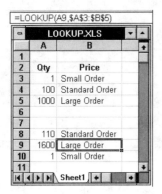

All I did was replace the cell *contents* in B3, B4 and B5 with text. That's the essence of table lookups. Consult the big books and on-line help for more information.

 TIP Lookup tables need not be on the same page or even the same sheet with the cells containing lookup formulas. Consider putting your lookup tables out of sight.

Controlling Recalculation

Normally, Excel recalculates each time you change any number in the worksheet. And, unless you instruct it otherwise, Excel always recalculates before saving. You can overrule these automatic recalculation options and others from the Calculation tab in the Options dialog box (shown in Figure 13.13), reached with the Calculation tab in the Tools ➤ Options dialog box.

You can override
Excel's automatic
recalculation by using
options on the
Calculation tab of the
Options dialog box.

When working on large, complex projects, consider shutting off automatic recalculation if lengthy recalculation delays bother you. Just remember that once you disable automatic recalculation, you become responsible for telling Excel when to recalculate. If you make changes to your worksheet and forget to recalculate manually, one or more cells containing equations may contain old, incorrect answers. To recalculate the worksheet manually, press the F9 function key. Stick a note on your monitor to remind you to recalculate before you save the worksheet, or use the Recalculate Before Save option.

Copying Entries and Equations to Minimize Typing

When creating a large worksheet it is time-consuming to type the same values over and over and over again. Why do it when Excel can do this for you? And, when creating similar formulas in different cells, sometimes the only things that change in the formulas are cell references. For instance, if you create an equation like =**A1-A2** in column A, you often want a similar equation like =**B1-B2** in column B and =**C1-C2** in column C. Excel provides a number of powerful features to minimize mindless typing like this. But you need to use these power tools with care! Take a look.

AutoFill

AutoFill is a tool that lets you select cells of interest and make relative copies of them in adjacent cells. While often used to create tables and forecasts, AutoFill can also be used to copy formulas. Figure 13.14 shows an example of AutoFill at work.

To use AutoFill, simply highlight the cell(s) of interest, then drag the *fill outline* using the square handle at the bottom corner of the active cell outline. (It's called the *fill handle.*) Your pointer turns into a large plus sign when it is able to drag the Fill handle (when the pointer is pointing at the lower-right corner of the last highlighted cell).

The *center* part of Figure 13.14 shows the results of autofilling. Excel has cleverly guessed that the second truck should be labeled **Truck 2** and the third **Truck 3**. It has noticed a trend. Not knowing any better, it has *copied* the beginning and ending odometer readings so that all three trucks have the same readings, and thus identical mileages. This is easy to fix by typing corrected odometer readings. (This problem could have been avoided altogether by placing zeros in column A before auto filling.)

The bottom screen in Figure 13.14 illustrates automatic equation modifications accomplished by AutoFill and other Excel equation-copying tools. Here, we've switched the Display Options to display the formulas created by Auto-Fill. Notice the formulas in row 4. Excel has altered the cell references in each column so that the formulas subtract the appropriate numbers in each column, because of the *relative addressing*. Remember, if you don't want Excel to do that for you, use *absolute addressing* instead, as discussed earlier.

FIGURE 13.14

Features like AutoFill minimize mindless retyping. Use them with care and inspect your work, or you will sometimes create hard-to-find errors.

Truck 3 ⬦	Truck 1			
	A	B	C	D
1		Truck 1		
2	Starting Odometer	1025.8		
3	Ending Odometer	1455.2		
4	Miles Travelled	=B3-B2		
5				
6	Cost Per Gallon	1.35		
7	Gallons Used	12.2		
8	Miles Per Gallon	=B4/B7		
9				
10	Cost Per Mile	=$B$6/B8		
11				

	A	B	C	D
1		Truck 1	Truck 2	Truck 3
2	Starting Odometer	1025.8	1025.8	1025.8
3	Ending Odometer	1455.2	1455.2	1455.2
4	Miles Travelled	=B3-B2	=C3-C2	=D3-D2
5				
6	Cost Per Gallon	1.35	1.35	1.35
7	Gallons Used	12.2	12.2	12.2
8	Miles Per Gallon	=B4/B7	=C4/C7	=D4/D7
9				
10	Cost Per Mile	=$B$6/B8	=$B$6/C8	=$B$6/D8

	A	B	C	D
1		Truck 1	Truck 2	Truck 3
2	Starting Odometer	1025.8	1025.8	1025.8
3	Ending Odometer	1455.2	1455.2	1455.2
4	Miles Travelled	429.4	429.4	429.4
5				
6	Cost Per Gallon	$1.35	$1.35	$1.35
7	Gallons Used	12.2	12.2	12.2
8	Miles Per Gallon	35.2	35.2	35.2
9				
10	Cost Per Mile	$0.04	$0.04	$0.04

More AutoFill Examples

AutoFill knows a number of tricks and you can teach it others. Take a look at this sampling:

	A	B	C	D	E	F	G	H	I	J
1	Jan	Feb	Mar	Apr	May	Jun	Jul	Aug	Sep	Oct
2	January	February	March	Q1	April	May	June	Q2	July	August
3										
4	1992									
5	1993									
6	1994									
7	1995									
8										
9	Monday	Tuesday	Wednesday	Thursday	Friday	Saturday	Sunday	Monday	Tuesday	Wednesday
10										
11	10	20	30	40	50	60	70	80	90	100
12	5	5	4	5	5	4	5	5	4	5
13	$10.00	$25.00	$40.00	$55.00	$70.00	$85.00	$100.00	$115.00	$130.00	$145.00
14										
15	10:00 AM	10:00:00								
16	11:00 AM	11:00:00								
17	12:00 PM	12:00:00								
18	1:00 PM	13:00:00								
19	2:00 PM	14:00:00								
20	Curly	Larry	Mo	Shep						
21	curly	larry	mo	shep						
22										

FILLS.XLS — Sheet1 / Sheet2 / Sheet3 / Sheet4 / Sheet5 / Sheet6

AutoFilling Days, Months and Years

Notice the months in rows 1 and 2 of the FILLS.XLS example. In row 1 I typed **Jan** and **Feb**, then AutoFilled, producing the rest of the months without typing them.

In Row 2, typing **January**, **February**, **March** and **Q1**, then AutoFilling, produced long versions of the rest of the months and appropriate quarters (Q2, Q3, etc.) Yes, you can enter years with your dates and they will change as necessary. So, when you extend **November 1993**, **December 1993**, the next cell will read January 1994. Include just as much of the date as you want to see (just years, months, days years, etc.). Row 9 shows what happens when you type just days. International date formats work here as well.

Notice how Excel duplicates the formatting used in the sample cells (Bold and Centering in rows 1 and 2).

Dates (and other things) can be AutoFilled down also. You can see an example of this in cells A4 through A7.

AutoFilling Time

Type the first two or more time examples, and Excel will follow. That's plain old American time in A15 through A 19 and 24-hour time with seconds to the right.

AutoFilling Numbers

Our example also shows some AutoFilled numbers. Rows 11 through 13 show an example of linear forecasting. Supply a few numbers to illustrate the trend, drag away, and Excel will extend the forecast on your behalf. Here too, formatting gets noticed. Since cells A, B and C12 were centered, so are their offspring. In row 13 dollar signs were included and so it is written.

Look carefully at row 12. Here we've *filled* with the numbers 4, 4, and 5 (handy if working with budgets where you care about the number of weeks in a month). You *can't* just type **4, 4,** and **5** in the first three cells, then AutoFill, however. This will produce a forecast along the lines of 5, 5.33333, 5.833333, and so on. To prevent forecasting (and to force filling) hold down the Ctrl key while dragging. The mouse pointer should contain an extra little + as you work.

Creating Custom Fill Lists

Excel's not a mind reader (although if you watch the Tip Wizard long enough you'll begin to wonder.) So, you might want to create some custom lists that Excel can use whenever it recognizes your request. For example (and with apologies), check out rows 20 and 21. After my setting up a custom list, my version of Excel now knows to add Mo and Shep when ever I type Curly and Larry and then choose AutoFill. A better use for this feature might be to

AutoFill department names, employee names, etc. Here are the general steps for creating your own custom lists:

1. Choose Options... from Excel's Tools menu.

2. Click on the Custom Lists tab if necessary to bring it foremost.

3. Click on New List.

4. When the insertion pointer moves to the List Entries area, type your list in the desired order:

5. Click OK when done.

6. The next time you type the first two or more items in your list and AutoFill, the rest will follow (assuming you drag far enough to include all the items in your list.

Excel handles capitalization quite cleverly. If you capitalize, it follows your lead. Check out rows 20 and 21 in the FILLS.XLS example to see what I mean.

TIP You can use an existing sample to create a list by typing its range in the Import List from Cells portion of the Custom List dialog. For example, if you have a ready list of product numbers in cells A1 through A10 you could enter $A$1:$A$10 to capture them without retyping.

Filling Right or Down

In addition to AutoFill, Excel offers a variety of fill commands on the Edit menu. You can use these to copy values or formulas in much the same way that you use AutoFill. Select the cell(s) to copy, then drag to highlight destination cells. This time, don't drag the Fill handle. Pick the appropriate fill method from the Edit ➤ Fill submenu, as illustrated in Figure 13.15.

FIGURE 13.15

You can exercise more control over the way you fill cells by using Edit ➤ Fill and choosing a fill option from the submenu.

Protecting and Unprotecting Documents and Cells

Sometimes you'll want to prevent others from gaining any kind of unauthorized access to a worksheet (say, a worksheet with your employees' salaries). Other times you'll want to let people see, but not change, your work—to prevent yourself or someone else from accidentally destroying a cell's formula or other contents with an inadvertent entry. Or you may want to authorize the changing of some cells but not others.

Excel

Preventing Others from Opening Your Documents

You can assign a password to an Excel document to prevent unauthorized people from opening it. This is done with the Save Options dialog box reached by choosing the Options button in the Save As dialog box (choose File ➤ Save As):

You can completely prevent unauthorized opening of documents from this dialog box, or you can permit people to open and even change things in a worksheet without allowing them to save the changes. It is also possible to let others save changes but only after a warning.

Excel's passwords are case-sensitive. That is to say, if you assign **Mickey** as the password, Excel will not accept **MICKEY** or **mickey** or any other variation. You are asked to confirm each password assignment by typing it a second time before it becomes "official."

Cell Protection

It is sometimes desirable to protect portions of your worksheets even from your own mistakes. For instance, it is very easy to accidentally enter a value into a cell containing a formula. When you do this, the formula is destroyed and your worksheet will no longer function properly.

For this reason, it's often a good idea to protect cells containing formulas and labels after you are happy with the functioning and appearance of your worksheet. See online help and the big books for details.

14

Rearranging Worksheets

R egardless of how carefully you plan a project, inevitably you'll wish you had put things in a slightly different order. You'll want to insert extra rows or columns, move things around, or just plain delete them. You'll be able to use Windows and Word skills learned earlier in this book to do so. You can use the cut-and-paste and drag-and-drop features, for instance.

NOTE When you move, insert, and delete cells, formulas are sometimes affected. The end of this chapter explores these issues.

Moving Cells

Moving the contents of a cell or cells and other items can be as simple as selecting the cell or cells, cutting with the Cut command on the Edit menu, and pasting with the Paste command. Any existing Clipboard contents will be replaced by the data you cut. You can also use the keyboard shortcuts Ctrl-X for cut and Ctrl-V for paste. (To see these and other shortcuts, use the right mouse button to reveal the shortcut menu.) Excel does not warn you if your pasting will overwrite the contents of a cell, so keep your eye on the screen. If you use Undo in time, you can undo any accidental overwrite.

You can also move cells, rows, and columns by selecting them and using drag-and-drop. Figure 14.1 shows the basic process.

1. Highlight cells you want to move.

2. Drag at their edges with the arrow-shaped pointer.

3. Release the mouse button to drop the selected items at the outlined position.

FIGURE 14.1

You can move cells, rows, and columns in Excel worksheets by using drag-and-drop.

4	Miles Travelled	429.4	429.4	429.4
5				
6	Cost Per Gallon	$1.35		
7				
8	Gallons Used	12.2	12.2	12.2
9	Miles Per Gallon	35.2	35.2	35.2

Unlike cut-and-paste, drag-and-drop *does* warn you if you are going to overwrite nonblank cells. Click OK to replace the previous cell contents with whatever you are dragging, or choose Cancel to abort the dragging and dropping.

NOTE **Normally, when you move the contents of cells, you also move their notes, formatting information, and equations if the cells contain them. Unless you've used absolute addressing (discussed in Chapter 13), the references in the moved cells will change. <u>Cutting</u> and pasting causes references to adjust to fit the new location; <u>copying</u> and pasting does not adjust references.**

Copying Cells

To copy cells, select them, then copy with the Edit menu's Copy command and paste with the Paste command. Any existing Clipboard contents will be replaced by the data you copy. You can also use the keyboard shortcuts Ctrl-C for copy and Ctrl-V for paste. Excel does not warn you if your copying or pasting will overwrite the contents of a cell, so keep your eye on the screen. If you use Undo in time, you can undo any accidental overwrite.

You can also copy with drag-and-drop. Figure 14.2 illustrates this.

1. Select the cells of interest.

2. Hold down the Ctrl key while dragging. The mouse pointer will have a small plus sign next to it.

Excel

FIGURE 14.2

To copy with drag-and-drop, select the desired items, then hold down the Ctrl key while dragging to where you want the copy to appear.

MPG1.XLS			
	A	**B**	**C**	**D**
1		**Truck 1**	**Truck 2**	**Truck 3**
2	Starting Odometer	1025.8	1025.8	1025.8
3	Ending Odometer	1455.2	1455.2	1455.2
4	**Miles Travelled**	429.4	429.4	429.4
5				
6				
7	**Cost Per Gallon**	$1.35		
8	**Gallons Used**	12.2	12.2	12.2
9	**Miles Per Gallon**	35.2	35.2	35.2
10				

Sheet1 / Sheet2 \ MP(

3. When you release the mouse the selected cells will be copied to the new location.

4. Excel will ask you to confirm the copy if it will cause cells to be overwritten. Click OK to confirm the changes.

Sorting Cell Data

You can sort groups of cells in ascending or descending order, using up to three sort keys at once. Excel will even use headings in your worksheet to "name" the sort keys. For instance, if you had a spreadsheet containing first names, last names, and test scores, you could simultaneously sort on scores (descending so that high scores are first), then last names, then first names, so that students with the same scores and last names would appear alphabetically by first name within their score group. Figure 14.3 illustrates this.

FIGURE 14.3

Excel lets you sort
on up to three keys
at once.

  Sorting in a spreadsheet is risky business. <u>You must remember to select everything you want to sort, and nothing else.</u> For instance, in Figure 14.3, if you select everyone's first and last names but forget to select their scores, the scores will not move, but the names will, giving some people wrong scores. You can use Undo to fix this, but you should save before you sort, so you can close a messed-up worksheet without saving, if necessary. Then you can reload the good, unsorted version (or make a copy and try your sort on <u>it</u>).

That said, here are the steps for sorting:

1. Select just the cells (or rows or columns) you want to sort. Include headings if you wish.

2. Choose Sort from Excel's Data menu.

3. Specify row or column sorting in the Sort Options dialog box (Data ➤ Sort ➤ Options).

4. If you want to use headings as sort keys, pick that option in the dialog box.

5. Pick the first sorting key. If you use headings for keys, you'll see them listed in drop-down lists.

6. Next, tell Excel whether you want the sort to produce ascending or descending results. (In Figure 14.3 we wanted the high scores first, so a descending sort was specified for scores, but ascending was used for the others.)

7. If you want to do additional sorts, move to the next key box and repeat the process. Do it again, if necessary, for a three-level sort.

8. When you've set up the sorting specifications, click OK and inspect the results.

 The Utility toolbar contains two sort buttons—Sort Ascending and Sort Descending.

Inserting Rows

It's easy to insert additional rows in a worksheet. One way is to select the entire row *below* the place where you want a new blank row. For example, click on the row number at the left edge of row number 4 to select row 4. Then choose Rows on Excel's Insert menu. You will see a new, blank row 4, and the old contents of row 4 will become row 5. All of the rows that follow will also be pushed down and renumbered. Formulas will usually accommodate insertions like this, but, as always, check your work.

The mouse shortcut menu offers a quick way to insert rows or columns into your worksheet: Click the right mouse button and choose Insert from the shortcut menu to display the Insert dialog box.

To insert multiple rows, *select* multiple rows before issuing the Insert command. For instance, to insert three rows in our earlier example, you could select rows 4, 5, and 6.

Inserting Columns

To insert a column, point to the label of the column where you want the new column to appear. For instance, if you want a blank column at column B, select it. Use the Columns command on Excel's Insert menu, or click the right mouse button and choose Insert from the shortcut menu. You will see a new, blank column B, whereupon the old contents of column B will become column C. All of the columns that follow will also be pushed right and renamed. Formulas will usually allow for insertions like this, but check your work to be sure.

To insert multiple columns, select multiple columns before using the Insert command. That is, to insert three columns in our example, you could select columns B, C, and D.

Inserting Cells

You can insert empty cells into an existing worksheet, thereby pushing existing cells either to the right of the insertion point or down from the insertion point. Highlight the area where you want to insert new blank cells and then use the Insert menu's Cells command (or click the right mouse button and choose Insert from the shortcut menu that appears). The Insert dialog box comes up, asking you if you want to shift cells right or down, or insert an entire row or entire column. This pushes cells as you might expect, although it

Excel

can ruin the appearance of your worksheet. Use Undo if you are unhappy with the results.

Inserting as You Paste

Sometimes you'll want to make room for items as you paste them. If so, select the items to be pasted, then copy or cut them to the Clipboard. A new Insert Cut Cells command will appear on the Edit menu. Activate the cell, row, or column where you want to insert the Clipboard contents, and choose the Insert Cut Cells command. Check the effect upon formulas and the overall worksheet appearance after pasting this way.

Deleting Parts of a Worksheet

The Delete command on the Edit menu is used to delete unwanted rows, columns, or cells. This places them on the Clipboard and closes up the space made by the deletion. For example, if you select all of column B and use the Edit menu's Delete command, the contents of column C will shift left and become column B, D will become C, etc., almost to infinity (or the maximum width of the worksheet).

The same basic process occurs when you delete rows. Deleting row 4 moves row 5's contents up, making those cells the new row 4, and so on.

 The mouse shortcut menu offers a quick way to delete rows or columns from your worksheet: Click the right mouse button and choose Delete from the shortcut menu.

If you select an irregular collection of cells (something other than a complete row or column), Excel will ask how you want remaining cells to move when they fill in the newly emptied space.

Deletions of rows, columns, or cells can affect formulas, particularly if you remove cells that are referenced by formulas. Check your work.

Clearing Parts of a Worksheet

Clearing removes cell contents but does not move the contents of other cells to fill in the newly emptied space. Highlight the cell or cells you want to clear, then use the Clear command on the Edit menu or press the Del key. Excel will ask if you want to clear every aspect of the cell or just selected features like formats, formulas, or notes.

How Formulas React to Worksheet Design Changes

We've mentioned the whole host of potential problems with formulas when modifying worksheet designs, but it's worth recapping them here. Some changes can have a profound effect on formulas, others are benign. But whenever you fiddle with a cell that is referenced in a formula (even if the formula is in some other worksheet or file), there is the potential for trouble. This is particularly true when you:

- Insert rows, columns or cells
- Delete rows, columns or cells
- Move cells, rows or columns referred to by formulas
- Clear cells referred to by formulas
- Change the data type of a cell (e.g., numbers to text)

Careful planning at the beginning of your projects, Excel's good nature and its paternal instincts should minimize problems. But you need to anticipate the effects of changes, then test modified worksheets carefully. Let's take the issues one at a time using the small payroll budget as an example. I've employed

Excel

the command Tools ➤ Options ➤ Formulas to display the formulas in their cells, making it easier to see what's going on:

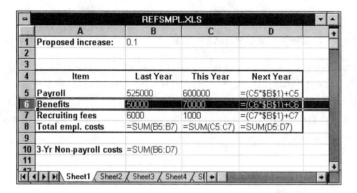

Effects of Inserting Rows

Inserting rows and columns can be either very straightforward or fiendishly tricky. For instance, if you were to insert a row between Payroll and Benefits (between rows 5 and 6), the SUM formulas that calculate Total empl. costs will automatically change to include the newly inserted row.

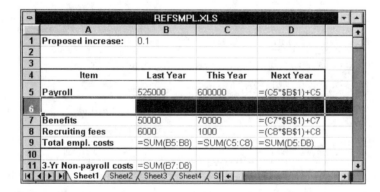

This is probably but *not always* what you want. In this example, if you are adding a new expense line like *Relocation costs*, perhaps, you are okay, since the SUM formulas are computing *total costs*. But, suppose you inserted the new row because you plan to put some non-expense items in the new row like the percent of change in the payroll costs. In that instance, you wouldn't want those newly-inserted percentages to be included in your subtotals below, where they would erroneously increase the subtotals. And, there's another potential gotcha. Can you spot it?

The formula that finds three-year non-payroll costs (in what is now cell B11) does not automatically refer to the newly inserted cells after you insert the row! So, if you *do* put additional non-payroll employee costs in the newly-inserted row, they will be ignored by the formula in B11, making for a too-small result. You need to modify the B11 formula.

TIP **Use named ranges to minimize insertion problems like the one in cell B11. For example, if you create a named range for the original non-payroll cells (named Non_Payroll, let's say), and used the range name in the B11 formula instead of the cell numbers;=SUM(Non_Payroll) instead of =SUM(B7:D8), for example, changes in the size and shape of the range will be reflected in the formula (assuming, of course that you redefine the range when necessary) Learn more about names at the beginning of Chapter 16.**

Check out the formulas in D5 through D9. As we already discussed, D9's references have changed to automatically include the new row. The formulas in D5, D7, and D8 now refer to cells C5, C7, and C8 respectively, properly reacting to the insertion. Because we used absolute addressing each time we specified cell B1, all three old formulas got that right too. Had we not used absolute addressing here, that might have been a problem, however. Check your work!

There is no formula in Cell D6 and it needs one. It can be copied (or filled down) from D5, or copied or filled up from D7. Alternately you can just type a new formula from scratch.

Incidentally; notice that the new row took on the non-standard row height from the neighboring row above. In fact, it took on all of the formatting options from the row above including things like number formatting.

Inserting at the Tops and Bottoms of Lists

Although inserting new rows in the middle of areas serviced by a range reference includes the new row in most formulas, inserting at the top or bottom
does not. Take a look at this:

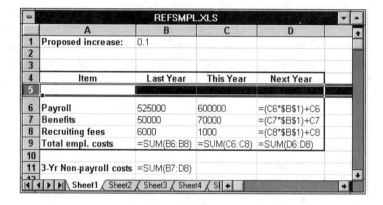

If you insert a new row directly above the Payroll line, Excel will not include
it in things like the SUM formulas used to create totals. You can see this by
examining the formulas in B9, B10, and B11. You'll have the same problem if
you insert a row or rows between the SUM formula line and the old *last* row.
You'll need to modify the references after inserting this way.

Effects of Inserting Columns

Excel reacts about the same way when you insert columns as it does when you
insert rows. Insertions in the middle of ranges are usually included in references to the range, those on the left and the right are not. Check your work
carefully.

Effects of Moving Rows, Columns, or Cells

Excel does a pretty good job of keeping track of things when you move them
around on the same worksheet. For example, you just saw Excel adjust formulas
when things got moved down during a row insertion. Even absolute addressing

can be maintained when referenced cells are moved. Here, the contents of cell B1 were cut, then pasted into cell A2. Notice that the absolute address references in Cells D5 through D7 were automatically modified, and are correct even after the move:

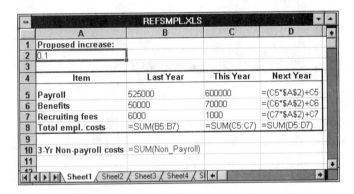

This will not work if you cut from one sheet and paste to another sheet in the same workbook, or to a different file, however. If you do move referenced items off of a worksheet, you'll often see the error message **#REF** in cells referencing the "lost" item. (This is when you're in normal view mode, not when you're viewing the formulas—if you're viewing the formulas, they'll look all right.) For example, here, I've moved the percentage info to Sheet2:

Excel

Notice the error message in each cell that depends upon the moved cell that was B2. I simply need to show Excel the way to the missing data. Here are the general steps:

1. Select a confused formula (D5, perhaps)

2. Select the REF error in the Formula bar (including the # and !):

3. Either type the correct cell address (including sheet name, etc.); or click on the new cell location, which is often much easier than typing the whole address. In this example, I've switched to Sheet2 and clicked on cell B1 there.

4. Switch back to the original worksheet by clicking on the original worksheet tab and save the formula changes by clicking the Enter box or pressing ↵.

5. Inspect the results from the new formula. If the problem is resolved, change other references as necessary.

Note that you may not need to correct each formula containing the #REF! error. This message will also appear in any cell affected by the results of another troubled cell. In our example, for instance, fixing the trouble in cells D5 through D7 will clear up the problem in B10.

Effects of Deleting Rows, Columns, or Cells

The major problem with deletions is the obvious one. If you delete rows, columns, or cells that are referenced in formulas, the formulas may not work. Or worse yet, they may still work, but using different, incorrect data, thereby providing incorrect results.

Effects of Data Type Changes

Formulas expect to see a specific type of data in cells. If you place text in a cell that is supposed to contain a number, for example, Excel will ignore the text when doing math and you will see #VALUE! in the cell(s) containing the formula. See Excel-specific books and on-line help for details.

Auditing Tools Help Spot Potential Problems

Before you insert, delete, or move things around, you can use several of Excel's auditing tools to help you see which cells are affected by each other. This can make it easier to understand what might happen if you redesign a worksheet. For example, by selecting the B1 cell in this example and choosing Tools ➤

Excel

Auditing ➤ Trace Dependents, arrows will radiate from the selected cell(s) to dependent cells:

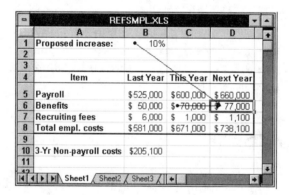

To see how a cell gets its results, you can use the Precedents command (Tools ➤ Auditing ➤ Trace Precedents) to see the other cells involved in the conspiracy. Here, Excel is telling us that cells B1 and C6 are involved in the results being displayed in D6:

You can use these commands repeatedly. The arrows will remain on-screen *and print on your printouts* until you issue the Remove All Arrows command from the Tools menu. To learn more about auditing, read Chapter 23.

That's the short course on rearranging worksheets. Practice on copies or unimportant projects. Save before making big changes. To learn more, check with on-line help and *Mastering Excel 5 for Windows,* by Thomas Chester (SYBEX 1994). Next stop: formatting tips and techniques.

Excel

Excel Formatting Tips and Techniques

Excel provides many formatting features that can enhance the appearance of your worksheets. Some of them will remind you of Microsoft Word's formatting tricks for characters, paragraphs, and tables. Others are unique to Excel. You'll be amazed at how quickly column widths and row heights can be adjusted with a simple mouse click or drag. And Excel's AutoFormat feature can make it look as if you've spent all day on a project, when all you did was make a menu choice. Even if you've used other versions of Excel, be sure to read this chapter carefully. There is plenty of new material here, including a way to center headings over multiple columns.

Excel Page Setup

Just a reminder—as with other Windows programs, it's a good idea to make at least preliminary printer and Page Setup decisions when you start a new project. This way you'll be able to see on-screen how your document will look when printed.

1. If you have more than one printer, pick the one you'll be using for the project.

2. Choose File ➤ Page Setup to get to the Page Setup dialog box.

3. Make any known changes to settings in the Page, Margins, Header/Footer, and Sheet tabs. (At a minimum, make preliminary page size, orientation, and margin settings.)

4. Later you can revisit Page Setup and fine-tune the settings to improve the final appearance of your document.

Changing Column Widths and Row Heights

Sometimes you'll need to change the width of columns or the height of rows. For instance, Excel often displays series of pound signs (#####) when the results of a calculation won't fit the cell width.

If an entry is too big to fit a cell, you *could* switch to a smaller font or otherwise change the cell's content and format. But frequently you'll want to increase the size of the cell instead. Excel offers a number of ways to adjust column widths and row heights. You can adjust a single row or column or select multiple rows or columns and change them simultaneously. You can make size changes by double-clicking or dragging, or you can visit dialog boxes. Figure 15.1 illustrates the various approaches, described next.

Using Best Fit to Automatically Adjust Columns and Rows

When you place the mouse pointer on or near the right edge of a *column label* (like the one between columns A and B in Figure 15.1), the pointer changes into a thick black bar with arrows pointing left and right. If you double-click, Excel's *Best Fit* feature will automatically make the left column (column A in our example) wider or narrower as necessary to accommodate the longest entry in that column. When you select multiple columns before double-clicking, *each* selected column will switch to its best fit, potentially making every column a different width.

Row heights automatically increase to accommodate the tallest character in a row. In addition, heights can be changed using techniques similar to the ones used for column widths. You can change single or multiple rows at once. Pointing to a row label changes the pointer to a thick horizontal bar with up- and down-pointing arrows. Double-clicking results in a best fit (taller or shorter rows).

While the mouse tricks just described are the most convenient way to adjust column widths and row heights, you can also use the AutoFit choices on the Row and Column submenus reached via the Format menu.

FIGURE 15.1

Double-click, drag, or use Column and Row dialog boxes to change column widths and row heights.

Double-click or drag for best fit, or just drag to change column width

Number of characters that will fit

Reach with Column Width commands on the Format menu

Before

After

Double-click or drag to change height

Height in points

Reach with Row Height commands on the Format menu

If you make changes to the contents of cells later (add or remove characters, for example), you may need to use AutoFit again, since the column widths will not automatically readjust.

Use Undo (Ctrl-Z) to restore column widths and row heights. Incidentally, AutoFits are computed using *screen fonts*. As a result, you may occasionally need to readjust columns and rows manually before printing. To see if this will be necessary, use Excel's Print Preview feature.

Dragging to Change Row and Column Sizes

If you'd rather make your own manual column width and row height decisions, drag with the pointers rather than double-clicking. As with the Best Fit trick, when you place the mouse pointer on or near the right edge of a row label (like the one between columns A and B in Figure 15.1), the pointer changes into a thick black bar with arrows pointing left and right. Dragging displays a light line showing the column width that will result when you release the mouse button. If you've selected multiple columns, dragging one will make all of them the same width. You can also drag to define your own row height using similar techniques.

Row Height and Column Width Submenu Commands

The Row Height and Column Width choices reached with Row and Column commands on the Format menu let you see and specify row heights and column widths. Column Width statistics refer to the number of characters that will fit in a cell, assuming they are formatted in "Normal" style. For instance, in Figure 15.1 the column will hold 28.43 characters. Row heights are displayed and entered in points. In Figure 15.1 the row height is 25.5 points.

AutoFormat

Excel's AutoFormat feature uses *Table Formats*, which are predefined collections of number formats, fonts, cell alignments, patterns, shading, column widths, and row heights to embellish ranges of cells you specify. You can use these formats as-is or overrule some of their characteristics.

TIP Because automatic formatting is sometimes difficult to undo, you should save worksheets before experimenting with the automatic formats. Then use the Save As command to save differently named copies as you experiment. Print before settling on formats, and don't forget to write the format style names on each printout until you can recognize them on sight.

Excel

Choosing Formats

1. Start by selecting the range of cells you wish to format. Typically, this is the entire worksheet, but it could be a small range of adjacent cells if you so choose.

2. Use the AutoFormat command on Excel's Format menu to reach the dialog box shown in Figure 15.2.

3. When you first open the AutoFormat dialog box, you'll see the short version, illustrated in the top of Figure 15.2. Click the Options>>>> button to show these extra check boxes:

4. Scroll through the list of table formats and click on the names in the list to see them demonstrated in the Sample window.

5. When you find a format of interest, click OK to apply it. (Use Undo to remove the formatting.) In the process of formatting your document this way, Excel sometimes changes decisions you've made. For instance, if you've made some cells bold, Excel may change them back to plain text or italicize them instead.

Formats to Apply

| ☒ Number | ☒ Font | ☒ Alignment |
| ☒ Border | ☒ Patterns | ☒ Width/Height |

---

6. To remove some aspect of a Table Format (borders, for example), remove the corresponding X from its name in the Formats To Apply section of the enlarged AutoFormat dialog box. The sample box will show you the effect of these changes as you experiment.

7. Click OK to do the actual formatting.

How Excel Makes Automatic Formatting Decisions

If you have only one cell selected when you issue the AutoFormat command, Excel looks for what it thinks is a logical range of cells to format. It will

FIGURE 15.2

Pick a format to apply to selected cells. The finished product is shown at the bottom of this illustration.

Before

After

highlight the proposed range. If you want to format a different range, cancel AutoFormat and select the desired range before trying again.

Different formats look for—and change—different things when formatting. For instance, the classic formats seek out cells containing totals and subtotals, which receive special formatting. The list-type formats use shading and patterns to make lists more readable. Excel considers outline information while formatting, if you've outlined your worksheet. (See Chapter 16 for more about outlines.)

Manual Formatting

You can make many common formatting changes from the Standard toolbar, from the Formatting toolbar, and with your keyboard. For instance, to make

Excel

selected text bold, you can click the Bold button (B) on the Standard or Formatting toolbars or use the Ctrl-B keyboard shortcut. The table at the back of this book lists Excel's buttons and their names and functions. And, remember that you can see a button's name by simply sliding the mouse pointer over it and waiting a moment.

Remember to select all of the cells you want to affect before using these buttons and keyboard shortcuts. Some style changes will affect the size of cell contents, which may necessitate subsequent changes in column widths, cell heights, and so on. For instance, if you increase a cell's font size and make it bold, text or numbers may be too big to fit within your current column width.

Using Styles

Styles are collections of formatting decisions that might include a number format, alignment instructions, border specifications, pattern selections, and cell protection decisions. Styles need not specify all of these things. For instance, a style might consist of just a number format and bold character formatting.

Excel provides a number of standard styles for things like currency. Don't confuse styles with number formats, which only specify commands, decimal places, currency symbols, and the like. You can use Excel's predefined styles or create your own. Styles are stored with the worksheets themselves. You can create new styles, edit existing ones, and copy styles from other worksheets.

Applying Styles

Excel 5 applies styles differently than earlier versions did. Unless you add it, there is no longer a style list on any of the toolbars. Instead, to apply an existing style:

1. Select the cell or cells you want to format.

2. Choose Style from the Format menu.

3. Pick the desired style from the drop-down Style Name list within the resulting Style dialog box, shown in Figure 15.3.

4. Click once on the name and once on OK to apply the style.

FIGURE 15.3

The Style dialog box

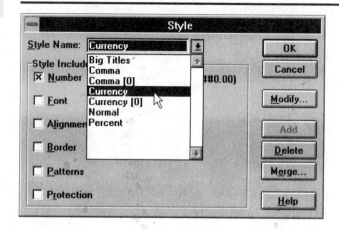

Normal Style

Excel's Normal style displays and prints numbers using the General format, 10-point sans-serif type, no borders, and no shading. It is possible to redefine the standard style just as you can redefine any other style using the steps described next.

Creating Styles

The easiest way to create a new style is to format a cell to meet your requirements (number format, font, borders, and the like) and then name it. Here are the steps:

1. Format the cell to your liking.
2. With that cell still the active cell, choose Style from Excel's Format menu.
3. Type a new style name in the Style Name portion of the Style dialog box, shown in Figure 15.3. Click the Modify button to set changes.
4. Click OK to save the style, which will be added to the drop-down list and saved with your document.

Excel

Modifying Styles

Modifying an existing style requires a visit to the Style dialog box and some typing:

1. Modify a cell containing the style of interest.

2. Choose Format ➤ Style to open the Style dialog box.

3. Click the drop-down list button to display the drop-down list and choose the old style name from it. Alternatively, type the old style name in.

4. Excel may ask if you want to redefine the style based on the changes you've just made. Answer Yes to redefine the style. Choose No or Cancel to leave the style unchanged.

For instance, if you activated a cell formatted with Percent style (named "Percent") and italicized the contents of the cell, then typed **Percent** (the name of the old style) in the drop-down Style list area and pressed Enter, you would be asked if you wanted to modify the Percent style.

When you redefine a style, all of the other cells formatted with the style change too. In our example, that would mean that all existing and new cells formatted with the Percent style would be italicized.

The Style dialog box lets you see which style elements are used by the style—number formats, borders, patterns, and so on. It also lets you change these style elements by clicking the Modify button and visiting the appropriate tabs in the resulting Format Cells dialog box, shown in Figure 15.4.

FIGURE 15.4

The Format Cells
dialog box

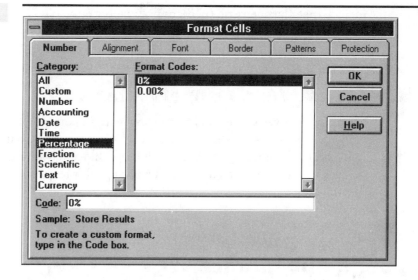

For example, to change font characteristics, click on the Font tab, shown in
Figure 15.5, and make the desired choices there:

Use the entry boxes, scrolling lists, and drop-down menus to pick font characteristics. No X next to an item indicates that the style currently does not

FIGURE 15.5

The Font tab in the
Format Cells dialog
box

include that characteristic (perhaps no superscripting has been specified, for instance). To include previously unspecified style attributes, click to place an X in the appropriate option box.

How Styles Affect Manual Formatting

Styles usually overrule manual formatting, with important exceptions. For example, if you use a style that specifies bold characters, cells that were originally not bold but were italicized will *become* bold and *not* italicized. You can go back to cells thus altered and manually apply (or reapply) characteristics like italics.

Format Codes Alter a Number's Appearance

As you've seen, you can use *styles* to alter a number's appearance (add commas, dollar signs, and so forth). Styles use *format codes* to determine how numbers will appear. You can apply format codes directly to selected cells without using styles. And, you can alter existing format codes or create your own. Let's take a look.

Applying Format Codes

Excel comes with a variety of format codes organized by type. You can get a sense of this from the list of code categories back in Figure 15.4. There are codes used to format percentages, other codes for currency, etc. To apply a code:

1. Select the cell or cells to be reformatted.

2. Choose Format ➤ Cells or use the Ctrl+1 shortcut.

3. Bring the Number tab forward if it's not already on top by clicking on the Numbers tab. Your screen will look something like Figure 15.4.

4. Click on a category to display the available format choices (Percentage is shown in Figure 15.4).

5. Double click on a format code to use it, or click once on the name of the code, and once on OK.

6. Reformat the columns if necessary to accommodate changes in the numbers' widths.

Creating and Modifying Format Codes

Suppose you want to display numbers in a format not offered by Excel. For example, suppose you wanted to format dollars with dollar signs before and the letter K after to signify thousands of dollars, like this:

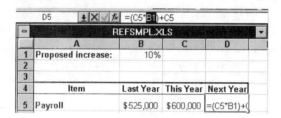

Pretty slick, huh? Here are the steps.

1. Select the cell or cells to be formatted if you like.

2. Choose Cells... from the Format menu or use the Ctrl+1 shortcut.

3. Bring the Number tab forward if it's not already on top by clicking on the Number tab.

4. Click on a category to display the available format choices.

5. Either select an existing format to use as a jumping-off place, or type your own in the Code text box. In Figure 15.6, I've selected a standard currency format and added the letter K and a leading space twice.

6. When you are finished, click OK. The new format codes will be saved in the list and you'll be returned to the worksheet. Selected cells should be formatted to your liking. If not, repeat steps 1–5 until there is joy. You can delete unwanted attempts by selecting them in the dialog box and using the Delete button.

Excel

FIGURE 15.6

Creating a new currency format in Format Cells dialog box

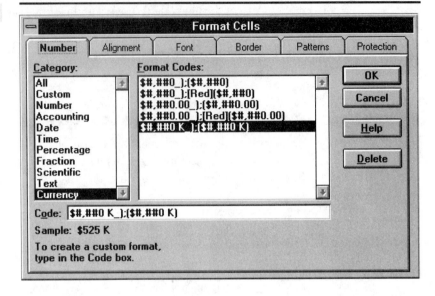

To learn more about the various formatting symbols (#, 0, ?, _, etc.) check the Number Format Codes topic in on-line help or crack the Excel-specific books.

WARNING

Remember, you are altering the <u>appearance</u> of the numbers here, not their actual values. Thus, if you format the number $1.00 with our K format trick, it will look like $1 K. There's a big difference! Unless you are consistent in the entry and formatting of numbers you can get into big trouble this way.

format Painter Speeds Format Copying

The Format Painter lets you quickly copy a cell's format (size, color, bold, format codes, etc.), then spread it around elsewhere. For example, suppose we wanted to use our new "K style" number formatting in the rest of the Payroll example. Here are the steps:

1. Select the cell containing the desired formatting (click in it).

2. Click upon the Format Painter button. It looks like a paintbrush.

3. The mouse pointer will change to a cross and a paintbrush. Drag with it to select the cells in need of reformatting:

Last Year	This Year	Next Year
$525 K	$ 600.00	$ 660.00
$ 50.00	$ 70.00	$ 77.00
$ 6.00	$ 10.00	$ 11.00
$ 581.00	$ 680.00	$ 748.00

4. Release the mouse button.

5. Paint other cells, as needed

6. Adjust column widths if necessary.

Copying Styles to and from Other Workbooks

You can either copy individual styles from one workbook to another or you can merge all of the styles from one workbook with those of another. In either case, start by opening and (optionally) displaying both workbooks. (Use the Arrange command on the Window menu to tile both workbooks if you like.)

With both workbooks open, to copy a single format from one workbook to another, copy a cell containing the desired style to the Clipboard, then switch to the destination workbook and paste the cell into it. The copied style will appear in the Style list and therefore become available in the destination workbook. If you don't want to paste a cell's contents—just formats, for instance—you can choose the Paste Special command from the Edit menu and specify Formats only.

To copy *all* of the styles from one workbook to another, do the following (practice on *copies* of important workbooks):

1. Switch to the workbook that is to receive the new styles (click in it or pick it from the Window menu).

2. Open the Style dialog box (use the Style command on the Format menu).

Excel

3. Use the Merge button to open the Merge Styles dialog box.

4. Select the name of the workbook containing the desired styles from the scrollable list in the Merge Styles dialog box.

5. Click OK to merge the styles of the selected workbook with the destination workbook.

Use Care when Merging Styles

Be warned that if the destination workbook and the source workbook have styles with identical names, Excel will want to replace the destination styles with the source styles. Excel will caution you about this and will give you a chance to keep all of the existing styles or to cancel the merge command. You will only be warned *once*—even if you have more than one identical style name!

Deleting Styles

When you delete unwanted styles, all cells formatted with the deleted style revert to the Normal style for the worksheet. You will not be able to use Undo here. Use care or, better still, save your worksheet before deleting styles, so that you can close the clobbered worksheet without saving and then reload the unmodified version. To delete styles, do the following:

1. Open the Style dialog box (use the Style command on the Format menu).

2. If necessary, select the name of the style you want to delete from the drop-down Style Name list in the Style dialog box.

3. Click the Delete button. Use care since you won't be asked to confirm the deletion.

Changing Font Sizes and Attributes

Use the Formatting toolbar's drop-down font name and size lists for their obvious intended purposes. Use the Bold, Italic, and Underline buttons to add those attributes to your worksheet.

For more advanced formatting options, use the Font tab in the Format Cells dialog box (reached with Format ➤ Cells or the Ctrl+1 shortcut).

Adjusting Alignment

A number of alignment buttons are available on the Standard and Formatting toolbars. Use these to shift the horizontal position of cell contents flush left, flush right, or to the center of cells. In addition, the Alignment tab in the Format Cells dialog box offers the choices shown in Figure 15.7.

From here you can also specify how text and numbers will be positioned vertically within selected cells. For instance, you can center short type in tall rows. Text can be flipped with the Orientation buttons, so that it runs top to bottom or bottom to top within cells. The buttons illustrate their effects. The Wrap option, also found here, is discussed next.

FIGURE 15.7

The Alignment tab in the Format Cells dialog box

Excel

Wrapping Text in Cells

Words can be made to wrap to fit the width of columns. Choose the Wrap Text option in the Alignment tab of the Format Cells dialog box.

Centering Text across Columns

Sometimes you'll need to position a cell's contents to float across more than one column. Figure 15.8 illustrates this concept.

1. Activate the cell you want to float.

2. Drag to select adjacent cells in the columns of interest, as shown in Figure 15.9. Don't AutoFill by mistake.

3. Click the Center Across Selection button, shown here, on the Standard toolbar. Alternatively, you can use the Center Across Selection option in the Alignment tab of the Format Cells dialog box. The text will center itself across the cells. Thereafter, if you change column widths, the text recenters properly.

FIGURE 15.8

Sometimes you will want to float a cell's contents over multiple columns.

FIGURE 15.9

Select the cells in which you want text to float, then click the Center Across Selection button.

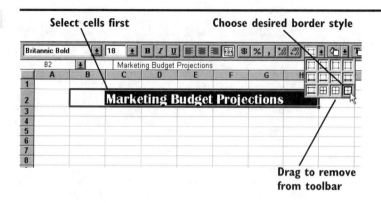

Select cells first

Choose desired border style

Drag to remove from toolbar

Using Border Buttons and Commands

Borders can be used to set apart related worksheet sections and to emphasize totals and subtotals. Or use them just for decoration, to enhance the worksheet's appearance.

Borders can be created using buttons on the Formatting toolbar:

1. Start by selecting the cell or cells you wish to embellish.

2. To outline selected cells with a border on the four extreme sides, simply click the Border button arrow, shown here, on the Formatting toolbar. The keyboard shortcut is Ctrl-Shift-&.

3. Pick the desired border setting by pointing to the desired border style in the small palette containing numerous border choices, shown in Figure 15.10.

You can drag the palette off of the toolbar and leave it displayed if you wish. This is handy if you will be creating numerous borders.

Excel

FIGURE 15.10

Click on the arrow
to see the border
choices, then click to
pick one.

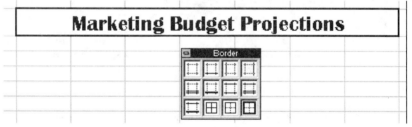

You can also construct custom borders in the Border tab of the Format Cells
dialog box using many of the same techniques you learned in Microsoft Word.

1. Select the cells you wish to pretty up.

2. Open the Style dialog box and click Modify.

3. Click the Border tab, shown in Figure 15.11.

4. Click to pick a border element (left, right, etc.).

5. Pick line types (thick, thin, single, double, or whatever).

FIGURE 15.11

The Border tab in
the Format Cells
dialog box

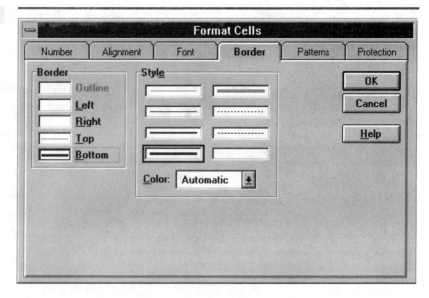

6. Repeat steps 4 and 5 until you are satisfied.

7. Click OK.

To remove all borders from a selected range or cell, use the Ctrl-Shift-under-
line (_) keyboard shortcut, or choose the No Borders choice in the Borders
palette.

Changing Colors and Shading

You can change the color of selected text, cell shading, and other items with
the Color button and Text Color button (and their drop-down palettes) found
on the Formatting toolbar, shown in Figure 15.12.

FIGURE 15.12

The Color drop-
down palette on the
Formatting toolbar

Excel

In addition, you can use the Patterns tab in the Format Cells dialog box, shown in Figure 15.13. Watch the sample in the dialog box while you fritter away.

FIGURE 15.13

Select cells to fill with patterns, then pick from the drop-down list of samples.

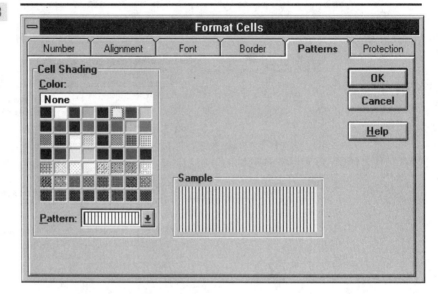

Inserting and Removing Page Breaks

Excel makes page break decisions automatically, but sometimes you'll want to force new pages elsewhere. Do this by activating the cell beneath and to the right of where you want a page break, then choose Set Page Break from the Insert menu. Dark dashed lines will mark the new page breaks. Figure 15.14 illustrates this.

To remove breaks, activate the cell below and to the right of the break lines and choose Remove Page Break, the command that replaces Page Break on the Insert menu.

FIGURE 15.14

Use the Insert ➤ Page
Break command to
insert page breaks
above and to the left
of the active cell.

Vertical break

Horizontal break

**The position of the active cell
determines the position of the break**

Hiding Rows and Columns

You can hide rows or columns without destroying their contents, then reveal
them later when you want to see or edit them.

1. Select the row(s) or column(s) you want to hide.

2. Choose the appropriate Hide and Unhide commands on the Format
   menu's Row and Column choices, shown in Figure 15.15.

You can also play hide-and-seek with your mouse, but it takes a steady hand
and some practice. If it's morning and you haven't had your second cup of coffee yet, forget it.

To hide rows with the mouse, select the row or rows of interest:

1. Place the mouse pointer beneath the heading of the row or rows you
   want to hide. For instance, if you want to hide rows 3 and 4, select
   both rows.

2. Point beneath the appropriate number at the left edge of the worksheet.

3. You'll see the pointer shape that indicates your ability to change row
   height.

Excel
CHAPTER 15

FIGURE 15.15

The Hide command is highlighted.

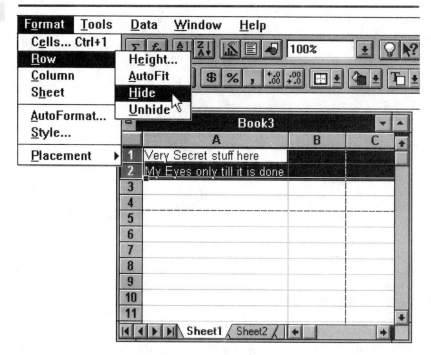

4. Drag up until the rows are so thin that they disappear. The line between the visible and invisible row labels will become darker than the rest, and the row numbers will no longer be consecutive (row numbers will jump from 1 to 5, for instance).

Use the same basic approach to hide columns, but drag to the right on column letters. To bring back hidden rows or columns, slowly move the pointer over the dark lines in row or column labels (indicating hidden rows or columns). Watch the pointer carefully. At some position, the dark bar between the two arrowheads will split, indicating that you can drag the rows or columns back to a useful size. Alternatively, you can select the columns or rows to either side of the hidden column or row and use the Unhide button in the Column Width and Row Height dialog boxes.

Time to Experiment

Go forth and multiply (and divide and format). You now have the basic skills needed to create and format powerful, great-looking spreadsheets. The chapters that follow deal with tools for managing large projects, charting, and other advanced topics. This would be a good point to create some of your own worksheets before continuing.

Excel

16

Organizing
Large Projects

Projects take many shapes and sizes. Sometimes you'll need to deal with a few big worksheets. Other times you'll need to work with lots of little ones. Excel offers a number of features to help you view, edit, navigate, and consolidate big projects. This chapter introduces you to them. You'll read about naming things in such a way that you can quickly locate and refer to them. You'll see how to split windows to make it easier to view widely separated parts of a document. Just as outlines can help you view and rearrange Word documents, they can also change the way you look at big Excel worksheets. And you'll see how those tabs at the bottom of workbook windows can help you keep related Excel information together, within easy reach.

Using Names

You can name ranges of cells, formulas, and more. Sometimes naming things this way makes it easier to refer to them. The names appear in the Name Box on the left side of the formula bar. Named items are also easy to find with Excel's Go To command on the Edit menu, or by using the F5 (Go To) function key.

Names can be up to 255 characters long. The first character in a name must be a letter or the underline character. Names cannot look like cell references (A$1, for instance).

You can *define* names yourself, or let Excel *create* names for you by using labels in your worksheets. Let's start by seeing how Excel can automatically *create* names.

Asking Excel to Create Names

Excel can create names for selected cells based on things like row and column headings. Take a look at Figure 16.1.

In this instance, Excel will use the selected column labels for columns A, B, C, and D, plus the selected labels for Rows 2, 3, 4, 5, and 6 to name ranges of cells *automatically*. Excel ignores empty cells when naming this way, and it "cleans up" names so that they conform to naming rules. Therefore, the resulting ranges will be labeled Air_related, California, Hawaii, Land_related, Rockies, and Water_related. Here are the general steps:

1. Select cells you wish to name. (Include their headings.)

2. Choose Name from the Insert menu.

Excel can use row and column labels to automatically name things.

Select the cells, then tell Excel where to get the names it will be creating

By clicking on the name of a range (in the Name Box's drop-down list), you can highlight the entire range

Excel

3. Choose Create from the resulting submenu. You'll see the Create Names dialog box illustrated in Figure 16.1.

4. Choose the label locations you wish to use as names. Excel will use those labels to assign names automatically, modifying them as necessary to fit the naming rules.

5. Repeat the steps as often as necessary to name different areas. The F4 (Repeat) shortcut works great for this.

Defining Names Yourself

Suppose you wanted to define something manually—like the range of cells containing all of the listing numbers in our example. You could use the following general steps:

1. Select cells you wish to name (just the listing numbers, in our example).

2. Choose Name from the Insert menu.

3. Choose Define from the resulting submenu.

4. You'll see the Define Name dialog box illustrated in Figure 16.2.

5. Excel proposes a name if it can. In this case it cannot.

6. Click OK to accept the proposed name, or type a name (**All_Listings** in this example), then click OK.

7. Repeat the steps as often as necessary to name different areas. The F4 (Repeat) shortcut works great for this.

  It is very important to thoroughly test your work when using names, since they won't always do what you'd expect. Consider, for example, how we selected ranges when naming them in this last example. If we later add numbers in row 3, they'll be included in the Hawaii, California, and Rockies ranges, but not in the All_Listings range. Why? Because we didn't include row 3 in our selection when we named that range. Folks lose their jobs when things like this happen in the real world.

FIGURE 16.2

Select cells you wish to name, then name them using the Define Name dialog box.

Seeing Named Items

It is important to understand what's included in a named item or range. The easy way to do that is to pick a name from the Name Box's drop-down list on the left side of the formula bar. Picking a name causes Excel to select (high-light) the named item or range in the worksheet. For instance, Figure 16.3 shows what happens when Hawaii is chosen.

Referring to Ranges by Name

Once you've created named items, they can be used in many ways. For instance, you can create equations like the one in cell B8, as illustrated in Figure 16.4.

As you can see, the formula

```
=B4/SUM(All_Listings)
```

Excel

Excel

CHAPTER 16

FIGURE 16.3

Excel highlights named
items and areas when
you choose them from
the drop-down list
on the equation bar.

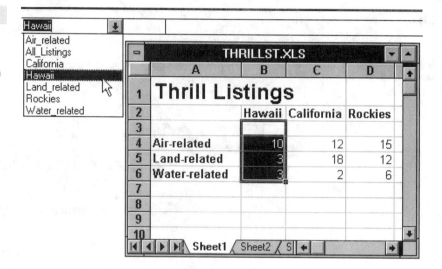

FIGURE 16.4

Named areas can be
used in equations, as
illustrated here in the
formula bar.

works in place of the traditional

`=B4/SUM(B4:D6)`

or the awkward

`=B4/(B4+C4+D4+B5+C5+D5+B6+C6+D6)`

It reads better, too, don't you think?

While our example is obviously overkill, you can see how constructing formulas this way in complex worksheets might make it easier to create and troubleshoot complex projects.

Inserting Names

You can type names out longhand, or visit the Paste Name dialog box reached via the Insert menu:

But the easiest way to insert names is to pick them from the Name Box's drop-down list in the formula bar. Here are the general steps for all three techniques:

1. Activate the cell where you want to insert the name.

2. Construct the equation, pausing whenever a name is required.

3. Either type the name, pick it from the Name Box's drop-down list, or open the Paste Name dialog box (Insert, Name, Paste...) and double-click on the name in the list. Excel will place the name at the insertion point in the equation.

4. Finish the equation (inserting other names if you wish).

Excel

Splitting Windows and Fixing Titles

Excel document windows can be split into two or four separately scrollable panes that make it easy to see different parts of your worksheet at the same time. Figure 16.5 illustrates this.

Use the *Split* command on the Window menu to create four panes in the neighborhood of the active cell. Each pane will have its own scroll tools, which can be used to position each pane's contents independently. Use the *Remove Split* command that appears in Excel's Window menu whenever a window is split.

Alternately, you can drag to create panes exactly where you want them. Here's how: in a single-pane worksheet, there are thick black lines just above the top of the vertical scroll arrow and to the right of the right horizontal scroll arrow. These are called *split boxes*. Drag on either one or both to create

---

FIGURE 16.5

Split an Excel window into panes to see widespread parts of your project simultaneously.

		C	D	E	F	G	H	I	J	K	
66	Air	131.4250	D		Aeronautical Radio, Inc.						
67	Air	131.5000	D		Aeronautical Radio, Inc.						
68	Air	131.5250	D		Aeronautical Radio, Inc.						
69	Air	131.5500	D		Aeronautical Radio, Inc.						
70	Air	131.6000	D		Aeronautical Radio, Inc.						
71	Air	131.6250	D		Aeronautical Radio, Inc.						
72	Air	131.6500	D		Aeronautical Radio, Inc.						
73	Air	131.7000	D		Aeronautical Radio, Inc.						
74	Air	131.7250	D		Aeronautical Radio, Inc.						
75	Air	131.7500	D		Aeronautical Radio, Inc.						
76	Air	131.8000	D		Aeronautical Radio, Inc.						
77	Air	131.8250	D		Aeronautical Radio, Inc.						
78	Air	131.8500	D		Aeronautical Radio, Inc.						
79	Air	131.8750	D		Aeronautical Radio, Inc.						
80	Air	131.9000	D		Aeronautical Radio, Inc.						
81	Air	131.9250	D		Aeronautical Radio, Inc.						
361	Highest	1104.0000									
362											

Split Boxes—Drag to move panes, double-click to remove panes

panes. Double-clicking on a split box removes its pane. The Window menu's Remove Split command also removes panes you've created by dragging.

Outlining Your Worksheets

Excel's *outline* feature lets you expand and collapse large worksheets. For instance, you could create an annual budget containing 12-month totals, monthly, and quarterly subtotals, then collapse it to view and print quarterly subtotals and annual totals. You could collapse it further to show only annual totals. You'll see an example of this in a moment. Moreover, once items have been collapsed, all formatting, cutting, pasting, and similar activities affect all of the subordinate (hidden) detail.

To create outlines, all of the references in your formulas must point in the same direction (for instance, every row's sum ranges should be either left to right or right to left).

Automatic Outlines

Excel will automatically outline for you, or allow you to define your own levels of detail. To outline automatically:

1. Start by selecting any *single* cell in the worksheet.

2. Use the Data ➤ Group and Outline ➤ Auto Outline command as shown in Figure 16.6.

3. Word will look for subtotals, titles, and other recognizable elements, create an outline, and display the worksheet with additional outline tools as illustrated in Figure 16.7.

Viewing, Printing, Promoting, and Demoting

Once you've outlined a document, you'll see outlining tools along the edges of the worksheet, as illustrated in Figure 16.7. (These can be hidden with the Outline Symbols choice in the View tab of the Tools ➤ Options dialog box.)

Excel

FIGURE 16.6

Excel will outline
automatically for you.

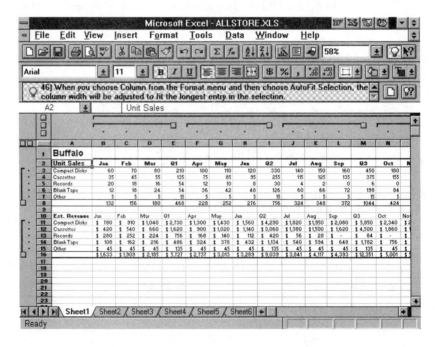

FIGURE 16.7

Use the outline tools to show or hide various levels of detail.

A	E	I	M	Q	R
1 **Buffalo**					
2 Unit Sales	Q1	Q2	Q3	Q4	Totals
3 Compact Disks	210	330	450	570	1560
4 Cassettes	135	255	375	495	1260
5 Records	54	30	6	0	90
6 Blank Tape	54	126	198	270	648
7 Other	15	15	15	15	60
8	468	756	1044	1350	3618
9					
10 Est. Revenue	Q1	Q2	Q3	Q4	Totals
11 Compact Disks	$ 2,730	$ 4,290	$ 5,850	$ 7,410	$ 20,280
12 Cassettes	$ 1,620	$ 3,060	$ 4,500	$ 5,940	$ 15,120
13 Records	$ 756	$ 420	$ 84	$ -	$ 1,260
14 Blank Tape	$ 486	$ 1,134	$ 1,782	$ 2,430	$ 5,832
15 Other	$ 135	$ 135	$ 135	$ 135	$ 540
16	$ 5,727	$ 9,039	$ 12,351	$ 15,915	$ 43,032
17					

In the bottom of Figure 16.6 you saw the worksheet shown at its full level of detail. Row-level and column-level symbols in the upper-left corner of the worksheet tell you that there are two levels of detail in this worksheet. It is possible to have up to eight levels.

Click on the column and row level buttons to show or hide detail. Hidden details don't print.

Manually Outlining

Although automatic outlines are much easier to create, you can use the Utility toolbar to outline manually. Consult the big books and online help for details.

Clearing Outline Structures

If you don't mind keeping the outline levels, but don't want to see the outline symbols, which rob some of your screen space, turn them off using the Ctrl+8 keyboard shortcut, which toggles the display of outline symbols, saving you a trip to the Options dialog box.

Excel

To actually clear (remove) outline levels from a worksheet without otherwise changing the contents of the worksheet, use the Clear Outline command found on the Group And Outline submenu of the Data menu.

Working with Multiple Worksheets

There are many reasons to work with multiple worksheets. You might need to combine departmental budgets into a company-wide total budget, for instance. Or you might have separate and detailed payroll, sales, and other budget worksheets containing totals that need to be included as line items on a summary worksheet for the top brass. Other times colleagues might send you their budgets on disk or over a network, and you need to combine them in order to work with them.

Starting with Excel 5 each new project can have multiple worksheets. That's what the tabs at the bottom of your screen indicate.

If you've ever worked on projects requiring dozens or even hundreds of related worksheets, you'll enjoy Excel's ability to "round up" related files even if they're in different workbooks. Ultimately, you may save a great deal of time as well.

Linking Worksheets

It is possible to *link* the contents of one worksheet with another regardless of whether it is in the same workbook. For instance, if you have a worksheet containing product prices, then decide to create a second worksheet in a different workbook containing unit sales forecasts and revenue projections based on the number of units sold times the prices on the pricing spreadsheet, you could link the two worksheets. Then, whenever you change prices on the pricing worksheet, the revenue forecasts will change on the forecast worksheet. Figure 16.8 shows a simplified example of this process.

Here are the general steps:

1. Start by opening both workbooks, if necessary, and switch to the appropriate worksheets.

FIGURE 16.8

When you use Paste Link, changes on one worksheet are updated on other linked worksheets.

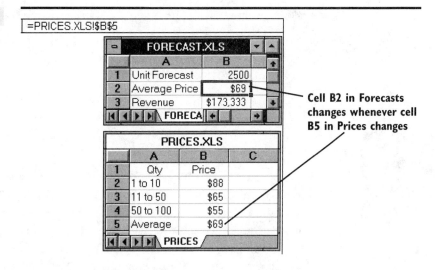

Cell B2 in Forecasts changes whenever cell B5 in Prices changes

2. Select and copy the cell or cells containing the numbers you want to link (cell B5 in the Prices worksheet in our example).

3. Switch to the worksheet where you want to paste the numbers (cell B2 in the Forecast worksheet in our example).

4. Select Edit ➤ Paste Special and choose the Paste Link option. The path to the linked item will appear in the formula bar. Henceforth, any change you make to the Prices worksheet will be reflected on the Forecast worksheet.

If you open a document that references a link (Forecast in our example), but the referenced document (Prices) is *not* open, Excel will ask whether you want to update from the unopened document.

Range names also work for linking (and, remember, you can link things besides numbers—text, graphics, charts, and so on).

Using Multiple Worksheets in a Workbook

When you use the New command (Ctrl+N), Excel 5 always opens a new workbook containing 16 worksheets. (You can change the actual number of worksheets created in new documents in the Option dialog box's General tab.)

To switch from worksheet to worksheet, click on the desired worksheet tab at the bottom of the workbook window, as shown in Figure 16.9. Use the scroll arrows if necessary to see the rest of the tabs:

A WHOLE NEW WAY TO WORK

OLE Tips for Excel

- It's a good idea to name portions of an Excel worksheet that you plan to use as a source when linking or embedding. This way if you insert rows or columns later, they will be included when you update the link. Name the cell range before you link, then open the Links dialog box and edit the link so that it refers to the named area rather than the cell range.

- If you think you'll want to edit worksheet data from within the destination document (a Word document, for example), embed the worksheet cells rather than linking them. Then you can just double-click in Word to work in the spreadsheet.

- It is possible to paste Excel cells into Word without creating a table. When you use the Paste Special command, pick the Un-formatted text option. You can always use Word's Text to Table command later if you like.

- Pasting Excel charts as pictures reduces the file size of the desti-nation file, but you won't be able to double-click on the chart to edit the chart or the related Excel data. When in doubt, embed.

Naming Worksheets and Tabs

To name a worksheet, double-click on its tab. You'll see the Rename Sheet dialog box shown in Figure 16.10. Type any name up to 31 characters includ-ing spaces. The tab will display the new name.

Click on a tab to pick a different worksheet, or on a scroll arrow if necessary to see the desired tab.

Click to see more tabs   Click on a tab to bring the worksheet forward

Double-click on worksheet tabs to rename sheets and their tabs.

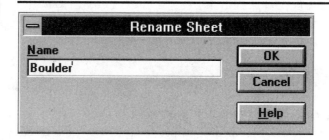

Moving Worksheets within a Workbook

To change the order of sheets in a workbook:

1. Click on the tab you wish to move. The mouse pointer will change shape, and a tiny black triangle will appear as shown here:

2. Drag the tab with the mouse while watching the little black triangle.

3. Release the mouse button when the triangle is pointing at the desired new tab location. The sheet and its tab will move.

Copying Worksheets within a Workbook

It's often handy to copy a worksheet's contents. For instance, you could set up a sample budget on worksheet 1 and then copy it to worksheet 2, worksheet 3, worksheet 4, etc.

Excel

1. Create the first worksheet.

2. Click on the tab for the worksheet you wish to copy.

3. Hold down the Ctrl key. The mouse pointer will change shape (it will look like the Move pointer with a plus sign inside). You'll also see a tiny black triangle like the one you see when moving sheets.

4. Drag the tab with the mouse while watching the little black triangle.

5. Release the mouse button when the triangle is pointing at the desired insertion tab location. Excel will insert a new copy of the worksheet, and uniquely name the new tab:

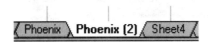

Notice that this adds an additional sheet to your workbook. To change the tab's name, double-click and proceed as previously discussed.

Copying and Moving Worksheets to Other Workbooks

Use the Move or Copy dialog box to copy or relocate selected worksheets to another workbook. Here are the general steps:

1. Open the workbook containing the sheets to be copied or moved.

2. Ctrl-click to select each sheet to be copied or moved. Selected tabs will be lighter than the others.

3. Choose Move or Copy Sheet from the Edit menu.

4. If you want to copy rather than move worksheets, be sure to select the Create a Copy option.

5. Choose the destination book and the desired insertion point as shown in Figure 16.11. To copy or move sheets to a new, as yet unopened workbook, choose *(new book)* from the To Book list.

FIGURE 16.11

Copying or moving
sheets to another
workbook

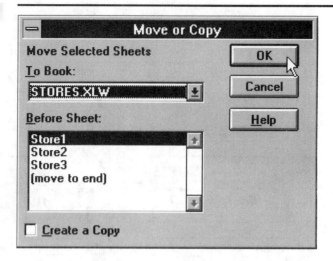

Viewing Multiple Windows

Sometimes it is useful to see more than one sheet or more than one workbook
on-screen. Use these general steps and techniques:

1. Choose New Window from the Excel Window menu for each additional
   window you wish to display.

2. Choose Arrange from the Window menu and make your desires known
   in the Arrange Windows dialog box. (For example, the windows in Figure 16.12 are tiled.) Experiment.

Excel

FIGURE 16.12

Use 3-D cell references to consolidate information from multiple sheets.

| B3 | ▼ | =SUM(Boston:Maui!B3) |

BKSTORE.XLS:2

	A	B	C	D
1				
2	**Boston**	*Plan*	*Actual*	
3	Sales (K)	$10.0	$12.6	
4	Cost (K)	$ 5.0	$ 6.2	
5	**Profit (K)**	$ 5.0	$ 6.4	
6				

◄ ◄ ► ►◄ \ **Boston** / Boulder / Maui /

BKSTORE.XLS:1

	A	B	C	D
1				
2	**Boulder**	*Plan*	*Actual*	
3	Sales (K)	$ 3.5	$ 4.2	
4	Cost (K)	$ 2.1	$ 1.8	
5	**Profit (K)**	$ 1.4	$ 2.4	
6				

◄ ◄ ► ►◄ \ Boston \ **Boulder** / Maui /

BKSTORE.XLS:3

	A	B	C	D
1				
2	**Maui**	*Plan*	*Actual*	
3	Sales (K)	$ 8.2	$ 9.1	
4	Cost (K)	$ 4.8	$ 5.6	
5	**Profit (K)**	$ 3.4	$ 3.5	
6				

◄ ◄ ► ►◄ \ **Maui** / Combined / Sheet2

BKSTORE.XLS:4

	A	B	C
1			
2	**Combined**	**Plan**	**Actual**
3	Sales (K)	$21.7	$25.9
4	Cost (K)	$11.9	$13.6
5	**Profit (K)**	$ 9.8	$12.3
6			

◄ ◄ ► ►◄ \ **Combine** ◄ ►

3. Drag the window borders or corners with your mouse if you wish to fine-tune.

Summarizing Information from Multiple Worksheets

Often, when you have a workbook containing a sheet for each of many offices or departments, or several workbooks containing related information, you might want to create a "top" summary sheet containing company-wide totals. This is often called *summarizing* or *consolidating*. In this book we will provide an overview of this complex topic and a simple example of one consolidation technique. Consult the big books and test your work if you need to consolidate important data!

Defining 3-D References

One way to consolidate information is to create an additional worksheet with equations that sum the data from the others. For instance, suppose you had stores in Boston, Maui, and Boulder. You've created a profit and loss (P&L) statement for each store on a separate sheet in the same workbook. Figure 16.12 illustrates this.

You might decide to create a *fourth* sheet that consolidates the data for the three stores. Here are the general steps:

1. Create the new sheet that will be used to contain the consolidated numbers (perhaps by copying one of the others to save some time and give the project a uniform look).

2. Activate a cell needing an equation in the consolidation sheet (B3 in the lower-right sheet in Figure 16.12).

3. Type an equal sign to begin the equation.

4. Continue the equation until you need to refer to a cell. (We used the SUM function in this example.)

5. When it is time to refer to a cell, click on the tab for the first sheet to be included in the consolidation (let's go with Boston here).

6. Click on the cell to be included in the equation (B3 in this case).

7. Shift-click on the tab for the last sheet to be included in the consolidation (let's go with Maui here).

8. Finish the equation back in the consolidation sheet. It should look like that shown in Figure 16.13.

Excel

FIGURE 16.13

The consolidation sheet showing the formula for cell B3 summing values from two other worksheets.

`=SUM(Boston:Maui!B3)`

BKSTORE.XLS:4

	A	B	C	D	E
1					
2	Combined	Plan	Actual		
3	Sales (K)	$21.7	$25.9		
4	Cost (K)	$11.9	$13.6		
5	**Profit (K)**	$ 9.8	$12.3		
6					
7					

Combined / Sheet2

9. Test the equation. In this example, cell B3 in the consolidated sheet should equal the sum of all of the stores' B3 cells. A change in cell B3 for any of the stores should properly update the consolidation.

10. Copy the working equation to establish other 3-D sums if desired (cells B3 through C5 in our example).

11. Test again, then save your work.

12. From now on, changes in any store's P&L will update the consolidated sheet.

There are many, many variations on this theme. You can use named ranges instead of cell addresses, for instance, and OLE will let you link cells or ranges in other workbooks. Again, check online help and the big books when you get stuck. Check your work carefully.

Printing Tips for Large Excel Projects

Excel's Print dialog box (Ctrl+P, or File ➤ Print) offers choices specific to spreadsheets. For instance, you can choose to print just selected cells, selected sheets, or the entire workbook:

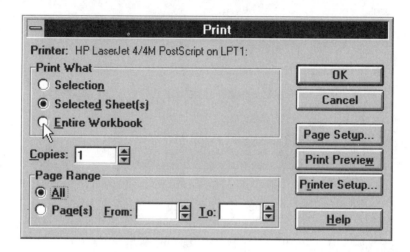

It is possible to have a different page setup for each sheet in a workbook, but that's not usually what you'll want. To change the page setup for a single sheet, click on the worksheet's tab to bring it forward, then choose Page Setup from the File menu.

To affect the page setups for multiple (or all) sheets, Shift-click on the sheet tabs before visiting the Page Setup dialog box.

Use the Scaling and Orientation choices in the Page tab of the Page Setup dialog box to have Excel automatically adjust the size of images so that your work will fit on the desired number of pages.

Excel

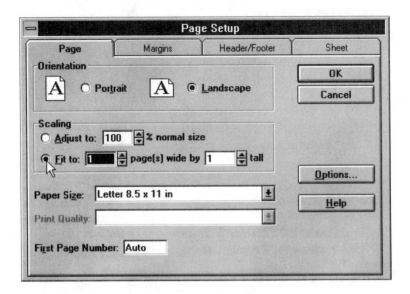

Use the Sheet tab in the Page Setup dialog box (Figure 16.14) to specify printing ranges (using either cell addresses or names). In addition, the Sheet tab lets you specify the printing of repeating rows, columns, and more.

Use Print Preview before beginning large printing jobs. It can be a real time-saver. If you find yourself creating complex reports containing just selected parts of your workbook, it would pay you to explore Excel's Reports features described in online help and in the bigger books.

FIGURE 16.14

The Sheet tab in the Page Setup dialog box lets you specify which rows or columns to repeat from page to page, which elements to include in the printout, and the order in which to arrange multiple worksheets.

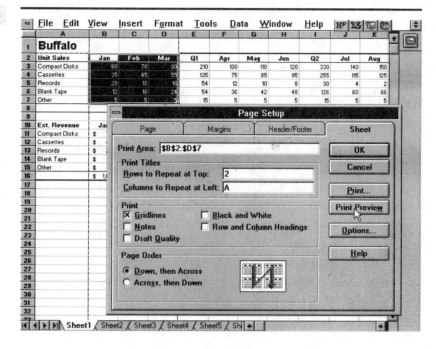

Excel

17

An Introduction
to Functions

Excel's worksheet functions are power tools that help you perform complex computations. Excel has hundreds of functions that facilitate engineering computations, manipulate text, and do much, much more. In addition, Excel offers over four hundred macro functions, which are discussed briefly in Chapter 20. This chapter deals only with *worksheet* functions.

Worksheet functions can often be used by themselves as stand-alone formulas, or they can be built into more complex formulas of your own creation. For instance, the SQRT() function finds the square root of a positive number. In the simplest case, you could type the formula **=SQRT(9)** into a cell and see the results (3). Or you could include the square root function in a more complex formula like **=SQRT(9)*9**.

Functions can often refer to other things in your worksheet. For instance, **=SQRT(A2)** would compute the square root of the contents of cell A2. If you use named items in your worksheets, functions can sometimes refer to them as well. For example, **=SQRT(SPEED)** might be a legal formula if your worksheet contains a positive number named SPEED or some other equation that computed speeds.

Some functions *inspect* things and take actions based on what they find. For example, the function ISNONTEXT() can check a cell and tell you if the cell contains text or not. Other functions *convert* things. The text function LOWER() converts text to all lower case, for instance. The engineering function CONVERT() transforms values from one unit of measure to another (Fahrenheit to Celsius, feet to meters, and so on). Most functions are already installed with Excel. Others (like CONVERT) may need to be installed as *add-ins*. You'll see how that is done later in this chapter.

Parts of a Function

Functions consist of *function names* and (usually) *arguments*. For instance, SQRT is the function name, while the value (the positive number) being evaluated is the argument. As you saw earlier in the square root example, arguments can be values, references, or names. They can also be text, logical values (TRUE and FALSE), or arrays. A function's *syntax* is illustrated by listing in documentation, as well as in Excel's Help windows, all the function's *argument names* in the order they should be used. For example, you might see the functions and their arguments expressed as

`SQRT(number)`

or

`SUM(number1,number2...)`

or

`FV(rate,nper,pmnt,pv,type)`

Notice that in the FV example some of the arguments are bold and others are not. This is how some documentation differentiates between *required* and *optional* arguments. Often, if you don't provide an argument, Excel uses the default argument for that function. For instance, the function

`DOLLAR(number,decimals)`

converts numbers into text with dollar signs and, optionally, decimal places for cents or pennies. The expression **=DOLLAR(10)** would yield $10.00. (Notice the default decimal point and two places for pennies even though no second argument was supplied.) The expression **=DOLLAR(10,1)** would create the text string $10.0, and **=DOLLAR(10,)** would yield $10 (neither decimal point nor pennies). In the first case, leaving out the optional second argument *and the comma* that separates it causes Excel to use the default argument (a decimal point and two places, in this case). In the second example, the comma separates the second argument, which specifies the number of decimal places (1). In the third example, where there is a comma and no second argument, the comma suggests to Excel that there *is* a second argument (an argument specifying neither decimal point nor decimal places). The lesson here is that commas are important in functions, and that sometimes there is a big difference in the results if you delete a comma instead of leaving it and not entering an argument after it.

Excel

You can frequently use *other functions* as arguments. For instance, you could combine the ROUND and SQRT functions to compute the square root of a number, then round the results. The formula

=ROUND(SQRT(A1),2)

would compute the square root of the contents of cell A1, then round the answer to two decimal places.

functions Requiring Add-Ins

Some functions require *add-ins*—additional software (such as a utility program) that is provided with Excel, but not automatically loaded when you run Excel. When you attempt to use functions that require add-ins, Excel loads the add-ins automatically for you. For example, the BESSELI statistical function needs the Analysis ToolPak. If Excel can't load the required add-in, it may be because you chose not to install add-ins when you initially installed Excel on your hard disk. Try rerunning the installer program to add these features.

Online Function Help

If we described each Excel function in detail here, the book's size would double, and its title would need to be changed to *The Not-So-Compact Guide*. Fortunately, you won't need to lug around some six hundred extra pages of function trivia. Excel's extensive online *help* feature and the Function Wizard will let you find and explore just the functions you're interested in. To expedite your searching, worksheet functions have been divided into eleven categories:

- Commands
- Database
- Date and Time
- Engineering
- Financial

- Information
- Logical
- Lookup and Reference
- Mathematical and Trigonometric
- Statistical
- Text

Use the Help menu's Search or Contents commands to get to the Search window shown in Figure 17.1.

For instance, if you want to learn more about the SUM function, you could type SUM in the Search dialog box, then show the topic list and pick the help topic SUM in the scrollable topic list and go to that topic.

If you'd rather browse, start with a general topic like functions, then pick a function category like Financial or Statistical.

FIGURE 17.1

Excel provides extensive online function help, complete with descriptions and examples of the functions at work.

Since some of the help provided for functions is often fairly detailed and complex, you might want to print out the information that you find. Use the Help window's Print Topic feature to do this. Reach it from the File menu within the Help window.

The Function Wizard

Excel's Function Wizard greatly simplifies the use of functions. It leads you through the necessary steps, shows the results as you work, and even provides examples of the functions in use.

1. Start by activating the cell where you want to paste the function.

2. Begin the formula with an equal sign (=), and place the insertion point where you want to insert the function.

3. Click the Function button on the Standard toolbar, or choose Insert ➤ Function. The Function Wizard's Step 1 window appears (see Figure 17.2). The Wizard lists functions within the eleven categories mentioned earlier (Database, Date and Time, and so on). In addition you'll see the *Most Recently Used* and *All* options.

FIGURE 17.2

The Function Wizard
Step 1 window

TIP The keyboard shortcut for the Function Wizard is Shift+F3.

4. Pick a category from the list on the left, then scroll in the list on the right to find the desired function.

5. Click to pick the function. Its name is displayed in the Name Box on the formula bar and its name and arguments show near the bottom-left corner of the Paste Function dialog box.

6. Read the Wizard's description of the function to be sure it's the one you want.

7. Click the Next button and you will see the second Wizard dialog box (see Figure 17.3). Here you see a list of arguments that are required and possibly some that are optional (and labeled as such). The arguments are explained on-screen, and the Help button provides real-life examples.

 NOTE Each dialog box is different and depends upon the function for its appearance and content. For instance, SQRT has only one argument, while PV has many.

8. You can type directly in the Wizard's entry boxes or use your mouse to point to cells containing the data you wish to use as arguments.

FIGURE 17.3

The Function Wizard
Step 2 dialog box

Excel

> **TIP** Entries can be the actual data (like the number 90), or cell addresses (like A1), or names (like SALES), or even other functions.

9. As you work, the Wizard will show the results of its calculations in the Value area at the top right corner of the dialog box.

10. Click Finish when your formula is complete. As you can see in Figure 17.4, when you click Finish, the Wizard pastes the function into the active cell and displays the results of the current arguments in the cell. You'll see the equation in the formula bar.

FIGURE 17.4

A function at work

An equation containing a function and an argument

The cell containing the equation and displaying the answer

The cell containing the data for the argument

Examples of Functions by Category

The best way to learn about functions is to experiment with them. Here are a few examples to get you started.

Date and Time Functions

Some of the Date and Time functions simply *return* the current date and/or time. Others do date-and-time math. Let's first look at a function that finds and reports the current time—the NOW() function. When you use it, NOW() inserts (returns) a new serial number corresponding to the current date and time whenever the worksheet is recalculated.

For example, if you simply paste the formula **=NOW()** into a cell, it will display the current date followed by the current time, then update the cell's contents every time the worksheet is recalculated (and *only* when it is recalculated).

The actual *appearance* of cells containing the NOW() or other Date and Time functions can be changed by using different date and time *format codes* found in the *Number Format* dialog box, reached from the Format menu. For instance, Excel's **Date** format will display date and time in the format

```
m/d/yy h:mm
```

or in a number of other variations with or without the time. If you want to see only the *time* portion of a date serial number, format the cell(s) with one of five predefined Time formats, or create your own.

Other Date and Time functions *compute* things using date serial numbers. For instance, the DAYS360 function computes the number of days between two dates assuming a 360-day year (used by many accounting folks).

When you do any kind of date math, check your work very, very carefully. It is quite easy to produce technically correct answers that are not the ones you need. For instance, when computing working days, Excel does not automatically know that December 25th is a holiday for many. Your equations will need to take things like this into consideration.

Engineering Functions

Engineering functions are available, but require the Analysis ToolPak add-in macro, which you will probably need to install manually (i.e., get out your installation disks) if you didn't opt to install it when you first installed Office. Consult online help and the big books for details.

Financial Functions

Excel's many financial functions are pretty well documented with online help. Many of them can be used together, or can be included as arguments, one within the other.

Here's an example of one way to use *PMT*, Excel's payment function. Officially, this function "Returns the periodic payment of an annuity based on constant payments and a constant interest rate." In other words, it will tell

Excel

you what your payments will be, given the loan amount, number of payments, and a fixed rate of interest. The function's syntax is

```
PMT(rate,nper,pv,fv,type)
```

Figure 17.5 illustrates PMT at work.

FIGURE 17.5

PMT is one of many useful financial functions.

`=PMT(B2/12,B3,B4)`

PMT.XLS

	A	B
1	**Loan payment calculator**	
2	Interest Rate	10.50%
3	Number of Payments	360
4	Loan Amount	$100,000
5	Monthly Payments	($914.74)
6		

PMT

Rate is the interest rate *per period*. For instance, if you borrow at an annual fixed interest rate of 10.5% and then make *monthly* payments, the interest rate is 10.5% divided by 12. That explains the division portion of the formula in Figure 17.5.

The argument *nper* needs the *total* number of payments. Thus, if you are borrowing for 30 years, and make monthly payments, you'll make 30*12 or 360 payments. *Pv* is the present value, or total amount that the series of payments is worth now—the loan amount, in this case. Notice that in our example the optional *fv* (future value) and *type* arguments were omitted. Future value is a desired cash balance after the last payment is made. *Type* is either a 0 (zero) or 1. Omitting the *type* argument or entering 0 indicates that you will make payments at the end of each period. Entering 1, on the other hand, tells Excel that the payments will be made at the beginning of the period.

Related financial functions include FV, IPMT, NPER, PPMT, PV, and RATE as separate functions.

Information Functions

Some functions inspect things and report back. For example, ISNONTEXT() will let your formulas know if a cell entry is not text. Other information functions can check things external to Excel, like the amount of RAM in your computer, or which DOS version you are using. Figure 17.6 shows INFO() at work. Its syntax is **INFO(type)**.

Cells B1 through B13 each have the same formula that refers to corresponding cells in column A, which contain the arguments that produce the results you see.

FIGURE 17.6

The INFO function can tell you much about your computer, Excel, and files in use.

```
| =INFO(A2)
```

	A	B
	INFOFUN.XLS	
1	**Argument**	**Results**
2	directory	C:\EXAMPLES\
3	memavail	18,360,096
4	memused	115,712
5	totmem	18475808
6	release	5.0
7	recalc	Automatic
8	release	5.0
9	numfile	1
10	origin	$A:$A$1
11	recalc	Automatic
12	system	pcdos
13	osversion	DOS Version 6.20

INFOFUN

Logical Functions

You use logic all the time. Chances are, you say things like "If the fruit at the market looks good, please pick up some peaches or grapes, if grapes are less than a dollar a pound." You can use logic in Excel, too. Take the IF function demonstrated in Figure 17.7. Its syntax is

```
IF(logical_test,value_if_true,value_if_false)
```

541

Excel
CHAPTER 17

FIGURE 17.7

Excel's IF function tests for conditions and does different things based on what it finds.

`=IF(B3>B2,(B3-B2),"Check OD")`

MPGLOGIC.XLS

	A	B
1		*Truck 1*
2	Starting Odometer	100
3	Ending Odometer	90
4	**Miles Travelled**	Check OD
5		
6	**Cost Per Gallon**	$1.35
7	**Gallons Used**	12.2
8	**Miles Per Gallon**	#VALUE!
9		
10	*Cost Per Mile*	#VALUE!

MPGLOGIC

The equation for cell B4 displays the message text only if the logical test is false

In this example, the IF() function checks to see if the ending odometer reading is greater than the starting reading. If it isn't, chances are that the user has made a typographical error when entering readings. Or perhaps the odometer has reached its limit and "rolled over" to start again at zero. If the readings look okay, the IF function causes Excel to subtract the beginning from the ending readings (B3–B2). If there seems to be an error, the function displays text in the cell (Check OD).

Lookup and Reference Functions

Like explorers, Lookup and Reference functions go to places that you send them and return with answers. They can be used to create invoices that look up and insert different unit prices based on quantities purchased, for instance. These features can inspect *rows*, *columns*, or *arrays*. Take the simple example in Figure 17.8, for instance.

The INDEX() function in Figure 17.8 has been asked to go to the array bounded by cell addresses A1 through D4, then get the value stored in the cell two rows down and three columns across.

Lookup and Reference functions can refer to ranges, names, specific cell addresses, or row and column counts.

FIGURE 17.8

Use Lookup and
Reference functions to
find an bring back
information

Math and Trig Functions

You've already seen several of the Mathematical functions in action—
SQRT() and SUM(), for example. There are many others, enough to make an
eighth-grade math teacher weep with joy. Most are quite straightforward, and
well documented with online help. Math and Trig functions can refer to cell
references, names, or plain old numbers.

Two of the Math and Trig functions simply produce *numbers* whenever a worksheet recalculates. RAND() produces evenly distributed random numbers
greater than or equal to 0 (zero) and less than 1 each time you recalculate—
handy if you play the lottery or need to check probabilities. The PI() function
inserts 3.141592654.

Statistical Functions

Pollsters and statisticians will want to check out the many statistical functions, from AVDEV() to ZTEST().

Text Functions

To manipulate or analyze strings of text in cells, use text functions. For example, CLEAN() will strip away any nonprinting characters stored in a cell.

Excel

UPPER( ) converts text to all uppercase. DOLLAR( ) converts numbers to their spelled-out dollar equivalents and formats them in currency format.

Error Messages from Functions

When you leave out or misuse arguments in functions, you will sometimes see cryptic error messages like **Error in formula**, or a message like **#NAME?** or **#NUM!** will appear in the cell containing the flawed argument.

It is common to get messages like these when you work with names or text strings as arguments. Text strings *must* be enclosed in quotation marks, while names (references to areas, for instance) must *not* be in quotes. For instance, suppose you are using a math function like SQRT. If you enter the formula argument **=SQRT(SALES)**, Excel expects to be able to find a named numeric value or range of cells in your worksheet called SALES. If it can't, you'll get the message **#NAME?** in the cell containing the formula. If you *do* have a positive numeric value named SALES, the formula will use its contents as the function's argument. If the value of SALES is negative, you'll see the error message **#NUM!**. Suppose you accidentally enclose the name SALES in quotes, then try to use it as an arithmetic argument. The expression **=SQRT("SALES")** will produce the error message **#VALUE!**, since SQRT needs a numeric value to do its thing, and material in quotes is treated as *text*.

To Learn More about Functions

There is clearly much more to know about Excel's functions. While you can learn a lot by experimenting and exploring Excel's online help, you may also benefit from seeing them all in one place—for which you should check out the *Microsoft Excel Function Reference* (at 500-plus pages) shipped with the program. Or for a tutorial approach to the entire topic of functions, check out *Mastering Excel 5 for Windows* by Thomas Chester (SYBEX, 1994).

18

Excel's
Chart Features

xcel helps you create charts in two or three dimensions based on data in a worksheet. You can take almost complete control over every aspect of your chart's appearance with Excel's Chart toolbar and menu choices, or you can let Excel's ChartWizard make most of the decisions for you.

Once you've created a chart, you can print it, hide it, spell check it, modify it, or even include it in your non-Excel projects (such as Word or PowerPoint documents).

Whenever you change data in a worksheet, Excel will update (or at least offer to update) charts that are linked to the changed data.

Chart Parts and Terminology

It's possible to fumble along without knowing the names of Excel's chart parts, and there is plenty of on-line help available while you create and edit charts. But you'll be much more productive if you take a moment to understand just a few concepts and terms.

Chart Data Series

A *chart data series* is a collection of *related* values that are plotted on the chart. For instance, in the chart in Figure 18.1 there are two one-data series—the numbers 300, 907.7, and 3300 make up one data series, while 133.8, 355.4, and 808.9 make up the other series.

FIGURE 18.1

Take a moment to learn the various names of chart parts and the concepts behind them.

Chart Wizard button

Tear-off palette

Chart toolbar

Category names

Data series markers

Legend

Data Markers

Data markers are the bars, pie wedges, dots, pictures, or other elements used to represent a particular data point (a single value in a series). For instance, the six shaded columns in Figure 18.1 are each separate data markers.

When charts have more than one data series, the markers for each series usually look different. This is also illustrated in Figure 18.1, where the consumer debt columns are one color (or shade of gray, or pattern) while government debt columns are another.

It is also possible to use different *types* of markers for different series in the same chart. You might, for instance, use *columns* for one series and *lines* for another. Think of data markers as the columns, bars, pie wedges, lines, and other elements used to represent values on a chart.

Axes

An axis is a reference line denoting one of the dimensions of a chart. Excel can plot in up to three axes: X, Y, and Z. Usually the X-axis runs horizontally (left to right) and the Y-axis runs vertically (bottom to top). For instance, in Figure 18.1 the years run along the X-axis and the billions of dollars run along the Y-axis. In three-dimensional charts, the Z-axis runs vertically, and the X- and Y-axes are at angles to display perspective.

Category Names

Category names usually correspond to worksheet labels for the data being plotted along the X-axis (horizontally along the chart). For instance, in Figure 18.1 the category names are 1970, 1980, and 1990. ChartWizard identifies and includes category names when it creates a new chart. Some chart types (like bar charts) place category names on the Y-axis.

Chart Data Series Names

Chart data series names usually correspond to worksheet labels for the data being plotted on the Y-axis. For instance, in Figure 18.1 the chart has two data series names, one for each series. Data series names are usually displayed in a box (called a *legend*) alongside a sample of the color, shade, or pattern used for each data series. ChartWizard automatically identifies category names and creates legends.

Tick Marks and Grid Lines

Tick marks are short lines that intersect an axis to separate parts of a series scale or category. You can also add optional, longer grid lines in any of a chart's dimensions using the Grid Lines choice on the Chart window's Chart command. Horizontal grid lines are illustrated in Figure 18.1.

Chart Text

The ChartWizard automatically adds text for things like chart and data labels. It is also possible to add your own text, like text boxes containing notes. Chart text is discussed later in the chapter, because by now you must be itching to create a chart. Let's cut to the chase.

Instant Charts with the ChartWizard

ChartWizard "looks" at the data you've selected to plot. It also "watches" as you drag to define the size and shape of the desired chart area. Next, it offers you a number of chart styles, and even lets you define chart titles. Faster than you can say, "Next year let's reduce the deficit," you'll have a great-looking chart. Here are the steps for a simple column chart, plus some insights into the other options you'll encounter along the way.

Starting and Assisting the Wizard

1. Start by creating a worksheet containing the data you wish to chart. In Figure 18.2 the cells A1 through D3 contain the necessary data and labels for a multiseries chart.

2. Select the data to be included in your chart (probably most easily by dragging to highlight the relevant cells). Don't include empty rows or columns. In the sample chart, cells A1 through D3 are surrounded by marching ants, indicating that they have been selected.

3. Click on the ChartWizard button, shown at the left.

4. Marching ants surround selected cells, and your pointer turns into crosshairs with a little chart trailing it around.

5. Drag with it, as illustrated in Figure 18.2, to define the size and shape of your new chart. To create a square, hold down the Shift key while you drag.

Excel

FIGURE 18.2

Start a worksheet, then let the ChartWizard help you size and shape it.

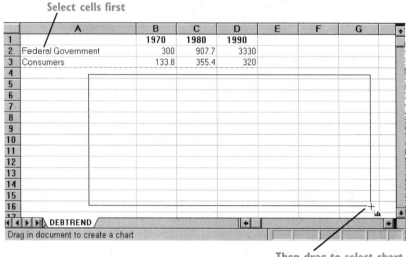

Select cells first

	A	B	C	D	E	F	G
1		1970	1980	1990			
2	Federal Government	300	907.7	3330			
3	Consumers	133.8	355.4	320			
4							
5							
6							
7							
8							
9							
10							
11							
12							
13							
14							
15							
16							

DEBTREND

Drag in document to create a chart

Then drag to select chart size and shape

6. When you release the mouse button, you will see the first of five ChartWizard Step dialog boxes, illustrated here:

ChartWizard - Step 1 of 5

If the selected cells do not contain the data you wish to chart, select a new range now.

Include the cells containing row and column labels if you want those labels to appear on the chart.

Range: =$A$1:$D$3

Help | Cancel | < Back | Next > | Finish

This box shows you the range of the data to be charted and gives you a chance to alter the selected range.

7. Normally, you'll click the Next>> button at this point, taking you to Step 2 of 5.

Picking the Right Chart Type

ChartWizard can create many different *chart types* and many different *formats* for each of those various types. The Step 2 window, shown in Figure 18.3, illustrates all the chart types and proposes one (Column, in our example).

ChartWizard presents samples of 14 chart types and suggests one by highlighting it (Column in this example).

It's usually obvious from the chart samples which ones are best for various projects. You can also just experiment, or read on-line help for each chart type. Use Help's Search feature to find information by chart type name (Radar, for instance).

When you've decided on a chart type, click its sample to highlight it, then click the Next>> button to continue. Don't worry if you pick the wrong type; you can easily change it later.

Once you've chosen a chart type, ChartWizard presents a Step 3 dialog box showing various *formatting* options, which are different for each chart type. Figure 18.4 shows the formatting options for column charts.

Don't lose any sleep over these choices, either. Formats can be tried on later like hats or mittens. Start with the choice the Wizard suggests, and experiment after you've seen those results. Click the Next>> button to continue.

In Step 4, you'll see the beginnings of your chart design in a *Sample Chart* box. If you like what you see, forge ahead. Don't worry about the actual shape of the chart at this point, and don't be alarmed if your labels are temporarily truncated (shortened) or replaced with words like "Series 1" and "Series 2."

TIP Watch the preview as you work. Think about the general presentation of the data at this point. Does the chart help you understand the data? Do you have the appropriate data on the right axis? Do you like the chart type? If not, you can use the <<Back button to return to the earlier steps and pick a different chart type or format. Sometimes the option buttons in Step 4 can improve your chart. Experiment.

FIGURE 18.4

Pick chart formats by clicking, after you've chosen a chart type. Format choices are different for each chart type.

As you'll soon see, the settings proposed by the ChartWizard (and shown in Figure 18.5) are just fine for this sample project.

The Wizard does a pretty good job of picking the right options most of the time. It also shows you your work-in-progress.

You're almost done. Step 5 gives you a chance to add chart titles for the chart itself, and for each axis. You will see the titles appear in the Sample Chart area as you type. The Add a Legend? option turns legends on and off. Figure 18.6 shows the Step 5 dialog box and the resulting chart.

Add optional titles and legends, then click the Finish button.

Excel

If you get cold feet before you click Finish, you can still go back to choose other options. When you click Finish, Excel will create a chart worksheet quicker than you can say "1040EZ" (see Figure 18.7).

FIGURE 18.7

The finished chart

	1970	1980	1990
Federal Government	300	907.7	3330
Consumers	133.8	355.4	320

Creating Charts on Separate Worksheets

Excel 5 is less confusing than earlier versions where charts are concerned. Now, when you create charts, they can either be an integral part of your current worksheet—or they can be separate *chart worksheets* in the workbook that are *linked* to selected worksheet data. ChartWizard usually creates chart objects on your current worksheet. The whole process is simple, clean, and automatic. But if you like, you can place charts on their own worksheets within a workbook.

Separate Chart Worksheets

To create a new chart on a separate worksheet:

1. Select the data to be charted.

2. Choose New (Chart) option from the Insert ➤ Chart ➤ As New Sheet command.

3. You'll see the ChartWizard. Use it as previously described.

4. The wizard will create a new sheet with a tab containing the word Chart and a sequential number.

5. Each new chart you create this way gets its own worksheet in the current workbook, and thus its own tab. Rename tabs just as you do any others—double-click on the tab.

Resizing and Moving Charts

You may need to change the size or shape of a finished chart, which is easily done by dragging the little handles that surround a selected chart like the one shown in Figure 18.8.

FIGURE 18.8

Drag the black handles to resize charts.

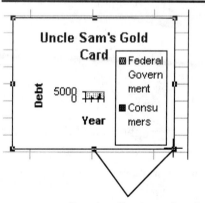

Drag handles to resize chart

Excel

Besides making room for previously cramped labels, resizing charts changes their size and shape, and thus the appearance of the chart markers and other chart elements. Resizing is particularly useful if your data labels are invisible or all scrunched up.

Adding Chart Notes and Arrows

Often it's nice to be able to draw attention to, or explain, certain items on your chart. The boxed note in Figure 18.9 is an example of this.

To create boxed text:

1. Click on the Text Box button, shown at the left. You'll find it in Excel's Standard toolbar.

2. Drag to create the outline of a text box in the approximate desired size and shape.

3. Type and edit your note using text-editing techniques that should be familiar to you by now.

Restyling and Resizing Text Boxes

To resize the box or move it, point and click on any edge. The outline will thicken and you'll see eight size handles. Drag and resize this outline as you do any similar Windows object.

To embellish text, select it and use the Standard toolbar or text-related menu commands. For instance, you might select text and then use the Bold Toolbar button to make it bold.

To change the outline or fill pattern used for the box, or to add a drop-shadow effect like the one shown earlier, double-click on the edge of the text box. You'll see the Format Object dialog box shown in Figure 18.10.

Choose the desired tab and options within the tab. For instance, the example shows the rounded corner and shadow options being added via the Patterns tab.

FIGURE 18.10

The Format Object dialog box lets you add patterns to your objects.

Excel

Drawing and Formatting Arrows

To draw an arrow:

1. Click the Standard toolbar's Drawing button (shown here) to display the Chart toolbar.

2. Click the Drawing Toolbar's Arrow button (it's the darker of the two arrow buttons and is illustrated at the left).

3. When your pointer turns into crosshairs, point where you want the arrow to start and drag to the ending point.

4. When you release the mouse button, an arrow will appear. You can drag either end of selected arrows to reposition them and/or change the length of the line.

Double-click exactly on an arrow to bring up the Format Object dialog box (see Figure 18.11), which lets you define arrow styles, line thicknesses, colors, and much more.

FIGURE 18.11

Using the Format
Object dialog box to
define an arrow.

This changes only the arrow that you've double-clicked upon. To reformat other arrows immediately afterwards, select them (by Shift-clicking, perhaps), and use the Repeat Format Object command on Excel's Edit menu.

Editing Charts

You could either get a life or spend the rest of your life exploring Excel's chart options. These are nearly endless. It's possible to change chart types and formats, embellish text, choose patterns or colors, add grid lines, insert notes with arrows, and much more. Here's the "compact" tour of Excel chartology.

Changing Chart Types and Formats

Once you've created a chart, you can quickly change its type by clicking on the chart type list on the Chart toolbar. This provides a palette of chart choices that can be "torn-off" if you like and moved to a convenient spot on your screen for repeated use (see Figure 18.12).

TIP **The right mouse button reveals a number of chart-related choices if you point and click on a chart. This is often the quickest way to edit charts.**

Changing Data Series Ranges

There are several ways to change the data series ranges. One is to select a chart, then click on the ChartWizard button. You'll see Step 1 of a 2 step procedure, which will let you specify a new data range by typing it or dragging with your mouse. The second step lets you change the appearance of the chart.

Selecting and Editing Chart Components

You can edit specific parts of a chart, like text, grid lines, the shading used for markers, and so on, by either single- or double-clicking on them. For instance, to change the appearance of a chart title you would double-click on it to bring up the Format Object dialog box.

Excel

Excel

FIGURE 18.12

You can tear off palettes of chart choices and place them in convenient spots on your screen.

To edit the content of the title object, click once to select the object, then select the text by dragging or waiting a moment before clicking or double-clicking on the text.

To select a *data series*, click on any marker in the series. For instance, to select the government spending series in your sample chart, you could click on any of the government columns in any year. You will then see a description of the data series in your Formula bar, where you can edit the series definition if you choose.

To select a *single data marker* (like the 1990 Federal borrowing column marker in your sample chart), hold down the Ctrl key while pointing.

To select a *grid line*, click exactly on a grid line. Clicking on any axis selects it. To select just the *plot area* (the columns without their category names, for instance), click in any part of the plot area not occupied by other things like grid lines or markers. There is also a Select Plot Area command on the Chart menu. To select the *entire chart*, click anywhere outside of the plot area, but not on other items like titles or legends. There is also a Select Chart command on the Chart menu.

General Formatting Techniques

Frequently, you can double-click on chart elements to quickly bring up relevant formatting options. If you double-click on a data marker, for instance, you'll soon see a Patterns dialog box that will let you select a new color or pattern for the marker. Double-clicking on a legend takes you to a dialog box where you can rearrange the appearance of the legends, and so on.

The other general editing technique is to select something, then use the appropriate menu commands and Toolbar buttons.

Rotating 3-D Charts

As you experiment with 3-D graphs, you will find that in some instances tall parts of a chart will obscure inner details. Other times you'll just want to tilt or rotate a 3-D object to get a more dramatic effect. In either case, select a 3-D chart, then choose 3-D View from the Format menu. You'll see a dialog box like the one in Figure 18.13. Use the Elevation buttons to tilt the chart and the rotation buttons to rotate it. Use the Apply button to preview your changes without closing the dialog box. OK applies the latest changes and closes the box.

Changing Worksheet Values by Dragging Chart Parts

Here's a neat way to "what-if," or to make your data fit a desired scenario:

1. Create a worksheet and a chart—your Debt worksheet, for instance.

2. Click once on the data marker you wish to resize (the 1990 Federal Government bar in Figure 18.14). Wait a second or two so as not to make Excel think step three is a double-click.

3. Click once again (after that brief pause just mentioned).

Excel

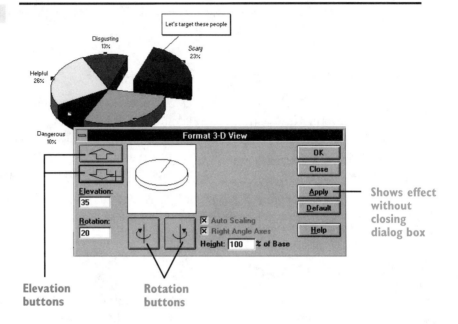

FIGURE 18.13

Try a 3-D chart to reveal inner details or to achieve a special effect.

Shows effect without closing dialog box

Elevation buttons

Rotation buttons

FIGURE 18.14

You can change worksheet cell values by dragging chart parts!

4. Just the data marker you clicked upon will be selected. And it will have some small, black selection markers.

5. When you *drag* on the top center black marker, you will be able to move that selected part of the chart *and* automatically change the numbers in the corresponding worksheet cell(s)!

I can hear the voice of corporate America now… "Jones, make the report say we did 26 percent of our sales in February, truth be damned."

Printing Charts

Unless you tell Excel to do otherwise, it prints all charts. To display but not print an embedded chart, select the chart, then remove the check mark from the Print Object option in the Object dialog box. Reach this box from the Object Properties command on the Format menu.

If a chart is a separate worksheet, print it like any other Excel worksheet. Remember to update it before printing if that's what you want. Use the Page Setup and Print Preview features to format these documents, add headers or footers, and so on.

Deleting Charts

To delete charts, simply select them and press the Del key or use the Clear command on Excel's Edit menu. Undo works here if you act promptly.

Delete separate *chart worksheets* as you would any other unwanted Windows worksheet. (Use Excel's Delete Worksheet command on the File menu.)

Setting the Default Chart Type

ChartWizard and the New Chart (F11) command normally create new charts using the Column chart type and format 1. This is the default *preferred chart style.* You can define a different preferred style this way:

1. Select a chart from the current worksheet that you would like to use as the default.

2. Select Options from the Tools menu.

3. Click the Chart tab.

4. Click on the Use the Current Chart button in the Default Chart area.

5. Give the chart a custom format name in the resulting dialog box.

Controlling Which Series Is on Which Axis

Excel considers the numbers of rows and columns you've selected when determining how to plot your data. While space prohibits showing each chart type and examples of the results with different row/column combinations, it's easy to watch the sample as you work with the Chart Wizard, and change the outcome. For example, look at Figure 18.15.

As you can see in Figure 18.15, Excel has plotted the months on the X-axis and the departments on the Y-axis because of the number of rows and columns selected. To overrule this choice, simply change the "Data Series in:"

FIGURE 18.15

Excel will automatically assign the X and Y axes based on the number of rows and columns you select. You can overrule Excel, however.

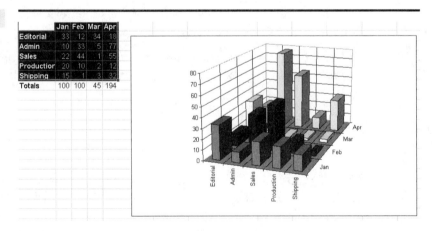

choice from columns to Rows in step 2 of the Chart Wizard. You can either do this while you are creating the chart, or later select the chart, then click on the Chart Wizard button and choose the Next > button to visit step 2. Figure 18.16 shows the same data plotted with the Data Series set to Rows.

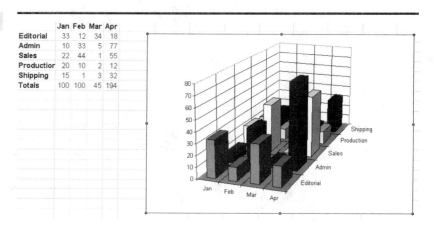

FIGURE 18.16

Here the same cells are being plotted as in Figure 18.15, but the "Data series in:" choice has been switched to Rows. Notice the new positions of months and departments.

	Jan	Feb	Mar	Apr
Editorial	33	12	34	18
Admin	10	33	5	77
Sales	22	44	1	55
Production	20	10	2	12
Shipping	15	1	3	32
Totals	100	100	45	194

Adding Overlay Charts

Sometimes you'll want to overlay one kind of chart data on top of another. For instance, you might want to add a totals line to a bar chart as shown in Figure 18.17.

The easy way to do this is to choose the Combination chart type. It creates two *layers* on the chart, displaying half of the layers as bars and the other half as lines. If there is an uneven number of series, the extra series is plotted as bars.

Creating Trendlines

Trendlines are used to plot the direction of data in a series. It's easy to add trendlines to Excel bar, column, area, and scatter charts. To create trendlines

FIGURE 18.17

Adding a totals line to a bar chart by overlaying one kind of data on top of another

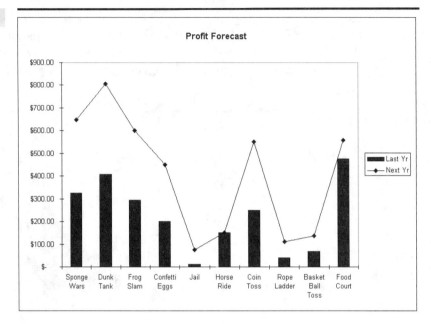

on charts, follow these general steps (we'll use a simple exercise to demonstrate the technique):

1. Double-click on a chart object if necessary to select it.

2. Select the data series for the trendline by double-clicking on one of its markers, as shown in Figure 18.18.

3. Choose Insert ➤ Trendline to display the Trendline dialog box.

4. In the Trendline dialog box, pick a Trend/Regression type, as shown in Figure 18.19.

5. If necessary, click the Options tab of the Trendline dialog box and change options. For example, in Figure 18.20 we are extending the trendline for two periods to create a forecast.

6. Click the OK button and admire your work (see Figure 18.21).

FIGURE 18.18

Double-click on one of
the markers for the
trendline to select the
data series for the
trendline.

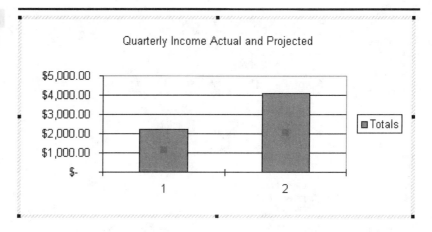

FIGURE 18.19

Pick a Trend/Regression
type from the Trendline
dialog box

Excel

FIGURE 18.20

Choose trendline options from the Options tab of the Trendline dialog box.

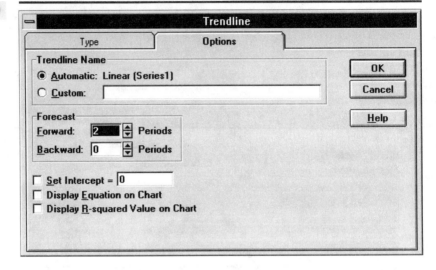

FIGURE 18.21

The finished product: The trendline extended for two periods to create a forecast.

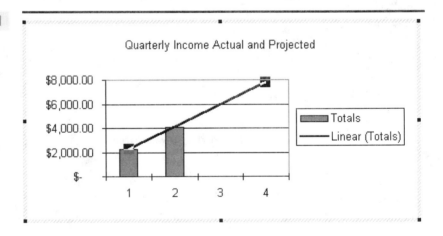

Tell Me More

These are the basics of Excel charting, and, as you can see, skills you learned in Windows and practiced in Word are often called for and applied in Excel. Many times, just reading the menu, dialog boxes, or the status bar will show you how to do new and useful things.

But there may be other charting details that are not so obvious. For instance, you can link a chart's text with worksheet cells so that chart notes or labels change when worksheet cells change. You can sometimes plot nonadjacent data. There is more to know about forcing axis values than you've read here. And so on.... If you don't find the answer to questions like these in Excel's on-line help, check out the hundred-plus pages on charts in your Excel manual, or pick up *Mastering Excel 5 for Windows by Thomas Chester (SYBEX, 1994)*.

Excel

19

Working with
Graphics in Excel

You can apply many of your Windows graphics skills to Excel worksheet projects. Worksheets can include imported graphic images, items you draw yourself, arrows, text boxes, and so on. You can use graphics to dress up the appearance of a document or as an integral part of a presentation. Figure 19.1 is an example of a worksheet drawn from many sources: The car is from the ClipArt Gallery Transportation section, the price tag was drawn using the Drawing toolbar, prices of the individual car options are entered into worksheet cells, and the *Added Cost* figure of $1,845 in the price tag is a worksheet cell containing a formula that adds up all the items.

Creating and Placing Graphic Objects

You can place graphics anywhere on a worksheet. Select graphics to move, resize, and restyle them. Copies of graphics can be pasted from your Clipboard into a worksheet or *linked* with the original objects so that changes in the original are reflected on the worksheet.

Importing Graphics

As a general rule, if you can get a graphic onto your Clipboard, you can paste it into an Excel worksheet. Sometimes it pays to visit Excel's Paste Special command rather than using the basic Paste command or the Ctrl-V keyboard shortcut when inserting graphics into Excel worksheets. For instance, if the source program supports object linking and embedding (OLE), you might want to Paste Link rather than Paste.

FIGURE 19.1

Excel worksheets can include imported graphics or graphics you create using Excel's drawing tools.

Any of Microsoft's object-creating tools (WordArt, the ClipArt Gallery, etc.) can provide graphic fodder. Simply use the Insert Object command to bring up the available list of object creators, shown in Figure 19.2. Then go for it.

Exporting Excel Graphics

You can also paste parts of your Excel worksheet into other types of documents. For instance, you can copy an Excel drawing or chart to your Clipboard, then switch to another program and paste (or Paste Link) the Clipboard contents either as a picture or often in other formats. The type of pasting that you do and the program you paste into determine how the pasted items will both appear and behave in the destination document.

Excel

FIGURE 19.2

Scroll through the Object Type list to choose which type of object you'd like to create.

WordArt in Excel Worksheets

A WHOLE NEW WAY TO WORK

You can insert just about any kind of graphic object into an Excel worksheet. For example, here's how to use WordArt to create stylized text for a logo on an invoice worksheet:

1. Use Excel's Insert ➤ Object command.

2. In the resulting Object dialog box, choose Microsoft WordArt Object from the Create New tab.

3. Type the word or words to be stylized in the text box.

4. Use the WordArt options on the WordArt toolbar and menus to change the appearance of the text (consult online help, or just have fun experimenting).

5. When you get the desired effect, click the Update Display button, then click in the Excel worksheet to insert the object.

6. Use your mouse to resize the resulting art if necessary and drag it into position.

7. To further embellish the WordArt, use the Format ➤ Object command to display the Format Object dialog box.

Excel

A WHOLE NEW WAY TO WORK

In this case, for instance, we've used it to remove the automatic border:

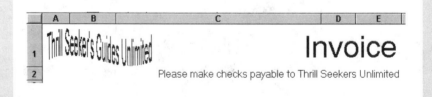

Resizing Graphics

Chances are, you already know how to resize Excel graphics:

1. Select a graphic by pointing with your mouse.

2. When the handles appear, drag on a handle to resize the graphic.

3. To change both dimensions at once, drag the corner handles.

Positioning Graphics on Worksheets

To move an object, select it and drag with your mouse. To move more than one object, Shift-click on each of them. Drag them all at once with your mouse and release. To align a graphic object's border with the worksheet cell grid, hold down the Alt key and drag one of the object's corner handles. You can also select graphics, copy or cut them to the Clipboard, and paste them elsewhere.

Drawing Lines and Shapes

Excel provides a number of drawing tools that will remind you of the ones in Microsoft Word's Draw feature as well as the Windows drawing packages described earlier in this book. Excel's tools were used to create the price tag and arrows in Figure 19.1. They work like most similar Windows-savvy drawing tools. Reach them by clicking the Drawing button, shown here, on Excel's Standard toolbar.

Since you've probably used similar drawing tools by now, we'll not waste paper here covering what must be familiar ground. If you forget what a tool does, point to the tool in question and read its description in Excel's status bar area. Incidentally, the polygon and oval tools were used to create the price tag in Figure 19.1.

Excel

Examples of Graphics in Excel

You can create invoices and other forms that include logos, as illustrated in Figure 19.3. The same basic technique could be used to place illustrations in order forms.

And how about this? Excel makes a great teaching tool. Set up some spreadsheets that illustrate concepts and let students explore, as illustrated in Figure 19.4.

How about sprucing up those budgeting exercises by creating "Org-chart–like" top sheets like the one in Figure 19.5. Link them to the detailed numbers using OLE.

FIGURE 19.3

Use Excel's graphics prowess to include logos in forms.

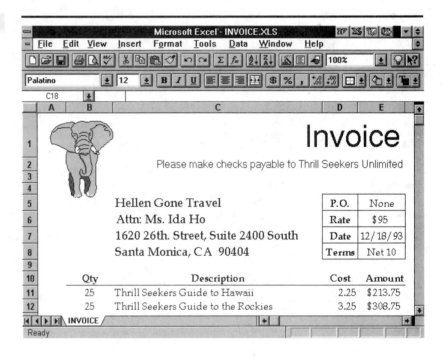

Excel

FIGURE 19.4

Changes in cells B9 or D* cause a corresponding change in the meter (cell D11).

FIGURE 19.5

Org charts can be used for things besides names and job functions.

Possible Sources of Excel Graphics

Here are just a few potential sources of Excel graphics and how to get them into your worksheet:

GRAPHIC SOURCE	HOW TO IMPORT
Bitmap graphics	The Windows Clipboard or OLE
DrawPerfect files	Insert Picture command or OLE
Encapsulated PostScript Files	Insert Picture command or OLE
TIF Files	Insert Picture command or OLE
Macintosh graphics	Insert Picture command or OLE
Windows Metafiles	Insert Picture command or OLE
PC Paintbrush	Insert Picture command or OLE
AutoCAD	Insert Picture command or OLE
CompuServe GIF files	Insert Picture command or OLE
CorelDRAW files	Insert Picture command or OLE
HP Plotter files	Insert Picture command or OLE
Kodak PhotoCD files	Insert Object command or OLE
Lotus 1-2-3 Graphics	Insert Object command or OLE
ImagePal screen dumps	Insert Object command or OLE
MS ClipArt Gallery items	Insert Object command or OLE
MS Graph graphs	Insert Object command or OLE
MS Org Charts	Insert Object command or OLE
MS Word Pictures	Insert Object command or OLE
MS WordArt	Insert Object command or OLE
MS PowerPoint objects	Insert Object command or OLE
Paintbrush objects	Insert Object command or OLE

Excel Slide Shows

Once you've created art and worksheet data charts (and sounds if your computer is properly equipped), you can use Excel's Slide feature to display this information as an animated and entertaining on-screen sequence that will remind you of a 35mm slide show. You'll need to install the Slide Show add-in to do this, but before you do, consider this:

Since you are probably a Microsoft Office owner, check out *Part Four: Presenting with PowerPoint* before spending a lot of time installing and learning about Excel's slide shows. PowerPoint is much more powerful and you can always use OLE to include Excel information in your PowerPoint presentations!

Excel

20

Introduction to Excel's Command Macros

Just as Microsoft Word lets you create macros to automate repetitive tasks, Microsoft Excel will record and play back *command macros*. When you record a series of steps, Excel watches you work and converts your actions into *Visual Basic*—a computer programming language that describes what you've done. You can then save this information as a named macro and run it whenever you wish.

For instance, if you find yourself continually creating twelve centered and bold column headings (Jan, Feb, and so on), you can record your typing, Auto-Filling, and formatting tasks *once*, then use the resulting macro in the future. Or you can use a macro to update past-due amounts in invoice worksheets.

There are several ways to run macros. You can assign keyboard shortcuts to macros. You can even create *macro buttons* or place macros on menus, as you will see in this chapter.

Advanced users can write and modify macros by working directly with the hundreds of macro functions (called programming commands) described in the *Microsoft Excel Visual Basic User's Guide* that comes with your Excel program. For now, let's stick with macros that don't require any programming skills, because you can accomplish quite a lot without knowing anything about ABSREFs or ZTESTMs or HENWAYs. (Don't ask.)

Recording Your Own Macros

1. Start by practicing what you intend to do a few times so you know what steps to take and are assured that they will work.

2. When you're done rehearsing, choose the Record Macro command from Excel's Tools menu. You'll see a dialog box like the one in Figure 20.1. Click the Options button to see the "big" version of the dialog box.

Name your macro and
decide where you
want to save it.

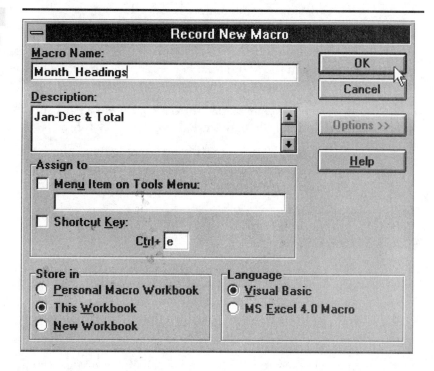

3. Excel will suggest a macro name that you will probably not like. Type a new name if you wish. Macro names must start with a letter, cannot contain spaces, and should not look like a reference (no A$1 names, for instance). In place of spaces, use an underline character (**Month_Headings**, for instance).

4. Add a note in the Description box if you like. It will help you remember what the macro does later on.

5. Decide where to save your macro—in the current workbook (the default), a new workbook, or a "personal" collection of macros. (Stick with the current workbook at first.)

6. Excel proposes a keyboard shortcut that you can use in combination with the Ctrl key, and sometimes the Shift key, to execute macros. In Figure 20.1, it is proposing Ctrl-e. Excel differentiates between upper- and lowercase keyboard shortcuts, so you can use both a Ctrl-e and a

Excel

Ctrl-Shift-e combination. Excel will not propose key combinations that are already used by Excel itself or by the open macro sheet.

7. You can also add the macro to your Tools menu by typing a menu item name in the Menu Item box and checking the Menu Item On Tools Menu choice.

8. Once you have named the macro, chosen a key combination for it, and told Excel where to store the macro, click OK to begin recording.

9. Live it up! Click, drag, format, enter text or values, construct formulas, use functions, and so on. When you are finished, click the Stop Recorder button, shown here.

Running Macros

Once you've recorded a macro, use either the keyboard shortcut, the Tools menu choice if you've added one, or the Macro command on Excel's Tools menu. If you use the keyboard shortcut, it will run immediately. The Macro command provides a list of macros like the one in Figure 20.2. Pick the one you want—either double-click on it or click once to select and once on Run.

Any way you start your macro, Excel will repeat your recorded steps, sometimes with surprising results. Remember that you may need to prepare your worksheet before running a macro: If a macro expects cell A1 to be the active cell, you may not like the results if Q7 is the active cell. And when you want your macro to sort a table of cells, there had better be the right data in them.

There is no short list of macro "gottas," as you will learn the hard way. And, as you will also discover, Undo may not always completely rectify the results of a macro's rampage. You should save your work *before* running powerful macros.

When you want to give some input into what Excel does when you start a macro, you can use Visual Basic (a programming language) to create dialog boxes, tests for specific conditions, and much more. You can even create your own on-line help for macros. Check out *Mastering Excel 5 for Windows* for details.

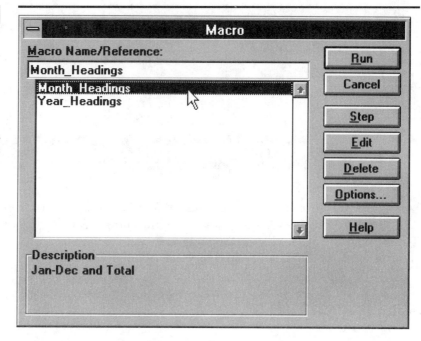

FIGURE 20.2

Use keyboard shortcuts or this dialog box to run macros. Note that each macro name is preceded by the letter of its Ctrl key shortcut.

Assigning Macros to Buttons

If you have a favorite macro or you want to make a complex task easy for other users, consider creating *macro buttons*. The process is surprisingly simple.

1. Start by displaying the Drawing toolbar. (Use Excel's Toolbars command on the View menu or the Drawing button on the Standard toolbar.)

2. Click the Create Button button.

3. When you click on the button tool, your pointer turns into crosshairs. Drag to create a button large enough to contain a descriptive label (Figure 20.3).

4. When you release the mouse button, you'll see a rectangle like the one at left. The box will contain the word Button and a number.

FIGURE 20.3

Drag to create the
desired button size
and shape, then label
the resulting button
and assign it to a
macro.

5. Once you've created the button, Excel will present a list of macros. Pick
   the one you want to assign to the button (double-click on the macro's
   name in the scrolling list).

6. Click on the button name and change it to something meaningful.

Past Due

Click on the button to run your macro. To move, resize, or otherwise change a
button *without* running the macro, hold down the Ctrl key when you point to
the button. The button will take on a by-now-familiar outline that will remind you of a graphic (it will be outlined with size handles). You can reposition a selected button by dragging with the pointer shaped like an arrowhead.
You can edit the button's size, shape, or name by holding down the Ctrl key while
you click on the button. (This selects the button without activating it.) Use Excel's formatting commands and tools to change the button's font, type size, style,
and other text attributes. Drag the button as you would any other graphic object
to change its size and shape. (See how this all starts to tie together?)

To delete a button (in order to free up some screen space, perhaps), select it
(Ctrl-click), then use the Del key or Edit menu's Clear command. Deleting a
button does *not* delete the macro that it is assigned to. To delete the macro,
open the Macro dialog box (reached with Tools ➤ Macro), select the macro
to be deleted, and click the Delete button.

To Learn More about Macros

You now know enough about macros to be dangerous. Through on-line help and trial and error, you will learn a lot more. Also check out the *Excel Users Guide 2* and *Excel Function Reference* that are packaged with your Excel program, or try *Mastering Excel 5 for Windows*.

If you are just curious about what the instructions look like for a macro, either check out Figure 20.4 or use the Macro dialog box to select a macro, then click the Edit button to see the Visual Basic programming instructions created by the recorder.

FIGURE 20.4

Some of the instructions Excel created for the Year_Heading macro.

589

21

Using Worksheets as Databases

"**W**hen you get a new hammer," the saying goes, "everything looks like a nail." Perhaps that's why many users (to say nothing of spreadsheet manufacturers) turn to spreadsheet packages when they really need a database-management program. It is true that Excel has a number of database *features*. It is also true that you can use these features to manage a Print Merge mailing list, to control your inventory, or to do a statistical analysis of complex opinion surveys. But *should* you?

Most spreadsheet programs, including Excel, have limits that can frustrate database users. For instance, you can only have 16,384 *records* in a single Excel worksheet. If you keep 16,385 people in your mailing list, you'll have a problem (though not an insurmountable one).

In any one field you can have a maximum of 256 *characters*. So, if you want to collect quotations from famous people in an Excel database, they'd better not be quotes from long-winded speakers. (This paragraph contains *294* characters, for example, so it wouldn't fit in an Excel database field.)

Excel limits you to three *sort levels* at any one time; so if you want to sort a list of employees by division, department, last name, and then first name, you will need to take extra (and sometimes confusing) steps.

The biggest concern about using spreadsheets as databases has to do with how easily the *integrity* of your data can be corrupted. For instance, in a worksheet, it is *far too easy* to sort a list of employees and their salaries only to find that you've given each worker someone else's earnings! You'll see an example of this later in the chapter. It's also pretty easy to think you've added records to an Excel database when you haven't.

Nonetheless, there *are* times when Excel's database features can be life-savers: you can use them to extract interesting reports from budgets and other "legitimate" spreadsheet data. The moral of this sermon is, Before you spend hours entering a mailing list into a worksheet, consider whether you wouldn't be better off with a real database program, like Microsoft *Access*. But if you have a large budget or other worksheet, Excel's database features can sometimes help you find and manage that information.

Database Concepts and Terms

You'll need to know several database terms to make sense of this chapter. Even if you've used "real" database programs before, it's worth browsing the next few topics, since Excel adds a few new wrinkles to "databasics." For instance, the Excel documentation often refers to databases as *lists*. Here are some other terms worth knowing.

Database Range

Even though your database can be a small part of a larger worksheet, Excel 5, unlike earlier versions, can often automatically define likely database ranges, like cells A2 through E8 in Figure 21.1.

FIGURE 21.1

Excel can often find and define database ranges, like cells A2 through E8 in this example.

	A	B	C	D	E	F	G	H	I
1									
2	**Name**	**Age**	**Sex**	**Dpt**	**Salary**				
3	Tina	52	Female	Sales	$47,000				
4	Ringo	45	Male	Sales	$62,000				
5	Paul	43	Male	Production	$30,000				
6	Mary	25	Female	Admin	$75,000				
7	John	25	Male	Shipping	$25,000				
8	George	30	Male	Admin	$40,000				
9									
10	January	February	March	April	May	June	July	August	September
11	$ 125.00	$ 125.00	$ 125.00	$ 125.00	$ 125.00	$ 125.00	$ 125.00	$ 125.00	$ 125.00
12	217	217	217	217	217	217	217	217	217
13	$ 309.00	$ 309.00	$ 309.00	$ 309.00	$ 309.00	$ 309.00	$ 309.00	$ 309.00	$ 309.00
14	401	401	401	401	401	401	401	401	401
15	$ 493.00	$ 493.00	$ 493.00	$ 493.00	$ 493.00	$ 493.00	$ 493.00	$ 493.00	$ 493.00
16	585	585	585	585	585	585	585	585	585
17									
18									

Records and Fields

Excel treats the contents of each *row* of a database range as a *record*. In Figure 21.1, row 4 is George's record, row 5 is John's record, and so on. The first row of any database range (row 3 in Figure 21.1) must always contains *column labels*, which Excel will use as *database field names*. These field names can contain spaces. The field name **Annual Salary** would be permitted, for instance.

Microsoft calls each *column* in a database a *field*, and *individual cells* in a database are also referred to as *fields*. You can enter text, numbers, dates, functions, and formulas in cells. When a field contains a function or formula, it is referred to as a *computed field*. For instance, if you had a **Quantity Ordered** field and a **Unit Price** field, you could create a **Total Cost** field containing a formula that computes total cost based on the other two fields.

Creating an Excel Database

When creating a database, set up a separate field (column) for any item you'll want to refer to separately. For instance, if you want to sort on first and last names separately, create a field for each. This is particularly important to remember if you plan to sort on, or search for, things like ZIP codes.

Set column widths right at the start, or change widths after you've entered the data by dragging or by using Column Width features (Best Fit, for instance).

Entering Data

You can enter, edit, and format the data in a database just as you would any other Excel cell contents, or you can use Excel's Data Form feature, which is described later in this chapter. Regardless of which method you use, there are some cautions worth mentioning.

■ Excel does *not* let you specify "field types," so it's possible to enter either a number or text or a date into any field. This can cause problems when entering numbers that you plan to display and sort as text. For instance, Excel strips off leading zeros in numeric entries. But some zip codes start with zero. If you want to see those "leading" zeros in zip codes, you'll need to enter each zip code as *text*, not as a number. To do this, you must type an apostrophe before each zip code—or any number you intend to enter as text. If you want ZIP codes to sort the way you normally expect to see them, you'll *always* need to enter *each* ZIP code this way.

■ Unlike fancier database products, Excel will *not* challenge you if you mix text, numeric, and date entries. Usually, you can see if there is a problem by looking at the appearance of the entries. For instance, unless you format them otherwise, text entries in cells will be left-justified, and general numeric entries will be right-justified.

Adding Records to a Database

Normally, you'll add new records beneath the last record in your database. You can either do this the way you add regular worksheet data (by activating cells in the next empty row and typing), or you can use a database *form* that "prompts" you for data entries and automatically places new records beneath your last record.

It is also possible to make space for records in the middle of your data range (insert empty rows), then make *mid-database* entries. There are advantages and disadvantages to each of these approaches. To weigh their pros and cons, you must understand what Excel does when new data won't fit in the data range you've defined. Read on.

Excel will automatically accommodate the addition of new records if it can—which brings us to the second problem:

If you plan to have anything in rows directly *beneath* the database cells, you will be inconvenienced when you have more data than will fit in the previously defined data range. Suppose, for instance, that in Figure 21.1 you've placed a worksheet equation in cell B10. If you used the data form to enter a new record, you'd get the message "Cannot extend database," since the data form feature will not write over or push down cell contents. (If the equation was in cell A10, however, you *could* continue appending records, since the equation would not be directly beneath the data range.)

In cases where there is insufficient room to easily extend the database, either you can opt to manually *insert* additional records mid-database, pushing everything else down, or you can insert blank lines at the end of the database range to *extend* it. Check your worksheet for formulas that no longer work as a result of your pushing things down this way.

You can also add fields to an existing database. For example, if you wanted to add a Last Name field in column A, you could simply type the field name in cell A3, then enter last names in cells A4 through A9. If you decided to insert a last name field between Name and Age (by selecting column C and using the Edit menu's Insert command), Excel will extend the database range for you.

Working with Data Forms

Data forms are handy for data entry, record viewing, and searching. A data form is automatically created whenever you choose the Form command on the Data menu. You can bring the form into view with Excel's Form command on the Data menu. As you can see from Figure 21.2, data forms are dialog boxes containing field names, text entry boxes, and buttons.

Field contents (or first portion of field contents)

Scroll to view different records.

Fields containing text and numbers can be edited; computed fields cannot.

Unfortunately, it is possible to design databases with so many fields that they won't all be visible on your form. You *cannot* scroll to overcome this. And, if you place multiple-line entries in fields by using the old Ctrl+Enter trick, you'll only see the first line of those entries in your form.

The width of the text areas in a data form (and the width of the dialog box itself) is based on the widest field (column) in your database. Thus, if you have an 80-character field in your database, you'll see a pretty big data form.

Use the scroll arrows to view different records. Enter and edit text in the data form's text boxes as you'd expect. You can use the Tab key to move from text box to text box (and to the buttons) in your data form. Shift-Tab moves you backwards.

Adding and Editing Records with the Data Form

To add a new record with the data form, click the New button, or scroll to the last record, which should be empty. Type as usual, making sure you put the right data in the right fields. Feel free to leave fields empty.

To edit records using the data form, scroll to (or otherwise locate) the record of interest and edit in the text boxes using standard Windows techniques (select and change). Computed fields *cannot* be edited. You cannot *format* text in a data form (the Bold and Italic toolbar buttons won't work here, for instance). Instead, format text in the worksheet itself.

Changes and additions made in the data form aren't reflected in the database until you move to a different record or close the data form.

  Even when changes have been made in the database, they reside only in your computer's RAM until you save the worksheet. Save early and often to avoid datus interruptus.

Deleting Records with the Data Form

To delete a record with the data form, bring the record into view and click the data form's Delete key. You will be asked to confirm the deletion. You cannot undo deletions performed from the data form. (If, instead, you delete directly in the database using Excel's Edit menu, then act immediately, you can undo those deletes.) To delete multiple records, it's usually best to round them up with AutoFilter (described in a moment) and then delete the records found.

Search Criteria

You can use the data form to create and then scroll through collections of records that meet specific criteria (for instance, all the women earning more than $50,000). Start by choosing the Criteria button in the data form. You'll see a dialog box like the one in Figure 21.3.

FIGURE 21.3

Specify search criteria to see a filtered list of records.

In this example, Excel will gather up just female employees who earn in excess of $50,000. Notice that dollar signs and commas are ignored, so you only need to enter **>>50000** for the Salary criterion.

If none of your records meet your criteria, frequently Excel will go ahead and display a record that does not meet the criteria.

This data form search feature can locate character strings (text), and it can locate records that fall within ranges of numbers or dates.

The comparison operators are:

=	Equal to
>>	Greater than
<<	Less than
>>=	Greater than or equal to
<<=	Less than or equal to
<>	Not equal to

When you use an equal sign with nothing after it as the single search criterion, only records with blank entries will appear.

These comparisons only work with numbers and dates, not with text. Thus, a search for ZIP codes entered as text, like **>>80000** or **>>**"80000," won't work.

Using Wildcards

You can use asterisks (*****) and question marks (**?**) as wildcards. But note that Excel adds an invisible asterisk to the end of any search criterion that uses wildcards. For instance, **Sm?th** finds Smith and Smyth, and also smithereens. The search criterion **Jo*** will find John and Job and joke, but then so will the string **jo**. The criterion ***mary** will find Mary and Queen Mary, while the criterion *** mary** (note the space) will find Queen Mary, but not Mary as the first name in a field.

To find an "exact text match," that is, a match of the same length (for example, **John** but not **Johnny**), precede the search string with an equal sign: **=John**. By now you may be suspicious that search criteria searches are *not* case-sensitive. You're right. The search criterion **=John** will also find **john**.

Use the Find Next and Find Previous buttons to review multiple found records.

Excel
CHAPTER 21

filtering—A Better Way to Find

Excel now offers a powerful database function that is a big improvement over the search criteria method just described. It comes in two flavors—AutoFilter and Advanced Filtering. We'll stick with AutoFilter here and leave Advanced Filtering to the bigger books.

When you choose AutoFilter from the Data menu's Filter submenu, Excel zips through your database looking for each unique entry in each column. For example, in our sample database it would find *three* unique departments in the Dpt column—Admin, Shipping, and Production. In the Sex column it would find *two* unique entries—Male and Female. It does this for each column and creates drop-down lists for each column, like the one shown in Figure 21.4.

FIGURE 21.4

AutoFilter creates drop-down lists for each column in the database.

	XTABFUN.XLS				
	B	**C**	**D**	**E**	**F**
3	Name	Ag	Sex	Dpt	Salary
4	George	30	Mal	(All)	$40,000
5	John	25	Mal	(Custom...)	$25,000
				Admin	
6	Mary	25	Fem	Production	$75,000
7	Paul	43	Mal	Sales	$30,000
8	Ringo	45	Mal	Shipping	$62,000
				(Blanks)	
9	Tina	52	Fem	(NonBlanks)	$47,000
10					

XTABFUN

The lists contain all the unique values for the column plus the choices (All), (Custom), (Blanks), and (Non Blanks).

When you drop down one of these menus and pick a choice, Excel will *filter* (hide) all records not containing the chosen value. For instance, if you choose Sales from the Dpt column, you will see only records that contain sales values in their Dpt field, as shown in Figure 21.5. (The other records are not deleted; they are just temporarily hidden from view.)

FIGURE 21.5

When you choose a
value from one of the
drop-down menus,
Excel hides all records
not containing the
chosen value.

	B	C	D	E	F
3	Name ↓	Ag ↓	Se↓	Dpt ↓	Salary ↓
8	Ringo	45	Male	Sales	$62,000
9	Tina	52	Female	Sales	$47,000
11					
12					
13					
14					
15					

XTABFUN.XLS · XTABFUN

The choices (Blanks) and (Non Blanks) show records with either blank and
nonblank entries, respectively. In other words, choosing (NonBlanks) will display (not filter out) any records that have something (anything) typed in the
field.

The (All) choice filters nothing for that column. In other words, if you
choose (All) in every column, you will see all of your records.

You can combine filters. For instance to find all of the males in the Production department, you could choose Male in Sex and Production in Dpt.

I promised not to get into advanced filtering, but there is one capability worth
noting. It's the (Custom) choice in the drop-down menus. With it you can
specify *ranges* of things you want to see. For instance, to see all of the employees that earn over $26,000, you could:

1. Choose (*Custom*) from the Salary drop-down list, as shown in Figure 21.6.

2. Specify **Greater Than** by picking the **>>** operator from the drop-
   down list.

3. Enter the dollar amount (dollar signs and commas are optional).

4. Click OK. Excel will filter out (hide) records for employees earning less
   than $26,000.

There are many more custom filtering features. For example, you can specify
ranges like "greater than 26,000 *and* less than 50,000." There are also text

FIGURE 21.6

Specifying ranges for filtering in the Custom AutoFilter dialog box

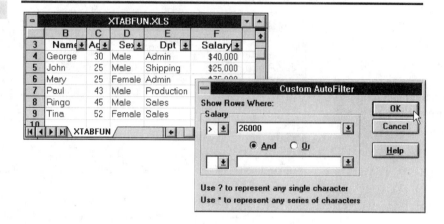

string specifiers. They work like those in the Criteria dialog box described earlier.

Showing All Records after AutoFiltering

There are two ways you can show all records after AutoFiltering. If you wish to leave the drop-down lists in-place for future use, you can display all your records by choosing Data ➤ Filter ➤ Show All.

Removing AutoFilter Lists

To remove the drop-down filter lists and redisplay all of your records, choose the AutoFilter choice from the Filter submenu a second time. This removes the checkmark next to the menu choice, deletes the drop-down menus, and redisplays all records.

Sorting Excel Databases

It's time to turn to sorting. Figure 21.7 shows a column typically chosen for sorting—the ages of your company's employees.

FIGURE 21.7

A typical column for
sorting

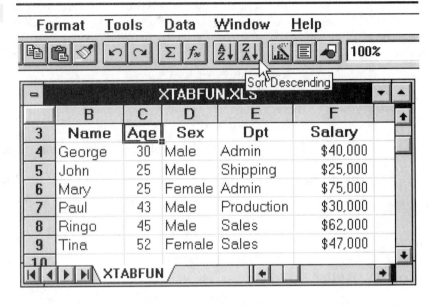

If you only have one database defined on your worksheet, sorting can be quite easy:

1. *Activate* any *one* cell in the field you wish to use as the sort key (Age, in
   our example).

**If you <u>select a range of cells</u>, rather than <u>activating a single
cell</u>, only those selected cells will be sorted. If you leave
columns out when you select prior to sorting, they will not
be rearranged. So, if you selected everything except column
F in our sample database, most of your employees would
end up with someone else's salary after the sort, and you
could have a riot on your hands. This sort error is very easy
to make if you have wide worksheets with fields that you
can't see. Out of sight, out of mind, as they say....**

2. With either a single cell or everything you want to sort selected, click either the Sort Ascending or Sort Descending button on the Standard toolbar:

3. Excel will sort, leaving the labels at the top of the list where they belong.

In the example shown in Figure 21.7, the data will be sorted in descending order, based on employees' ages, resulting in the oldest person being first in the database and the youngest at the end. You could just as easily sort the list by department, using cell E4 as the first key (in the 1st Key box).

Multilevel Sorts

Suppose you had a bigger database and wanted to sort it by department to see staffers listed alphabetically *within* their departments. You could do this in one pass by using the Sort dialog box shown in Figure 21.8 (reached with the Sort command on the Data menu).

You would make *Dpt* the first sort key (1st Key) and *Name* the second sort key (2nd Key). Pick names from the drop-down lists or specify cell addresses.

In a still more complex database, if you have several people with the *same names* in the *same department*, you could use their age or sex as the tie breaker by specifying one of those criteria as the third sort key (3rd Key).

Incidentally, you can choose to sort by column instead of row, which is one way to rearrange the order in which fields appear in your database. If you rearrange a database this way, be sure to include the field names in the selection so that the names move with the data.

Excel ignores capitalization when sorting text. Furthermore, numbers entered as numbers sort before numbers entered as text. (International versions of Excel may use slightly different sort orders.)

FIGURE 21.8

The Sort dialog box
lets you sort with up
to three sort keys.

Crosstabulating Databases

"How many women do we have in each department? How do salaries break down by sex around here?" If you ask, or are asked, questions like these, you may want to check out Excel's PivotTable Wizard. With a minimum of groaning, you should be able to create crosstabulated tables like the one in Figure 21.9. Complex crosstabulation can also be performed on budgets and other large documents.

FIGURE 21.9

Use the PivotTable
Wizard to create
tables like this from
databases.

XTABFUN.XLS							
A	B	C	D	E	F	G	H
1 Count of Dpt	Dpt						
2 Sex	Admin	Production	Sales	Shipping	(blank)	Grand Total	
3 Female	1	0	1	0	0	2	
4 Male	1	1	1	1	0	4	
5 (blank)	0	0	0	0	0	0	
6 Grand Total	2	1	2	1	0	6	

Ages / XTABFUN /

Excel

The PivotTable Wizard is a big improvement over the Crosstab Wizard from earlier versions of Excel. It is quick, intuitive, and powerful. It seems more reliable than its predecessor too. Just the same, save your work before using Pivot-Table Wizard.

1. After saving your work, click anywhere in your database.

2. Choose PivotTable from Excel's Data menu.

3. Specify a data source. (You can use your Excel database or external sources.)

4. Drag items in the PivotTable Wizard Step 2 of 4 dialog box to set up the report. By default the Wizard counts things, but if you double-click on an item, you can choose other actions such as sums (totals). Figure 21.10 shows a typical report and the settings that produced it.

Whenever you change data in your database, you'll need to *refresh* the data. The easiest way to do this is with the Refresh data button on the Query and Pivot toolbar that appears when you are working with PivotTable Wizard:

It is very easy to receive far more detail than you need, so get in the habit of visiting the Options dialog boxes, where you can customize your reports to show desired crosstabs only, ranges instead of each specific value, and so on.

Adding Subtotals to Databases

While many Wizards automatically create subtotals for you, Excel's Subtotal command on the Data menu lets you add your own subtotals to any sorted list of data. Subtotals will be created each time the data in a specified differs from

FIGURE 21.10

Use the PivotTable
Wizard to set up
reports like these.

Sum of Salary			Salary							
Age	Dpt	Sex	25000	30000	40000	47000	62000	75000	(blank)	Grand Total
25	Admin	Female	0	0	0	0	0	75000	0	75000
	Admin Total		0	0	0	0	0	75000	0	75000
	Shipping	Male	25000	0	0	0	0	0	0	25000
	Shipping Total		25000	0	0	0	0	0	0	25000
25 Total			25000	0	0	0	0	75000	0	100000
30	Admin	Male	0	0	40000	0	0	0	0	40000
	Admin Total		0	0	40000	0	0	0	0	40000
30 Total			0	0	40000	0	0	0	0	40000
43	Production	Male	0	30000	0	0	0	0	0	30000
	Production Total		0	30000	0	0	0	0	0	30000
43 Total			0	30000	0	0	0	0	0	30000
45	Sales	Male	0	0	0	0	62000	0	0	62000
	Sales Total		0	0	0	0	62000	0	0	62000
45 Total			0	0	0	0	62000	0	0	62000
52	Sales	Female	0	0	0	47000	0	0	0	47000
	Sales Total		0	0	0	47000	0	0	0	47000
52 Total			0	0	0	47000	0	0	0	47000
(blank)	(blank)	(blank)	0	0	0	0	0	0	0	0
	(blank) Total		0	0	0	0	0	0	0	0
(blank) Total			0	0	0	0	0	0	0	0
Grand Total			25000	30000	40000	47000	62000	75000	0	279000

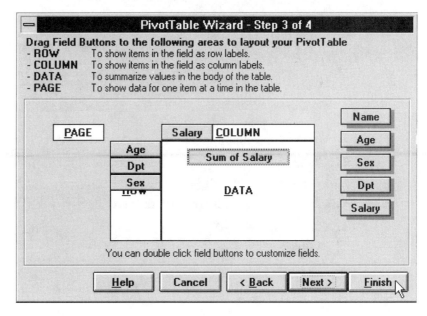

PivotTable Wizard - Step 3 of 4

Drag Field Buttons to the following areas to layout your PivotTable
- **ROW**   To show items in the field as row labels.
- **COLUMN**   To show items in the field as column labels.
- **DATA**   To summarize values in the body of the table.
- **PAGE**   To show data for one item at a time in the table.

PAGE

Salary COLUMN

Sum of Salary

DATA

Age
Dpt
Sex
ROW

Name
Age
Sex
Dpt
Salary

You can double click field buttons to customize fields.

Help   Cancel   < Back   Next >   Finish

that in the row above. For example, we could sort our sample employee database by department and get salary subtotals by department. Here are the general steps for creating subtotals:

1. Sort the data in an order that will produce the subtotals you desire (we've sorted on Department for the example in Figure 21.11).

FIGURE 21.11

Sort your data then choose Subtotals from the Data menu.

2. Choose the column to be monitored for changes (Dpt in this example).

3. Choose the function to be used (typically SUM for numeric subtotals or COUNT for counting things).

4. Choose the columns you wish to subtotal (Salary in this example).

5. Choose the other appearance options you desire. The defaults are shown in this example.

6. Click OK

7. Reformat the columns if the subtotals exceed the old column widths (a common occurrence).

8. You should see subtotals something like the ones in Figure 21.2.

	Name	Age	Sex	Dpt	Salary
1	Name	Age	Sex	Dpt	Salary
2	George	30	Male	Admin	$ 40,000
3	Mary	25	Female	Admin	$ 75,000
4				**Admin Total**	**$ 115,000**
5	Paul	43	Male	Production	$ 30,000
6				**Production Total**	**$ 30,000**
7	Ringo	45	Male	Sales	$ 62,000
8	Tina	52	Female	Sales	$ 47,000
9				**Sales Total**	**$ 109,000**
10	John	25	Male	Shipping	$ 25,000
11				**Shipping Total**	**$ 25,000**
12				**Grand Total**	**$ 279,000**

9. You can show or hide detail with the new outline controls that appear on the left of the worksheet. For example, in Figure 21.13, only totals and subtotals are displayed.

	Name	Age	Sex	Dpt	Salary
1	Name	Age	Sex	Dpt	Salary
3				**Admin Total**	**$ 40,000**
5				**Shipping Total**	**$ 25,000**
7				**Admin Total**	**$ 75,000**
9				**Production Total**	**$ 30,000**
12				**Sales Total**	**$ 109,000**
13				**Grand Total**	**$ 279,000**

Excel

609

Removing Subtotals

To remove all subtotals, select the data of interest, and use the Subtotals command on the Data menu. (You can select just part of a worksheet if you only want to remove some of the subtotals.) Click on the Remove All button.

22

Automating "What-If" Projects

Excel

you know the drill. "What are the effects of changing sales commissions to 3 percent, 2 percent, or 4 percent?" Or "What if mortgage rates fall to 7.25 percent?" It is questions like these that inspired someone to invent computerized spreadsheets. But the process of preparing them can be pretty tedious, particularly when juggling multiple variables. Excel provides a number of features designed to speed up complex "what-if" questions. They include the *Scenario Manager*, *What-If add-in macros*, the *Solver*, and related *reporting features*. This chapter introduces you to those tools. Excel's online help, sample worksheets shipped with the program, and the documentation or bigger books can fill in the details.

General Organizational Tips

When you design worksheets that will be used regularly, it is a good idea to organize them logically, in a top-down manner. Place introductory text and instructions at the top, followed by the assumptions you'll most likely want to change. Label them clearly. This makes it easy for other people to see and understand your methodology.

If colleagues will be changing or examining your formulas, consider using names (like SALES and COMMISSION) rather than more obscure cell references (like B14 or $Q$13). As you will see, this can also automatically improve the appearance of your reports.

Protect critical equations so that people don't accidentally overwrite them. Consider breaking complex formulas up into smaller, easier-to-understand parts that display helpful intermediate answers. Test. Test some more. Test again. Dust off that pocket calculator.

Scenario Manager

Scenarios are named sets of assumptions (inputs) and the resulting computations (results) that you ask a worksheet to compute. For instance, suppose you wanted to explore the impact of interest rates on mortgage payments and total interest paid. You might also want to see the effect of borrowing for 15 rather than 30 years. Scenario Manager can make short work of this and can even create nice summary reports.

Defining Scenarios

Select or Ctrl+select the cells that you want to be able to change in the scenario. In the following example we want to be able to explore changes in interest rates, the number of payments, and the loan amounts; so cells B2 through B4 have been selected. (To select nonadjacent cells, Ctrl+click.)

With the appropriate cells selected, use the Scenarios command on Excel's Tools menu. You'll see the Scenario Manager dialog box telling you that no scenarios have been defined yet. Click the Add button to define some. You'll see an Add Scenario box something like the one in Figure 22.1.

FIGURE 22.1

Use the Add Scenario dialog box to define multiple scenarios.

Select the assumptions you want to use in your "what-if?" (Ctrl-click to select nonadjacent cells)

Click OK to continue

Excel

Create as many named scenarios as you want by typing distinct scenario names and different values (in the Scenario Values dialog box) for one or all of the assumptions in each scenario. Click Add each time you want to save one scenario and start another. When you are done adding scenarios, click OK. You will see a Scenario Manager dialog box like the one in Figure 22.2.

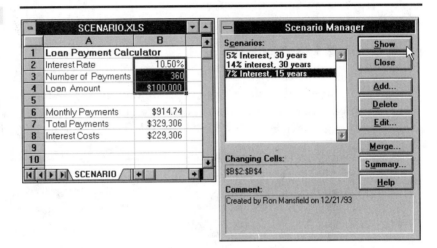

Viewing Scenarios

In Figure 22.2 there are three possible scenarios for cells B2 through B4: 5% Interest 30 Years, 14% Interest 30 Years, and 7% Interest 15 Years. To see the effect of a scenario, select it from the list and click Show. Your worksheet will reflect the chosen assumptions.

Obtaining Scenario Summaries

It is also easy to obtain summary reports that show the assumptions for each scenario and the results of each scenario. Figure 22.3 illustrates an example of this.

FIGURE 22.3

A scenario summary
shows you multiple
assumptions and their
results in an
easy-to-read report.

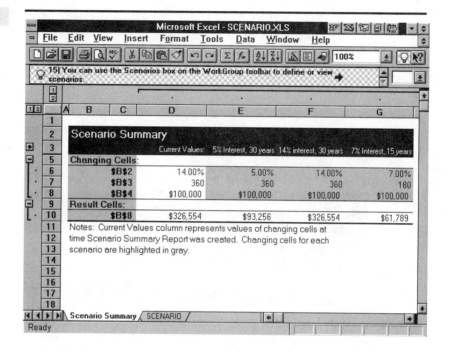

Start by clicking the Summary button in the Scenario Manager dialog box.
Excel asks you to define the changing cells to be displayed. It proposes a range
for you.

The proposed range usually contains formulas that refer to the changing assumption. You can keep the suggested range or define your own. Click OK
when you are satisfied with the results range.

You can ask Excel to create a summary report (the default) or, by clicking on the appropriate button, request a Scenario Pivot table. (See Chapter 21 for more about PivotTables.)

Excel then creates and formats a report (a separate worksheet in your workbook, actually), showing the various scenarios and their results. Notice that Scenario Manager labels rows with cell addresses ($B$2, $B$3, etc.). It makes for pretty obscure reading. You can overcome this by *naming* cells back in your model worksheet. (Use the Insert ➤ Name ➤ Define command to do this.) The names will appear in the reports as seen here:

Scenario Summary	
	Current Values:
Changing Cells:	
Interest_Rate	14.00%
Number_of__Payments	360
Loan__Amount	$100,000

Notice also that Excel may not propose all of the result cells that you'll want to see. You can overrule the proposed range by entering your own.

Changing Scenarios

Visit the Scenario Manager dialog box to add, delete, or edit scenarios. You cannot undo scenario deletions.

finding the Right Number with Solver

Solver helps you find combinations that reach a goal. For instance, have you ever said, "If interest rates are 7 percent, and I can afford monthly payments of $1000 a month, how much can I borrow?" Or have you ever needed to find the most profitable product mix, or examine sales commission scenarios to find the mix that is most profitable. Excel's Solver add-in program can help.

Suppose you know you can spend $1000 per month for 360 months, and you know that interest rates are 7%. Solver will help you determine the maximum loan amount.

1. Start by constructing and testing your model (a worksheet built around Excel's PMT function in this case).

B6	↓	=PMT(B2/12,B3,B4)*-1	
	A	**B**	**C**
1	Loan Payment Calculator		
2	Interest Rate	6.00%	
3	Number of Payments	360	
4	Loan Amount	$100,000	
5			
6	Monthly Payments	$599.55	
7	Total Payments	$215,838	
8	Interest Costs	$115,838	

2. When you know the model works right, save it.

3. Choose Solver from Excel's Tools menu. It's an add-in, so the command may take a moment to load itself the first time you use it each session.

4. Soon you'll see a Solver Parameters dialog box (shown here).

5. Tell Solver which cell you want to solve for (**Monthly Payments**, or **$B$6** in this example). Then define the *constraints*, or the rules to be used. For instance, you know you don't want to spend more than $1000 per month, and you don't want Solver to change the interest rates or number of payments, so you must add constraints for all three of these items. Create each constraint separately by using the Add button to build constraints like the ones shown here:

Constraints can refer to cell locations ($B$6, for instance), or to names if you've defined them (like Interest for cell B2).

6. When you've created all the appropriate constraints, use the Solve button to search for a solution. Eventually the hourglass that pops up will disappear. If your model worksheet is in view, you'll see a solution:

B4		150307.658064803

	A	B	C
1	**Loan Payment Calculator**		
2	Interest Rate	7.00%	
3	Number of Payments	360	
4	Loan Amount	$150,308	
5			
6	Monthly Payments	$1,000.00	
7	Total Payments	$360,000	
8	Interest Costs	$209,693	

and you will see a Solver dialog box like this one:

7. Choose Answer in the Reports list to see a report like the one in
Figure 22.4.

FIGURE 22.4

The Answer report
created by Solver for
the preceding exercise.

Microsoft Excel 5.0 Answer Report
Worksheet: [WHAT-IF.XLS]WHAT-IF
Report Created: 12/21/93 13:53

Target Cell (Max)

Cell	Name	Original Value	Final Value
$B$6	FALSE	$599.55	$1,000.00

Adjustable Cells

Cell	Name	Original Value	Final Value
$B$2	Interest	6.00%	7.00%
$B$3	Months	360	360
$B$4	FALSE	$100,000	$150,308

Constraints

Cell	Name	Cell Value	Formula	Status	Slack
$B$6	FALSE	$1,000.00	$B$6=1000	Not Binding	$0.00
$B$2	Interest	7.00%	$B$2=0.07	Binding	0.00%
$B$3	Months	360	$B$3=360	Binding	0

Solver lets you view your solutions, change the rules, and create reports. You can save solutions for later reuse.

To Learn More about Solver

This chapter illustrates a very simple Solver example that admittedly could be accomplished other ways. But it illustrates the concepts nicely. To see Solver at work on a bigger problem, open the SOLVEREX.XLS worksheet found in your EXCEL\EXAMPLES\SOLVER subdirectory.

23

Auditing and Troubleshooting Worksheets

Nothing is more embarrassing than handing someone an important worksheet page containing an error or omission. Blunders can be expensive, both financially and career-wise. But errors are inevitable, particularly on large worksheets or in projects in which one worksheet refers to another. Excel will help you catch some errors, while others can lurk undetected for years. Make it a habit to test new worksheets using real data. Do the numbers look *reasonable* under a wide range of conditions? If you have time, set the work aside for a day or two and revisit it when you are fresh. Ask a knowledgeable associate to inspect and test your worksheet. Sometimes we get so close to a project that we overlook obvious problems.

Incidentally, just because a worksheet is operating properly on the day you create it does not mean it always will. It's very easy, for instance, to accidentally replace a formula with a value. This is particularly common when you share worksheet files with people who didn't create and don't fully understand them. That's why it is an especially good idea to protect your worksheets—and your formulas in particular—using the techniques described earlier in this book.

Excel provides a number of devices designed to help you locate and stamp out errors whenever they crop up. These include *Error values*, *iteration*, the *Info window*, and *Auditing tools*.

Using Error Values to Locate Problems

Occasionally you will see the following error values in cells. They always start with the pound sign (#):

#DIV/0!

#N/A

#NAME?

#NULL!

#NUM!

#REF!

#VALUE!

These values appear both in cells *containing* erroneous formulas and in cells with formulas that *refer* to the erroneous formulas. Thus, you may need to inspect more than one cell to find the real source of the problem. Although they should never be *completely* ignored, error values like these sometimes appear simply because you are not finished creating the worksheet. For instance, if you create a formula that performs division using the contents of a cell as the divisor, and if that referenced cell is empty because you haven't entered a value into it yet, you'll see Excel's #DIV/0! value. The error value should disappear when you place an appropriate divisor in the referenced cell.

Let's look at each of the error values and consider what they mean and what to do when you see them.

#DIV/0!

You'll see this error when Excel tries to divide by zero, or if a referenced cell is blank when it needs to contain a divisor. Some Excel functions return the value of zero under certain circumstances. If your division formula looks to a cell containing a function for a divisor, then the function itself, or one of its arguments, may be causing the problem. Fix the formula if it is referring to the wrong cell, or fix the cell being referenced or the erroneous function or argument.

#N/A

N/A stands for "No Value Is Available." Under certain circumstances, Excel inserts this error value in cells (when you've improperly used certain function arguments, for instance). Other times, you may want to type **#N/A** into cells yourself as a reminder that you need to obtain and enter missing data. Suppose, for instance, that you were creating a worksheet that computes sales commissions for many salespeople and that the commission percentages were still being negotiated for some of them. You could enter #N/A as the commission percentages for the "problem" reps. Then, any formulas that rely upon those missing percentages will display #N/A. The #N/A will "ripple through" the rest of your worksheet and be seen in any cell that can't be computed properly without the missing data (totals and subtotals of sales commissions, for example).

#NAME?

The #NAME? error message usually appears because you've referred to a *named item* improperly. For instance, if you define a cell name **Sales** and create a formula like **=SQRT(Sails)**, you'll get the #NAME? error message. (Unless, of course, you also have an item named Sails in your worksheet, in which case Excel will attempt to find the square root of *it*.)

If you name an item, then delete or change its name, you will also get the #NAME? message. Solution: Either rename the item or fix the affected formulas.

You might also see #NAME? if you enter a *function's* name improperly. For instance, the formula **=Sqr(9)** will produce a name error.

Forgetting to place a colon between cell addresses in a cell range will make Excel think you are referring to a name rather than a range. For example, **=SUM(B1B3)** will make Excel think you meant an item named B1B3 instead of the range B1:B3.

#NULL!

The #NULL! message means that you've specified the intersection of two areas that don't intersect, usually in a range specifier. For example, the formula **SUM(A1:D1 A3:D3)** produces a null error. Use a comma to separate referenced areas that don't intersect. For instance, **SUM(A1:D1,A3:D3)** is permitted.

#NUM!

You will see the #NUM! error value for several reasons. Unacceptable numeric arguments in functions will produce the error. For instance, trying to find the square root of negative numbers will produce the #NUM! error value.

When worksheet functions that use iterations to solve problems can't reach a workable result, you will also see the #NUM! error value. See the section "Using Iteration to Solve Circular References" to learn more about iteration.

#REF!

The #REF! message is commonly seen after you delete something to which other formulas refer. For instance, if you delete rows or columns containing things that remaining formulas need, you'll see the #REF! value in all affected formulas. Either use Undo to restore the deleted items or fix the formulas.

#VALUE!

You'll get a value reminder whenever you use the wrong type of argument, value, or operand. For instance, if you have a cell named Sales and you type the formula =**"Sales"***2, Excel will see the quotation marks and treat sales as text rather than a name.

Sometimes, however, Excel will convert text automatically. For instance, if you make the cell entry **' 10.5** (notice the leading apostrophe) in cell A1, the entry will be formatted and entered as text. You can tell this because it will be left-justified. If you then type the formula =**A1/2** in another cell, Excel will continue to display and treat cell A1 as text, but will convert it to a number for purposes of the formula. Thus, the formula will return the answer 5.25.

Excel

Using Iteration to Solve Circular References

It is not uncommon to see a dialog box warning that Excel "Cannot resolve circular references." That's not completely true. Excel *can* resolve circular references; you just need to use iteration (multiple passes) to do it. First, here's a review of what a circular reference is. Take a look at Figure 23.1.

A circular reference is a bit like a Catch 22— for example, telling a young actress you'll give her a role in your play if she has experience, but she can't gain experience till she gets her first role.

In worksheet terms, suppose you wanted to pay sales commissions based on company profitability, and wished to include commissions as one of the expenses affecting profit. You might create a profit formula in cell B3 that subtracted the contents of both cells B2 and B4 from the gross sales cell (B1). This would result in a circular reference, since profit will change when sales commissions change. Since commissions change with profit changes, commissions will need to be changed again, and so on. The first time you create a formula like this, and each time you load (open) a worksheet containing such a circular reference, you will see a warning like the one in Figure 23.1.

FIGURE 23.1

Use iteration to resolve circular references, or redesign your worksheet.

	B3	⬇		=B1-(B2+B4)			
	A	B	C	D	E	F	
1	Gross sales	$100,000					
2	Total costs	$50,000					
3	Profit	=B1-(B2+B4)					
4	Commission	$ 9,000					
5							
6							
7							
8							
9							
10							
11							
12							

Microsoft Excel

(!) **Cannot resolve circular references.**

[OK]   [Help]

There are several ways to work around circular reference problems. One way is to redesign the worksheet (and perhaps your commission policy) so that there is a precommission profit line, then a commission line, then an actual profit line that takes commissions into consideration.

Another approach is to use iteration to resolve the circular reference.

1. Start by selecting the cell containing the circular formula (B4 in our example).

2. Choose Options from the Tools menu.

3. Choose the Calculation tab in the resulting dialog box. You'll see the dialog box illustrated in Figure 23.2.

4. Choose the Iteration check box and specify the Maximum Iterations and the Maximum Change options if you don't like the values shown.

5. You can see the results without closing the Calculation Options dialog box by using the Calc Now button or the F9 function key. Clicking OK will also run the iteration routine and display an answer in the affected cell(s).

FIGURE 23.2

Switch to the Calculation tab in the Options dialog box to control iteration.

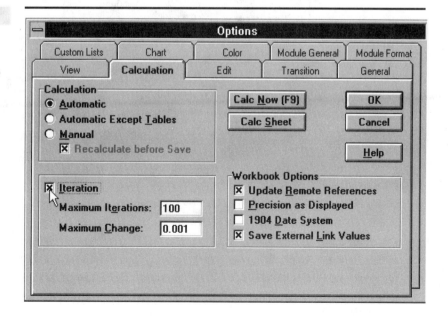

Using the Info Window to Find Errors

The Info window gives you another useful troubleshooting tool. It can tell you a lot about the active cell. Here's how to open and use the Info window:

1. Activate the cell of interest.

2. Choose Options from the Tools menu.

3. Click on the View tab (see Figure 23.3) if necessary to bring it topmost.

4. Click OK.

5. Visit the Windows menu and choose Arrange.

FIGURE 23.3

Choose Info Window in the Show section of the Options dialog box View tab.

6. You'll see a window such as the one in Figure 23.4, containing information about the active cell. Resize and move the window as you would any other.

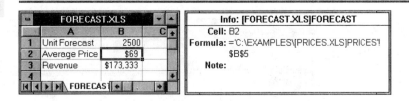

Most of the displayed items are self-explanatory. What you see varies with the cell contents. "Cell" is the cell reference of the active cell, for instance. "Formula" shows the formula, and so on. In this case, the selected cell is linked to another, so you see the path to the other cell (C:\EXAMPLES\ [PRICES.XLS]PRICES'!$B$5).

"Precedents" lists all the cells referred to by the formula in the active cell. "Dependents" lists all other cells containing formulas that rely upon the contents of the active cell. This is particularly useful information when working with multiple worksheets that are consolidated. To display things like precedents and dependents, go to the View menu and select the items you want to see.

To print information about a range of cells:

1. Select all cells of interest.

2. Open or activate (click in) the Info window.

3. Choose Print from the File menu.

Using the Auditing Command to Troubleshoot

Errors can be particularly elusive in large worksheets. Get in the habit of double-checking your work, and don't forget to expand outlined worksheets when examining them. You can also use Excel's Auditing command to help you. Among other things, it can show you which cells are used by which others.

Excel

Excel

Do you remember the bookstore workbook with three store worksheets and a summary worksheet? Here it is again in Figure 23.5. The Auditing command can find all of the cells referenced by the summary equations—including the ones in other worksheets.

FIGURE 23.5

Excel's Audit features let you see cell dependencies.

To try auditing on your own, open a worksheet and follow these steps:

1. Choose Auditing from the Tools menu.

2. Choose Trace Precedents (or Trace Dependents) from the resulting submenu.

3. Excel will show you cells that depend upon (or affect) the active cell. You'll see a little arrow as well.

4. To visit the cells, double-click on the arrowhead and you will get a list of possible places to go in the Go To dialog box, shown below:

5. Double-click on the location of interest.

Finding the Source of Error Messages

The Trace Error choice on the Auditing submenu will take you to the worksheet and cell containing the equation responsible for an error message. For instance, if you are looking at the "combined" bookstore worksheet and see an error like #####, choose Trace Error to take you to the offending cell (B5 in the Boston worksheet here):

Excel

Troubleshooting OLE Links

Problem: Linked items don't update

If you get this message, check to see that you've actually established links, and that they are set to update when you expect. For example, if you choose Locked as a link option, changes in the source will not be reflected in the destination document.

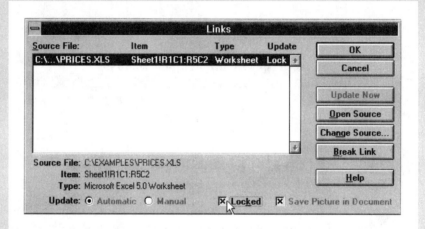

Make sure that the source document still exists. Make sure it hasn't been moved. If the document exists, you can reestablish the link by doing the following:

1. Switch to the destination document (a Word document, perhaps).

2. Choose Links from the Edit menu.

3. Select the troublesome link from the Source file list.

A WHOLE NEW WAY TO WORK

4. Click on the Change Source button.

5. Use the Change Source dialog box (shown here) to find the source document, and click OK.

Change Source

File **N**ame:
prices.xls

gasscen.xls
infofun.xls
invoice.xls
median.xls
mpglogic.xls
nm_store.xls
ohmslaw.xls
olexl.xls
pmt.xls
prices.xls
rain.xls
ranges.xls

Directories:
c:\examples

c:\
examples

Drives:
c: ast

List Files of **T**ype:
Microsoft Excel Files [*.xl*]

Item: Sheet1!R1C1:R5C2

OK
Cancel
Find File...
Help

Problem: Object types not available

If you don't see an object type that you think should be available in the Object Type list used to insert objects, try reinstalling the application that generates the object type. For instance, if you expect to see Microsoft WordArt listed and you don't, try reinstalling Microsoft Word from the original Microsoft disks, and if you do a custom installation, make certain that WordArt is one of the items specified.

Excel

A WHOLE NEW WAY TO WORK

Problem: You get a "Can't Find Application" error message

You might get the "Can't Find Application" message if you've moved a source application to a different subdirectory or driver. If the source application resides on the server, you'll get this message if you have network problems. Remember that in order to edit embedded objects you must have the application that was used to create the object. For instance, if a co-worker gives you a worksheet containing a PowerPoint slide, you'll need PowerPoint on your machine to edit the slide.

PART FOUR

Presenting with PowerPoint

There was a time when you could stand up, speak your piece, get a yes or a no, and sit down. But it's the nineties now, and you are expected to give "awesome" meeting presentations to the MTV generation. Your audience expects to be dazzled. They want to see color, motion, and special effects. To a large extent how a presentation looks is often as important as what it says.

PowerPoint is Microsoft's answer to that need. It will help you create good-looking overhead transparencies, 35mm slides, and even video slide shows. And while it is true that most of what PowerPoint does can also be done by Word and Excel, PowerPoint streamlines a few of the tasks, and provides some handy prefabricated layouts, color schemes, and font choices. Let's take a look.

PowerPoint Toolbar Reference

BUTTON	DESCRIPTION

Buttons on PowerPoint's Standard Toolbar

New: Creates new presentation. [File ➤ New] *Shortcut:* Ctrl+N

Open: Opens existing presentations. [File ➤ Open] *Shortcut:* Ctrl+O

Save: Saves current presentation. [File ➤ Save] *Shortcut:* Ctrl+S

Print: Prints single copy of *slides* (does not bring up Print dialog box).

Spelling: Runs the spelling checker. [Tools ➤ Spelling] *Shortcut:* F7

Cut: Cuts selected item(s). [Edit ➤ Cut] *Shortcut:* Ctrl+X

Copy: Copies selected item(s). [Edit ➤ Copy] *Shortcut:* Ctrl+C

Paste: Pastes from Clipboard. [Edit ➤ Paste] *Shortcut:* Ctrl+V

Format Painter: Copies then applies format of selected item. Not for graphics or pictures.

Undo: Performs a single undo (no list). [Edit ➤ Undo] *Shortcut:* Ctrl+Z

Insert New Slide: Inserts a new slide after current slide. [Insert ➤ New Slide] *Shortcut:* Ctrl+M

Insert Microsoft Word Table: Inserts a Word table. [Insert ➤ Microsoft Table]

Insert Microsoft Excel Worksheet: Inserts an Excel *worksheet* (not a workbook).

Insert Graph: Creates a Graph object. [Insert ➤ Microsoft Graph]

BUTTON	DESCRIPTION

Insert Org Chart: Creates an org-chart object. [Insert ➤ Object ➤ Microsoft Organization Chart]

Insert Clip Art: Opens the ClipArt Gallery. [Insert ➤ Clip Art]

Pick A Look Wizard: Runs the Pick A Look Wizard. [Format ➤ Pick A Look Wizard]

Report It: Saves slides as a Word outline sans graphics.

Help: Click then point to item of interest for online help.

Buttons on PowerPoint's Drawing Toolbar

Selection: Click on objects while this button is depressed.

Text: Drag with this button depressed to create text objects.

Line: Use to draw lines

Rectangle: Use to draw rectangles.

Ellipse: Use to draw circles and ellipses.

Arc: Use to draw arcs.

Freeform: Use to draw freeform shapes.

Free Rotate: Use to rotate selected drawn objects.

Autoshapes: Reveals tear-off AutoShape palette.

Fill On/Off: Turns automatic drawing fill on or off. Will add or remove fill from an existing object.

PowerPoint

PowerPoint Toolbar Reference

BUTTON	DESCRIPTION

Buttons on PowerPoint's Drawing Toolbar (continued)

 Line On/Off: Applies the default line style to an object or removes the line.

 Shadow On/Off: Adds or removes shadow effects from selected objects.

Buttons on PowerPoint's Slide Sorter Toolbar

Transition: Opens Transition dialog box. [Tools ➤ Transition]

Build: Opens Build dialog box. [Tools ➤ Build]

Hide Slide: Hides current slide. [Tools ➤ Hide Slide]

Rehearse Timings: Times rehersals and shows times on-screen. [View ➤ Slide Show]

Show/Hide Formatting: In Outline view, this toggles display of character formatting (bold, italic, etc).

Buttons on PowerPoint's Outline Toolbar

Promote (Indent Less): Moves item up one level in outline. *Shortcut:* Ctrl+←

Demote (Indent More): Moves item down one level in outline. *Shortcut:* Ctrl+→

Move Up: Places selected text nearer to the beginning of your outline. Alt+Shift+↑

Move Down: Places selected text nearer to the bottom of your outline. Alt+Shift+↓

Collapse Selection: Hides all but slide title for selected slides. Alt+Shift+minus

Expand Selection: Shows all text and headings in selected slides. Alt+Shift+plus

Show Titles: Shows titles only. *Shortcut:* Alt+Shift+1.

Show All: Shows all text and headings. *Shortcut:* Alt+Shift+A

Show Formatting: Displays and hides text formatting (bold, italic, etc).

PowerPoint's Slide Show Toolbar

Drawing: Turns on-screen drawing on and off.

PowerPoint's Formatting Toolbar

Increase Font Size

Decrease Font Size

Bold

Italic

PowerPoint Toolbar Reference

BUTTON	DESCRIPTION
PowerPoint's Formatting Toolbar (continued)	
	Underline
	Text Shadow
	Text Color
	Left Alignment
	Center Alignment
	Bullets On/Off
	Promote (Indent Less)
	Demote (Indent More)

24

PowerPoint Basics

PowerPoint helps you quickly create, update, and sort "slide-based" professional-looking presentation materials, even if you are not a graphic arts designer.

PowerPoint is no replacement for multimedia development programs, and it is probably not the tool you should choose for creating a brochure or proposal booklet, because it does not have the page layout capabilities of Word. Rather, PowerPoint is a program that helps you quickly create:

- Black-and-white overhead transparencies
- Color overhead transparencies
- 35mm slides
- Computer screen and video slide shows complete with special effects
- Presentation files that you can send to coworkers for their review, even if they don't own PowerPoint
- Printed meeting handouts
- Detailed speaker's notes
- Printed and on-screen presentation *outlines*

Figure 24.1 shows some examples of items you can create using PowerPoint.

While creating and modifying your presentation materials, you will use techniques that should be familiar by now, because PowerPoint "behaves" much like Word and Excel. Moreover, you can use cut and paste or OLE to include Word and Excel information such as worksheets, charts, and text in your presentations.

PowerPoint provides rehearsal tools that let you practice your presentation at your desk. It lets you quickly rearrange presentation materials by dragging them around on your screen with your mouse. It also offers "drill-down" capabilities

FIGURE 24.1

Examples of presentation materials PowerPoint can help you create

People to see

- Hopi Indians
- White Water Wizards
- For Four Wheel drivers, Inc.
- Don Flaps @ Old Plane graveyard
- The Friday crowd at Crazy Larry's Pub

Places to go

- Sedona
- Four corners
- Johnson Speedway
- Sun Lakes Golf Cart Rentals
- Sleepy corner Pizza and Donuts

Arizona Thrill Seeker's Guide

- Indian culture
- Off-road adventures
- Great glider rides
- White water
- Dude ranches

PowerPoint

OLE Tips for PowerPoint

A WHOLE NEW WAY TO WORK

- Switch to the slide you want to use as the destination before linking or embedding into a PowerPoint document.
- PowerPoint lets you resize, restyle, and move embedded and linked items. These changes will not be altered when you update links.
- You can embed slides in Word documents. Select and copy the one(s) you want to embed in Slide Sorter view.

---

that let you pull up supporting documents. For example, if you are presenting a budget summary, PowerPoint makes it easy to pull up the supporting detail numbers from a worksheet or other source. This assumes, of course, that you have your computer with you and that it has the necessary data on it. And, as you will see if you experiment with this feature, there may be quicker ways to accomplish the same thing.

Terminology

Well, we can't have a new program without some new buzzwords, now, can we? Here's everything you need to know about PowerPointSpeak:

Slides

You create and edit individual pages called *slides*. For instance, in a sales presentation you might have a slide titled Competition, another called Pricing, and so on. For example, Figure 24.2 shows six typical PowerPoint slides.

Speaker's Notes

Use speaker's notes when you present. They are usually printed on paper and can be either the exact text of the speech, reminder notes, back-up information, or combinations thereof. Figure 24.3 shows an example of speaker's notes.

FIGURE 24.2

PowerPoint lets you create and arrange slides for use with overhead projectors and video display systems.

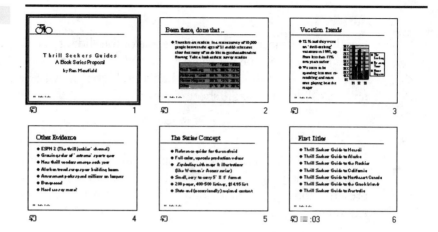

FIGURE 24.3

Speaker's notes are used when rehearsing and giving presentations.

Handouts

Handouts are paper copies of all or some of the slides to be given to the audience. They can be one per page or reduced so that three or six fit on a sheet of paper. Figure 24.4 shows a typical handout. Notice how PowerPoint will place up to six slides on a single sheet of paper.

Presentation Files

All of the PowerPoint slides for a particular project (a sales pitch, for instance) are kept in a single PowerPoint file called a *presentation file*. These presentation files normally end with the extension .PPT (SALES.PPT, for example).

A presentation file might have just a few slides or many. If you've recorded sounds as part of your presentation or added speaker's notes, those presentation elements will also be stored in the presentation file. In other words, each presentation consists of only one file, making it easy to copy and pass around presentations.

Masters

You create *masters* (also called master slides) to hold information that will appear on multiple slides in your presentation. For instance, if you wanted to put your name, company logo, or some other decoration on each slide, you'd add it to the master for that presentation.

You can also create separate masters for handouts and speaker's notes within each presentation. PowerPoint comes with a variety of preprogrammed masters to get you started. You can use these as-is, modify them, or create your own masters from scratch. Figure 24.5 shows one master—designed to make it easy to create slides with bulleted lists.

Color Schemes

PowerPoint lets you define rules used for applying colors or shades of gray to the various components of your presentation. For instance, you can specify a slide's background colors, the colors used for major headings,

FIGURE 24.4

Print handouts for your audience and perhaps for yourself.

Thrill Seekers Guide

Thrill Seekers Guides

A Book Series Proposal

by Ron Mansfield

Thrill Seekers Guide   12/29/93   1

Been there, done that ...

♦ Travelers are restless. In a recent survey of 10,000 people between the ages of 21 and 65 it became clear that many of us *do* like to get that adrenaline flowing. Take a look at these survey results:

	1991	1992	1993
Thrill Seeking	12%	38%	72%
Relaxing Travel	88%	78%	15%
Home Repairs	33%	15%	23%
Other	21%	31%	28%

Thrill Seekers Guide   12/29/93   2

Vacation Trends

♦ 72 % said they went on "thrill-seeking" vacations in 1993, up from less than 13% two years earlier.

♦ We seem to be spending less time re-modeling and more time playing beat the reaper.

Thrill Seekers Guide   12/29/93   3

Other Evidence

♦ ESPN 2 (The thrill junkies' channel)
♦ Growing sales of "extreme" sports gear
♦ New thrill vendors emerge each year
♦ Alaskan travel surge spurs building boom
♦ Amusement parks spend millions on loopers
♦ Bungeeeee!
♦ Need we say more?

Thrill Seekers Guide   12/29/93   4

The Series Concept

♦ Reference guides for the unafraid
♦ Full color, upscale production values
♦ *Exploding* with maps & illustrations (like Wurman's Access series)
♦ Small, easy to carry 5" X 8" format
♦ 200 pages, 400-500 listings, $14.95 list
♦ State and (occasionally) regional content

Thrill Seekers Guide   12/29/93   5

First Titles

♦ Thrill Seekers Guide to Hawaii
♦ Thrill Seekers Guide to Alaska
♦ Thrill Seekers Guide to the Rockies
♦ Thrill Seekers Guide to California
♦ Thrill Seekers Guide to Northwest Canada
♦ Thrill Seekers Guide to the Greek Islands
♦ Thrill Seekers Guide to Australia

Thrill Seekers Guide   12/29/93   6

Microsoft

FIGURE 24.5

This master makes it easy to create bulleted lists.

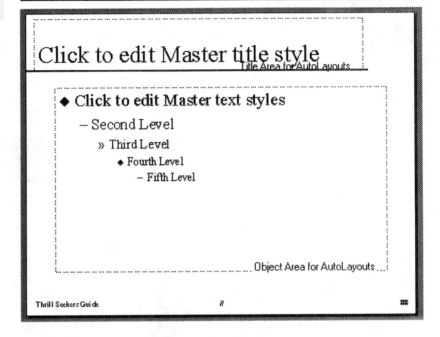

and so on. PowerPoint comes with many predefined color schemes, which you can use as-is or modify to taste. Chapter 30 explores colors and shades of gray in more detail.

PowerPoint Templates

A PowerPoint *template* consists of a master and a color scheme. PowerPoint comes with 160 predefined templates. For example, the slide in Figure 24.6 was created with a template that includes a diamond-shaped graphic and changes the colors of headings and bullets.

If you've created presentations containing your own custom masters and color schemes, you can use these as templates. To change the *look* of a presentation, you need merely apply a different template to an existing presentation to completely change the presentation's appearance. PowerPoint makes all the necessary changes in colors, fonts, and so on. (You'll see how this all works in Chapter 26.)

FIGURE 24.6

Templates make it easy to apply professionally designed "looks."

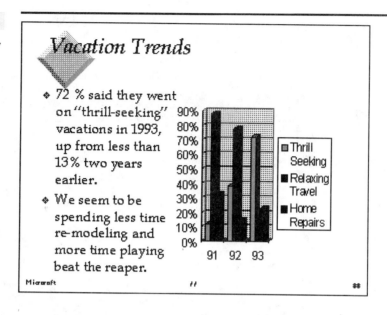

Getting Started

No surprises here: Start PowerPoint as you would any other Office program. One way is to click on the PowerPoint button, shown below, in the Office Manager toolbar:

TIP

If you create and show on-screen presentations, you may find that the Office Manager toolbar gets in the way of the presentation. To turn it off, quit the Office Manager by clicking on the Office Manager toolbar button (the right-most) and choosing Exit.

You can also start PowerPoint from the Windows Program Manager by double-clicking on the PowerPoint icon or using the Run command (File ➤ Run **c:\powerpnt\powerpnt.exe**, for instance).

Unless you turn this feature off, you will be greeted with a PowerPoint Tip of the Day, like the one shown in Figure 24.7.

FIGURE 24.7

A PowerPoint Tip of the Day

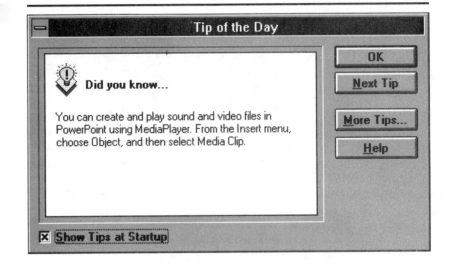

When you dismiss the tip dialog box by clicking on the OK button, you will see a second dialog box, shown in Figure 24.8.

It wants to know if you'd like to create a new presentation or work with an existing one. Notice that, if creating a new presentation, you have the options of using several wizards and template choices. Chapter 25 will explore these choices in detail.

Views

Like other Microsoft Office products, PowerPoint offers different views for entering, editing, and previewing your information. For instance, PowerPoint's Outline view is handy for entering text and for rearranging the text in a given slide, but once you have done the bulk of the typing, you'll want to switch to other PowerPoint views. They include:

- Slide view
- Slide Sorter view

FIGURE 24.8

The PowerPoint
dialog box

- Notes Pages view
- Slide Show view

Switching Views

You can switch views by using the View menu or the view buttons (shown below) at the bottom left of the PowerPoint window. You may want to try switching views as you read about them.

The buttons are named (from left to right) Slide View, Outline View, Slide Sorter View, Notes Pages View, and Slide Show View.

PowerPoint

Outline View

It's easy to rearrange the individual line items while in Outline view. And you can collapse items in this view so that you can see just headings or just the names of each slide. For example, to show just the title for each slide you could use the Show Titles button, shown in Figure 24.9.

It's easy to move collapsed slides to different places in your presentations. You work with outline buttons in much the same way you do in Word's Outline view. Chapter 27 has the details.

FIGURE 24.9

Use Outline view to rearrange slides or entire presentations.

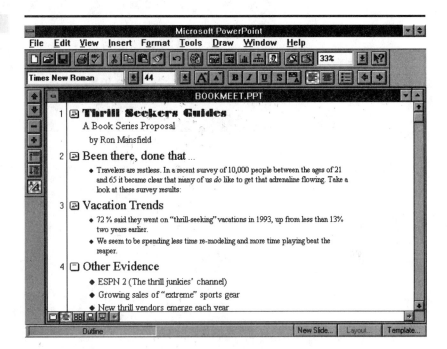

Slide View

Slide view shows you how your finished slides will look. You'll see the backgrounds, colors or shades of gray, and so forth. Figure 24.10 illustrates a typical slide in Slide view.

FIGURE 24.10

Slide view shows you
how your slides will
actually look.

Typical Categories & Listings

Air Thrills	Helicopters, Aerobatics, Gliders, Vintage aircraft ...
Water Thrills	Highspeed cats, Renting skeedoos, Parasailing ...
Water Adventures	Alaskan ferrys, Freighter adventures, Sail to Hawaii ...
Underwater Thrills	Submarine rides, Shark dives, SNUBA, Best dive shops ...
Four Wheels	Rent exotic cars, Off-roading, Pro stockcar lessons ...

Thrill Seekers Guide   1/13/94

Notice that PowerPoint has wrapped long lines whenever necessary. You can move from slide to slide with the Page Up and Page Down keys or the scroll box.

You can edit text and other slide elements while in Slide view, as you will learn in Chapter 26.

Slide Sorter View

The Slide Sorter view lets you see "thumbnails" (reduced-size slide images) like those shown in Figure 24.11.

While in Slide Sorter view you can drag slides to move them. Chapter 27 shows how this is done. The Slide Sorter view is also where you specify types of slide transitions. For example, you can make one slide dissolve into another or make slides appear and disappear using venetian blind effects. You can also specify how individual bullet points on a slide are revealed to the audience (all at once or one at a time). Slide Sorter is an excellent view to use for this purpose because you get a preview of the effects as you choose them.

FIGURE 24.11

Slide Sorter view lets
you see and move
miniature slides,
sometimes called
thumbnails.

Notes Pages View

Use the Notes Pages view to create and see notes to the presenter. It shows a
miniature slide image and provides a text area for presenter's notes, as shown
in Figure 24.12.

To enter a note:

1. Click in the text area beneath the slide. The box outline will change
appearance.

2. Type and edit in the note box as you would any other.

As you will see in Chapter 28, you can print these notes if you like.

FIGURE 24.12

Use Notes Pages view
to edit and review
your notes.

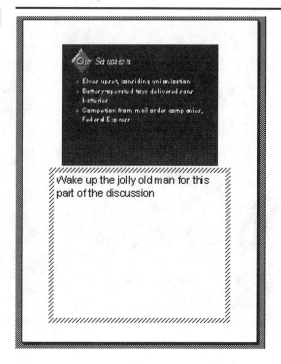

Slide Show View

Use Slide Show view to help you rehearse, or for actual video presentations of
finished shows. It removes all of the PowerPoint clutter and places a small
pencil icon at the bottom right of the screen, as shown in Figure 24.13.

When you switch to Slide Show view, you'll see the slide you were working on
in the previous view. To move forward (to see higher numbered slides), either
press the space bar, click the primary mouse button, or use the → key. Use the
← key to move backwards.

If you click on the little pencil icon, you can use the mouse to draw temporary
lines on the screen. Use the lines to emphasize things on the screen as you
talk. These lines are not saved with the presentation, and might remind you
of chalk marks—visible only during the current presentation or rehearsal.

To leave the Slide Show view, press Esc. You'll be switched to the previous
view you were using. You'll learn more about slide shows in Chapter 28.

PowerPoint
CHAPTER 24

FIGURE 24.13

Click the Slide Show

Our Situation slide content:

- Elves upset, considing unionization
- Battery-operated toys delivered sans batteries
- Competion from mail order companies, Federal Express

25

Creating Presentations the Easy Way

I t's the Wizards, templates, layouts, and masters that put the *power* in PowerPoint. While you *could* format each slide manually, the combination of wizardly automation and predesigned layouts greatly simplifies the task. There's even a Wizard called *AutoContent* that will help you develop a presentation's content and organization. So let's get off on the right foot by looking at automation first. You'll learn about manual techniques in later chapters.

AutoContent Wizard

The AutoContent Wizard asks you several questions and then uses a predefined template containing suggested topics and tips to help you tell your story. There are templates for:

- Breaking bad news (BADNEWS.PPT)
- Progress reports (PROGRESS.PPT)
- Sales presentations (SELLING.PPT)
- Strategy meetings (STRATEGY.PPT)
- Training sessions (TRAINING.PPT)
- General presentations (GENERAL.PPT)

When you start PowerPoint and dismiss the tip of the day, you will be presented with the PowerPoint dialog box. It offers a number of choices. If you desire help with the content of your presentation, click on the AutoContent Wizard button, shown in Figure 25.1, and then on the OK button to get started.

FIGURE 25.1

Using the AutoContent
Wizard

 TIP You can start a new Wizard-driven presentation at any time by choosing New from the File menu.

After you read the Wizard's greeting, click the Next button (or press Enter). You'll see the Step 2 dialog box, shown in Figure 25.2.

Here, you are asked to provide information for the title slide (the opening slide in your presentation). Type a topic, change the name in the name box if necessary, and place other text in the Other Information You'd Like To Include? text area, if you wish. When you click Next, you will see a list of presentation types (Strategy, Selling, Training, etc.). A small status area at the left side of the dialog box will show sample text from each template as you click

PowerPoint

FIGURE 25.2

Add information that will appear on the title slide.

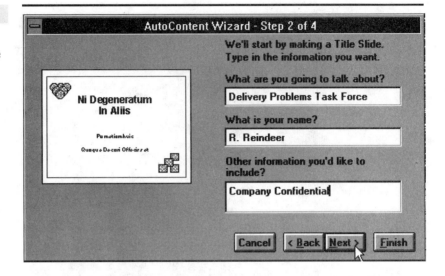

on a presentation type. For instance, Figure 25.3 shows what the Communicating Bad News choice looks like.

When you settle on a topic (Communicating Bad News in this example), click the Next button to move on. You will get the racing flag dialog box (Step 4 of 4). Click Finish to begin to create the actual presentation. You

FIGURE 25.3

Step 4 of the AutoContent Wizard

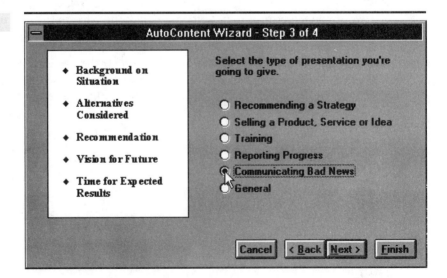

should see an outline of a presentation. For example, Figure 25.4 shows the beginnings of a Communicating Bad News presentation.

The Wizard automatically switches to PowerPoint's Outline view. You will see a number of slides. In Outline view, the slides are numbered along the left edge of the windows. Notice that the Wizard has already edited the title slide for you. It inserts the topic and presenter's name information that you typed earlier (*Delivery Problems Task Force* and *R. Reindeer* in Figure 25.4).

FIGURE 25.4

The Wizard will provide an initial outline for your presentation, complete with content suggestions.

Editing the Wizard's Work

Edit PowerPoint text just as you do Word or Excel text. As you can see in Figure 25.4, the PowerPoint window has scroll bars, toolbars, and all the other things you've come to expect. Select text to edit or replace it. Figure 25.5 shows some edited text.

FIGURE 25.5

It's easy to edit text in PowerPoint's Outline view.

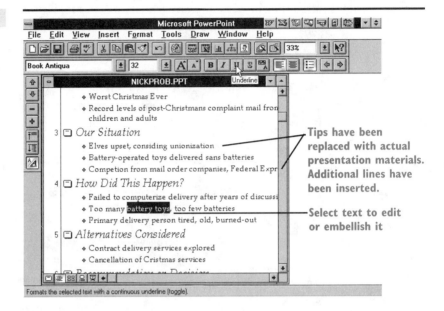

Tips have been replaced with actual presentation materials. Additional lines have been inserted.

Select text to edit or embellish it

You already know the important text editing techniques well if you've ever used another Windows program. Here's a brief review. (Details can be found in Chapter 26.)

- Select text by dragging or double-clicking.
- Type to replace selected text.
- Use toolbar buttons and drop-down lists to embellish (bold, underline, etc.).
- To insert text, point and click to move the insertion point and then start typing.
- Press ↵ to insert new bullet items.
- Use the delete key to remove text and bullets.
- Most other tools (like drag and drop or cut and paste) work in PowerPoint.

The Pick a Look Wizard

You can *manually* change the background, typestyles, and other design elements on slides by using techniques discussed in Chapter 26. But when you want to change the look of *all* the slides, it is better to change masters. This changes design elements for all the slides in a presentation. PowerPoint's Pick a Look Wizard makes this easy to do. You can run the Pick a Look Wizard at any time on an existing or new presentation. And since you can run the Wizard at any time, it is possible to try multiple looks on the same presentation until you find the one you like.

1. Begin by opening the presentation you wish to improve.

2. Choose Pick a Look Wizard from PowerPoint's Format menu.

3. Click the Next button to dismiss the Wizard's general information (Step 1) screen.

4. Choose an output format from the choices shown in Figure 25.6.

    PowerPoint uses your answer to this question to select appropriate height and width settings for your slides. It also makes color decisions based on your choices. You can always revisit this dialog box later to try different output settings.

FIGURE 25.6

The Pick a Look Wizard lets you change the overall appearance of your entire presentation.

PowerPoint

5. Click Next to move to Step 3, where you will be given a choice of four templates offering different "looks" (see Figure 25.7) and an opportunity to choose additional templates.

6. When you click to enable a template you'll see a thumbnail of the resulting look in the preview area at the left of the dialog box. It's not very detailed, but it will give you a general idea of what to expect.

FIGURE 25.7

To see additional templates, click the More button.

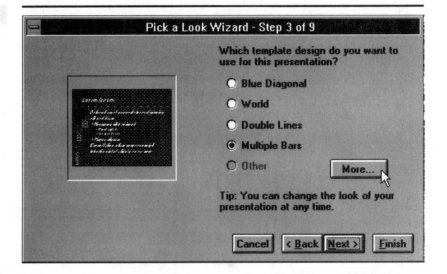

7. To preview additional templates, click the More button. The More button takes you to the Presentation Template dialog box, shown in Figure 25.8, which lets you locate and preview additional templates.

8. Use the dialog box to locate templates of interest. It behaves like the Open dialog box in most Windows applications (select a disk drive, then a directory, and so on).

9. When you click on a template's name in the scrolling File Name list, you'll get a preview in the lower-right corner of the dialog box.

10. When you find a look you want to try, click Apply.

FIGURE 25.8

Pick templates in the
scrolling list and pre-
view them right in this
dialog box.

TIP   If you've created presentations with looks that you like, you
can locate and preview those in addition to PowerPoint's
predefined looks.

11. You'll be returned to the Wizard's Step 3. You'll see the chosen template
in the preview area.

12. Click the Next button. Step 4, shown in Figure 25.9, will ask which
types of output you'll need for the project.

13. Click to remove the x from any item(s) you won't need, then click Next
to continue. You'll see Wizard Step 5.

14. At this step you can type text you wish to have appear on each slide.
You can also turn page numbering and date stamping on and off. Click
Next when you are done, as shown in Figure 25.10.

15. You will be given similar choices for each of the other output types
you've chosen (handout pages, speaker's notes, etc.). If you want the
same choices for all output types, click the Finish button. Otherwise
click Next to visit each of the remaining Steps.

PowerPoint

FIGURE 25.9

Choose the desired
printout types here.

FIGURE 25.10

Things you choose
here appear on all
slides.

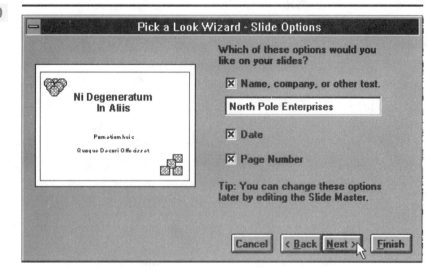

16. There will be a heart-stopping pause while the Wiz thinks this all over. In a moment (sometimes after a *kilomoment*) you will see one of your slides, such as the one shown in Figure 25.11, strutting the new look.

The font(s) may have changed. The image should be in the right proportions for the given task. (35mm slides are a different shape than overhead transparencies, for instance.) If the template calls for shadowed text, you'll see shadows. The type of bullets might have changed in bulleted lists.

FIGURE 25.11

The slide after the Pick a Look Wizard has done its work.

  Occasionally, all of the Wizard's font changing, margin changing, and other remodeling will cause some problems. Slide headings that once fit on a single line now might take two lines. Text that fit on the slide may fit no longer. Graphics inserted by the new template may obliterate something important on one or all of your slides. Therefore, it is very important that you inspect each slide in Slide View or with the Slide Show feature after using the Look Wiz!

PowerPoint

Masters

Masters make it easy for you to specify common design elements that you wish to include throughout your presentation. Masters can contain elements like backgrounds, logos, font choices, color schemes, date and time stamps, page numbers, etc. Each presentation has a master for:

- Slides
- Outlines
- Handouts
- Speaker's notes

PowerPoint comes with a variety of predefined masters. They are stored in templates. You can pick the masters you wish to use for each presentation and even change to different masters after you've created your presentation.

Changes that you make to masters in a presentation affect all of the slides or pages in your current presentation. For instance, if you add a big logo to a presentation's slide master and a little logo to the presentation's handout master, the big logos will appear on all of your slides and the small logos will print on handouts, but not on the outline or speaker's notes.

You can "overrule" master settings for individual slides (or printout pages). PowerPoint will remember these exceptions even if you switch masters in a production.

Typical elements of a master include:

- Title text
- Body text (in a variety of indent levels)
- Color schemes
- Background shading and other "wallpaper" art
- Presentation title or other marginal text
- Date stamp
- Time stamp

Figure 25.12 shows a typical slide master.

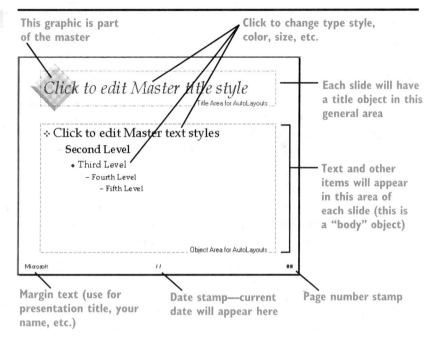

FIGURE 25.12

Masters contain common elements for all slides or report pages. This is a typical slide master.

This graphic is part of the master

Click to change type style, color, size, etc.

Click to edit Master title style

Title Area for AutoLayouts

Each slide will have a title object in this general area

❖ Click to edit Master text styles
— Second Level
  ♦ Third Level
    – Fourth Level
      – Fifth Level

Text and other items will appear in this area of each slide (this is a "body" object)

Object Area for AutoLayouts

Microsoft / / ##

Margin text (use for presentation title, your name, etc.)

Date stamp—current date will appear here

Page number stamp

Editing Your Masters

To change something in a master, follow these steps:

1. Open the presentation.

2. Choose Master from the View menu.

3. Choose the type of master you wish to edit from the resulting submenu (Slide Master, Handout Master, or Notes Master).

4. Make changes as you would in most Microsoft Office programs. For instance, to change the font of the title style, click on the master's title and choose a new font from the Formatting toolbar or Font menu. (Chapter 26 has details.)

5. To move items on a master, click to select, then drag them with the mouse pointer. Notice how the border surrounding the object changes appearance when selected. Figure 25.13 illustrates this.

FIGURE 25.13

You can drag master elements after selecting them.

Click to select and drag objects on masters to reposition them. The appearance of outlines will change when they are able to be moved.

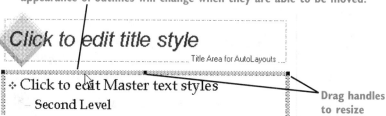

6. To *resize* master elements (like the areas that contain text and cause it to wrap), select the object as in step 5, then drag the *black handles* to change the object's size and shape.

7. Look at *all* the slides in your presentation to see the effect of the changes.

TIP

If you've spent a long time creating a presentation and then decide to make major changes to the masters for that presentation, experiment on a copy of your presentation (made with the Save As command) rather than working on your original presentation file. It's often easier to abandon an experiment and revert to the old file than it is to undo everything.

Using Masters from Different Presentations

Since all presentations have masters, it is possible to have a wide variety of different looks. And it is very easy to reuse looks once you've developed them. Two ways to do this include the Pick a Look Wizard (which you learned about earlier in this chapter) and the Presentation Template command. To apply different masters to an existing presentation:

1. Open the presentation.

2. Choose Presentation Template from PowerPoint's Format menu.

3. Choose a drive and directory containing presentations whose masters you'd like to use.

4. Click on file names and see a tiny preview of each in the lower-right corner of the dialog box, as shown in Figure 25.14.

5. Click Apply to try the new look with your existing presentation.

FIGURE 25.14

Click to pick and
preview templates.

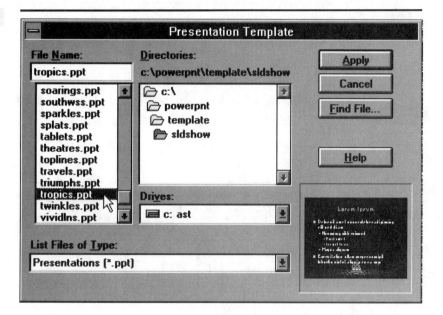

Adding Slides

You can add (insert) new slides while in the Outline, Slides, or Slide Sorter views. The new slides can be created by inserting an AutoLayout to help with the format and then typing, or you can insert slides from other presentations. Moreover, by using OLE and other techniques, you can insert elements from other programs including Word outlines, Excel charts, and much more. You'll learn more about this in Chapter 27. For now let's stick with manually inserting and typing slides.

PowerPoint

Specifying the New Slide's Insertion Point

New slides are always inserted *after* the current slide in a presentation. The easiest way to see this is in Slide Sorter view, but the concept is the same in Slide and Outline views. Here are the steps:

1. Switch to one of the three views (Slide, Slide Sorter, or Outline view).

2. Click to select the slide just before the point where you want the new slide. For instance, to place a new slide after slide 2 in Figure 25.15, you would click on slide 2 to select it.

 TIP To insert slides while in Outline view, simply click on the slide icon next to the slide you wish to select.

FIGURE 25.15

The new slide will be inserted between slides 2 and 3.

3. Use the New Slide command on PowerPoint's Insert menu.

4. If you are in Outline view, PowerPoint inserts a new slide using the same layout as the preceding slide. (You'll learn more about layouts in a moment.) If you are in Slide view or Slide Sorter view, you will be presented with the New Slide (AutoLayout) dialog box, which will be explained in a moment. Select an AutoLayout and click OK.

5. The new slide will be inserted and the slides following it will be renumbered, as shown in Figure 25.16.

FIGURE 25.16

New Slide inserted a new, blank slide.

AutoLayout—Simple Slide Design

Chances are, your presentations have many things in common with those of other people. *You* need a title slide, *they* need a title slide. You create bulleted lists, they need bulleted lists. They show graphs with some explanatory text and so do you. Organizational charts are often important in presentations, as are photos, clip art, and other embellishments. Knowing this, Microsoft has developed a number of *slide layouts* for common slide-making tasks. These layouts have text boxes, places to insert graphics, bullet list formatting, and so on. AutoLayout takes care of things like margins, line spacing, etc. Each slide in a presentation can use the same or different layout.

There are two very similar dialog boxes to help you automatically lay out slides. You see the New Slide dialog box automatically when you insert new slides in Slide and Slide Sorter views, or you can call for the Slide Layout dialog box, shown in Figure 25.17, by choosing the Slide Layout command on PowerPoint's Format menu while in Slide view.

Except for one button, these two dialog boxes are identical. In both instances, each AutoFormat choice is illustrated in a thumbnail example. You can select a layout by clicking on its thumbnail. This surrounds the thumbnail with a

PowerPoint

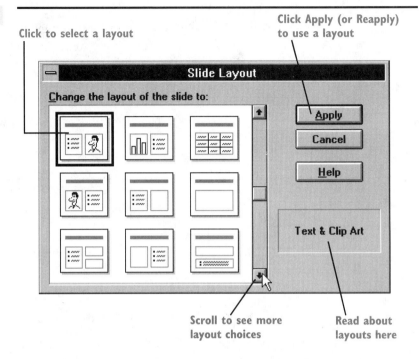

FIGURE 25.17

The Slide Layout (aka
New Slide) dialog box

dark border. The text box in the lower-right corner of the dialog box contains
a brief description of the selected layout.

Scroll to see the rest of the AutoLayout choices. Click on different choices to
read about them.

TIP To see which layout was used for a particular existing slide
(in someone else's presentation for instance), select the
slide in any view, then choose the Slide Layout command.
The Slide Layout dialog box will open with the current
slide's layout thumbnail selected (surrounded by a dark
border).

Click on the Apply button in the New Slide dialog box or on the Reapply button in the Slide Layout dialog box to apply the chosen layout to the current
slide in your presentation. Let's see an example of this at work.

Using AutoLayout when Inserting a Slide

Suppose we wanted to add a new slide after slide 10 in an exisiting presentation. The slide will contain a bulleted list and some clip art. Here's one way to do that:

1. Open the presentation.

2. Switch to Slide view (or the Slide Sorter) and go to the slide just before the insertion point (slide 10 in our example).

3. Choose New Slide from the Insert menu.

4. Peruse the AutoLayout choices until you find one that offers a design layout you like—a combination of text and clip art in our example. (Notice that there are *two* layout choices in this instance.)

5. Click on the desired choice to select it, then click OK.

6. PowerPoint will insert a new empty slide (numbered 11 in Figure 25.18) and renumber the slides that follow it.

7. The new slide will take on the general characteristics of the current presentation, including things like marginal text (Thrill Seekers Guide in our example), page numbering options, etc.

8. Click in the various areas of the slide blank to add and edit things, or double-click if that's what the on-screen instructions say to do. For instance, to add a title, click in the title area and start typing. To create a bulleted list, click in a text area and type. Pressing ↵ will start a new bulleted line.

9. Save your presentation (Ctrl+S) when you are happy with the changes.

FIGURE 25.18

AutoLayout contains
a number of layout
choices. This one is
ideal for slides needing
a title, text, and clip art.

 Some layouts (including the one in our example) facilitate
Object Linking and Embedding and the inclusion of
graphics—topics covered in more detail in Chapter 27.
OLE is also discussed in Part Seven.

Deleting Slides

To delete an unwanted slide, select it in any view and then choose the Delete
Slide choice on PowerPoint's Edit menu.

 You won't be asked to confirm slide deletions, and Undo will
only work if you catch your mistake immediately.

26

*Working with
Text in
PowerPoint*

P owerPoint does a pretty good job of formatting text for you. But if you get the urge to one-up your co-presenters, you can reach deeper into PowerPoint's bag of tricks. In fact, you could probably fritter away days playing with typestyles, shadow effects, and more.

Nothing's worse than spotting a five-foot-tall misspelling. That's why it's a good idea to let PowerPoint check your work *before* you present.

Last-minute changes in content and organization are a snap with PowerPoint's outlining and text-editing features. Most of the techniques will seem familiar if you've already used Microsoft Word. The odd thing is, there are text tools in PowerPoint you'll wish you had in Word (like the Periods command), and some tools in Word that you sure could use in PowerPoint (like Insert Symbol).

Editing and Moving Text

As you've already seen, PowerPoint requires familiar text-editing skills. Text is kept in things called *title objects* and *body objects*. These objects are rectangular areas surrounded by nonprinting lines. First you select an object, then you select text within the object to work with it. Work in Slide view, Outline view, or Note Pages view.

Inserting Text

Point-and-click within a title object or body object to move the insertion point to the place in the text where you want to make the addition. Begin typing. Text to the right of the insertion point will be pushed forward and down.

NOTE Unlike Word, PowerPoint does not automatically scroll text onto the next "page" (a new slide) if you run out of room on the current slide, so watch the screen as you type.

Keep your writing terse. Insert additional slides if necessary. While you *can* decrease type sizes and line spacing to make things fit, you shouldn't make text too much smaller or tighter than the AutoFormat defaults, or it will be difficult for audiences to read your words of wisdom.

Inserting New Bullet Items

Place the insertion point where you want the new item and press ↵. PowerPoint will add a new line preceded by a bullet, as shown in Figure 26.1.

Remember, since PowerPoint won't add new pages or "spill" text onto slides that follow, your bulleted line insertion can force text to fall outside of the body object. You'll need to create additional slides or use other techniques in this chapter to make the words fit.

FIGURE 26.1

Press ↵ to insert a new bulleted line.

◆ **Reference guides for the unafraid** I

◆

◆ **Full color, upscale production values**

◆ *Exploding* **with maps & illustrations (like Wurman's Access series)**

◆ **Small, easy to carry 5" X 8" format**

◆ **200 pages, 400-500 listings, $14.95 list**

◆ **State and (occassionally) regional content**

PowerPoint

Deleting Text

Select the unwanted text and press the Del key. Text below will snake up to take its place. To delete bullets, select them and delete them like other text. Alternately you can use the Edit menu's Cut command (Ctrl+X) or the scissors-like Cut button on the Formatting toolbar.

Moving Text

The technique you use to move text will vary depending upon how much you need to move, and how far you wish to move it. When reorganizing multiple items, it is often best to work in Outline view (using techniques described in a moment). But for minor alterations, like moving a little text from one point in a title or body object to another place within the same object, you can work in Slide view. Simply select text, then drag and drop as in Microsoft Word.

To move a little text to other objects, or to other slides or even to other presentations while in Slides view, it is best to:

1. Select the text to be moved.
2. Cut it (Ctrl+X).
3. Switch to the destination slide if it's not the current slide.
4. Select the title or body object to receive the text.
5. Click to position the insertion point where you want to place the incoming text.
6. Paste (Ctrl+V).

  Double-clicking on a word selects the entire word. Dragging after double-clicking selects subsequent words.

A WHOLE NEW WAY TO WORK

Converting PowerPoint Slides to Word Reports

Here's a cute trick. You can convert the text from your PowerPoint presentations into a Word document.

1. Open the PowerPoint presentation you wish to create a report from.

2. Use the Report-It button on the PowerPoint toolbar.

3. In a moment or three Word will appear with a new untitled document containing the text of each PowerPoint slide. It will not contain tables or other objects.

A WHOLE NEW WAY TO WORK

4. Save the Word document.

5. Switch back to PowerPoint if you wish and copy or link objects of interest with the Word document.

Working in Outline View

Outline view is *the place* to make major renovations to the content and organization of your text. It will remind you of Word's Outline view, but there are differences. Figure 26.2 shows a typical presentation in Outline view.

Outline view lets you see all text or just selected heading levels. You can rearrange the order of slides by dragging them from place to place. You

FIGURE 26.2

Work in Outline view when reorganizing or making major revisions.

Drag selected items to move them.

can move text around on its slide or move text from one slide to another. Let's take a closer look.

Expanding and Collapsing Outline Views

You can increase and decrease the amount of information displayed by clicking on the buttons on the left edge of the Outline view screen. For example, to hide all the text and show just slide titles, you'd click the Show Titles button as illustrated here.

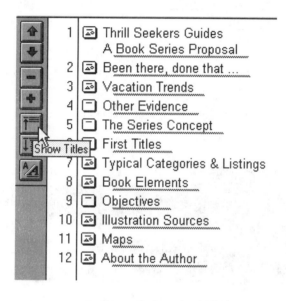

To reveal all the text, click on the Show All button (just beneath the Show Titles button). This will bring all the text back into view.

To expand or collapse details for selected slides only (or even portions of slides):

1. Select the slide or slides, or portions thereof (Shift+click to select multiple slides or lines).

2. To expand (reveal) information in the selected area, use the Expand Selection button (the plus sign):

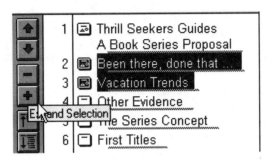

PowerPoint will expand the selected area so that you can see additional detail.

3. To collapse (hide detail), use the Collapse selection button (the minus sign).

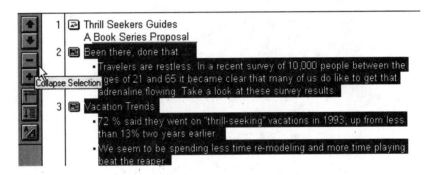

Promoting and Demoting Headings

Like Word headings, PowerPoint titles and headings can have different levels. These let you quickly create multilevel indented lists like this:

▣ About the Author

- Ron has written 16 books
- Is a columnist
- Has appeared on CNN
- Has traveled to:
  - 49 states
  - Europe
  - Japan
- Is a glider pilot
- Is a photographer

The top level is the slide title itself. The next level is for the usual bullet lists, and the next indent (49 states, Europe, and Japan in this example) are the next level down. As you saw in Figure 26.2, different levels have their own appearance (different type size, fonts, etc.). To move items from one level to another, follow these steps:

1. Select an item to promote or demote.

2. Point at the left edge of the item. The mouse pointer will change to a four-headed arrow.

3. Drag left to promote or right to demote the selected item.

4. A vertical line will appear to show you the pending new level of the item being dragged.

5. Release the mouse button. The item will take on its new indent level and appearance.

You could also just select the item to promote or demote and then click on the up or down arrowheads in the Outlining tools collection on the left side of the screen.

Showing and Hiding Text Formatting

Sometimes it's desirable to see Outline views without text formatting. You can get more information on the screen this way, and it may speed scrolling. Use the Show Formatting button to toggle on-screen text formatting. It's the bottom button in the Outlining toolbar collection.

Spell-Checking

PowerPoint's spelling checker dialog box should look familiar. It's a lot like those in Word and Excel, though not identical. The PowerPoint spelling checker shares dictionaries with your other Office applications. It doesn't, however, let you check just selected parts of your presentation. It always checks all of the words in your slides, notes, and other printouts—with one important exception: It will not check words in your drawings.

You can work in Outline or Slide views when checking spelling. To start the checker, press F7, use the Standard toolbar button, or use the Spelling command on the Tools menu. The checker will scan your whole presentation looking for unfamiliar words (unrecognized collections of text surrounded by spaces, actually). When it finds one, it will highlight it in your presentation and place it in the Not In Dictionary section of the Spelling dialog box, as shown in Figure 26.3.

FIGURE 26.3

The spelling checker highlights unfamiliar text strings and offers suggestions.

Unfamiliar words are highlighted on screen and appear in the Spelling dialog box.

PowerPoint shares your other Office dictionaries.

You can accept PowerPoint's suggestions, type a correction of your own, add the unfamiliar word to a custom dictionary, or skip the word by clicking the appropriate buttons. When making changes, you can have PowerPoint always make the same correction without asking you again whenever it occurs later in the same spell-checking session. Unlike Word, if you run the spell checker more than once on the same presentation without quitting PowerPoint, it will stop each time on the same unfamiliar words.

Run the checker after you've entered all of your text but before doing your final formatting, and before running the Look wizard or applying new Look templates, etc., since some corrections will change line endings, affecting the amount of room available on a slide and so on.

Finding and Replacing Text

PowerPoint lets you do basic text searching and replacement, though not to the degree that Word permits. (Wildcards are not supported, for instance.) The Edit menu contains a simple Find command that lets you search for text; and a Replace command that lets you search for and change text. The usual cautions apply here. Automatic replacements can make guacamole out of a great presentation, so save your work before replacing, then check to see how it went.

Replacing

Replacing is pretty self-explanatory. For instance, to replace all occurrences of *travelled* with *traveled* you would:

1. Save your presentation.
2. Choose Replace from the Edit menu.
3. Enter **travelled** in the Find What box.
4. Enter **traveled** in the Replace With box.

5. If you want to find only words with matching capitalization, choose Match Case.

6. To find only exact word matches (*Ron* but not elec*tron*ic, for instance) choose Find Whole Words Only.

7. Click Find Next. PowerPoint will search for a match.

8. Click Replace to replace the first match, and Find Next to continue, or Replace All to replace all occurrences.

9. Check your work.

Finding

Finding is actually a subset of replacing—the Find dialog box in PowerPoint includes a Replace button if you decide to expand your Find operation into a Replace operation.

1. Choose Find from the Edit menu.

2. Specify the text you are looking for.

3. Specify any restrictions (Match Case or Whole Word).

4. Use the Find Next button to find matches, or Close to quit.

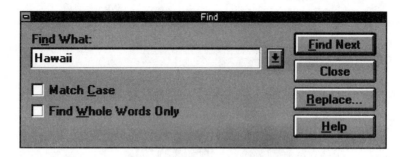

If you wish to replace a word after finding this way, click the Replace button. You'll be visited by the Replace dialog box, discussed in the preceding section.

 As you'll see in Chapter 28, PowerPoint does not have a Go To feature like Word or Excel's. Find can be of some help here, though: Enter things like slide titles or unique text that you know is on a particular slide, and you can scoot from place to place that way.

Adding and Removing Periods in Sentences

Here's a trick Word can't do that PowerPoint can—and it's a nice one. If you are like me, you can never decide whether or not to end each bullet list item with a period. Or perhaps you are combining the works of multiple authors with different styles. Either way, the Periods command can help.

1. Select the text you wish to conform.
2. Choose Periods from the Format menu.
3. Choose Add Periods or Remove Periods to suit your taste.

As illustrated in Figure 26.4, you should check your work after using this command. After all, computers are just dumb servants. They will obediently remove periods even after abbreviations like *etc.*, so you will have to put those periods back in after running the Periods command.

PowerPoint

FIGURE 26.4

You can quickly add or
remove periods at the
end of bulleted lines.

All periods at the end of an item
will be removed—including ones
at the end of abbreviations

formatting Text

While PowerPoint automatically chooses fonts, colors, character sizes, and
the like, you can overrule these choices on individual slides and reports or for
entire templates. You use toolbars, menu choices, and dialog boxes that will
seem familiar from your work with other programs in the Office package.

Changing Fonts and Sizes

You have the usual tools at your disposal:

- The Formatting toolbar buttons
- Keyboard shortcuts
- The Font command
- The Replace Font command

Select the text of interest and then apply the desired formatting. PowerPoint will tell you if you need to switch views. Let's see some examples of the less obvious formatting choices.

Shadow Effects

Perhaps you've noticed those shadow effects applied by some of the Microsoft AutoFormat features. You can also add them manually. Work in full-size views (choose 100% on the Standard toolbar) to get the best understanding of the effect:

1. Select the text.

2. Click the shadow button on the Formatting menu for default shadow effects, or choose Shadows from the Format menu.

3. Make your choices in the resulting Shadow dialog box. Usually just a few points of Offset is all that's required.

4. Click OK. You may need to deselect the text to see the results.

5. Experiment with different amounts of Offset.

> **Moderation is a good thing when applying shadows. Nobody likes a show-off, and too much shadow effect makes text difficult to read.**

Embossing Text

Select the text and choose Emboss from the Font dialog box.

Underlining Text

To underline text, select it and use the Formatting toolbar's Underline button or the Ctrl+U keyboard shortcut.

You may notice that the Underline feature in PowerPoint uses a continuous underline by default (that is, it includes the spaces and any punctuation between words). To underline single words, you must select and underline them one at a time.

These commands toggle; using them on underlined text removes the underline.

Font Colors

Here are the steps to changing the color of text in PowerPoint:

1. Select the text.

 2. Either click the Text Color button or choose Font from the Formatting menu.

3. In the dialog box that appears, click on the Color list arrow.

 4. Choose one of the basic colors shown on the palette, or choose Other Color.

5. If you chose Other Color, click on the desired color in the Other Color dialog box (shown in Figure 26.5).

6. Click OK to finish up. You may need to deselect the text to experience the resulting show of color.

Incidentally, you need not have a color display to use color. If you plan to print your output on a color printer, or send files out to a slide-making company, you can specify colors on your black-and-white screen and get color output.

WARNING Picking colors for slides and overheads can be tricky. That's why PowerPoint makes many of those choices for you. If you plan to get creative, test your work using the output device and preferably the projection system you plan to use in your final presentations. The wrong color combinations can make things hard to read, and might make things seem to disappear entirely.

PowerPoint

FIGURE 26.5

A larger variety of colors is offered through the Other Color dialog box, reached from the Color drop-down list in the Formatting ➤ Font dialog box.

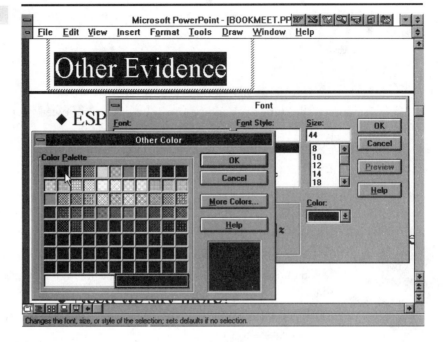

Changing Case

PowerPoint lets you change the case of selected text. For instance, you can switch all text to upper case, or automatically create "capitalized" sentences. Use the Format menu's Change Case command to do this. The resulting dialog box illustrates the effect of each available choice (including the rather interesting "tOGGLE cASE").

Alas, there is no Small Caps option; and this feature cares not a whit about the content of your document. So if you select a sentence containing acronyms like ASAP, you'll end up with things like asap or Asap. ...Check your work.

Replacing One Font with Another

When you change templates or use the Pick a Look Wizard, PowerPoint automatically changes fonts for you. You can also choose fonts on your own by using the Replace Fonts command on the Tools menu.

1. Choose Replace Fonts from the Tools menu.

2. Choose the font that you wish to replace from the drop-down list, or type the font name.

3. Choose the replacement font from the second list, or type its name.

4. Click OK.

Behold. Check your slides; you may need to reformat some things (perhaps enlarge a title or body object here and there, or tighten line spacing to make things fit). If you hate the results, just replace the new font with the old font and try something else.

Line and Paragraph Spacing

You can change the amount of space between lines and before and after paragraphs in body objects and title objects. You can change all of the paragraphs in a text object, or just selected lines.

1. Select the line(s) or text object(s) you wish to reformat.

2. Choose the Line Spacing command from the Formatting menu.

3. Use the resulting dialog box (Figure 26.6) to specify new settings in either lines or points.

4. Click Preview to see the effect of your choices.

5. Click OK to make the changes.

FIGURE 26.6

Use the Line Spacing dialog box to change the amount of space above and below selected lines or paragraphs.

Copying Text Styles

There are two ways to copy text formatting. One uses the Pick Up and Apply commands on the Format menu; the other uses a toolbar button.

To copy text formatting with the menu commands:

1. Select the text containing the formatting you'd like to copy.

2. Choose Pick Up Text Style from the Format menu.

3. Select the text you wish to reformat.

4. Choose Apply Text Style from the Format menu. (This choice is visible only after you've picked up some formatting.) The selected text will be reformatted.

If you don't select multiple words for reformatting, only the word containing the insertion point will be reformatted.

To use the Format Painter toolbar button on the formatting menu:

1. Select the text containing the formatting you want to copy.

2. Click on the Format Painting toolbar button. It looks like a paintbrush.

3. The mouse pointer changes shape. (It will look like a paintbrush also.)

4. Click the text you wish to reformat. The selected text will be reformatted.

Picking Bullets for Lists

You can use virtually any character from any font as a bullet in the bullet lists. You have control over the size and color of bullets as well.

1. Select the bulleted items you wish to modify.

2. Choose Bullet from the Format list to open the Bullets dialog box.

3. Choose a font to explore in the Bullets From list.

4. To get an enlarged view of your candidates while still in the dialog box, click on individual symbols (as shown in Figure 26.7).

5. Specify a different color if you wish.

6. Click the Preview button to see the proposed changes at work.

7. The size of the bullets is specified as a percentage of the text size. Use the Size text box to change this percentage if you wish.

8. Click OK to make the change or Cancel to abort.

FIGURE 26.7

Use the Bullet dialog box to choose from a collection of special symbols.

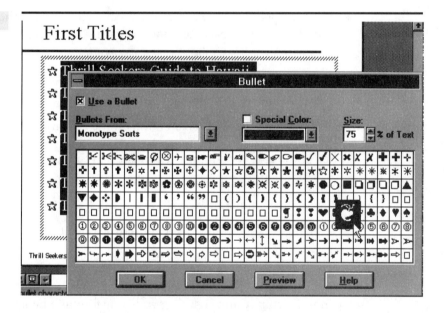

Aligning Text

You can right-align, left-align, center, or justify text just as you would in Word. There are even similar-looking toolbar buttons. Start by selecting text, then apply the desired formatting.

The Format menu's Alignment command offers the most options—found on a submenu, as illustrated in Figure 26.8.

Alternatively, you can use the Left and Center toolbar buttons, also shown in Figure 26.8.

First select the text to be aligned, then use the Alignment command or toolbar buttons to align it.

Here too, temperance is called for. PowerPoint does a pretty good job of aligning text all on its own. But excessive white space between justified words bothers some people. You can manually hyphenate words to minimize this.

◆ Computer-generated regional maps will be provided by GEOSys.

◆ Useful local maps will be included as well.

◆ Each will contain numbers which correspond to listings.

Word Tables in PowerPoint

A WHOLE NEW WAY TO WORK

There are several ways to include Word tables in PowerPoint presentations. The obvious way is to copy text from the Word document and paste it into a PowerPoint slide. But a more intriguing technique uses OLE to temporarily add *Word commands* to your *PowerPoint menu* so that you can create tables in slides using the Word techniques described in Chapter 7! Here are the steps. Refer back to Chapter 7 for help with Word table techniques.

1. If you've created slides without saving yet, save your PowerPoint presentation just in case.

2. Use PowerPoint's New Slide command (Ctrl+M) and the resulting AutoLayout icons to create a blank slide containing a table object:

A WHOLE NEW WAY TO WORK

3. Double-click on the table icon in the resulting new slide to start the table design process.

4. In a (long) moment, you'll see a table dialog box asking how many rows and cells you'd like to start with. Choose reasonable numbers, realizing that you can change your mind as you work. Click OK.

5. After your hard disk grunts and groans for a while, you'll see changes in your PowerPoint window. It will still say PowerPoint, but you'll see Word's menus and toolbars. Create and edit the

A WHOLE NEW WAY TO WORK

table as if you were working in Word.

6. Use all of your Word table tricks. Add borders, employ Auto-Format, merge cells, have at it. When you are finished, click in the slide portion of your screen (outside of the table) to return to PowerPoint sans Word.

7. Use PowerPoint to make changes to the non-table portion of the slide (like the slide title), and double-click on the table to bring back Word and its wonderful table toys.

27

Working with Graphics in PowerPoint

T hese days, what's a presentation without graphics? You can include in a PowerPoint presentation virtually any graphic created with other programs. Examples include:

- Clip art from the ClipArt Gallery
- Excel charts
- Microsoft OrgChart objects
- Pictures created with Word's Drawing features
- Kodak Photo CD images
- Paintbrush pictures
- Windows bitmap images of all kinds
- DrawPerfect images
- Encapsulated PostScript images
- TIF images
- Macintosh pictures and drawings
- Scanned images
- AutoCad images
- and more

Moreover, PowerPoint has a nifty AutoShape feature that can make even *me* seem like an artist. If you happen to be able to draw, you'll find the usual collection of more traditional tools in PowerPoint as well. Let's take a look at the various options.

Importing Images from the Outside World

The general steps for importing, sizing, and positioning images for use with PowerPoint are pretty straightforward. Here they are in a nutshell, followed by a couple of examples.

1. Open the PowerPoint presentation needing a graphic image.

2. Go to the slide needing the image or insert a new slide to receive the image. (Choose either a slide layout specifically designed for graphics or any other.)

3. Use any of these commands: Insert Picture, Insert Clip Art, or Insert Object.

4. Choose the type of graphic element you wish to import, if more than one type is offered (PhotoCD, TIF, bitmap, etc.).

5. Choose the file name of the desired image.

6. Click OK and PowerPoint will insert a full-size copy of the chosen image, converting its file format, if necessary.

7. Use your mouse to resize and reposition the graphic as desired.

8. To edit the image, you can just double-click on it.

With those general steps in mind, let's see some actual examples. We'll start with inserting clip art from Microsoft's ClipArt Gallery.

The ClipArt Gallery

Suppose we wanted to add some clip art to the slide in Figure 27.1.

1. After switching to the slide and perhaps dragging the text object's bottom edge up to make room for the graphic on the slide, you could click on the George Jetson-looking Insert ClipArt button, shown at left, in PowerPoint's Formatting menu.

2. You'll see the ClipArt Gallery, shown in Figure 27.2.

PowerPoint

FIGURE 27.1

Use the Insert ClipArt button to add predrawn artwork to your slides.

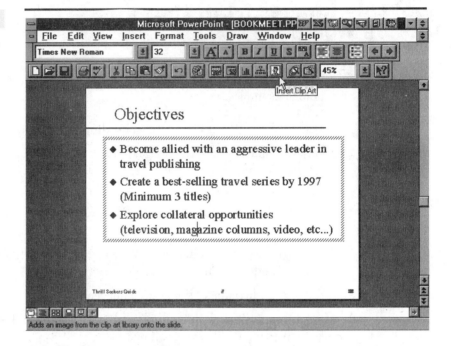

FIGURE 27.2

The ClipArt Gallery

3. Browse the various categories and images and double-click on the chosen picture. A copy of the picture will appear on your slide, as shown in Figure 27.3.

FIGURE 27.3

Imported pictures arrive in their original size.

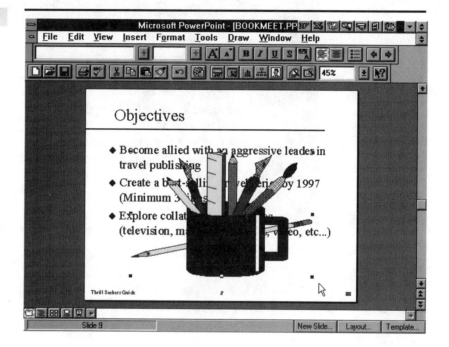

4. Drag a corner of the image to reduce its size, then drag the image itself, if necessary, to reposition it. In Figure 27.4, the image has been resized and repositioned.

5. Later, if you want to substitute a different image from the ClipArt Gallery, simply double-click on the graphic in your slide. This will bring up

PowerPoint

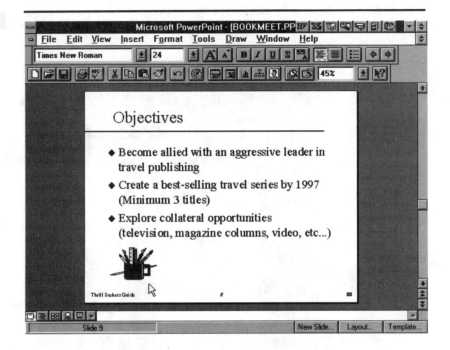

the Gallery. When you choose a *new* image from the Gallery it will automatically shrink and position itself as a replacement for the old one.
Too easy!

◆ **Explore collateral opportunities**
(television, magazine columns, video, etc...)

Drawing in PowerPoint

There are a number of drawing tools available in PowerPoint. Use the Tool-bars choice on the View menu to turn on the Drawing toolbar, Drawing+ tool-bar, or both. The toolbars can be reshaped and moved, as is always the case.

Most of the drawing tools and concepts should be familiar to you if you've read Parts One and Two of this book, or used other Microsoft Windows pro-grams. Others may not be so well known.

Manually Drawing Shapes and Lines

You've already learned how to use some Microsoft drawing facilities in Chap-ters 8 and 16, so we'll not kill another tree on that subject here. It's enough to know that you can:

1. Switch to a slide where you want to insert a drawing or insert a new slide. (If you use the Insert New Slide command, choose an AutoLayout that in-cludes an object area and double-click in it, as shown in Figure 27.5.)

FIGURE 27.5

Double-click to add an object.

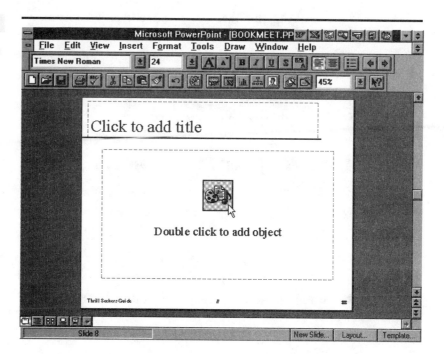

PowerPoint

2. Use the resulting dialog box to choose your favorite object type and related tools (PaintBrush, Word 6 Picture—whatever). Some of your options are shown in Figure 27.6.

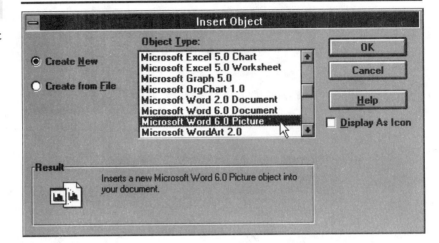

3. Draw using the line, shape, text, and other drawing tools. Figure 27.7 shows a sample drawing.

4. When you close the drawing window (by clicking in the slide), your masterpiece will be inserted into the slide (see Figure 27.8) where it can be resized and moved with your mouse.

5. To edit the drawing, just double-click on it.

AutoShape for Everyday Objects

PowerPoint offers a nifty AutoShape drawing feature that's worth a look. It's less complicated than Draw and combines a small collection of clip art with some text tools.

1. Use the Toolbars command on the View menu to display either of the drawing toolbars or just the AutoShape toolbar.

2. Switch to the slide needing artwork or insert a new slide.

FIGURE 27.7

Use the drawing tools
to create drawings.

FIGURE 27.8

Finished drawings can
be placed with text on
slides.

PowerPoint

3. Click on the AutoShape button in the toolbar.

4. Pick a shape from the AutoShape toolbar (like the cartoon balloon in Figure 27.9).

FIGURE 27.9

AutoShapes make it easy to draw arrows, stars, and other complex shapes.

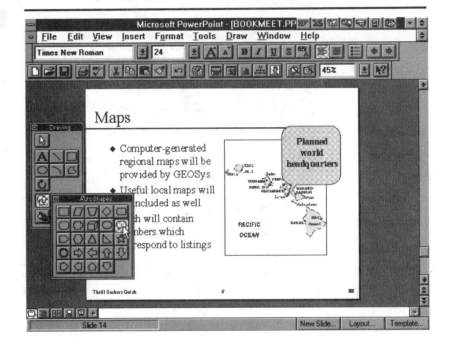

5. Drag with your mouse to define the desired size of the chosen graphic.

6. Position the graphic by selecting it and then dragging it.

7. Use the toolbar's text tools to add text, then use the Format toolbar to embellish the text, if you like. For instance, the example shows centered bold text in the balloon graphic.

8. Resize them if necessary to make things fit by dragging on handles.

9. Group the text and graphic if you wish, to make them easier to move simultaneously.

10. Drag the drawn object and/or text objects to move them.

Creating Organizational Charts

Use the OrgChart toolbar button on the PowerPoint toolbar to add organizational charts to your slides. See Chapter 8 for details.

Inserting Photos in Your PowerPoint Presentation

You can insert scanned photos into PowerPoint slides, but there are some things you should know.

First of all, photos take *lots* of disk space, particularly if the images are large and in color. This is particularly important to know if you plan to pass around your PowerPoint presentations on floppies.

Photos slow down the loading of slides and the process of switching from slide to slide in an electronic presentation, particularly if you are using a slow machine. Rehearse on the machine you'll use for the presentation to see if this will be a problem.

Large photos can also slow you when editing a presentation, since it takes time for the photos to be displayed. Consider leaving "holes" where the photos will go, then insert the actual images at the end of your creation process.

Photos may *print* better than they look *on screen* if you do not have a high-resolution monitor. For instance, compare the on-screen image and the printed companion beneath it in Figure 27.10. This is not a big problem unless you plan to give on-screen presentations. If you do, consider investing in a high-resolution monitor and display card. Preview before the audience arrives to see what to expect.

Save early and often when working with photos. The memory gods will get you sooner or later. In fact, this happened even as I wrote these words.... Fortunately, the presentation had been saved prior to my attempting to print the illustration.

It takes a long time to print slides containing photos. Leave yourself plenty of extra time for printing if your presentation has photos.

PowerPoint

FIGURE 27.10

Photos often look better printed than they do on-screen.

About the Author

- ◆ Ron has written 16 books
- ◆ Is a columnist
- ◆ Has appeared on CNN
- ◆ Has traveled to:
  - ↠ 49 states
  - ↠ Europe
  - ↠ Japan
- ◆ Is a glider pilot
- ◆ Is a photographer
- ◆ *Is* a thrill seeker

Thrill Seekers Guide

A WHOLE NEW WAY TO WORK

Excel Charts in PowerPoint

Treat Excel charts just as you would any other inserted object in PowerPoint. If you link the chart and your PowerPoint slide, Power-Point will get an updated copy of the chart at intervals you specify (when you open the PowerPoint presentation, for instance).

A WHOLE NEW WAY TO WORK

You can either create the chart in Excel and then copy it to Power-Point or work with Excel's chart features right in Excel. To create a chart while in Excel:

1. Click on the Insert Chart button. You'll see a small data sheet.
2. Enter your data and labels.
3. Click in the slide.
4. Resize and reposition the graph.
5. Double-click on the graph to edit it.

28

Showtime!

■

I
t's almost time for those sweaty palms. You've combined your greatest thoughts with wonderful graphics and a color scheme that yells "promote me, dammit!"

But before you jump into the spotlight, it might be worth taking some extra time to polish your work, rehearse, prepare for unexpected questions, and create some handouts. That's what this chapter is all about.

If We Can Put a Man on the Moon...

Why can't we give a presentation without some kind of audio-visual equipment meltdown? You've seen it. Rhodes scholars, award-winning scientists, doctors, lawyers—all looking like idiots because their slide show's screwed up.

Chances are they all have one thing in common. They didn't rehearse with their final material in the room where the presentation was to be given on the equipment that was to be used for the real show (preferably on the *day of the show*).

I know, you can't always do that. But whenever possible, TRY. Some projectors don't throw certain colors very well. If you are using someone else's computer for an electronic presentation, does it have enough RAM for that beefy slide number 12 with the full color photo, or will it lock up? Does the borrowed or rented computer have the proper fonts, or are you headed for disaster? The *only* way to minimize embarrassment is rehearsal. There. That's off my chest.

Arranging, Previewing, and Rehearsing

The sequence of information in a presentation is often as important as the content itself. PowerPoint makes it easy for you to try out different slide sequences by yourself or with friendly coworkers in rehearsals. Start with a desktop slide show, then switch to the Slide Sorter to move things around, or even delete unnecessary slides. Here's how.

Desktop Slide Shows

Unless you have a monster monitor on your computer, desktop slide shows are best for rehearsing and for very small group huddles. Here are the steps to present a desktop slide show.

After opening the presentation file, switch to the first slide. You can do this in any view, but the technique varies:

■ In *Slide Sorter View*, click on the first slide, as shown in Figure 28.1.

FIGURE 28.1

In Slide Sorter View, you would click on the first slide.

■ In *Outline View*, click on the first slide's icon, as shown in Figure 28.2.

■ In *Slide View*, drag the scroll box at the left of your screen all the way to the top, as shown in Figure 28.3. Watch the slide numbers that appear as you drag.

FIGURE 28.2

In Outline View, you would click on the first slide's icon.

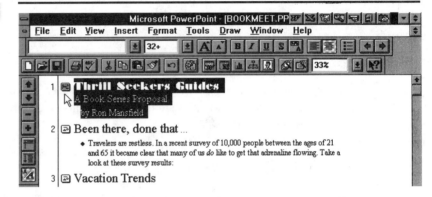

FIGURE 28.3

In Slide View, you would drag the scroll box at the left of your screen all the way to the top.

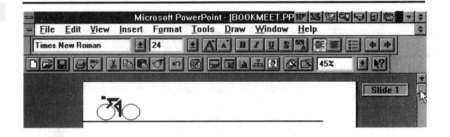

Begin the slide show either by picking Slide Show from PowerPoint's View menu or clicking on the Slide Show button illustrated on the left.

All of PowerPoint's familiar menus and other tools will disappear. If you've been running the Office Manger, that toolbar will still be visible. To remove it, quit the Manager as shown in Figure 28.4.

In the bottom right corner of Figure 28.4 you'll see a new button used for drawing. It controls a piece of electronic "chalk" with which you can scribble temporary on-screen lines while presenting:

To draw with it, click so that the button is depressed and surrounded by a dark border. Hold down either mouse button while you drag.

FIGURE 28.4

On-screen slide shows needn't be obscured by the Office Manager. Close it.

The scribbles do not permanently scar your masterpieces. Press the E key on your keyboard to erase all on-screen marks. And, when you switch to another slide, the drawings will vanish. That's the good news and the bad. If someone "chalks" something important, *make notes*, because the electronic chalk marks will be squirted like watermelon seeds out of the universe when you change slides.

TIP You can also use your mouse pointer while presenting. Move it around the screen to point to things you wish to emphasize. To hide the mouse pointer (and the little drawing button) press A or the equal sign (=).

Manually Advancing Slides

To manually move from slide to slide during a slide show, you can do any of the following:

- To advance to the next slide, press the spacebar, click the primary (usually the left) mouse button, or press N, → or ↓, or Page Down.

- To go back one slide, press the backspace key, click the non-primary (usually the right) mouse button, or press P, ← or ↑, or Page Up.

- To go to a specific slide, type the slide number, and press ⏎. For example, to go to slide 5, you'd type **5**⏎.

- To go to the first slide in your presentation, simultaneously press and hold *both* mouse buttons for at least two seconds, then release them both.

- To quit a slide show and return to the previous view press Esc, Ctrl+Break, or either of your computer's minus keys.

TIP If a slide is distracting your audience and you want to temporarily hide it without advancing to the next slide, press B to blacken the screen or W to make the screen all white. These choices toggle, so pressing B when the screen is black or W when the screen is white will bring your slide back into view.

Transition and Build Effects

You know those fancy video transition effects weather forecasters use on the television news? Some remind you of venetian blinds, others look like confetti.... Or a nearly blank slide fades up, then lines of text reveal themselves one at a time to *build* the completed slide. PowerPoint provides its own suite of transition and build effects, which you can add to your on-screen shows. Here's how.

Transitions

Transition effects dictate how one slide leaves the screen and how the next arrives.

1. Switch to Slide Sorter view.

2. Select the slide that you want to transition *from* (or pick the first slide if you want to transition *into* your presentation).

3. Pick a transition effect from the drop-down list shown in Figure 28.5.

4. Watch the *selected slide* in Slide Sorter view as you pick the effect. It will demonstrate the transition for you.

5. Select the next slide and choose another effect.

FIGURE 28.5

Choose the transition effect you want from the drop-down list.

PowerPoint

725

6. You may need to switch to Slide Show to understand the full impact of these transitions, then switch back to Slide Sorter and try other effects until you see one you like. Some combinations work well together on adjacent slides, like Cover Right and Uncover Left. Experiment.

You can select multiple slides and apply the same effect to all of them at once. Simply hold down the Shift key while you click on each of the slides you wish to influence.

Removing Transitions

To remove transitions, select the slide or slides of interest and choose No Transition from the transition list.

Changing the Speed of Transitions

To change the speed of transitions, use the Transition button (next to the transition list) to reveal the Transition dialog box, shown in Figure 28.6.

FIGURE 28.6

The Transition dialog box offers further options for controlling the transition.

Pick Slow, Medium, or Fast from the Speed section. Faster is usually better.

Automatically Advancing Slides

While most speakers like to manually advance slides in order to maintain full control over their presentations, you can ask PowerPoint to change slides at timed intervals. This works well for trade shows where you want to let a presentation run continuously and unattended, or when you have a precise presentation time limit that you cannot exceed.

Even when you let PowerPoint advance slides at timed intervals, you can intervene. Here's how automatic advancing is accomplished:

1. Open your presentation in Slide Sorter View.

2. Click or Shift-click to select the slide or slides for which you plan to specify an on-screen time.

3. Click on the Transition button to reveal the Transition dialog box illustrated a moment ago.

4. Click in the box next to the word Seconds and enter the desired on-screen time. (The Automatically After button will darken automatically for you.)

5. Pick a transition effect while in this dialog box, if you haven't already.

6. Click OK.

7. To rehearse, run the slide show and see how the timings feel to you. Remember you can always use the keyboard and mouse buttons to advance or go back.

8. There's another keyboard trick worth knowing: To pause the automatic advance feature, press the **S** key.

TIP If you forget the keyboard controls while presenting in Slide Show mode, press the F1 function key for an on-screen list of shortcuts. Don't be embarrassed. Remember: Nobody <u>else</u> in the room can run "AV" equipment either. Click OK or press Enter to make the help screen disappear.

PowerPoint

Running a Presentation Continuously

To run a presentation over nonstop (in a trade show booth, for instance):

1. Open the presentation.

2. Make sure all your slides have transition times assigned to them.

3. Choose Slide Show from the View menu. You'll see the Slide Show dialog box, shown in Figure 28.7.

4. Select the range of slides to be shown (or use the All default).

5. Select Use Slide Timings in the Advance section of the Slide Show dialog box.

6. Click the Show button.

7. The show will run continuously until you press the Esc key (but watch it in its entirety before going on that coffee break just in case.)

FIGURE 28.7

Use the Slide Show dialog box, reached from the View menu, to run your presentation.

8. Move the keyboard and mouse out of sight and out of reach to frustrate the mischievous, but *don't* (even though the Microsoft manual suggests this) unplug the keyboard and/or mouse with your computer running.

Changing Slide Timing

After you've rehearsed or presented a show a few times, you may decide to "tweak" slide timing. In fact, PowerPoint can "watch" you give the show and "learn" the timings. (Just don't stop to answer the phone while doing this.)

1. Choose Slide Show from the View menu.

2. Pick Rehearse New Times from the Advance options.

3. Click the Show button. A little clock/button, shown in Figure 28.8, appears in the lower-left screen corner.

4. When the current slide's been on-screen long enough, click the clock/button to advance to the next.

FIGURE 28.8

The clock button here keeps track of the amount of time you keep a slide on-screen; clicking on it advances to the next slide but keeps the clock running.

	1991	1992	1993
Thrill Seeking	12%	38%	72%
Relaxing Travel	88%	78%	15%
Home Repairs	33%	15%	23%
Other	21%	31%	26%

 Guide   1/5/94

PowerPoint

5. Continue this way through the entire show. At the end of the show, PowerPoint will tell you the total running time, and ask if you want to save the timings:

6. If you switch to Slide Sorter view, you'll also see the times. (You can change individual times here as well.)

Using Build Slides

Don't you hate when you project a slide and half the room reads ahead and then interrupts with questions on topics you were going to cover in a moment anyway? Build slides can help you avoid this.

 The quickest way to specify builds is to select the material that you wish to reveal in a series of steps, then click the Build button illustrated at left. It's located on the Standard toolbar.

For example, suppose you wanted to reveal the list of book titles shown in Figure 28.9 one at a time.

FIGURE 28.9

You could reveal the titles in this book title list one at a time by using PowerPoint's build effect.

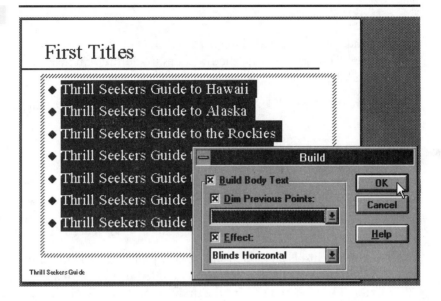

1. Switch to the slide of interest in Slide View.

2. Select the text you wish to reveal in builds.

3. Choose Build from the View menu.

4. If you'd like previous items to dim and/or change color when new items appear, choose the desired effects in the Build dialog box.

5. Click OK. Switch to the Slide Show to see the build effect.

First Titles

◆ Thrill Seekers Guide to Hawaii

◆ Thrill Seekers Guide to Alaska

Each time you advance one "slide" (by clicking, using the space bar, etc.) the screen will contain an additional bulleted line, until the entire build is complete.

Hiding Slides

Slides can be included in your presentation file but not shown in the presentation. Simply select the slide or slides in Outline, Slide Sorter, or Slide views, and then choose Hide Slide on the Tools menu.

 There's also a Hide Slide button in Slide Sorter view. It's illustrated to the left.

 Hidden slides don't get displayed in your shows unless you force them, but the slide numbers do not change, so savvy audience members may notice that your on-screen slide numbers jump from 10 to 12 and challenge you. Be ready to show the hidden slide or explain why you're not showing it.

 You can display a hidden slide at any time by typing its number and pressing ↵. Moreover, the slide before any hidden line has a small button at the bottom of the screen next to the drawing button. It looks like an asterisk, and is shown at left. Click on it to reveal the hidden slide.

Showing Slides Out of Order

From time to time you may need to present slides out of sequence ("branch," in PowerPoint parlance) in response to questions from your audience or to reiterate a point, or you might want to resequence your show entirely because you've discovered a better way to present your information. These are standard orders of business for any good presentation package, and PowerPoint makes it easy to do both.

Branching and "Drilling Down"

During your presentation you can branch to a slide out of sequence whenever the need arises by simply typing the slide number and pressing ↵. You can also "drill down" to reach the source of the information on the current slide if you've included linked, embedded objects (like Excel worksheets, Word tables, or PowerPoint slides from other presentations). Simply double-click on them and bring up the source document. (This assumes of course that the source document is on the computer being used for the presentation.)

Realize too that the process can sometimes be painfully slow. So rehearse first if you plan to show off this way in a big meeting.

Resequencing

To change the order of slides permanently:

1. Switch to Slide Sorter view or Outline view.
2. Point to a slide (or its icon in Outline view).
3. Hold down the mouse button and drag. The mouse pointer's shape will change and you'll see a line indicating the proposed new position of the slide.
4. Release the mouse button when the line indicates the correct slide position. The slide will move and be renumbered automatically along with those that follow it.

Deleting Slides

To delete a slide or slides:

1. Switch to Slide Sorter view or Outline view.
2. Click to select the slide (or its icon in Outline view).
3. Press the Delete key.

To delete multiple slides at once, Shift-click to select them, then press the Delete key.

Printing Presentation Elements

PowerPoint's Print dialog box, shown in Figure 28.10, offers choices not found in other Office applications. You can access the Print dialog box using the Print command on the File menu, the Ctrl+P shortcut, or the Print toolbar button.

FIGURE 28.10

The Print dialog box in PowerPoint offers more options than the Print dialog box for the other Office programs.

Most of the choices are pretty obvious. Select the desired item to be printed from the drop-down Print What list (slides, handouts, etc.). Here are some printing tips:

- You can specify a range of slides either by typing the numbers in the range (**3-6**, for instance) or by selecting slides in Sorter or Outline views and then specifying printing of selected items.

- If you are making overhead transparencies and plan to mount them in cardboard or plastic frames, be sure the frames won't cut off information in your slides. If necessary, change the margins in the slide master to make the images fall within the frames' openings.

- When printing handouts of slides, you can request reduced size copies (2, 3, or 6 slides per page) from the Print What list, as shown in Figure 28.11. The s6 slide choice usually provides very legible results and saves some paper.

Thrill Seekers Guide

Thrill Seekers Guides
A Book Series Proposal

by Ron Mansfield

Thrill Seekers Guide   1/22/94   1

Been there, done that ...

- Travelers are restless. In a recent survey of 10,000 people between the ages of 21 and 65 it became clear that many of us *do* like to get that adrenaline flowing. Take a look at these survey results:

	1991	1992	1993
Thrill Seeking	12%	38%	72%
Relaxing Travel	88%	76%	15%
Home Repairs	33%	15%	23%
Other	21%	31%	26%

Thrill Seekers Guide   1/22/94   2

Vacation Trends

- 72 % said they went on "thrill-seeking" vacations in 1993, up from less than 13% two years earlier.
- We seem to be spending less time re-modeling and more time playing beat the reaper.

Thrill Seekers Guide   1/22/94   3

Competitive Books

Competition	
Title	**Publisher**
Go Ahead. Jump!	Bungee Books
No Fear, No Fun	Two Crazy Guys Unlimited
Faster, Faster	Pisano Publications

Thrill Seekers Guide   1/22/94   4

Other Evidence

- ESPN 2 (The thrill junkies' channel)
- Growing sales of "extreme" sports gear
- New thrill vendors emerge each year
- Alaskan travel surge spurs building boom
- Amusement parks spend millions on loopers
- Bungeeeee!
- Need we say more?

Thrill Seekers Guide   1/22/94   5

Typical Categories & Listings

Air Thrills	Helicopters, Aerobatics, Gliders, Vintage aircraft ...
Water Thrills	Highspeed cats, Renting skeedoos, Parasailing ...
Water Adventures	Alaskan ferryn, Freighter adventures, Sail to Hawaii ...
Underwater Thrills	Submarine rides, Shark dives, SNUBA, Best dive shops ...
Four Wheels	Rent exotic cars, Off-roading, Pro stockcar lessons ...

Thrill Seekers Guide   1/22/94   6

1/22/94   1

- Multiple sets will come out of the printer faster if you don't ask the computer to collate. Then you'll need to hand collate, so only you can decide which approach is quicker overall.

- If you pick the Slides [without Builds] choice on the Print dialog box's Print What drop-down list, you'll get *one* copy of build slides, containing all the slide's lines. Choosing Slides [with Builds] will give you multiple copies of the slides, one at each build stage.

- When printing handouts or overhead masters from presentations designed with 35mm slide settings, use the Scale to Fit Paper option.

- To change the orientation and margins of slide, outline, and note printouts, choose Slide Setup on the File menu. You'll see the dialog box shown in Figure 28.12.

FIGURE 28.12

The Slide Setup dialog box from the File menu

Creating Overhead Transparencies

A number of companies sell overhead transparency materials for laser and inkjet printers. Since not all transparency materials work in all printers, do some research ahead of time. Test print and test project, if possible. Follow the printer and material manufacturers' suggestions for loading transparency material. There is usually only one side of the material that is designed to accept an image.

TIP

Consider whether you want your hidden slides to be included in handouts. If you want to print hidden slides, check (×) the Print Hidden Slides choice in PowerPoint's Print dialog box before printing.

Obtaining Color 35mm Slides

Many service bureaus can convert PowerPoint files into 35mm slides. In fact, PowerPoint comes with special GraphicsLink™ software for use with Genigraphics slide delivery services. Expect to pay around $9.00 per slide for non-rush service, more if you are in a panic. It's even possible to send PowerPoint files to Genigraphics through your modem, and get the slides back the next day via express courier. Your PowerPoint software came with a brochure explaining these services. If you need more information or assistance, you can contact Genigraphics at 800-638-7348.

Here are the general steps for using the Genigraphics driver; refer to the Genigraphics literature for details.

1. Open the presentation and select the first slide.

2. Choose Print from the File menu (Ctrl+P).

3. Click on the Printer button in the Print dialog box.

4. Choose the Genigraphics Driver On FILE option in PowerPoint's Print Setup dialog box.

5. If you want to create 4 × 5 or 7 × 9 film images, click the Options button to visit the Genigraphics Setup dialog box.

6. Click OK in the Print Setup dialog box. You'll see the dialog box shown in Figure 28.13.

7. Click OK to print the slides to disk or to use the modem connection, depending on which you've selected in the Send Via area of the dialog box.

 TIP

It's a good idea to do a test run with your slide-making vendor before sending a large, important project. And be sure you understand all of the costs involved (one-time setup fees, costs for duplicates, dial-in surcharges, etc.).

PowerPoint

FIGURE 28.13

The Genigraphics Job
Instructions dialog box

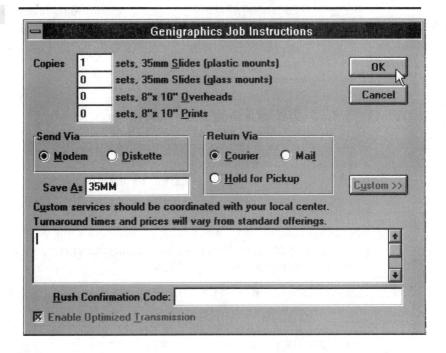

Sharing Presentation Files with Others

You can share your presentations with other computer users in several ways. The most obvious is to play "pass the floppy" or to send a copy of the presentation file via network or modem. These straightforward approaches will work if the other user has PowerPoint Version 4 on his or her computer, along with all the fonts you've used in your presentation.

If you've used only TrueType fonts in your presentation and think the recipient might not have the fonts, you can send them along with your presentation by clicking the Embed TrueType Fonts option in the Save As dialog box:

Sending along embedded fonts can greatly increase the size of a presentation file, so do it only when necessary. Not all TrueType fonts can be embedded this way. Experiment.

 When sharing presentations with others on a network, it is sometimes possible to share "downloadable" fonts stored on the server. Check with your network administrator or help desk for assistance.

Obviously, if you plan to exchange presentations on floppy disks, they'll need to fit, or you'll need to use some file compression or backup and restore scheme. For instance, the main 12-slide Thrill Seeker example shown in this book is about 1.2 MB in size, due mainly to the map and small grayscale photo at the end. If we added another large graphic or embedded fonts, it would be too big for most floppy formats.

 Users without PowerPoint on their computers can play your presentations (but not edit them) if you send along the Viewer. You'll need one 1.44MB floppy for the Viewer and its installer, and another disk or disks for your presentation. See online help for details.

PowerPoint

PART FIVE

Delivering Information with Microsoft Mail

Microsoft Mail makes it possible for networked users to exchange messages and files. Depending on your network, you can communicate with other users in the same department, the same building, or even world-wide. Here you will find out how to use Mail to join the e-mail revolution.

Mail Toolbar Reference

BUTTON	DESCRIPTION
Buttons on Mail's Standard Toolbar	

Compose: Write a new message. [Mail ➤ Compose] *Shortcut:* Ctrl+N

Reply: Reply to the sender of an open message. [Mail ➤ Reply] *Shortcut:* Ctrl+R

ReplyAll: Reply to the sender and all recipients of an open message. [Mail ➤ Reply To All] *Shortcut:* Ctrl+A

Forward: Forward a message to another user on the mail system. [Mail ➤ Forward] *Shortcut:* Ctrl+F

Move: Move a message to another folder. [File ➤ Move] *Shortcut:* Ctrl+M

Delete: Delete selected item of mail. [File ➤ Delete] *Shortcut:* Ctrl+D

Previous: View previous mail item in folder. [View ➤ Previous] *Shortcut:* Ctrl+<

Next: View next mail item in folder. [View ➤ Next] *Shortcut:* Ctrl+>

Directory: Display a list of user directories on Mail system. *Shortcut:* Ctrl+L

BUTTON	DESCRIPTION
	Buttons for Managing Address Books in Mail
	Personal Address Book: Display members of personal address book. *Shortcut:* Ctrl+P
	Find: Find a member in current user directory. *Shortcut:* Ctrl+F
	New Address: Add an entry to personal address book.
	Add Names: Add entries in selected directory list to personal address book.

29

Mail Basics

Mail

With all the wires being strung everywhere, this truly is the decade of networking. Even small businesses are entangling their computers. E-mail is replacing in-house memos, *While You Where Out* notes, and even office supply order forms. Let's take a look at how a network might work for you.

What's Microsoft Mail?

Microsoft mail is a collection of programs that make it possible for coworkers to exchange messages and files over computer networks. Networked users can be in the same room, the same building, or stretched world-wide. Who you can exchange mail with depends on your network setup and decisions made by the person in charge of your network and mail services.

Your Microsoft Office package comes with a license (a piece of paper, actually) permitting you to use Microsoft Mail software. The software itself is not shipped with the rest of your Office software. Rather, it is shipped with the Microsoft Mail system, a separate product.

What's Required to Get Started?

At least one of the computers on the network acts as a mail server. Microsoft now calls these *postoffices*. The postoffice is where the mail server and related administration software have been installed by the mail administrator. It is also where lists of authorized users and groups are stored. (And it may or may not be where your messages are stored.) Check with your administrator for details.

Your mail administrator will need to set up *access rights* for you and your *mailbox* in the postoffice or postoffices you'll access. You will also need to know the security procedures, and probably set up a password.

Your computer needs some mail software too, though not the same kind as is on the server. It will probably be installed on your hard disk by your mail administrator. Remember, the Office package only contains a license agreement for Mail. The software itself is shipped with the Mail server program and thus, is *not* installed automatically when you install the Office.

Your computer will need to be connected to the same network with the postoffice or postoffices you wish to access.

Starting Mail from the Office Manager

Once everything is properly set up, you can start Microsoft mail (or switch to it if it is already running) by clicking on the Mail button in the Office Manager toolbar. The button's shown at the left.

To start mail from the Program Manager, double-click on the Microsoft Mail icon in the Microsoft Applications Group (or perhaps the Office group).

Signing In and Out

You will be asked to enter your name and password (unless Mail has been set up to do this automatically for you—this process will be described later in the chapter).

1. Type your mail box name exactly as you and the administrator agreed to set it up.

2. Press Tab.

3. Enter the mail password. Capitalization counts. HoHoHo, hohoho, and HOHOHO are all different passwords.

4. Click OK or press ↵.

To quit Mail, choose either Exit (which maintains your network connection with the postoffice) or choose Exit and Sign Out, which disconnects you from the postoffice.

Getting On-Line Help

Mail, like the other Office programs, has context-sensitive on-line help. Reach it from Mail's Help menu or with the F1 function key.

Running the Demo

There are two demonstrations worth viewing if you've never used mail before. Here's how to reach them:

1. Start Mail.

2. Choose Contents from Mail's Help menu.

3. Click on the Getting Started with Mail button, shown below.

4. Click on one of the resulting demo buttons, shown below.

Getting Started with Mail
- Demo Overview Demo
- Demo Highlights Demo
- ☐ Signing Into or Out of Mail
- ☐ Changing Your Password
- ☐ Sending a Message
- ☐ Reading a Message
- ☐ Deleting or Retrieving a Message

Sending Mail

There are a few basic steps to sending mail. All but four are optional:

- Bring up the Send Note dialog box.
- Pick the intended recipient(s) and *address* your message.
- Type the text of the message.
- Spell check if you like (optional).
- Attach a file if you wish to send one along (optional).
- Send away.

Let's look at those steps in more detail. Realize that specific procedures at your site may vary, so don't be afraid to ask for help if things go wrong.

Sending a Note

Begin by opening Microsoft Mail and clicking on the Compose button, shown at left. You will see the Send Note dialog box, illustrated in Figure 29.1.

Mail

FIGURE 29.1

This is where you compose, address, and send mail.

Click to begin composing a new message

Click to see the names of people in your post office

Click here to send the finished message

Type your message here

Addressing Mail

Microsoft Mail needs to know where to send your message. You can either type the name of the recipient in the To: box or look it up by clicking on the Address button in the Send Note dialog box. If you click the Address button, you'll see the Address dialog box, shown in Figure 29.2.

Pick a name in any of the following ways:

■ Type the first few characters of a name to scroll the list into "the right neighborhood," and then use the up and down arrow keys to select the desired name and press ↵, OR

■ Double-click on the name in the list, OR

■ Select a name and click the To: button.

FIGURE 29.2

Choose names in the
Address dialog box.

In any case, the name will be added to the To: list. You can place more than
one name in the To box this way.

To place names in the CC: (carbon copy) list, tab or click to move the insertion point there, then pick names as before.

When finished adding names to the To: and CC: lists, click OK.

 TIP Send mail to yourself—it's a good way to practice, and a
way to confirm that the post office is working properly.

Composing Mail

You compose mail in the large white box illustrated in Figure 29.1.

1. Begin by adding a subject in the Subject box (tab or click to move the insertion point there).

2. When you've finished typing the subject, tab again or click in the message area.

3. Type and edit text as you would in any good Windows program. Text will wrap, so only press ↵ when you want to start a new paragraph. You can't embellish text with attributes like bold and italics or use drag-and-drop, etc. You *can* indent with the tab key, however, and use the Change Font choice on the View menu to change the appearance of the text on your screen.

4. When text fills the screen, it will scroll. Use Page Up, Page Down, and the arrow keys to navigate.

5. To delete text, select it and press the Delete key.

6. Move text by cutting and pasting.

Spell Checking Messages

To spell check messages before sending them, press the F7 function key or choose Spelling from the Edit menu. Your entire message, including the subject line, will be checked. To check just a word or just part of your text, select it first. Mail's Spell Checker is a lot like Word's, which is described in Chapter 10 (see the "Spelling Checker" section).

Attaching Files

You can attach a file that will be sent along with your message by clicking the Attach button in the Send Note dialog box. This will reveal an Attach dialog box, shown in Figure 29.3, that will remind you of most Windows Open dialog boxes. We will explore variations on this process in Chapter 30.

FIGURE 29.3

Select the file you wish to send in the Attach dialog box.

Sending Messages

Once the message is addressed and typed, click on the Send button, or use the keyboard shortcut Alt+S, to send it.

Sending Urgent Messages

The Options button in the Send Note dialog box will bring up another dialog box that you can use to change the priority of the messages you send. To make a message high priority (and add that exclamation mark to the recipient's incoming mail list):

1. Create the message.
2. Click on the Options button in the message window.
3. You'll see the Options dialog box illustrated in Figure 29.4.
4. Choose High priority.
5. Click OK.
6. Click Send to send the message. Messages sent this way appear with an ! next to them in recipients' mail lists.

Requesting a Return Receipt

To learn if and when a recipient read your message, choose the Return Receipt option in the Options dialog box:

1. Create the message.

2. Click on the Options button in the message window. You'll see the Options dialog box.

3. Choose Return Receipt.

4. Click OK.

5. Click Send to send the message. When the recipient(s) read your message, you will receive a return message detailing the time and date the message was read, even if a recipient does not reply.

Saving Copies of Messages You Send

To save copies of messages you send, choose the Save Sent Messages option in the Options dialog box:

1. Create the message.

2. Click on the Options button in the message window. You'll see the Options dialog box.

3. Choose Save sent messages.

4. Click OK.

5. Click Send to send the message. A copy of the message will be placed in your Sent mail folder.

Aborting a Message before Sending

If you have a change of heart before sending a message, close the Send Note window (Ctrl+F4) and answer No to the Save Changes? prompt.

Receiving and Reading Mail

Inbox

Incoming mail is stored in your *inbox*. How you are alerted to incoming mail depends on which options you've specified. (See the section "Personalizing Microsoft Mail Settings" later in this chapter.)

To look inside your inbox, open Mail and double-click on the icon shown at left. You'll see an inbox like the one in Figure 29.5.

The mail inbox tells you what mail you've received and its status. Unread messages have unopened envelopes next to them, as shown in Figure 29.5. Urgent messages have exclamation points to the left of the envelope icons.

FIGURE 29.5

The Mail inbox

Double-click to open
different folders

Double-click
on a message
to read it

Unopened envelopes
indicate unread mail

Opened envelopes indicate
the mail has been read

To read a message, double-click anywhere on its listing in the inbox. The message will appear on-screen, complete with a header describing the sender, date, subject, and so on.

Scroll if necessary to read the entire message.

TIP

If you have a lot of mail in your inbox, you can sort it by sender's name, subject, or time and date received. Simply check on the headings From, Subject, or Received above the list of mail.

Printing Mail

To print a message or messages:

1. Select a message name in the message list by clicking on it, or select multiple names by holding the Ctrl key while you click.

2. Choose Print from the File menu or use the usual Ctrl+P shortcut. You'll be given a chance to print multiple messages on a page, and you can select print quality (High is the best choice).

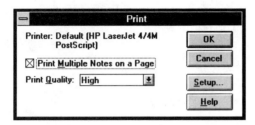

3. Click OK to print the message(s).

Responding to Mail

To reply to a message, click on the Reply button in the message window. To reply to all messages, use the ReplyAll button:

Microsoft Mail will automatically address the reply message, but you can add or delete names from the address lists if you like.

The subject box will contain the subject of the original message preceded by RE:. This can also be edited.

You'll see the original message in the text area with the reply area separated by a solid line. Type the reply and click Send or use the Alt+S shortcut.

Saving and Deleting Mail

You'll want to delete unwanted messages to delete the clutter from your in-box. There may also be times when you want to save copies of messages on your disk. Here's how to do both.

Deleting Messages

To delete messages:

1. Select a message name in the message list by clicking on it or select multiple names by holding the Ctrl key while you click.

2. Press the Delete key, choose Delete from the File menu, or drag the message from the list to the wastebasket folder in your Private Folders list. (See Figure 29.5.)

3. If you drag items to the wastebasket folder and then change your mind, double-click on the folder to retrieve messages. Unless you tell MS Mail otherwise (in the Options dialog box) the wastebasket will be emptied when you exit Mail.

Personalizing Microsoft Mail Settings

You have some control over how Mail behaves. For instance, you can choose whether to be alerted to incoming mail with a chime. To see and select mail options, choose Options from the Mail menu. You'll see the Options dialog box shown in Figure 29.6.

FIGURE 29.6

Use the Options dialog box to personalize your mail settings.

Working Off-Line

While you'll usually want to work with Microsoft Mail while connected to the network and postoffice, there are times when that won't be possible—for instance, if you have a portable computer and take it out of the office, or if the network or mail server are inoperative.

Under these conditions, it is sometimes possible to accomplish some mail tasks—like composing mail. You may also be able to read some unread mail and review saved mail. Check with on-line help and your mail administrator for details.

30

Microsoft Mail and Office Applications

I n this chapter, we'll look at Word, Excel, and PowerPoint features for both *mailing* and *routing* files on a network. Mailing simply sends copies of files to recipients, while routing lets you control who gets the copy when, and then lets you collect and include the work of others in your finished project. Typically, you'll *mail multiple* copies of files to many people at once or *route a single copy* of a document from one person to another and often back to you.

In order to exchange and work with documents this way, you and the recipients must have the Office applications used to create the documents and Microsoft Mail or a compatible mail program installed on your computers.

The exact steps for mailing and routing vary slightly from application to application. Let's look at Microsoft Word first, since it has some annotation and merging features not found in the other applications.

Word Documents and E-Mail

Word offers two menu commands (File ➤ Add Routing Slip and File ➤ Send) that you can use to send and return copies of Word documents. You can also add toolbar buttons for some mail and routing tasks.

If the Add Routing Slip and Send commands do not appear on your File menu or if they are dim, contact your Mail manager or network administrator. You may have an improperly installed mail program, an incompatible mail program, or network problems.

Sending Word documents via electronic mail is pretty simple:

1. Open the document you want to send.

■ If the document's already open because you've just created or altered it, make sure it's saved.

2. Select File ➤ Add Routing Slip. The Routing Slip dialog box, shown in Figure 30.1, will appear.

FIGURE 30.1

The Routing Slip
dialog box

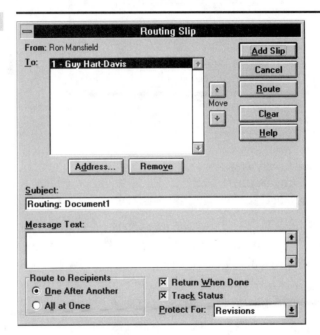

3. Click the Address button. In the Address dialog box (see Figure 30.2), select the names of the people you want to send the document to and choose the Add button.

■ To route the document to one recipient after another (we'll get into this in a minute), arrange the names in the appropriate order using the arrow buttons.

4. Click OK to return to the Routing Slip dialog box. The names you entered will appear in the To box.

FIGURE 30.2

The Address dialog box. Choose your victims here.

5. Type the subject of your communiqué in the Subject box and any message in the Message Text box. Each recipient will get the same subject and message, so don't get too personal.

- If the To box shows you that you've added someone you shouldn't have, click the Remove button and remove that person from the list.

- Word will automatically add to your message instructions that tell the recipients to select File ➤ Send when finished with the document you send, so you don't need to write that in your message.

6. In the Route to Recipients area, choose whether you want the document to be sent to the recipients One after Another or All at Once.

TIP   If you send a document to the recipients One After Another, each successive recipient will see his or her predecessors' comments. This way, you may be able to avoid duplicate comments. If you send multiple copies All At Once, everyone's comments will be between them and you (until you put them in the ultimate document and attribute them to their maker!). You'll probably also get quicker answers this way.

7. If you're ready to send your document, choose the Route button. The document will be sent to recipients as an attached Word file.

■ To further edit your document before you send it, click the Add Slip button again, do your editing, and then select File ➤ Send to send the document. Click Yes in the confirmation dialog box.

Let's look quickly at three further options in the Routing Slip dialog box: Return When Done, Track Status, and Protect For.

Return When Done	Check the Return When Done check box to have the document sent back to you when the last recipient finishes with the document and chooses File ➤ Send.
Track Status	Check the Track Status check box to keep track of where your document has been routed. Word will send you a message each time the document is sent on to the next person in the To list.
Protect For	Select protection for your document from the drop-down list: **Annotations** allows recipients to add only annotations to the document, **Revisions** allows them to make changes (forcibly marked with revision marks) and add annotations, and **Forms** lets recipients enter information only in form fields.

Revising and Returning a Mailed Document

If you're the target of an e-mailed Word document, here's how you do your bit:

1. Retrieve the document from your mail program in the usual way for that program and open the document in Word.

2. Revise the document depending on how the sender has protected it:

   ■ If the document allows annotations only, select Insert ➤ Annotation, type your annotation into the annotation pane, and click Close when you're done.

   ■ If the document allows both revisions and annotations, just go ahead and make your revisions. Word will use revision marks to mark your revisions.

   ■ If the document is protected as a form, you're wearing a strait-jacket. Fill in the fields (*all* the fields—be good) and don't try to do anything else.

3. Choose File ➤ Send. The Send dialog box will appear (see below), asking if you want to use the routing slip or send the document without using the routing slip. To send it, choose the Route Document option and click OK.

   ■ If the original sender chose to route the document to recipients All At Once, this will return the document to the sender.

   ■ If the original sender chose to route the document to recipients One after Another, this will pass the document on to its next victim—unless you're the last, in which case the document will be returned to the sender.

■ If the original sender checked Track Status, Word will let the sender know when you send the document on to its next recipient. Yup, Big Brother is e-mailing about you.

 NOTE If you choose the Send Copy of Document Without Using the Routing Slip option, all protection the original sender chose remains in effect.

Merging Annotations and Revisions

So you sent out—all at once—seven copies of your latest marketing proposal for industrial-strength deodorant, *Hang-Gliding off Power Pylons*, and everyone got back to you with helpful comments. Well, sort of helpful. Most of them, anyway. Bunch of cynics, the lot of them. Now you need to merge the annotations and revisions into one copy so that you can pick out the best and trash the rest.

 WARNING You can't merge annotations and revisions back into the original document unless they're marked. Makes sense if you think about it. This is another good reason for protecting your document for revisions or annotations before sending it out. If you forget to protect your document, try using Tools ➤ Revisions and using the Compare Versions feature.

To merge all those pesky revision marks and annotations:

1. Retrieve your returned document from your mail program. Word will automatically ask you if you want to merge revisions with the original document.

2. Click OK. The Merge Revisions dialog box, shown in Figure 30.3, will appear (well, what did you expect?).

3. Select the original file and click OK. The original document will open and the revisions will be merged into it.

4. Repeat as necessary with the other six copies of the report.

NOTE   When you merge revisions or annotations from multiple documents into the original, Word will use a different color for each reviewer (up to eight—after that, Word will cycle through the colors again).

FIGURE 30.3

The Merge Revisions dialog box. Select the original file here and click OK. Change drives and directories just as you would in the Open dialog box.

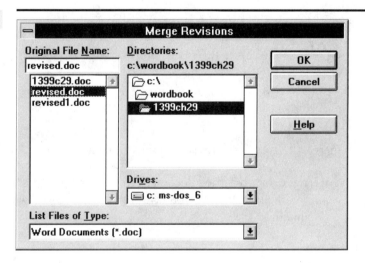

Mail

For Additional Help with Mail in Word

Mail and network connections can be confusing, particularly on the complex networks that have been proliferating recently. Read your mail program's user guide to glean further information, or go harass your friendly network administrator or hallway guru.

Network Security Considerations

Networks can be a source of security problems. While there's no way that you can absolutely safeguard all your work, remember to take the following obvious precautions:

- Protect your documents from changes.
- Save your documents frequently, and back them up to a safe medium frequently.
- If you store your documents on a network drive, be careful about whom you give access to them. If necessary, make your documents read-only.

If you're sharing documents a lot, here are a few things to think about first:

- Don't use templates that the other people in the group don't have.
- If you share templates, keep them clean. Don't redefine built-in key combinations—you may confuse your coworkers, or worse.
- Don't use fonts that the other people in the group don't have. (But remember that you can embed TrueType fonts in shared documents so that other users who don't have the fonts installed can see the fonts and print them. Select Tools ➤ Options, click the Save tab in the Options dialog box, and check the Embed TrueType Fonts check box.)
- Don't lose your file-protection password.

Excel and Mail

 Excel lets you both mail and route workbooks (collections of worksheets). The process is virtually the same as that described for mailing and routing Word documents. You can use File ➤ Add Routing Slip and File ➤ Send on Excel's File menu, or the Routing Slip and Send Mail buttons, shown at left, on the WorkGroup toolbar.

Remember: When you mail someone a copy of a workbook (or route a workbook copy) the original file stays in your possession. It is not modified. The copy or copies and original are not linked.

PowerPoint and Mail

As with Word and Excel, you can mail or route copies of Powerpoint presentation files over the network to others that have Mail and PowerPoint installed. As with Word and Excel, PowerPoint will display File ➤ Add Routing Slip and File ➤ Send choices on your File menu if you have a compatible mail program installed and running.

You can add Mail buttons to your PowerPoint toolbars if you wish. The process is illustrated in Figure 30.4.

Here are the steps:

1. Choose Customize from PowerPoint's Tools menu.

2. Highlight the File category if it isn't already highlighted.

3. Point to the button you wish to add (the Send Mail button, for instance).

4. Hold down the primary mouse button and drag the button to the desired location on a PowerPoint toolbar.

5. When you release the mouse button, the toolbar will make room for the new button. For instance, here's the PowerPoint Standard toolbar with the Send Mail and Routing Slip buttons inserted:

FIGURE 30.4

Drag buttons to add them to your PowerPoint toolbar.

Drag buttons from the Customize Toolbars dialog box

Send Mail button   Routing Slip button

Managing Your Data with Access

As you have seen in the chapters describing Word's mail-merge features, PowerPoint's outlining abilities, Excel's database tools, and Mail's address books, Office provides many different ways to collect and organize business and personal information. But while Word and Excel are fine for small to medium projects, you may need the extra features, speed, and flexibility provided by Microsoft Access for larger jobs.

Access is an integral part of Microsoft Office Professional; if you have the Standard version of Office you can purchase Access separately and add it to the Standard version. We'll take a look in these next few chapters at how this database management system can help you collect, find, and use mountains of data.

Access Toolbar Reference

New Database: Creates a new database.

Open Database: Brings up the Open dialog box.

Attach Table: Click to attach tables from other database.

Print: Opens the Print dialog box to let you print the active object (table, form, etc.). *Shortcut:* Ctrl+P

Print Preview: Takes you to the Print Preview window.

Code: Lets programmers edit and create Access BASIC modules.

Cut: Cuts selected object(s). *Shortcut:* Ctrl+X

Copy: Copies selected object(s). *Shortcut:* Ctrl+C

Paste: Pastes Clipboard contents. *Shortcut:* Ctrl+V

Relationships: Displays the Relationships window where you view and change relationships.

Import: Opens the Import dialog box.

Export: Opens the Export dialog box.

BUTTON	DESCRIPTION

Buttons on Access's Database Window Toolbar (continued)

BUTTON	DESCRIPTION
	Merge It: Opens the MS Word Mail-Merge Wizard to link data for mail-merges.
	Analyze It with MS Excel: Saves contents of current table, form, report, or module as an Excel worksheet (.XLS), opening Excel in the process.
	New Query: Creates a new query based on currently active table or query.
	New Form: Creates a new form based on currently active table or query.
	New Report: Creates a new report based on currently active table or query.
	Database Window: Switches you to the Database window.
	AutoForm: Creates a new form containing all fields and records in the current table or query.
	AutoReport: Creates a new report containing all fields and records in the current table or query.
	Undo: Attempts to undo last action.
	Cue Cards: Activates Access tutorial help.
	Help: Offers help for the *next* item that you click on.

Access

Access Toolbar Reference

BUTTON	DESCRIPTION
Buttons on Access's Form View Toolbar (Form, Datasheet Views)	
	Design View: Switches to Design view.
	Form View: Switches to Form view.
	Datasheet View: Switches to Datasheet view.
	Print: Opens the Print dialog box to let you print the active object (table, form, etc.). *Shortcut:* Ctrl+P
	Print Preview: Takes you to the Print Preview window.
	New Record: Creates a new record.
	Cut: Cuts selected object(s). *Shortcut:* Ctrl+X
	Copy: Copies selected object(s). *Shortcut:* Ctrl+C
	Paste: Pastes Clipboard contents. *Shortcut:* Ctrl+V
	Find: Opens the Find dialog box, permitting you to search the database.
	Sort Ascending: Sorts records from small to large based on selected field(s).
	Sort Descending: Sorts records form large to small based on selected field(s).
	Edit Filter/Sort: Opens the Filter window, enabling you to create or edit a filter for restricting and/or sorting records displayed.
	Apply Sort/Filter: Uses the current filter.
	Show All Records: Shows all records (removes any filters).

BUTTON	DESCRIPTION

Database Window: Switches you to the Database window.

Undo Current Field/Record: Reverses all changes made to current field or record.

Undo: Attempts to undo last action.

Cue Cards: Activates Access tutorial help.

Help: Offers help for the *next* item that you click on.

Buttons on Access's Table Design Toolbar (Design View)

Design View: Switches to Design view.

Datasheet View: Switches to Datasheet view.

Save: Saves current design (layout) only, not data. *Shortcut:* Ctrl+S

Properties: Shows and hides Properties sheet for selected control, section, or other object.

Indexes: Opens Indexes window where you can add, remove, or review field indexes.

Set Primary Key: Makes selected field the Primary key.

Insert Row: Inserts a new row above the current row.

Delete Row: Deletes the selected row(s).

New Query: Creates a new query based on currently active table.

Access

Access Toolbar Reference

BUTTON	DESCRIPTION
Buttons on Access's Table Design Toolbar (Design View) (continued)	
	New Form: Creates a new Form based on currently active table.
	New Report: Creates a new Report based on currently active table.
	Database Window: Switches you to the Database window.
	Build: Opens the Build window to let you pick items to add to an expression or procedure.
	Undo: Attempts to undo last action.
	Cue Cards: Activates Access tutorial help.
	Help: Offers help for the *next* item that you click on.
Buttons on Access's Print Preview Toolbar	
	Close: Closes the active window.
	Print: Opens the Print dialog box to let you print the active document (the one in the Preview window). *Shortcut:* Ctrl+P
	Print Setup: Opens the Print Setup dialog box where you adjust margins, etc.
	Zoom: Switches between close-up and bird's-eye views of document being previewed.
	Publish It with MS Word: Saves contents of current table, form, report, or module as a Word Rich Text Format document (.RTF), opening Word in the process.

BUTTON	DESCRIPTION

Buttons on Access's Print Preview Toolbar (continued)

Analyze It with Excel: Saves contents of current table, form, report, or module as an Excel worksheet (.XLS), opening Excel in the process.

Mail It: Lets you add the current table, query, report etc. to a Mail message.

Database Window: Switches you to the Database window.

Cue Cards: Activates Access tutorial help.

Help: Offers help for the *next* item that you click on.

Buttons on Access's Relationships Toolbar

Save: Saves design (layout) only, not data. *Shortcut:* Ctrl+S

Add Table: Lets you add a table to the Relationships window.

Show Direct Relationships: Shows only relationships that have a direct relationship with the current table.

Show All Relationships: Shows every relationship in the database.

Database Window: Switches you to the Database window.

Cue Cards: Activates Access tutorial help.

Help: Offers help for the *next* item that you click on.

Access

Access Toolbar Reference

BUTTON	DESCRIPTION
Buttons on Access's Macro Toolbar	

Save: Saves current macro. *Shortcut:* Ctrl+S

Macro Names: Shows or hides the Macro Names column in the Macro window.

Conditions: Shows or hides the Conditions column in the Macro window.

Run: Runs the macro.

Single Step: Runs the macro a step at a time for easy troubleshooting.

Database Window: Switches you to the Database window.

Build: Opens the Build window to let you pick items to add to an expression or procedure.

Undo: Attempts to undo last action.

Cue Cards: Activates Access tutorial help.

Help: Offers help for the *next* item that you click on.

Select Objects: Use to select objects.

Label: Lets you create labels.

Option Group: Lets you create option *groups*.

Option Button: Lets you create a *single* option button.

Combo Box : Lets you create a combo box (drop-down list).

BUTTON	DESCRIPTION

Buttons in Access's Form and Report Toolbox (continued)

Graph: Starts the Graph Wizard.

Object Frame: Lets you create unbound frames for things like logos in headers.

Line: Lets you draw lines.

Page Break: Inserts forced page breaks in reports and forms.

Control Wizards: Turns Control Wizards on and off.

Text Box: Use to create controls that display data, bound or unbound.

Toggle Button: Use to create toggle buttons.

Checkbox: Use to create checkboxes.

List Box: Use to create scrolling lists of choices.

Subform/Subreport: Creates a frame to display an embedded form or report.

Bound Object Frame: Lets you create frames for bound objects that are "connected" to records in a table (like promotional photos or multimedia film clips in a videotape database).

Rectangle: Draw rectangles with this button.

Command Button: Create command buttons with this tool to run a macro or Access BASIC function.

Tool Lock: Keeps the current tool as the active tool so you can use it over and over.

Access

31

Introduction to Access

■

Access

Microsoft Access is a fully featured *database management system* (*DBMS*) that lets you collect, organize, find, display, and print information about your personal and business life. The amount and variety of information it can deal with is huge. Since folks at Microsoft have done much of the setup work for a variety of common database management tasks, it's easy for you to start working with simple, professional looking information systems in a matter of moments. Access comes with Wizards and a variety of predefined database elements that let you set up the following common tools with only a few clicks of your mouse:

- Billable-time trackers
- Book inventories
- Contacts lists (personal and business)
- Customer lists
- Delivery systems
- Diet logs
- Employee record-keeping systems
- Event trackers
- Exercise logs
- Expense trackers
- Film and photograph inventories
- Fixed-asset trackers
- Guest lists
- Household inventories
- Investment tracking sytems
- Invoices

- Mailing lists
- Music-collection inventories
- Order-taking and tracking systems
- Payment tracking systems
- Planting and flower records
- Product lists
- Project trackers
- Recipe collections
- Reservation-taking and tracking systems
- Service records
- Student records
- Supplier lists
- Video collection inventories
- Wine inventories

Of course, you can create your own tools, or modify any of these for your own situations. Moreover, you can combine tools to form complex systems. For instance, while the video collection tools in Access were designed for personal use, they can quite easily be combined with other elements like reservation and invoicing tools to run a video rental store. You'll see examples of this shortly.

But we are getting ahead of ourselves. Let's start with some basics.

Access System Requirements

Let's face it. Computer programs are getting bigger and slower. (But then, aren't we all?) Access is no exception. Here are Microsoft's minimum and recommended system configurations for Access:

COMPONENT	MINIMUM	RECOMMENDED
Computer	80386 SX or greater	80386/20 or greater
RAM	6 MB	8 MB

COMPONENT	MINIMUM	RECOMMENDED
Hard disk space (for programs)	5 MB (Minimum installation)	19 MB+ (Typical installation)
Monitor	EGA	VGA or higher
DOS Version	3.1	Current MS-DOS Version
Other	Windows 3.1	Windows 3.1 or Windows for Workgroups or Windows NT 3.1 or later

In addition, you'll need a mouse or other compatible pointing device (like a trackball), and plenty of hard disk space for your database files. Access works with virtually all printers supported by Windows. A tape drive or other device capable of backing up large files would also be a good idea.

Upgrading from Earlier Access Versions

TIP

Hard disk space permitting, if you have an earlier version of Access installed on your PC (Access 1.0 or 1.1), you might initially want to keep it installed, and place Access Version 2 in a separate directory. This is particularly important if you share databases over a network with people who have not yet upgraded to Version 2.

While Version 2.0 can open and use databases created with earlier versions of Access, the reverse is not true. And, since once you've used an old database with Version 2, you won't be able to open it directly with earlier Access versions, eventually you'll probably want to convert all of your databases (and co-workers) to Version 2. Think of it as contributing to the economy, at least in and around Redmond, Washington, if that makes the investment in new software less painful.

Access Concepts and Terms

Microsoft has its own take on certain standard DBMS terms, and has added a few new terms to the database world, so even if you're a seasoned pro you should skim this next section.

Database

A *database* is simply a collection of useful data. The phone book is an example. So's your office filing cabinet, or a Rolodex full of cards. Access databases include such "objects" as tables, queries, forms, and more.

Tables

In Access-ese, *tables* are collections of *similar data*. For instance, if you ran a videotape rental store, you might have an Access table that collects information about each tape you own (title, running length, date purchased, tape inventory number, and so on). A portion of it might look like this:

You might also have a *different* table that collects customer's names, phone numbers, membership numbers, addresses, and so on:

There might be yet another table where you keep information about which customer has reserved which tape for which night, and so on. With Access, all of these tables would be organized differently, and contain mostly different information; but they'd all be in the *same* database file.

For instance, you might have a database file called *VID_STOR* containing tables named *Members*, *Tapes*, *Reservations*, etc. These tables are stored in the same database file because they are often used together to create reports, to help you fill out on-screen forms, etc. Figure 31.1 shows how parts of a simple Access video store database might look as separate tables.

Relational Databases

Access is a *relational database*, which means that it allows data that has been stored in different places (normally in various Access tables) to be *linked*. (The "relational" part of the term actually refers to a class of operations described by a branch of mathematics called *set theory* rather than from the relatedness of the data, but that needn't concern us here.) For instance, whenever your video store employee enters a customer's phone number into an on-screen invoice form, Access could look up the customer's name, address, and membership number from the tables that contain that data.

You'll learn more about this concept in Chapter 37. For now it's enough to know that relational database tools like Access can help you manage information in three important ways, by helping you in:

- Reducing redundancy.
- Facilitating the sharing of information.
- Keeping data accurate.

We'll talk about all of these in the upcoming chapters.

Records

A *record* is all the information contained in *one row* of an Access datasheet table. In the video store example, the store's employee records might include a row (a record) for each employee as shown in Figure 31.2.

FIGURE 31.2

Access data are kept in tables. Each row is a record. Records are broken down into fields.

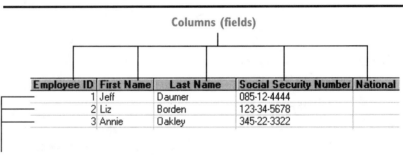

Fields

Fields are places in a table where you store individual chunks of information. If you look at Figure 31.2, for instance, you'll see that there's a field called Employee ID, another called First Name, and so on.

Primary Key and Other Indexed Fields

Access uses *key fields* and *indexing* to help speed many database operations. You can tell Access which fields should be key fields or Access can assign them automatically. You'll learn more about these later.

Controls and Objects

Controls are Access *objects* that help you display, print, and use your data. They can be things like field labels that you drag around when designing reports, for instance. Or they can be boxes containing the results of calculations. Or pictures, or titles for reports.

NOTE As you'll see, Microsoft refers to a rather confusing collection of things as controls and objects. Even though the terms are not synonymous, often the terms are used interchangeably in Microsoft's documentation. Don't fret. Such terms will make more sense later.

Queries and Dynasets

When you request a list of all videotapes that were due back yesterday and did not arrive, that's a *query*. Queries are *requests* to Access for information.

When Access *responds* with its list of overdue tapes, that response constitutes a *dynaset*—a dynamic set of data meeting your query criteria.

Because of the way Access is designed, dynasets are updated even after you've made your query. So, if your video store has networked computers, and if you display a list of overdue tapes, and then someone checks in an overdue tape on another computer, your dynaset will *automatically* update to reflect the returned tape. (This works in theory, anyway. In practice it seems to make a difference just how your machines are networked. In some cases you have to *ask* Access to update your dynaset, by pressing Shift+F9.)

Forms

Forms are on-screen arrangements that make it easy to enter and read data. You can also print out the forms if you wish. You can design forms yourself, or let the Access *AutoForm* feature do it for you. Here's a sample AutoForm for the Reservations table in our video store database:

Reservations
Reservations
Reservation ID: 1
Customer ID:
Reservation Date: 11/7/95
Confirmed: ☐
Employee ID: 1
Video Collection ID: 1
Movie Title: Thelma and Lassie
◀◀ ◀ Record: 1 of 1 ▶ ▶▶

Reports

Reports are (usually) paper copies of dynasets. You can also print reports "to disk," if you like. Here too, Access can help create the reports. There are even Wizards for complex printouts like Crosstab reports—reports in which the data is cross-tabulated. You'll learn much more about reports in Chapter 36.

Properties

Properties are the specifications (or characteristics) you assign to parts of your database design. For instance, each field's properties can include things like the type of data (text, numbers, etc.) and the format of the data (number of decimal places, typestyle, color, and so on). You can define properties for fields, forms, controls, and most other Access objects.

Calculations, Expressions, and Functions

If you own a store and decide to give certain customers a discount on rentals, you can have Access do the calculations as required. You instruct Access to perform specific calculations by building *expressions* using built-in *functions* (which will remind you of those in Excel). You'll learn how in Chapter 38.

Wizards

Unless you've just picked up this book, you've already met some *Wizards*. These are built-in assistants that know how to guide you through steps necessary for common tasks.

Access Wizards can help you create:

- Queries
- Tables
- Forms
- Reports
- Mailing labels
- Controls and buttons

Macros

Macros are tools that can help automate complex or time-consuming repetitive manual tasks. Consultants and advanced users often set up macros to help simplify things for less experienced users and to "bullet-proof" databases. You get an introduction to macros in Chapter 38.

Command Buttons

Command buttons are on-screen objects that you can click on to run macros. You'll get a chance to create your own buttons in Chapter 38.

Modules and Access Basic

Modules are programs that advanced users create with *Access Basic*, a programming language. These programs can perform complex operations not possible with Access alone or even Access with macros. While a full treatment of Access Basic is beyond the scope of this book, you'll get a glimpse of how it can be used with macros in Chapter 38.

Starting and Quitting Access

Enough theory, Mansfield, let's process some data! Once you've properly installed Access (see our installation instructions in Appendix A, if necessary), you start it in the usual ways. That is, with Windows already running, either:

■ *In the Office Manager toolbar,* click on the Access button (the one with the image of the key):

■ *or, in the Office Manager toolbar,* click on the Office Manager button then choose Access from the menu that it displays:

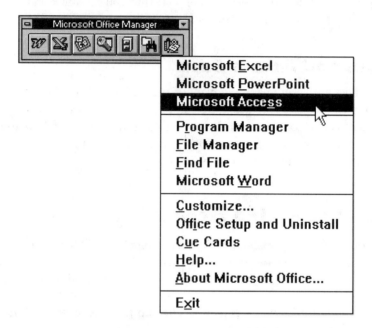

■ *or, in Windows' Program Manager,* double-click on the Access icon in the MS Office group:

■ *or, in Windows' File Manager,* double-click on the Access application file:

■ *or, in Windows' File Manager,* double-click on an Access database file (any file with an *MDB* extension):

When you first start Access, you might be invited to take a tour with Microsoft's electronic coaching tool, the Access Cue Cards (as shown in Figure 31.3):

FIGURE 31.3

You can take advantage of Microsoft's Cue Cards to coach you as you try out various operations in Access.

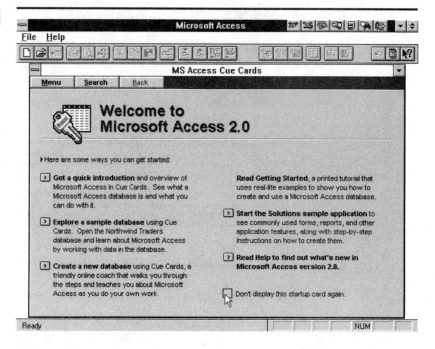

You can use Cue Cards to get an introduction, explore a sample database, create your own database, and more. You'll be greeted by the Cue Card screen until and unless someone shuts it off. To do this, click to place an X in the Don't Display This Startup Card Again box.

Quitting Access

Always use the Exit command on the Access File menu (or Alt+F,X) to quit Access. This provides for an orderly shut-down and will prompt you to save any recent changes to database elements.

If you attempt to quit Windows with Access still running, Access will also prompt you for any necessary saves, then shut down properly.

The Access Workspace and Tools

In addition to the usual Windows tools (a menu bar, control boxes, and so on, the Access window (shown in Figure 31.4) contains some other items of interest.

FIGURE 31.4

The Access window and a typical Database window

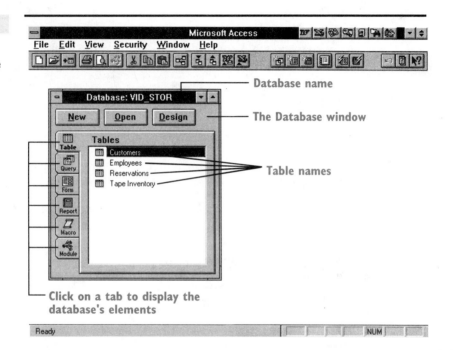

Access

The Access Window

The Access window contains the menu, toolbars, and other windows you use to create and use data.

The Database Window

The Database window lets you both create and see database elements (tables, queries, forms, and so on). In Figure 31.4 you can see the Database window for our video store example. Clicking on the various tabs in the window reveals lists of the various tables, forms, reports, and other elements that have been created for the database.

The Status Area

As with other Microsoft applications, get in the habit of checking the status area at the bottom of the Access window. It can often tell you what's going on, what the tool you are pointing to will do, or what's going wrong.

Menus

Menus work as you'd expect, but they change quite often in Access, depending on what you are doing at the time. As in other well-behaved programs, there are keyboard shortcuts (like Ctrl+S for Save); the shortcuts are displayed on the menus. There are mouseless ways to issue virtually all the menu commands.

Shortcut Menus

In most situations, holding down the non-primary mouse button (usually the right one) produces a short list of actions that can be taken at that time.

For example, if you right-click on a table name in the Database window, you'll see a menu that allows you to rename the table, print its contents, and so on:

Toolbars

Access has toolbars galore, many of them appearing automatically when you need them. You can resize and reposition them by dragging, as with other Microsoft applications. Moreover, you can customize them just as you can with the other Office programs. Check out our Access Toolbar Reference (found just before this chapter), which lists all the buttons and their functions.

Views

The term *views* can be a little confusing in Access, because there is so much on-screen commotion. The three "official" views are *Datasheet view*, *Design view*, and *Form view*. They all have to do with the way the data you're looking at is arranged on screen. Unfortunately, there is also a View menu, which has to do with the different lists of database objects (Tables, Queries, Forms, Reports, and so on) that you can see in the Database window. The View menu lets you switch these lists; but since the tabs along the side of the Database window do the same thing, you won't be losing anything if you conveniently forget that the View menu exists.

In any case, Access usually switches views for you as needed anyway (when you click on a particular toolbar button, for instance).

Online Help for Access

The usual, comprehensive Microsoft online help is available in Access, and it's described in Chapter 2, so I'll not kill more trees redescribing it in detail. Like the Help menu in the other Office programs, the Help menu in Access offers a table of contents and allows you to search by keywords, launch Cue Cards, or obtain information about Microsoft's technical support programs. This is also where you go for the About Access command, which provides version, owner, serial number, and system information.

Access

In addition to the Help menu, the *Access Help button* lets you explore the various Access tools by pointing and clicking. As a review, in case you've forgotten how this works in other programs:

1. Click on the Help button (at the right end of the Database toolbar).

2. Click on the on-screen item of interest.

3. Read the resulting on-screen help.

4. Close the Help window by picking Exit from Help's File menu or by double-clicking on the Help window's Control-menu box; or use the key sequence Alt+F,X.

Microsoft's Sample Databases

Access comes with three sample database files worth exploring. These are NWIND.MDB, ORDERS.MDB, and SOLUTION.MDB. They can be found in the SAMPAPPS subdirectory of the ACCESS directory. If you are new at database management, let the Cue Cards walk you through NWIND.MDB, a collection of information used by a fictitious worldwide gourmet food company.

Experienced database users will also want to poke at the ORDERS and SOLUTION database files to see what makes them tick.

When you're ready to create your own database, turn the page and let's get started.

32

Creating a Simple Database and Tables

Tables are key ingredients to an Access database. In this chapter you'll first see how to create a new database, and then you'll use a Wizard to create a new table. Next, you'll learn how to create a table from scratch without the Wizard. Once you've got that under your belt, you'll learn about field properties, and how to view and print detailed design descriptions.

Exercise: Creating a Contacts Database with the Wiz

If you are near your computer, work along with this exercise.

1. With Access running, choose New Database from Access's File menu, or use the Ctrl+N keyboard shortcut.

2. When you see the New Database dialog box shown here, type a new, legal DOS filename (eight characters max, no spaces—you know the song). There's no need to add the file extension *MDB* since Access will do this for you. Let's call the exercise database **FRIENDS**:

3. Notice where Access plans to store your new database (in this example, on drive C: in the SAMPAPPS subdirectory of the ACCESS directory). Change the drive and/or directory in the usual way, if necessary.

4. Click OK.

5. Soon you'll see a new, empty Database window like this one:

6. Click the New button. You'll be offered the choice of using the Table Wizard, or rolling your own. Click on the Wizard's button:

The Access Table Wizard

Before you can enter a single datum into a database (sorry, I just *had* to use that word), you must set up a field in which to store it. In Access, these fields will become *columns* in your database *tables*. The Table Wizard already knows how to create a bunch of tables for various tasks. These sample tables have been subdivided into Business and Personal categories, but if your life's like mine, the distinctions often blur.

When you activate the Table Wizard (as we just did in Step 6 back there), you'll see a dialog box like the one in Figure 32.1.

FIGURE 32.1

The Table Wizard knows how to design many useful tables.

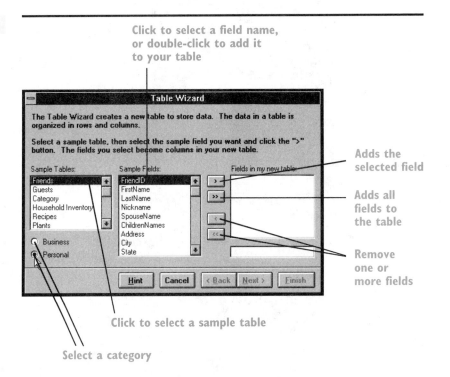

To use the Table Wiz:

1. Select either Business or Personal. (Click on the appropriate button.)
2. Scroll the Sample Tables list see the available table types.

3. Click once on a table of interest to select it, and view the sample field in the Sample Fields list. For example, in Figure 32.1, we've chosen the Personal category, the Friends sample table; we can see some of the fields for that table in the Sample Fields list. Scroll if necessary to see all of the fields in the list.

4. After you've had a chance to browse the available tables and their fields, make your screen look like Figure 32.1. That is to say, when you find a table you like (Friends, in our example), click to select it.

5. To add fields from the sample list to your new table, you can either double-click on a field name or click on the > button between the two windows. To add *all* of the fields from the sample to your table click on the >> button.

   Add all of the fields now. Your screen should look like the following illustration:

6. To remove a field from your table, scroll up or down to it in the right-most list, click to select, then click on the **<** button. For example, here we're removing the Region field from our table:

Clicking on the **<<** button—you guessed it—removes all of the fields from your table.

You can use fields from different sample tables by clicking on different sample table names while "building" your new table.

7. When you are satisfied with the new table list, click on the Wizard's Next> button to continue.

8. You'll be asked to name your table. Here you can use longer names that include spaces. The Wizard proposes **Friends,** which is fine, but suppose you and a spouse want to keep separate friends tables in the *same* friends database? You could both have your own tables. So let's personalize your table's name. Type the new name as shown here (**Ron's Friends**—what did you expect?). Table names can be up to 64 characters long and can include spaces.

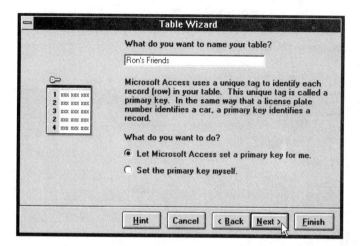

9. Access databases always need a *primary key*, which you'll learn about later. For now, leave things well enough alone, and let the Wiz create the primary key by clicking on the Next> button.

10. At this point, you *could* start entering data right into the table that the Wiz will create, but you can also have the Wiz create an on-screen *form* for data entry. Since this costs no more, what the heck? Click the Enter Data Into The Table... choice as shown here, then click the Finish button.

11. In a moment (or in a flash if you are a Pentium junkie) you'll see a form, and under that form, the Database window updated to include the name of your first table. Drag things around if necessary to see what the Wiz has done. Slick, no?

12. Save the form by clicking on it to select it if it isn't already the active window, then choose Save Form from Access's File menu or use the Ctrl+S shortcut. Form names, like table names, can be up to 64 characters long and can include spaces. (You'll learn all about forms in the next chapter.)

 TIP You can add your own favorite table designs to the Wiz by using the techniques outlined in Chapter 40.

Creating Databases without the Wiz

Designing tables from scratch requires considerable attention to detail. You'll need to decide which information to collect and what names to give each field, and you'll need to specify the types of fields you'll be using, and their properties, among other things. So before you can create your own table you'll need to know about these concepts.

  If this is your first-ever database, or if you like to take things slowly, you might want to jump ahead now to Chapter 34, and return to the remainder of this chapter and Chapter 33 only when you need to know how to mess with table designs, or how to create your own tables and forms without the Wizard's help.

Plan Ahead

Still with me, gluttons? Start by trying to imagine all of the ways you plan to use the data. Sketch out *all* of the screens and reports you hope to create. Pretend you are creating a paper, computerless system. Pencil it out. What would each of the blanks on the forms contain?

If you are creating a mailing list, for instance, will you need to sort by postal code? If so, you'd better have a separate field for that piece of information rather than one big field that holds the recipient's name, address, city, state, and zip as one big block of information.

Database designing is an art, and there are many books and seminars on the subject. Before you spend hundreds or even thousands of hours entering data into a huge database, learn the basics. Start small and experiment. Talk to others about blunders they've made.

Designing Your Table

When you are ready to take a stab at designing a table without the Wizard:

1. Open the database that needs a new table, or create a new database (Ctrl+N).

2. If necessary, click on the Table tab to bring it to the forefront.

3. Click the New button in the Database window:

4. Click the New Table button in the New Table box.

5. You will see an *empty* table window like the one used to create Figure 32.2. It is here that you type field names and put into effect other design decisions.

To create a table you follow these general steps (we'll look at the specifics in a moment):

1. Type a field name.

2. Pick a data type.

3. Specify any necessary properties. (You may need to save the table first.)

4. Repeat steps 1 through 3 for the remaining fields.

5. Save the table if you haven't already done so.

field Names

Field names can be up to 64 characters long, and include spaces and numbers. Simply click in the first empty field name box and type a unique, meaningful field name as illustrated just a minute ago in Figure 32.2.

FIGURE 32.2

Specify field names, types, and properties in the Table window.

Type field names here

Make notes to yourself here

Click to see the list of field types, then pick one for each field

Read about your options here

Notice how properties change with different field types

Specify field properties here

Shorter field names without spaces are often better, particularly if you are planning to write expressions that refer to field names, or are planning to use SQL statements or Access Basic.

Data Types and Properties

Access offers eight *data types* for its fields, and each type offers a variety of options called *properties*. It is important to understand what the different types and properties do; and when to make which choices. Sometimes the answers are not obvious. For example, although postal zip codes are numbers, you'll probably *not* want to put them in a numeric field. Same goes for telephone numbers, part numbers, Social Security numbers, etc. Read on to find out why.

You choose a field's data type by clicking on the little arrow in the current field's Data Type column. This displays a list, from which you choose an appropriate type. You can see this list back in Figure 32.2, where a data type is being chosen for the Notes field.

Once you've chosen a field's *data type*, its *property list* is displayed in the bottom half of the dialog box. Different data types offer different properties.

Properties let you specify things like the maximum length of entries, how the entries will be formatted, whether an entry is required or not, and so on. For example, in the following illustration, the Unit Price field is a *Number* data type with properties that specify a Currency format and a default value of 0. Moreover, the number entered must be a positive number (as you can see from the >0—greater than zero—requirement in the Validation Rule property). If the user forgets to enter a unit price (or enters an invalid value, such as zero or a negative number in this case), Access will display the text "Please enter a valid unit price."

Field Name	Data Type	
ID	Counter	
Order ID	Number	
Unit price	Number	

Field Size	Double
Format	Currency
Decimal Places	Auto
Input Mask	
Caption	
Default Value	0
Validation Rule	>0
Validation Text	Please enter a valid unit price
Required	No
Indexed	No

Properties can also force things like all uppercase letters. And you can use properties to insert characters for you, like the hyphens in Social Security numbers or slashes in phone numbers.

 Explore the field types and properties assigned in Microsoft's NWIND and other sample databases to see which choices the pros have made. You'll learn how to do this in a moment.

Here's an overview of the various data types, their properties, and examples of their application:

Text Fields

Text is the default data type. You use the Text data type when you need to store words, obviously. But it is also a good type to use for fields that will contain part numbers, Social Security numbers, or zip codes. Why? Well, when you enter numbers beginning with zeros into an Access *Number* field, Access strips off the leading zeros, and doesn't like hyphens or other nonnumeric characters. So when you enter a Social Security number like 085-98-9999 into a numeric field, it becomes 85989999—the zero disappears! Likewise, the zip code 01234 becomes 1234. Use of the Text data type prevents this phenomenon.

Text fields can be *indexed* (a process you'll learn about later), so that Access can find pieces of it quite quickly. Unfortunately, a Text field cannot contain more than 255 characters; for longer text entries, you must use the Memo data type (described in a moment).

There are ten possible Text field properties. You do not need to specify them all. They include

- Field Size
- Format
- Input Mask
- Caption
- Default Value

Access

- Validation Rule
- Validation Text
- Required
- Allow Zero Length
- Indexed

Field Size

The Field Size of a Text field can be anything between 1 and 255 characters. Smaller sizes save disk space, but you shouldn't make the setting too small unless disk space is at a premium. Also, be careful when changing the length of a Text field to smaller values after data has been entered into your table. You run the risk of truncating (shortening) long entries.

 NOTE If you expect that in some cases you will be filling a field with just a phrase or a few words, while in other cases you will fill the same field with whole lines or even paragraphs, use a Memo field instead of a Text field for maximum flexibility. A Memo field will "shrink to fit" each entry on a record-by-record basis. If you opt for a Text field, remember that you have to define a Text field at the largest size you estimate any of the field's entries to be (and no greater than 255 characters).

Format

The Format property forces entries to appear according to the characteristics you specify. For instance, to force all text to upper case, regardless of how it is entered, you can place a > (greater-than sign) in the space next to Format. Conversely, a < (less-than sign) forces all text to lower case.

To force a specific character to appear in a particular place (for example, a hyphen after the second digit of a six-digit part number, perhaps), use the @ sign as a placeholder for the digits and type the special character itself in the position where you want it to always appear, for example, @@-@@@@.

Use an & character to tell Access that text is not required. Check out the examples in online help to see how this works.

Input Mask

Input Masks provide things like parentheses around area codes in telephone numbers; time and date formats, etc. The Input Mask Wizard can help you pick and experiment with predefined masks:

The Wizard will launch when you click on the small button at the right edge of the Input Mask property box as shown here:

NOTE You will need to save the table at least once before you can use the Wizard, and will be prompted to do so if necessary.

Caption

The Caption property lets you specify replacement text for the name of the field as it appears *on screen*. Captions thus have the same effect as *labels*. For instance, if you have a field named "PostalCode" you might want the on-screen caption or label to read "ZIP Code." Type the desired label in the space for the Caption property.

Default Value

This property lets you specify a value that will be automatically entered into the field whenever you create a new record. For instance, if you want the word "Member" to appear in the field you would type **Member** in the space for Default Value. Although the default entry will then appear automatically whenever a user is entering new records, the user can edit, replace, or delete it.

Validation Rule

This property lets you specify error checks. For instance, if an entry must be at least 12 characters long, you can create an expression here to check for this. See online help and Chapter 38 for details.

Validation Text

Place your desired error message here, like "Oops! Part numbers are always 12 characters in length." When an entry violates the validation rule, the error message text will appear on-screen.

Required

Use this Yes/No field to tell Access if an entry is required in the field you are designing. You can change the setting here by clicking on the space next to Required and then picking Yes or No from the drop-down list.

Allow Zero Length Characters

As any homicide detective will tell you, there's a big difference between "nothing" and "I don't know." Sometimes, when entering data, users leave a field empty because there is no data for that particular field in that particular record. Other times users leave a field empty because they don't know the correct data to enter. For example, when entering data in an employee database, you might leave a particular field empty for one employee—say a field for Assigned Parking Space—either because she does not have an assigned space or because you don't know her parking space number. In databases, this subtle but important difference, between "None" and "I don't know," is frequently distinguished as follows:

- For "None," the user enters a *zero length*, or *null*, character by typing two double quote marks with no spaces between them ("").
- For "I don't know," the user simply skips the field.

Although there are other ways, like simply entering **None** for "None" and **Unknown** for "I don't know," many of your users may already be familiar with the traditional DBMS approach outlined here. To make Access recognize the "" choice, set the Allow Zero Length Characters option to Yes, the Required option to No, and the Default Value option blank. Then instruct your users to enter the "" null character when the value for the field is none, null, not applicable, or whatever. See online help and the bigger books if this intrigues you.

Indexed

Use this Yes/No field to tell Access if a field is to be indexed for speedy lookups. (See "Indexing" later in this chapter or online help for details.) You can change the setting here by clicking on the space next to Indexed and then picking Yes or No from the drop-down list. You can also choose to permit or prohibit duplicate records.

Memo Fields

A field of the Memo data type can hold up to 64,000 characters. However, it can't be indexed, so use it only for data that will exceed 255 characters per entry.

Other than maximum character counts and the fact that it does not offer an Input Mask property, the Memo field's property options are identical to those of the Text field.

Number Fields

The Number data type should be used:

- When you are collecting data to be used in computations.
- When you want to require someone to enter only numbers (as opposed to letters).
- When you want to format entries with things like decimal places and currency symbols.

Number field properties affect both the precision of numbers *and* their appearance.

Field Size

The table that follows summarizes the available Field Size choices and their specifications. As you can see, some field sizes use more disk space than others, with a resulting increase in precision:

FIELD SIZE	NOTES
Double	(The default) Stores numbers with 15 digits of precision, from −1.79769313486232E308 to +1.79769313486232E308, in 8 bytes.
Single	Stores numbers with 7 digits of precision, from −3.402823E38 to +3.402823E38 in 4 bytes.
Byte	Uses 1 byte to store whole numbers (no fractions) from 0 to 255.
Integer	Uses 2 bytes to store whole numbers (no fractions) from −32,768 to +32,767.
Long Integer	Uses 4 bytes to store whole numbers (again, no fractions) from −2,147,483,648 to +2,147,483,647.

NOTE When you want to change the way numbers are stored, change the Field Size setting. To change how a number appears on the display and in printouts, change the Field Format, which is discussed next.

Format

The Format property lets you choose the on-screen and printed appearance of numbers. This does not change the internal precision of the numbers, thus it does not affect things like storage and computations.

There is a drop-down list that lets you see and pick the desired formats, which include commas, currency symbols, scientific notation, etc. You can also define your own formats. See online help and the bigger books for details.

Decimal Place

This property tells Access how to *display* numbers. For example, with the Format set to Fixed, if you enter **1.1234** in a field and the Decimal Place option is set to 1, Access will only display **1.1**. This does not affect the precision of data or computations the way choosing a Field Size does. Leave the default Auto setting, type a number from 0 to 15, or pick a number from the available drop-down list.

Input Mask

Although Input Mask appears as a property option in Number fields, it only applies in Text and Date/Time fields. Access will remind you of this if you forget.

Other Number Properties

The remaining number properties (Caption, Default Value, Validation Text, Validation Rule, Required, and Indexed) are identical to those previously described under "Text Fields."

Date/Time Fields

The Date/Time data type lets you enter dates and times in a variety of formats as illustrated here:

Format	Short Date	
Input Mask	General Date	6/19/94 5:34:23 PM
Caption	Long Date	Sunday, June 19, 1994
Default Value	Medium Date	19-Jun-94
Validation Rule	Short Date	6/19/94
Validation Text	Long Time	5:34:23 PM
Required	Medium Time	5:34 PM
Indexed	Short Time	17:34

Although Access supports a wide range of date and time formats, the options available are based on the International settings in your Windows Control Panel.

Available Date/Time properties include many you will recognize from earlier field types:

- Format
- Input Mask
- Caption
- Default Value
- Validation Rule
- Validation Text
- Required
- Indexed

Since the features and functions of most of these properties have already been discussed in this chapter, we'll spare you a rehash.

Use the Input Mask Wizard if you want users to enter dates and times in pre-defined formats. Here's how:

1. Click on the button next to the Date Field's Input Mask property.

2. Answer Yes if asked to save the table first.

3. Pick the desired date format in the resulting dialog box:

4. Try entering a date if you like, by clicking in the white portion of the "Try it:" portion of the dialog box.

5. If you want to personalize the input mask, click the Next > button; otherwise, click Finish.

Currency Fields

Use the Currency data type when you want to store information about money. The options listed are based on the International settings found in your Windows Control Panel.

Standard American currency options include General Numbers, numbers with dollar signs, etc., but you'll probably want to leave it at the default setting (which provides dollar signs, commas, and two decimal places). If you wish, you can create your own custom settings.

You can have Access worry about decimal place location in displays and print-outs, or you can specify a decimal position in the Decimal Places section of the Field Properties list.

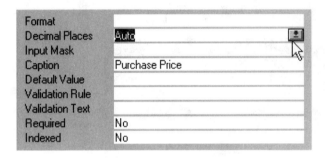

To choose a specific decimal setting, either type the desired number of decimal places to replace the default setting Auto, or click on the drop-down list to see the options available.

The rest of the Currency field properties (Caption, Default Value, etc.) work as you'd expect.

Counter Fields

To have Access automatically number each record as you add them, use the Counter data type. Many users define the Primary Key field as a counter field. (In fact, Access does this automatically if you let it create the Primary Key field for you.)

Counter field properties include Format, Caption, and Indexed. Normally you'll leave them alone, except perhaps for the Caption property.

Yes/No Field

Use the Yes/No data type when you want to give users a field with only two entry choices, like Yes or No, On or Off, or True or False, or perhaps Male or Female, Paid or Unpaid—in short, any either/or value you want. You can specify a default answer (like No).

▶ Okay to Sell Used?	Yes/No	⬇

	Field Properties
Format	Yes/No
Caption	Sell Used?
Default Value	No
Validation Rule	
Validation Text	
Required	No
Indexed	No

In addition, you can specify a caption for the field if you don't want to use the field name as a caption. Validation rules are possible.

You'll see Yes/No fields at work later in this chapter.

OLE Object Field

Finally, you can define a field as an OLE Object field. This makes it possible to round up and use OLE objects like video clips, audio clips, graphs, etc. See Chapter 39 for details.

Adding or Deleting Fields in Tables

Even the best-designed tables will need an additional field occasionally. Or you may wish to delete an unnecessary field. Access makes it easy to do this.

Adding Fields

Begin by opening a table (if it's not already open), then switch to Design View, and add or delete the necessary field, and/or field properties. Here's a specific example of that process:

1. Open the appropriate database with the Open Database command on Access's File menu.

2. Open the table you wish to alter. Your screen will look something like Figure 32.3.

FIGURE 32.3

Click on the Design View button to alter a table.

3. Click on the Design View button at the left edge of the toolbar. Your table will disappear and the field list will appear in its place:

4. To add a field, scroll through the field list until you see an empty Field Name row, then type your new field name (**Send Mailings?** in this example):

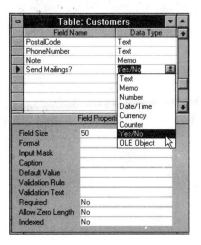

5. Tab to the Data Type area (or click there), then click on the arrow button to reveal the field type list.

6. Pick the appropriate type from the drop-down list.

7. Make any necessary changes to the field's properties.

8. If you want to add additional fields, repeat steps 4 through 7 as necessary.

 9. Click on the Datasheet View button on the toolbar when you have finished.

10. You'll be asked if you want to save the table changes. Agree to do this, if that's what you want.

Renaming Fields and Their Captions

When you change a field *name*, you actually change the way Access internally refers to the field. When you change a field's *caption*, however, you only change the on-screen and report labels for the field.

While the process of *renaming* a field is quite easy, it can have far-reaching effects. For instance, if you've created expressions that reference the field (see Chapter 38), or if you have a database using multiple tables (discussed in Chapter 37), changes to field names may require changes in the expressions and/or related tables. That's why it's a good idea to leave the field *names* alone whenever possible, and change the field *captions*, instead.

Changing Captions

Begin by opening a table (if it's not already open), then switch to Design View, and change the entry in the Caption area of the Field Properties list. Here's a specific example of that process:

1. Open the appropriate database with the Open Database command on Access's File menu.

2. Open the table you wish to alter.

3. Click on the Design View button at the left edge of the toolbar. Your table will disappear and the field list will appear in its place:

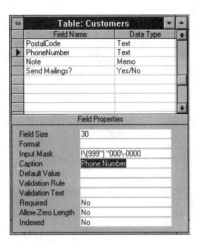

4. Scroll in the field list if necessary until you see the field whose caption you wish to change. Click on that field name. You'll see a black triangle at the left edge of the selected field.

5. Click in the white Caption area of the Field Properties section of the dialog box. (This should select the current caption if there is one.)

6. Type a new caption.

7. Make any other necessary changes to the field's properties.

8. If you want to change captions for additional fields, repeat steps 4 through 7 as necessary.

9. Click on the Datasheet View button (second from the left in the toolbar) when you have finished.

10. You'll be asked if you want to save the table changes. Agree to do this, if that's what you want.

Changing Field Names

Begin by opening a table (if it's not already open), then switch to Design View, and change the field name in the Field Name column of the dialog box.

Here's a specific example of that process:

1. Open the appropriate database with Open Database command on Access's File menu.

2. Open the table you wish to alter.

3. Click on the Design View button at the left edge of the toolbar. Your table will disappear and the field list will appear in its place:

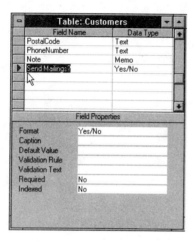

4. Scroll in the field list if necessary until you see the field whose name you wish to change. Click on that field name. You'll see a black triangle at the left edge of the selected field.

5. Select all or a portion of the field name in order to edit or delete it, and make your changes.

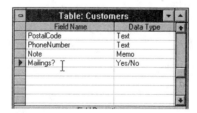

6. Make any other changes you need to the field's properties (a new caption, perhaps?).

7. If you want to change field names for additional fields, repeat steps 4 through 6 as necessary.

8. Click on the Datasheet View button (second from the left on the toolbar) when you are done.

9. You'll be asked if you want to save the table changes. Agree to do this, if that's what you want.

Moving Fields (Rearranging Tables)

To rearrange the order of fields in tables, you can simply switch to the table of interest, view it in Design View, select the field you wish to move, then drag it to the desired location. Suppose, for instance, we want to move the Note field so that it is last on the list:

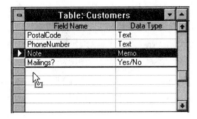

1. Open the appropriate database with the Open Database command on Access's File menu.

2. Open the table you wish to alter (Customers in this example).

3. Click on the Design View button at the left edge of the toolbar. Your table will disappear and the field list will appear in its place.

4. Scroll in the field list if necessary until you see the field you wish to move. Click to the left of that field name. You'll see a white triangle at the left edge of the selected field.

5. Click a second time on the left edge and hold down the mouse button. You'll see a new pointer shape (the drag-and-drop pointer).

6. Drag the field to a new location in the field list and release the mouse button.

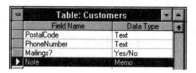

7. Click on the Datasheet View button (second from the left in the toolbar) when you are done.

8. You'll be asked if you want to save the table changes. Agree to do this, if that's what you want.

Deleting Fields in Tables

Deleting fields in tables should not be taken lightly. When you delete a field, you also delete all of the information in that field for each record in your database. For example, if you have 100 employees, and you delete the SocialSecurityNumber field in your employee database, you will delete all 100 Social Security numbers! While Undo can save you if you catch your mistake in time, use caution, and whenever possible, back up your database before deleting things!

Also, realize that if you delete a field that is related to other tables (see Chapter 37), or a field that is referred to in expressions (see Chapter 38), you may cause additional problems that will need to be solved somehow. That said, here are the steps:

1. Open the appropriate database with the Open Database command on Access's File menu.

2. Open the table you wish to alter (Customers in this example).

3. Click on the Design View button at the left edge of the toolbar. Your table will disappear and the field list will appear in its place.

4. Scroll in the field list if necessary until you see the field you wish to delete. Click to the left of that field name. You'll see a white triangle at the left edge of the selected field.

5. Press the Del key.

6. Access will ask if that's what you really want to do (Figure 32.4).

7. Click on the Datasheet View button (second from the left in the Datasheet toolbar) when you are done.

8. You'll be asked to Save the Table Changes. Agree to do this, if that's what you want.

FIGURE 32.4

Access reminds you that deleting a field deletes the data in that field. In fact, it deletes it from every record in your database, so be sure that this is what you want to do!

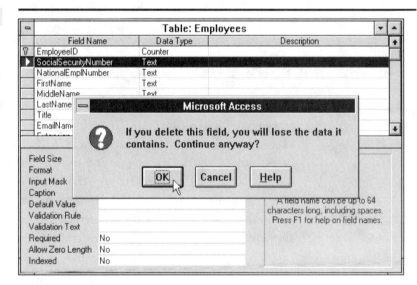

Resizing Fields

There are several field-sizing concepts worth understanding. Here are a couple of basic ones.

First, there is the actual size of the field you define in the Field Properties area of a table in Design view. For instance, Text fields can have a maximum field size of 255 characters, but you may define smaller sizes (like 10 characters) if that's all you ever want users to enter into a particular field. This offers two benefits:

- Access will warn users if they attempt to enter more characters than the defined field size permits.

- Smaller fields take up less disk space, and may actually improve the speed of certain database tasks.

Second, sometimes you'll want to leave the definition of a field's size large (20 characters, for example) but *display* only a smaller portion of the available field size when viewing the table in Datasheet view.

Let's start by reminding you how to change a field's size by altering the field's Size property.

Changing a Field's Size Property

  If you reduce the size of a field using the steps that follow, you may truncate (lose) any portions of your data that exceed the new field length. For instance, if you shorten a field from 20 to 15 characters, and have already entered items that are 20 characters long, the last 5 characters of those long entries will be deleted. However, Access will remind you of this potential problem when you attempt to save the changed table.

1. Open the appropriate database with the Open Database command on Access's File menu.

2. Open the table you wish to alter (Employees in this example).

3. Click on the Design View button at the left edge of the toolbar. Your table will disappear and the field list will appear in its place.

4. Scroll in the field list if necessary until you see the field you wish to resize. Click to the left of that field name.

5. Click in the white area next to the Field Size property in the dialog box.

6. Enter a new field size (that is, type a number):

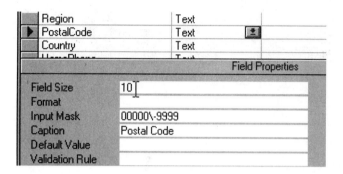

7. Click on the Datasheet View button (second from the left in the tool-bar) when you have finished.

8. You'll be asked if you want to save the table changes (and warned if your changes may cause problems). Agree to save the changes, if that's what you want.

Changing Column Widths in Tables

As mentioned a moment ago, sometimes it's useful to change the *display* of column widths in your tables without actually changing the field properties of the table. For instance, if you wish to keep the Middle Name field, but can get by with seeing only middle initials (to make more room on the screen for other items of more interest), you can drag the column widths much as you do in Excel:

1. Open the appropriate database with the Open Database command on Access's File menu.

2. Open the table you wish to alter (Employees in this example).

3. Scroll in the table window if necessary until you see the field you wish to resize (Middle Name in this example). Point at the right edge of the

heading of the field to be changed, and watch the pointer change to a
two-headed arrow:

4. Drag the two-headed arrow to change the column width to the desired size:

Here, the column has been made so small that only the first character
can be seen. *The data's still there, it is just hidden.*

5. Next time you attempt to close the table, you'll be asked if you want to
save the table changes. Agree to do this, if that's what you want.

Increasing a Column's Width to "Autofit"

To avoid wasting screen space while still being able to see all of the characters
of the longest entry (record), try this simple trick:

1. In Datasheet view, place the pointer at the right edge of the field
to be resized (Movie Title in this example). The pointer shape

changes to a double-headed arrow:

ID	Movie Title	Actr
17	Abbott And Costello Meet Frank	
18	Above The Law	
19	Abyss, The	
20	Accident	
21	Accused, The	
22	Adam's Rib	
23	Adventures In Babysitting	
24	Adventures Of Baron Munchaus	

2. Double-click on the line between the two columns. The Field will expand or contract just enough to display the longest entry (or just enough to show the full field name if it's longer than any of the entries):

ID	Movie Title	Actr
17	Abbott And Costello Meet Frankenstein	
18	Above The Law	
19	Abyss, The	
20	Accident	
21	Accused, The	
22	Adam's Rib	
23	Adventures In Babysitting	
24	Adventures Of Baron Munchausen, The	

3. You may need to do this again later if you add or remove long entries.

Changing the Appearance of Text in Tables

You have some control over the appearance of text in tables, via the Access Format menu. For instance, you can change the font used for all columns by using the Format ➤ Font command. In Figure 32.5 I've selected Engravers-Gothic, Regular, 10 Point.

FIGURE 32.5

The Font command on Access's Format menu lets you choose fonts, font sizes, and styles for the text in your Access tables.

Access will adjust row heights to accommodate new fonts and font sizes, but you may need to change the widths of columns.

TIP Rather than changing the appearance of your tables, consider creating different forms for different uses, as described in the next chapter.

Freezing Columns

Sometimes it is useful to freeze one or more columns so that they stay in view when you scroll through the rest of the table. For instance, here I've selected the first two columns (ID and Movie Title) and chosen Format ➤ Freeze

Columns so that these two columns will stay in view when I scroll to see the columns for other fields:

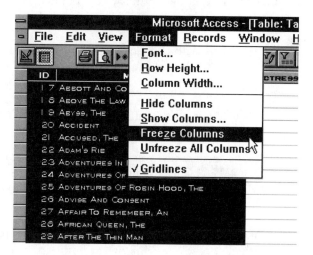

Primary Key Field(s)

Access needs a unique way to identify each record in your tables. To do this either you or Access must create what is called a *primary key*. There can only be one primary key in a table, but a primary key can use multiple fields. (This will make sense in a moment.)

If you let Access automatically create the primary key for you (a good idea, particularly for beginners), Access will add a Counter field that will assign a unique number to each new record that you create. If you wish, you can sometimes rename (or at least recaption) this field and use it for additional purposes. For instance, in the video store example, you could take the numbers generated by Access in the Primary Key field and print them on the tapes themselves as "inventory control numbers."

Defining Your Own Primary Key Field

If you're bold and decide to create your own Primary key (or change the existing primary key to some other field), here are the general steps:

1. Open the appropriate database with the Open Database command on Access's File menu.

2. Open the table you wish to alter (Employees in this example).

3. Click on the Design View button at the left edge of the toolbar. Your table will disappear and the field list will appear in its place.

4. Scroll in the field list if necessary until you see the field you wish to define as the primary key (SocialSecurityNumber, perhaps). Click to the left of that field name. You'll see a white triangle at the left edge of the selected field.

5. Click on the Set Primary Key button on the toolbar, as shown here to the left, or, if you'd rather, choose Set Primary Key from Access's Edit menu instead:

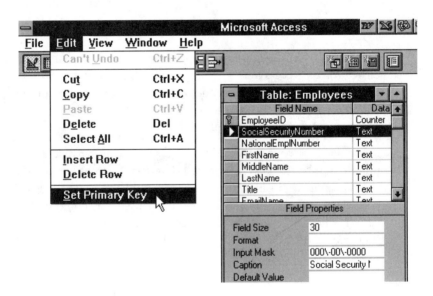

6. A little key icon will appear next to the new field, indicating that it is now the primary key:

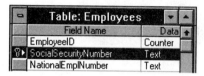

7. When you get around to closing the table or switching to Datasheet view, you'll be asked if you want to save the table changes. Agree to do this, if that's what you want.

Creating Multiple-Field Primary Keys

Sometimes you'll want to create a primary key by using multiple fields (FirstName, LastName, and PhoneNumber, for instance). To do this:

1. Select multiple fields by holding down the Ctrl key while clicking on them:

 2. Click on the Set Primary Key button from the toolbar or choose Set Primary Key from Access's Edit menu as we did in the last section.

3. Notice that the key icon now appears next to all the fields you selected:

	Field Name	Data Type
	CustomerID	Counter
🔑▶	FirstName	Text
🔑	LastName	Text
	Address	Text
	City	Text
	State	Text
	PostalCode	Text
🔑	PhoneNumber	Text

4. Save or cancel the table changes them when asked to do so.

Indexing Fields

Often, you can speed up searches (queries) and reporting by telling Access to *index* certain fields. Indexing is the procedure by which Access orders a field's entries in some way that makes it easier to search. For example, it can find text entries faster if it keeps track of them alphabetically than if it keeps them in the more or less random order in which users enter them. There's a trade-off to indexing, however: Indexes sometimes slow the data-entry process.

Access always indexes the primary key field(s). You can specify other fields for indexing. My suggestion is that you don't do that, however, until you are unhappy with the speed of things like finding and sorting information (discussed in Chapters 35 and 36). When you are ready to experiment with field indexing, follow this example:

1. Open the appropriate database (Tape Inventory in this example) with the Open Database command on Access's File menu.

2. Open the table containing the field(s) you wish to index (MovieTitle in this example).

3. Click on the Design View button at the left edge of the toolbar. Your table will disappear and the field list will appear in its place.

4. Scroll in the field list if necessary until you see the field you wish to move (MovieTitle in this example). Click to the left of that field name. You'll see a black triangle at the left edge of the selected field.

5. Click in the Indexed area of the Field Properties list, as shown in Figure 32.6. You'll see an arrow button indicating that there is a list of choices for this property.

6. Click on the button to reveal the indexing options and pick one.

7. Click on the Datasheet View button (second from the left in the toolbar) when you are done.

8. You'll be asked if you want to save the table changes. Agree to do this, if that's what you want.

FIGURE 32.6

The Indexed field property can be set for No, Yes (Duplicates OK), or Yes (No Duplicates). The choices are explained in the area to the right of the Field Properties list.

Viewing a List of Table Properties

To see (and, optionally, print) a detailed description of your tables and their field properties:

1. Open the database and select the table whose definitions you want to see.

2. Switch to Design view.

3. Choose Print Definition... from the File menu.

4. Specify the desired level of detail in the resulting dialog box:

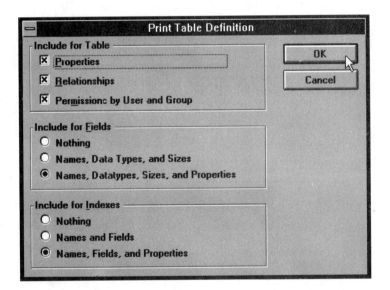

5. Click OK.

6. In a moment or two, you'll see the first page of the report of field properties in a print preview-like window, as shown in Figure 32.7.

7. Either scroll to read the report on screen or click on the Print button to print it.

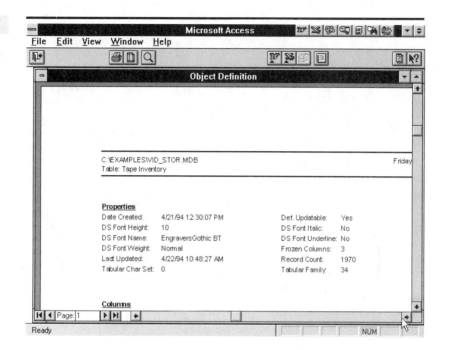

FIGURE 32.7

You can view a detailed list of your field's properties by choosing Print Definition from the File menu while in Design view.

Where to Go from Here

If you feel you are ready to enter a little data and experiment with some simple tables, you should still at least skim Chapter 33 to learn something about forms in Access, and then jump into Chapter 34 where you'll learn how to enter and edit data. You can return to Chapter 33 later after you get some experience playing with the program.

If you are already a database pro and want to get going in a hurry, take a few minutes first to check out Chapter 40, which shows you how to use existing data from other databases like dBASE and Paradox.

Because forms are such a powerful and attractive part of Access, I suggest, regardless of your ability level, that you find the time at some point to read the following chapter. It will make a difference in your work.

33

Forms

n their simplest implementations, forms are designs (layouts) you create to improve the appearance of data from your tables. Although forms can be both displayed and printed, the main use of forms is on screen, to improve the interface for data entry. You can add graphics to them, and specify shading, colors, type styles, and more. Access forms will often remind you of paper forms. For example, you might have a form that you use for the on-screen entry and editing of employee records:

Or, you might create a form that is used on screen to make and check videotape reservations. Notice how this form provides a drop-down list of customers:

As you will see in Chapter 37, forms can use information from multiple tables. So, when designing a video-store system you might combine information from the Reservation table, Tape Inventory table, and Customer table to create a single on-screen form and perhaps a report or two. It's even possible to combine information from different databases on the same form. And as you'll learn in Chapter 38, you can compute and control things in your forms by means of expressions and other forms of automation.

With Access, you can limit access: you can control how much information your users can see on your forms, permitting them to see only information that they need to know. For example, you might want to lock out all but selected employees from forms that display confidential salary information. You'll learn how in Chapter 41.

Let's start off slowly in this chapter. If you've already created a database, you may wish to open it now and work along with us as we explore the basics.

The Form Wizard

Fortunately there are Wizards and other tools to help you create forms. It's a good way to get started.

The Form Wizard asks you questions, then helps you create good-looking forms. You can run the Form Wizard at any time after creating a new table. In this example the Wiz and I will show you how to create a couple of forms from a database I call CONTACTS:

1. Open the database of your choice (CONTACTS, in this example).

2. Click on the Form tab, if necessary to bring it forward. Unless you've already created some forms for this database, you'll see an empty list like this:

3. In any case, click the New button in the Forms window.

4. You will be asked to select a table. Choose your Contacts table from the drop-down list (Ron's Contacts in this example).

5. After selecting a table, click on the (rather large) Wizard button as shown here:

6. You'll be presented with a choice of five Form Wizards (Single-Column, Tabular, etc.). You can click once on a Wizard's name to display a brief description of its function at the bottom of the dialog box. Double-clicking on a name selects the Wizard *and* continues the process of creating a form. (Or you can click once to select a Wizard, then click the OK button to continue.) For this exercise, double-click on the *Tabular* Form Wizard.

7. You'll be given the opportunity to choose which of your tables' fields will appear on the new form. To choose fields, select them in the Available fields list (the one on the left) and click on the > button between the two lists, or ouble-click on the fields. To remove fields from the form list (the "Field order on form" list, on the right), double-click on them or use the < button.

Access

8. When you've moved all of the desired fields to the Form list, click on the Next button to continue. For this example I'll be making a Birthday Reminders form by choosing the field for birthdate and the fields necessary for first and last names, phone numbers, CompuServe ID, mailing address info, and notes.

9. The Wiz will offer some predefined style choices. They are chosen by clicking on the appropriate radio button. Chosen styles are demonstrated in the upper left corner of the dialog box. Explore them all, if you like. Then choose one and click on the Next button.

10. You'll be presented with the Wizard's final dialog box, which gives you a chance to modify the form or see it with your contacts data. This is also where you create a title for your form. Access proposes a tile which you can edit. I've changed my title to "Birthday Reminders."

11. After you've titled yours, be sure the choice "Open the form with data in it" is marked (click on it if it's not), and click on the Finish button.

12. In a moment you'll see your new Birthday Reminders form with your Contacts data displayed in it. Here's how mine looks. (I chose the Embossed style in step 9.)

NOTE Using familiar Windows tools, you can resize the window that contains a form so that it reveals more or less information, and you can scroll to see additional fields that are currently out of view. Navigation keys, like PgUp, PgDn, and Home, work as you'd expect in form windows.

Saving Forms

It's a good idea to save new forms right after you create them *and* after you modify them. Use the Save command, or the Save As… command. If you wish to "clone" a form before modifying it further, give the form a different name when you save it.

TIP Experiment on <u>copies</u> of your favorite forms, keeping the original in its unmodified state. It's often easier to delete an unsuccessful form and start over with the original than to manually undo a lot of changes. Use Save As… to do this.

Modifying Forms

Alas, Form Wizards are not perfect; nor are they mind readers (thankfully). Inevitably, you'll want to do some fine-tuning. For instance, I find the space that separates records in some multirecord reports a little wasteful. That can be fixed easily. But in the Birthday Reminders form there are more subtle problems as well. For instance, birthdays appear in an almost useless order. Using the Sort button in the toolbar to sort by year won't help; we really don't care much about the *year* someone was born. We want a list sorted by *month* then by *day* so we can buy birthday cards, make phone calls, and send e-mail on time. Looks like we'll need to take things into our own hands. Before we can, you'll need to know some more buzzwords.

Design View

You modify forms in *Design view*, which you can reach by clicking on the Design View button. The button contains a little ruler, a drafting triangle, and a pencil. Cute.

Clicking on the button displays the underpinnings—the controls and objects—of your current form. You can mess with these controls and objects to get the desired effect. Figure 33.1 shows what my Birthday Reminders form looked like immediately after the Wizard created it. (Notice the toolbar that also appears when you switch to Design view.)

FIGURE 33.1

Forms contain header detail and footer sections.

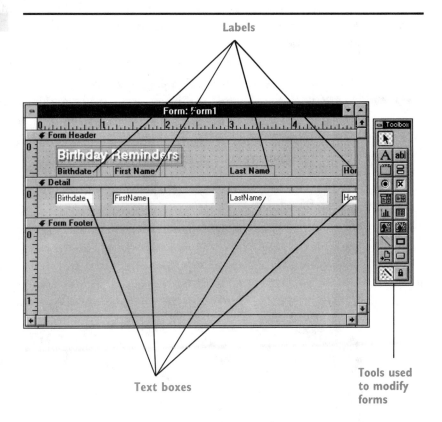

Labels

Text boxes

Tools used to modify forms

Forms are broken down into three sections:

- Header
- Detail
- Footer

It's pretty obvious which section does which jobs. Headers and footers contain things like form titles, page numbers, etc., at either the head or foot of the page. The Detail section is where you specify which fields will be displayed, what they will look like, and so forth. You can also place labels (captions), graphics, lines, and other design elements in any of the three section types.

You move things around by selecting and dragging them. (See "Moving Items in a Form," below.) There are alignment tools to help; and, while the editing techniques are not identical to those used in other Office programs, working in Design view will probably seem familiar, and often intuitive.

 Alas, some things like page numbering and adding dates are not as familiar and intuitive as they could be. You'll learn about them in Chapter 38. Perhaps the designers of Access and Word and Excel should have lunch together more often...

Moving Items in Forms

The brute-force method of moving things in Design view is to select an item (or Shift-select multiple items), then drag the selected item(s) with your mouse:

 To select multiple, adjacent items (controls), drag with your mouse to form a rectangle around the desired controls. You'll see a rectangle as you drag. Items within the rectangle will be selected when you release the mouse button.

Notice how the mouse pointer turns into a little hand when it can move things. Keep an eye on that mouse pointer when working in Design view—it goes through a lot of changes.

There are grids to help you keep things lined up, and a variety of alignment tools that can be used to put multiple items on the same, straight line. For example, to align the bottoms of multiple labels you can shift-click to select them then choose Format → Align → Bottom:

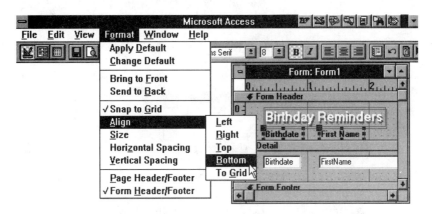

Changing the Appearance of Text in Forms

As you'd expect, you can change the appearance of text by selecting items, then using the available arsenal of menu choices, buttons, and keyboard shortcuts to embellish text. For example, to change the font used to display birthdates, names, and other data you might select all of the boxes containing text you wish to reformat:

Then make new font, size, and alignment choices from the toolbar and menus. If the new font choices make text considerably larger or smaller you may need to resize the objects using the techniques discussed next.

Resizing Items in Forms

To resize something, select it (and items related to it, like lines or shadow boxes) and drag the appropriate handles. For example, here's how to make FirstName box and the white and black special effect lines smaller:

1. Drag to select the FirstName box *and* the white and black lines that are beneath it:

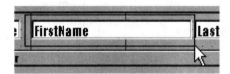

2. With the necessary items (and nothing else) selected, drag on one of the end handles with the cursor shaped like a two-headed arrow:

3. If necessary, resize related items (like LastName) by repeating the steps above. For instance, here's an example of the box for FirstName shorter and LastName longer:

4. To see how things are going, switch back to Form view from time to time, by clicking on the Form View button.

Colors and Patterns in Forms

 Use the Palette button to bring up the tools necessary to modify a selected object's color, shading, etc. Here's what the tools look like:

While the choices are pretty obvious, you can get more information by pointing to a choice in the palette and reading the status area's description of that item.

You can tell which choices have been made by selecting an object on the form, then looking in its related palette. For example, by selecting the Birthday Reminders text box you can see its choices outlined with thicker borders in the palette. Look at the choices the Wizard used to format the title text:

Notice how the type (Fore Color) is white, the background is clear (letting you see the form's background), and the text border is clear (invisible). You can explore other sample forms this way to see how the pros create their effects.

Select some objects on your form and experiment with the palette. Be sure to try the Normal, Raised, and Sunken Appearance buttons in the upper left corner of the palette. These are nifty effects. Incidentally, Undo is available if you hate what you've done, but as mentioned before, you should experiment only on copies of your favorite forms.

Lines and Boxes in Forms

You can either add borders to objects by using the Border buttons in the palette. You can also draw lines and rectangles using the Line and Rectangle tools in the Design toolbar. You'll learn more about this in Chapter 39.

Adding Fields in Forms

To add additional fields to a form you drag them from the field list. Here are the specific steps:

1. Open the form if necessary and switch to Design view.

2. Click on the Field list button in the toolbar. A field list will appear.

3. Scroll in the Form window to the area where you want to insert the new field, as shown in Figure 33.2.

4. Click on the desired field name (scroll to see it if necessary), then drag it to the place on the form where you want the field to reside. Your mouse pointer will take on a rectangular shape as shown in Figure 33.2.

5. When you release the mouse button, the field will take up residence.

6. Use the techniques described in this chapter to resize and reformat the field and its caption if necessary.

FIGURE 33.2

Notice the retangular mouse pointer. It is in the lower right corner of the Detail section of the form.

1. Click here...

...to show the field list

2. Drag the name to the form. (Notice the rectangular pointer?)

Learning More about Form Design

There is much more to know. Most of the upcoming chapters in this book discuss form design topics as they arise. You can also learn a lot from online Help, and by examining some of the sample forms Microsoft has provided. Moreover, larger books like *Microsoft Access 2 Roadmap* and *Understanding Access 2* have hundreds of pages of information on topics relating to form design.

34

Entering and Editing Data

I n this chapter you'll see how easy it is to enter, save, and edit new records using your keyboard. Many of the techniques will be familiar if you've used other Microsoft Office products like Word or Excel. You'll need the skills presented in this chapter to help you add new records and edit information in your databases.

TIP Before spending hours retyping information you've already entered into your computer (dBASE files, or Word or Excel tables, for instance), at least skim Chapter 40. You may be able to avoid a lot of retyping by <u>importing</u> or <u>attaching</u> data from existing files.

There aren't many surprises here. You can enter and edit text directly in tables in Datasheet view, or you can enter and edit in forms you have created (from scratch or with the Wizard).

If you've been working along with the Contacts database exercise, you might want to continue to do so in this chapter.

Adding Records

To add records to a table:

1. Open the database and the table of interest (in this example, the "Ron's Contacts" *table* in the more general Contacts *database*).

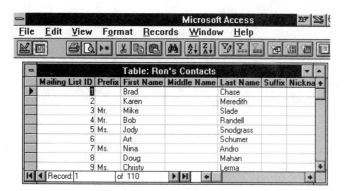

2. Choose *Data Entry* from the Records menu.

3. You'll see a blank row with a triangle at its left edge, indicating that the empty row is the *current record*. You may also see "(Counter)," indicating that Access will be automatically assigning a record number for possible use as the primary key.

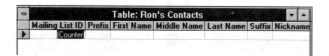

4. Tab to the first field into which you want to enter something. Watch the flashing insertion point as you do this. It will tell which field you have activated. When you get to the desired field, start typing. Press Tab or ↵ to move to the next field of interest (or to skip a field without placing anything in it). (Incidentally, pressing Shift+Tab will move you *back* one field each time you do it.)

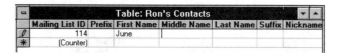

5. When you reach the last field in the last record and press Tab or ↵, Access will take you to the first field in a *new*, blank record. Or, also from the last record, you can also start a new record by clicking anywhere in the row beneath the current record. Or, you can click on the New record button in the toolbar. All three techniques are illustrated in Figure 34.1.

The Current Selection Symbols

By now you may have noticed two of the three little icons Access places at the left of tables to indicate the status of a record:

ICON	MEANING
▶	This is the current record
𝆑	You are editing this record
⊘	This is a *locked* record, which means it cannot be edited

FIGURE 34.1

Tab or click to start a new record.

Clicking on the New button starts a
new record and takes you to its first field

Clicking in the
New Record row
starts a new record

Tabbing in the
last field takes
you to the first
field in a
new record

Once you know their purposes, the visual meanings of these icons are fairly obvious. If you see a "record locked" symbol and you think you should be able to edit the record, check Chapter 41. It deals with security issues.

When entering data into new records, it is often best to use the table's Datasheet view or a form that includes <u>all</u> fields, so that you don't forget to enter something. By the same token, if you find yourself entering or editing just the same few fields in a table with many fields, you may want to create a small form containing only the necessary fields, to reduce on-screen clutter. Remember, forms needn't contain all of a table's fields.

Entering When Fields Have Masks

Some fields may have *input masks*. Masks, which are common for entries like phone numbers, part numbers, etc., help force consistent entries. You'll normally see the mask when you activate a field. For instance, most date fields created with the Access Wizards contain masks. The Birthdate field is an example:

When you encounter fields like these, there is no need to add slashes, dashes, or parentheses. When you type a date in the Birthdate field, for instance, you can just type 110747 and Access will add the slashes to produce 11/07/47.

Entry Error Messages

You'll often be expected to enter data in a specific way (with leading zeros, for instance), and Access may scold you if you try to break an entry rule. For instance, here I've committed the crime of entering a day of the month (7) without the necessary leading zero:

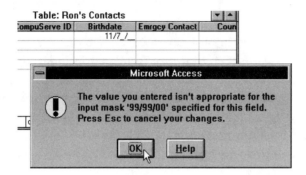

Sometimes the rules are imposed by the type of field you've specified (you can't type letters in number fields, for example). Other times, rules are added by the database designer. You'll see this in action in Chapter 38. Just follow the rules and you won't get hurt. (They're usually meant to help you.)

Seriously, if the Wiz or some database designer sets up masks and rules you dislike, you might be able to change them using the information in Chapter 38 or by consulting online help and rummaging the bigger books. Rule and mask changes are risky, however; changing rules and masks can create seemingly mysterious problems in things like expressions, searches, and sorting.

Duplicating Previous Entries without Retyping

Sometimes, when entering or editing multiple records. it's nice to be able to duplicate previous entries without retyping them. For instance, here I am getting ready to type my dog Murph's last name into my Contacts table, since I don't want to forget her birthday:

June		Mansfield
Adam		Mansfield
Scott		Mansfield
Murphy		

I could *retype* Mansfield, of course, but the key combination Ctrl+' (Control + apostrophe) will duplicate the data from the field above (Mansfield, in this case).

Switching Out of Data Entry Mode

When you're working in Data Entry mode, you see only the new records you've just added. Eventually, you'll want to leave Data Entry mode and see your entire table again (to edit old records, for instance.) To do this, choose Show All Records from the Records menu.

When Do Entries Get Saved?

Entries and edits get saved automatically when you move to the next record. The record you were last working on will also get saved if you use the Show All Records command. There is no need to do anything special.

If it makes you feel better, however, the keyboard shortcut Shift+Enter saves the current record without switching to another record.

 NOTE As you will see when you learn more about relational databases and "relational integrity", sometimes it is desirable to force automatic updates (or deletions) in other tables when you make changes in the current table. For now it is enough to know that you can do this. You'll learn how later, in Chapter 37.

Undo

There are a number of Undo choices that may or may not be available on the Access File menu when you are entering and editing records. These choices and their keyboard shortcuts include:

Undo Typing	Ctrl+Z
Undo Current Field	Esc
Undo Current Record	Esc
Undo Saved Record	Ctrl+Z

Unfortunately, Access Undo's are not as intuitive as, say, those in Word's drop-down Undo list. However, you will usually be given a chance to cancel an Undo, or undo the Undo if that's what you "wan' do."

Obviously, when choices are dimmed or invisible they are unavailable.

Correcting Entries

You can correct entries with the usual Windows text editing techniques. Select the text to be edited or replaced and "have at it." For instance, to replace all or part an entry, select some or all of the old entry, then type the replacement text.

To add information to an existing text entry, click at the desired insertion point and begin typing. The mouse pointer becomes a text editing I-bar at the insertion point, unless you've landed it in a field that is protected or can't be edited.

The Backspace key munches characters to the left of the insertion point, and Copy (Ctrl+C), Cut (Ctrl+X), and Paste (Ctrl+V) commands work both within Access and between applications just as you'd expect based on your Windows experience. For instance, you can Copy text from a table in Word or Excel then Paste it into an Access table.

As mentioned earlier, there's a great shortcut for entering duplicate data (use this if you're entering the same city's name in a number of records, for example): Press Ctrl+' (Ctrl and an apostrophe) to copy the data from the same field in the previous record.

Global Replacements

There are several ways to make replacements in multiple records. Some of the more powerful techniques require the creation of expressions, so they will need to wait until Chapter 38. But suppose you wanted to do something simple, like replace all those politically incorrect "Miss" prefixes with "Ms." in your Contacts database. You could use the Replace command to do that.

1. Click anywhere in a field to select it (for instance, the Prefix field in your Contacts database).

2. Choose Replace from the Access Edit menu.

3. When you see the resulting dialog box, enter the text string you wish to find, and the replacement string. (Miss and Ms., perhaps). Be sure to include spaces and punctuation as needed.

4. Tell Access if you wish to search and replace in just the selected field (the default) or table-wide.

5. If you want to force Microsoft Access to change only those entries that have exactly matching capitalization, choose Match Case.

6. To force changes only when the text string exactly matches the field's *entire* contents, choose the Match Whole Field option. (This will prevent things like changing Mississippi to Ms.issippi, which would also be considered politically incorrect.)

7. When you are ready, click Find Next.

8. Access will highlight the first proposed change. Click Replace to make the change, then Find Next to continue.

WARNING When you select Replace All, Access will make all changes, but will display a warning: "You won't be able to undo this replace operation." Select OK or Cancel at that point to seal your fate.

Moving from Record to Record in a Table

The bottom of a table window provides some handy arrow buttons that can make it easy to move from record to record—that is to say, to make a different record the *active* record. Figure 34.2 illustrates them.

In addition, there are keyboard shortcuts for locomotion:

TO MAKE...	...DO THIS
The next record down the active record	Press ↓
The next record up the active record	Press ↑
The next window full of records appear	Press PgUp or PgDn

FIGURE 34.2

Click on these arrows to move from one record to another.

Current record number

Total record count for table

Move to first record

Move to previous record

Move to next record

Move to last record

TO MAKE...	...DO THIS
The first field in the first record active	Press Ctrl+Home
The last field in the last record active	Press Ctrl+End
A specific record active	Click in the ID field, press F5, type the record number, and press ↵. Or, it may be faster, especially if you want to remain in the same field, to select the current record number, type the record number you want to see, and press ↵.

Entry and Navigational Shortcuts

There are a number of *entry* shortcuts and *navigational* shortcuts that will bounce you around more quickly from field to field within a record. Here is a table listing those shortcuts:

TO DO THIS...	...DO THIS
Move to the next field	Press Tab, →, or ↵ (Enter)
Move back one field	Press Shift+Tab or ←
Move to the current field in the next record	Press ↓
Move to the current field in the previous record	Press ↑
Move to the current field in the last record	Press Ctrl+↓
Move to the current field in the first record	Press Ctrl+↑
Scroll right	Press Ctrl+PgDn
Scroll Left	Press Ctrl+PgUp

What Now?

Since the next exercise will involve searching for and sorting data, you might want to practice what you've learned in this chapter by typing a few of your favorite names and addresses before continuing.

35

Finding, Sorting, and Displaying Data

m icrosoft Access lets you search for, sort, and display data in a variety of ways. To minimize needless repetition, you can even save commonly executed searches for later reuse. In this chapter you'll learn about these features. But first, a few more buzzwords.

Queries and Dynasets

It seems like *everybody* in the DBMS business feels compelled to invent fancy new words for age-old concepts. Not wanting to be outdone, Microsoft has coined a few new phrases themselves.

Queries are simply requests you make when searching your data (for instance: show me all employees who make under $50,000).

Access responds to queries by corralling and displaying all of the records that match your query (a collection of everybody making less than $50K, for example). These results are called *dynasets* (see Chapter 31). When you *query* Access, you'll receive a *dynaset*. If you are on a network and someone changes a record that affects your query, you will see the change as soon as the network gods decide to pass it along.

So... you query, "What kinds of queries are there, and how do I query?" Well, campers, there are six kinds:

TYPE	USE
Select	Lets you specify desired search criteria (like all the records with a last name of Schnicklegruber).

TYPE	USE
Crosstab	Lets you see data with row and column headings—like a breakdown of voters by age and sex, with age in rows and sex in columns.
Action	Lets you automate tasks you do frequently. These queries change or delete records meeting your criteria. (See Chapter 38.)
Union	Takes a 15-minute coffee break every four hours. (Actually, Union queries are those that can span multiple tables.)
Pass-through	Sends commands to SQL databases (see Chapter 40).
Data-Definition	Is another type that's SQL-related (see Chapter 40).

If you've entered some records into your Contacts database, run Access now and open the Contacts database if you'd like to follow along. Otherwise, just keep an eye on the profuse illustrations the back cover of this book promised.

Creating and Using Select Queries

Suppose you wanted to locate and display a list of all immediate family members and their birthdays from your Contacts database. You'd start by building the query in something called the Query by Example (QBE) grid. Here are the general steps:

1. Open the appropriate database (Contacts, in this example) if it's not already open.

2. Switch to the appropriate table (Ron's Contacts, for instance).

Access

3. Click on the New Query button as shown here:

Database:
CONTACTS

4. Choose New Query from the resulting little dialog box:

5. This will bring up a large dialog box (containing the QBE grid) where you will both design the query and enter your search criteria as illustrated in Figure 35.1.

6. Add fields you wish to include by scrolling through the field list and double-clicking on each field you wish to display in your results. (Alternately, you can click once on a field name and drag it to the desired position in the grid.)

FIGURE 35.1

Design your query and enter search criteria in this dialog box.

Double-click on the asterisk to add all fields (but see text for restrictions first)

Double-click to add a field

Drag to change size of window panes

The Query by Example (QBE) grid

Specify sort order (if any)

Type search criteria in this row. Access will add the quote marks.

When building a query, instead of double-clicking on field names, you can click then drag them into position. To select multiple fields, Ctrl-click to select before dragging. If you wish to add all fields to a query, either Ctrl-click on all of the field names (the suggested method) or double-click on the asterisk (*) at the top of the field list. Note that if you use the asterisk shortcut you may not be able to sort or specify search criteria for fields added via the asterisk trick. On the other hand, if you add fields this way, then change the design of the underlying table(s), those changes will be reflected in the query. That is to say if you Ctrl-click to add all of a table's fields, then add fields to the table later, those new fields won't automatically show up in the query.

Access

7. Be sure to include the field or fields you wish to use to specify search criteria, and any additional fields you'll want to look at when Access finds the records of interest. For example, in Figure 35.1, I've included the LastName field since that's what I will use to tell Access to display only records with the same last name as mine. And, in Figure 35.1, we are including FirstName and Birthdate fields since we'll want to see the information they contain.

8. Specify sorting options, if you wish. For example, to see your list sorted by first names (in our exercise this is important because all the last names will be identical), add a sort request to the FirstName field. Do this by clicking in the Sort: row in the FirstName column. Pick Ascending (or another option) from the drop-down list that is revealed when you click on the arrow box:

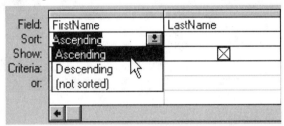

9. If you wish to limit the display of records to only those meeting search criteria (last names of *Mansfield*, for instance), type the search criteria in the appropriate Criteria box. Access will add quotation marks to your entry. For this exercise, I've put **Mansfield** in the LastName box:

10. Once you've completed your query, click on the Run button (which looks like an exclamation point) to run the query and display the resulting dynaset:

Well, there's good news and bad. The query produced a list of Mansfields, but I haven't yet entered birthdates for everyone. This missing information is easily added, since you can type directly into the dynaset. Except in special cases (which are discussed in Chapter 37), changes that you make in a dynaset update the table(s) from which the dynaset was built. So I can type in the dates now or later.

There are a few other things I'd like to fix first, however. None of my extended family members are listed, for example, since their last names are different than mine. And there are some duplicate records (two *Scotts* and two *Nancys*). Finally, in an informal list like this, there really is no need to display the last names, since first names are good enough identifiers, but we need the LastName field to do the searching. Let's tackle one problem at a time.

Returning to the Query Design

 To modify the query we need to return to Design view by clicking on the left-most toolbar button containing the ruler, pencil, and triangle.

We'll modify this query to explore additional tools and techniques.

Multiple Search Criteria

To search for multiple matches (like two or three different last names) you can simply add the desired search criteria in the query as shown here:

Field:	FirstName	LastName	Birthdate
Sort:	Ascending		
Show:	☒		☒
Criteria:		"Mansfield"	
or:		"Chernus"	
		"Frederick"	

WARNING Carefully check your specifications and the results they produce! In our example, Access will display records with last names of <u>Mansfield</u>, <u>Chernus</u>, and <u>Frederick</u>, but <u>not</u> variations like <u>Chernus-Mansfield</u>. See "Finding Incomplete Matches" (next).

Finding Incomplete Matches

Suppose you have a database containing film names, and you want to find a film with the word *town* in its title, but you don't remember the *exact* title. With some DBMS products you can just enter the text string **town** and you'd see all the near matches. Not so with Access.

Instead, entering **town** is liable to turn up absolutely nothing! So, you need to use the little-known asterisk trick that I share only with my closest friends and readers.

To find text even if you don't know the exact field contents, precede and follow the text with a single asterisk. Thus, you'd type ***town*** in our example.

When you type asterisks into a search criterion this way, Access converts the criterion to a "LIKE" statement which it then uses to find your stuff. Figure 35.2 shows an example of this. It was created by typing ***town*** in the MovieTitle Criteria box.

FIGURE 35.2

Surround partial text
strings with asterisks,
and Access will find
the strings.

This criterion...

...finds these records

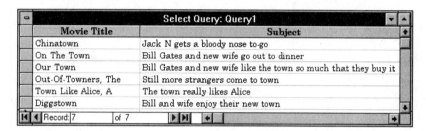

You can look in more than one place this way as well. For example, to find occurrences of *town* in either the MovieTitle or Subject fields, you could type
town twice—once in the MovieTitle criteria and once in the Or box under
Subject. (You'll learn more about advanced searching techniques like this
later in the chapter.)

Using Wildcards in Queries

Besides using the asterisk wildcard character just described, you can include
other wildcard characters in your search criteria. For example, the criterion
R?n will find *Ron*, *run*, and *ran*.

If you've ever used wildcard characters with other programs (or even DOS) before, they will seem familiar. The asterisk (*), question mark (?), number sign
(#), exclamation point (!), hyphen (-), and brackets ([ ]) are all Access wildcard characters.

You can use wildcard characters in queries, commands, and expressions; you
can also use them to further refine searches.

WILDCARD	SAMPLE	NOTES
*	***all** finds *ball*, *call*, and *fall*	The asterisk matches any number of characters. You can use it as the first or last character in the character string, or you can use one on each end of the text string.
?	**b?ll** finds *ball*, *bell*, and *bill*	The question mark matches any single character. You can use more than one question mark, for instance, **b??k** will find *beak* and *book*.
#	**2#4** finds *204, 214, 224*	The pound sign matches any single digit.
[ ]	**b[ae]ll** finds *ball* and *bell* but not *bill*	This wildcard combination matches any single character (and only the characters) placed within the brackets.
!	**b[!ae]ll** finds *bill* and *bull* but not *bell*	The exclamation mark means *not*; in the combination shown it matches any character *not* in the brackets.
-	**b[a-c]d** finds *bad*, *bbd*, and *bcd*	The hyphen indicates a range of characters; in the combination shown it matches any one of a range of characters from A through C.

To search for the wildcard characters themselves, that is, the * (asterisk), ? (question mark), # (number sign), and [(opening bracket) characters, enclose them in brackets. For example, to search for an asterisk, you would type **[*]**.

Requesting Ranges of Records

You can Request ranges of records, like "all the customers over 25 years old but under 40," or "all past-due payments that are more than 60 days late," or "all the names of customers after 'Smith' in the alphabet." You do this by using *expressions* in your search criteria. And, while I vow to spare you the gory details of expressions until Chapter 38, a few simple examples are in order here.

Suppose for instance your video store took a straw poll to see who liked VHS, 8mm, and laserdisc formats. People as young as 22 and as old as 49 responded. After entering the data, you wish to see how people over the age of 25 and less than 40 years old voted. You could create a query like the one in Figure 35.3 to find the answers.

FIGURE 35.3

You can include ranges in Queries.

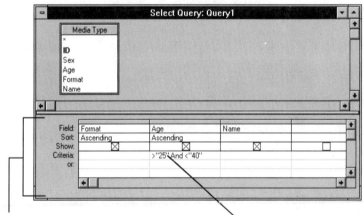

These criteria produce the results below

Entering a range limits the records shown (in this case to those older than 25 and under 40)

Format	Age	Name
8MM	32	Meredith
8MM	33	Manson
8MM	35	Andro
8MM	36	Lieber
Laser Disc	30	King
Laser Disc	35	Nixon
Laser Disc	36	Snodgrass
Laser Disc	39	Miller
VHS	28	Knight

All that was necessary was to type **>25 and <40** as the age criterion. Access added the quotation marks and capitalized the word *and*.

The > symbol before 25 tells Access to find souls *greater than* 25 years of age and <40 stands for *less than* 40. These and other operators used in expressions will remind you of those found in Excel and in Word's Print Merge features. Check online help and Chapter 38 for details.

Hiding Columns

To hide a column (so that you can use it to generate a query, but not display it in your dynaset), click to remove the X from the appropriate "Show" box.

When you're done changing the query, click the Run (!) button again to see the results.

First Name	Birthdate
Adam	
Fran	
Fran	
Julie	
June	
Ken	
Murphy	2/3/90
Nancy	
Nancy	
Scott	
Scott	

There you have it, a list of family members sorted by first name and displayed without last name.

Reformatting Dynasets

You can reformat dynasets in much the same way you change the appearance of Access Tables or Excel worksheets. Here are some commonly used techniques.

Column Widths and Heights

Double-click on the lines separating columns to "autofit" column widths, or drag to set widths manually. (The mouse pointer's shape will change when you have pointed to the correct spot.)

First Name	Birthdate
▶ Adam	
Fran	
Fran	
Julie	
June	
Ken	
Murphy	2/3/90
Nancy	
Nancy	
Scott	
Scott	
✳	

The same basic technique works for row heights. Point to the lines separating rows at the left edge of the dynaset and either double-click or drag when the pointer shape changes.

Moving Columns

To move a column:

1. Click once on the column (Field) name to select the entire column.

2. Click again and hold down the mouse button. The pointer shape will change to include a box:

First Name	Birthdate
▶ Adam	
Fran	
Fran	
Julie	
June	
Ken	
Murphy	2/3/90
Nancy	

3. Drag the column to its new location and release the mouse button.

4. The Column will move:

	Birthdate	First Name
▶		Adam
		Fran
		Fran
		Julie
		June
		Ken
	2/3/90	Murphy
		Nancy
		Nancy
		Scott
		Scott
*		

Changing Fonts

While dynasets are not usually meant to look "pretty" (you'll use reports and forms to keep up appearances), you can change the font and size for the entire dynaset by using the familiar Font... choice on the Access Format menu.

"Freezing" Columns

When a query reaches epic proportions and exceeds your screen width, it is often useful to "nail down" the first column or two, so that the data there can be used as labels while you scroll horizontally. Take the video tape example in Figure 35.4, for instance.

To accomplish this, select one or more columns (fields), and choose Freeze Columns from the Access Format menu. The Unfreeze Columns command returns things to normal.

FIGURE 35.4

The Movie Title and ID columns will remain in view while you scroll the rest of the window left or right.

Select one or more columns first

These columns won't move after freezing

These arrows will scroll only non-frozen columns

Access

Multilevel Sorts

Access lets you do limited—but useful—multilevel sorts in queries. For instance, if you wanted to sort a query so that it broke out people by sex then, within that, by age, you might set up a query like this:

Since Access *always* uses the *leftmost* sort request (sex in this example) as the first sort level, be sure to arrange the query with this in mind. Remember, you can rearrange the location of the fields in the dynaset if you wish. Here are the results of a two-level sort with sex as the top level and age as the next level:

Sex	Age	Name
M	32	Meredith
M	33	Manson
M	35	Andro
M	36	Lieber
M	40	Slade
M	40	Brody
M	40	Chase
M	41	Mahan
M	42	Jackson
M	42	Schumer
M	44	Bishop
M	49	Kennedy
F	22	Randell
F	23	Lerma
F	24	Lincoln
F	28	Knight
F	30	King
F	35	Nixon
F	36	Snodgrass
F	39	Miller

You could easily add another layer of sorting to this query to make the names alphabetical within age group, and so on. Remember, this does not affect the order of the records in your table, it just specifies the way they will be displayed for this query.

Showing All Records after a Query

Eventually you'll want to see all of your records again as opposed to just those in your query. Don't panic. Unless you've deleted them while querying, they

are there, albeit sometimes a little hard to find. You just need to switch from the Query window to the Table window. If you are lucky, you can just choose the table from the Access Window menu.

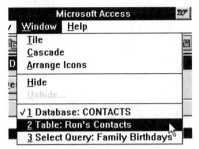

In some cases you may need to choose the database from the Window menu (since the table may not be listed there if you've closed it). In this case, Choose the database name from the window menu, then click on the Table tab in the Database dialog box, and then click on the table of interest.

Hey. We asked for graphical computers, we got graphical computers. Okay?

If you have a big enough screen, you can display the Database window, and the table and the Query window all at once with the Window Tile command, as in Figure 35.5.

Access

FIGURE 35.5

Use the Tile command on the Window menu to display all the windows you're working with.

FIGURE 35.5

Use the Tile command on the Window menu to display all the windows you're working with.

Saving Queries for Later Reuse

One of the nice things about queries is that, after you spend time creating them, you can easily save them for use again and again. There is only one very important gotcha, which deserves its own box:

  Never (ever, _ever_) give a query the same name as a table when you are saving the query. If you do, it is likely that the query will replace the table; and records not meeting the query criteria will be squirted like watermelon seeds right out of the universe. Gone. Lost. Think of those watermelon seeds whenever you get ready to save a query, then pick a clever, distinct name.

That seed planted, here are the steps for saving and reusing queries:

1. Switch to the Query window if you are not already there.

2. Choose Save from the File menu or use the Ctrl+S shortcut. (Sometimes you may see the command Save Query ... listed instead. They are the same thing.)

3. Type a unique query name:

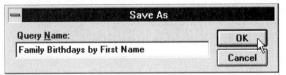

4. Click OK.

5. The query will be saved.

Crosstab Queries

Sometimes it is nice to see the results of queries summarized and or arranged into meaningful groups. Crosstab queries can do this. Remember our video tape customers, who voted on which formats they liked? Crosstab queries can help you see data like that in a whole new light. For example, here are the voting results in a Crosstab table that illustrates format preference broken down by age and sex:

Format	Sex	Row Summary	22	23	24	28	30	32	33	35	36	39	40	41	42	44	49
Laser Disc	F	4					1			1	1	1					
VHS	F	4	1	1	1	1											
8MM	M	5						1	1	1	1		1				
Laser Disc	M	4											2		1	1	
VHS	M	3											1		1		1

Each age is listed along the top of the dynaset. Formats and sexes are listed along the left. (Notice that there is no row for female 8mm voters, since no women voted for that media format.) The Row summary adds up all of the entries for each row. For instance, four women chose VHS.

This intriguing dynaset was created with the Crosstab Query Wizard. Here is the QBE (Query by Example) the Wizard created:

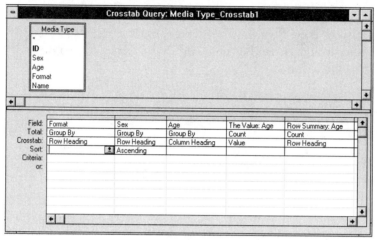

Let's walk through the steps fir using the Wizard:

1. Start a New Query using the database of interest (click on the Query tab, then the New button:

2. Choose the Wiz:

3. Pick Crosstab (double-click on the choice).

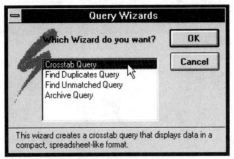

4. Start reading the Wizard dialogs, as shown in Figure 35.6, making choices and watching the example develop. Sometimes the Hint button provides very helpful advice.

5. Pick the field or fields to be shown at the left edge of the dynaset (Do this by double-clicking or by clicking once and then using the > button). Watch the sample area of the dialog box change as you work.

Try to imagine how the data will look given the choices you are proposing. Remember you can use the Back (<) button to reverse earlier decisions.

6. Specify the field type you want to use to create columns (Age, in this example). Double-click to select it. You will get a list of function choices (Count, Average, etc.) Pick one. If you want Summary rows (like the ones in our example) be sure there's an X in the Calculate Summary for Each Row box, as shown in Figure 35.7, then click Next.

7. Name the query if you like, then click Finish.

8. This will create the basic dynaset, which you will then probably want to embellish. (In the example, I changed the column widths and added a sort request so that the Female and Male choices were clustered together.) Click on the Design View toolbar button to get to the QBE where you can do the fiddling.

Access

FIGURE 35.6

Click around a bit with the Crosstab Query Wizards and see what develops, using the Hint button to explore different possibilities.

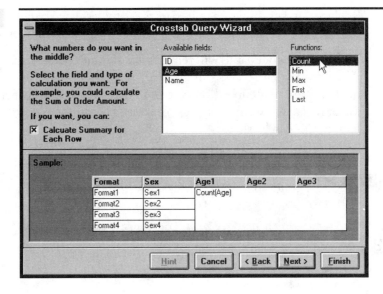

FIGURE 35.7

Select the type of function you want for each field, and decide if you want to have a summary calculated at the end of each column.

find and Replace

The Find… command (located on the Edit menu) lets you locate text and numbers in tables. It is particularly helpful when you have lots of data. For example, here, I've asked the Find… command to locate the text string *Jody* in the First Name field. It has located and highlighted (selected) the first occurrence:

Replace… takes things once step further and lets you change found items. For instance you could change "Mrs." to "Ms." with the Replace… command.

Both of these commands will remind you of their counterparts in Microsoft Word. By default, Access searches only the current field (the selected field or field containing the insertion point), so click in a field to select it before finding or replacing. While it is possible to search entire tables with the All Fields option, this can be slow.

 NOTE You may see the term <u>filter</u> in the Microsoft documentation and online help. Filters are simple queries that apply to a single open table. Filters can be applied to forms, however, which may be <u>based</u> on more than one table.

36

Printing Reports, Forms, Letters, and Labels

Access
CHAPTER 36

ccess provides a number of ways to put data on paper. Options include:

- The Print command in Table view
- The Print command in Form view
- The Print command in Query view
- The Print command in the Database window
- The AutoReport feature
- The Report Wizards (for common report and label types)
- The exporting data capabilities (for use with Word's Print Merge features)

Simple Table, Form, and Database Printing

The Print command available in Table, Form, and Query views, and in the Database window, is great for quick-and-dirty tree killing. Basically, you put what you want to print on your screen and print it. Access even adds page numbers, dates, and a title. The general steps are almost self-evident:

1. Visit Print Setup and pick the desired page size, orientation, and other available printing options. (You can't do this when you use the Print command in the Database window.)

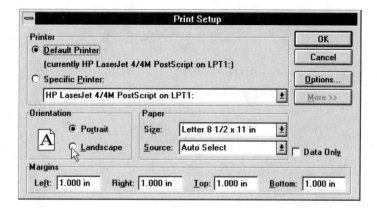

2. Open the Form, Table, or Query window (Figure 36.1) from which you plan to print.

3. Make any necessary changes to the on-screen layout (column widths, locations, font choices, etc.).

4. Use the Print Preview command to save a tree. (See Figure 36.2.)

FIGURE 36.1

The table I'll be printing

FIGURE 36.2

Print Preview lets you
see your work before
printing and potentially
saves some paper.

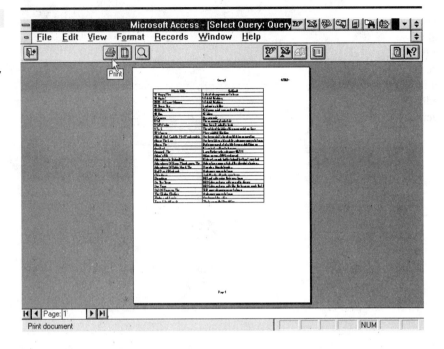

5. When you're happy with your decisions, click the Print button, or choose Print from the File menu, or press Ctrl+P.

6. Make any last-minute choices (number of copies, etc.).

7. Click OK and let 'er rip. The table I printed using these steps appears in Figure 36.3.

AutoReport

AutoReport is another quick way to create basic reports containing headings, page numbers, etc. Execute it with the AutoReport button.

Your satisfaction with this feature will depend upon the type of data you work with and how agreeable you are to having machines run your life and arrange your printouts.

FIGURE 36.3

Actual unretouched result (well, okay, reduced to fit in the book) from the preceding step-by-step instructions

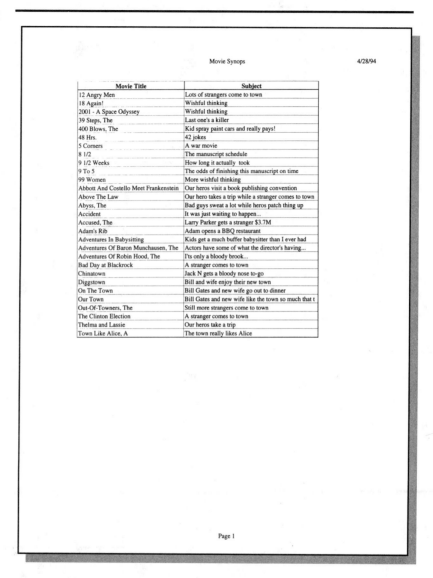

Movie Synops   4/28/94

Movie Title	Subject
12 Angry Men	Lots of strangers come to town
18 Again!	Wishful thinking
2001 - A Space Odyssey	Wishful thinking
39 Steps, The	Last one's a killer
400 Blows, The	Kid spray paint cars and really pays!
48 Hrs.	42 jokes
5 Corners	A war movie
8 1/2	The manuscript schedule
9 1/2 Weeks	How long it actually took
9 To 5	The odds of finishing this manuscript on time
99 Women	More wishful thinking
Abbott And Costello Meet Frankenstein	Our heros visit a book publishing convention
Above The Law	Our hero takes a trip while a stranger comes to town
Abyss, The	Bad guys sweat a lot while heros patch thing up
Accident	It was just waiting to happen...
Accused, The	Larry Parker gets a stranger $3.7M
Adam's Rib	Adam opens a BBQ restaurant
Adventures In Babysitting	Kids get a much buffer babysitter than I ever had
Adventures Of Baron Munchausen, The	Actors have some of what the director's having...
Adventures Of Robin Hood, The	I'ts only a bloody brook...
Bad Day at Blackrock	A stranger comes to town
Chinatown	Jack N gets a bloody nose to-go
Diggstown	Bill and wife enjoy their new town
On The Town	Bill Gates and new wife go out to dinner
Our Town	Bill Gates and new wife like the town so much that t
Out-Of-Towners, The	Still more strangers come to town
The Clinton Election	A stranger comes to town
Thelma and Lassie	Our heros take a trip
Town Like Alice, A	The town really likes Alice

Page 1

For example, Figure 36.4 shows one page of an AutoReport created using the same query that created the previous example. Notice how *this* layout adds a lot of white space and creates many more pages per table or query than the regular old Print command.

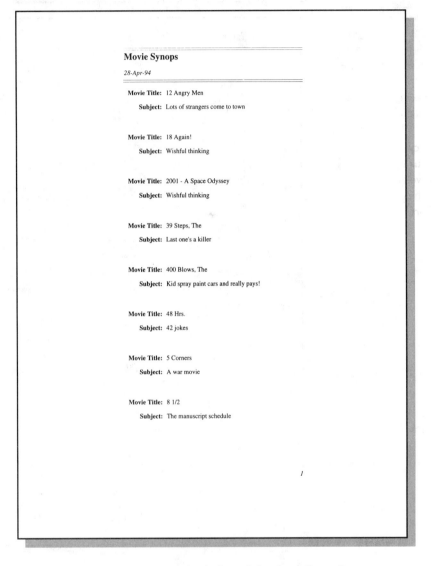

Go ahead and experiment. Just get in the habit of checking Print Preview when you do.

Defining Advanced Reports

While the Print commands and AutoReport feature are fine for basic reports, eventually you'll want to create fancy ones like the list of expenses, sorted by expense category (Account) and Payee, shown in Figure 36.5.

A fancy report with various type sizes and line weights, created with help from the Report Wizard

Accounting

28-Apr-94

Account	Date	Payee	Amount
Auto:Fuel	3/21/92	RMI (TEXACO)	($30.15)
	1/30/92	UNOCAL 76	($70.00)
	2/26/92	UNOCAL 76	($110.90)
	3/21/92	UNOCAL 76	($200.00)
			($411.05)
			0.37%
Auto:Registration	6/26/92	DMV	($367.00)
			($367.00)
			0.33%
Capital	4/22/94	Background Engineers	($529.86)
	11/16/93	CS	($2,478.93)
	5/28/93	ST Research	($1,500.00)
	7/22/93	The Computer Store	($393.61)
			($4,902.40)
			4.43%
Charity	12/7/93	American Red Cross	($50.00)
	2/11/94	KLON	($50.00)
			($100.00)
			0.09%
Credit Pay	1/15/92	AMERICAN EXPRESS	($48.04)
	2/14/92	AMERICAN EXPRESS	($151.87)
	3/21/92	AMERICAN EXPRESS	($428.41)
	4/15/92	AMERICAN EXPRESS	($241.82)
	5/27/92	AMERICAN EXPRESS	($170.05)
	6/12/92	AMERICAN EXPRESS	($430.73)
	7/11/92	AMERICAN EXPRESS	($395.12)
	8/21/92	AMERICAN EXPRESS	($88.11)
	9/17/92	AMERICAN EXPRESS	($207.60)
	10/12/92	AMERICAN EXPRESS	($420.39)
	12/11/92	AMERICAN EXPRESS	($172.95)
	1/14/93	AMERICAN EXPRESS	($216.74)
	2/12/93	AMERICAN EXPRESS	($738.40)

1

There are subtotals, and the percentages have been calculated. There are nice lines and boxes of various weights used to separate the various groups, titles, dates, and page numbers. The best part is that it was all done with a Wizard. Here are the general steps:

1. Open (or simply select) the desired database and table.

2. Click on the New Report button.

3. Make sure the desired table or query name (Accounting in this example) is visible in the dialog box. Click on the Report Wizards button.

4. Choose the desired report type (Groups/Totals in this example) from the scrolling list. Watch the bottom of the dialog box for descriptions of each Wizard type.

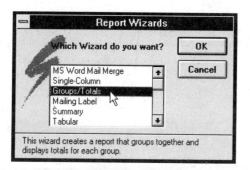

5. Read each subsequent screen and watch the example build as you make decisions. Here fields are being specified along with the order in which they'll appear.

6. If the Wizard you've chosen can create subtotals you will be asked how you want the report "grouped." You may also need to decide how to group data in each field. Here, for example, subtotals will be grouped by Account (expense category):

7. You may also be asked if you wish to sort by additional groups. Pick the sort levels by double-clicking on possible choices to move them from the Available list to the Sort list:

8. If given a style choice, click on each button and watch the example change until you find the one you like. The Ledger style is handy for financial reporting, and was used for the example.

9. You might be asked to title your report. When you're done, click on the Wizard's Finish button and Print Preview the work.

Access

Manual Reporting and Modifying

While it is nice to let Access handle the details for you, you'll eventually want to mess with them yourself. Or perhaps your boss will ask for something the Wizard can't deliver. That's when you will need to dig into the report design itself. Space prohibits a complete treatment of report features in this book, so we'll look at the general principles and you can either experiment, use online help, or crack the bigger books on Access for additional wisdom.

You can also learn a lot about reporting by peeking behind the scenes in the sample reports supplied with the NWIND database in the ACCESS\SAMPAPPS subdirectory.

You make changes to reports by adding or deleting report sections and controls, and by changing their properties.

1. Begin by switching to the Database window. Click on the Report tab, and then on the Design button:

2. Your screen will erupt with graphical nonsense as you enter the *Design view* (Figure 36.6).

The different report sections (headers, footers, detail sections) can be customized from here

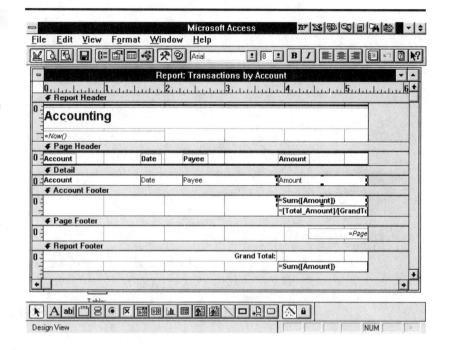

3. Take a deep breath and a long look. The Design View window is divided into many *report sections* (six, in this example—other reports will have more or fewer sections). Each section contains *controls* like text boxes, expressions, etc. You make changes to the report by altering these controls and their properties.

Let's take a look at the various sections that were set up by the Wizard when we asked for that Accounting report.

Report Header

The report header contains a label with the report's title, and often other controls like the expression =now(), which prints the current date, in a text box.

Page Header

Page headers contain information that will repeat on every page—like column headings. In our example there are the bold headers Date, Payee, Account, and Amount.

Detail Section

The detail section contains labels and field controls (Date, Payee, and Amount) that specify which data will be printed. Don't confuse the field controls with labels.

Group Footers

Group footers (like the Account footer in our example) are used to specify things like subtotals. These frequently use expressions—like **=sum([Amount])** in our example. You'll learn more about expressions in Chapter 38. Depending upon your report design you may have more than one group footer or none at all.

Page Footer

The page footer contains text and expressions that print on each page. In our example, there's an expression (**=page**) that prints page numbers. You can just as easily have labels that say "Confidential" on each page. There are other expressions worth exploring for page footers; you may want one that prints the message "page *n* of *x*." See Chapter 38.

Report Footer

The report footer contains items that appear only at the end of a report, like grand totals or instructive text like "Please report all errors to EX 251."

Modifying Section Contents

By now you have most of the skills necessary to modify report sections. You can increase and decrease the height of a section by dragging on its top and bottom boundaries. To change the size of control boxes, click on them and drag their handles. To move text boxes and other controls, click to select them, then drag with the mouse when the pointer looks like a little hand.

To change the appearance of text in a report, select the control box or boxes of interest, then choose new settings from the toolbar and menus. For instance, to change the font(s) used in a report you might:

1. Use the Select All command on the Edit menu to select all controls, or Shift-click to select just a few controls.

2. Choose a new font from the drop-down Font Name list in the Report Design toolbar. Here, just the controls in the Page Header have been selected and the font is being changed:

3. To accommodate the font differences, you may need to resize some or all of the control boxes by dragging. Here, since four controls are selected,

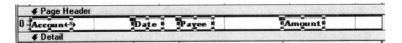

resizing one resizes all four (notice the shape of the mouse pointer—it's over the leftmost control):

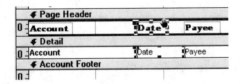

4. Move controls by dragging them to tighten things up, or make more room as necessary. Slide the mouse pointer around a selected object until the pointer turns into a small hand, indicating that you can move objects. Again, if multiple items are selected, they will all move in unison. This is a handy way to move entire rows or columns. Here, both the heading in the Page Header section and the field control in the detail section will move as one:

Incredibly, you can use the choices on the Format menu to alter the appearance of selected items.

Properties in Reports

There are many, many *properties* (characteristics) in reports. There are report-wide properties, and section properties, and properties for individual controls. When you use a toolbar to change the font used in a control, or if you drag a control with your mouse to move it elsewhere on the screen, or if you change source of the data to be printed, you are changing properties.

In general, to see (and perhaps to change manually) a property, select the item (the control) of interest and use the Properties... command on the View menu or click on the Properties button. Here as an example are the properties for the page numbering control:

To change a property, click in the white box next to the property you wish to change, and either type a new property, or choose one from the resulting drop-down list. To add a normal black border around the date field, for example, you'd choose Normal from the Border Style list, and pick Black as the Border color if that's not already chosen.

You can sometimes watch the effect of property changes as you work. For instance, here we've changed the page number so that the numbers will be white and centered in a black box:

Click on the Palette button to change these options.

Online help is available to assist you with changing properties, and the bigger books review the mind-boggling options in detail.

Saving Report Formats for Reuse

Once you have a report that you like, use the Save command to save it. Report names can be long and have spaces.

To make variations on the same report, use the Save As... command.

Printing Mailing Labels

Access provides a "Mailing Label" Wizard that can speed the creation of all kinds of labels. Don't be fooled by the Mailing Label Wizard's name. You can use it for creating name tags, file folder labels, floppy disk labels, video and audio tape labels—you name it.

Since the Wizard "knows" the standard layout sizes for many commercially available labels (Avery and others) you can often get the labels you need with

one or two dozen mouse clicks. Here are the general steps, using mailing labels as an example:

1. Open the desired database (we will use Contacts for this example, in
   case you want to follow along on your own.)

2. If necessary, create a Query that rounds up just the records for which you
   want labels (we've invented a newsletter subscribers' query here.)

3. Start a new report, either with the New Report toolbar button shown to
   the left, or by picking New in the File menu then Report in the resulting
   submenu.

4. Pick the Report Wizard.

5. When the Wizard gives you a choice of report types, pick Mailing Label,
   as shown here:

6. Select the fields that will appear in your labels, and add text or punctuation in the dialog box shown in Figure 36.7.

Now build the label design by clicking on the desired elements. For example,
to construct a full name line from the fields Prefix, FirstName, and LastName,
you'd double click on the Prefix field, click on the Space button (to place a
space between the Prefix and FirstName, then double-click on the FirstName
field name, or select a field and click on the > button, click on the space button again, and double-click on the LastName field.

FIGURE 36.7

Pick label fields, and
add punctuation and
text here.

Type text here

Double-click to add a field to the label

**Click these to place spaces
or punctuation between fields**

**Watch the label
design evolve here**

FIGURE 36.8

Telling the Wiz to sort
first by zip code and
then by street address
within zip code

7. To start a new line in the label design, click the Newline button.

8. To add punctuation, click on the desired character button (comma, period, etc.).

9. To add repeating text (like "Your subscription is about to expire") type it in the long white text box and then click on the Text > button.

10. When you are happy with your label click on the Next > button.

11. You'll be asked to pick fields for sorting. Here, we've specified a two-level sort starting with zip code and using street address as the tie-breaker:

12. Next, the Wiz will ask you to pick a label size and type, and units of measure. Scroll, if necessary, to find the desired label type, and click Next > when done.

13. You get to make some label-wide font choices (which can be tweaked later). Start with a small font size if you are at all concerned about fitting everything on the chosen label size.

14. Click Next > and if you are in luck, the Wiz will continue. On the other hand, not all of the fields will fit, you will be informed.. If this happens, go back and change the label or font sizes at this point.

15. Click Finish when you are ready to preview your new label layout.

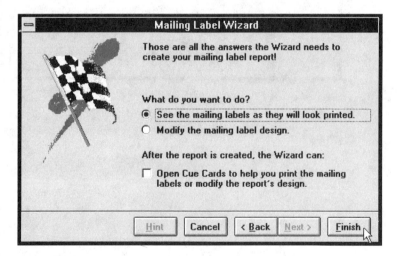

16. You'll see (an often uninspired-looking) print preview, as illustrated in Figure 36.9.

17. Use the Zoom button to take a closer look, or click on the Print button to see how the design looks on paper.

> **TIP** Always print at least a reasonable sampling of your labels (perhaps 20% of them) on cheap, plain, white paper before you print on the more expensive label stock. Check for things like horizontal and vertical alignment problems, fields that have been truncated, and so on.

18. Save the label design the way you would any other report, with the Save command. Label report names can be long and can include spaces.

FIGURE 36.9

A print preview of our mailing labels layout

Changing Label Designs

To embellish your labels (by adding a logo, changing type styles, etc.) you'll use techniques that will probably seem familiar by now.

1. Open the label design by switching to the Database window, clicking on the Report tab, selecting the desired label "report," and then clicking on the Design button:

2. When you see the report design it will contain controls for each line of the label (a control for the first line, another for the second, and so on). The Wizard constructs these controls using your specified desires and expressions (as discussed in Chapter 38). You can change these controls and their properties. (This takes some care and some knowledge, so make sure you have a backup copy before you begin.)

3. Select a control by clicking on it, then change properties with toolbar tools or menu choices. Or, select a control, choose Properties… from the View menu, and make changes using the property editing techniques discussed earlier in this chapter.

4. You can add art, repeating text, etc., to your report. For instance, Figure 36.10 shows a label logo under construction. It is being created by inserting a graphic object from the ClipArt gallery, a label, and, in a moment, I'll add a line and some text. (You already know how to create text objects in Access reports, and you can probably figure out how to insert graphic objects and lines from your previous Windows experience. If not, turn to Chapter 39, where we'll play with graphics and lines.)

5. Save the changes when you are happy with them.

When you experiment with redesigning reports, use the Save As... command to save the new designs. Then you'll have copies of both the old design and the new ones. If you don't like the new ones, you can always go back and use the old design.

FIGURE 36.10

Creating a label logo is easy using clip art and a Wizard

Here's a print preview of our finished label masterpiece:

Using Access Data with Word's Mail Merge

One of the Report Wizard choices is *Microsoft Word Mail Merge* You can use it to link data from your database to a new or existing MS Word Mail Merge document. Simply save your query or Access table with the Save command then run the Access Report Wizard, choosing MS Word Mail Merge when the choice is offered. Follow the resulting dialog boxes and obtain online help if necessary. The Wizard will launch Word as needed and will lead you through the appropriate steps. Unless you have a fast computer with plenty of RAM this can take a while. Be patient.

Other Printing Topics to Explore

There is more to know about Access printing, of course, but if you've read this chapter and have used other Windows programs, you already have the skills necessary to create impressive reports.

Many of the things you'll learn in Chapters 38 and 39 will also be useful when printing. For example, you can use expressions to control printing. You can use macros to automate printing tasks, and so on. But next, let's turn briefly to relational databases.

Access

37

Relational Databases

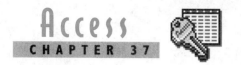

There are two general ways to organize databases: as flat files or as relational databases. In this chapter we'll explore the relational approach.

Flat vs. Relational

If you keep all of your information in one table in a single database file, it is called a *flat file*. Simple projects like a personal collection of names and addresses are often good flat-file candidates. Flat files are easy to maintain. There is very little chance of misplacing or duplicating data.

Other times, however, it is wise to put data in different tables or even different database files and then to create links between the tables or database files. These multiple tables and database files, when used together, create something called a *relational database*.

Relational databases allow you to store and use large amounts of data efficiently. Frequently used information like the names, addresses, and phone numbers of your customers can be stored in one table, while other information—data concerning orders, for example—is stored in another table. This way, there's no need to keep the name, address, and phone number of each customer as part of the record for each order; instead, a link between the two tables allows that data to be stored in one table and accessed for use in the other. A third table, for invoices, could then be linked so it could pull data from each of the first two tables.

This not only minimizes the amount of storage space needed for large, complex databases, but can also minimize the need for retyping of frequently used information, and can reduce the chance that you'll use out-of-date information or make typographical errors. Good database designs like this break complex collections of data into "chunks" that can be managed by different groups of people and used by everyone for the common good.

As you may recall, in our sample video store database (Vid_Stor) we created the four tables illustrated in Figure 37.1.

One table is called *Customers*. It contains each customer's name, address, phone number, customer ID number, etc.

The second table is called *Tape Inventory*. It's a list of tapes, containing each tape's (movie) title, a unique number to identify each copy of that title, a brief plot description (subject), and so on. In addition, there is a field in the Tape table designed to track which *customer* has rented that particular tape for today. For example, in Figure 37.1, Customer 7 has the film $8\frac{1}{2}$, and customer 6 has *The 39 Steps*.

There's another table that tracks which tapes have been reserved by which customers. This table (called *Reservations*) collects reservation dates, tape numbers, the ID of the employee making the reservation, etc.

Finally there is the Employees table containing employee ID numbers, names, and the other usual data contained in employee records.

As you probably know from your trips to the video store, employees routinely call customers from lists (printed or on-screen) to confirm reservations, to ask for overdue tapes, and so on. Linking these four tables in our Vid_Stor database

FIGURE 37.1

The tables we created earlier for our sample video store database

927

means that the parts become more than the whole. For instance, looking at all four tables long enough back in Figure 37.1, you *could* figure out that Abe Sea (Customer 3) reserved the film *The 39 Steps* (Tape ID 9) for 12/22/94; and you'd know that the employee Liz Borden (Employee 2) made the reservation. This takes a lot of hunting through different windows and lots of irrelevant data, a process that can eventually make you blind or crazy.

Obviously, you could have employees type all the full names of things in each table, but there is a better way. You can create queries, reports, and data entry forms that compile the data into meaningful information and display it in a more usable fashion. For instance, here's a query that uses not only the four tables in the Vid_Stor database, but an external table from another database:

	Date	Movie Title	Last Name	Phone Number	Desired Format	Confirmed	BY
	12/21/94	Bad Day at Blackrock	Gone	(714) 555-8765	Laser Disc	No	Liz
	12/21/94	Thelma and Lassie	Rather-Knot	(818) 555-1234	VHS	Yes	Liz
▶	12/22/94	39 Steps, The	Sea	(310) 555-9876	VHS	No	Liz
	12/23/94	8 1/2	Foolz-Day	(310) 555-5555	8MM	Yes	Jeff

Ah, much better! Those shorthand numbers for tapes, customers, and employees have been replaced by real names. And we've pulled the customer's phone number from the customer file, so there's less chance of an accidental typo. Notice the column *Desired Format*. It contains information from that separate database called Voters we explored earlier. It collected customers' last names and their preferred media type. While, as you'll see later, it isn't always good database design to relate things this way, I thought I'd show off, and make an important point at the same time: You can relate multiple *database files* to form relationships between them when the need arises. Sometimes, you can even use non-Access database files.

Once you've properly established links to form relationships between tables, you can create a variety of reports and queries. For instance, here's a report showing who has which tape and when it is due back. Notice that we've added first names here:

Tape #	Due Back	Movie Title	Last Name	First Name	Phone Number
11	Thursday, November 10, 1994	48 Hrs.	Gone	Hellen	(714) 555-8765
1	Friday, December 02, 1994	Thelma and Lassie	Rather-Knot	Ida	(818) 555-1234
10	Friday, December 02, 1994	400 Blows, The	Rather-Knot	Ida	(818) 555-1234
9	Thursday, December 22, 1994	39 Steps, The	Johnson	J. J.	(818) 555-2018
7	Thursday, December 22, 1994	2001 - A Space Odyssey	Reed-Moor	Wanda	(818) 555-4567
4	Thursday, December 22, 1994	12 Angry Men	Foolz-Day	April	(310) 555-5555

We'd better give J. J. a call or Abe will be disappointed. Notice that this report uses the long date format, which includes the names of days, and different headings (captions) for some of the fields (columns). Remember, once you understand how to change field properties, you can make these and other changes in reports, queries, and elsewhere.

How Relationships Work

This is one of those chicken-and-egg things. It's hard to understand how relationships work until you know how to create them, and it's hard to create them until you understand them. So, let's look at the insides of the Vid_Stor relationships, then try one or two of your own. Don't worry if this Vid_Stor tour doesn't make complete sense. It will after you create your own relationships. Let's look at the "Who has the Videos" query first. It's pretty straightforward.

When you design a query or report, you start by "opening" the various tables you wish to use. (You will learn how later). For our first example we'll need the tables *Tape Inventory* and *Customers*.

We need the Tape Inventory table because it contains, among other things, a field that tell us who has which tape. This information is stored in the field called *Who Has?*. When a customer picks up a tape, the store's employees enter the customer's ID number into this field.

Obviously, a customer could pick up one tape, or many tapes; but no two customers can have the same tape at the same time. If more than one tape is rented by the same customer, the customer's ID number is placed in each appropriate tape record.

So far, so good? If not, reread the preceding four paragraphs.

Now, the *Customer* table has a field that corresponds to (is related to) the *Who Has?* field in the Tape Inventory table. The field is called *CustomerID*. This table contains a single, unique number for each customer. No two customers have the same ID number.

The numbers in the CustomerID field and in the Who Has? fields *match*. That is to say, they are *related*. We tell Access about this relationship using a simple technique you'll soon use yourself. Since we've already related the two fields in the example, Microsoft Access has drawn a line between them. (For extra credit, look back at the diagram and see if you can figure out why there is a *1* at the Customers end of the line, and the sign for infinity—indicating many—at the Tape inventory end of the line.)

Once you've established one or more relationships like this you can use them to create meaningful reports and queries. For example, take a look at the design for the *Who Has the Videos?* query:

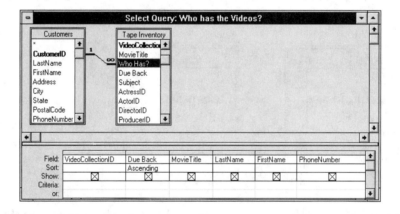

We have told Access to display information from the two tables. The first field that will be displayed is from the Tape Inventory table. It's the tape ID number (VideoCollectionID). The next two fields are also from the Tape Inventory table (Due Back and MovieTitle).

The next three fields to be displayed (LastName, FirstName, and PhoneNumber) are from the Customers database. The last field is Who Has. Notice that the related fields (Who Has? and CustomerID) won't even show up on the screen! In this case, they do their work of linking the tables in the background.

In other words, when we run this query, Access looks for all tape records that have a customer ID in the Who Has? field. Whenever it finds one, it displays the requested tape information (VideoCollectionID, Due Back, and Movie-Title) *along with the requested information from the Customers table* (names and phone numbers). It matches the numbers in the Who Has? field with the numbers in the CustomerID field to know what to display in the name and phone fields.

Take a peek at some more complex relationships, before you create one of your own.

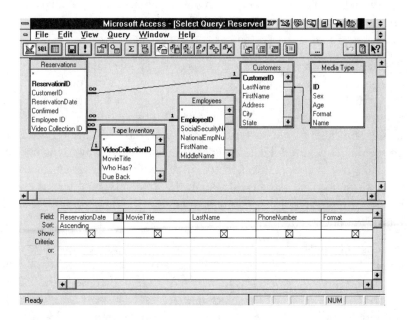

Holy cow! *The Compact Guide to Rocket Science....* Actually, this is easier than it looks. We have *five* tables this time, four from the Vid_Stor database, and the fifth (Media Type) from the Voters database.

We are using the relationship formed by the link between the EmployeeID in Reservations and EmployeeID in Employees to look up and display the employees' first names (FirstName) in the query.

And we are using the two VideoCollectionID fields in Reservations and Tape Inventory together to display the Movie Title field contents from the Tape Inventory database. The relationship between the two CustomerID fields in the Reservations and Customers tables is used to display the customer's names (LastName) and phone numbers. These relationships were made all the easier to see and understand by naming the fields in the different tables with the same names (CustomerID in Reservations and CustomerID in Customers, for example). That's a good habit to establish, where possible.

Finally, we have taken the risky step of relating the Customers table in the Vid_Stor database with the Media Type table from the Voters database. The theory is, that if customers voted in our imaginary straw poll, we could learn and display their preferred media type by relating their last names from the Customer list with the last names from Voters.

Besides illustrating the point that data from outside databases can be related, this gives me an opportunity to point out the pitfalls of sloppy relationships. First, what happens if you have two customers with the last name Smith? Or what if a visiting nonmember votes? What if two members of the Smith family vote for different media types? People will find the darndest ways to screw up seemingly wonderful database designs. The proper way to include survey results like this is to ask customers to write down their customer numbers, and enter those into a CustomerID field in the Media Type table of the Voters database, or have an employee look up and enter ID numbers after the survey has been conducted.

Forcing *referential integrity* is another step you can take to minimize the risk of events like this. Basically, you ask Access to enforce the validity of data in related tables. For instance, if you change or add or delete something in one table that affects another table, you want Access to at least warn you of potential problems. This technique is discussed later in this chapter.

Exercise: Creating a Simple Relationship

Let's create a simple relational database together. How about a Little League Roster and some stats?

1. With Access running, start by closing any database you might have open with the Close Database command, then pick New Database from the File menu (or use the Ctrl+N keyboard shortcut).

2. Pick a name and location for the new database. My team's going to be the *1994 Sybex Pirates*, but database names must adhere to DOS filename rules (8 characters, no spaces, etc.), so I'll just call the file **Pirates** and store it in my Examples subdirectory. Access will take care of adding the filename extension:

3. Now we need a couple of tables. Let's start with a Players table. When Access displays the empty Database window, click the Table tab if it isn't already foremost, then click the New button to create a new table.

4. Let's roll our own here, without the help of a Wizard. Click the big New Table button.

5. Create a Player Number field and a Name field, specifying the appropriate data type for each:

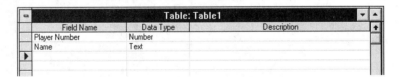

6. Make the Player Number field the primary key by clicking in the field name and then choosing Set Primary Key from the Edit menu. A small image of a key will appear at the left of the field:

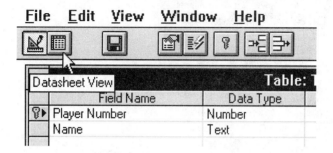

7. To enter a few team numbers and names you will need to switch to Datasheet View by clicking on the Datasheet View toolbar button, but you'll be asked to save the table when you switch views. Here you can use longer names and spaces:

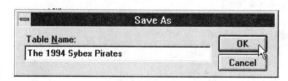

8. Enter a few uniform numbers and names. To do this, tab from field to field, typing in the appropriate information in each field. (Notice that Access won't let you assign duplicate player numbers, since this is the Primary Key field.) You can adjust the column widths if you like.

935

9. To create a second table to use for collecting game stats, select File ➤ New ➤ Table.

10. Include a numeric field for Player Number field, a text field for Game Date, a text field for What Happened, and a numeric field to collect Runs Batted In (RBI).

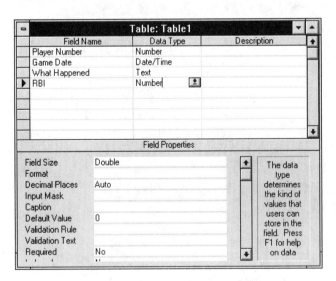

11. Save the table as Game Stats. Let Access create an index field for you when it asks permission.

12. Make four or five entries like those shown here:

ID	Player Number	Game Date	What Happened	RBI
1	1	5/4/94	HR	0
2	2	5/4/94	BH	0
3	3	5/4/94	BH	0
4	5	5/4/94	HR	2
＊ter)	0			0

Table: Game Stats

TIP **To enter today's date without typing it, use the key combination Ctrl+: (Ctrl+semicolon).**

Now that you have two tables with some data let's relate them while creating a simple query.

1. Choose New Query from that multilevel New command in the File menu.

2. Click the big New Query button (not the New Query *Wizards* button).

3. You'll see the beginnings of a query, probably with only the Game Stats table in view:

Access

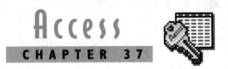

4. To add a table to the query design, use the Add Table toolbar button. In this case we want the Pirates table. Select it in the Add Table dialog box:

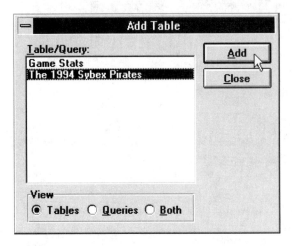

5. Now click the Add button and the Pirates table will appear in your Query window. Close the Add Table dialog box by clicking on the Close button.

 You can drag the corners of the tables to resize them if you like. Dragging on the table titles will move them.

Look at that! Since we used the same field *name* and field *type* in both tables, Access has inferred a relationship, which it has indicated by drawing that line representing the link from Player Number in Game Stats to Player Number in the other table. You can create additional relationships by pointing to one field in a table and dragging to a field in another table, drawing new relationship lines in the process. But don't do that now, since none of the other fields are meant to be related. (And in fact there is a problem with the way Access has related the two fields for us, as you will soon see.) For now, you've done what you came to do. You have created a relational database!

Let's check out this relationship by creating a query that shows events from Game Stats with players' names from the Pirates table.

1. To include the players' names in the query, double-click on *Name* in the Pirates table:

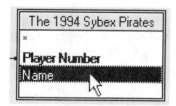

2. Next, add other fields you'd like to see in your query (perhaps Game Date, What Happened, and RBI).

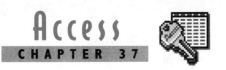

3. Save the query, if you like, with the File Menu's Save Query command or the Ctrl+S shortcut. Long spacey names are okay here. (I called mine Player Performance.)

4. Click on the Datasheet View toolbar button to see the results of your first query:

Name	Game Date	What Happened	RBI
▶ Big Al	5/4/94	HR	0
Rudolf Motzart Langer	5/4/94	BH	0
Sarah Sidbar Wadsworth	5/4/94	BH	0
✱			

That's pretty neat, but if you are paying attention, you've noticed a problem. There were *four* entries in our sample Game Stats table, but only *three* of them are showing in the query. Wat gives? Looking at the data in both tables together will shed some light:

One of the Game Stats is credited to a player number 5, but there is no player number 5 in the Pirates roster (the 1994 Sybex Pirates table). We forgot to enter one of our heavy hitters—Julie "the Slugger" Simmons. With Julie in the table the query produces the desired results.

The lesson is: *Check your work.* Get in the habit of knowing how many items you should be seeing when you perform a new query or create a new report, and consider building in data entry *tests* that will warn you if entries are out of range. (This is discussed in Chapter 38.)

You can also minimize the chances of problems like the one that just occurred by defining *relationship types* and using Access's ability to enforce *referential integrity.* So, this near-disaster we just experienced is a good excuse to explore these concepts.

Types of Relationships

Let's look at the types of relationships first then learn how to specify them. The three types of relationships are (take notes, this'll be on the test):

- One-to-Many
- Many-to-Many
- One-to-One

I'll pass on the opportunity to slip in a promiscuity joke here, and cut to the chase. Here are examples of the different types of relationships and why you would use them.

One to Many

"One-to-many" is the most common type of relationship. The Pirates database includes what should be a one-to-many relationship. Each player listed in the Pirates table has a unique Player Number. Any given Player Number can be found only *once* in the Pirates table. That is to say, there are never duplicate Player Numbers in the Pirates table.

In the Game Stats table, however, there can be *many* entries containing the same Player Number, because players make many plays each year. (By the way—there can only be only one Player Number in any single game stat.)

...Got all that?

- There must be one and only one player number for each player in the Pirates table—no duplicate player numbers are permitted in this table.

- Many Game Stat entries in the Game Stats table can contain duplicate player numbers since one player makes many plays.

- Only one player number is stored in any one Game Stats record since there is only one field to hold a player number in a Game Stat record.

That's a classic one-to-many relationship. There are other examples of one-to-manys in the Vid_Stor example. Each tape can only be rented by one person at a time, but one person can rent many tapes at the same time. One employee can make many reservations, but each reservation can be taken by only one employee, and so on.

Whenever possible, it's a good idea to create one-to-many relationships (as opposed to many-to-many relationships, which are discussed next).

Many to Many

If you are a novice database user, you may want to skim this section, and study it later, along with bigger books on the subject, if and when you ever need to set up a complex database on your own.

Occasionally, many-to-many relationships are unavoidable, or at least troublesome to do without. A classic example of a many-to-many relationship is illustrated in The Microsoft Northwind Orders database, as illustrated on the following page.

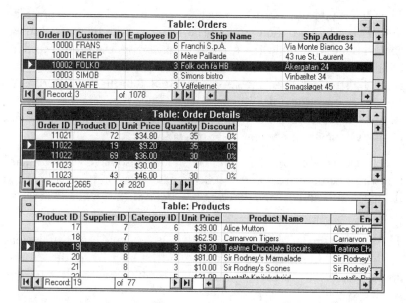

The Orders *table* (I know it's confusing; there's an Orders table in the Orders database) …anyhow, the Orders *table* collects things like Order ID numbers, Customer ID numbers, Employee ID numbers, Shipping addresses, and so on. There is only one record for each order. Each has a unique order *number*.

In addition, there's a second table called Order Details. Here, each row (record) contains the details of a single item that has been ordered by a customer. As you can see, this table has multiple rows (records), with each record containing a customer's purchase order number, the part number (Product ID) for the ordered item, the quantity ordered, etc. Some records have the same Order ID numbers. You might have thousands of these records with many records for each purchase order number. (We'll get back to this table in a moment.)

Finally, you see a table called Products. It contains product information, with one and only one record for each product. Each record has a field for Product ID, a description, unit pricing, and so on.

The Orders table and the Order Details table have a one-to-many relationship. This is because there can only be a single Order ID number in each record in the Orders table, but it's okay to have more than one record in the Order Details table with the same Order ID number. Take a moment to look at the illustration. There are two highlighted items in the Order Details table. They both have the order number 11022. Since there can be only one Order ID entry in a record in the Order Details table, the relationship is—one-to-many. (Or maybe one *too* many, at this point.)

The Products table and the Order Detail table also have a one-to-many relationship. Each line item in the Order Detail table can have only one Product ID, but there can be many different line items with the same Product ID in the Order Details table, making this a one-to-many relationship.

The many-to-many relationship is developed because there can be many Order IDs in the Order Details table that match Order IDs in the Orders table, and many Product IDs in the Order Details table that match entries in the Products table.

The advantage to this arrangement is that you needn't bog down tables with needless repetition. You could live without the Order Details table, and clutter up your Products table with an entry each time someone ordered the product. Or you could clutter up the Orders table with a lot of repetitive product descriptions and such. But this way is cleaner.

Again: Don't try to figure this out for the first time by yourself a few hours before an important deadline. It takes time to develop, test, and trust complex relationships. Doesn't it?

One to One

I'll mention one-to-one relationships, but if you are clever, you'll probably never use them. In a one-to-one relationship, there can only be one matching record in each of the related tables. For instance, in our Vid_Store and Voters example, if you had a CustomerID field in both Vid_Stor and Voters, there should probably never be multiple occurrences of a customer's ID in either table (assuming of course that customers only vote once, know their customer ID numbers, and that noncustomers didn't vote.) Almost inconceivable, but in unlikely cases like this, Customer ID 1 would occur only once in the Customer table and only once in the Voter table, forming a one-to-one relationship.

When you spot potential relationships like this, consider adding a field to an existing table rather than creating a new table. For instance, it would probably be better to add a Media field to the Customer table rather than to create that whole Voter table just to capture customer media preferences.

Viewing Relationships

The types of relationships between tables are graphically indicated by special symbols in Relations tables:

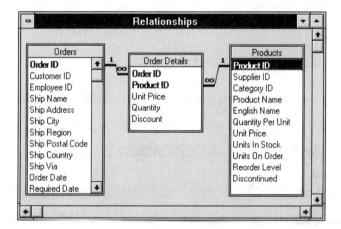

The one-to-many relationships have a number 1 at one end and the infinity sign at the other, indicating many. As you will see when you get to referential integrity, the thick connecting bars have a special meaning.

You can view relationships by following these steps:

1. Open the Database of interest (NWIND, in this example).

2. Click the Relations toolbar button as shown here:

3. When you see the Relations window, click on the Show All Relationships button:

4. If necessary, drag to resize and rearrange the table lists so that the lists don't clutter or cover lines and obscure your understanding of the relationships.

5. Click once on a relationship line to select (darken) the line.

6. Double-click on a selected line to display the Relationships dialog box, which is where you can view and modify relationship settings. (You'll actually do this with your Pirates database in a moment.)

7. When you're done, close the Relationships dialog box (if it is open) by double-clicking on its close box. Close the larger Relations diagram window in the same way.

Defining and Redefining Relationships

You'll frequently need to define or modify relationships. For instance, the relationship Access established automatically when we created the Sybex Pirates database needs some work. That's because Access failed to establish a one-to-many relationship, and it doesn't do an integrity check that would be helpful.

In general, you create the links that represent relationships by dragging new lines from a field name in one table list to a field name in a different table list. The first field (where you start dragging) is referred to as the *primary key field*. The second (the one you drag to) is called the *foreign key field*.

You edit a relationship by first selecting the relationship's line, then double-clicking on the line (this makes a total of 3 clicks) and changing the rules in a dialog box or two.

This next bit is going to take some concentration. Take a break if that will help. Then let's experiment:

1. Open your Pirates database and use the Relationships toolbar button to open the Relationships window:

2. You should see both tables in the Relationships window and a line indicating the relationship between the two Player Number fields. Your screen arrangement may look a little different than mine, but you should see all three of these elements:

3. If you don't see all of the tables you want to work with, use the Add Table toolbar button to bring up the Add Table dialog box. Double-click on the names of tables you wish to add to the Relationships window, then close the Add Table dialog box. (You actually should not have to do this for the current exercise.)

Deleting Relationships

In a moment we are going to add—and then modify—a relationship in the Pirates database. But first it's time for a brief side trip.

From time to time you'll need to delete relationships. For instance, Access might create unwanted relationships when you set up a new database, or you might try to change a field type (from number to text or from one number type to another, for instance), only to find that relationships exist and that they will have to be deleted before you can make the type changes.

To delete a relationship:

1. Display the Relations window showing the relationship(s) to be deleted.

2. Click once, carefully, upon the relationship line to select it. The line will thicken when you hit the sweet spot:

3. Press the Del key to remove the relationship. You will be asked to confirm the deletion. The line should disappear.

Try deleting the relationship in your Pirates database if you haven't already done so.

Creating Relationships

The process of creating links to form relationships is also called *Joining*. The actual steps for joining will vary based on the *type* of relationship you wish to establish, and the *source* of the tables and databases you need to relate. You'll also need to give some thought to which will be the *primary field* and which will be the *foreign field*. And, sometimes you'll need to tell Access what to do when there are, or are not, matches between the two tables. Finally, there are ways to ask Access to help you maintain the *integrity* of your database. Here are the general steps for enforcing integrity, using a Pirates relationship as an example.

1. Open the Relations window for the database of interest and make sure all of the necessary tables are visible.

2. Decide which field you wish to be the primary key field and locate it in the field list (by scrolling, if necessary). In the Pirates example, you'll want to use the *Player Number* field from the Pirates table.

3. Decide which field you wish to be the foreign key field and locate it in the field list (by scrolling, if necessary). In this exercise we want to use the Player Number field in the Game Stats field list.

4. To begin the actual joining process, click on the primary field name (the Player Number field from the Pirates table) and hold down the mouse button. The mouse pointer will change into a rectangle. If you look carefully you can see the funny new pointer shape hovering over the Player Number field name here:

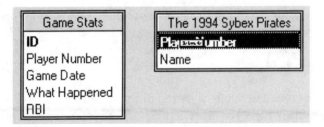

5. Hold down the mouse button and drag until the pointer is over the field name in the destination table (the Player Number field in the Game Stats field list). It's okay that the mouse pointer changes shape while moving between table lists.

6. When you reach the destination field (the Player Number field in the Game Stats field list) release the mouse button. You'll see a Relationships dialog box:

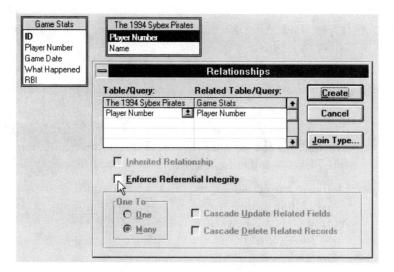

7. The Relations window displays the primary table and field on the left and the foreign table and field on the right. (If you've made a mistake and pointed to the wrong field you can use the drop-down lists to choose different field names.)

With the desired field names showing in the Relations window, clicking Create will establish a one-to-one relationship between the two tables. But don't click Create if you are following along with the Pirates exercise. To define the *type* of relationship you wish to establish, you must first specify whether or not to enforce referential integrity and pick a relationship type. Read on.

Referential Integrity

When you choose the Enforce Referential Integrity option in the Relations window you tell Access that there must be appropriate matches between the two tables. This is one way to prevent things like that missing player problem we had earlier in the chapter. In that example, if the relationship between the Player Number fields in the roster and Game Stats tables had been defined as "one-to-many with enforced referential integrity," we would have seen an error message when trying to enter a game stat for an undefined player. That is to say, we can force Access to make sure there is a match in the primary key field for entries in the foreign key field, by demanding the enforcement of referential integrity.

Here are the steps for establishing this kind of relationship in general, using the Pirates database as an example:

1. With the Relations window open for the relationship of interest (the two Player Name fields, in our example), choose the Enforce Referential Integrity option.

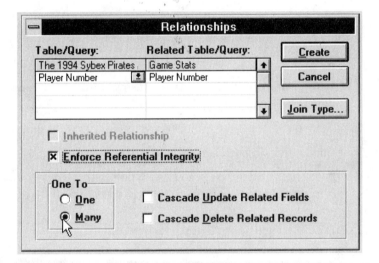

2. You will be faced with the one-to-one vs. one-to-many choice. Pick one or the other radio button. In the case of the Pirates database we want one-to-many, since there can be only unique Player Numbers in the Pirates table, but many of the same Player Numbers in the Game Stats table. Click on the Many button.

3. To create the actual relationship, click the Create button in the Relations window. This will establish the relationship and close the Relations window.

4. Notice that the relationship is now graphically represented with thicker lines, indicating enforced referential integrity, and that the indicators for a one-to-many relationship appear:

To test the results of your work, switch back to the Game Stats table and try to enter a record using a player number that you've not defined in your other table:

1. Choose Database:PIRATES from the Window menu to make the Pirates Database window active.

2. Click on the Table tab, if necessary, to see the list of tables.

3. Double-click on the Game Stats table to view it.

4. Try to enter a record with a Player Number that has not been defined yet in the 1994 Sybex Pirates table (Player Number 16 in this example):

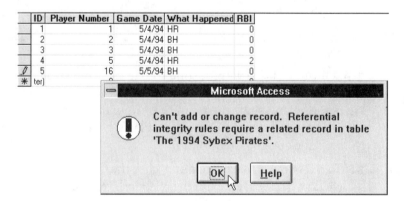

5. When you try to leave the record, Access will display an alert telling you about the integrity problem. You can correct the Player Number in the Game Stats entry, or you can switch to the Pirates table and add a player with the number causing the problem.

Troubleshooting

It's common when setting up new relationships or changing field types to be scolded by Access for type mismatches. Access expects that if you are going to relate two fields from different tables, both fields have compatible definitions (both number fields with double field sizes, or both text fields 50 characters in length, for instance). That's why it is a good idea to plan ahead when you are creating tables. Think about the potential relationships before defining fields.

What Next?

There's much more to know about relationships if you plan to develop databases, so if that's the case, you'll need to grab some books devoted to Access. You might try *Microsoft Access 2 Roadmap*, or *Your First Access Database*, or *Understanding Microsoft Access 2, Special Edition*, all from SYBEX. You can then begin experimenting on some small databases of your own, and you can always check out the sample databases in the ACCESS\SAMPAPPS directory.

You'll also need a firm understanding of expressions, and other Access automation tools. These are the topics of our next chapter.

38

Expressions, Macros, and Other Automation

Database management often requires a number of specific steps that must be carried out in a definite order. Access provides tools that can be used to automate these complex tasks, making experienced users more productive, and enabling novices to accomplish things with a minimum of technical expertise.

There are risks, of course. Computers take their instructions quite literally; they are known for their lack of good judgment. When you automate your databases, it is your responsibility to anticipate (and test for) all the things that can and will go wrong.

Let's take a look at expressions, macros, Action queries, Control Wizards, buttons and other forms of Access automation.

NOTE If you are an experienced user of Access version 1, be sure to check out the online help topic <u>New Approaches for Statements</u>, <u>Functions Methods</u>, and <u>Properties</u>. Many things have changed in version 2.

Expressions

We use *expressions* every day when we ask questions or give instructions like:

- Let's raise prices on all accessories by 10%.
- Who are the top ten sales people?
- Be sure to get each customer's phone number, including area code.
- If customers want to purchase more than ten of those, sell them for $1.50 each.

■ Change the vendor name for "Air-O-Mass" products to "Aeromass" throughout the database.

■ We need a list of all the customers who purchased propellers with serial numbers in the range of 11198 to 11225.

Access lets you create computerized expressions analogous to the ones just listed. These expressions can be used in reports, forms, queries, and even while creating new fields in tables. They let you find or compute information. For example, expressions let you:

■ Change property settings based on calculations or validation rules

■ Enter and use *calculations* in queries and filters

■ Set the stage for different actions in macros

■ Add arguments to Access Basic procedures

■ Change properties in SQL queries

If you've worked with Excel, Access's expressions will remind you of *formulas*. Unfortunately, Access expressions and Excel formulas are not identical. Neither are the buzzwords used to describe their parts.

Parts of an Expression

Access expressions always begin with an equal sign (=) and are entered into "text boxes" or directly into property sheets, as you'll see in a moment. Expressions contain some or all of the following parts:

■ Control names (names of text boxes, buttons, etc.)

■ Operators (+, -, *, AND, OR, <, >, etc.)

■ Identifiers (field and table names)

■ Function names (DATE, SUM, etc.)

■ Literals (numbers, dates, or text strings)

■ Constants (unchanging values)

■ Criteria (>10, etc.)

Control Names

A *control name* is a name you define for the control that will contain the results of your formula. For example, if you create an expression to compute a 10% discount on list prices, the Control name might be **Discounted Price** and the expression could be **=[List Price]*.9**. When Access uses this expression it will place the results of the computation in the *Discounted Price* control.

Operators

Operators do the necessary calculations and comparisons. For instance, you might use an operator to find all the records with a price of *greater than* (**>**) $1.00, or you might use the operator ***** to *multiply* the contents of one field by another. Online help along with the examples in this book and the Microsoft sample databases will help you explore the categories of Access operators:

- Arithmetic
- Comparison
- Concatenation
- Logical
- Pattern matching
- Miscellaneous

The following are listings of all the operators by group:

Arithmetic Operators   Arithmetic operators let you perform computations like addition and subtraction.

OPERATOR	OPERATION
^	Exponentiation
*	Multiplication
+	Addition
-	Subtraction
/	Division

OPERATOR	OPERATION
Mod	Modulo arithmetic
\	Integer division

Comparison Operators Comparison operators let you determine relative values, posing questions like, Is the number greater than 10? Less than another?

OPERATOR	MEANING
<	Less than
<=	Less than or equal to
<>	Not equal to
=	Equal to
>	Greater than
>=	Greater than or equal to

Concatenation Operator Use the concatenation operator to manipulate text strings.

OPERATOR	OPERATION
&	used for text string concatenation (for example: **FirstName & ", "&LastName**)

Logical Operators Use logical operators when building logic statements.

OPERATOR	OPERATION
And	Conjunction
Eqv	Equivalence
Imp	Implication
Not	Negation
Or	Disjunction (inclusive Or)
Xor	Exclusion (exclusive Or)

Pattern Matching Operator   The Pattern Matching operator is used for text searching.

OPERATOR	OPERATION
Like	String comparison

Miscellaneous Operators   The remaining operators perform a variety of functions.

OPERATOR	DESCRIPTION
!	Separates parts in an identifier; tells Access that the object name that follows it refers to a user-defined object
.(dot)	Separates parts in an identifier; precedes the name of the object, method, or property
Between…And	Determines whether the value of an expression lies within a specified range of values
In	Determines whether the value of an expression is equal to any of several values in a specified list
Is	Used with the reserved word "Null," determines whether an expression is Null.

Using Operators

You can use operators in reports, property statements, and many other places. For example, in the Voters database, adding the simple expression **>17** to the Age field's property sheet will check to make certain that voters are 18 or older, as shown on the following page.

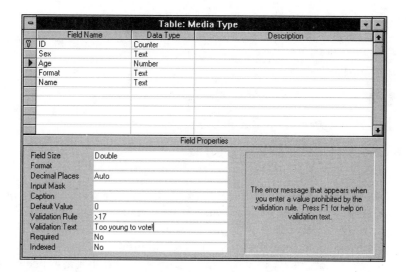

Notice that we've also added the text "Too young to vote!" to the Validation text box. This text will be displayed in a dialog box whenever someone attempts to enter an age of less than 18.

Identifiers: Field and Table Names

Identifiers help you "point" Access in the direction of the desired data. Identifiers might be the name of an object or collection of objects, a form name, a table name, a property name, etc. You must enclose an object's name in brackets when typing it in an expression; **[Unit Price]** is an example. See online help and the big books for more about identifiers.

Functions

Functions are built-in tools that can be used for specific, often complex tasks. For instance, there's a function that computes the square root of a number you specify. Other functions simply "return" current information, like the present time or date.

Functions fall into four general categories:

- Conversion
- Date/Time
- Math
- Text

Conversion functions do things like convert numbers to integers, or days of the week like Sunday to their numeric equivalent (1), etc.

Date and Time functions either perform date and time computations or they return current system dates and times. For instance, the function **Now ()** uses or returns the current date and time from your computer's built-in clock/calendar. Math functions let you perform calculations, like adding sales tax to an invoice. Text functions let you find and manipulate text. For instance, you can use them to change all of the characters to upper case in a specified field.

Literals

Literals are values you type into expressions not for the purpose of computing, but rather to be taken literally. For instance in the expression **=[Price]*1.065** the number 1.065 is a literal. In that case, the price is being multiplied literally by the number 1.065. Text is also permitted as a literal; for example, the text **"Too young to vote!"** (which we saw typed into a Validation text box a few paragraphs ago) is a literal.

Criteria

Criteria tell Access which records are of interest. You enter criteria in queries, reports and expressions. For example, **="Langer"** means you are interested in records that meet the criteria *Langer*.

Using Expressions in Reports

Most reports contain expressions. Either you put them there or a report Wizard does it for you. Take this report for instance:

Accounting

10-May-94

Account	Date	Payee	Amount
Auto:Fuel	3/21/92	RMI (TEXACO)	($30.15)
	1/30/92	UNOCAL 76	($70.00)
	2/26/92	UNOCAL 76	($110.90)
	3/21/92	UNOCAL 76	($200.00)
			($411.05)
			0.37%
Auto:Registration	6/26/92	DMV	($367.00)
			($367.00)
			0.33%
Capital	4/22/94	Background Engineers	($529.86)
	11/16/93	CS	($2,478.93)
	5/28/93	ST Research	($1,500.00)
	7/22/93	The Computer Store	($393.61)
			($4,902.40)
			4.43%
Charity	12/7/93	American Red Cross	($50.00)
	2/11/94	KLON	($50.00)
			($100.00)
			0.09%
Credit Pay	1/15/92	AMERICAN EXPRESS	($48.04)
	2/14/92	AMERICAN EXPRESS	($151.87)
	3/21/92	AMERICAN EXPRESS	($428.41)
	4/15/92	AMERICAN EXPRESS	($241.82)
	5/27/92	AMERICAN EXPRESS	($170.05)
	6/12/92	AMERICAN EXPRESS	($430.73)
	7/11/92	AMERICAN EXPRESS	($395.12)
	8/21/92	AMERICAN EXPRESS	($88.11)
	9/17/92	AMERICAN EXPRESS	($207.60)
	10/12/92	AMERICAN EXPRESS	($420.39)
	12/11/92	AMERICAN EXPRESS	($172.95)
	1/14/93	AMERICAN EXPRESS	($216.74)
	2/12/93	AMERICAN EXPRESS	($738.40)

1

Figure 38.1 shows the five expressions used to create the Accounting report.

The first expression, **=NOW()**, appears near the top left corner of the report. It tells Access to insert the current date whenever it creates a report.

There's a similar expression, **=[Page]**, in the Page Footer section of the report. It simply tells Access to place a page number in the footer. A variation of this expression will produce page numbers in the format *Page 1 of 5*. That expression is "**=**"**Page** "**&[Page]&**" of "**&[Pages].**"

FIGURE 38.1

Expressions in the
Accounting report
example

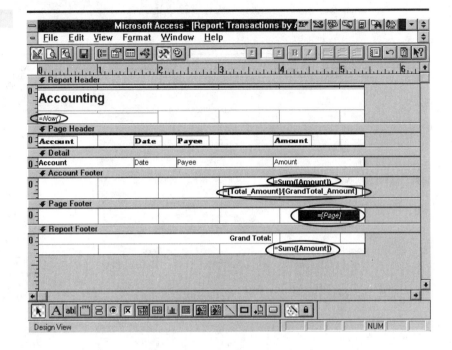

The remaining expressions in the sample report create totals, subtotals, and percentages. For example, **=Total_Amount]/[GrandTotal_Amount]** computes the percentage of total expenditures for each category's subtotal. Properties are then used to format the results as percentages.

Using Expressions in Queries

You can also add expressions to queries, or let Wizards add them for you. For instance, the "Like" expression shown on the next page will round *up* only those records with the text string *phone* in the Account field.

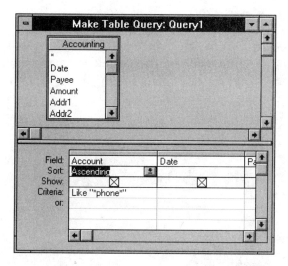

Running the query produces results like these:

It is interesting to note that Access will sometimes insert the necessary Expression minutia for you. In the last example, if I had just typed ***phone*** in the text box, Access would have taken the initiative to change it to **=Like"*phone*"**.

Using Expressions in Forms

Forms can also contain expressions, which are often added to the form's text boxes. In the following illustration, for instance, a field will use the current date as the default entry whenever a new form is created in Data Entry mode (thanks to the **=Now()** function in the Date field's Default Value property):

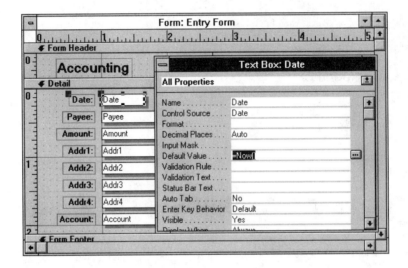

Expression Builders

While you can build expressions by simply typing them, you may want to use the Expression Builders. These often cluttered dialog boxes contain lists and buttons offering available options for use in expressions. For example, in the following illustration is the Expression Builder you'll see if you click on the Build button on a properties sheet like the one for the Date field previously discussed.

This Expression builder lets you construct expressions either by typing them directly or by clicking on the desired operators, field names, etc. To open a list, double-click on the leftmost choice of interest. For instance, to see a list of the fields available in a table, double-click first on the Tables choice, then on a table. Here, the contents of the Accounting table are visible:

> **TIP** The Expression Builder can be a little confusing. Don't forget use the Help button if you get stuck.

Option Groups, Check Boxes, and Option and Toggle Buttons

Access lets you create a variety of buttons on forms and in reports that make it easy for users to make choices. In addition, you can add, delete, and modify toolbar buttons. But let's leave the discussion of toolbar buttons to Chapter 41. For now, let's look at option groups, check boxes, and option and toggle buttons.

Buttons

Suppose you were designing an on-screen form that permitted users to choose their favorite media for watching home videos (VHS, laserdisc, etc.) Instead of having users type their choices via the keyboard, (using lord-knows-how-many different spellings of laserdisc), you could provide them with on-screen buttons like these:

The buttons on the left are called *toggle buttons*. The center controls are called *option buttons*. The rightmost controls are called *check boxes*. This can be very sophisticated—toggle buttons can include graphics. Here, for instance, pictures are displayed instead of names for the various media. (You will learn how to do this in Chapter 39.)

Access toggle buttons, option buttons, and check boxes should seem familiar. They all behave like their Windows counterparts. When you click on a toggle button, it depresses, indicating that you've activated the choice. An X in a check box or a dot in an option button indicate that it's activated.

When selected or deselected, these items *all* indicate yes/no decisions (or, in other words, true/false conditions) to the program. To use these items effectively, (and before you can add them to your database) you must understand *option groups*, so that's the next stop.

Option Groups

Option groups provide users with a finite number of choices. Option groups consist of a *group frame* which contains the buttons or boxes used to make the choices, and a *frame label*.

You can create option groups yourself or get some help from a Wizard. Option groups are often *bound* to a particular field, but they need not be. (This should make sense in a moment.) You manipulate the properties of groups, buttons, and fields to get the desired effects. This too should make sense after you've defined a group or two of your own, so let's try it.

Access

Creating Button Groups with the Wizard

Suppose you want to create a form containing buttons to be used for entering game stats for the Sybex Pirates. Using a Wizard to set up this form is so much easier than doing it by hand that it's the only way to go.

1. Start by opening the appropriate database (Pirates, in this example).

2. Choose the Forms tab.

3. Click the New button (or select a form to which you wish to add buttons):

4. Select a table or query (Game Stats, perhaps).

5. Choose either the Form Wizard or Blank Form option (Blank Form for this example). You will see a new, blank form window (or you'll see an existing form you'll modify, if that's what you are doing).

6. Make sure the Control Wizards are available at the bottom of the tool box. If they are not, choose Control Wizards in the View menu or click on the control Wizards button.

7. Click the Option Group button.

8. Point to one corner of the area where you wish to create the options group, and drag to outline the approximate desired size and shape of the group as shown here. Notice the new mouse-pointer shape:

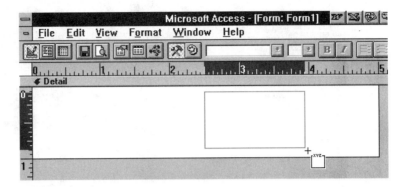

9. Type the list of options you wish to display, tabbing to move from one row to the next; then click the Next> button:

10. Pick a default entry choice if you want one, or just click Next> again, as shown in the following illustration.

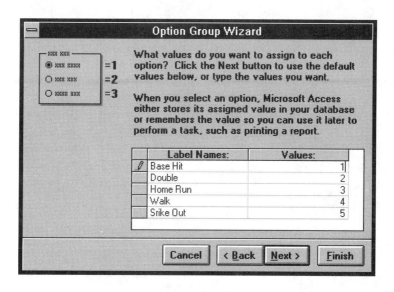

11. The Wizard suggests values for each choice. Sometimes you can change these depending upon the type of field being used. Usually the Wiz will display suggested numbers for each choice—the best (and often only way) to go. Either accept the suggestions or attempt entries of your own by typing changes in the appropriate boxes. Click Next> when you're ready to continue.

12. Pick a field to be updated (this is called binding the field). Here, the *What Happened* field will be updated. Click Next>.

13. Design the appearance of the new buttons and related elements by making the desired choices. Watch the sample change as you experiment:

Click Next>.

14. When you move to the last Wizard screen you'll be asked to name the group. This name will appear at the top of the group frame. Type a group name (**What Happened**, perhaps), and click the Finish button. You'll see the resulting group:

15. To change things in the group (like the misspelling of *Strike*), select the item of interest and change its properties. While you are at it, you can change other properties, like color and so on:

16. Move the group or its individual elements by selecting one or more items and dragging.

17. Add other fields to your form if you like, as described in earlier chapters.

18. Change fonts and type sizes if you desire. Maybe you could include graphics (as described in the next chapter).

19. When you're ready to see the finished form, click the Form View button.

20. Make some test entries and check the table you expect to be updating to make sure everything is working properly.

Notice how, in this example, the button group inserts a different number for each thing that happens (1 for base hits, 2 for doubles, etc.) You might want to create a second, related table that contains the numbers and their meanings, then use that table (rather than the space saving—but cryptic—numbers) to display the names for various events in your forms, queries, and reports.

List and Combo Boxes

Another way to automate choices is to provide lists from which users pick. This is particularly useful when there are more choices than will fit on the screen if you devote button space to each. For example, the following illustration shows a version of the Stats data entry form with a list box containing the players' names and numbers.

Creating List Boxes

To enter a player's Player Number in a record, the user scrolls to the player's name and clicks. Access then puts the player's number in the Player Number field.

There's a Wizard that helps you create lists like these. Here's how a list like the Player list is created:

1. Switch to the Design view.
2. Click the List Box button, as shown on the next page.

3. Drag to indicate the approximate desired size, shape, and location of the list box. Notice the unique mouse pointer shape:

4. The Wizard asks if you want to type entries or use values in an existing table or query to create the drop-down list. Here, an existing table will be used:

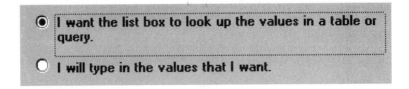

Click Next>.

5. Specify the table or query that will be the source of the items in your list:

Click Next>.

6. Choose the fields that you want to *see* in the list. More than one field can be displayed side-by-side. For instance, both the player's number and name can be shown:

7. The Wizard will show you samples of the list and ask you to size the columns. Drag or double-click to specify the desired relative widths.

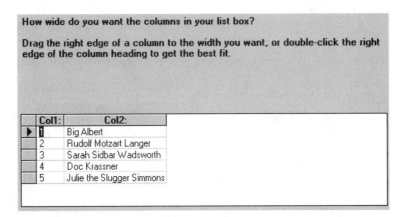

How wide do you want the columns in your list box?

Drag the right edge of a column to the width you want, or double-click the right edge of the column heading to get the best fit.

Col1:	Col2:
1	Big Albert
2	Rudolf Motzart Langer
3	Sarah Sidbar Wadsworth
4	Doc Krassner
5	Julie the Slugger Simmons

Click Next>.

8. Only one value can be entered in a field when the user makes a choice from the list. For example, here we want the Player Number to be entered, and so we specify:

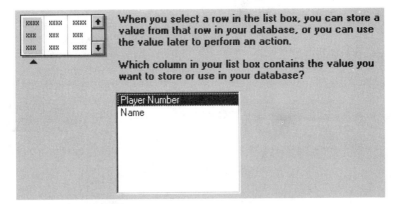

When you select a row in the list box, you can store a value from that row in your database, or you can use the value later to perform an action.

Which column in your list box contains the value you want to store or use in your database?

Player Number
Name

Then click Next>.

9. Access needs to know which field is to contain the entry. Here it will be the Player Number field:

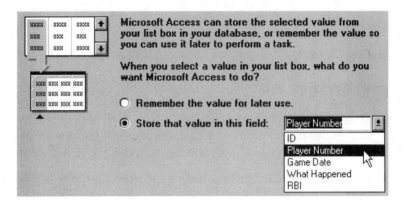

Click Next>.

10. Finally, you'll be asked to name the list. You can leave the proposed name or type one of your own; then click Finish.

11. The Wizard will switch to Design view and create a list object. Either change its location, shape, and appearance, or switch to Form view to test it.

Creating Combo Boxes

Combo boxes provide drop-down lists like this one:

The entry is visible in a small box and the arrow can be used to reveal a drop-down list from which to pick things. Combo boxes are created using techniques that are almost identical to those used for list boxes. The only difference is that you use the Combo Box Wizard. Its button is to the left of the List Box Wizard's.

Command Buttons

Command buttons let you make it obvious how to perform tasks necessary for your application. This often makes things easier for novices and pros alike. A Wizard can lead you through the steps necessary to create command buttons.

For instance, suppose you wanted to add a button to the Sybex Sluggers Game Stats data entry form that would create a new record each time someone clicked on it:

1. In Design mode, click on the Command button. Make sure Control Wizards is selected. Use the new mouse pointer to drag a button shape to the desired location on your form. The beginnings of a new, numbered button will appear (Button 29 in our illustration), and you'll see the first Wizard dialog box:

2. Choose the category of action you wish the button to perform (Record Operations in our example), and the action from the displayed list for the chosen category (Add New Record in this example). Click Next>.

3. You will be asked to specify a button name or a graphic to use on the button's face. Explore the picture options first and if you don't find one that screams the function the button will perform, consider using text, as illustrated here on the following page.

Access

CHAPTER 38

4. You will be asked to give your button a meaningful name (like New Record) or accept the automatic, incremental name (Button 30, for example). Descriptive names are nice if you wish to reuse the button design later. Click the Finish button to see your masterpiece in place.

5. Move it, resize it, change it's priorities to alter the appearance, or just leave it alone.

6. Switch to Form view and test the button.

To learn more about buttons, consult online help and the bigger books.

Action Queries

Action queries do things like delete records or make new tables, or update one field when criteria in another field are met. There are Wizards for some, and you can write your own.

You can screw up bigtime when using Action queries. There is a warning that lets you cancel an action query, but lots of people fall into the habit of clicking right through the warning without looking at it. To safeguard your data, work only on <u>copies</u> of your important databases. Then if you accidentally delete a truckload of records, you'll be able to keep your job.

Finding Duplicates with a Query Wizard

One common desire in database management is to locate duplicate (or potentially duplicate) records. Access provides an Action Query Wizard that can help you do this. It's called the *Find Duplicates Query Wizard*.

1. Begin by opening the database of interest and switching to the Query tab.

2. Pick New and then the Query Wizards button:

3. Double-click on Find Duplicates Query.

4. The Wiz will ask which table to examine (Tape Inventory in this example).

5. Tell Access which field(s) to check for duplicate entries (Movie Titles in this example).

6. Ask to see additional fields in the report if they will help you determine true duplicates from similar but not identical records. For instance, The Tape ID numbers would help here:

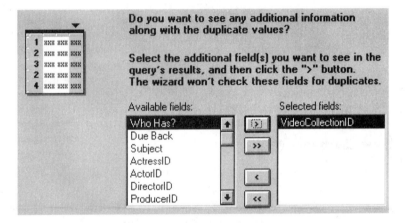

7. Click Finish, and Access will display possible duplicates, as shown on the following page.

Select Query: Find duplicates for Tape	
Movie Title	**ID**
Abbott And Costello Meet Frankenstein	115
Abbott And Costello Meet Frankenstein	17
Above The Law	116
Above The Law	18
Abyss, The	117
Abyss, The	19
Accident	118
Accident	20
Accused, The	119
Accused, The	21
Adam's Rib	120
Adam's Rib	22
Adventures In Babysitting	121
Adventures In Babysitting	23

Record: 1   of 238

As you can see by this example, Access sometimes collects records that are not exact duplicates. That's why it is important to specify enough fields to narrow the search. Eliminating duplicates always requires some careful inspection and hand work. There is no perfect automated solution. Even the pros get it wrong sometimes. Have you ever received two or more invitations from the Publishers Clearinghouse?

Other Action Queries

Other action queries you can perform include appending records to a table, creating a new table, deleting groups of records, and updating groups of records. Search online help for the topic *Action*, or check the bigger books for details. And remember to practice on backup copies of your important databases!

Macros

Macros are like mini-programs that record and automate repetitive database tasks. When you create a macro, Access will "watch" you work and record the steps you take to accomplish something. Then when you run (play back) the resulting macro, it will repeat the steps. Macros are just dumb servants, so if you don't anticipate all of the possible variations in a day's work, some mighty strange things can happen when you or others run poorly designed and untested macros. Be patient, and repeat the process you went through to create the macro; it should all work out in the end.

Sometimes, Access creates macros behind your back without you realizing it. For example, Command buttons like the ones you just read about run macros that you and the Wizard create together.

Much of what can be done with macros can also be accomplished by cleverly applying other skills you've learned already (like properly designed queries). Space prohibits a complete tour of Access macro capabilities and the underlying *Access Basic* language used to create macros, but a few highlights seem in order. Then, if you get bitten by the macro bug, and have plenty of time to invest, check out the big (really, really big) books for details.

A Sample Macro

Suppose your Vid_Stor database includes a query called *Old Tapes* that searches the Tapes Inventory table for tapes that were purchased more than a year ago. Suppose further that when rental tapes get to be a year old you want to make them available for sale. You *could* use the existing query to find the old tapes, then change the contents of each *OK to Sell?* field from No to Yes manually. Or, you could create a macro to do that for you. Before we deal with the mechanics of a macro, think about the manual steps you would follow:

1. You'd open the Old Tapes query (which would locate just the old tapes).

2. You would choose Replace... from the Edit menu.

3. Using the Replace dialog box, you'd tell Access you want it to search for *No*.

4. You'd tell Access you want to replace *No* with *Yes*.

5. You'd tell Access where to search.

6. You'd click the Replace All button to start the process.

7. You'd inspect the results. (You would, wouldn't you?)

Well, you can write an Access macro to do the first six of those seven steps for you. As is so often the case, there are even many versions of a macro that will do the same thing. Computer lovers often spend hours finding the most elegant solutions to problems. For this exercise, however, we will use the brute force approach just to make it easier to see what's going on. In the process we'll point out some potentially nasty problems.

Here are the steps for creating a macro:

1. Open the database and click on the Macros tab (if necessary), to bring it foremost.

2. Click the New button. You'll see an empty, two-column list into which you'll place commands and optional notes of explanation.

3. Click in the first Action cell and choose the first desired action. In our
example, the first thing we want to do is open a query:

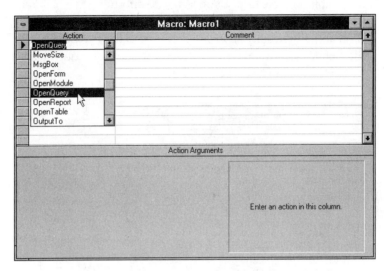

4. Action Arguments will appear in the bottom half of the dialog box. The
actual choices available will change with the type of action you have selected. In this case, we need to select a query from the resulting drop-
down list:

That's the essence of macro building; you can add additional steps, arguments, and (optionally) notes to build a reliable macro. You can add steps switch you from table to table or from one view to another, or to pick menu items. In fact, there are commands you can include in your macros to copy, delete, navigate, and do virtually anything Access can do. For example, here we are using the SendKey command to tell Access to send the equivalent of a Tab keystroke (notice how it is enclosed in braces):

Macro: Macro1	
Action	
OpenQuery	Opens the Old Tapes Query, Dyna
DoMenuItem	Open the Replace dialog box
SendKeys	Type "No" in the Find What: box
▶ SendKeys	Tab to the Replace With: box

Action Arguments	
Keystrokes	{TAB}
Wait	No

Regular keystrokes (like No or Yes) are simply typed as action arguments. Key *combinations* like (Alt+A) are sent using special characters. For example, Alt is represented by the percent sign, so to specify Alt+A you'd enter the argument %A. (See online help and the bigger books for details.)

5. When you've finished entering steps, save the macro with the File Menu's Save… command (Ctrl+S), and test it. Here's an example of a completed (but imperfect) macro:

Macro: Approve sale of old tapes	
Action	**Comment**
OpenQuery	Opens the Old Tapes Query, Dynaset contains only tapes > 1 year old
DoMenuItem	Open the Replace dialog box
SendKeys	Type "No" in the Find What: box
SendKeys	Tab to the Replace With: box
SendKeys	Type "Yes" in the Replace With: box
SendKeys	Type Alt+I to choose the All Fields option
▶ SendKeys	Type Alt+A to press the Replace All button

Action Arguments	
Keystrokes	%A
Wait	No

Do us all a favor. If you work at a nuclear power plant, don't just read this chapter and then try automating your workplace. Marketing hoopla notwithstanding, when you create macros you are <u>programming</u>. Test your work on copies of your important databases rather than the original. Dig into the big books, and get help from experienced Access Basic macro writers, at least for your first few important projects.

Troubleshooting Macros

It is often difficult to spot potential problems with macros. The strangest things can happen. For instance, in our sample macro, we asked Access to search for all occurrences of *No* in the Dynaset, and then replace *No* with *Yes*. Since the Dynaset contains only old tapes, you might think that a safe move, but look at what happened to the film titles *No Holds Barred* and *No Way Out*.

Select Query: Old Tapes		
Movie Title	**Date Acquired**	**Sell Used?**
12 Angry Men	1/5/93	Yes
20,000 Leagues Under The Sea	3/4/21	Yes
▶ Yes Holds Barred	3/3/91	Yes
Yes Way Out	1/2/93	Yes
101 Dalmatians	10/12/92	Yes
1492: Conquest Of Paradise	2/2/93	Yes

Record: 3 of 6

Ho, boy; it's drawingboard time. Remember—computers are very unimaginative, and often (under the guise of being helpful) a little quirky. For instance, you might get away with that "Swap Yes for No" trick we pulled in the Replace dialog box regularly as long as the Match Whole Field box option is selected, since it would only change things in fields where it found only the word *No* all by itself.

But the Replace dialog box, and some others, "remember" settings from their prior uses. So if, after you create your macro, you or a coworker use the Replace dialog box for some other task, changing the options, new settings may be retained, which could affect the outcome next time you run your macro, which will use the altered dialog box.

That's what happened here. We never told Access to look just in the Sell Used? field, but got away with it because the other occurrences of *No* in the database were not exact. That is to say, the occurrences of *No* in the Movie Title field had other words with them. But later, with the *Match Whole Field* option cleared, Access felt justified—*compelled*, actually, to replace all occurrences of *No* with *Yes*.

The moral? When in doubt, include instructions in your macro to specify all important options. Or better yet—unless you have the time and disposition to become a programmer, keep your day job and leave the programming to a pro. Next stop, something fun: graphics in Access.

39

Graphics
in Databases

It's a graphical world, and Access has some of the tools you need to live in it. You've already seen examples of clip art embellishing Access forms and reports. You can also insert or link charts, drawings, photos, and other graphics into records, reports, and forms. It's even possible to link multimedia files.

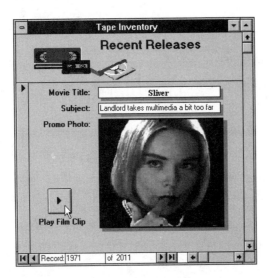

You'll spot many similarities between the use of graphics in Access and in the rest of the Office suite, but there are significant differences. Let's dig in.

Objects: Linked, Embedded, Bound, and Unbound

We might as well get this out of the way up front. In Access graphics are *objects*, so you'll need to brush up on the Object Linking and Embedding concepts explored in Chapter 3 of this book. You'll also need to know a few more terms.

All Access graphics are placed in *object frames*. Think of frames as containers for graphics and other objects. You manipulate a frame to change the size, shape, location, and cropping of the graphic it contains. (Some of the techniques will seem familiar. Others won't work as you'd expect. For example, to switch between cropping and resizing a graphic, you'll have to modify the frame's *properties* (characteristics) as you will see in a moment.)

Bound vs. Unbound

There are two types of object frames: *bound* object frames and *unbound* object frames. When graphics are stored in a *table* they are referred to as *bound objects*. For example, in Figure 39.1, the promotional photo for each film in the Tape Inventory database is a bound image.

The three pictures that make up the logo art in Figure 39.1 are examples of unbound objects.

Access

FIGURE 39.1

Bound objects are stored in tables. Unbound objects (like the logo art) are not stored in tables.

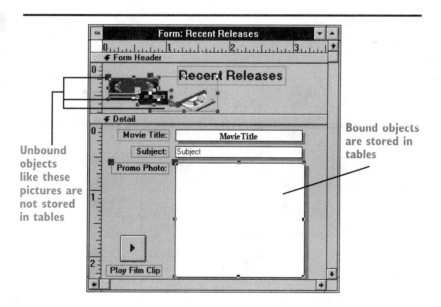

Unbound objects like these pictures are not stored in tables

Bound objects are stored in tables

Embedded vs. Linked

An Access graphic (object) can be *embedded*, meaning that it is stored within the Access database; or it can be *linked*, meaning that the object is stored in some other file, but used by Access. That should sound familiar.

As you embed photos, the size of your database file (the .mdb file) increases significantly, telling you that the graphic objects are being stored within the file itself. That is to say, embedded objects are stored with (stored within)the main database file.

Linked objects are stored outside of the Access main database file. Because Access supports OLE2, you can edit both embedded and linked graphics using the general techniques discussed in Chapter 3.

Unbound Graphics as Form and Report Embellishments

You can round up graphics from the usual sources (Office's ClipArt Gallery, art disks, etc.) and use them in Access. Graphics can be either inserted from your Clipboard or with the Insert Object... command, then resized, moved, piled one-on-top-of-the-other, etc. For example, here's a picture from the Office Clipart Gallery and a line created with the Access line tool:

Sybex Pirates
Game Stats
Entry Form

Game Date:	5/4/94
Player Number:	4
RBI:	0

What Happened
- ☐ Base Hit
- ☐ Double
- ☐ Home Run
- ☐ Walk
- ☒ Strike Out

Here are the general steps taken to create unbound graphics on a form or report:

1. Open the form or report of interest and switch to Design view.

2. If necessary, make room for the new graphics in the appropriate section (header, detail, etc.) In this example the art will be added to the Detail section of the form, but it is also common to place art in headers and footers.

3. To add an unbound object, click on the Object Frame button as shown here:

4. Note that the mouse pointer changes shape. Drag to define the desired location, size, and shape of the frame.

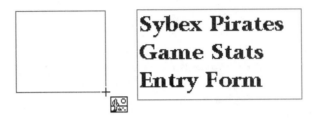

5. When you release the mouse button, Access will insert the frame and display the Insert Object dialog box, listing a choice of object sources.

6. When you release the mouse button, Access will insert the frame and display the Insert Object dialog box, listing a choice of object sources:

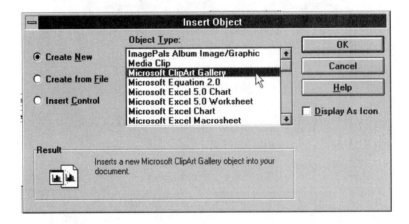

7. Pick one (Microsoft ClipArt Gallery in this example).

8. Select (or create) the desired image and return to Access. The exact steps vary with the graphic source. Check Chapter 3 and other documentation as required to see how best to insert the finished image—various techniques will work. For example, selecting and clicking OK or double-clicking both work in the Microsoft Clipart Gallery:

9. Back in the Access Design View window, you'll see all or part of your graphic surrounded by the frame handles. The function of the handles changes based on the frame's Size Mode selection in the Frame's Layout Properties dialog box. Reach the dialog box by choosing Properties... from the View menu with the frame selected:

Clip displays as much of the object as will fit in the frame. Stretch makes the graphic fit the frame's shape and size, distorting the graphic in the process. Zoom re-sizes the image proportionally to fit either the height or width, sometimes leaving part of the frame empty.

10. If necessary, change the Size Mode property and drag the frame handles to get the desired effect.

11. Switch to Form View (or Print Preview when working with reports) to see how the project is coming. Switch back to Design view to alter your work or to continue designing. For example, to reposition a graphic, switch to Design view, select the graphic, move the mouse pointer until it turns into a hand, then use it to move the frame.

Bound Graphics in Records

Sometimes it's useful to have graphics for each record. The promotional photos and film clips are examples in the Vid_Tape database. Employee databases sometimes contain photos. Real estate databases can contain photos, floor plans, videotape walk-throughs, etc.

The technical realities of using this capability are sometimes lost by the folks marketing the products—it's not quite as simple as it may seem from the demos—so you'll want to experiment to see if you're ready for big graphics-intensive databases and visa versa. There are some pitfalls. For starters, collections of photos and multimedia "show" files consume *acres* of disk space, and they can slow even the most enthusiastic Pentium machine to a crawl. Moreover, it's been my experience (even when working with the final version of Access and other applications) that the OLE links required to pull this off can be a little funky at times. They might hang your machine, or produce unexpected formatting results, for example. But if you are in the mood to experiment, come along on this short journey. The steps are very similar to those used to include unbound graphics.

Suppose you want to collect and display promotional photos in a videotape database.

1. Start by opening table that will contain the bound graphic or other element (the Vid-Stor Tape Inventory table in this example).

2. Switch to Design view.

3. Add the necessary field or fields (three fields in this example, one for video clips, one for photos, and a third for Excel charts).

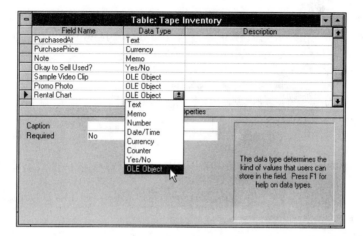

4. Switch to the Table view and select the record and field where you want to insert your first bound graphic. For example, here we will be inserting a photo into the Promo Photo field of the *Hot Enough for June* record in the Tape Inventory table:

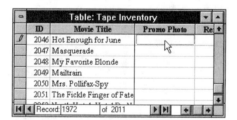

5. Get thee to a graphic of interest. You can use the Access Insert Object command, or launch another application like Paintbrush, then copy the image to the Clipboard. One or another (or many) of the techniques described in Chapter 3 will work, depending upon the mood of the "Different Way to Work" gods.

6. Switch to the Access table, if you are not already there, and insert the graphic (this will happen for you automatically in some cases, other times you'll need to use Paste Special....

7. You'll know you are on the right track if a description of the item you've attempted to insert appears in the table. You might see the word *Picture*, for instance, as seen here:

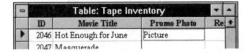

8. Since you can't see graphics in Table view, you'll need to switch to a form or report containing a frame for the graphic—or you can create one. For instance, this Form design has a bound field frame for the Promo Photo:

9. In Form or Report view, your graphics should appear, all cropped or zoomed or whatever, depending on how you've set the Picture Properties back in Design view. Here's a typical record containing a bound graphic in both Table and Form views.

You can use similar techniques to include charts, movies, or other objects from various applications. For example, here's a collection of Excel charts bound to Access records:

In this case Excel Chart objects were inserted into Access records. Again, your mileage may vary. Combining object linking, embedding, and Access is all going to take some experimenting. Even the big books can't cover all of the possible approaches and pitfalls, but take a look at them for more coverage.

Adding Graphics to Buttons

Here's a quick trick you can use to spruce-up buttons on your Access screens. Remember the *Play Film Clip* command button in the Recent Releases form?

It started out life as a boring Command button like this:

To change its face, all you need to do is:

1. Select the button in Design view.

2. Visit the button's properties and choose Picture.

3. Scroll through the resulting list of button names, clicking once on those that sound interesting and watching the sample as you work:

4. When you see a button you like, click OK.

5. The graphic will appear on the button's face.

If you don't like the "stock" selection of button faces, you can roam your hard disk looking for other bitmap graphics (the extension for these is BMP) by using the Browse button. For instance, you can use the bitmap graphics in your Windows directory as button faces, or you can create your own bitmap graphics in a paint program. Then follow steps 1 through 5 above.

Graph Wizard: Charting Your Data

The Access Chart Wizard lets you use Microsoft Graph to create graph objects that can be included in Access reports. Once created, the charts can be further embellished using Microsoft Graph itself.

Suppose, for instance, that you wanted to create a new form containing a graph depicting video media preference by sex. Here are the *general* steps.

Access

(Check online help, the other information on Microsoft Graph in Chapter 18, and the big books for more details on using this powerful feature.)

1. Start a new form design.

2. Click on the Graph button.

3. Drag to define the desired size and shape of the finished graph. When you release the mouse you'll see the Graph Wizard dialog box:

4. Double-click to select the fields you wish to include in your graph (Sex and Format in our example).

5. Answer the other questions posed by the Wizard, clicking Next > to move forward. The questions you are asked will change based on your previous choices.

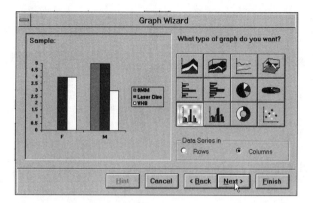

6. Watch the sample develop as you work. Use the < Back button if you want to try different approaches.

7. When you click Finish, the Wizard will insert a graph object in your report, like the one shown here:

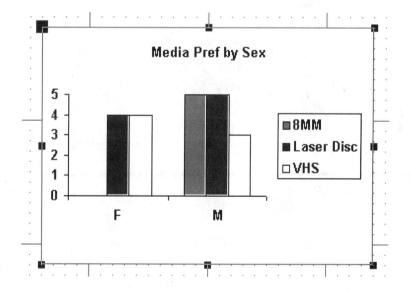

8. To modify the graph, double-click on it and you will see a Microsoft Graph window like this one.

Access

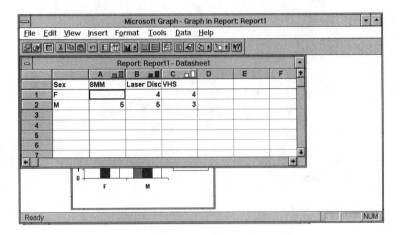

9. Use Graph's options to change the appearance of the finished graph object. For instance, here I've used the Chart Type command and the Options button to change to stacked columns:

40

Attaching, Importing, and Exporting Records

f requently the biggest consumer of your time when you're creating a new database is data entry—just typing in all of the information for each record. Access provides ways to minimize this if you've already put the data on disk for some other purpose. For example, if you've already typed a parts list in Word, you might be able to avoid re-keyboarding all those part numbers and descriptions. With Access you can *import* data from other databases, spreadsheets, and word processing documents, or you can *attach* non-Access files as tables.

Moreover, you'll sometimes want to *export* all or some of your Access records for use by some other program. For example, you might want to export names and mailing addresses to be used in a Word Print Merge project, or export financial transaction details for an Excel budgeting project. Here are some examples of data sources and destinations:

- Other Microsoft Access database files
- Microsoft FoxPro version 2.0, 2.5, and 2.6 database files
- Paradox version 3.x and 4.x tables
- dBASE III and IV files
- Btrieve tables
- SQL database files
- Microsoft Excel and Lotus 1-2-3 spreadsheets
- Fixed-width and delimited text files
- Microsoft Word for Windows mail-merge data files (export only)
- Most other applications that can create and/or read fixed-length records
- Most other applications that can create and/or read comma-separated or tab-separated records

While Access makes this all pretty easy, there are some potential "gotchas." Welcome to Chapter 40.

  Once you "upgrade" an Access database with a newer version, for example, the database will not be usable "as is" with older versions. That is to say, you can't simply open a version 2 database with Access version 1.0 or 1.1. You'll have to export the tables from version 2 to the older versions. (Access will convert the tables in the course of exporting.) To avoid confusion and inconvenience, you might need to purchase new software for your home and coworkers. Test before making the commitment, and <u>always make backup copies of your old databases</u> and store them in a safe place before you attempt any kind of conversion, importing, or exporting.

Using Records from Earlier Access Versions

If you or your coworkers have created Access version 1.x database files, you will probably want to convert them to Access 2 database files. This will make it possible for you to use the new features in version 2, and probably will improve the overall performance of the database. Conversion will not affect attached tables. Attached tables will need to be converted separately if that's your intention. The steps for converting from Access version 1.x to version 2 are pretty straightforward:

1. Back up your old database file and confirm that the backup was successful.

2. Quit the old version of Access (thereby closing the old database file).

3. If you are on a network, make sure no one else is using the database you plan to convert. (Access will display a message alerting you to the fact that there is another user; if this happens, you will either need to ask the other user to close the file or wait until he or she is finished with it.)

4. Run the new version of Access (2.x).

Access

5. Choose Convert Database from the Access File menu.

6. Select the database file you wish to convert.

7. Give the database file a new name or, if you choose to keep the old name, specify a new location (different subdirectory) for it to occupy once it's converted.

8. Click OK to run the converter.

9. Convert related database files as well if that's part of the plan.

10. Test the converted database.

Testing after Conversion

It is important to test your converted database file(s). Access version 2 does some things differently than earlier versions. Look for the obvious. Are all of your records there? Do the queries work properly? How about reports, buttons, macros, etc. Do they run properly and match earlier results with the old database? Can other networked users access the new database? (Did you move it to a new subdirectory on the server and forget to tell them?) Poke at the security features and make certain only users with a need to know have access.

If you are an advanced user/tester, pay particular attention to the more advanced issues:

- Attached tables
- Validation rules for data entry and integrity checking
- Fields containing null characters and zero-length text strings
- The "Visible" property
- Fields containing the backquote character (')
- List boxes
- Subforms

If you have data that was created with other programs (like dBASE, Paradox, or Microsoft Word) you can convert (import) the data to Access tables or you can *attach* the unconverted tables so that Access can use them without converting. (This is a good idea when some users will be working with the data with Access, while others will be working with the data in the original program—dBASE, Paradox, or Word, perhaps.) In choosing whether to import or attach, there are important trade-offs to consider.

Importing definitely has its advantages. Converted databases generally run faster than attached ones. There will be fewer compatibility issues once the data have been converted. And some changes that you can make to Access tables can't be made to attached tables. For instance, you can't create Access Primary Keys in attached tables (although you can sometimes use keys from the creating database application).

Attaching, however, lets you keep the data in its old format for use with the old tools. For example, if you attach a Word file, you can still use Word to make changes to the file. Or, if most of the people in your company still use dBASE, you can share the data with them and even alter it without the need for them to purchase Access.

Consider testing the same database using both converted and attached tables to see which best-suits your needs.

TIP

If possible, test with a few hundred or even a few thousand records. Smaller samples will not give you a good indication of how quickly (or slowly) the database (as it's designed) will perform in the real world. If you test with tens-of-thousands or millions of records and the design is such that the thing runs slowly, the wait will seem endless.

Attaching Other Databases as Tables

Let's look at the general steps for attaching a non-Access database as a table, then turn to importing as an alternative. To attach:

1. Open the Access database to which you plan to attach the non-Access database. (Or open a new Access database if you are starting from scratch.) In either case, bring the Table Tab Forward and choose Attach Table from the File menu, as shown in Figure 40.1.

2. Tell Access the type and version of source file (Paradox 3.x, dBASE IV, etc.):

3. Locate the file you wish to attach:

4. If the file has an index (built by its application) sometimes Access can use it. Locate the index file if there is one and attempt to attach it, as shown on the following page.

5. Click Attach. Faster than you can recite the Academy Awards voting rules, there you'll have it—an attached non-Access database, usable as an Access table. In this case we've attached 307,659 FCC radio frequency assignment records:

6. Notice the listing for this attached table in the Table tab of the Database window. The → with the DB preceding the table name (FREQUENC) tells you that this table is an attached database.

Working with Attached Tables

You can do a surprising number of things to an attached table, including add, change, and delete records. Remember this when you are experimenting, particularly when working with someone else's database (or when permitting someone else to attach *your data* to *their* Access databases). Normally, Access will obey security rules if they've been properly established. But again—back up and test.

  To make certain that Access will not make your existing databases unusable with their original applications, <u>test</u> by using backup copies. After using them with Access (deleting, adding, and modifying records, for example), try to reuse the altered databases with their original program (dBASE, or whatever). As long as you're doing this with backup copies, if and when something goes wrong, you'll be covered—you'll still have the original.

There are, naturally, things you cannot do with an attached database. For example, you cannot change certain of the table's properties. Access warns you of this whenever you switch to Design view while in an attached table:

You cannot change field names (although you can add *captions* for your own use. And you can't change field types (from Text to Number, for instance).

But you can do things like change the appearance of numbers in the table. For example, in some circles, it's considered fashionable to display radio frequencies rounded to four decimal places. This you can do:

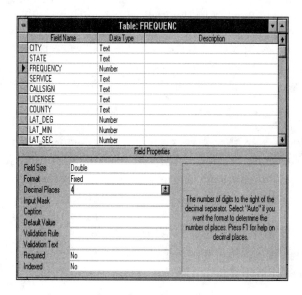

Watch the note box to the right of properties as you select them. Red notes tell you that you can't make property changes, blue notes tell you that you can. (User of monochrome displays and the colorblind will need to break down and actually *read* the on-screen notes.)

Incidentally, when Access warns that you can't make many specific property changes, it often lets you enter your illegal desires in the various property boxes, then scolds you and ignores the forbidden requests when you attempt to switch back to Table view.

Importing Data from dBASE and Other DBMS Programs

As you read earlier, Access almost always performs more quickly when using imported (as opposed to attached) data. Let's look at the general steps for importing a non-Access database as a table. The steps vary somewhat based on the database that created the original database, so we'll leave those intricacies to online help and the bigger books.

1. Make sure you have enough extra room on your hard disk for a new version of the database file, since the Import feature makes a completely new copy of all your records.

2. Open the Access database to which you plan to import the non-Access database. (Or open a new Access database if you are starting from scratch.) With the Table Tab top-most, choose Import from the File menu.

3. Tell Access the type and version of source file (Paradox 3.x, dBASE IV, etc.)

4. Locate the file you wish to attach, changing the List Files of Type, if necessary. For instance, to see just Word files, pick Word Documents (*.DOC).

5. Click Import. In a while (perhaps a *long* while) Access will convert the database and place its name in the table list.

6. Notice the listing for this converted table in the Table tab of the Database window. There is no → or DB preceding the table name (FREQUENC) because you've created a real Access table.

7. Examine the table, create indexes if necessary (see chapter 41), and set up desired queries, forms, reports, etc.

8. Once satisfied with the conversion (and only then, and only if you've backed up the old database) you can delete the old database from your hard disk or the server unless you will need it again with the original application (dBASE, or whatever).

Importing Delimited and Fixed-Length Records

The computer industry has established a number of data format standards over the past decades. The intent has been to enable transfer of data between competitive systems. Even antique programs and scientific instruments usually offer ways to export their data as *comma-separated* or *tab-separated* or *fixed-length* records.

Tab- and comma-separated records use tab marks or commas to separate fields. For instance tab-separated records might look like this:

```
Ruldolph{Tab}Langer{Tab}SYBEX, Inc.{CR}
Bob{Tab}Wernikowski{Tab}U. S. Department of Redundancy Dpt.{CR}
```

A *comma-separated* record almost always includes quotation marks around text so that commas used in the data aren't confused with the commas used for separation. So comma-separated records might look like this:

```
"Ruldolph","Langer","SYBEX, Inc." {CR}
"Bob","Wernikowski","U. S. Department of Redundancy Dpt."{CR}
```

Fixed-length records store the same number of characters for each record, even if this means filling with spaces. You can specify desired field lengths in the Import/Export Setup dialog box. There are usually no separators as such. Here's an example of fixed-length records. Notice what happens when an entry is too long to fit the fixed-width:

```
RuldolphLanger SYBEX, Inc. {CR}
BobWernikowski U. S. Department o{CR}
```

Access can import data using any of these standards. You can use this imported data to create new tables or you can append it to existing tables. Here are the general steps:

1. Open the database to which you want to add the records (or create a new one).

2. Choose Import from the Access File menu.

3. Select the type of file you'd like to import—either Text (Delimited) or Text (Fixed Width):

4. Locate the file to be imported and click the Import button:

5. When you see the Import Options dialog box, click the Options >> button to see the full range of choices.

6. Some programs export field names as the first row of an exported file. If you want to import that first row and have Access use it to create field names for a new table, click to place an X in the First Row Contains Field Names box.

7. Tell Access if you want to create a new file or append the records being imported to an existing table. (Sometimes it is easier to troubleshoot before the import step, then append the cleaned-up data after inspecting it.)

8. If the incoming data has unusual text delimiting characters, change the default Text Delimiter setting. Choose the appropriate Field Separator character (usually comma or tab).

9. Tell Access how incoming dates and times are organized (whether there will be leading zeros, etc.).

10. Save the import specification, if you plan to reuse it later, by clicking the Save As button.

11. When you're ready to import, click OK

12. Inspect the imported records.

13. Create a primary key if there isn't one already, and have Access index one or more fields if you like. (See Chapter 41.)

Import Error Tables

If all goes well, you will be notified that the import was successful. But if any of the data you imported was flawed, you'll get an alert. For example, if there is text in a numeric field Access will spot it. Data that shouldn't be duplicated in a field will also cause an alert. There are many potential problems. Here's a typical report:

When problems are spotted, Access creates a table containing the faulty records and places the table in your Database Table list:

Open the problem report table and have a look. For instance, here's the Import Error table from our example:

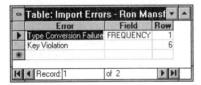

Since the error notes can be a little cryptic, it's often useful to look at the actual file you tried to import. Here we've opened it in Microsoft Word:

```
TERR. OF GRA  →  US      →      42·MHz    →  CF  →  WSM·79  →  SOUTH·CENTRAL
TERR. OF GRA  →  US      →      5925.0000 →  CF  →  WSM·79  →  SOUTH·CENTRAL
TERR. OF GRA  →  US      →      6425.0000 →  CF  →  WSM·79  →  SOUTH·CENTRAL
TERR. OF GRA  →  US      →      10700.0000 → CF  →  WSM·79  →  SOUTH·CENTRAL
DALLAS    →    US        →      2470.3000 →  IP  →  WEG534  →  MOBIL·OIL·TELCC
¶
```

The first reported error (Type Conversion Failure in the FREQUENCY field of Row 1) resulted from text (MHz) in what should be a numeric field. The second error—Key violation—resulted from that unwanted Paragraph mark at the end of the data being imported—Access confused this with an empty record.

 TIP When you're done with the error table you can delete it by selecting its name in the Table list and pressing the Delete key.

Importing Data from Spreadsheet Files

Access will attempt to import data from a variety of spreadsheet formats including Excel, Lotus 1-2-3, and clones thereof. Use the same importing techniques just described, except choose the appropriate spreadsheet file type when given the opportunity. (You can specify just a range to be imported if you don't want the whole spreadsheet.) Access attempts to name fields and pick appropriate data types based on the spreadsheet's contents and specifications. If you don't like the results, you can always change the data types later, by altering the appropriate Access table properties.

Importing Data from Word Files

To import Word files, either save the files as text and use the text importing techniques described earlier in this chapter, or take the following steps.

1. Place the Word data in Word tables organized in the same way as tables in your Access database file.

2. Copy from the Word table to your Clipboard.

3. Switch to the Access table window.

4. Select the first field in the "new" record at the end of your Access table.

5. Select Paste Append from the Edit menu . Access will import each Word table row as a record.

Exporting Access Data

Exporting is much like importing in reverse. Here are the general steps:

1. Open the Access database file containing the data you wish to export.

2. Choose Export from the Access File menu.

3. Specify the desired export format:

4. Use the Select Microsoft Access Object dialog box to determine which records will be exported. For example, if you choose a table, the entire table's contents will be exported. Selecting a query will export the results of that query.

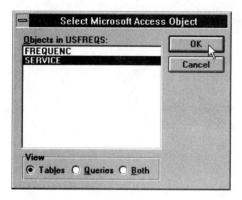

5. Specify a name and location for the new file Access will create when it exports:

6. Tell Access how you want the data formatted (types of delimiters, etc.).

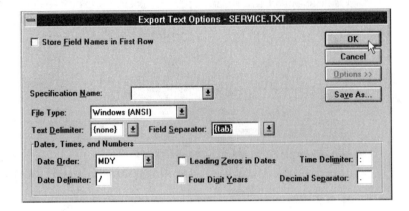

7. Click OK.

8. Check the finished file with an application that can read it, like MS Word.

Access Records as Word Merge Source Data

You can use Access records as Microsoft Word Merge data sources, making it possible to create personalized Word form letters and other documents containing Access data. Word has a Wizard that you can use for this purpose. It is described in Chapter 12. Alternatively, you can use the Merge It toolbar button. Consult online help and the bigger books for details.

Analyze with Excel

There are times when it might be helpful to export Access records to create Excel worksheets. You can export the contents of a datasheet, form, or report. The resulting file will have a file name that ends in .XLS, and you'll be able to open the file with Excel. Use the Output to MS Excel toolbar button to create Excel files. See the bigger books for details.

Access and SQL

Access is SQL-savvy; it can both use and create SQL-style data. That is to say, if your computer is properly connected to a network, Access can work with external, compatible Structured Query Language databases like those resident on Microsoft SQL or ORACLE servers. Not all SQL servers are Microsoft Access compatible.

Before Access can work with SQL server data, you or your network administrator will need to run the Open Database Connectivity (ODBC) Setup program that came with Microsoft Access. Moreover, ODBC drivers are required. Again, you'll probably need assistance from your network support people to install the appropriate driver software on your computer. Finally, you will need to be granted permission to use the appropriate SQL databases.

Unfortunately, space does not permit full coverage of this topic, so you will need to check with the big books and your network administrator if you plan to use Access for SQL tasks.

Access

41

Troubleshooting, Maintaining, and Protecting Databases

$\int$ etting up a database is just the beginning. You must maintain it, protect it, and occasionally fix it. Welcome to the real world, and the last chapter of database ownership.

We'll look at ways to speed up database operations, troubleshoot common problems, and set up security restrictions. We will start with some general troubleshooting tips first, and then turn to speed and security issues.

Troubleshooting

Kaaboom! ...Always when you are in a hurry, some cryptic message fills your screen. "Can't do this. Can't do that. Inappropriate data type." Relational databases are perhaps the most complex computer organisms that "average" users are permitted to alter, and that means you're as likely to run into trouble as to have things go smoothly.

The first thing to realize is that keeping your database designs simple is often better. If you design a complex, show-offish, gee-whiz database and then spend the rest of your life trying to make it work or explaining the missing data and faulty reports, you are not a more productive worker. (And you know what happens to even the marginally unproductive these days.) So step one is to *keep it simple*. If things don't work well when they're automated, rethink them. Imagine a peaceful Japanese rock garden and create the computer equivalent.

Getting Help in a Hurry

Okay, you can't simplify things any further. You are going about your business and up jumps the devil—an alert box like the example in the middle of Figure 41.1.

FIGURE 41.1

Read error messages carefully. Get online help if necessary.

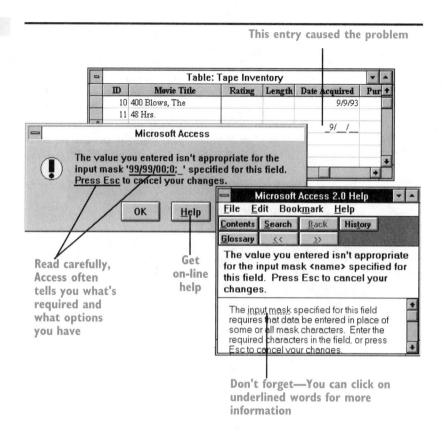

This entry caused the problem

Read carefully, Access often tells you what's required and what options you have

Get on-line help

Don't forget—You can click on underlined words for more information

In Figure 41.1 the date entered does not match the required format for the field. If you click OK and then try to do anything other than fix the date at this point, you'll probably see the error message again, as if you're trapped in a vicious circle. The alert box has given you an escape route, however, by telling you that you can press *Esc*. Read error messages carefully; they're there to help you. And don't forget to check the online help.

Common Error Messages and What They Mean

There are a few messages that you'll see so often that it is worth reading about them here. They are particularly common when designing new queries, forms, and reports, but you'll see some of them at other times.

Referential Integrity Warnings

Referential integrity messages come in a number of varieties, but they are all telling you something similar: "You can't do that because of forced integrity relationships that you or the database designer have specified."

For instance, in the Pirates database, if you try to delete a player from the roster (the 1994 Sybex Pirates table) and the player has records in the Game Stats table, and *if you've specified referential integrity*, Access won't let you delete the player. You'll get a message like this one:

That's because if you delete the record for a player, the reports and queries that look up players' names won't find a name for the deleted player. You have perhaps three choices at this point: Don't delete the player, turn off referential integrity, or rethink the design of your database so it doesn't do this type of "look-up."

Can't Edit or Save Changes to a Record

You'll get various messages like this one about not being able to make or save changes to records:

The reason might be any of several. The changes you are attempting may break Access's rules (like trying to type text in a numeric field), for example, or you may not have permission to change the record in question. Contact the owner of the database or your network administrator if you think you should be able to make changes to shared records and you can't.

Can't Change a Property Data Type or Field Size

There are many things that stand in the way of changing established Properties, data types, and field designs. If a field is related to others, you'll often see messages like this:

Your best bet is to delete the offending relationships, change the data type and/or size, then reestablish the relationships.

Can't Change a Table, Form or Query Design

If you try to switch to Design view and you see a message like the one that follows (offering read-only access), there can be a number of reasons.

Perhaps the most common problem is that you have a query or form open that is bound to the table. Simply close your Query or Form window and you can try again. If you share this database with others over a network, perhaps someone else is using the table, or a form or query that is bound to the table. Try to make design changes when others are not using the database. Finally, in a secured database, you may not have permission to make design changes. Contact the database owner or network administrator for help.

The Database Documentor

There is a Database Documentor in Access that will print out a description of your database, including field names, properties, relationships, and more. You should be able to reach it from the Add-ins command on the Access File menu:

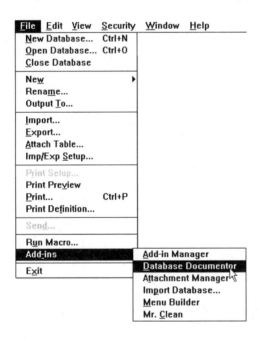

If you don't see this choice on your menu, run the Access Installer again and add it. Documentor reports can get quite long, so to avoid having to read through a lot of stuff you don't care about, you can specify which items you'd like to document:

Use the Options button to fine-tune the report. When you run the report, it may span many pages (the simple Pirates report was 5 pages long). Figure 41.2 shows just one typical page.

It's a good idea to run a final version of the report and store it after your database is up, running, and tested. Then you can refer back to it if future changes foul things up. The finished report may be displayed in Print Preview, giving you the option to print or not to print, or even *what* to print.

TIP You can print the details of a single, specific object (a form, or table or whatever) by choosing Print Definition from the File menu.

Recovering a Damaged Database

If you do not close your database and Access properly (because a power failure has crashed your system, for example), there may be damage to the database. Usually, Access detects this damage the next time you attempt to open the database and automatically attempts to repair it. If this does not happen, you can

FIGURE 41.2

A typical report page

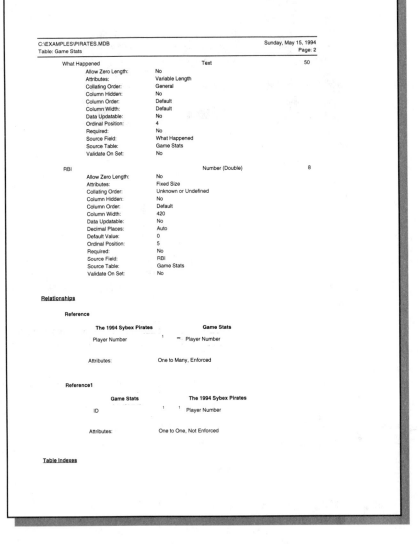

choose Repair Database from the opening File menu. Choose the database of interest from the list that appears, then click OK:

With luck the computer gods will give you back your data. On rare occasions you might need to revert to your most recent backup of the database (you *do* have a backup, right?) and re-enter or re-edit changes made since the last backup.

 WARNING   Shared databases have an important file called the SYSTEM.MDA file. This is where security settings live. It's a good idea to back up this file regularly. Otherwise, you'll need to reinstall Access and reestablish security privileges if the file gets damaged or lost.

Maintaining Your Databases

Databases are like gardens. They need care and attention. Besides the obvious task of keeping records up to date (changing people's phone numbers, etc.) there are some other things you can do to "tune up" your masterpiece.

Indexing

If you've ever waited endlessly while Access slogs through ten thousand records looking for Mr. Right, it may be because the database has grown to the point where one or more fields need *indexing*. The process helps Access keeps track of where records are stored in a way that speeds searches and other tasks.

For example, this radio frequency database has a number of text fields and contains almost 55,000 records.

CITY	STATE	FREQUENCY	SERVICE	CALLSIGN	LICENSEE
HOUSTON	US	1.7050	RS	KJV862	RACAL DATACOM INC
HOUSTON	US	1.7050	RS	KNDV993	WIMPOL INC
HOUSTON	US	1.7050	RS	KNDV993	WIMPOL INC
HARAHAN	US	1.7054	RS	KB64186	OFFSHORE NAVIGATION INC
HARAHAN	US	1.7060	RS	KB64186	OFFSHORE NAVIGATION INC
HOUSTON	US	1.7070	RS	KNEP618	NCS INTERNATIONAL INC
HOUSTON	US	1.7070	RS	KNEP618	NCS INTERNATIONAL INC

Record: 1 of 54979

Searching for a text string in an *unindexed* field using a 60MHz Pentium machine takes about two minutes, while doing the same search on the same field after *indexing* takes less than two *seconds*....

Here are the steps for indexing a field:

1. Open the database file.
2. Select the table containing the field to be indexed.
3. Switch to Design view.
4. Select the field to be indexed (Frequency in this example).

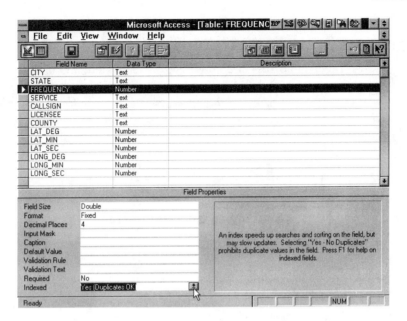

5. In the field properties area of the dialog box, click in the Indexed area and choose the desired indexing option—Yes or No (duplicates permitted or not).

6. Change other field properties (index other fields by repeating steps 1-5, for instance).

7. Save the table (Ctrl+S).

8. Switch back to Datasheet view and test the results. Remember, you can always "unindex" a field if you like.

Index Strategies

Since indexes take extra disk space, and slow down some data entry and importing tasks, don't get carried away. Experiment on a field or two, and only add indexes to fields that you regularly search in or sort. Sorting and searching speed should improve noticeably.

Compacting a Database

Over time, databases get flabby. As you delete, add, and modify records the data gets fragmented. Compacting makes a smaller, leaner, better-performing database, but the process requires enough disk space for the old file and the new one, at least temporarily. Here are the steps:

1. Close the database file.

2. Make sure there is enough disk space for an additional copy of the .MDB file nearly the size of your existing database file.

3. In a multiuser environment, make sure others have closed the database file.

4. Consider backing up the database file to separate media (tape or whatever) just in case.

5. From the initial Access File menu (the one you see when you first launch Access) choose Compact Database....

6. Pick the database file you wish to compact:

7. Choose a destination name (and location) for the compacted database file. It can be the same name as the old database, in which case, Access will delete the old database file automatically after compacting. You'll be asked to confirm the overwriting. (Unless you have made a backup of the database, it's a good idea to use a new name for the new file.)

8. Unless Access has done so for you in step 7, delete the old database file.

Security: Protecting Your Information

Some information needs to be kept private. If you doubt this, post a list of employees and their salaries on a bulletin board and see what happens. The very things that make Access easy to use make it possible for inquiring minds to know things they shouldn't. You'll need different levels of security for different situations. Typical security requirements include:

- Preventing others from opening your Access databases with Access whether sitting at their computer or yours

- Preventing others from opening your Access databases with other programs (like Word or dBASE)

- Preventing others from changing or deleting data

- Preventing others form changing or deleting database design elements (forms, relationships, etc.)

CHAPTER 41

TIP Check with your network administrator if you have questions about Microsoft Access security levels. Also be aware that some organizations have policies regarding passwords. Make certain that you understand your organization's policies.

A Security Overview

When you create a new database, it starts out life available to everyone. You secure a database by removing permission to do various things (like open tables, change records, etc.) There are five concepts you'll need to understand if you wish to use the various possible levels of Access security:

- Workgroups
- User Accounts
- Group Accounts
- Administrator and Owner Accounts
- Permission Assignments

Jeez. More buzzwords and concepts. Complexity is the price of privacy.

Workgroups, User Accounts, and Group Accounts let you specify which information can be seen and changed by various people in your organization. While normally associated with network operations, these security tools can also be used if different people share your computer, or if you are afraid that people might sit at your desk for the electronic equivalent of after-hours dumpster-diving.

Workgroups

Access Workgroup information lets you specify which people can potentially work with your database. When you installed Access, the installation program created a default Workgroup with some generic entries (accounts, actually) with names like Admins and Guest. You can add more specific accounts as you'll see in a moment. While it is possible to create and use Workgroups other than the default one (the one created by the installation program), let's leave those gory details to the bigger books.

User Accounts

Users are people that can have access to your database. You are a user. Different users can have different levels of security clearance. The information about a specific user's privileges is stored in a *User Account*. You will see how to create these in a moment.

Group Accounts

Groups make it easy to set up and change specific security levels for more than one person simultaneously. for instance, you might let everyone in accounting *see* employee payroll information, but only let accounting *managers* change pay rates. The quick way to do this is to split accounting people into two groups (managers and bookkeepers, for instance), then assign different security levels to the two *groups* instead of to each individual user. The information about a group's privileges is stored in a *Group Account*. When you install Access some group accounts are automatically set up. These include:

- Admins
- Users
- Guests

Permission Assignments

Permission assignments are stored with your database. They collect the nitty-gritty details like who gets to see and change what. Different permissions can be granted to individual users, but it is often better to grant permissions to groups, then add selected people to the appropriate group(s). See the big books for more information on personalizing permission.

Owners and Administrators

By default, the person that creates a new database is its *owner*. The owner can always have complete run of the database, and is free to make changes, deletions, redesign things, and so on. By default, the Admin account is the owner of each database when it is created, and remains the owner unless you change ownership. Unless you want the administrator of your system to be able to modify the database *you* have created, you should change the ownership of the database to yourself. Remember, as a matter of policy, some organizations require that multiple people know passwords. This way, if you get hit by a commuter train or win the lottery, your fellow employees will be able to pick up where you left off. Be certain you understand and adhere to your organization's policies in this regard.

WARNING Since the initial Admin account is exactly the same for each copy of Access shipped by Microsoft, it is important that you change the Administrator (owner) for your system, and create unique passwords for these accounts. Until you do this, everyone will have access to your data. You'll see how to change Admin and ownership information next.

Creating and Changing an Administrator Account

To change the Administrator account, follow these steps:

1. Open any Access database file.

2. Choose Users from the Security menu.

3. Click the New button.

4. Type a new account name and a personal ID. (account names can be 20 characters long and can include most characters except for " / | [ ] : | < > + = ; , ? * or ' (I know it's limiting, but don't shoot me— I'm just the messenger.) The personal ID can contain a minimum of four and a maximum of 20 characters:

  Write down exact account names and personal ID numbers and store them in a safe place. Remember: Capitalization counts!

5. Click OK.

6. When you see the Users dialog box again, it will contain the new account name. Select Admins from the Available Groups list and click Add>>, then click Close.

Now that you've activated security, you can start to take *real* control.

Forcing Log-on Challenges

Until you activate the Logon feature, anybody can run Access just by starting it, thanks to the Admin account. The default password for the Admin account is—well, there is no password.

You need to change that next.

1. Open a database file if there isn't one open already.

2. Choose Change Password from the Security menu.

3. Don't type anything in the Old Password portion of the resulting dialog box:

4. Tab to move to the New Password blank (or click on it) and enter the desired password, which can be up to 14 characters long and include anything except the Null character. (Most of us don't know how to type that, anyway.) Incidentally, Access cares about capitalization here.

5. Tab to the Verify box (or click on it) and reenter the new password using identical spelling and capitalization.

6. Click OK.

7. If all goes well the dialog box will disappear and not much else that is visible will happen. If you get a dialog box telling you "No permission for (account name)", you mistyped either the password or verification, or someone else got there first and changed the password from nothing to something.

8. Quit Access to test the log on feature.

Be sure you know the name and password including capitalization. Write it down and seal it in a mayo jar.

 To remove password protection, repeat steps 1 through 8 in the preceding exercise, clicking the Clear Password button instead of entering a new password.

Logging On after Protecting Access

Once you've established a password for the Admin account, you'll need to supply the name and password whenever you run Access.

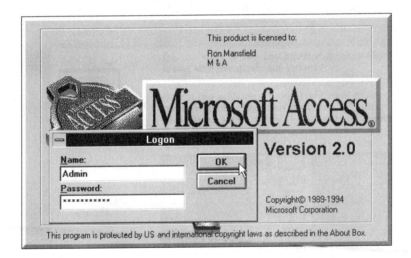

The password created is for the Admin account. You need to type Admin and password, or your new user name and no password. Once you are in Access, open a database and select Security, Change Password, type in a password for the new user, and check that user name shows the correct name.

Creating and Deleting Groups

Since it's a good idea to store users in groups (to minimize the need to redefine the same security parameters over and over again), you'll want to set up

Access

some groups. Here are the general steps:

1. Open a database file.

2. Choose Groups from the Security menu.

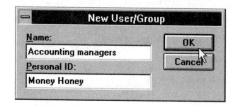

3. Type a meaningful group name and personal ID.

4. Add other groups if you wish.

Deleting a Group

If you find it necessary to delete a group (when a project is completed, or a department disbanded, for example), follow these simple steps.

1. Open a database file.

2. Choose Groups from the Security menu.

3. Pick a group name from the drop-down list.

4. Click the Delete button.

5. Confirm the deletion.

Creating Users

The steps for adding users will remind you of adding groups. The difference is you'll probably want to assign users to groups as you go:

1. Open a database file.

2. Choose Users from the Security menu.

3. Click New.

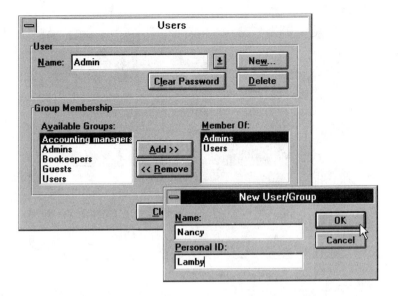

4. Type a meaningful user name and personal ID in the resulting dialog box.

5. Click OK.

6. Add other users if you wish, then click Close.

Assigning Users to Groups

1. Open a database file.

2. Choose Users from the Security menu.

3. Pick a user from the drop-down name list.

4. Pick a group name from the scrollable Available Groups list.

5. Click the Add>> button (or just double-click on the group name).

6. Add the user to other groups if you wish.

7. Pick a new user and perform steps 4 through 6, if you wish, then click Close when you're done.

Granting Permission

Once you've set up users (and probably groups), you can specify what they can and cannot do. Here are the general steps:

1. Open a database file.

2. Choose Permissions from the Security menu.

3. Pick a user or group from the User/Group name list. You will need to click the appropriate list button (Users or Groups) to display lists of either users or groups. Here we are looking at groups:

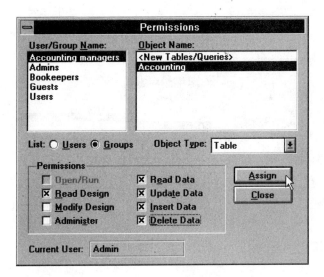

4. Click to add or remove permission for things like reading and updating data.

5. Click the Assign button when you've finished specifying permission.

6. Change permission for other users and groups if you wish.

7. Click Close when you're done.

8. Test to verify that security is what you expect.

 Access Version 2 has new security features not found in Version 1. To take advantages of these new features, after converting old database files, you'll need to recreate User Accounts and group accounts using the techniques described next.

Protecting Forms, Tables and Data

You can choose who gets to see and use each table, query, form, etc. Here are the general steps:

1. In the Database window, select the item you wish to secure

2. Pick the Permissions choice(s) from the Security menu:

3. Click Assign.

4. Grant permission to others, if you like; then click Close when you're done.

Encryption

After you've done all that security defining and assigning, some wonk down the hall can *still* open your database without even the electronic equivalent of a crowbar: a program as mundane as a word processor can do it. For example, here's part of our financial transactions database file opened in Microsoft Word:

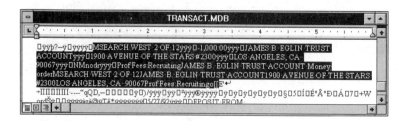

You don't need to be a financial guru to see that we are looking at a check in the amount of $1,000 for—well, I'll let you figure it out. Sure there's lots of garbage in there, but there's plenty of interesting info too.

So to be really paranoid—I mean "secure," *encrypt* your important stuff. This scrambles contents of your database (.MDB file) so that only you and folks you authorize (and perhaps Bill Gates) can make any sense of it. Here are the steps:

1. Close the database file if it is open.

2. Make sure you have room on the old hard disk for a second copy of this database file, albeit an encrypted one.

3. Back up, then hide the backup copy of the original database (the .MDB file) in a very secure place—your bank safe-deposit box, perhaps.

4. From the initial Access File menu (the one you first see when you run Access), choose Encrypt/Decrypt Database.

5. Locate the database you wish to encrypt and select it:

6. Click OK and pick a name for the new encrypted database.

7. Click OK and let 'er rip.

8. Test the encrypted database.

9. Delete the old database file. (You'll need to use something like Norton Utilities to *really* wipe it out. The DOS and Windows file deletion commands don't really wipe things from your hard disk.)

Does it work? You be the judge. Here's another financial transaction entry *after* encryption. Can you figure out how much it was for, and to whom it was written this time?

Sharing Info with OLE

Throughout the other parts of this book you've run into specially marked sections ("A Whole New Way to Work") illustrating techniques for sharing information among Office's component programs. Object Linking and Embedding are perhaps the two most powerful ways to share information between documents. Known collectively as OLE, these techniques are available to all of the component programs of Microsoft Office. With OLE you could create a graph in Excel or Microsoft Graph and then insert it in a Word document. In your PowerPoint slides you could include items from Word, Excel, and other OLE-savvy applications. You even have the choice of having the inserted data updated automatically or remain static. All of these and more are available with the OLE capabilities of Microsoft Office.

42

An Overview
of Object Linking
and Embedding

OLE

Object Linking and Embedding let you share information between applications. With OLE you can cause information to be updated automatically whenever the source is changed, updated only when you want it updated, or left forever as it was when you inserted it.

For example, suppose you publish a monthly newsletter, in Word, that shows company safety statistics, new product lists, etc. that you're getting from other files or objects. Let's call the newsletter the *destination* document. The other files or objects are called *source* documents. Since the information in the source documents we just mentioned is being updated regularly, you probably want your newsletter to use the most recently updated version of that information. You could **link** a framed area in the newsletter with information kept in an Excel spreadsheet and an Access database. Word can automatically **update** the newsletter each month to include changes made to the linked source documents.

Other types of information that you might want to put into your newsletter would not fall into the update category. Photographs, cartoons, the news stories themselves—these are essentially used only once, and hence do not need to be linked. They can simply be **embedded**. And if you have an application that can open the embedded object separately (don't worry; if it was created in Office, you've got the application) you can also **edit** the embedded object—you can touch up a dark photograph, or correct a mistake in your lead story.

Technical Requirements for OLE

In order to *link* an object created in another application to another file, you need to be running both applications in the same environment (e.g., in Windows with MS-DOS). Both applications must support either Object Linking and Embedding (OLE) or Dynamic Data Exchange (DDE—an earlier form of linking). If your setup doesn't match these requirements, you won't be able to link. All of the Office programs support some kind of OLE, although actual capabilities vary.

Embedded objects cannot be <u>edited</u> on computers that do not have the applications that were used to create them. For example, if you embed an Excel worksheet and give the resulting file to a coworker, the coworker will not be able to edit the embedded worksheet unless she or he has Excel.

The next three pages contain a sample newsletter created with Word 6.0. In this and the following chapter, you'll see how the linked and embedded objects in that newsletter were created.

What Is Linking?

Linking is a way of attaching information. For example, when you *link* an object to a Word document, the Word document stores the *location* of the object and its source application in a *field* in the document. Linking leaves the source document available to be used or updated on its own, by you or another user. Your Word document, to which is attached the linked object, can then be updated at your convenience to include the latest information in the source document—you can choose to update it manually (just when you want to update it), or to have it updated automatically (whenever the source changes). You can lock the links when the document and the object it contains are finalized, and you can break the links so that objects cannot be updated any further.

In our newsletter example, the injuries graph from Excel, the weigh-in worksheet from Excel, and the slides from PowerPoint are all linked. (The "Book Heap" letter is also linked to the newsletter, just to show that it's possible to link Word documents with *other* Word documents.)

OLE

OLE

FIGURE 42.1

Page 1 of our sample newsletter

The *Thicker* Gazette

Volume 12 Issue 7	A Thicker Publication Publication	December 1995

SAFETY CORNER

Editorial Still Riskier Than Shipping Dpt...

Hernias led last month's list of on-the-job injuries at Thicker, followed by head trauma, mostly among editors.

Here are the departmental breakdowns:

"I must have hit my bloody forehead on my bloody desk six times in the last ten days," Editor Guy Friendly observed.

Deadlines, tedium and lack of sleep were most often cited as causes of head injuries; with "I can't believe s/he/I wrote that" syndrome a close 4th. This month's safety slogan is:

**LIFT OUR BOOKS
WITH YOUR KNEES—
NEVER WITH YOUR BACK!**

JUST HIRED

NEW MAJOR ACCOUNTS REP MAKES LEAP OF FAITH

Our new major accounts rep will be literally on-board starting Monday.

"We've got a *lot* of preachin to do," smiled the Reverend Jack B. Shure. "People just need to get the word about how bigger is better, and it's gonna take a really big effort!"

The former child-preacher turned sales rep will soon call upon accounts from coast to coast. A special bus has been added to the Thicker Publishing, Inc. fleet to make life away from home more comfortable for the Reverend and regional reps who will accompany him on major accounts visits.

**PRAISE THE LORD AND
FIRE UP THE FORKLIFT!**

COMING SOON

New Obsession Series Ships!

The new Thicker Publications, Inc. Obsession series will soon buckle shelves everywhere, starting with a 2,000 page book titled:

*Obsessing Over
Word 12 for Windows
for Workgroups*

Starting with the history of typewriting, our new, 18-pound reference covers all 6,000 Microsoft Word commands; 12,000 keyboard shortcuts (including those illusive four-fingered ones), and much, much more. History buffs will even find an appendix listing all 600 of Word's programmers *and* their children's names.

"Finding the names of those kids was the hard part," confessed author Q. Group. "Fortunately there weren't many. *Very few* Microsoft employees have time to procreate. In fact, it's discourged," Group confided.

OTHER FORTHCOMING TITLES:

Title	Due
Windows for Buttheads	Spring
DOS Boot bist Jetz Gut	Spring
Mastering BIOS ROM	Spring
Upgrade That Commodore Pet!	Whenever
101 Computer Excuses Your Boss Will Believe	Summer
Pervert's Guide to the Internet	Summer
Stay Home & Vacation on the Internet	Fall
What's all this Fuss About Internet?	ASAP

Inside this issue:

1	Our older authors recall a time when books had no pictures and weighed less than computers!
2	Cafeteria now open all night. (Coin changer fixed.)
3	How Crown Books converted the entire *Grand Canyon* into "the world's first GigaSuperStore"

FIGURE 42.2

Page 2 of our sample newsletter

FIGURE 42.3

Page 3 of our sample newsletter

Our Readers Right

We always love getting letters from our readers and booksellers. Sometimes we even learn things. Check out this great idea from the Book Heap in Stinking Bog, California:

The Book Heap
1425 Foothill Lane
Stinking Bog, CA 95555

June 9, 1994

Thicker Publication, Inc.
2323 Fifth Avenue
New York, NY 14567

Dear Thicksters;

Thanks for the swell shipment of new Thick books. We've run out of shelf space, but, we find that when stacked, your hefty books make swell room dividers, sales counters and couches. The Special Editions are particulary useful.

We are wondering how high the books can be piled in earthquake country. Any advice would be much appreciated (the sooner the better).

Sincerely,

S. I. Jest

Shirley I. Jest
SIJ/mos

What Is Embedding?

Embedding, like linking, is a way of attaching information. When you *embed* information, the information becomes part of the destination document and is stored in that destination document. You can double-click on the information in the destination document to open the source object in its original application, ready for editing if you so desire.

Embedded objects in our newsletter example include the photo (originally a multimedia video frame, turned into a Word Picture object), the "Forthcoming Titles" list (from an Access table), and the logos in the "New Logo" section of the newsletter.

Oh yes, there's one more embedded item—the logo in the "Book Heap" letter. Yes, you can have embedded items *within* linked items, and the embedded items can still be edited.

  Embedding an object increases the size of the destination file. Considerably. If you embed a whole bunch of big objects (TIFF true-gray files, for example), your files will bloat. This can adversely affect the speed of editing, scrolling, and other tasks.

To Link or to Embed?

If you link objects in documents to their sources, you can either update the objects whenever it suits you or have them update automatically whenever the source objects change. When your document is finalized or ready for distribution, you can lock or break the links and freeze the document in final form.

If you embed objects in documents, you can enjoy the quality of the originals within the destination documents *and* have the convenience of being able to edit the objects in the original application (by double-clicking on them). No need to remember which object came from which source application—OLE keeps track of that information for you.

Remember that whereas *linked* information is still stored in the *source* file in the source application, *embedded* information becomes part of the *destination* document (and is stored in it). When you link, OLE records the location of the information in the source file and displays a picture of the information in the destination document. So here's the bottom line:

Link when you will need to share information with another file. Embed when you know you will not need to share information with another file.

Below are a couple of other considerations to keep in mind:

■ Linking is a complicated operation, even with the improvements in OLE 2. Although your computer may be a thundering 486 DX or a Pentium with more megs of RAM than you have fingers, updating large, linked files will take a while. If you have a slow computer, plan a few coffee breaks.

■ Linking creates a number of temporary files (for example, ~wrf001f.tmp). Check your computer every now and then for stray temp files and erase them (see the tip below). You're most likely to have leftover temp files if your computer crashes while you're working with linked files.

TIP

Temp files (~dft064f.tmp and the like) are files created by Windows applications for temporary storage. They're supposed to be deleted automatically when you exit the application that produced them or when you quit Windows (depending on what produced them). Every now and then, check your disk for stray temp files after loading Windows and before running any Windows applications—that is, before your applications get a chance to create new temp files. Run File Manager, select File ➤ Search and specify ~*.tmp. This will round up the usual suspects. Don't trash temp files unless you know what you are doing, however.

OLE Tips and Techniques

- Experiment on *copies* of the source and destination documents! Check both documents regularly as you work.

- The exact keystrokes and menu choices for OLE vary from program to program. Some OLE-capable programs don't even have menu bars. So you will need to consult online help and maybe even experiment a little.

- Whereas the Undo command often works, it may not work completely. For instance, if you use drag-and-drop to move information from an Excel cell to a Word document, Undo in Word may remove the insertion, but it won't necessarily restore the item to its original location in the source document. Check for this!

- Get in the habit of clicking on the Microsoft Office toolbar buttons to switch back and forth when setting up links. Consider adding other OLE-savvy programs (like CorelDRAW) to the Office toolbar if you link with them regularly.

With that said, let's get to the specifics. Linking is the topic of Chapter 43. Embedding is the topic of Chapter 44.

43

Linking

OLE

CHAPTER 43

you can either link an existing object or you can create a
new object and then link it. Start by learning to link the
easy way. Later you can graduate to the more sophisticated way if you wish.

Establishing a Link the Easy Way

The simplest way to link an object to a destination file is as follows:

1. Open the documents you want to link.

2. Select the object you want to link and copy it to the Clipboard (select Edit ➤ Copy, press Ctrl+C or Ctrl+Ins, or click on any Copy button the application offers).

3. Switch back to the destination application by pressing Alt+Tab, by clicking in the appropriate window, or by hauling down the Task List (press Ctrl+Esc, or click the appropriate button in the Office Manager toolbar).

4. Put the insertion point at a suitable place in your destination document and select Edit ➤ Paste Special to open the Paste Special dialog box:

5. In the Paste Special dialog box, select the Paste Link option button to link the object to your Word file. (The Paste Link option button description will be dimmed if it's not available—that is, if the object copied to the Clipboard is in an application that doesn't support OLE.)

OLE

6. In the As: box, select the form in which you want the linked object to appear. The Result box explains the effect of the option selected in the As: box.

7. Leave the Display As Icon checkbox unchecked for now. We'll discuss it in a moment.

8. Click OK. The object will be paste-linked into your document.

9. If necessary, reformat the pasted item, frame it, change its border, and otherwise work with it using Word techniques.

Notice how, since we pasted the chart into a narrow column, Word automatically resized it to fit. Alas, life is not often that easy. Sometimes you'll need to crop, resize, change table settings, font sizes, etc. In fact, I had to add one point of space above the chart to make the border show properly. So it goes in the OLE jungle. Save your destination document *before* inserting new objects, then, if things get too frustrating, close the destination document without saving, then reopen and try again.

TIP Give your destination application (Word, or whatever) a moment to "digest" new objects after you insert them. On slower computers, in particular, things will look pretty bad immediately after inserting. Sometimes all it takes is some repagination time to fix things up. Experiment when you are not in a hurry.

To Link an Existing Object

Here's how to link an existing object to a document:

1. In your destination document, put the insertion point where you want to insert the linked object.

2. Choose Insert ➤ Object. The Object dialog box will appear.

3. As you're linking an existing object, choose the Create From File tab:

4. Locate the file that contains the object you want to link.

5. Leave the Display As Icon checkbox unchecked for now. We'll discuss it in a moment.

6. Check the Link To File checkbox and choose the OK button. The selected object will be inserted and linked to your destination file.

7. Reformat if necessary.

The primary advantage of this technique is that you don't have to open up the source application. The primary disadvantage is that the whole business can be so slow that you hardly save any time over opening the source application yourself and editing manually.

Displaying the Linked Object as an Icon

You can save display space by displaying the linked object as an *icon* in the destination document. Your readers can then decide on their own whether they want to see the information or not, by clicking on it or not.

To display the linked object as an icon, check the Display As Icon checkbox in whichever dialog box you are using to link the object (the Paste Special dialog box or one of the Create tabs in the Insert ➤ Object dialog box). The standard icon for the source application will appear below the checkbox, along with a Change Icon button, should you want to use a different one.

If you want to display a different icon for your object, select the Change Icon button in the Program Manager. In the Change Icon dialog box, select one of the icons the application offers or click the Browse button to check out the icons from different applications. When you've finished browsing, click OK to return to the Change Icon dialog box, and OK again to accept the icon you chose. That icon will now appear in the Object dialog box.

When Are Linked Documents Updated?

Links can be updated in any of three ways:

Automatically   The default. Links are created with automatic updating; you'll have to change them to one of the following if you want something else.

Manually   You update any or all links only when you want to.

On Printing   All links will be updated at the point that you print the document.

The following sections explain these three options and how to choose them.

Updating a Link

Updating a link is straightforward and intuitive:

1. Select Edit ➤ Links.

2. In the Links dialog box, select the link or links that you want to update:

 TIP To update several links, hold down the Ctrl key while you click on each link, or hold down Shift and click on the first and last links of the desired range to select all the links in between.

3. Choose how you want the selected links to be updated:

   ■ Choose the Automatic option button to update linked information every time the source file is changed.

   ■ Choose the Manual option button to update links only when you choose to do so.

4. Choose OK to close the Links dialog box and accept the changes you've made.

To Update a Link Manually

To retain the most control over your document and its linked objects, you can update your links manually. Here's how:

1. Select Edit ➤ Links.

2. In the Links dialog box, select the link or links that you want to update.

3. Choose the Update Now button to update the links.

 TIP To update links quickly, select the links you want to update and press F9.

To Update Links Every Time You Print

To make sure your documents are up-to-date whenever you print them, arrange for their links to be updated each time you print.

1. Select Tools ➤ Options.

2. In the Options dialog box, select the Print tab.

3. Choose the Update Links checkbox.

4. Click the OK button to close the dialog box. Links in your documents will now be updated whenever you print.

Editing Linked Information

You're best off editing linked information in its source file so that your changes will be reflected in both the source file and the destination documents.

To edit linked information, follow these steps:

1. In the destination document, right-click the linked information to edit.

2. Select Edit ➤ Object (this menu item will vary depending on what kind of object you have selected). Choose Edit from the mini-menu that appears. The source application will open with the selected information displayed.

3. Make the changes you want in the source file.

4. Select File ➤ Exit And Return to get back to your destination document. The edits you made in the source file will be reflected in the destination file.

Breaking Links—Careful Here!

To prevent linked information from being updated ever again, you can break a link. Before you do this, though, make sure that that's what you want to do. Once you've broken a link, the only way to reconnect it is by choosing the Undo command, and that only works if you haven't done anything else since you broke the link. So you only get one chance to fix your mistake—and you have to fix it *pronto*!

  If you only want to temporarily prevent linked information from being updated, you need to lock a link, not break it. Locking is the topic of the section following this one.

To break a link, follow the steps below:

1. Select Edit ➤ Links.
2. In the Link dialog box, select the link or links that you want to break.
3. Choose the Break Link button. A dialog box will appear, asking for confirmation.
4. Choose Yes. The link or links will be broken.

 To break a link quickly using the keyboard, press Ctrl+Shift+F9.

Locking and Unlocking Links

You can *temporarily* prevent linked information from being updated by *locking* links. When you want to update the information again, you just unlock the links. Here's how it works:

1. Select Edit ➤ Links.
2. In the Links dialog box, select the link or links that you want to lock or unlock.

3. To lock a link or links, check the Locked checkbox. To unlock a link or links, uncheck the Locked checkbox.

4. Choose OK to leave the Links dialog box and save your changes.

TIP To lock links quickly using the keyboard, first select the links and press Ctrl+F11. To unlock links, press Ctrl+Shift+F11.

Reconnecting Lost Links

It's pretty easy to lose a link. For instance, you might rename or move the source file, forgetting that information in it was linked to another file. Someone else might even do this and forget to tell you.

If you lose links in a document, don't despair—you *can* reconnect lost links. Here's how:

1. Choose Edit ➤ Links.

2. In the Links dialog box, choose the link you want to reconnect.

3. Choose the Change Source button.

4. In the File Name box of the Change Source dialog box, select the file to which you want to reconnect the link. Then click OK. If your document contains other links to the same source file, you will be asked whether you want to change all links from the previous source file to the new source file. Choose Yes or No.

Troubleshooting Links

Problem: Linked Items Don't Update

If you get this message, check to see that you've actually established links, and that they are set to update when you expect. For example, if you choose Locked as a link option, changes in the source will not be reflected in the destination document.

Make sure that the source document still exists. Then make sure it hasn't been moved. If the document exists, you can reestablish the link by doing the following:

1. Switch to the destination document (a Word document, perhaps).
2. Choose Links from the Edit menu.
3. Select the troublesome link from the Source file list.
4. Click on the Change Source button.
5. Use the resulting Change Source dialog box to find the source document, and click OK.

Problem: Object Types Not Available

If you don't see an object type that you think should be available in the Object Type list used to insert objects, try reinstalling the application that generates the object type. For instance, if you expect to see Microsoft WordArt objects listed and you don't, try reinstalling Microsoft Word from the original Microsoft disks, and if you do a custom installation, make certain that WordArt is one of the items specified.

44

Embedding

A s you should remember by now, *embedding* actually puts objects into your destination documents, as opposed to *linking*, which only keeps track of objects in other files, in order to position them in a frame in the document you're viewing or printing. The difference between the two is borne out by the difference in file size: embedding objects into a file adds considerably to the destination document's size. Examples of embedded objects in our newsletter (Chapter 42) include the logos, the "Book Heap" letter, and the photograph. Many of the other objects (like the Excel "Weigh-In" worksheet) *could* have been embedded but they were not.

NOTE Remember that embedded objects are only "updated" when you choose to edit them or replace them with more recent versions. And remember, when you edit embedded objects, you need to have the application or applications that created them loaded on the computer you're using.

How to Embed

You can choose either to embed an existing object or to create an object and then embed it. There's a simple way to embed objects, and then there's a more complicated way. Simple first:

Embedding with the Insert Object Command

Here are the steps to follow to create, then embed an object:

1. Position the insertion point where you want to insert the new object.

2. Use the Insert ➤ Object command, to select an object type. (Here, I've chosen Microsoft WordArt 2.0 from the list in the Create New tab in the Object dialog box).

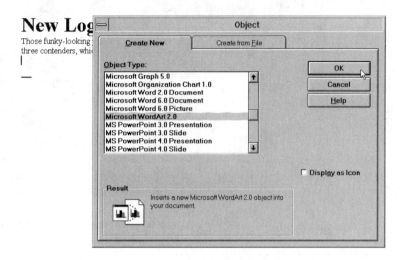

3. Create the object using the appropriate techniques for the application you are using.

4. Close the finished object, and return to the destination document. (Sometimes you'll use a Close command on the File menu, other times just clicking in the destination document will close the source application and insert the new object, as is the case with WordArt 2.0.)

Embedding Existing Objects

1. Position the insertion point where you want to insert the new object.

2. Choose Insert ➤ Object.

3. Click on the Create From File tab to bring it frontmost if it isn't already.

Our Read

We always love getting
from the Book Heap in

4. Locate the desired file and double-click on it.

5. The source document will be embedded in your destination.

The results can be a little frustrating, particularly if the destination document's margins can't accommodate the source document. You'll need to experiment.

Editing Embedded Objects

You edit embedded objects just as you would edit them in their original applications. Suppose, for example, that we had embedded that Excel worksheet instead of linking it, and wanted to make some changes:

1. Click the object to select it. Selection handles and a frame will appear around the object, as shown on the following page.

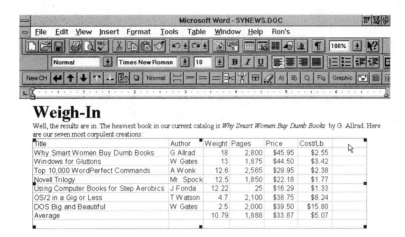

2. You guessed it. Double-click the object. Your computer will chug and whir for a while (quite a while if your object is something complicated, like a drawing). Then the application in which the object was created will open, with the object ready for editing. Notice how the window is titled Microsoft Word, but Excel's menus and toolbars are available:

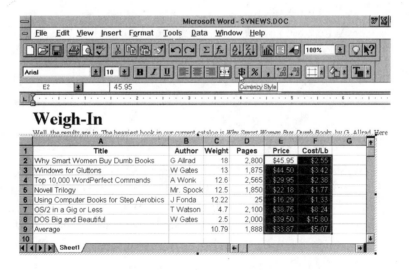

3. Edit the object, as you wish.

4. Select File ➤ Exit And Return to quit the source application and return to the destination document, which will reappear with the object updated to reflect your changes. (You may need to use different techniques for different object types. Esc often works too.)

Editing Sound and Video Clips

If you've been using sound and video clips, you will have spotted the fallacy in the preceding section. If you double-click a sound or video clip, you'll run it. These objects object to being edited this way. They wanna play instead.

In such cases (and in others, if you like), you can edit the embedded objects using the Object command:

1. Select the object you want to edit.

2. Select Edit ➤ Object. Choose the name of the object you want to edit, then choose Edit. (If you are offered the choice of Edit or Open, choose Edit if you want to edit the object in the destination application window, choose Open to open the application to which the object belongs and edit it there.)

3. When you've finished editing the object, select File ➤ Exit And Return to get back to the destination document, which will reappear with the edited object in place.

Converting an Embedded Object to a Different Format

You may run into situations where you need to convert an embedded object to a different format. You might want to do this if you receive a file containing an embedded object that was created in an application you do not have, or if you take a file that contains embedded objects to a colleague who does not have the relevant application.

To change an embedded object's source application, follow these steps:

1. Select the object you want to change.

2. Select Edit ➤ Object, choose the object you want to convert, and select Convert from the extension menu.

3. In the Convert dialog box, specify the format to which you want to convert the file.

   ■ Select the **Convert To** button to *permanently* convert the embedded object to the format you specify.

   ■ Select the **Activate As** button to *temporarily* convert the embedded object to the format you specify. You can then edit the object in that format, but when you save it, it will be saved in its original format.

4. Click OK.

Converting an Embedded Object to a Graphic

If you've been embedding objects and you want to save some space, you can reduce the size of your file by converting the embedded objects to graphics. Any text in the object will no longer actually exist as text, so its readability may suffer at smaller sizes, and you will no longer be able to edit the object except with graphics editing tools. Also, you cannot convert the graphic back to an embedded object.

Still want to do it? Here's how:

1. Select the object you want to convert to a graphic.

2. Select Edit ➤ Object and select the object in the Object dialog box.

3. Choose Convert.

4. In the Object Type box, select Picture. Click OK. The object will be displayed as a picture.

310

> **NOTE** If you have field codes displayed, you will also see the field {Embed Word Drawing}. This is helpful when you're sharing documents with people who may not have the same graphics applications.

Removing Embedded Objects

This being the end of the chapter, it seems like the natural place to mention how to start over. If your embedded object has served its purpose and is no longer needed, you can get rid of it, greatly reducing the size of your file.

Removing an embedded object is easy. Select it and press Delete. Or right-click on the object to pop up the shortcut menu, and choose Cut.

Installing
Microsoft Office

You can install Microsoft Office Manager and the Office applications on any machine that runs Windows 3.1. Office is composed of the following applications: *Microsoft Office Manager*, *Word*, *Excel*, *PowerPoint*, and, if you have Office Professional, *Access*. It also provides you a license to use *Microsoft Mail*. You'll need an absolute minimum of 4 MB of RAM, but that's only if you're not running Access, which requires a minimum of 8 MB. Realistically, to use multiple programs or OLE, you should consider upgrading to 16 MB or more.

NOTE The license to use Mail will only be useful to you if you plan to connect with an existing network that is running Mail. Contact your organization's network administrator or Mail administrator to get the necessary instructions, and assistance, in installing the network's software on your machine.

You'll need an EGA or better display. You really should have a mouse or trackball, though this is not a requirement. Disk space estimates vary with your needs. You can specify which features you wish to install. Microsoft's installer offers three suggested "packages" of features, or you can pick and choose on your own.

A *minimum installation* (also called a *laptop installation*) of Office requires around 16 MB of disk space. You'll get just the bare bones—mostly programs, usually with little or no online help. Travelers, listen up: You are going to wish you had the online help at midnight in some hotel room, so think twice about choosing the minimum installation. If you have the room, do a *complete installation* and then use the Setup program remove the parts you'll never use or don't need, like Word's Grammar Checker and Equation Editor. A full installation of the Office components requires about 62 MB.

Network users can choose a *workstation installation*, which requires much less local hard disk real estate. The trade-off is usually speed. Ask your network manager if this is an option where *you* work and if it makes sense for you. The instructions in this appendix assume that you will use floppies and *not* a workstation installation.

Word's installer will check to see if you have enough disk space for the requested installations, but you can save some time by assuring that there is room beforehand.

Table A.1 summarizes the *approximate* disk space required for the Office Manager and the Office components.

TABLE A.1: Disk Space Requirements for MS Office Applications

PRODUCT	APPROXIMATE DISK SPACE
Office Manager	
No options	0.7 MB
Word	
Program	5.9 MB
Proofing tools	2.4 MB
Online help, examples, and demos	4.8 MB
Wizards, templates, and letters	3.3 MB
Tools	0.2 MB
Excel	
Program	7.5 MB
Online Help	7.5 MB
Data Access	5.4 MB
Graphic Filters	0.4 MB

TABLE A.1: Disk Space Requirements for MS Office Applications (continued)

PRODUCT	APPROXIMATE DISK SPACE
Excel (continued)	
Add-ins	2.0 MB
Tools	1.1 MB
PowerPoint	
Program	9.6 MB
Help Tutorials and Cue Cards	0.6 MB
Applets	8.0 MB
Converters, Filters, and Translators	2.2 MB
Spelling	0.3 MB
Templates	6.3 MB
Clip Art	8.2 MB
Media Player	0.5 MB
TrueType fonts	1.4 MB
Tools	1.0 MB
Genigraphics tools	0.4 MB
Access	
Program	5.5 MB
Help/Cue Cards	5.7 MB
Wizards	3.7 MB
ISAM Drivers	.7 MB

TABLE A.1:   Disk Space Requirements for MS Office Applications (continued)

PRODUCT	APPROXIMATE DISK SPACE
Access (continued)	
ODBC Support	1.2 MB
MS Graph (may already be installed)	2.4 MB
Sample Apps	2.7 MB
Tools (Setup and Info)	1 MB
Common Tools	
Spelling	0.6 MB
Converters, Filters, and Data Access	5.0 MB
Graph	0.9 MB
ClipArt Gallery	1.1 MB
Equation Editor	0.6 MB
WordArt	1.2 MB
Setup Files	1.2 MB
Fonts	2.1 MB

Installing Microsoft Office Manager

If you purchase Microsoft Office or Microsoft Office Pro, the Office installer will install all of the applications at once (Office Manager, Word, Excel, Power-Point, and if you have Office Professional, Access.)

Appendix

Running Installers from Floppies

The files on the installation floppies are compressed—thus they cannot simply be dragged onto your hard disk. You need to run the Installer program, which will walk you through the simple installation steps. Microsoft Office does not come with Windows, so if you don't already have Windows on your machine, you must install Windows first (version 3.1 or later) and then run it for all Office-related installations.

1. Start Windows if it's not already running. Quit any other applications that you are running.

2. Unpackage and stack the disks in order. If you've purchased Office Pro, notice that there are two types of installation disks: Office and Access disks. Stack them separately and don't get them mixed up when playing feed the floppy drive.

3. Insert the first Microsoft Office Setup disk in a floppy drive (not the first Access disk).

4. Choose the Run choice on the Program Manger's File menu.

5. Type the disk drive name (**A:** or **B:**) and **Setup**, as shown in Figure A.1. In a (long) moment, you will see a Setup dialog box similar, but not necessarily identical, to Figure A.2.

FIGURE A.1

Start Setup with the
Windows Program
Manager's Run
command.

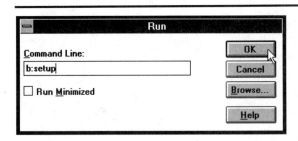

FIGURE A.2

Read the information
screen carefully as
you work.

You can also double-click on the SETUP.EXE file in File
Manager to start the installation process.

6. The choices you will be given from here on will vary with your situation.
   For example, the installer will propose disk drive and directory locations
   for the various programs. Read each choice carefully before clicking the
   OK button. You can also refer to online help.

7. When asked if you want a typical, minimum (laptop), or complete installation (see Figure A.3), opt for complete if you have the required disk
   space. You can always remove unwanted elements after you've had a
   chance to explore them. The installer will keep you abreast of progress
   and splash Microsoft propaganda on-screen as it starts the installation.
   It's worth reading and you'll have plenty of time to do so.

8. From time to time (up to 16 or more times), you'll be asked to swap
   disks. The beeper will beep a second or more before the disk drive light

Appendix

FIGURE A.3

If you have enough
disk space, do a
complete installation.
Delete unwanted
features after
trying them.

goes out. *Always* wait for the disk light to go out before swapping disks. Tap the ↵ key rather than reaching for the mouse and clicking OK every time. Eventually, you'll be returned to the Program Manager when the installation is complete.

9. Double-click on the new Office Readme Help file icon if there is one to learn about last-minute news.

Running the Installer from a Server

If your company has a network and is licensed to do so, you may be able to install Office programs from the server (over the network) without the need for floppy shuffling. Contact your network administrator for details.

Custom Installations

If you choose not to do a complete installation, you can tell the Installer which items you want to install. And you can revisit the Setup program later to remove items you don't use. This option is helpful if you have limited disk space or if one of your nonessential disks is damaged. In either case, you'll see a series of dialog boxes, each with lists of items that can be added or removed. Most of the dialog boxes also contain Change Option buttons that give you more detailed control. For example, the first dialog box in a Word custom installation lets you add or delete all Proofing tools, while the next level down lets you pick and choose from options like Spelling, Hyphenation, Thesaurus, and Grammar.

As you add or remove checkmarks in the various option boxes, Word revises its estimation of the required disk space and displays the statistics at the bottom of dialog boxes. The "top" dialog box looks like the one in Figure A.4.

To reach the detailed choices, click the Change Option button. You'll see choices like those in Figure A.5.

FIGURE A.4

Begin by selecting an application.

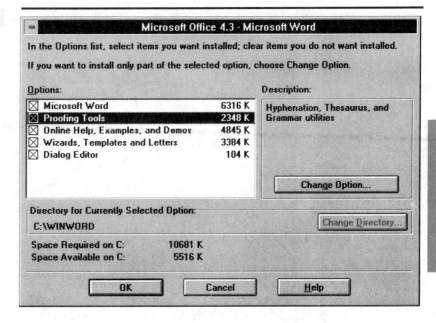

Appendix

FIGURE A.5

The Change Option
button lets you see
additional lists of
installation options.

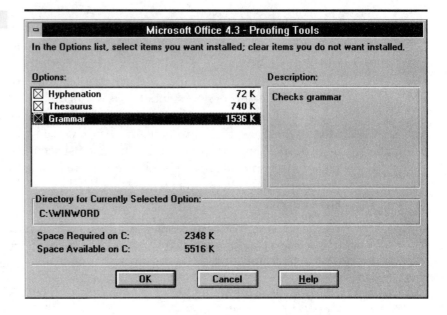

FIGURE A.5
The Change Option button lets you see additional lists of installation options.

It's a good idea to install the templates and sample documents, because they contain helpful files and examples. If you choose *not* to install certain features, they will either not appear on your Word menus or will always be dimmed. You can always return to the Installer later and install just the items you left off when you last did a custom installation.

Upgrading to New Software Versions

Eventually you'll need to upgrade from one version of an Office program to a newer version. (Bill Gates recently built a new house and he needs the income.) More to the point, without new software, there wouldn't be new computer books like these for me to write. When the big day comes:

1. Start Windows if it's not already running. Quit any other applications that you are running.

2. Unpackage the new disks and stack them in order.

3. Insert the new program's first disk (Setup) in a floppy drive.

4. Choose the Run choice on the Program Manager's File menu.

5. Type the disk drive name (A: or B:) and **Setup**.

6. You'll be asked if you wish to replace the old software with the new. Normally you will, so click OK.

7. The choices you will be given from here on will vary with your situation. Read each choice carefully before clicking the OK button. You can also refer to online help.

Appendix

The Toolbars
Reference

BUTTON	DESCRIPTION

Buttons on the Microsoft Office Manager Toolbar

Launches or switches to Microsoft Word.

Launches or switches to Microsoft Excel.

Launches or switches to Microsoft PowerPoint.

Launches or switches to Microsoft Mail.

Launches or switches to Microsoft Access.

You can add non-Office buttons, like this one for the Windows File Manager.

Brings down the Microsoft Office menu.

BUTTON	DESCRIPTION

Buttons on Word's Standard Toolbar

Opens a new document. [File ➤ New] *Shortcut:* Ctrl+N

Opens an existing document. [File ➤ Open] *Shortcut:* Ctrl+O or Ctrl+F12

Saves your work. [File ➤ Save] *Shortcut:* Ctrl+S or Shift+F12

Prints one copy using default settings. [Similar, but not identical to, File ➤ Print]

Switches to Print Preview. [File ➤ Print Preview] *Shortcut:* Ctrl+F2 or Alt+Ctrl+i

Checks spelling. [Tools ➤ Spelling] *Shortcut:* F7

Cuts selected material and places it on the Clipboard. [Edit ➤ Cut] *Shortcut:* Ctrl+X or Shift+Delete

Copies selected items to Clipboard. [Edit ➤ Copy] *Shortcut:* Ctrl+C or Ctrl+Insert

Pastes (inserts) Clipboard contents at insertion point. [Edit ➤ Paste] *Shortcut:* Ctrl+V or Shift+Insert

Copies character formatting.

Provides a list of actions that can be undone. [Similar, but not identical to, Edit ➤ Undo] *Shortcut:* Ctrl+Z or Alt+Backspace

Provides a list of actions that can be redone. [Similar, but not identical to, Edit ➤ Redo] *Shortcut:* Ctrl+Y or Alt+Enter

Automatically formats the document. [Format ➤ AutoFormat]

BUTTON	DESCRIPTION

Buttons on Word's Standard Toolbar (continued)

Creates or inserts AutoText entries. [Similar, but not identical to, Edit ➤ AutoText] *Shortcut:* F3 or Alt+Ctrl+V

Inserts (helps you create) new tables. [Table ➤ Insert Table]

Inserts MS Excel worksheet objects. [Insert ➤ Object ➤ Microsoft Excel 5.0 Worksheet]

Lets you define number of text columns. [Similar, but not identical to, Format ➤ Columns]

Shows and hides the Drawing toolbar.

Lets you create new charts (MS Graph Objects). [Insert ➤ Object ➤ Microsoft Graph 5.0]

Toggles display of paragraph marks and other nonprinting characters.

(Help tool) Lets you point to see on-screen command help and text property information. *Shortcut:* Shift+F1

Buttons on Word's Drawing Toolbar

Creates straight lines.

Creates rectangles.

Creates ellipses.

Creates arcs.

Creates freeform shapes.

BUTTON	DESCRIPTION
Buttons on Word's Drawing Toolbar (continued)	

	Creates text boxes.
	Creates callouts.
	Lets you format callouts.
	Lets you choose fill colors.
	Lets you choose line colors.
	Lets you choose line styles.
	Lets you select drawing objects or surround objects by dragging.
	Brings selected drawn objects forward.
	Moves selected drawn objects back.
	Brings selected objects in front of text.
	Moves selected drawn objects behind text.
	Groups selected items.
	Ungroups selected items.
	Flips selected items from left to right (horizontally).
	Flips selected items from top to bottom (vertically).
	Rotates selected objects 90 degrees to the right.
	Lets you reshape freeform objects by dragging points.
	Establishes a grid to which objects are attracted.

BUTTON	DESCRIPTION

Buttons on Word's Drawing Toolbar (continued)

Aligns multiple drawn objects.

Opens a new picture object window or inserts selected drawing into a picture object.

Inserts a new frame or encloses selected objects in a frame. [Insert ➤ Frame]

Buttons on Word's Formatting Toolbar

Toggles Bold formatting. [Format ➤ Font ➤ Bold (on Font Style list)] *Shortcut:* Ctrl+B or Ctrl+Shift+B

Toggles Italic formatting. [Format ➤ Font ➤ Italic (on Font Style list)] *Shortcut:* Ctrl+i or Ctrl+Shift+i

Toggles single underline formatting. [Format ➤ Font ➤ Single (on Underline list)] *Shortcut:* Ctrl+U or Ctrl+Shift+U

Makes selected paragraph(s) left-aligned. [Format ➤ Paragraph ➤ Left (on Alignment list)] *Shortcut:* Ctrl+←

Centers selected paragraph(s). [Format ➤ Paragraph ➤ Centered (on Alignment list)] *Shortcut:* Ctrl+E

Makes selected paragraph(s) right-aligned. [Format ➤ Paragraph ➤ Right (on Alignment list)] *Shortcut:* Ctrl+R

Aligns (justifies) left and right sides of selected paragraph(s). [Format ➤ Paragraph ➤ Justified (on Alignment list)] *Shortcut:* Ctrl+J

Creates numbered lists. [Similar, but not identical to, Format ➤ Bullets and Numbering (Numbered tab)]

BUTTON	DESCRIPTION

Buttons on Word's Formatting Toolbar (continued)

Creates bulleted lists. [Similar, but not identical to, Format ➤ Bullets and Numbering (Bulleted tab)] *Shortcut:* Ctrl+Shift+L

Decreases indent or promotes headings one level. *Shortcut:* Ctrl+Shift+M

Increases indent or demotes headings one level. *Shortcut:* Ctrl+M

Shows and hides the Borders toolbar.

Buttons on Word's Borders Toolbar

Changes top border of selected item(s). [Format ➤ Borders and Shading ➤ Borders tab]

Changes bottom border of selected item(s). [Format ➤ Borders and Shading ➤ Borders tab]

Changes left border of selected item(s). [Format ➤ Borders and Shading ➤ Borders tab]

Changes right border of selected item(s). [Format ➤ Borders and Shading ➤ Borders tab]

Changes inside border(s) of selected item(s). [Format ➤ Borders and Shading ➤ Borders tab]

Changes outside (surrounding) border of selected item(s). [Format ➤ Borders and Shading ➤ Borders tab]

Removes borders from selected item(s). [Format ➤ Borders and Shading ➤ Borders tab ➤ None]

BUTTON	DESCRIPTION

Buttons on Word's Forms Toolbar

ab|	Inserts a text field.
⊠	Creates a box field.
🔲	Creates a drop-down field.
📝	Displays the Text Forms Field Options dialog box.
🔲	Inserts a new table. [Table ➤ Insert Table]
🔲	Inserts a frame. [Insert ➤ Frame]
🔲	Lets you shade fields.
🔒	Lets you protect forms. [Tools ➤ Protect Document ➤ Forms option]

Buttons on Word's Database Toolbar

📝	Edits or creates a data form from a list or table.
📝	Lets you add, remove, or rename fields.
🔲	Adds a new, blank record to a database.
🔲	Deletes selected records from a database.
A↓Z	Sorts lists in ascending order.
Z↓A	Sorts lists in descending order.
🔲	Inserts a database. [Insert ➤ Database]
📄	Updates selected fields. *Shortcut:* F9 or Alt+Shift+U

BUTTON	DESCRIPTION
Buttons on Word's Database Toolbar (continued)	
	Displays Find In Field dialog box.
	Switches to a mail merge main document.
Buttons on Word's MailMerge Toolbar	
	Toggles between displaying merge fields and actual data.
	Displays your first record from the data source.
	Takes you to the previous record in the data source.
	Takes you to the next record in the data source.
	Takes you to the last record in the data source.
	Runs Mail Merge Helper and creates a main document. [Tools ➤ Mail Merge]
	Checks for mail merge errors. *Shortcut:* Alt+Shift+K
	Merges to a new Word document. *Shortcut:* Alt+Shift+N
	Merges to your printer. *Shortcut:* Alt+Shift+M
	Displays the Merge dialog box.
	Displays the Find In Field dialog box.
	Opens or takes you to the data source for editing. *Shortcut:* Alt+Shift+E

BUTTON	DESCRIPTION
Buttons on Excel's Standard Toolbar	

Opens a new workbook. [File ➤ New] *Shortcut:* Ctrl+N

Displays the Open dialog box to open a file. [File ➤ Open] *Shortcut:* Ctrl+O

Saves the current workbook. [File ➤ Save] *Shortcut:* Ctrl+S

Prints the current worksheet. [File ➤ Print] *Shortcut:* Ctrl+P

Displays each page as it will print. [File ➤ Print Preview]

Checks spelling in the current worksheet. [Tools ➤ Spelling] *Shortcut:* F7

Cuts the selection to the Clipboard. [Edit ➤ Cut] *Shortcut:* Ctrl+X

Copies the selection to the Clipboard. [Edit ➤ Copy] *Shortcut:* Ctrl+C

Pastes the Clipboard contents. [Edit ➤ Paste] *Shortcut:* Ctrl+V

Copies the format of the selection. [Edit ➤ Paste Special]

Reverses the last command or action. [Edit ➤ Undo] *Shortcut:* Ctrl+Z

Repeats the last command. [Edit ➤ Repeat] *Shortcut:* F4

Implements the SUM function. *Shortcut:* Alt+=

Displays the Function Wizard dialog box. [Insert ➤ Function] *Shortcut:* Shift+F3

BUTTON	DESCRIPTION

Buttons on Excel's Standard Toolbar (continued)

Arranges a selected list from minimum to maximum. [Data ➤ Sort]

Arranges a selected list from maximum to minimum. [Data ➤ Sort]

Runs the Chart Wizard. Click in the worksheet to display the Chart Wizard dialog box. [Insert ➤ Chart]

Draws a text box on the current sheet.

Displays the Drawing toolbar.

Displays the Tip Wizard, which shows hints about the current task.

Changes the pointer into the Help pointer. When double-clicked, displays the Search dialog box. [Help ➤ Search for Help on] *Shortcut:* Shift+F1.

Buttons on Excel's Chart Toolbar

Creates an embedded chart of the type displayed on the button. Click the drop-down list button to display a palette of available chart types to change the selected chart. This command is only available if the chart is activated—you must double-click on the chart to activate it. [Format ➤ Chart Type]

Changes the selected or active chart to the default chart type.

Runs the Chart Wizard to create or edit an existing chart. [Insert ➤ Chart]

BUTTON	DESCRIPTION

Buttons on Excel's Chart Toolbar (continued)

 Toggles major horizontal gridlines on and off the active chart. This command is only available on the activated chart's shortcut menu. [Shortcut menu ➤ Insert Gridlines]

 Toggles the display of the selected chart's legend.

Buttons on Excel's Formatting Toolbar

B Applies bold formatting to selected characters. [Format ➤ Cells ➤ Font] *Shortcut:* Ctrl+B

I Applies italic format to selected characters. [Format ➤ Cells ➤ Font] *Shortcut:* Ctrl+I

U Applies a single underline to selected characters. [Format ➤ Cells ➤ Font] *Shortcut:* Ctrl+U

Aligns selected characters to the left of the cell, text box, button, or chart. [Format ➤ Cells ➤ Alignment] *Shortcut:* Ctrl+1, Alignment

Centers selected characters within a cell, text box, button, or chart. [Format ➤ Cells ➤ Alignment] *Shortcut:* Ctrl+1, Alignment

Aligns selected characters to the right of the cell, text box, button, or chart. [Format ➤ Cells ➤ Alignment] *Shortcut:* Ctrl+1, Alignment

Centers the contents of the first cell in a selection horizontally across selected cells. [Format ➤ Cells ➤ Alignment] *Shortcut:* Ctrl+1, Alignment

$ Applies the current currency style to selected cells. [Format ➤ Cells ➤ Number] *Shortcut:* Ctrl+1, Number

BUTTON	**DESCRIPTION**

Buttons on Excel's Formatting Toolbar (continued)

%	Applies the current percent style to selected cells. [Format ➤ Cells ➤ Number] *Shortcut:* Ctrl+1, Number
,	Applies the current comma style to selected cells. [Format ➤ Cells ➤ Number] *Shortcut:* Ctrl+1, Number
+.0 .00	Adds a decimal place to the selection's number format. [Format ➤ Cells ➤ Number] *Shortcut:* Ctrl+1, Number
.00 +.0	Removes a decimal place from the selection's number format. [Format ➤ Cells ➤ Number] *Shortcut:* Ctrl+1, Number
	Adds the cell format displayed to the selected cell. Click the drop-down list button to display a palette of borders. [Format ➤ Cells ➤ Border] *Shortcut:* Ctrl+1, Border
	Changes the background color of the selection to the displayed color. Click on the drop-down list button to display a color palette. [Format ➤ Cells ➤ Patterns] *Shortcut:* Ctrl+1, Patterns
	Changes the color of the characters in the selection to the displayed color. Click on the drop-down list button to display a color palette. [Format ➤ Cells ➤ Font] *Shortcut:* Ctrl+1, Font

Buttons on Excel's Auditing Toolbar

	Draws an arrow from each cell that supplies a value to the formula in the active cell. [Tools ➤ Auditing ➤ Trace Precedents]
	Deletes the level of precedent tracer arrows farthest from the active cell.
	Draws arrows from the active cell to each cell that contains a formula using the value in the active cell. [Tools ➤ Auditing ➤ Trace Dependents]

BUTTON	DESCRIPTION

Buttons on Excel's Auditing Toolbar (continued)

	Deletes the level of dependent tracer arrows farthest from the active cell.
	Deletes all precedent and dependent tracer arrows in the worksheet. [Tools ➤ Auditing ➤ Remove All Arrows]
	Draws an arrow from each cell that might have caused the error in the active cell. [Tools ➤ Auditing ➤ Trace Error]
	Displays the Cell Note dialog box used to attach a note to the active cell. [Insert ➤ Note]
	Displays the selected cell's Info window. [Tools ➤ Options ➤ View]

Buttons on Excel's Drawing Toolbar

	Creates straight lines on a worksheet, macro sheet, or chart.
	Creates empty rectangles on a worksheet, macro sheet, or chart.
	Creates empty ellipses on a worksheet, macro sheet, or chart.
	Creates empty arcs on a worksheet, macro sheet, or chart.
	Creates empty freehand polygon objects on a worksheet, macro sheet, or chart.
	Creates empty text boxes on a worksheet, macro sheet, or chart.
	Creates arrows on a worksheet, macro sheet, or chart.
	Creates freehand lines on a worksheet, macro sheet, or chart.

BUTTON	DESCRIPTION

Buttons on Excel's Drawing Toolbar (continued)

Creates filled rectangles on a worksheet, macro sheet, or chart.

Creates filled ellipses on a worksheet, macro sheet, or chart.

Creates filled arcs on a worksheet, macro sheet, or chart.

Creates filled freeform polygons on a worksheet, macro sheet, or chart.

Creates blank buttons to which you can assign macros.

Changes the pointer into a selection arrow.

Places selected objects in front of any other objects. [Format ➤ Placement ➤ Bring to Front]

Places selected objects in back of any other objects. [Format ➤ Placement ➤ Send to Back]

Changes multiple selected objects into a single group. [Format ➤ Placement ➤ Group]

Divides a group into separate objects. [Format ➤ Placement ➤ Ungroup]

Changes the shape of a selected polygon.

Creates a dark border along the right and bottom edges of a selected object or range.

Changes the fill pattern and color in selected cells, chart items, or objects. [Format ➤ Cells ➤ Patterns; Format ➤ Selected *chart item* ➤ Patterns; or Format ➤ Cells ➤ Object ➤ Patterns] *Shortcut:* Ctrl+1, Patterns

BUTTON	DESCRIPTION

Buttons on Excel's Query and Pivot Toolbar

Displays the Pivot Table Wizard, used to create or edit a pivot table. [Data ➤ Pivot Table]

Changes the properties of the data area or options for a field. [Data ➤ PivotTable Field]

Divides a category group into separate items. [Shortcut menu ➤ Group and Outline ➤ Ungroup] (Right-click on the pivot table to display the shortcut menu.) *Shortcut:* Alt+Shift+←

Changes multiple items in a pivot table into a single grouped item. [Shortcut menu ➤ Group and Outline ➤ Group] *Shortcut:* Alt+Shift+→

Collapses the outer item in a row or column field to hide subordinate data. [Shortcut menu ➤ Group and Outline ➤ Hide Detail] *Shortcut:* Double-click on the item

Displays hidden subordinate data in a pivot table. [Shortcut menu ➤ Group and Outline ➤ Show Detail] *Shortcut:* Double-click on the item.

Copies each page of a pivot table to a different worksheet in the current workbook. [Shortcut menu ➤ Show Pages]

Updates the pivot table of the results of a query. [Shortcut menu ➤ Refresh Data]

BUTTON	DESCRIPTION

Buttons on PowerPoint's Standard Toolbar

New: Creates new presentation. [File ➤ New] *Shortcut:* Ctrl+N

Open: Opens existing presentations. [File ➤ Open] *Shortcut:* Ctrl+O

Save: Saves current presentation. [File ➤ Save] *Shortcut:* Ctrl+S

Print: Prints single copy of *slides* (does not bring up Print dialog box).

Spelling: Runs the spelling checker. [Tools ➤ Spelling] *Shortcut:* F7

Cut: Cuts selected item(s). [Edit ➤ Cut] *Shortcut:* Ctrl+X

Copy: Copies selected item(s). [Edit ➤ Copy] *Shortcut:* Ctrl+C

Paste: Pastes from Clipboard. [Edit ➤ Paste] *Shortcut:* Ctrl+V

Format Painter: Copies then applies format of selected item. Not for graphics or pictures.

Undo: Performs a single undo (no list). [Edit ➤ Undo] *Shortcut:* Ctrl+Z

Insert New Slide: Inserts a new slide after current slide. [Insert ➤ New Slide] *Shortcut:* Ctrl+M

Insert Microsoft Word Table: Inserts a Word table. [Insert ➤ Microsoft Table]

Insert Microsoft Excel Worksheet: Inserts an Excel *worksheet* (not a workbook).

Insert Graph: Creates a Graph object. [Insert ➤ Microsoft Graph]

BUTTON	DESCRIPTION
Buttons on PowerPoint's Standard Toolbar (continued)	

Insert Org Chart: Creates an org-chart object. [Insert ➤ Object ➤ Microsoft Organization Chart]

Insert Clip Art: Opens the ClipArt Gallery. [Insert ➤ Clip Art]

Pick A Look Wizard: Runs the Pick A Look Wizard. [Format ➤ Pick A Look Wizard]

Report It: Saves slides as a Word outline sans graphics.

Help: Click then point to item of interest for online help.

Buttons on PowerPoint's Drawing Toolbar

Selection: Click on objects while this button is depressed.

Text: Drag with this button depressed to create text objects.

Line: Use to draw lines

Rectangle: Use to draw rectangles.

Ellipse: Use to draw circles and ellipses.

Arc: Use to draw arcs.

Freeform: Use to draw freeform shapes.

Free Rotate: Use to rotate selected drawn objects.

Autoshapes: Reveals tear-off AutoShape palette.

Fill On/Off: Turns automatic drawing fill on or off. Will add or remove fill from an existing object.

BUTTON	DESCRIPTION

Buttons on PowerPoint's Drawing Toolbar (continued)

 Line On/Off: Applies the default line style to an object or removes the line.

Shadow On/Off: Adds or removes shadow effects from selected objects.

Buttons on PowerPoint's Slide Sorter Toolbar

Transition: Opens Transition dialog box. [Tools ➤ Transition]

Build: Opens Build dialog box. [Tools ➤ Build]

Hide Slide: Hides current slide. [Tools ➤ Hide Slide]

Rehearse Timings: Times rehersals and shows times on-screen. [View ➤ Slide Show]

Show/Hide Formatting: In Outline view, this toggles display of character formatting (bold, italic, etc).

Buttons on PowerPoint's Outline Toolbar

Promote (Indent Less): Moves item up one level in outline. *Shortcut:* Ctrl+←

Demote (Indent More): Moves item down one level in outline. *Shortcut:* Ctrl+→

Move Up: Places selected text nearer to the beginning of your outline. Alt+Shift+↑

BUTTON	DESCRIPTION

Buttons on PowerPoint's Outline Toolbar (continued)

Move Down: Places selected text nearer to the bottom of your outline. Alt+Shift+↓

Collapse Selection: Hides all but slide title for selected slides. Alt+Shift+minus

Expand Selection: Shows all text and headings in selected slides. Alt+Shift+plus

Show Titles: Shows titles only. *Shortcut:* Alt+Shift+1.

Show All: Shows all text and headings. *Shortcut:* Alt+Shift+A

Show Formatting: Displays and hides text formatting (bold, italic, etc).

PowerPoint's Slide Show Toolbar

Drawing: Turns on-screen drawing on and off.

PowerPoint's Formatting Toolbar

Increase Font Size

Decrease Font Size

Bold

Italic

BUTTON	DESCRIPTION
PowerPoint's Formatting Toolbar (continued)	
U	Underline
S	Text Shadow
A	Text Color
≡	Left Alignment
≡	Center Alignment
≔	Bullets On/Off
←	Promote (Indent Less)
→	Demote (Indent More)

BUTTON	DESCRIPTION
Buttons on Mail's Standard Toolbar	

Compose: Write a new message. [Mail ➤ Compose] *Shortcut:* Ctrl+N

Reply: Reply to the sender of an open message. [Mail ➤ Reply] *Shortcut:* Ctrl+R

ReplyAll: Reply to the sender and all recipients of an open message. [Mail ➤ Reply To All] *Shortcut:* Ctrl+A

Forward: Forward a message to another user on the mail system. [Mail ➤ Forward] *Shortcut:* Ctrl+F

Move: Move a message to another folder. [File ➤ Move] *Shortcut:* Ctrl+M

Delete: Delete selected item of mail. [File ➤ Delete] *Shortcut:* Ctrl+D

Previous: View previous mail item in folder. [View ➤ Previous] *Shortcut:* Ctrl+<

Next: View next mail item in folder. [View ➤ Next] *Shortcut:* Ctrl+>

Directory: Display a list of user directories on Mail system. *Shortcut:* Ctrl+L

BUTTON	DESCRIPTION
Buttons for Managing Address Books in Mail	
	Personal Address Book: Display members of personal address book. *Shortcut:* Ctrl+P
	Find: Find a member in current user directory. *Shortcut:* Ctrl+F
	New Address: Add an entry to personal address book.
	Add Names: Add entries in selected directory list to personal address book.

BUTTON	DESCRIPTION
Buttons on Access's Database Window Toolbar	
	New Database: Creates a new database.
	Open Database: Brings up the Open dialog box.
	Attach Table: Click to attach tables from other database.
	Print: Opens the Print dialog box to let you print the active object (table, form, etc.). *Shortcut:* Ctrl+P
	Print Preview: Takes you to the Print Preview window.
	Code: Lets programmers edit and create Access BASIC modules.
	Cut: Cuts selected object(s). *Shortcut:* Ctrl+X
	Copy: Copies selected object(s). *Shortcut:* Ctrl+C
	Paste: Pastes Clipboard contents. *Shortcut:* Ctrl+V
	Relationships: Displays the Relationships window where you view and change relationships.
	Import: Opens the Import dialog box.
	Export: Opens the Export dialog box.

BUTTON	DESCRIPTION
Buttons on Access's Database Window Toolbar (continued)	
	Merge It: Opens the MS Word Mail-Merge Wizard to link data for mail-merges.
	Analyze It with MS Excel: Saves contents of current table, form, report, or module as an Excel worksheet (.XLS), opening Excel in the process.
	New Query: Creates a new query based on currently active table or query.
	New Form: Creates a new form based on currently active table or query.
	New Report: Creates a new report based on currently active table or query.
	Database Window: Switches you to the Database window.
	AutoForm: Creates a new form containing all fields and records in the current table or query.
	AutoReport: Creates a new report containing all fields and records in the current table or query.
	Undo: Attempts to undo last action.
	Cue Cards: Activates Access tutorial help.
	Help: Offers help for the *next* item that you click on.

BUTTON	DESCRIPTION
	Buttons on Access's Form View Toolbar (Form, Datasheet Views)
	Design View: Switches to Design view.
	Form View: Switches to Form view.
	Datasheet View: Switches to Datasheet view.
	Print: Opens the Print dialog box to let you print the active object (table, form, etc.). *Shortcut:* Ctrl+P
	Print Preview: Takes you to the Print Preview window.
	New Record: Creates a new record.
	Cut: Cuts selected object(s). *Shortcut:* Ctrl+X
	Copy: Copies selected object(s). *Shortcut:* Ctrl+C
	Paste: Pastes Clipboard contents. *Shortcut:* Ctrl+V
	Find: Opens the Find dialog box, permitting you to search the database.
	Sort Ascending: Sorts records from small to large based on selected field(s).
	Sort Descending: Sorts records form large to small based on selected field(s).
	Edit Filter/Sort: Opens the Filter window, enabling you to create or edit a filter for restricting and/or sorting records displayed.
	Apply Sort/Filter: Uses the current filter.
	Show All Records: Shows all records (removes any filters).

BUTTON	DESCRIPTION

Buttons on Access's Form View Toolbar (Form, Datasheet Views) (continued)

	Database Window: Switches you to the Database window.
	Undo Current Field/Record: Reverses all changes made to current field or record.
	Undo: Attempts to undo last action.
	Cue Cards: Activates Access tutorial help.
	Help: Offers help for the *next* item that you click on.

Buttons on Access's Table Design Toolbar (Design View)

	Design View: Switches to Design view.
	Datasheet View: Switches to Datasheet view.
	Save: Saves current design (layout) only, not data. *Shortcut:* Ctrl+S
	Properties: Shows and hides Properties sheet for selected control, section, or other object.
	Indexes: Opens Indexes window where you can add, remove, or review field indexes.
	Set Primary Key: Makes selected field the Primary key.
	Insert Row: Inserts a new row above the current row.
	Delete Row: Deletes the selected row(s).
	New Query: Creates a new query based on currently active table.

BUTTON	DESCRIPTION
	Buttons on Access's Table Design Toolbar (Design View) (continued)
	New Form: Creates a new Form based on currently active table.
	New Report: Creates a new Report based on currently active table.
	Database Window: Switches you to the Database window.
	Build: Opens the Build window to let you pick items to add to an expression or procedure.
	Undo: Attempts to undo last action.
	Cue Cards: Activates Access tutorial help.
	Help: Offers help for the *next* item that you click on.
	Buttons on Access's Print Preview Toolbar
	Close: Closes the active window.
	Print: Opens the Print dialog box to let you print the active document (the one in the Preview window). *Shortcut:* Ctrl+P
	Print Setup: Opens the Print Setup dialog box where you adjust margins, etc.
	Zoom: Switches between close-up and bird's-eye views of document being previewed.
	Publish It with MS Word: Saves contents of current table, form, report, or module as a Word Rich Text Format document (.RTF), opening Word in the process.

BUTTON	DESCRIPTION

Buttons on Access's Print Preview Toolbar (continued)

Analyze It with Excel: Saves contents of current table, form, report, or module as an Excel worksheet (.XLS), opening Excel in the process.

Mail It: Lets you add the current table, query, report etc. to a Mail message.

Database Window: Switches you to the Database window.

Cue Cards: Activates Access tutorial help.

Help: Offers help for the *next* item that you click on.

Buttons on Access's Relationships Toolbar

Save: Saves design (layout) only, not data. *Shortcut:* Ctrl+S

Add Table: Lets you add a table to the Relationships window.

Show Direct Relationships: Shows only relationships that have a direct relationship with the current table.

Show All Relationships: Shows every relationship in the database.

Database Window: Switches you to the Database window.

Cue Cards: Activates Access tutorial help.

Help: Offers help for the *next* item that you click on.

BUTTON	DESCRIPTION
Buttons on Access's Macro Toolbar	
	Save: Saves current macro. *Shortcut:* Ctrl+S
	Macro Names: Shows or hides the Macro Names column in the Macro window.
	Conditions: Shows or hides the Conditions column in the Macro window.
	Run: Runs the macro.
	Single Step: Runs the macro a step at a time for easy troubleshooting.
	Database Window: Switches you to the Database window.
	Build: Opens the Build window to let you pick items to add to an expression or procedure.
	Undo: Attempts to undo last action.
	Cue Cards: Activates Access tutorial help.
	Help: Offers help for the *next* item that you click on.
Buttons in Access's Form and Report Toolbox	
	Select Objects: Use to select objects.
	Label: Lets you create labels.
	Option Group: Lets you create option *groups*.
	Option Button: Lets you create a *single* option button.
	Combo Box : Lets you create a combo box (drop-down list).

BUTTON	DESCRIPTION
Buttons in Access's Form and Report Toolbox (continued)	
	Graph: Starts the Graph Wizard.
	Object Frame: Lets you create unbound frames for things like logos in headers.
	Line: Lets you draw lines.
	Page Break: Inserts forced page breaks in reports and forms.
	Control Wizards: Turns Control Wizards on and off.
	Text Box: Use to create controls that display data, bound or unbound.
	Toggle Button: Use to create toggle buttons.
	Checkbox: Use to create checkboxes.
	List Box: Use to create scrolling lists of choices.
	Subform/Subreport: Creates a frame to display an embedded form or report.
	Bound Object Frame: Lets you create frames for bound objects that are "connected" to records in a table (like promotional photos or multimedia film clips in a videotape database).
	Rectangle: Draw rectangles with this button.
	Command Button: Create command buttons with this tool to run a macro or Access BASIC function.
	Tool Lock: Keeps the current tool as the active tool so you can use it over and over.

Index

NOTE TO THE READER: **Boldfaced** numbers indicate pages where the term is defined or where you'll find the principal discussion of the topic. *Italic* numbers indicate pages where the topic is illustrated in a figure.

A

About Microsoft Office command (Office Manager), 23
absolute references in Excel, **447–448**
accented characters in Word, **290**, *292*
Access, **784–785**
    buttons in. *See* buttons
    combo boxes in, **983–984**
    compacting databases in, **1046–1047**
    damaged databases in, **1041**, **1043**
    Database Documentor for, **1040–1041**, *1041–1042*
    disk space requirements for, 1096–1097
    dynasets in. *See* dynasets in Access
    error messages in, **1037–1040**, *1038–1039*
    exporting in, 1014, **1030–1032**, *1030–1032*
    expressions in. *See* expressions in Access
    fields in. *See* fields
    finding data in, **895–896**. *See also* queries in Access; select queries in Access
    forms in. *See* forms
    graphics in. *See* graphics
    graphs in, **1009–1012**, *1011–1012*
    help in, **799–800**, **1036–1037**, *1037*
    importing in. *See* importing
    list boxes in, **978–983**, *980–983*
    macros in, **990–996**
    mailing labels in. *See* mailing labels
    option groups in, **971–978**
    overview, **14–16**, *15*
    printing in. *See* printing
    queries in. *See* queries in Access; select queries in Access
    quitting, 796
    records in. *See* records
    relational databases in. *See* relational databases in Access
    replacing data in, **896**
    reports in. *See* reports in Access
    sample databases in, 800
    security in. *See* security
    starting, **793–796**
    system requirements for, **785–786**
    tables in. *See* tables
    terms in, **787–793**
    text in. *See* text
    typing in, 862
    upgrading, **786**, **1015–1016**
    views in, 799
    window for, **797–799**, *797*
Access Basic, 793, 991
Access button, 793, *793*
Access icon, 794, *794*
access rights in Mail, 747

Bold page numbers: Primary discussion of the topic.   Italic page numbers: The topic is illustrated in a figure.

Bold page numbers: Primary discussion of the topic.   Italic page numbers: The topic is illustrated in a figure.

Bold page numbers: Primary discussion of the topic.   Italic page numbers: The topic is illustrated in a figure.

Bold page numbers: Primary discussion of the topic.   Italic page numbers: The topic is illustrated in a figure.

Index

Bold page numbers: Primary discussion of the topic. Italic page numbers: The topic is illustrated in a figure.

Bold page numbers: Primary discussion of the topic.   Italic page numbers: The topic is illustrated in a figure.

Bold page numbers: Primary discussion of the topic.   Italic page numbers: The topic is illustrated in a figure.

Bold page numbers: Primary discussion of the topic.   Italic page numbers: The topic is illustrated in a figure.

Bold page numbers: Primary discussion of the topic.   Italic page numbers: The topic is illustrated in a figure.

Bold page numbers: Primary discussion of the topic.   Italic page numbers: The topic is illustrated in a figure.

Index

Bold page numbers: Primary discussion of the topic.   Italic page numbers: The topic is illustrated in a figure.

Bold page numbers: Primary discussion of the topic. Italic page numbers: The topic is illustrated in a figure.

Index

Bold page numbers: Primary discussion of the topic.   Italic page numbers: The topic is illustrated in a figure.

Bold page numbers: Primary discussion of the topic.   Italic page numbers: The topic is illustrated in a figure.

Bold page numbers: Primary discussion of the topic.   Italic page numbers: The topic is illustrated in a figure.

Index

Bold page numbers: Primary discussion of the topic.   Italic page numbers: The topic is illustrated in a figure.

Bold page numbers: Primary discussion of the topic.   Italic page numbers: The topic is illustrated in a figure.

Bold page numbers: Primary discussion of the topic.   Italic page numbers: The topic is illustrated in a figure.

Bold page numbers: Primary discussion of the topic.   Italic page numbers: The topic is illustrated in a figure.

Bold page numbers: Primary discussion of the topic.   Italic page numbers: The topic is illustrated in a figure.

Index

Bold page numbers: Primary discussion of the topic.   Italic page numbers: The topic is illustrated in a figure.

Bold page numbers: Primary discussion of the topic.   Italic page numbers: The topic is illustrated in a figure.

Index

Bold page numbers: Primary discussion of the topic.   Italic page numbers: The topic is illustrated in a figure.

Bold page numbers: Primary discussion of the topic.   Italic page numbers: The topic is illustrated in a figure.

Index

Bold page numbers: Primary discussion of the topic.   Italic page numbers: The topic is illustrated in a figure.

Bold page numbers: Primary discussion of the topic.   Italic page numbers: The topic is illustrated in a figure.

Bold page numbers: Primary discussion of the topic.   Italic page numbers: The topic is illustrated in a figure.

Bold page numbers: Primary discussion of the topic.   Italic page numbers: The topic is illustrated in a figure.

Bold page numbers: Primary discussion of the topic.　Italic page numbers: The topic is illustrated in a figure.

Bold page numbers: Primary discussion of the topic.   Italic page numbers: The topic is illustrated in a figure.

Bold page numbers: Primary discussion of the topic.   Italic page numbers: The topic is illustrated in a figure.

Bold page numbers: Primary discussion of the topic.   Italic page numbers: The topic is illustrated in a figure.

Index

Bold page numbers: Primary discussion of the topic.   Italic page numbers: The topic is illustrated in a figure.

Bold page numbers: Primary discussion of the topic.   Italic page numbers: The topic is illustrated in a figure.

Index

Bold page numbers: Primary discussion of the topic.   Italic page numbers: The topic is illustrated in a figure.

Bold page numbers: Primary discussion of the topic.   Italic page numbers: The topic is illustrated in a figure.

Bold page numbers: Primary discussion of the topic.   Italic page numbers: The topic is illustrated in a figure.

Bold page numbers: Primary discussion of the topic.   Italic page numbers: The topic is illustrated in a figure.

Index

Bold page numbers: Primary discussion of the topic.   Italic page numbers: The topic is illustrated in a figure.

Bold page numbers: Primary discussion of the topic.   Italic page numbers: The topic is illustrated in a figure.

Bold page numbers: Primary discussion of the topic.   Italic page numbers: The topic is illustrated in a figure.

Bold page numbers: Primary discussion of the topic. Italic page numbers: The topic is illustrated in a figure.

Bold page numbers: Primary discussion of the topic.   Italic page numbers: The topic is illustrated in a figure.

Bold page numbers: Primary discussion of the topic. Italic page numbers: The topic is illustrated in a figure.

Index

Bold page numbers: Primary discussion of the topic.   Italic page numbers: The topic is illustrated in a figure.

Bold page numbers: Primary discussion of the topic.   Italic page numbers: The topic is illustrated in a figure.

Index

Bold page numbers: Primary discussion of the topic.   Italic page numbers: The topic is illustrated in a figure.

Bold page numbers: Primary discussion of the topic. Italic page numbers: The topic is illustrated in a figure.

Index

Bold page numbers: Primary discussion of the topic.   Italic page numbers: The topic is illustrated in a figure.

Bold page numbers: Primary discussion of the topic.   Italic page numbers: The topic is illustrated in a figure.

Bold page numbers: Primary discussion of the topic.   Italic page numbers: The topic is illustrated in a figure.

Bold page numbers: Primary discussion of the topic.   Italic page numbers: The topic is illustrated in a figure.

Index

Bold page numbers: Primary discussion of the topic.   Italic page numbers: The topic is illustrated in a figure.

Index

Bold page numbers: Primary discussion of the topic.   Italic page numbers: The topic is illustrated in a figure.

Word Quick Reference *(continued from next page)*

Command	Shortcut	Command	Shortcut
Reset character formatting	Ctrl+spacebar or Ctrl+Shift+Z	Superscript	Ctrl+plus
		Symbol font	Ctrl+Shift+Q
Reset paragraph formatting	Ctrl+Q	System Info	Ctrl+Alt+F1
		Thesaurus	Shift+F7
Save	Shift+F12 or Ctrl+S or Alt+Shift+F2	Underline	Ctrl+U or Alt+U
		Underline: double	Ctrl+Shift+D
Save as	F12	Undo	Ctrl+Z or Alt+Backspace
Select all	Ctrl+A or Ctrl+(Num)5	Unindent	Ctrl+Shift+M
Select column	Ctrl+Shift+F8	Unlink fields	Ctrl+6 or Ctrl+Shift+F9
Select table	Alt+(Num)5	Unlock fields	Ctrl+4 or Ctrl+Shift+F11
Show all headings	Alt+Shift+A	Update fields	F9 or Alt+Shift+U
Show Heading	Alt+Shift+*heading number*	Update source	Ctrl+Shift+F7
Spell-check	F7	View field codes	Alt+F9
Spike	Ctrl+F3	View normal	Ctrl+Alt+N
Split document	Ctrl+Alt+S	View outline	Ctrl+Alt+O
Style	Ctrl+Shift+S	View page	Ctrl+Alt+P
Subscript	Ctrl+=		

NOTE: *The expression* **(Num)** *denotes that you must press the following number key on the numeric keypad, not a number key from the top row of the regular keyboard.*

Word Quick Reference

Command	Shortcut
Align center	Ctrl+E
Align justify	Ctrl+R
Align left	Ctrl+←
Align right	Ctrl+→
All caps	Ctrl+Shift+A
Apply Heading	Ctrl+Alt+*heading number*
Apply list bullet	Ctrl+Shift+L
AutoFormat	Ctrl+K
AutoText	F3 or Ctrl+Alt+V
Begin selection	F8
Bold	Ctrl+B
Change case	Shift+F3
Citation	Alt+Shift+I
Close current pane	Alt+Shift+C
Close document	Ctrl+W or Ctrl+F4
Copy format	Ctrl+Shift+C
Delete previous word	Ctrl+Backspace
Delete word	Ctrl+Delete
Extend selection	Shift+*GoTo keys* (see *Go To* entries in this list)
Field display (toggle)	Shift+F9
Find	Ctrl+F
Font	Ctrl+Shift+F
Font size	Ctrl+Shift+P
Go back	Shift+F5 or Ctrl+Alt+Z
Go To annotation	Alt+F11
Go To end of column	Alt+PgDn or Alt+Shift+PgDn
Go To end of document	Ctrl+End
Go To end of line	End
Go To end of row	Alt+End or Alt+Shift+End
Go To end of window	Ctrl+PgDn
Go To list of location choices	Ctrl+G or F5
Go To next page	Ctrl+Alt+PgDn
Go To previous page	Ctrl+Alt+PgUp
Go To start of column	Alt+PgUp, Alt+Shift+PgUp
Go To start of document	Ctrl+Home
Go To start of line	Home

Command	Shortcut
Go To start of row	Alt+Home or Alt+Shift+Home
Go To start of window	Ctrl+PgUp
Hanging indent on	Ctrl+T
Hanging indent off	Ctrl+Shift+T
Header/footer	Alt+Shift+R
Hidden	Ctrl+Shift+H
Increase or close up paragraph space	Ctrl+O
Indent	Ctrl+M
Insert annotation	Ctrl+Alt+A
Insert column break	Ctrl+Shift+↵
Insert date field	Alt+Shift+D
Insert endnote	Ctrl+Alt+E
Insert field	Ctrl+F9
Insert footnote	Ctrl+Alt+F
Insert merge field	Alt+Shift+F
Insert page break	Ctrl+↵
Insert page field	Alt+Shift+P
Insert Spike	Ctrl+Shift+F3
Insert time	Alt+Shift+T
Italic	Ctrl+I or Ctrl+Shift+I
Justify	Ctrl+J
Move text	F2
New document	Ctrl+N
Next field	F11, Alt+F1
Next object	Alt+↓
Next window	Ctrl+F6 or Alt+F6
Normal style	Ctrl+Shift+N or Alt+Shift+(Num)5
Open a saved file	Ctrl+O or Ctrl+F12
Other pane	F6 or Shift+F6
Previous object	Alt+U
Previous field	Shift+F11 or Alt+Shift+F1
Print	Ctrl+P or Ctrl+Shift+F12
Print preview	Ctrl+F2 or Ctrl+Alt+I
Redo	Alt+Shift+Backspace
Redo or repeat	Ctrl+Y or F4 or Alt+↵
Repeat find	Shift+F4 or Ctrl+Alt+Y
Replace	Ctrl+H

continues on previous page